AI, Transparency, and Organizational Change

Abdelfattah Jamal
Cadi Ayyad University, Morocco

Karima Aissaoui
Mohammed First University, Morocco

Lhoussaine Alla
Sidi Mohamed Ben Abdellah University, Morocco

Bouchra Alj
Hassan II University, Morocco

Badr Bentalha
Sidi Mohammed Ben Abdellah University, Morocco

IGI Global
Scientific Publishing
Publishing Tomorrow's Research Today

Vice President of Editorial	Melissa Wagner
Director of Acquisitions	Mikaela Felty
Director of Book Development	Jocelynn Hessler
Production Manager	Mike Brehm
Cover Design	Jose Rosado

Published in the United States of America by
IGI Global Scientific Publishing
701 East Chocolate Avenue
Hershey, PA, 17033, USA
Tel: 717-533-8845
Fax: 717-533-7115
Website: https://www.igi-global.com E-mail: cust@igi-global.com

Library of Congress Cataloging-in-Publication Data

Names: Jamal, Abdelfattah, 1980- editor | Aissaoui, Karima, 1987- editor | Alla, Lhoussaine, 1969- editor | Alj, Bouchra editor | Bentalha, Badr, 1985- editor
Title: AI, transparency, and organizational change / [edited by] Abdelfattah Jamal, Cadi Ayyad University, Morocco, Karima Aissaoui, Mohammed First University, Morocco, Lhoussaine Alla, Sidi Mohammed Ben Abdellah University, Morocco, Bouchra Alj, Hassan II University, Morocco, Badr Bentalha, Sidi Mohammed Ben Abdellah University, Morocco.
Other titles: Artificial intelligence, transparency, and organizational change
Description: Hershey, PA : IGI Global Scientific Publishing, [2026] | Includes bibliographical references (pages 453-505) and index. | Summary: "This book aims to discuss the merge between AI and management decisions"-- Provided by publisher.
Identifiers: LCCN 2025027628 (print) | LCCN 2025027629 (ebook) | ISBN 9798337354996 hardcover | ISBN 9798337355009 paperback | ISBN 9798337355016 ebook
Subjects: LCSH: Organizational change--Technological innovations | Artificial intelligence--Business applications
Classification: LCC HD58.8 .A48 2026 (print) | LCC HD58.8 (ebook) | DDC 658.4/06--dc23/eng/20251215
LC record available at https://lccn.loc.gov/2025027628
LC ebook record available at https://lccn.loc.gov/2025027629

British Cataloguing in Publication Data
A Cataloguing in Publication record for this book is available from the British Library.

Table of Contents

Detailed Table of Contents

Digital transformation acts as a lever for redefining ways of working, going far beyond the simple introduction of new technological tools. And therein lies the challenge: the ability of employees to embrace these changes and integrate them into their working environment. This chapter focuses on an aspect that is often overlooked in digital transformation projects: the actual place of employees in the technology adoption process. Through an analysis of 44 scientific articles listed in Scopus. One thing is clear: without the active involvement of employees, digital transformation loses its scope and remains largely unachieved. Employee readiness is a key success factor in digital transformation initiatives (Susanti & al.2023). Alignment between IT capabilities and employee engagement is decisive, companies that are able to align IT capabilities with employee engagement will be more likely to succeed, (Nwankpa & Roumani. 2016). This chapter offers an integrative reading of these contributions, and discusses the human levers of successful integration of AI and digital transformation.

Artificial technologies are evolving exponentially within organizations in a variety of managerial practices. The integration of artificial intelligence has been a growing trend in recent years, particularly for streamlining human resources processes and boosting employee performance. Organizations face a variety of challenges in successfully introducing AI to managerial practices, including boosting work motivation in the age of artificial technology. This study aims to examine the effect of artificial intelligence on work motivation. A systematic literature methodology was used, based on artificial intelligence and work motivation. The systematic literature review provided an analytical, critical and synthetic examination of the articles included in the database, following a rigorous examination according to the Prisma 2020 diagram. The results imply a significant effect of AI on work motivation. It is also worth highlighting the scarcity of research on the integration of artificial intelligence and its effect on organizational behavior, particularly work motivation.

Thc adoption of artificial intelligence (AI) technologies in the workplace has generated both concerns and optimism among employees. In response, scholars have dedicated considerable attention to understand the mechanisms through which AI may affect employee will-being, producing a significant number of publications in recent years. This chapter aims to map the current state of knowledge and to propose future research directions. To this end, an analysis was conducted on 313 articles sourced from Scopus and Web of Science. The results identify two approaches that explain how AI can assist in improving employee well-being. The first approach considers AI as a tool available to managers, enabling them to continuously monitor well-being indicators and take the necessary actions. While, the second approach views AI as a catalyst for transformation in the way work is organized and carried out by employees. These changes are not without challenges, thus opening new research avenues.

In a context of accelerated transformation of professional environments by AI, this research proposes an in-depth analysis. The analysis is of its effects on well-being at work. It uses a theoretical framework called the BIAT (Bien-être au travail et Intelligence Artificielle) model, which combines the PERMA model and information about how organizations work, especially how much job demands vary and how much decision-making latitude there is. Based on a hypothetical-deductive approach and a positivist epistemology, the study adopts a mixed methodology: a qualitative exploratory phase involving company directors and founders, and a quantitative confirmatory phase involving employees. The results show that PD and DL play a mediating role between AI use and the five components of well-being (positivity, commitment, relationships, meaning, fulfillment). Decision latitude has a particularly notable mediating effect. The study makes empirical contributions. It also proposes operational avenues. These avenues are for the ethical and sustainable integration of AI in organizations.

The aim of this research is to explore how artificial intelligence strengthens the individual resilience of entrepreneurs. To achieve this, we undertook a literature review, drawing on social cognitive theory (Bandura, 1986), to analyze the links between artificial intelligence and entrepreneurial resilience. Next, an exploratory qualitative study was conducted with ten entrepreneurs operating in the ICT sector. The results show that artificial intelligence is a tool that enables entrepreneurs to be more innovative and productive. In addition, AI strengthens the individual resilience of entrepreneurs, optimizing time management and promoting more effective post-adversity learning. Additionally, the present research makes two major contributions. Theoretically, this research relates artificial intelligence to the individual resilience of entrepreneurs. From an empirical point of view, shedding light on how artificial intelligence enhances entrepreneurial resilience as an indispensable point on which Moroccan entrepreneurial actors can draw, particularly in times of adversity.

This scoping review examines the ethical implications of AI in digital marketing strategies, focusing on personalization and customer experience optimization. As AI becomes increasingly integrated into marketing practices, concerns arise regarding privacy, transparency, and the ethical use of data. The study analyzes 144 academic sources to identify key themes, theoretical perspectives, and practical challenges at the intersection of AI ethics and marketing. Findings reveal four primary ethical tensions: the personalization-privacy paradox, algorithmic biases in customer segmentation, transparency deficits in automated decision-making, and accountability gaps in AI-driven marketing systems. The review proposes a framework for ethical AI marketing that balances business objectives with consumer rights protection, offering practical guidelines for implementing transparent and accountable AI systems in marketing contexts. This study contributes to ongoing discussions on responsible innovation in digital marketing and provides direction for future research in this emerging field.

This research investigates the perceived authenticity of Instagram influencers and its impact on Moroccan consumers, focusing on the duality between human and AI-generated influencers. A dyadic qualitative approach was used, incorporating both influencers and consumers through semi-structured interviews, considering their cultural context. Results show that authenticity is a key factor for both groups. Influencers view it as vital for credibility and trust with followers, while consumers consider it fundamental in shaping their purchasing behavior, though paid collaborations can undermine perceived authenticity. The study also explores the rise of AI-generated influencers, known as virtual influencers (VI), suggesting that their lack of authenticity may limit their effectiveness in Moroccan influencer marketing. This research underscores the importance of human influence in marketing strategies and highlights the tension between technological innovation and consumer demand for authenticity.

This chapter examines the critical challenge of uncertainty in risk management, a persistent issue for organizations operating in dynamic and complex environments. It explores the strategic integration of Artificial Intelligence (AI) with risk management processes, focusing on Bayesian Networks (BNs) as a robust analytical framework. BNs enable probabilistic modeling of risk factor dependencies, providing a systematic approach to anticipate, assess, and mitigate threats before they escalate. By combining AI's predictive capabilities with BNs' structured reasoning, organizations can enhance decision-making resilience and agility. The chapter establishes a triangular relationship between uncertainty, AI-driven solutions, and BN models, demonstrating their collective contribution to robust risk mitigation.

This study introduces an artificial intelligence system which predicts used car prices in Morocco to overcome the weaknesses of conventional valuation techniques that produce subjective and inconsistent results. The evaluation of multiple machine learning models resulted in CatBoost being chosen as the most effective model for prediction purposes. The final model reached an R^2 score of 91.35% after processing a web-scraped dataset from local automotive platforms through extensive preprocessing and hyperparameter tuning. The application of SHapley Additive exPlanations (SHAP) ensured model transparency. The system operates through a web-based interface which provides instant price forecasts together with analytical explanations and automated systems for monitoring data shifts and market adjustments. The study shows that combining advanced prediction capabilities with transparent models and ongoing monitoring systems enhances fairness, accountability, and user trust in AI-based pricing systems for emerging markets like Morocco.

The present chapter examines the effect of artificial intelligence (AI), particularly the ChatGPT-3 and ChatGPT-4 models, on the efficiency of the Moroccan stock market. The chapter is founded upon an empirical approach mobilizing quantile regression analysis. Through this empirical approach, the chapter explores the contribution of AI tools to market efficiency, thereby offering a novel perspective on the Adaptive Market Hypothesis (AMH). The findings of the study reveal a varied effect of AI on the efficiency of the Moroccan stock market, accompanied by noteworthy observations and discernible distinctions between the two models examined. This chapter is intended to stimulate further reflection on the effect of artificial intelligence (AI) on financial markets and the potential for technological advancement in this domain to enhance overall market efficiency.

Preface

The integration of artificial intelligence (AI) into organizational life is transforming the way institutions operate, make decisions, and engage with stakeholders. At the heart of these transformations lies a complex interplay between technological advancement, human behavior, and institutional values—most notably, transparency. As editors of AI, Transparency, and Organizational Change, we are proud to present this volume as a scholarly response to this rapidly evolving intersection. The chapters within offer multi-dimensional analyses of AI's influence on human resource management, organizational transformation, employee motivation and well-being, resilience, ethical marketing, financial systems, and even public governance.

This book emerged from a shared recognition among scholars and practitioners that AI is not simply a set of tools or techniques—it is a driver of profound systemic change. Yet these changes are often misunderstood or unevenly implemented, especially when it comes to maintaining trust, ensuring fairness, and fostering human well-being within organizations. With contributions from researchers across Morocco, Tunisia, France, and Ethiopia, this collection emphasizes both local insights and global implications. Each chapter is grounded in empirical evidence or systematic literature review, bringing together research rigor and contextual relevance.

What binds these contributions together is a focus on transparency—not only in the outputs and decisions generated by AI systems, but also in the processes of organizational transformation they prompt. Whether in human resources, marketing, taxation, or healthcare, the consistent message is clear: the ethical and effective integration of AI demands clarity, accountability, and a human-centered perspective. We hope this volume contributes meaningfully to ongoing conversations about the balance between innovation and responsibility.

CHAPTER OVERVIEW

Chapter 1: A Systematic Review of Employees' Behavior in Adopting Innovative Technologies: Aligning AI and Digital Transformation Projects

Kamar Reda, Abdelfattah Jamal, and Bouchra Benraïss

This chapter explores the human dimension of digital transformation by systematically reviewing employee behavior in the adoption of innovative technologies, particularly artificial intelligence (AI). Drawing on 44 scientific articles from Scopus, the authors emphasize that technological initiatives often fail when they neglect the crucial role of employee engagement. The chapter identifies employee readiness and alignment between IT capabilities and organizational culture as decisive factors in the success of digital transformation. Through an integrative analysis, the study highlights strategic ways to enhance adoption by focusing on employee involvement, engagement, and trust.

Chapter 2: Artificial Intelligence in Human Resource Management and Work Motivation: A Systematic Review

Sabah Laflafli and Charaf Saidi

Focusing on the intersection of AI and human resource management, this chapter systematically reviews how AI technologies influence employee motivation. The authors conduct a detailed literature review using the PRISMA 2020 methodology, analyzing research on AI's application in HR and its psychological effects on workers. The findings reveal that AI can positively influence motivation by streamlining HR processes and improving task alignment, though research in this domain remains sparse. The chapter calls for expanded inquiry into the behavioral impacts of AI on work environments and proposes new research directions to bridge the existing gaps.

Chapter 3: AI-Assisted Management and Employee Well-being: Review and Future Research Directions

FARAH Asmaa and Yassine Bamalk

This chapter investigates how AI technologies are shaping the future of workplace well-being. Based on a comprehensive review of 313 articles from Scopus and Web of Science, the authors identify two key paradigms: AI as a managerial tool for monitoring well-being and AI as a driver of structural work transformation. Both approaches reveal opportunities and tensions surrounding AI's role in supporting psychological health and job satisfaction. The chapter concludes by outlining priority areas for future research, including ethical AI design, organizational adaptability, and employee resilience.

Chapter 4: Revolutionizing Workplace Well-being through Artificial Intelligence with the BIAT Model

Cherkaoui Roquia and Salma Aarab

Introducing the BIAT model (Bien-être au travail et Intelligence Artificielle), this chapter presents a new theoretical framework that integrates psychological and organizational dimensions to assess workplace well-being in the age of AI. Using a mixed-methods approach involving both qualitative interviews and quantitative surveys, the study examines how decision latitude (DL) and psychological demand (PD) mediate AI's impact on five core elements of well-being: positivity, engagement, relationships, meaning, and accomplishment. The findings offer operational insights and actionable strategies for ethically embedding AI into the workplace.

Chapter 5: The Contribution of Artificial Intelligence to the Entrepreneur's Resilience

Hafsa Ouahi, Mohamed Bouikiker, and Majda El Agy

This chapter explores the role of AI in enhancing the resilience of entrepreneurs, particularly in Morocco's ICT sector. Combining literature review and qualitative interviews, the study applies social cognitive theory to understand how AI fosters innovation, time efficiency, and adaptive learning. The results show that AI is not only a productivity enhancer but also a psychological support tool that helps entrepreneurs navigate uncertainty and recover from adversity. The chapter emphasizes the strategic value of AI in strengthening individual resilience and highlights its relevance in emerging entrepreneurial ecosystems.

Chapter 6: Ethical Implications of Transparency in AI-Driven Marketing Strategies: A Scoping Review

Yasmine Benimma and Amina Bennouna

This scoping review critically examines the ethical dilemmas associated with AI-powered marketing, with a focus on transparency, privacy, and data governance. Analyzing 144 academic sources, the authors identify four central ethical tensions: the personalization-privacy paradox, algorithmic bias, opacity in decision-making, and lack of accountability. The chapter proposes a practical framework for ethical AI marketing, emphasizing the need to balance consumer rights with corporate objectives. This contribution offers strategic guidance for responsible marketing innovation and outlines future research needs at the intersection of AI and business ethics.

Chapter 7: The Authenticity of Influencers in the Age of Artificial Intelligence – Effect on Moroccan Consumers' Behavior: Dyadic Approach

Imane Margom and Mohammed Ben Amar

This chapter investigates the impact of perceived authenticity among human and AI-generated influencers on Moroccan consumer behavior. Using a dyadic qualitative methodology that includes both influencers and followers, the study finds that authenticity is a critical factor for building trust and shaping purchasing decisions. While human influencers are generally seen as more credible, AI-generated "virtual influencers" are often viewed with skepticism. The findings highlight a cultural preference for genuine, transparent communication and underscore the challenges of integrating synthetic personas into local marketing strategies.

Chapter 8: A Bayesian Network Framework for AI-Driven Risk Mitigation

Wissem Ennouri

Focusing on the strategic application of AI in risk management, this chapter introduces Bayesian Networks (BNs) as a powerful framework for mitigating organizational uncertainty. The author demonstrates how BNs, combined with AI's predictive capabilities, can model complex interdependencies among risk factors to support proactive decision-making. The chapter articulates a triangular relationship between uncertainty, AI tools, and BN models, offering a comprehensive methodology for enhancing organizational resilience and agility in volatile environments.

Chapter 9: Transparent AI for Car Price Prediction: Balancing Accuracy and Interpretability

Abdelhafid Ayaou, Fouad El Otmani, and Mohamed Atounti

This chapter presents an AI-based solution for predicting used car prices in Morocco, using CatBoost as the leading model for accuracy. Leveraging SHAP (SHapley Additive exPlanations) for interpretability, the authors show how transparency can enhance user trust and system accountability. The proposed model is accessible through a web interface, offering real-time predictions alongside explanations and automated monitoring features. The chapter illustrates how transparent, explainable AI can deliver both commercial utility and public trust in high-stakes consumer applications.

Chapter 10: The Artificial Intelligence Revolution and the Moroccan Stock Market's Efficiency: GPT-3 Versus GPT-4

Youness Ait Oummou and Driss Omerani

Investigating the role of generative AI models in financial forecasting, this chapter analyzes the impact of GPT-3 and GPT-4 on the efficiency of Morocco's stock market. Using quantile regression, the study tests the Adaptive Market Hypothesis (AMH) in light of AI-driven insights. The findings reveal nuanced differences between the two models in terms of predictive power and market behavior response. This chapter contributes to emerging research on AI's transformative influence in finance and offers data-driven insights for policymakers and market analysts.

Chapter 11: Privacy Concerns and Ethical Considerations in Integrating AI into Tax Control Processes: A Systematic Literature Review

Hicham Chanqaoui, Abdelouahab El Boukhari, and Doha Sahraoui

This chapter critically reviews the ethical and privacy challenges associated with using AI in tax administration. Based on 91 peer-reviewed studies and the PRISMA methodology, the authors identify concerns related to data protection, algorithmic fairness, and decision-making transparency. The study underscores the risk of eroding taxpayer trust in the absence of human oversight and legal safeguards. It concludes with actionable policy recommendations aimed at ensuring fair, compliant, and transparent AI deployment in digital taxation systems.

Chapter 12: Artificial Intelligence Effect on Renovation of Managerial Practices through Organizational Transformation of Health Care Sector in Horn of Africa

Wako Jio, Shashi Kant, and Hirut Assegid

Focusing on healthcare transformation in the Horn of Africa, this chapter investigates how AI is reshaping managerial practices in hospitals and medical institutions. Based on survey data from 385 healthcare professionals and analyzed through CFA and SEM models, the study confirms that AI integration enhances operational performance and decision-making capacity. The findings demonstrate that AI fosters innovation and data-driven management while improving service quality. This research offers practical insights for health sector leaders aiming to modernize operations through ethical and efficient AI adoption.

As editors, we are grateful to the contributing authors for their rigorous research and thoughtful perspectives. We are especially proud that this volume showcases both North African leadership in AI scholarship and meaningful collaboration across borders and disciplines. The work assembled here demonstrates that Moroccan universities, in partnership with international institutions, are contributing actively to global AI discourse—not only through technical innovation, but through critical inquiry into the social and ethical dimensions of AI adoption.

We also recognize that the conversation on AI, transparency, and organizational change is far from complete. The rapid pace of technological advancement ensures that new challenges will continue to emerge. This volume, therefore, is not an endpoint but a foundation—a step toward a deeper, more inclusive understanding of how AI can serve not only efficiency, but equity, well-being, and democratic integrity. Our hope is that readers will use these insights to inform future research, policy, and practice in their own institutions and communities.

Finally, we extend our thanks to the reviewers who supported this project, and to the scholars whose dedication and vision made it possible. As AI continues to evolve and permeate every facet of organizational life, it is our collective responsibility to ensure that these systems are transparent, trustworthy, and beneficial to all. May this book be a guide, a resource, and an invitation to continue that vital work.

Abdelfattah Jamal
Cadi Ayyad University, Morocco

Karima Aissaoui
Mohammed First University, Morocco

Lhoussaine Alla
Sidi Mohamed Ben Abdellah University, Morocco

Bouchra Alj
Hassan II University, Morocco

Badr Bentalha
Sidi Mohammed Ben Abdellah University, Morocco

Chapter 1

A Systematic Review of Employees' Behavior in Adopting Innovative Technologies:

Aligning AI and Digital Transformation Projects

Kamar Reda
https://orcid.org/0009-0002-1991-3240
Cadi Ayyad University, Morocco

Abdelfattah Jamal
https://orcid.org/0000-0002-8118-5638
Cadi Ayyad University, Morocco

Bouchra Benraïss
Sidi Mohamed Ben Abdellah University, Morocco

ABSTRACT

Digital transformation acts as a lever for redefining ways of working, going far beyond the simple introduction of new technological tools. And therein lies the challenge: the ability of employees to embrace these changes and integrate them into their working environment. This chapter focuses on an aspect that is often overlooked in digital transformation projects: the actual place of employees in the technology adoption process. Through an analysis of 44 scientific articles listed in Scopus. One thing is clear: without the active involvement of employees, digital transformation loses its scope and remains largely unachieved. Employee readiness

DOI: 10.4018/979-8-3373-5499-6.ch001

is a key success factor in digital transformation initiatives (Susanti & al.2023). Alignment between IT capabilities and employee engagement is decisive, companies that are able to align IT capabilities with employee engagement will be more likely to succeed, (Nwankpa & Roumani. 2016). This chapter offers an integrative reading of these contributions, and discusses the human levers of successful integration of AI and digital transformation.

INTRODUCTION

Nowadays, the driving force behind organizational revolutions is not only structural reforms and managerial initiatives, but also the gradual implementation of predictive and autonomous digital technologies. Work organization is undergoing profound changes, decision-making processes are being called into question and the very foundations of human behavior are being challenged (Forcina, 2024). The integration of technologies such as artificial intelligence (AI), automated systems and predictive modeling tools can have a significant impact on human-machine interactions, often without adequate support from companies (Volberda & Khanagha, 2021).

Implementing these tools in the workplace has proven to bring a number of notable benefits, including increased efficiency and reduced cognitive load. It also influences how employees perceive their work, their value and their ability to make a difference.

With the widespread emergence of automated tasks, algorithmic recommendations and intelligent dashboards, the boundaries of individual responsibility are blurring, particularly when these changes are not guided by a regulatory framework. The resulting change in attitude, though often subtle, has an impact on commitment, initiative and trust within teams.

In a collective environment, users' choices regarding the adoption of a digital tool are rarely purely rational. The transition to a new tool is a process that takes time and involves adjustments, interpretations and sometimes resistance (Bibi, 2024). If the objectives of the transformation are not sufficiently clear, or if measures are imposed without consultation, employees may reject the change.

The tool may be used formally, but remain marginal in practice. Real commitment then depends less on technical performance than on the system's ability to fit into a recognized business logic. The acceptability of a technological innovation depends on how it is introduced and articulated in relation to user expectations. (Nguyen, 2024)

When technology is positioned as a working partner rather than a substitute, it is perceived more favorably. Conversely, its introduction as a control, monitoring or evaluation tool has been shown to elicit a range of reactions, including mistrust or withdrawal (Jamal & al., 2024). Establishing legitimacy depends on clear objectives, transparent decision-making processes and the ability to interact with the system. In the absence of these elements, the tool is perceived as an "alien entity" to day-to-day professional activities.

Moreover, trust in a digital system is not acquired instantly; it develops with familiarity and experience, as well as with the organization's ability to anticipate its implications. Opaque, arbitrary or unfair technology poses considerable challenges to integration, even if performance targets are met.

This process relies on the principles of transparency of criteria, the ability to explain algorithmic choices and consistency between managerial discourse and practice. Legitimacy cannot be decreed; it is proven in the relationship between the tool and individuals. This relationship with the digital system becomes even more complex when the tools implemented have not been developed with their field of use in mind. What's more, the gap between developers, who are rarely aware of the realities on the ground, and end-users, who are subject to specific constraints, can lead to serious misunderstandings (Broo & Schooling, 2023). This can lead to under-use, misuse or abuse of the tool. This approach is not in itself sabotage, but rather reflects employees' desire to adapt and, in some cases, defend themselves.

The system is then partially integrated, its operation modified or symbolically neutralized.

On the one hand, the impression given by a technology is influenced not only by its technical properties, but also by the organizational structure in which it is implemented. The adoption process is often facilitated when the context allows for dialogue, the expression of uncertainties and the negotiation of use. Lack of communication and an autocratic management style are generally the most effective strategies for combating resistance (Zhao & al., 2024). Organizational culture plays a mediating role in the dynamics of goal appropriation and transformation. When people feel recognized, listened to and appreciated for their work, their well-being and performance can improve considerably.

Conversely, failure to take account of the local context is one of the main challenges of transformation projects. In some cases, digital systems are created for specific sectors, populations and practices, without taking into account the uniqueness of stereotypes. The widespread deployment of technical solutions often overlooks the diversity of contexts in which they are used (Ciruela-Lorenzo & al., 2020).

he relevance of a system depends on a number of factors external to its functionality. For example, a tool that works well in one organization may be harmful in another. The problem is not always the technology itself, but the fact that it is not adapted to the environment in which it is implemented.

This observation ties in with the idea that adopting an innovation is a process that involves intention (Xiao & al. 2024).

It encompasses representations, feelings, predispositions, social relations and systems of power. The integration of a technical system within an organization involves political, symbolic and identity-related elements (Díaz-Arancibia & al., 2024). Digital technologies are not just tools; they imply framing, hierarchy and normativity. Their very use modifies processes and norms.

In this case, the sociological aspect is not plausible as an adjustment factor. It plays a central role in the success or failure of change transformation programs. The usefulness of a system depends not only on its technological suitability, but also on the way it is adopted and perceived by its users. Clearly, recognition of constructive adaptation, continuous and sustained transition, ongoing support and participatory design are essential for sustainable integration. In their absence, systems are viewed too externally to understand the realities of best practice.

Many questions have arisen about AI (artificial intelligence) and other technological advances. These questions have also been answered in many publications about digital transformation. As far as we know, there are differences in the ideas of management, organizational science, and sociotechnical science. This gap in integration between disciplines can be explained by a lack of multidisciplinary integration, as noted in several studies (Elhaj & al., 2025; Santhi & Kumar, 2025; Jiang & al., 2024).

Research on how individuals and technology interact with their environment and how organizations use technology is limited. This gap makes it hard to build and predict the body of literature (Bui & Ali 2023; Zahoor & al., 2024). Most of these studies focus on large companies in developed countries (Zahoor & al., 2024; Wu & al., 2023; Ramanathan, 2025).

These studies don't consider situations where digital maturity is low and institutional frameworks, organizational structures, and capabilities are limiting.

Also, there are not enough studies that look at the details of why people adopt technology. Research shows that these gaps can be filled in two ways. First, when working together, it's important to consider how the data relates to the situation it's from, how things change over time, and why they change. To understand this, this study aims to address the gaps in both sides of the issue.

In the context of these findings, this chapter presents three key objectives:

- It is essential to identify the personal and social attributes of individuals that determine their willingness to adopt new technological innovations.
- A critique of the existing theoretical framework and its explanatory gaps is required.
- It is essential to identify practical strategies for aligning strategic technological goals with the human factors that make them possible.

The key question can be formulated as follows: ***How can employee behavior influence the adoption of innovative technologies such as AI with the aim of aligning "employee behavior and digital transformation projects"?***

To this end, we have chosen the systematic review approach, as it enables us to explore in detail the behavioral, social or cultural dimensions of initiatives, particularly those involving AI, aimed at the effective implementation of disruptive technologies.

This chapter analyzes 46 articles published on Scopus. The aim of this literature review is to analyze how psychological, organizational and structural elements influence workers' acceptance or resistance to digital innovations. It also explores the theories used in the literature on the subject and critically assesses the data presented.

REVIEW

1. Conceptual Framework

The objective of this conceptual framework is to define and articulate key concepts used in this research. It Is an analytical tool designed to provide a structure for analyzing the study subject: the adoption of innovative digital technologies, especially artificial intelligence, in organizations.

This framework does not draw on formal theories, but rather clarifies key concepts based on the findings of existing literature and their contextualization.

Four interdependent concepts have been selected: digital transformation, technology adoption, artificial intelligence, and organizational performance.

Each of these concepts will be presented in a manner that explains and defines it, identifying its constituent dimensions, conditions for emergence, and expected effects in the contemporary organizational context.

The objective is to provide a clear reference framework to guide empirical analysis and facilitate the operationalization of the dimensions studied.

Digital Transformation

Integration and digital transformation should not be viewed solely as technological enhancements because they constitute a fundamental reorganization of the logic of production, collaboration, and governance. Also, it differs from digitization, which simply refers to the process of converting an analog document or process into digital form. With digital transformation, professional frameworks and routines are reorganized as a result of smart interconnected technologies (Díaz-Arancibia & al.,).

There seems to be an emerging literature that converges around the prevailing agreement that this transformation is a systemic organizational phenomenon in which technology, culture, and people impact the organization simultaneously. Ciruela-Lorenzo & al. (2020) argues that for digital transformation to be achieved, the objectives must be rooted in technology and organizational culture and integrated with the work of the organization's members.

In most cases, this shift is aligned with some increase with the customer's demand pertaining to the organizational performance, efficiency, or competitiveness. Nonetheless, several authors agree that this also increases the risk of internal destabilization, especially when accompanied by a lack of employee guidance due to directional technological innovations. Volberda & Khanagha, (2021) note that in certain unprepared contexts, digital transformation may potentially result in unease and even muted resistance towards new technologies. The idea of technostress, as researched by Wach & al. (2023), elegantly encapsulates these burdens: limited attention spans, the need to operate within unforgiving deadlines, rapid shifts, and the fear of incompetence concerning opaque technologies.

The focus is the culture of the organization undergoing changes on the digital transformation. As cultures exist in organizations, for an organization to successfully integrate sophisticated digital systems in the long run, they have to embrace a collective culture that appreciates change, collective learning, and practical knowledge. Anning-Dorson & Zulu (2025) support this.

These authors emphasize that such cultures are not imposed, they need to be nurtured through participatory training and appreciation processes. Lower or absent digital cultures decrease cross-functional collaboration within an organization, and the range of technology-driven initiatives. The adoption of digital transformation shifts along with dismantles layered hierarchies and centralized decision-making within an organization. For example, the application of intelligent technologies in human resources and operational planning modifies professional strata, reorganizes processes, guides relationships through algorithms, and automates engagements (Jamal & al., 2024). Such automation triggers perceptions of a loss of discretion or the encroachment of AI where machines are commandeering areas once reserved for human autonomy. As Altrock & al. (2023) demonstrate, technology perception —whether it is considered an enabler or a means of control— demonstrates how strongly digital transformation relates to an enterprise's broader strategy.

Digital transformation in the context of their research establishes both possibilities and boundaries. Kelm & Lee (2022) identified a gap on how digital competencies preservice teachers interact with advanced digital systems, suggesting rethinking professional training. It is not a matter of only changing tools, as Bibi & al. (2024) argues; there is also a change in the users of the tools.

Zhao & al., (2024) posits that the lack of suitable strategic and educational support is one of the principal factors why the digital initiatives of agri-food SMEs fail. On the other hand, a supportive, incremental, participatory transformation enhances the adoption of appropriate technologies and the alignment of human resources and strategic initiatives at the level of their execution.

Technology Adoption

The adoption of technology constitutes the very first phase in the continuum of steps associated with executing digital innovations (Xiao & al. 2024).

It can be referred to as the stage in which the individual makes a decision to accept and utilize a specific technology in their work routines. This individual acceptance and use of technology is influenced by broad factors such as the organizational processes which occur in the workplace (Broo & Schooling, 2023). Acquiring new technologies has social intuition systems beyond mere calculated choices. It has various paths exploring social norms; ambiguity, search, and at times an apathy (Díaz-Arancibia & al., 2024).

The two primary explanations to this phenomenon are the Unified Theory of Acceptance and Use of Technology (UTAUT) and the Technology Acceptance Model (TAM). They reflect on why it is critical to take into account ease of use, perceived usefulness, and peer influence when deciding to adopt something new (Zhao & al., 2024).

These models have faced criticism for neglecting the social and cultural dimensions of adoption contour. Numerous studies have established that firm-level factors such as organizational climate, managerial structure, and prevailing employee perceptions impact the rate of technology adoption (Wach & al., 2023; Ramanathan & al., 2024).

Other significant factors comprise of users' digital competencies, receptiveness to novel concepts, and self-efficacy. Forcina & Mauro's research (2024) demonstrates that confidence in one's digital skills facilitates greater ease in employing technology. On the contrary, skill deficits combined with inadequate training tend to result in a substantial implicit rejection rate even for technologies that are regarded as beneficial.

Effective leadership regarding organizational commitment, continuous innovation, and addressing staff concerns is important at the organizational level. As Volberda & Khanagha, (2021) note, technological initiatives must have unified goals along with good practices in change management.

Every workplace's specific circumstances also impact the frequency with which they are adopted. In the more regulated fields, such as education or healthcare, the manner in which things are adopted is shaped not only by the policies in place, but also the compliance of the individuals bound to those policies, as well as some debates regarding morality (Ciruela-Lorenzo & al., 2020). Other sorts of organizations, such as the creative industries or tech SMEs, tend to offer greater autonomy to their personnel. This occurs because local constituents, who tend to be the company's “digital gurus,” shape the philosophy (Altrock & al., 2023).

As pointed out, people are not only utilizing technology for the very first time. It also encompasses becoming sedimented with discipliner, incorporating practices into habitual activities, as well as modifying business processes. Jada & Mayayise (2024) support that adoption should be regarded as cyclical with phases in which each cycle consists of three phases: uncertainty, reinforcement, and abandonment. The existence of community of practice, and sites of exchange enables this in so far as they provide space for people to gather and reflect on their experiences.

It follows that the adoption of technology is in this case a single, multilayer phenomenon that intersects with the personal, organizational, and the contextual frameworks in which the person operates. Existing models of acceptance will still apply, but seek understanding of the cultures, social structures, and sentiments individuals encounter within organizations (Anning-Dorson & Zulu, 2025). In this case, sustaining long-term employee engagement requires robust frameworks to support them, acknowledgement of successful knowledge, and clarifying the meaning, action, and consequences of the technology involved.

Artificial Intelligence (AI)

The incorporation of artificial intelligence (AI) has become vital for all organizations that leverage digital tools. As defined by Matamoros-Echeverria & al. (2025), AI is a collection of technologies that can perform human activities such as decision making, forecasting, and learning. Automated AI systems have been integrated into the workplace through task automation and enhancement of efficiency within processes. Moreover, AI has facilitated large-scale organizational restructuring.

Processing massive data sets, drawing novel insights, and making non-intuitive decisions are capabilities of AI systems that learn continuously and improve over time (Jamal, & al., 2024). The obscurity of AI systems is a bottleneck for people looking to leverage its usefulness, as the inner workings of AI tools remain shrouded in mystery. This is, however, a major challenge when attempting to deploy these systems in an organizational context (Forcina, & al., 2024).

People have differing opinions about AI and its impact. Some are enthusiastic, while others are apprehensive. Wang & Su (2021) demonstrate how AI can enhance productivity, reduce cognitive load, and streamline steps in various tasks. On the contrary, Bibi & al (2024) discuss the fear of role obsolescence, loss of autonomy, heightened surveillance, and other shattering influences AI may impose on employees. Ramanathan & al. (2024) also suggest that the manner in which AI is integrated into organizations, particularly whether it is ascribed the role of a support tool or a supervisory device, functions as a decisive factor on employee conduct.

Previous authors suggest that trust issues are pivotal in the attempts to integrate AI systems into existing organizational structures. Lack of clear rules regarding how data is processed and how decisions are made leads users to perceive biased systems as arbitrary and capricious, which can lower acceptance (Jamal & al., 2024). Matamoros-Echeverria & al (2025) show that algorithm transparency, providing the rationale behind outputs, and the revisability of the outcomes enhance acceptability.

Moreover, the use of AI technology profoundly shifts the anticipated competencies in companies. In particular, it has a demand for interpreters of information systems, as well as controllers and interactors with these systems (Díaz-Arancibia, & al., 2024). Such a change requires not only an updating of retraining policies, but also considers implicit understanding and social competencies.

AI technologies also contribute to inclusion problems. Some workers, for instance those in lower paying positions with no digital competencies, may be disregarded by systems which do not cater to their level or are overly complex (Mocanu, & al., 2024). People may perceive this lack of consideration as rude indifference, especially if the technologies are meant to be widely available and there is no effort to accommodate diverse demographics (Broo, & Schooling, 2023).

Most troubling are the ethical issues raised by the use of automated AI technologies in sensitive human resource functions like hiring and evaluating employees. The matter is further complicated when the decision-making process is automated because such systems lack built-in accountability, require strict regulatory controls, privacy protection, responsibility frameworks, and social accountability mechanisms (Ciruela-Lorenzo, & al., 2020).

Other researchers point out that more evenly distributed AI development would abide by principles of justice, responsiveness, participation, and provided rationale with explanations would address concerns for their governance (Ramanathan, & al., 2024).

Socially and human wise, AI is a source of promise and contention for workplace transformation. Some of the social and human factors are trust in the outcome, mechanisms, training and skills development, and day-to-day value-added tasks. All of these acceptance-and-quality centric factors tilt the balance toward AI developed or accepted by professionals.

Acceptance and Adoption of Technologies

Integrating digital technologies into an organization usually requires their initial adoption. It is the stage at which people make a decision to implement a certain technology in their day-to-day routines. This decision is influenced by the specific technology, its implementation, and its introduction in the organization (Broo & Schooling, 2023). Adoption is not a one-off or purely rational act. It is a journey often riddled with doubt, trial, and at times, quiet defiance (Díaz-Arancibia & al., 2024).

Perhaps the most common explains this phenomenon through the Technology Acceptance Model (TAM) and the Unified Theory of Acceptance and Use of Technology (UTAUT). They place great emphasis on the importance of the perceived value of the new tool, its usability, and social influence in the decision-making process of accepting the technology (Zhao & al., 2024). However, these theories have been criticized for ignoring the socio-cultural context of adoption. There is substantial evidence that the climate, leadership, and employee perceptions within an organization have profound effects in the adoption process (Wach & al., 2023; Ramanathan & al., 2024).

Effective use of digital technologies correlates with a person's familiarity regarding its use, acceptance of different concepts, and self-efficacy. Forcina and Mauro (2024) assert that having confidence in one's digital abilities encourages technology utilization. On the contrary, in regions where people's experience tends to be undertrained and/or poorly trained, they may foster much higher rates of implicit rejection for technology, even if they consider it beneficial.

At the organizational level, critical factors include secured management buy-in, effective persistent communication concerning innovation, and addressing employee feedback. Volberda & Khanagha, (2021) state the need for technology projects to be undertaken in alignment with effective change management strategies.

The states of each sector influence their adoption pace. In the more regulated sectors such as healthcare and education, the way things are adopted is aligned with regulations, stakeholder compliance, and sometimes there are conflicts of compliance (Ciruela-Lorenzo & al., 2020). People working in tech SMEs and in the creative industries have more freedom and less bureaucratic red tape because local "digital champions" elect what is reasonable.

This is possible because technology wasn't utilized as a static function. (Not their practice a stable thing, it is their practice for a while as an add-on until it is integrated into a routine, and sometimes re-engineering business practices.) As Jada and Mayayise (2024) describe, "adoption or up-take is a cyclical process with multiple waves of doubt, reinforcement, abandonment, and so forth."

The existence of a community of practice and exchange spaces supports this process by enabling employees to talk about the adjustments, share experiences, and assist with the modifications.

Implementing new technology is crucial for an individual, an organization, or a circumstance and requires everything to be considered in detail. The standard methods of accepting new things are still relevant, however, we also need to understand the interplay of emotions in organizations on a deeper level (Anning-Dorson & Zulu, 2025). Offering the proper backing and appreciation of their skills and knowledge plays a great role in ensuring that workers are happy and willing to perform optimally.

Technology Adoption and Organizational Performance

The application of new heterogeneous technologies, especially artificial Intelligence, is becoming increasingly relevant in the modern context of studying management and information systems. Most empirical or conceptual studies draw a link between digital technologies and organizational productivity, beginning with AI adoption, through digital transformation, to automation systems.

The integration of new technologies improves an organization's agility and productivity, enhancing internal processes as well. Yoo and Kim (2018) studied the cloud computing adoption phenomena and its impact of decision use cloud computing, where they show that the cloud computing acceptance stem from the structural hierarchy of the organization, its technological fit, and executive's sponsorship. In a similar vein, Ramanathan (2024) expounds on the repercussions of AI on organizations' capacity to effectively respond to crises. He underscores the potential of AI to bolster organizational resilience, defined as the capacity to effectively manage and recover from crises.

The integration of novel technologies invariably precipitates a transformation in the competitive landscape. Pereira & al. (2021) expounded on the potential of artificial intelligence (AI) and big data for market analysis and customized service provision, enhance customer experiences, and make data-driven decisions at every level of the organization. With these technologies, organizations have the power to maneuver change and impact their purpose, governance structure, and business model.

From the other side of the coin, not all businesses are likely to benefit from them. Focus on capability posits that firm-specific resources and activities must be scrutinized to align with technology strategy. Wu & al. (2023), through a multi-case study, demonstrated that for manufacturing firms in China, multidisciplinary performance is dependent on the execution of digital transformation accompanied by deep internal organizational structural overhaul, workforce reskilling, and comprehensive change management at the organizational level. In other words, firms seeking enhanced performance through mere technological adoption are deeply mistaken; a holistic systems approach is crucial.

To articulate it more simply, the literature exploring these unintended impacts of technologies paints a vivid picture of uncontrolled information flow resulting in increased organizational stagnation or disconnection from work—an overabundance of democratic movements centering around technologies perceived to be hostile toward traditional employees.

Social and cultural innovations, along with human innovations, greatly impact an organization's performance innovation (Santhi & Kumar, 2025).

The corpus data shows a conditional causal correlation between the use of technology and performance enhancement within a business. Some contextual factors, like the kind of technology, the sector, organizational culture, and the level of commitment to change, influence this relationship. Rather than a straightforward correlation, the relationship is complicated appropriation. Digital performance tools may serve as performance enhancers only when they are a part of a comprehensive strategy and integrated into the right internal environment.

2. Theoretical Framework

The use of technology in any organization cannot be understood from a psychocognitive or technical approach and more from pluralistic that incorporates individual, structural, and institutional factors. This understanding focuses on the dynamics of AI as a pluralistic construct. There was no an a priori normative choice of theories for this research. Rather, these theories surfaced from patterns and themes noticed during the literature review. Such theories will assist in answering the addressing the central research question of the study.

Theories Most Commonly Used in the Literature

Institutional Theory

Institutional theory provides a fundamental explanatory framework for understanding the adoption of innovative technologies in organizations, beyond purely technical or utilitarian considerations. Innovation adoption still relies heavily on social frameworks; thus, institutional theory is paramount. Anning-Dorson and Zulu noted in their 2023 research that organizational behavior shifts under the force of environment upon compliance at the cost of social legitimacy.

My analysis revealed that many articles did not adopt certain technologies only because that they did not contribute to the operational aspect, which is the conventional understanding. Rather, the technology was acquired due to compliance or institutional image, also referred to as Fregano Theory. Anning-Dorson and Zulu expands on that with technology not contributing to manipulative, operational enhancement but image-enhancement conducted via Fregano and Harwood's institutional theory, which builds on resemblance, violation and control of operational standards. It is also noted that the operational adoption of such macroscopic technology generally exceeds its compliance, thereby resulting in the manipulation of the social reputation as a dominant effect.

The works of Ciruela-Lorenzo & al. (2020) and Matamoros-Echeverria & al. (2025) illuminate the adoption of AI or digital tools in organizations, particularly in cooperatives, public institutions, or educational companies, where the implementations can be primarily symbolic. Some structures, for example, showcase the deployment of AI solutions to enhance their image as modern or innovative, projecting this image externally while internally, there is no real change in practice. Here, what is captured by institutional theory as "mimetic isomorphism" illustrates a tendency to adopt technological systems already in use by competitors deemed as credible or mainstream, devoid of any meaningful analysis on relevance.

Immediately, however, the theory structures how exogenous legitimation factors that determine adoption impact it. These can include funders, regulatory agencies, or political factors. In the case of AI technologies applied to H.R., as an example, in the work of Jamal & al. (2024), some companies appear to use explainable XAI tools not because they hope to improve selection processes but rather to fulfill expectations for transparency and compliance perceived as indispensable for organizational reputation sustenance.

The integration of institutional theory into this work is justified by its capacity to explain constraining or strategic adoption out of context with a direct logic of performance. It accounts for discrepancies within the corpus where there is stated discourse, such as "transformation strategies" or "digital alignment", and actual practices which are more resistant or superficial Furthermore, it explores the extent to which social norms, sectoral dynamics, and regulatory constructs influence technological pathways, often in more implicit ways.

Within the framework of this study, the theory proffers a macro-sociological perspective on the deliberated integration of technology, thus offering a complementary interpretation to models such as TAM or TOE. It makes it possible to examine micro analysis of employee actions and consider organizational appropriation at a higher level where institutional factors dominate and intervene as frameworks. It contributes to the discussion on the acceptance and rejection of novel technologies like AI in contemporary organizations by providing empirical evidence and powerful explanations.

Diffusion of Innovations Theory

Diffusion of innovations theory made by Everett Rogers (2003) serves as an important foundation for grasping how new technologies spread within organizations. It assumes that the adoption of innovation is determined by the qualities of the innovation itself and its social acceptance, social network acceptance, and relay actors' integration such as opinion leaders, or 'champions of innovation.' This view emerged multiple times in the analyzed corpus, especially with regard to social legitimacy, reputation, inter-organizational influence, and domestic support for the adoption (Matamoros-Echeverria & al., 2025).

This theory elucidates the factors that contribute to the successful integration of certain technologies into the workplace, while others face challenges in achieving the same level of acceptance. For instance, Jamal & al. (2024) discuss the utilization of artificial intelligence (AI) in the hiring process by companies such as X. This practice is not merely a means of enhancing their professional effectiveness; it is also a means of projecting an image of modernity, advanced thinking, and fairness. This is illustrative of what diffusion theory describes as social or symbolic adoption logic, where the perception of innovation may be more critical than its measurable utility.

Another important element of diffusion is the classification of adopters: Rogers made a distinction between the innovators, early adopters, the early majority, the late majority, and the laggards. This taxonomy resounds in several texts from the corpus which speak of users' profiles based on their readiness to shift to newer technologies. An example is that of Ciruela-Lorenzo & al. (2020), who investigate adoption behavior in digitized agricultural cooperatives and assert that diffusion is strongly moderated by internal constituents who understand innovation and can sell it to the colleagues.

This account underscores the "digital champions" highlighted in several studies, who mediate between technical innovation and organizational culture. Their efforts further the collective technologies and legitimizes the use of such technologies in professional routines.

Incorporating the supporting theory into this research enables analyzing the appropriation process as a gradual social construction rather than an irrational, or top-down unilateral decision. It helps investigate the social barriers for AI circulation where escalation circumstances like the network effect, sectoral imitation, and barriers tied to the absence of mediators, communication, or recognition exist.

In attempts to understand the dynamics of AI adoption within organizations, innovation diffusion theory provides important meso-social dimensions that go under-researched. It adds to the individual (TAM, TRI) and system (TOE) perspectives by cross-sectionally analyzing the interrelations, causative intersections, and channels of technological innovation diffusion throughout time. Employing the theory answers the demand for discovering the mechanisms operating between the intention to adopt and the change in practices.

Organizational Climate and Technological Readiness Theory

The organizational climate framework and its extension via Technology Readiness Index (TRI) reveals a critical collection of resources toward developing a comprehensive understanding of the contextual and psychological drivers regarding one's ability to engage with technology innovation. Unlike UTAUT or TAM models which concentrate strictly on the behavioral intention or feature of the technological interaction as a rational choice, this theory incorporates the workplace affective and cognitive predispositions (Parasuraman, 2000). As supported by literature, many studies emphasize perceptions of usefulness alongside socio-emotional climates as foundational components to implementing digital technologies, most notably those with AI capability. All these ideas have been studied with regard to the various technology introductions (Volberda & Khanagha, 2021; Ciruela-Lorenzo & al., 2020).

The TRI model consists of four components: individual innovation, optimism, discomfort, and insecurity which provide systematic classification around an individual's propensity towards newer technologies. For more details, refer to the works of Zhao & al. (2024) and Bibi & al. (2024). The former showed that people have a higher likelihood of dropping out in situations where they perceive low autonomy, no surveillance, and minimal task complexity. In contexts where digital transformation appears to be imperative but lacks support, this form of demobilization poses a major danger, highlighting the duality between technological concern and apparent denial of new approaches.

In the same vein, appropriate organizational development, which includes praise, managerial follow-up, training, and open communication, galvanizes buy-in and a positive view of the tool. In these circumstances, the existence of "digital champions" significantly influences the context and pace of system adoption and thus fosters a favorable disposition toward technology in the long term. Readiness, it seems, is not an adaptable factor, ecosystems differ more than expected, and individual circumstances cannot dictate the organizational climate that governs the journey through digital transformation.

Thus, the theory attempts to connect micro-attitudes with organizational behavior and attempts to explain why some work units' internal cultures adopt changes in a different sequential order within the workflow. It also strengthens the contributions of the TOE model by adding subjective experience with focus structures. In addition, the blending of TRI and TAM (as some scholars make these blends in the literature) makes it possible to expand "perceived usefulness" to consider emotion-based elements that are important but usually overlooked.

In this study, the use of TRI, together with aspects of organizational climate, allows for deeper exploration of the engagement-resistance spectrum regarding AI by focusing design not just on the technology but on the broader contextual narrative surrounding its implementation, as well as employee perception regarding the portrayal of the AI system. This model highlights trust and psychological safety alongside mutual acknowledgement as critical factors enabling rational adoption of new technology within the group.

Conceptual Models Most Commonly Used in the Literature

Theories developed to understand how innovative technologies are adopted within organizations are based on information systems and management sciences. However, they cannot be applied in a general way, as they must be contextualized. Indeed, the processes of appropriation, rejection, or misappropriation of technologies are shaped by regional, industrial, institutional, and cultural factors. It is therefore essential to question conceptual models in order to assess their contexts, limitations, and potential for adaptation.

Southern countries, emerging economies, and labor-intensive industries such as agriculture and public services have organizational environments that are structurally, technologically, and humanly different from those of large Western multinationals in the technology sector.

To illustrate this point, consider the ease with which a given tool can be used within the TAM framework. The success of these efforts depends on the availability of technological training, the level of trust in institutions, and social norms. A similar argument can be made for the UTAUT model, in which social influence and facilitators play a central role, and which must also take into account implicit conformity or institutional imitation, typical of highly regulated environments or those subject to symbolically superior pressures.

The TOE framework tends to gain relevance when combined with specific sectoral variables, such as infrastructure skills, local governance systems, or the impact of integration into regional value chains. Similarly, institutional models such as TRI and others reveal their explanatory potential only in empirical contexts where the adoption of new technologies is mediated by legitimation, reputation, or compliance with social norms.

This articulated, context-specific approach therefore seeks to enrich the application of analytical frameworks by seeking to anchor these frameworks in specific realities rather than applying them indiscriminately. Only then can analysis shed light on the complex dynamics of technology adoption in diverse and changing organizational contexts.

From an analytical perspective, these theoretical models will be reexamined in light of the specific conditions identified in the cases analyzed, whether industrial, institutional, or geographical.

Technology Acceptance Model (TAM)

The Technology Acceptance Model (TAM) is one of the models that has been applied in recent years to provide a workplace implementation intention of workplace technology. This model has a psychocognitive component concerning adoption behavior based on perceived ease of use and perceived utility. It has been proven to be relevant in many deployment environments, especially in systems with a greater degree of algorithmic autonomy (Zhao, Y. & al. 2024).

Regarding generative technologies like ChatGPT, it was noted that the system's transparency directly correlates to a user's sense of usefulness. The authors claim that the willingness of users to engage with AI tools tends to hinge on the transparency of the system. Xia & Shannon (2025) within an industrial context provided an empirical study on TAM alongside contextual variables such as managerial encouragement and instructional training. The authors of the study emphasize a discrepancy between the perceived utility of specific technologies by individuals and the level of support these technologies receive from their users. This notion is further substantiated by Volberda & Khanagha, (2021), who observed that transformational leadership fosters the utilization of digital technologies and fosters favorable attitudes toward their adoption.

Specific studies focus on culture and relationships as parts of the tools that help to adapt TAM to organization's context. From the perspective of digitally-altered agricultural cooperatives, Ciruela-Lorenzo, A.M. & al. (2020) demonstrate that collective mental models of innovation strongly influence employee actions.

The adoption of new technology is facilitated by cultures that view its implementation as collective value add. Conversely, when an innovation is viewed as a rigid external control imposed from Outside, the value assigned to it, irrespective of the technical usefulness, is greatly diminished. "Techscopes" refers to practices associated with technology co-development that Forcina & al. analyze in 2024. These participants report being in the tool configuration stage and cognizant of structure, affording greater ease of use.

Within broader-scope arguments, Jamal & al. (2025) posit that XAI" explaining" tools calibrated into recruitment processes enhance the usefulness of human resources for clients and enhance perceived value when contextualization of the algorithm's outputs is provided. In critical analysis, Díaz-Arancibia & al. make an effort to counter the other side of the framework by proposing that the foundational components of the TAM of the AI ecosystem require refinement.

In this argument, estimated utility equates, to an extent, to trust, organizational backing for the initiative, and a prominent figure able to skillfully orchestrate the story behind the digital transformation. On higher education institutions the usefulness of the TAM framework for integrating hybrid models that consider organizational logics and collective skills. Critique of a particular technology encompasses much more than its practical use, functionality, ease of use, and accessibility.

The steps taken by TAM should not be dismissed as no effort has been made in constructing a rationale for adoption since the absence of such a rationale can be greatly broadened beyond plausible limits. In digital environments, trust that is co-created with anchor cultures that are noticed to fetch value enhances perceived utility. No matter how aggressively the model is deemed dead, it offers a robust basis for understanding the acceptance or rejection of new technologies by employees, and can be seamlessly integrated with other frameworks.

Unified Theory of Acceptance and Use of Technology (UTAUT)

The UTAUT model was developed by Venkatesh and his team in 2003. The study sought to synthesize a variety of theoretical frameworks that attempt to explain why individuals adopt technology. The model is predicated on four fundamental factors: the usefulness and ease of use of a given object or concept, the influence of social networks, and the conditions that facilitate its use. Moreover, it includes age, gender, experience, and intention to utilize the technology as moderating factors (Zhao & al., 2024).

Using the UTAUT framework, Zhao & al. (2024) conducted a quantitative study on generative AI acceptance perception amongst students, finding social influence and performance perceptions to be the primary factors. Even though these findings come from the educational context, they illustrate intricate social and collective acceptance dynamics in professional environments where one's intention to use such technologies is heavily supported.

Relationship aspects of the TAM model do not consider the context affecting such a structure. Some authors claim interrelationships and managerial attitude relationships, along with supporting organizational structures, influence the adoption of technology, Volberda & Khanagha, (2021) claim These factors shape the defined perception toward a resource in terms of value or effort through the lived experience of an everyday user.

One problem with this model is that it focuses too much on what people plan to do and not enough on later stages of the usage cycle. In a study on adoption dynamics, Bibi & al., (2024) argue that changes after adoption, like how tools are used, how they are customized, and recognizing the digital work done, have a strong impact on the belief that usage always stays the same. Such components make the original UTAUT model incomplete.

Additionally, contemporary organizational environments contain contradictory paradoxes pertaining to cultivating innovation. Some contexts may accept technology as strategic compliance or implicit coercive choice as opposed to compliance. Standard iterations of the UTAUT model do not incorporate these structurally tacit logics of constraint or organizational alignment.

Aside from these considerations, the model remains applicable in situations where integrated analytic frameworks coupled with qualitative approaches situated within a social organization, like the TOE model, are employed. Volberda & Khanagha, (2021) note that due to the model's versatility in handling multifaceted endeavors, it is also flexible to fundamental constituents of digital transformations, such as leadership, trust, and strategic alignment.

Technology–Organization–Environment (TOE) Framework

The Tornatzky and Fleischer TWG is reconsidering its model for technology acceptance at the organizational level by employing a Technology-Organization-Environment (TOE) framework. Unlike models centered on the individual, the TOE framework possesses a broad organizational level focus that encompasses "technology attributes (T), organizational resources and processes (O), and other factors such as other industry players or politics (E)" (Wang, & Su, 2021).

Insights gathered regarding the digital transformation of manufacturing companies indicates that synchronization of internal assets, with external surrounding conditions, provides a competitive edge in the application of such technologies as AI (Wang, & Su, 2021).

This implies that TOE framework includes sophisticated associations such as organizational governance frameworks, organizational competencies, and outside the region and external constituents.

Various other works corroborate the refinement potential of the study by employing the TOE approach for AI integrations in more deeply scoped projects of technology-integration. In more rigid institutional frameworks, AI is mostly driven by innovation, funding, and publicly held views (Ciruela-Lorenzo, & al., 2020).

Keeping this in mind, the particular strength of the TOE framework lies in the explanation of gaps created between organizational strategy and the defined strategic objectives.

Jamal, & al. (2024) review the impact of policies concerning the integration of AI at the organizational level on its application within human resources functions. Although this attempts to resolve some issues, it does not reveal organizational sponsorship and organizational control.

As an example, communication and change management as internal factors have been analyzed and documented by Díaz-Arancibia, & al. (2024) and are integral parts of an organization's training scheme; they ascribe to the effective or non-effective deployment of technology. Their results suggest that the climate within an organization has a profound enabling or constraining effect on technology.

These researchers brought forth the notion that unbridled competition might give rise to a plethora of external sophisticated technological activities which, due to the organization's structure-dynamic capabilities paradox, increase resistance and make appropriation difficult.

The above-mentioned proponents and critics help structure and formulate my thoughts towards the definition of technological organizational environment (TOE) which is useful for framing and understanding the IT architecture as an assemblage of components, yet for my heels-digging critics out there, it is at best rudimentary and overly simplistic. The emphatic support claim although providing a robust framework does tend to overstructure the surprisingly intricate interplay between several factors.

Wang & Su (2021) and Diaz-Arancibia & al. (2024) underscores the point that it is more beneficial to incorporate social and individual variables by integrating them into frameworks like the Technology Acceptance Model (TAM) and the Unified Theory of Acceptance and Use of Technology (UTAUT).

Technology Readiness Index (TRI)

The TRI, or Technological Readiness Index, attempts to gauge the psychological aspects of a person's readiness to adopt a specific technology. A character like Parasuraman would likely view such readiness as stemming from one's level of optimism, personal innovation, discomfort, and even insecurity.

As AI-assisted tools are noted to be utilized within organizational contexts, as Zhao & al. (2024) indicated, such factors will most likely influence the willingness to adopt them.

The organizational context seems to be primarily hindered by discomfort and lack of security. Employees who feel that a system is overly complex or violates their autonomy disengage, leading to systematic disengagement which diminishes the potential value derived from digital investments, even in scenarios where significant returns are anticipated (Bibi & al., 2024).

With the application of ChatGPT, the case of its adoption added to the IRR model along with a proposition rooted in the Technology Acceptance Model (TAM). Under TAM, insecurity placed within anticipatory behavior negatively affects the perceived ease of use, while optimism about technology enhances attitudes toward acceptance in the model. These results indicate that technology affects people's affection for it just as much as they for the technology (Zhao & al., 2024).

Every person has their unique choices regarding profiles while adopting. Through behavioral segmentation, various groups (enthusiasts, skeptics, resisters and pragmatists) are defined.

These groups are differentiated by the level of particularized help they require, specially tailored guidance they lacking help must overcome. To help deal with potential resistance, contextual and tangible proof is essential (Volberda & Khanagha, 2021).

Under IRT an organizational climate is directly associated with a readiness level for adopting a certain technology. For instance, if the work environment is perceived as unfavorable or even hostile, it doesn't matter how ready an employee is; he will avoid any active engagement with digitization tools.

This inertia is a silence, lack of communication, teaching, lack of effort towards integration, adoption recognition, and reaffirming the status quo (Ciruela-Lorenzo & al., 2020).

That cozy atmosphere may on the contrary serve as a source of great pain. Non-threatening surroundings, along with support groups and gradual introduction to scaffolding technology, with non-threatening environments, can, that subsequently improve attitude towards integration.

Institutional Theories and the Diffusion of Innovation

It is apparent that an institutional framework can explain the technology adoption processes within an organization (Anning-Dorson, & Zulu, 2025). Industry norms, processes of legitimation, and even political dictates have significant integration selection consequences. Technological adoption for any organization stems from a blend of its pragmatic advantages and the institutional constraining and enabling requirements of pressure emanating from funders, constituents, governance, and other entities (Anning-Dorson, & Zulu, 2025).

For the most part, organizations try to use new technologies either as a self-marketing tool aimed at showing compliance with international standards or an attempt to subscribe to a prevailing norm, albeit such choices may not be accompanied by corresponding actual behavioral change. Is referred to as "symbolic" adoption deliberately conceals profoundly shallow implementation and change that is relegated to a facade of a new organizational strategy rather than authentic structural metamorphosis (Ciruela-Lorenzo, & al., 2020).

Mimicry as an institution deals with this particular dynamic. When a particular technology is considered an emerging standard, or possible indicator of development, organizations try to adopt it, even if only at a cosmetic level, so as not to lag behind (Matamoros-Echeverria, & al., 2025). This often happens within social sectors, or in shadowed-over areas of social attention, such as education or medicine.

The existing literature on AI and the hiring processes serves perfectly to exemplify this rationale. AI is marketed to some companies as a panacea, a marketing one since it does not only automate the process of applications' perusal, but also projects an image of the organization as equitable, transparent, and progressive

(Jamal, & al., 2024). Reputation —and even strategic diversification— AI fosters, but its primary advantages are often ignored.

Like any technology, AI systems do have some limitations, Michael & al. (2023) describes nuances and differences AI offers calling it 'discouraging.' Without direct involvement from organizational managers, employees are bound to lose motivation. Employees can be entitled to some level of context which alongside preconceptions can limit an employee's willingness to trust problem-solving technologies.

Despite addressing these formal misconceptions, Matamoros-Echeverria & al. (2025) explanation on technology's circulation through and within social and professional scaffolds describes their innovation diffusion theory with emphasis on the circulation of media as well as attention grabbing public figures, notably endorsers and their role aiding in the diffusion of technologies. In organizational contexts, these individuals help sway and manage those that initially oppose adapting a new system.

Through internal advocacy, these processes are often led by so-called "digital champions" who actively promote and validate new ideas. Successful diffusion still relies heavily on scaffolding the provided training and recognition.

As previously stated, the formal approaches to technology adoption compliance, mimicry, and legitimation deal with issues that constitute the puzzlement of many organizations. Nonetheless, we still must understand the reasoned dynamics of actual use, as the above approaches alone are not sufficient to explain this situation. This solution calls for study-designs featuring unbounded ethnographic techniques alongside the observation of daily life centered on change—and resistance to it, reinterpretation, and personal narratives of appropriation.

RESEARCH DESIGN

In order to preserve the integrity of the literature, a rigorous process was implemented, involving a systematic and methodical approach. The present process follows the guidelines of the PRISMA protocol (Preferred Reporting Items for Systematic Reviews and Meta-Analyses).

The analysis corpus consists exclusively of the Scopus database due to its extensive coverage of various academic subjects, the rigor of its material (which includes articles from peer-reviewed journals only), and its sophisticated filtering and bibliometric evaluation capabilities, which make it optimal for academic journals. In addition, a large number of methodological studies have emerged that support the use of Scopus, citing its reputation for metadata quality and interoperability with analytical software such as VOSviewer.

The Boolean query yielded a collection of articles for the period 2015-2025, which was intentionally left open, although it corresponds to the period during which relevant work on the subject was published. The criteria were meticulously defined, with an emphasis on scientific work published in peer-reviewed journals. This work focuses exclusively on the adoption of emerging technologies, such as artificial intelligence, in organizational settings.

The corpus was subjected to a systematic process divided into two consecutive stages. In the initial phase, the analysis took a qualitative approach, involving manual thematic review of the texts. This method was used to identify the dominant theoretical frameworks and critical components of the phenomenon under study.

In the next phase, a bibliometric analysis was carried out, in which co-occurrences and collaboration networks of authors were mapped using VOSviewer software.

This approach integrates exploratory quantitative analysis and qualitative interpretation, facilitating understanding of the results within a framework of methodological rigor and analytical depth.

1. Data Collection

The selection of sources is based on a systematic review in accordance with the Preferred Reporting Items for Systematic Reviews and Meta-Analyses (***PRISMA***) framework. This protocol was followed in order to structure the process of searching, filtering, and including articles, thus ensuring the transparency and reproducibility of the study.

The database used to identify articles is Scopus, recognized for its multidisciplinary coverage and academic reliability. The searches were conducted using key concepts related to the review topic: technology adoption, artificial intelligence, appropriation, employees, organizational environment, and digital transformation. Applying these keywords yielded an initial total of **80** documents.

An initial filter was applied based on the scientific fields relevant to the issue under study. The fields selected were:

- Business, Management and Accounting
- Social Sciences
- Economics, Econometrics and Finance

This thematic sorting reduced the corpus to **47** documents.

A second filter was applied based on the languages of publication. Given that the work is based on a critical content analysis requiring expert reading, only articles in English and French were retained. Publications in other languages, although potentially relevant, were not included due to a lack of sufficient linguistic competence for reliable scientific interpretation. This linguistic criterion eliminated a single document in Spanish, bringing the final corpus to **46** articles.

Finally, the accessibility of the full texts was the last inclusion criterion. Of the **46** publications selected, **28** full articles were obtained, either directly via Scopus, through open academic platforms such as ResearchGate (after requesting permission from the authors), or via Google Scholar and institutional archives.

It should be noted that no time restrictions were imposed a priori during the search. However, the publications ultimately included cover the period from 2015 to 2025, which naturally reflects the topicality of the subject and the recent rise of artificial intelligence in professional environments.

The following Scopus search was conducted, with the most recent search conducted on *April 30, 2025*. This was done to identify relevant literature based on important words related to the research topic:

(((TITLE-ABS-KEY("Digital Transformation") AND TITLE-ABS-KEY("technology adoption") AND TITLE-ABS-KEY("artificial intelligence"))) AND (LIMIT-TO (PUBSTAGE,"final")) AND (LIMIT-TO (SUBJAREA,"BUSI") OR LIMIT-TO (SUBJAREA,"SOCI") OR LIMIT-TO (SUBJAREA,"ECON")))

Table 1. Inclusion and exclusion criteria applied to selected articles

CRITERIA	INCLUSION	EXCLUSION	JUSTIFICATION
DATABASE	Scopus only	Other databases (e.g., Web of Science, IEEE, Springer)	Scopus offers broad multidisciplinary cover, high-quality metadata, and is compatible for use in bibliometric tools such as VOSviewer.
LANGUAGE	English and French	Articles in other languages	The content analysis requires expert-level reading; limited linguistic skills made it impossible to give a reliable interpretation of the other languages.
PUBLICATION PERIOD	No restrictions a priori; the resulting period covers the period 2015-2025.	—	The range reflects the natural progression of the query and takes into account the latest developments in the field.
DOCUMENT TYPE	Peer-reviewed journal articles	–	To ensure academic rigor and comparability, only peer-reviewed journal articles were selected.

continued on following page

Table 1. Continued

CRITERIA	INCLUSION	EXCLUSION	JUSTIFICATION
THEMATIC RELEVANCE	Adoption of technological tools, artificial intelligence, digital transformation, organizational environment, employees.	Studies focused solely on consumers, technical engineering, or algorithm design	This analysis focuses on the adoption of AI technology by employees within organizations, rather than consumer behavior or technical progress in the AI sector.
FULL-TEXT AVAILABILITY	Articles whose full text is accessible (via Scopus, official archives, ResearchGate, etc.)	Articles without accessible full text	Full access to the text is necessary for in-depth thematic and bibliometric analysis.

Source: Authors

Figure 1. PRISMA diagram showing the steps involved in searching, filtering, and selecting the 26 articles included in the literature review

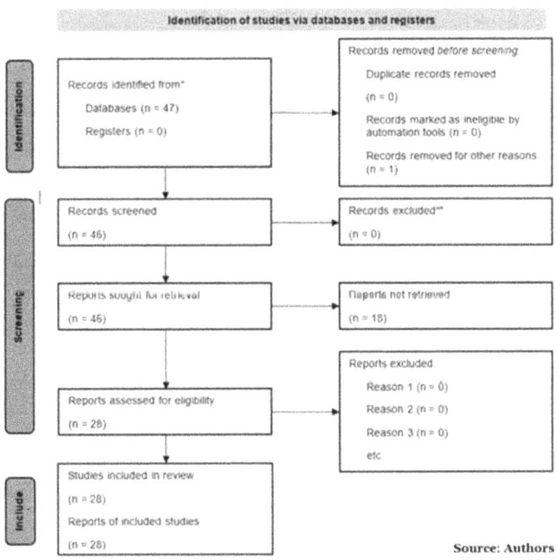

Source: Authors

2. Data Analysis

The analysis of the corpus of **28** articles was performed in two complementary stages that combine qualitative reasoning with computer-aided semantic analysis.

Document Analysis Qualitative

Every text has its central conceptual, empirical, and theoretical aspects, which were determined after a preliminary reading of the texts. For the introduction, methodology, and results sections, the authors' statements were coded, which resulted in a manual analysis. The excerpts were classified into thematic categories according to their recurrence and degree of convergence so as to delineate key issues elaborated upon in the literature, the theoretical frameworks employed like TAM, TOE, UTAUT, along with the key gaps and contradictions.

Lexicometric Analysis of Data Using VOSviewer

Furthermore, the analysis was extended to include co-word analysis using VOSviewer software which creates bibliometric maps from textual metadata and abstracts, or keywords.

This lexicometric analysis is aimed at revealing the dominant clusters of the concepts, their relationship with one another, and the underlying semantic structure of the domain.

Bearing this in mind, co-occurrence analysis was performed with VOSviewer software with the data taken from the articles' textual metadata (keywords, abstracts, titles). This software retrieves the bibliometric maps by determining terms that appear most frequently and their associates within the corpus. Terms are relationships visualized as nodes in a network and the links as the frequency of co-occurrence of these terms in the documents.

Clustering: Methods and Interpretation

The **VOSviewer** analysis operates based on a clustering algorithm known as VOS clustering. The aim of this process is to identify term clusters which suggests strong association, called as clusters that represent structuring themes within the area of interest. Every cluster is formed automatically based on the degree of association between words calculated by the method called "strength association," which is also the basis of coloring the cluster on the map.

This method is especially effective in allowing groupings along semantic lines without prejudice during the grouping stage.

The resolution parameter embedded in the software permits the grouping to be modified: higher value increases segmentation while lower value creates more global sets. During the analysis, multiple coherent thematic groupings were identified, each corresponding with the specific direction of the scientific literature pertaining to the adoption of innovative technologies.

This clustering is one of the steps in the analysis that requires arrangement, which enables the technic reading of the corpus.

It allows determining not only the prevailing themes, but also their interrelations, which help in determining the areas of convergence, as well as polarization or fragmentation. The described clusters will form the foundations of the subsequent section dedicated to results analysis.

RESULTS

The examination of 28 articles shows that there is striking variation, although some sectoral and regional biases do appear. In terms of geography, the principal focus of most research concerns developing Asian economies, primarily China and India, where the application of modern technologies like artificial intelligence (AI), digital twins, and automation is fully integrated with industrial transformation and digital ("governance") strategies (Wu & al., 2023; Anning-Dorson & Zulu, 2025). Studies on Southeast Asia and Middle Eastern countries, particularly the Gulf region, also look at the so-called modernization of procurement processes or the use of AI in public sector governance (Ashal & Morshed 2024).

At the same time, some European studies more critical in nature or more academic in their approach cover such delicate issues as generative AI risk (ChatGPT), psychosocial hazards in electronic workplaces, and semiotic politics of innovation in HRM (Bibi & al., 2024; Jamal & al., 2024). This research focuses the attention on adopting technologies constrained by culture, mimicry, and practices of heavy-danda (severe reputational damage) social surveillance.

The productivity and safety assessments of the manufacturing industries continue to be the most covered industry business studies (Forcina, & al., 2024; Broo, & Schooling, 2023). These studies elaborate on the integration of the various technological instruments in a given industrial workplace. Followed by service sectors like healthcare and education where AI functions primarily as a supportive tool for decision making or service delivery (Mauro, & al., 2024; Zhao & al., 2024). Furthermore, a branch of digital marketing exists that focuses on analyzing the interactions of customers through chatbots and recommendation systems (Xia, & Shannon, 2025).

From the organizational viewpoint, the scant literature tends to center on market-leading large corporations, presumably because they are the ones with the resources to try out or implement new technologies. There is little consideration given to SMEs or the other side, developing countries (Diaz, & al., 2024). These are remarkable exceptions. Some accessible literature stemming from a public institution and agricultural cooperative adopt curriculum critiques centered around the so-called digitally dominative technological legitimation discourse (Ciruela-Lorenzo & al., 2020; Djatmiko, & al., 2025).

The analyzed environments highlight a sharp differentiation between the, on one hand, formal well-defined environments where AI is used with purpose as a strategic lever, and on the other, more loosely defined environments related to acknowledgment, appeasement, or soft politics. This range of contexts is a methodological strength that allows for the combination of the methodological serving, critical, and institutional approaches to strategy or the use of technology within an organization.

This geographical, sectoral or organizational diversity defines the bounds of the issues covered by the studies which were analyzed. By superimposing these contexts of research with the empirical findings employed in the studies, a number of prevailing themes emerge which, in combination, point to some dominant areas of convergence synthesizing the literature along with considerable interpretative divergence based on the disciplines, methodologies or theoretical frames adopted.

The first point we would like to make, which many seem to share, is that the adoption of new technologies, especially those that involve artificial intelligence, is an issue of a strategy, organization, and human behavior, and as such, is not merely an issue of capital expenditure.

The literature is remarkably clear that the use of technology is largely determined by its perceived value, ease of utilization, and the quality of organizational services offered to employees during the change process. Those factors are completely in line with the contributions of the TAM model and which is quite frequently applied in the studies within the corpus (Zhao & al., 2024; Xia & Shannon, 2025).

In this case, some studies stress the efficiency of continuous training, explainability of automated systems, and the roles of intermediaries such as "digital champions" in maintaining employee engagement (Volberda & Khanagha, 2021). This suggests that automated systems and clarity of goals linked to a new technology are crucial for fostering trust, acceptance, and ownership of the digital tools.

Nonetheless, this more straightforward and sensible perspective on the acceptance of technology is balanced, if not outright contradicted, by other studies focusing on the adverse psychological impacts—known as technostress—that these changes can evoke. For instance, research conducted in highly controlling environments or poorly supportive contexts exposes unsettling dynamics in anxiety, stress, job insecurity, or disengagement from increasingly threatening systems (Bibi & al., 2024; Matamoros-Echeverria & al., 2025).

These effects seem to be significantly exacerbated in situations where consultation is absent before the implementation of innovations, or when unsubstantiated claims from company leaders accompany the changes.

The lack of unity around a single guiding rationale raises concerns as to why AI is viewed as a tool for achieving positive business results. First, there's an over-optimistic and purely functional attitude where AI is portrayed as a magic wand that enhances drives efficiency, optimization, and innovation. The other pole takes a rather derivative stance and addresses the social, professional, and ethical dimensions of these technologies, particularly for clients in the lower-tier decision-making or clerical administrative roles. This gap of divergence represents a more diverse set of further theoretical and methodological angles: some quantitative studies focus on the measurement of intention, while the opposite side, frequently qualitative and critical in nature, study appropriation, resistance, or legitimation mechanisms.

The portrayal of an unequivocal positive effect of technology stems from ignoring its social implications. Such attempts lead to oversimplification since every change is multifaceted. Therefore, the gap in understanding the different conditions required for successful adoption makes the hostility gap toward AI adoption entirely predictable. This rationalization of practice requires further investigation of the employees' emotional aspects, which we will analyze next based on the principles we have outlined in this study.

Focusing on these matters, a considerable portion of the literature analyzed focuses the individual level psychosocial reactions induced by new workplace technologies. These effects are not simply random. They drive, good or bad, acceptance or rejection of new technologies, and reveal to us the subjective realities silencing or unsilencing an organization's digital transformation.

Parts of the corpus document the development of anxiety, discomfort, and even passive resistance, especially in those cases where Technologies are perceived as tyrannical or dehumanizing powerful presence in the work environment. "Bibi and colleagues (2024) argue strongly that highly automated digital environments increase stress and meaninglessness for people performing judgmental or selection profile functions, even turning them into recruitment algorithms." Employees who hold such views tend to think their professional expertise is unappreciated and develop intense anxiety about becoming obsolete.

This understanding has significant implications when communications regarding instructions are lacking or when middle management discussions primarily focus on addressing concerns related to performance. The research conducted by Ciruela-Lorenzo & al. (2020) on agricultural cooperatives emphasizes that the acceptance of technologies largely relies on the organizational culture that sustains a positive collective utility rather than merely recognizing the technological compliance as a mere command issued from some higher echelon of authority.

These clusters, especially the one revolving around the Technology Readiness Index (TRI), attempt to explain the aforementioned biases attempt to explain in detail. The employees placed firmly in the technology embrace group are likely to be those with stable employment, vibrant, persistent constancy, and have a work environment where innovations are not only provided, but also explained, acknowledged, and celebrated in an orderly manner. An opposite extreme is comprised of anxious, skeptical, or resistant (Zhao & al., 2024) who have very particular support, emotional, guidance demands that in the context of their complaints, dominates the environment devoid of the technical support.

In addition to these peculiar differences, some researchers emphasize how the organizational culture might rhythmically determine the degree to which sentiments are either expressed or restrained. Generally, negative emotion tends to be dampened when changes occur in trustful, collaborative, and effort-recognizing inter-hierarchical relations (Volberda & Khanagha, 2021). On the other hand, in organizations where decision-making processes remain opaque or where a dominating pressure culture prevails, technological innovation heightens ambiguity and sometimes leads to passive disengagement.

The synthesis of this empirical evidence with the other theorical literature is, in one way or another, an illustration on how the application of technology cannot be regarded exclusively from structural or productivity perspectives. It also involves an emotional and identity-based negotiation in which fear, stress, pride, enthusiasm, and weariness emerge as decisive factors. Therefore, concerning these issues, the psychological well-being of employees is not just an ancillary concern, but rather understanding the processes of success or failure on adoption hinges on this factor.

Table 2. Summary of the empirical and contextual aspects of the articles reviewed

Analytical Aspect	Findings	Comments and References
Dominant themes	Adoption, training, transparency, trust, performance, automation	Consensus on core elements of technological acceptance and usability. Zhao & al. (2024); Xia & Shannon (2025); (Volberda & Khanagha, 2021); (Bohari & al., 2024)
Psychological reactions	Anxiety, stress, insecurity, skepticism, disengagement	Psychological responses linked to lack of support, transparency, or job clarity. Bibi & al. (2024), Wash & al. (2023); Silva & Bonetti, (2021); Lorenzo & al. (2020); (Volberda & Khanagha, 2021).
Empirical convergence	Need for human support, organizational climate influence, presence of 'digital champions'	Widespread agreement on enabling conditions for successful AI adoption. (Volberda & Khanagha, 2021); Sirimal & Bonetti (2021); Díaz-Arancibia & al. (2024), Mauro, & al., (2024); Ciruela-Lorenzo & al. (2020).

continued on following page

Table 2. Continued

Analytical Aspect	Findings	Comments and References
Empirical divergence	Positive vs. negative impacts on job roles; resistance vs. compliance; performance enhancement vs. loss of meaning	Dual narratives of digital transformation: empowerment vs. alienation. Bibi & al. (2024); Matamoros-Echeverria & al. (2025), Digital Marketing Trends and AI; Volberda & Khanagha, (2021); Michael & al. (2023), Fairness and AI Disruption.
Geographical regions	Asia (China, India), Europe, Gulf, Africa, North America	Strong representation of emerging and industrial economies; limited studies in informal or low-resource environments. Wu & al. (2023), Wang & Su (2021); Matamoros-Echeverria & al, (2025)
Sectors studied	Industry, healthcare, education, marketing, public administration	Manufacturing and public services dominate; underrepresentation of small-scale or informal sectors. Forcina & al. (2024); Mauro & al. (2024); (Díaz-Arancibia & al., 2024); (Xia & Shannon, 2025).
Organizational types	Large enterprises, cooperatives, public institutions	Micro-enterprises are rarely studied; growing interest in hybrid governance structures. Ciruela-Lorenzo & al. (2020); Jamal & al. (2024).

Source: Authors

Along with manual thematic analysis, a bibliometric approach was applied to lexically and conceptually analyze the literature on the selected topic. The analysis was performed with the aid of VOSviewer, a software tool specifically designed for creating visual representations of the semantic relationships between terms. This analysis is based on the examination of keyword co-occurrences in extracted bibliographic metadata (title, abstract, author keywords), which allows for the construction of thematic clusters that organize a particular scientific domain.

The goal is to reveal the most frequent nodes, their dominant conceptual connections, and the central organizing lines around which research on the adoption of innovative technologies is structured. The discussion that follows draws on the image supplied by VOSviewer, which was generated using the 28 selected articles.

The image is a semantic co-occurrence map where each node is a meaningful keyword. Every node's size is proportionate to its occurrence within a given corpus which indicates its importance. The connections between the nodes demonstrate semantic relationships Furthermore, the node's colors represent conceptual clusters which are frequently found in association with the articles.

Figure 2. Co-occurrence network of author keywords in the selected corpus

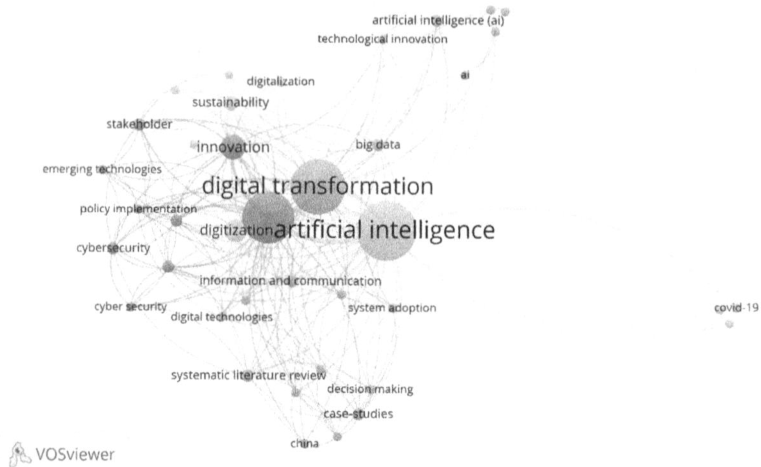

Source: Authors

This network visualization **(Fig.2.)** illustrates the co-occurrence relationships among keywords from the authors of the **28** selected articles. Each keyword has its own node. The proximity of the nodes suggests how closely related the keywords are. The lines between the keywords indicate the degree of co-occurrence, with thicker lines suggesting stronger relationships. The various colors represent clusters formed by the VOSviewer algorithm, which have been identified as thematic subdomains of the literature. Additionally, the most used and recognized keywords in the overarching research areas include "artificial intelligence," "digital transformation," and "system adoption," which characterize the semantic structure of the domain.

This analysis shows five main thematic clusters:

1. Light blue cluster: focused upon artificial intelligence alongside several system adoption strategies, decision making, COVID-19, case studies, and systematic literature review. The focus centers around organizational adoption in conjunction with case-based model analysis, particularly through TAM or UTAUT frameworks in tandem with pandemic impacts.
2. Red cluster: structured around "digital transformation" policies, digitization, implementation policy, cybersecurity, policy change, and emerging technologies. This reflects a more public policy-oriented approach to cybersecurity policy and structural reform focused ones. This cluster depicts spheres in which compliance or institutional-driven mandates dominate the technology adoption discourse.

3. Green cluster: characterized by “big data”, technological innovation, ai, and sustainability. This cluster integrates strategic innovation discourse concerning artificial intelligence exploitation and optimization, anchored to ethical and sustainability examination. It borders on TOE or institutional frameworks.
4. Yellow cluster: smaller but more integrated, centered on digitalization and stakeholders. It connects technological innovation with stakeholder engagement, and therefore may be considered as a cross-cutting pivot between organizational and institutional clusters.
5. Dark blue cluster: focused on research methods (systematic literature review, China, case studies). It demonstrates increasing attention to methodological rigor and area analyses.

Figure 3. Thematic clustering of indexed keywords related to technology adoption and artificial intelligence

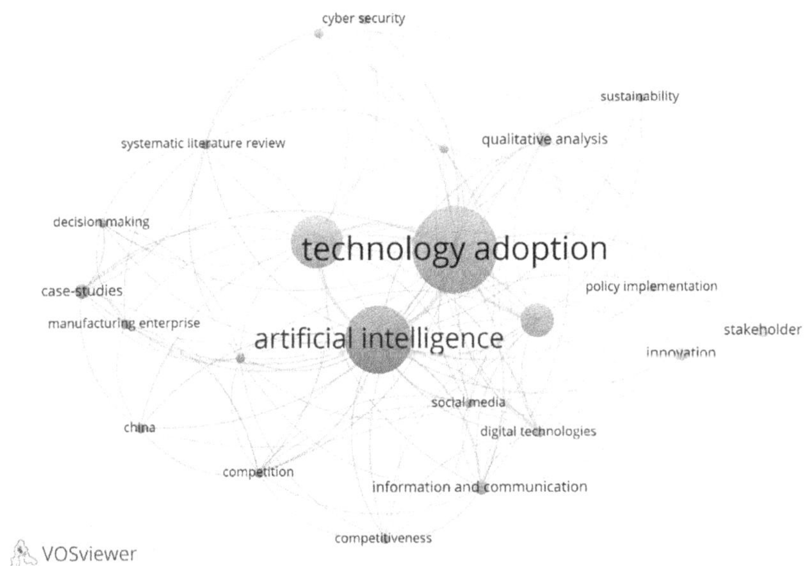

Source: Authors

The **figure 3** depicts how indexed keywords associated with particular literature are organized based on their co-occurrence. It shows the primary conceptual domains associated with ‘technology adoption’ ‘artificial intelligence,’ which were organized into five thematic groups. The node sizes correspond to the keyword occurrences, while the group colors signify thematic relations such as performance, decision making, organizational context, cybersecurity, and stakeholder participation. The map illustrates the socio-technical discourse in science concerning the adoption of artificial intelligence and its organizational factors.

This bibliometric map demonstrates a framework organized in five main clusters:

Purple cluster: Technology adoption as the main core

Related keywords: "Technology adoption," "qualitative analysis," "policy implementation," "stakeholder," "sustainability."

This cluster captures organizational and social impact analysis of adoption and consideration surrounding its participation and especially its institutional.

This is the main theoretical framework of the field highlighting peripheral institutional approaches and networks. It underscores an emphasis on sociopolitical governance underlying the use of innovative technologies.

Red cluster: Artificial Intelligence" and the industrial context

Keywords Artificial intelligence, manufacturing enterprise, China, case studies, decision making, competition.

This cluster is focused toward the more tangible, practical implementation contexts, especially in the industrial or manufacturing areas. AI is seen as a means for automating processes, decision making, and competitiveness.

These terms suggest strong empirical underpinning for the work, especially in sectoral case studies with focus on performance and strategic optimization (often in China, as noted in several articles in your corpus).

Green cluster: Security, methodology, and scientific rigor

Related keywords cyber security, systematic literature review

This cluster connects analytical methods (systematic reviews) to issues of digital security. It captures the development of a structured, rigorous, and reflective approach toward technological adoption.

It supports the notion that the field of AI and adoption research is progressively, scientifically institutionalized with standards for empirical validation. This justifies the approach you have taken in your own systematic review.

Blue cluster: Communication in a Digital Environment and Framework

Related keywords: social media, digital technologies, information and communication, global competitiveness.

A cluster focusing on tools and channels for dissemination. This includes the digitization of processes, social media, and competitive activities at a global level.

This captures organizational practices regarding social relations within and outside the workplace, particularly in terms of reputation management and visibility in the digital space.

Yellow cluster: Institutional Actors and Innovation

Related keywords: innovation, stakeholder

A linking cluster that attaches innovations with stakeholders' interest and involvement. It is positioned at the boundary of adoption logic and institutions' expectations.

This demonstrates the governance of innovation inclusiveness in other entities bound by compliance or transparency frameworks.

Figure 4. Network visualization of document citation links among selected articles

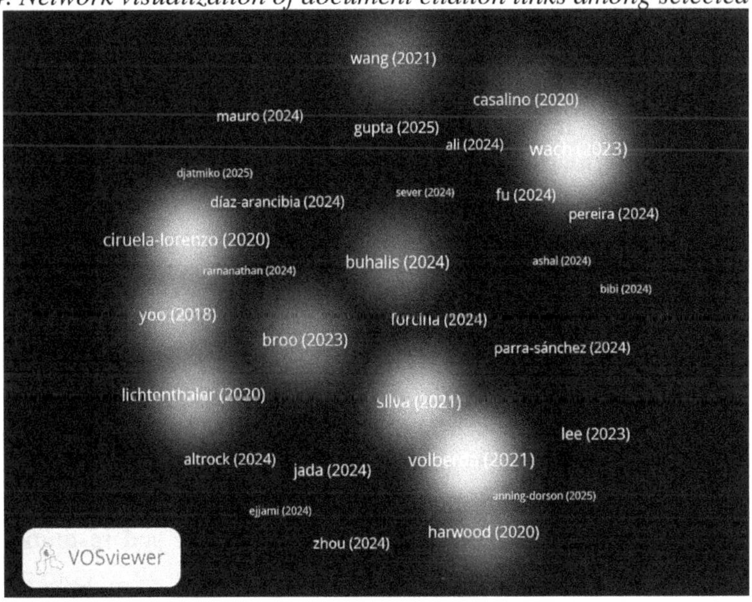

Source: Authors

This network visualization portrays the citation relationships of the 28 selected articles. The first author and year of each publication (node) is represented along with the label's size that indicates the publication's core and citation prevalence within the corpus. Nodes on the perimeter of the network and with minimal interconnections are less important. Different colors represent the groups of documents which are mutually interconnected with citations, indicating closeness in themes or methodologies. This diagram has been constructed using the VOSviewer clustering algorithm to enhance visualization of the intellectual landscape of the domain.

As shown in Figure 4, the document citation map integrates the intellectual framework of the literature by depicting articles interconnections based on citation relations. The overview reveals clusters comprising highly interconnected documents based on thematic or methodological criteria.

Central nodes in the network such as Broo (2023), Volberda (2021), and Ciruela-Lorenzo (2020) demonstrate significant interconnections suggesting these scholars have been cited by multiple studies and therefore occupy prominent positions in the network. These studies serve as foundational concepts for many others who provide scant or no attribution, offering conceptual intellectuals, theoretical ideas, or empirical frameworks on which they build. In some capacity, it appears that Broo heavily focuses on innovation strategies, while Volberda and Ciruela-Lorenzo bind organizational transformation with collective learning.

The map depicts other tighter knit sub-communities of authors as follows:

- One subset: studies organizational governance and leadership pertaining to the digital transformation within enterprises, Harwood, Volberda, Silva.
- Another subset analyzes the application of AI to institutions, industries or regions, mainly focused on tourism cooperatives, Buhalis, Díaz-Arancibia, Ciruela-Lorenzo.
- A third subset focuses on the public sector, including human resources, explainable AI, and policy making, Wach, Pereira.
- Gupta (2025) and Wang (2021) appear peripheral due to their focus on user acceptance through TAM and UTAUT but apply broader peripheral framing.

This evidence of divergence in primary themes alongside the interconnectedness of multiple lines reveals an emerging domain of research that has been considered from many diverse angles. The emphasis on orthogonality, where so many different angles—technological, organizational, psychological, and institutional—are increasingly coming together, highlighted the embrace Finial: to dominate pivot: bounded flexibility in the agnostic stretch agile innovation- adoption frameworks bounded stretch frameworks innovation agility.

Figure 5. Annual scientific output on technology adoption and artificial intelligence (2015–2025)

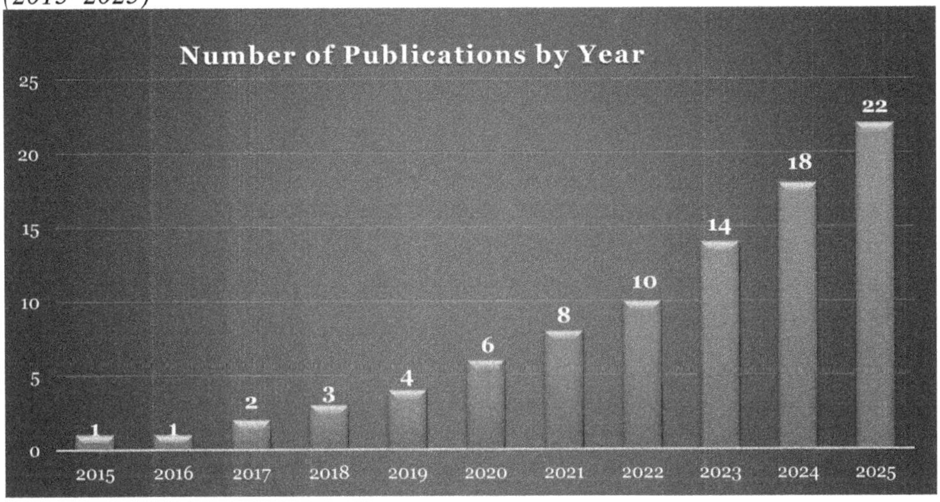

Source: Authors

This histogram demonstrates the development of the volume of scientific publications concerning the implementation of emerging technologies and artificial intelligence in relation to organizations from the perspective of Scopus indexed literature. Data is available until April 30 2025. The steady rise supports the notion of research interest increasing, especially in the past five years.

The publication output (Figure 5) shows the yearly collection of scientific publications which showcases a remarkable increase in the volume of research focused on the implementation of emerging technologies, especially artificial intelligence, in organizational settings. Publication activity during 2015-2019 was rather low, as fewer than five articles were published per year, but an increase has been noticeable since 2020. This increase coincides with the acceleration of digital transformation activities triggered by internal strategic needs and external shocks, particularly the COVID-19 pandemic.

As of April 30, Scopus marks 2025 with 22 identified publications which not only exceed the count of previous full years, but is also not yet complete. This observation as of April, assuming no further publications structure in the topic, indicates that researchers and practitioners have, or are presumed to have, sustained interest in the topic - and perhaps even increased interest as time progresses. The unprecedented rise from 6 articles in 2020 to 22 in 2025 elucidates further the deepening attention towards the intersectionally human, organizational, and technological facets of AI adoption. This also strengthens the need and timeliness of conducting this systematic review, which aims to explore, and determine the central concepts and theoretical frameworks dominant in this emerging body of knowledge.

DISCUSSION OF RESULTS

The incorporation of new technologies within firms is more than a mere technical exercise; it is a phenomenon that evokes situational understanding, socio-psychological processes, and some theoretical framing. As a part of the literature review and bibliometric analysis, the leading review suggested considerable attention regarding technology acceptance, particularly for artificial intelligence (AI), is captured in the volatile interaction of the cognitive, emotional, institutional, and strategic architecture.

The emerging trends in technology, alongside the contemporary issues of concern such as economic recession and increased competition, have now availed a unique set of solutions for the firms and industries. The way in which firms use technology has dramatically changed. It is not merely about technology anymore, and this represents a fundamental shift regarding the ways in which technology is used, integrated into, and affects society as a whole. With the advent of AI and other new technologies, the distinction between human and machine possible, controlled, controlled, efficient, and employee autonomy is swiftly changing (Zaid, 2025). Many reasons have shown that these changes are not universally valid, neither in all social systems nor under any conditions. Employees' perception, experiences, and practice of technology in the organizational context is shaped by a broad range of aspects such as cultural context, the organization's digital maturity, or the predominant leadership style (Santhi 2023; Wach 2023).

Most discussions on the success or failure of any digital initiative seldom link the thoughts to the technology used. More often, failure results from a disconnect between the system's implementations and the intended human and organizational contexts (Bohari & al., 2024; Díaz-Arancibia & al, 2024). This is where appropriation comes into play. Even where a social system exists, use, acknowledgment, or recognition of the system is not assured. Acceptance of digital technologies hinges on the social construction of meaning, undergirded by trust, transparency, and the provision of relations.

This complexity lends itself to a variety of literature. Models such as TAM and UTAUT are still being used for intention-based behavioral analyses focused on perceived usefulness, ease of use, and social influence (Zhao & al., 2024; Volberda & Khanagha, 2021). However, in many contexts, these models are often regarded as lacking sensitivity. Jamal & al. (2024) Bibi & al. (2024) extend the TRI model using empathy, emotional risk, and user assurance from a psychological standpoint. Within the TOE framework, Wang and Su (2021) add organizational readiness to the structural and contextual factors, whereas institutional theory alongside the diffusion of innovation offers explanatory models for adoption framed by noncompliance, legitimacy, and sectoral influence (Ciruela-Lorenzo & al., 2020; Anning-Dorson & Zulu, 2025).

The assessment of the documents corresponding to the 28 selected articles reveals some common themes and contradictions. Some works celebrate the efficiency and impact of AI on an institution's decision-making processes and operations while others raise serious issues about surveillance, transparency, and autonomy erosion of professional sociometers (Matamoros-Echeverria & al, 2025, Ramanathan & al, 2024). Toward changes, one dominant strategy which most stakeholders seem to embrace is disengagement that stems from insufficient transparency and absence of meaningful interaction. Organizational approaches to technologies as design autobiographies infused trust and adaptive learning frameworks offer clearly new perspectives (Forcina & Mauro, 2024).

One particularly important insight is that employee adoption cannot be reduced to individual behavior alone. There are social, institutional, and historical factors that shaped them. How innovations are received is mediated by leadership, organizational culture, communication, and strategic clarity (Volberda & Khanagha, 2021). more regulated professions like health care and education, adoption is determined as much by legal and ethical frameworks as it is by motivating performance (Broo & Schooling, 2023).

Differential inclusion also arises as an important issue. Some articles point to differences in digital competence, age, and resource availability as critical impediments to inclusive transformative change (Jada & Mayayise, 2024). Without appropriate support mechanisms, some segments of the workforce face the risk of being marginalized, which leads to either technological resistance or under-utilization. These gaps are often proposed to be filled through tailored training, co-designing processes, and active involvement of leadership.

The thematic conclusions of the study are also supported by the bibliometric analysis. The Keyword Co-occurrence maps (Figures 2 and 3) indicate the existence of dominant clusters around digital transformation, technology adoption, and AI. At the same time, document citation mapping (Figure 4) shows the most important contributions along with the converging and diverging lines of thought. The graphic representation of publication activity depicted in Figure 5 underscores the high level of scholarly activity and attention that these subjects have been commanding. Significantly, as of April 2025, publications regarding this topic have outnumbered those published in the preceding years, showcasing the increased interest in this field of research.

In addition to the theoretical frameworks and the empirical case studies which are part of the documents analyzed, the outcomes from the bibliometric analysis—specifically those using VOSviewer—offer an insightful pathway to visualize the field's structure and its dynamics. The keyword co-occurrence maps (Figures 2 and 3) demonstrate semantic convergence around keywords AI, technology adoption and digital transformation. These clusters confirm the proximity of the managerial, technological and organizational debates, while also providing additional insights regarding the debates' differences.

The citation map (Figure 4) pinpoints the landmark works that anchor the discipline. Scholars Broo (2023), Volberda (2021), and Ciruela-Lorenzo (2020) constitute vital intellectual nodes. The empirical and conceptual bears telling relevance to appropriation, digital resistance, and institutional isomorphism concerning his work in enduring frameworks. So many authors ascribed such importance to them that it is likely that their work is emerging canon of reference which legitimizes research directions, and pluralistic methodologies construct appropriation.

The corpus sheds light on the political and ethical aspects of the digital transformation. A group of authors led by Jamal & al. argues about the control, monitoring, and governance implications of Technological instruments like explainable AI (XAI). Organizational settings where performance evaluation is conducted through automized or opaque mechanisms devoid of ethical and participatory safeguards or oversight often raises ethical concerns. One predominant suggestion focuses on the blurring of discursive boundaries to fair technical and ungoverned discourse whilst transcending the borders of speaking about technical issues only towards fairness and inclusive governance.

Simultaneously, an important issue common to several articles is the relevance of training and cognitive scaffolding towards effective appropriation. The literature suggests that organizational readiness should not stop at the infrastructure level, but that organizational emotional and didactic supports must also be provided. As Bibi & al. (2024) and Volberda & Khanagha, (2021) point out, employees appreciate innovation much more when they feel management cares about their development and when they are able to slowly discover the system's affordances in a manageable, low-stakes setting.

In this regard, organizational culture appears to surface as a critical moderator of technological change. Structures that promote conversation, innovation, and appreciation are more favorable in attaining digital transformations as sustaining routines. On the other hand, compliance-based, top-down models are more likely to engender superficial compliance while pursuing denial of authentic participation. As Forcina & Mauro (2024) observes, the successful fulfillment of AI system's integration most of the time does not depend on technical execution, but rather on ostensible congruence peripheral to the organization's values and identity.

In addition, several contributions argue that the adoption of technology, especially, should be understood as a life-cycle process rather than an adoption or rejection event. Successful digital transitions are characterized by learning loops, trial phases, redesign, and appropriation rituals. These technologies for organizations only become 'real' after interpretation, testing, modification, and gradual embedding into practice is done. This requires greater micro-dynamics and narrative analysis focus within transformation studies.

From these considerations, we see that the worth of technology is not inherent, but rather co-constructed. Whether an AI tool is perceived as enabling or alienating is not solely dependent on its practicality—its engagement, control, and purpose within the organization also determine its value. This perspective overlooks the symbolic and cultural aspects.

As this review highlights, there is a need to integrate psychological variables at the individual level with organizational meso models and macro institutional ones. It is only with such combing frameworks that one can address the diversity of user experiences and the multilayered nature of digital transformations. In the same way, practitioners are encouraged to broaden their approaches beyond systems development to strategies that include trust cultivation, co-construction, and the establishment of enduring legitimacy processes.

CONCLUSION

This systematic review confirms that the adoption of new organizational technologies, especially artificial intelligence, cannot be treated exclusively as a technological challenge. An analysis of twenty-eight articles indicates that technology adoption is an emotionally charged and contentious process shaped by numerous psychological, structural, institutional, and other influences. The foremost theoretical frameworks—TAM, UTAUT, TRI, TOE, and even institutional theory—offer compelling but fragmented explanations regarding the enabling and constraining aspects of digital transformation.

Through keyword co-occurrence analysis in VOSviewer, Figures 2 and 3 reveal the semantic structure and predominant attention areas in the field. Besides the focal concepts "digital transformation," "artificial intelligence," "technology adoption," and others that are starting to take shape such as stakeholder participation, organizational trust, trust in organizations, and cybersecurity. The document citation network in Figure 4 illustrates further evidence of the scientific intertextuality of foundational contributions by showing which works anchor the field along with Figure 5's publication benchmarks chart showing the increasing scholarly interest from 2024 into early 2025. This rise showcases the relevance and context of the discourse.

This research exemplifies, from a theoretical perspective, the additional value brought by pluralist integration. While TAM and UTAUT continue to work in explaining user intentions and behavioral drivers (Zhao & al., 2024; Xia & Shannon, 2025), they require supplementation with context and institutional frameworks such as TRI and institutional theory, which encompass emotions, social norms, and compliance reflexes (Volberda & Khanagha, 2021; Matamoros-Echeverria & al., 2025). More precisely, the TRI framework shows that AI engagement is severely disabled by unease and insecurity in socially constrained resource-depleted or acutely hierarchical dominator settings (Bibi & al., 2024).

While this review incorporates methodological triangulation, some gaps still exist. First, the review is based on 28 articles sourced from the Scopus database. While comprehensive, this selection may miss relevant works published in non-indexed periodicals or other languages. Second, a majority of the studies included in the review concentrate on formally occupational sectors with pre-existing institutional arrangements, focusing primarily on large public and private enterprises and public sector institutions, which neglects the informal sector and SMEs from poorer regions (Wu & al., 2023; Anning-Dorson & Zulu, 2025). Third, many of the models—especially TAM and UTAUT—rest on rational choice theory, thus inhibiting the incorporation of emotional, ethical, and symbolic elements pertaining to technological change.

Regarding the future perspectives of the project, the following research directions can be outlined:

1. The informal economy poses significant challenges for sociological research. The studied regions focus primarily on social innovation phenomena, where innovation, resistance and appropriation are prominent features.
2. The overlaps of anxiety, burnout, and TRI studied identity loss are relevant for the development of technology acceptance models. It would be preferable to integrate them into the readiness and well-being frameworks.
3. A qualitative approach combined with quantitative methods significantly contributes to broadening the interpretation of intention to action by incorporating organizational and narrative perspectives alongside informal feedback systems.
4. Normative ethics on AR include social and ethical relevance such as focus, unfair transparency, and responsibility concerning the use of concealed social AI systems (Jamal & al., 2024; Díaz-Arancibia & al, 2024).

Ultimately, economic and digital sustainability, alongside social inclusivity, cannot rely solely on the efficacy of technology. It needs a strategy that is participant focused and takes into account organizational behavior. With the growing proliferation of digital systems, research and studies must incorporate emotional, contextual, and institutional intricacies into their frameworks.

REFERENCES

Altrock, S., Mention, A.-L., & Aas, T. H. (2023). Being Human in the Digitally Enabled Workplace: Insights From the Robo-Advice Literature, in IEEE Transactions on Engineering Management, vol. 71, pp. 7876-7891, 2024, Doi: DOI: 10.1109/TEM.2023.3291820

Ashal, N., & Morshed, A. (2024). Transforming Procurement in the Arab Gulf: Integrating AI, Blockchain, and BI Tools for Enhanced Efficiency and Strategic Decision-Making Journal of Logistics. *Informatics and Service Science, 11*(9), 266–279. DOI: 10.33168/JLISS.2024.0917

Bibi, M., Ajaz, M. A., Akaak, A. S., Noureen, S., & Alghizzawi, M. (2024). How the family business hotels of Europe are reshaping business models with AI and big data. In *Strategies and Approaches of Corporate Social Responsibility and Governance*. IGI Global.

Bohari, A., Wider, W., Udang, L. N., Jiang, L., & Tang, Y. (2024). Transformational leadership's role in shaping Education 4.0 within higher education. Journal of Infrastructure. *Policy and Development, 8*(8), 4900. Advance online publication. DOI: 10.24294/jipd.v8i8.4900

Broo, D. G., & Schooling, J. (2023). Digital twins in infrastructure: Definitions, current practices, challenges and strategies. *International Journal of Construction Management, 23*(4), 1–16. DOI: 10.1080/15623599.2021.1966980

Buhalis, D., Efthymiou, L., Uzunboylu, N., & Thrassou, A. (2024). Charting the progress of technology adoption in tourism and hospitality in the era of industry 4.0. *EuroMed Journal of Business, 19*(1), 1–20. DOI: 10.1108/EMJB-11-2023-0310

Ciruela-Lorenzo, A. M., Del-Aguila-Obra, A. R., Padilla-Meléndez, A., & Fernández-Portal, M. (2020). Digitalization of agri-cooperatives in the smart agriculture context: Proposal of a digital diagnosis tool. *Sustainability (Basel), 15*(12), 9999. Advance online publication. DOI: 10.3390/su12041325

Díaz-Arancibia, J., Hochstetter-Diez, J., Bustamante-Mora, A., Sepúlveda-Cuevas, S., Albayay, I., & Arango-López, J. (2024). Bustamante- Mora, A.; Sepúlveda-Cuevas, S.; Albayay, I.; Arango-López, J. (2024). Navigating Digital Transformation and Technology Adoption: A Literature Review from Small and Medium-Sized Enterprises in Developing Countries. *Sustainability (Basel), 16*(14), 5946. DOI: 10.3390/su16145946

Djatmiko, G. H., Sinaga, O., & Pawirosumarto, S. (2025). Digital Transformation and Social Inclusion in Public Services: A Qualitative Analysis of E-Government Adoption for Marginalized Communities in Sustainable Governance. *Sustainability (Basel), 17*(7), 2908. DOI: 10.3390/su17072908

Forcina, A., Silvestri, L., De Felice, F., & Falcone, D. (2024). Exploring Industry 4.0 technologies to improve industrial resilience: A sociotechnical perspective. *Safety Science, 169*, 106351. Advance online publication. DOI: 10.1016/j.ssci.2023.106351

Harwood, S., & Eaves, S. (2020). Conceptualising technology, its development and future: The six genres of technology. *Technological Forecasting and Social Change, 160*, 120174. DOI: 10.1016/j.techfore.2020.120174 PMID: 32904525

Jamal, A., Aissaoui, K., & Kassal, S. (2024). Enhancing Recruitment Transparency and Efficiency with Explainable AI (XAI). In 2024 3rd International Conference on Embedded Systems and Artificial Intelligence (ESAI) (pp. 1-6). IEEE.

Matamoros-Echeverria, K. L., Sanchez-Leon, E. R., & Toledo-Orozco, M. (2025). The Impact of Artificial Intelligence on the Digital Economy: A Review of Economic, Social and Technological Dimensions. *Journal of Posthumanism, 3*(1), 23–38. DOI: 10.33182/joph.v3i1.3368

Mauro, M., Noto, G., Prenestini, A., & Sarto, F. (2024). Digital transformation in healthcare: Assessing the role of digital technologies for managerial support processes. *Technological Forecasting and Social Change, 209*, 123781. Advance online publication. DOI: 10.1016/j.techfore.2024.123781

Mocanu, C., Matei, M. M. M., & Năstasă, A. (2024). Patterns of Artificial Intelligence Adoption in Small and Medium Businesses. In Fotea, S. L., Văduva, S. A., & Fotea, I. Ş. (Eds.), *Reimagining Capitalism in a Post-Globalization World. GSMAC 2023. Springer Proceedings in Business and Economics*. Springer., DOI: 10.1007/978-3-031-59858-6_26

Pereira, L., Resio, M., Costa, R., Dias, Á., & Gonçalves, R. (2021). Artificial Intelligence in Strategic Business Management: The Case of Auditing. *International Journal of Business Information Systems, 1*(1), 10039269. Advance online publication. DOI: 10.1504/IJBIS.2021.10039269

Ramanathan, S., Tang, S. G. H., Afzal, M. M., & Ker, P. J. (2024). Artificial Intelligence and Socioeconomic Impacts of Pandemic: Key Roles and Potentials. World Journal of Science. *Technology and Sustainable Development, 19*(3–4), 205–218. DOI: 10.1108/WJSTSD-01-2023-0002

Sang, N. M. (2024). Bibliometric insights into the evolution of digital marketing trends. *Innovative Marketing*, *20*(2), 1–14. DOI: 10.21511/im.20(2).2024.01

Santhi, R., Tang, S. G. H., Afzal, M. M., & Ker, P. J. (2023). The relevance of artificial intelligence in mitigating socio-economic impacts of COVID-19 and future epidemics. *World Sustainable Development Outlook*, *21*, 105–118.

Silva, E. S., & Bonetti, F. (2021). Digital humans in fashion: Will consumers interact? *Journal of Retailing and Consumer Services*, *60*, 102430. Advance online publication. DOI: 10.1016/j.jretconser.2020.102430

Volberda, H. W., Khanagha, S., Baden-Fuller, C., Mihalache, O. R., & Birkinshaw, J. (2021). Strategizing in a digital world: Overcoming cognitive barriers, reconfiguring routines and introducing new organizational forms. *Long Range Planning*, *54*(5), 102110. DOI: 10.1016/j.lrp.2021.102110

Wach, K., Duong, C. D., Ejdys, J., Kazlauskaitė, R., & Simionescu, M. (2023). The dark side of generative artificial intelligence: The risk of "technostress" among employees in Europe. *Entrepreneurial Business and Economics Review*, *11*(2), 7–24. DOI: 10.15678/EBER.2023.110201

Wang, Y.-Y., & Su, X. (2021). Driving factors of digital transformation for manufacturing enterprises: A multi-case study from China. *International Journal of Technology Management*, *87*(2/3/4), 229. DOI: 10.1504/IJTM.2021.120932

Xia, Z., & Shannon, R. (2025). Navigating the Digital Frontier. Exploring the Dynamics of Customer–Brand Relationships Through AI Chatbots. *Sustainability (Basel)*, *2025*(17), 2173. DOI: 10.3390/su17052173

Xiao, J. Xu, Z. Xiao, A. Wang, X. Skare, M. (2024);Overcoming barriers and seizing opportunities in the innovative adoption of next-generation digital technologies, Journal of Innovation & Knowledge, Volume 9, Issue 4, .DOI: 10.1016/j.jik.2024.100622

Yoo, S.-K., & Kim, B.-Y. (2018). A Decision-Making Model for Adopting a Cloud Computing System. *Sustainability (Basel)*, *10*(8), 2952. Advance online publication. DOI: 10.3390/su10082952

Zaid, M., Farooqi, R., & Azmi, S. N. (2025). Driving sustainable supply chain performance through artificial intelligence and big data analytics. In *Handbook of Research on Big Data and Artificial Intelligence in the Supply Chain* (pp. xx–xx). IGI Global., DOI: 10.4018/978-1-6684-6810-3.ch011

Zhao, Y., Li, Y., Xiao, Y., Chang, H., & Liu, B. (2024). Factors influencing the acceptance of ChatGPT in higher education: A quantitative analysis of student attitudes and behavioral intentions. *SAGE Open*, *14*(1). Advance online publication. DOI: 10.1177/21582440241234567

Chapter 2
Artificial Intelligence in Human Resource Management and Work Motivation: A Systematic Review

Sabah Laflafli
https://orcid.org/0009-0000-4560-5503
Cadi Ayyad University, Morocco

Charaf Saidi
https://orcid.org/0009-0007-3125-7561
Cadi Ayyad University, Morocco

ABSTRACT

Artificial technologies are evolving exponentially within organizations in a variety of managerial practices. The integration of artificial intelligence has been a growing trend in recent years, particularly for streamlining human resources processes and boosting employee performance. Organizations face a variety of challenges in successfully introducing AI to managerial practices, including boosting work motivation in the age of artificial technology. This study aims to examine the effect of artificial intelligence on work motivation. A systematic literature methodology was used, based on artificial intelligence and work motivation. The systematic literature review provided an analytical, critical and synthetic examination of the articles included in the database, following a rigorous examination according to the Prisma 2020 diagram. The results imply a significant effect of AI on work motivation. It is also worth highlighting the scarcity of research on the integration of artificial

DOI: 10.4018/979-8-3373-5499-6.ch002

intelligence and its effect on organizational behavior, particularly work motivation.

INTRODUCTION

Artificial intelligence is rapidly emerging in a variety of fields, including education, healthcare and finance. It is also reaching a stage where it can rival humans in terms of creativity, thanks to its rapid learning in various fields and possession of a vast database (Lin, 2023). In the age of digital transformation, human resources management is currently undergoing changes, including the introduction of artificial intelligence, with the aim of streamlining human resources processes and boosting employee efficiency and performance. In effect, the integration of artificial intelligence tools within organizations makes it possible to optimize the recruitment process, improve performance appraisal management and facilitate the rationalization of employee professional training (Almaraghin, 2024). However, organizations are currently facing major challenges resulting from the introduction of new information technologies such as artificial intelligence, in terms of adapting human capital to exponential technological change, which will have a considerable impact on positive work outcomes through positive employee behaviors and attitudes, including work motivation. In this context, the integration of these new technologies requires respect for fundamental human values (Binns et al., 2018). From the above, it is worth highlighting the importance of the effect of introducing artificial technology on individual attitudes and behaviors, to ensure consistency and alignment between rapid technological change and positive workplace outcomes. Some studies on artificial intelligence and managerial practices, particularly in the field of human resource management, has highlighted the existing relationship between artificial intelligence and employee motivation in an organizational context (Almaraghi, 2024; Allam, 2024; Lin, 2023).

Employee motivation is a key to individual and collective efficiency and performance, which in turn strengthens and improves overall performance in both private and public organizations. Motivation is a key element contributing to more sustainable performance (Deci & Ryan, 1985). Many other studies have established a positive link between motivation and individual performance (Vansteenkiste et al., 2004; Gillet & Vallerand, 2016). However, the introduction of artificial intelligence into the organizational environment is likely to affect employee motivation at work and, indirectly, individual performance. Therefore, it seems important to highlight the effect of the introduction of these technologies on work motivation (Budhwar et al., 2022; Chowdhury et al., 2023). This study aims to investigate the effect of the integration of artificial intelligence on employee motivation, particularly in the field of human resource management. A systematic literature review will be conducted to identify the potential impact of this introduction on work motivation, in the light of previous empirical work from a database selected from academic databases.

The introduction of artificial intelligence into a given environment or domain is likely to influence employee motivation accordingly. Therefore, the introduction of this technological trend in human resources management can contribute to strengthening motivation at work, through organizational equity, which can manifest itself, for example, in the process of evaluating employee performance and skills (Lin, 2023). Conversely, a study of 20 employees in a company sampled as «junior staff», « level managers» and « department managers», reveals that the introduction of artificial intelligence may contribute to a decline in work motivation due to reduced remuneration, increased managerial and professional demands, and the increased requirement for a high level of knowledge and post-graduate training. The aim of the present study is therefore to expose the potential link between the key variables identified, and to highlight the mechanisms involved in improving work motivation in the era of the emergence of artificial technologies in an organizational context.

To explore the link between the introduction of artificial intelligence in human resource management and work motivation, our research adopts a systematic literature review methodology, enabling us to conduct a structured and rigorous literature review of scientific articles that address the effect of artificial intelligence on work motivation. To this end, an in-depth search will be carried out in several academic databases, to ensure the quality and relevance of the articles making up our database. In addition, our systematic literature review will focus on work published over the last five years. It should be noted that our study adopts inclusion and exclusion criteria, which will be presented in detail in the methodology section of our scientific article. Next, the data extracted from this systematic review will be the subject of a Prisma 2020 diagram and an analysis of the data by year and continent. This article will be structured in two distinct parts. In the first part, the focus is on the conceptual foundations of artificial intelligence and work motivation. The second part focuses on the methodology applied and the analysis of the data generated by the systematic review approach. Finally, the results obtained will be discussed, followed by perspectives for future research.

1. CONCEPTUAL AND THEORETICAL FRAMEWORK

1.1. Artificial Intelligence

Artificial intelligence is one of the essential tools for resolving complex malfunctions. Historically, artificial intelligence technology emerged in the early 1950s with the introduction of Alan Turing's Turing Test (1950), which assessed the intelligence of technological systems (machines) by answering the question « Can machines think? » This test confirms the intelligence of machines and their ability to mimic the human cognitive mind (Parveen & Palaniammal, 2019; AL-thabhawee, 2025). Since the 1950s, the concept of artificial intelligence has continued to develop right up to the present day (XXth century), thanks to the development of various tools such as the ability to process and analyze bigdata, also known as cloud computing, and deep learning (Al-Talidi, 2021).

In his book « life3.0: being human in the age of artificial intelligence», Max tegmark (2017) points out that artificial intelligence is an algorithmic component that enables even the most complex goals to be achieved (Max tegmark, 2017). On the other hand, Alan Turing (1950), the founding father of artificial intelligence (AI), sees artificial intelligence technology as a science and engineering that tends towards the production of computer programs characterized by human intelligence. According to Boubay (2022), artificial intelligence refers to the ability of machines or robots to perform acts that were previously necessarily performed by human beings, such as logical reasoning, learning and generalizing past experiences. In 2023, the European Parliament describes artificial intelligence as a technology able to process and analyse large databases by adopting human reasoning and machine learning, with a view to generating specific solutions.

For Marvin Minsky (1960), one of the pioneers of artificial intelligence, the latter is defined as the programming of computing machines able to perform tasks requiring a high level of intellectual intelligence, which have always been performed by human beings, such as machine learning, intellectual reasoning and decision-making (Russell & Norvig, 2016). In this sense, artificial intelligence tends towards the development of intelligent machines with a high rational capacity to solve complex problems and automate their learning. Indeed, it has demonstrated its ultimate ability to surpass human intelligence in terms of efficiency in accomplishing tasks in various domains and within reduced timeframes, while underlining its inability to absolutely mimic human intelligence (Moustaid, 2025).

Generally, artificial intelligence is nothing more than systems that mimic the cognitive processes of human beings using mathematical algorithms (Sutton & Barto, 2018). Technically, artificial intelligence technology is a set of advanced technologies that enable systems to process big data and improve their performance through the process of automatic algorithmic learning (Goodfellow et al., 2016). In addition, it has proved its crucial ability to simulate, rather than replace, the human cognitive process by performing complex actions in the analysis of massive data in various business sectors (Brynjolfsson & McAfee, 2014). Artificial intelligence technology refers to a series of emerging tools that help streamline and optimize processes to achieve a high level of efficiency in various fields. This technology is also emerging in the field of human resources management, with a view to facilitating various processes such as recruitment, competency management and performance appraisal, with a view to streamlining and optimizing these decision-making processes (Davenport et al., 2020).

Artificial intelligence constitutes a science of ideas attributed to machines in order to improve the latter's ability to think, judge and criticize by mimicking human cognitive intelligence (Ashe, 2019). In addition, the integration of artificial intelligence into computing machines makes them more capable of adopting logical reasoning close to that of human beings, enabling these machines to perform tasks that had for decades been achieved through human dependence and intelligence (Khattab, 2021). Consequently, the field of human resources management is modernizing its processes, integrating various types of artificial intelligence, in order to benefit from its characteristics of objectivity and transparency in decision-making. These features are likely to boost confidence and job satisfaction, in turn stimulating employee motivation to generate more effective results.

1.2. Artificial Intelligence: Theoretical Framework

Theoretically, artificial intelligence is a multi-disciplinary concept that is rooted in several theoretical currents. Neural network theory was developed in 1969 by two theorists, Minsky and Papert. Their work aimed to create computer models with the ability to learn automatically from data, in order to make the machine more adaptable to solving malfunctions and more complex problems, while drawing inspiration from the way the human brain works. This theoretical trend has contributed to the creation of applications based on neural networks, enabling intelligent task execution and problem solving in various fields of activity. Long after the advent of neural network modeling, machine learning theory (Hastie, Tibshirani, & Friedman, 2001) developed. This theory has made considerable and significant progress in the field of artificial technologies, particularly in the areas of data analysis, prediction and natural language processing. In fact, this trend aims to develop algorithms and models capable of learning and improving their decision-making capacity through experience, which is known as « machine learning ».

By 2003, the discipline of artificial intelligence had moved beyond the analysis and processing of data to the processing of visual data in autonomous systems such as autonomous vehicles and robots. In this perspective, computer vision theory (Hartley & Zisserman, 2003), through deep learning, has enabled the development of computer models for the automatic recognition of more complex objects and scenes. This rapid evolution of artificial intelligence technologies has proven their considerable and significant contribution to the improvement of various fields such as health, education and business.

The development of artificial technologies in various fields has given rise to a number of debates on the question of ethics and transparency. In this respect, the Ethical Artificial Intelligence Theory has emerged as a result of various works that have attempted to highlight the importance of this reflection (Hanson, 2016; Müller, 2020). This theory highlights the ethical issues involved in the design and use of artificial intelligence technologies. It also emphasizes the responsibility and accountability of artificial intelligence systems, in addition to highlighting the mechanisms that ensure fair and ethical use and decision-making on the part of users. Certainly, artificial intelligence technologies help to improve decision-making, efficiency and task automation, but they can also generate risks and challenges associated with their implementation, and can sometimes be a source of value destruction (Wamba-Taguimdje et al., 2020). The literature has highlighted a number of principles and mechanisms involved in ensuring digital ethics, including transparency, accountability, security, confidentiality and fairness (De Laat, 2021; Rivero et al., 2022).

As a result, it is essential to emphasize that artificial intelligence technologies have undergone progressive developments in various fields, aiming to invest their advantages in improving task efficiency and automated, rapid resolution of complex problems by adopting human cognitive processes and machine learning (machine learning theory (Hastie, Tibshirani, & Friedman, 2001)). Artificial transition is also emerging in the field of human resources management, with the aim of automating tasks, guaranteeing transparency and fairness in individual performance evaluation processes, as well as efficient decision-making by managers in terms of training needs, talent management and recruitment processes. It is therefore interesting to see how these technologies contribute to the development of human resources management processes in a work environment.

1.3. Artificial Intelligence in HR Processes

The emergence of artificial intelligence has given rise to various artificial technologies, such as machine learning and natural language processing (NLP). First of all, machine learning is an integral part of artificial intelligence, which is able to analyze and exploit voluminous data (big data) and automatically learning continuously to progressively improve its performance in resolving malfunctions and completing tasks (Jordan & Mitchell, 2015). So, these new artificial technologies adopt a human intelligence process based on reflection and automatic learning from experience. Human resources management also benefits from this new artificial technology, with the aim of improving and optimizing its human capital management processes. Based on algorithms for voluminous analysis of the organization's employee history in terms of training, job performance, professional behavior, personality traits and envisaged needs. From the above, it is necessary to emphasize that machine learning systems help organizations to enhance individual performance, by proposing personalized and rational competency management strategies for training engineering, skills development and employees' professional careers. Furthermore, the emergence of artificial intelligence in the field of human resources is making a major contribution to enhancing the transparency and ethical nature of human resources processes in terms of recruitment, talent management and the objective, ethical assessment of individual employee performance.

Machine learning systems also contribute, on the basis of algorithms, to providing personalized recommendations based on received databases (Ricci et al., 2015). The present logic tends to analyze a behavioral database, then to understand it intelligently, in order to provide personalized instructions and actions for each user and this, according to needs and detected malfunctions. As a result, this sub-domain offers a range of benefits for human resources management, for example by proposing training programs that are mutually consistent with employees' needs and the organization's strategy (Sparrow, 2016), while taking into account the well-being of human capital in terms of work motivation, career development and skills enhancement, which directly affects their performance at work as much as organizational performance.

In this perspective, the sub-domains of artificial intelligence, through their systems for personalizing recommendations and actions, can contribute to the objective and optimal improvement of human capital management strategies in terms of commitment and motivation at work, based on an individualized approach which in turn contributes to a global and efficient management of human resources with a view to facilitating access to organizational performance. These sub-domains also include AI support as an integral and innovative branch of artificial intelligence, referred to as « natural language processing» (NLP). The latter is an artificial conversational system that mimics the understanding and interpretation of human language, in addition to its ability to facilitate human interaction (Manning & Schütze, 1999).

Effectively, the integration of this type of innovative technology into human capital management facilitates interactions with employees and ensures accessibility and availability at all times, 24/7 and on a variety of subjects (leave, benefits, salary, training, career development), which is likely to boost motivation, satisfaction and commitment at work (Bersin, 2018). This intelligent interaction process, such as HR chatbots, results in increased trust in the organization thanks to their objective, transparent and more ethical nature. So, it's worth pointing out the close link between artificial intelligence tools in human resources management, citing AI assistance as an example, and motivation at work thanks to the transparent and ethical character perceived by employees during intelligent interactions. What's more, self-determination theory (SDT) has shown that satisfying the three psychological needs, including the need for competence, considerably helps to develop and maintain motivation at work. It follows that integrating new artificial technologies for the satisfaction of psychological needs at work, through the personalized and individual treatment of employee needs, can further contribute to the reinforcement and development of motivation at work.

Briefly, artificial intelligence is a science of ideas attributed to machines in order to improve their ability to think, judge and criticize by mimicking human cognitive intelligence (Ashe, 2019). What's more, the integration of these new artificial technologies into computing machines has made them more capable of adopting logical reasoning close to that of human beings, enabling these machines to perform tasks that have for decades been carried out through human dependence and intelligence (Khattab, 2021). As a result, the field of human resources management is modernizing its processes, integrating various types of artificial intelligence, in order to benefit from its characteristics of objectivity and transparency in decision-making, which is likely to overturn knowledge and findings in work psychology with regard to commitment, performance and motivation at work. These characteristics are likely to boost confidence and job satisfaction, in turn stimulating employee motivation and producing higher-performance results, or on the contrary to diminish employee motivation by affecting their well-being and mental health at work in terms of technostress, technological insecurity, resistance to change and habit.

1.4. Artificial Intelligence and Work Motivation

The integration of artificial intelligence technology into human resources practices remains a favorable practice in large organizations, thanks to its perceived contribution in terms of optimization, facilitation and its anticipatory approach to the fair and effective management of motivation at work. Indeed, the integration of artificial intelligence into human resources practices helps to improve the analysis of employee performance and behavior, by proposing personalized objectives for each profile in line with the organization's short and long-term strategy, thanks to advanced artificial intelligence algorithms. To this end, personalizing the treatment of employees in terms of defined actions and performance to be assessed, identified rewards and preferred climate helps boost motivation at work (Davenport et al., 2020).

The ability demonstrated by artificial intelligence systems in various fields, including big data analysis, recommendation systems and natural language processing, can enable the organization to gain in terms of efficiency in the management of human resources, which can have a stimulating effect on their motivation at work. The American multinational « International Business Machines Corporation » (IBM), for example, has mobilized artificial intelligence to quickly and easily identify signs of employee disengagement, with a view to strengthening their commitment to the organization (Liptak, 2022). In turn, the Google team has taken advantage of the anticipatory approach of artificial intelligence to boost employee engagement and motivation at work. For this, they are focusing their efforts on recognition processes and employee well-being in their work environment (Bersin, 2019).

In this context, the integration of artificial intelligence into human resources management enables anticipatory management of human capital by optimizing HR processes (recruitment, performance evaluation, competency management) and proposing proactive corrective actions, based on the continuous analysis of big data, with a view to improving the human capital management strategy, which can have an impact on job satisfaction, commitment and motivation. On the other hand, the positive effect of integrating artificial intelligence on employee motivation (intrinsic, extrinsic), is likely to be conditioned by its use in an ethical and transparent way, which can motivate individuals to perform their tasks perfectly, thanks to the feeling of trust towards the reliability and transparency of their performance assessment and HRM decisions (Allam et al., 2024).

Personalized human resources management, or the automation of daily tasks based on artificial intelligence technologies, are all new mechanisms for managing human resources processes that can help increase motivation at work (Manzoor et al., 2021; Almaraghi, 2024). Furthermore, Prasetyo (2021) highlight various benefits of using artificial intelligence technologies within organizations, including the reduction of transactional costs, the rationalization and objectification of management mechanisms, and above all the facilitation of internal communication, to make it more fluid and efficient. AI-based information systems represent a real revolution for human resources management, due to their ability to influence individual and collective organizational behaviors and attitudes through fluid and personalized internal communication, not to mention the sense of real support they provide to employees (Welch & Brantmeier, 2021), which can have a significant impact on employee motivation.

Following this line of thought, this article will highlight the existing links between these two key concepts in the light of a literature review, by using a systematic literature review. In an era of increasing artificial transition, it is important to draw attention to the significant effects of the emergence of artificial technologies on work psychology, such as employee well-being, job satisfaction and organizational commitment. Consequently, our work focuses particularly on the concept of work motivation following the introduction of artificial intelligence technologies in human resource management. While the field of human resource management has for decades highlighted a number of organizational behaviors that contribute to organizational development and performance, the notion of work motivation remains one of the ultimate factors in motivating individuals to perform tasks perfectly, and above all in boosting individual performance.

2. METHODOLOGICAL FRAMEWORK

2.1. Search Strategy

In order to answer the research question, we decided to follow a systematic literature review, in order to achieve a more structured and rigorous analysis rather than a conventional review. This study will define the temporal and partial dimension, and highlight the results generated by the main works in the database, selected according to the Prisma guidelines. The research will be structured as a systematic literature review, focusing on the main journals in our field of research: the field of social and management sciences, in particular the field of human resource management. As part of this research, we collect a database of academic articles, in particular indexed journals, to guarantee the reliability of the information gathered. These international academic databases cover various disciplines, including the social sciences, in particular the sub-disciplines of work motivation, human resource management and artificial intelligence.

In order to clarify and include as much research as possible, we focused on the new artificial technology known as « artificial intelligence», and on work motivation as key factors in human resource management. In our research, we focused on human resource motivation, because of its considerable effects, according to the literature, on stimulating individual and collective employee effectiveness and performance, which is a key element for more sustainable performance (Deci & Ryan, 1985). Consequently, this work focuses on academic work that simultaneously includes the effect of artificial intelligence on work motivation. To do this, the academic articles that will be used in this research are identified by using the appropriate keywords in English and French. This choice is motivated by the predominance of the English language in international scientific research on artificial intelligence, particularly in China, the USA and Asia. In addition, in order to broaden the linguistic field, we aim to include studies carried out in francophone countries. The aim of this linguistic field is to optimize the comprehensiveness of research on different continents.

By analyzing the literature, we identified the key concepts for formulating the search function using Boolean operators. Indeed, the first domain concerns artificial technology and includes the following keywords: « artificial intelligence », « AI » and « intelligence artificielle ». The second area focuses on keywords such as « work motivation » and « motivation au travail ». The third area concerns human resources management, and includes « Human Resource Management », « HRM », and «Gestion des ressources humaines ». As a result, these keywords were combined using the Boolean operators AND/OR, under the following formula: ("Artificial Intelligence" OR "Intelligence artificielle" OR "AI") AND ("Work motivation"

OR "Motivation au travail") AND ("Human Resource Management" OR "HRM" OR "Gestion des ressources humaines").

2.2. Study Selection

In this study, we opted for a systematic literature review, recognized by a rigorous and structured methodology compared to a classic literature review. This review involves a structured and rigorous examination of the collected articles in order to select only those that remain relevant to answer the research question, based on keywords, title and abstract. This critical approach also requires the definition of exclusion and inclusion criteria to limit the scope of the search. These allow us to select scientific articles that perfectly answer the research question, and consequently, the article database included in the analysis remains relevant and of high quality, helping to specifically address the research problem. To this end, the inclusion and exclusion criteria are presented as follows:

2.2.1. Inclusion Criteria

Based on the research objective, which concerns the effect of the introduction of artificial intelligence in human resource management on motivation at work, we chose to highlight the inclusion of publications, published both in English and in French, in order to guarantee the comprehensiveness of research work around this topic, and this choice is explained by the dominance of scientific publications in English, while French is also used in various Francophone journals and countries. For greater precision, our search focused on publications covering the period 2020-2025, given the growing advent of artificial intelligence technologies after 2020. Aligning with the temporal and linguistic framework, the inclusion of publications in our database implies taking into consideration scientific works that illustrate certain criteria, namely: publications examining the effect and link between artificial intelligence and motivation, accessibility of research results for evaluation, as well as the inclusion of predefined keywords in the title, abstract, keywords.

2.2.2. Exclusion Criteria

To ensure the relevance of the articles included, the definition of exclusion criteria also remains essential according to the systematic approach to the literature. Thus, publications excluded from the selected database are those that include certain keywords but do not focus on artificial intelligence and work motivation, and articles that focus exclusively on artificial intelligence or work motivation.

Furthermore, it should be noted that books and book chapters are excluded because they are not peer-reviewed or only lightly peer-reviewed and/or often do not include an empirical part of the research (Dekker & Bekkers, 2015). To guarantee the scientific rigor of our systematic approach, we opted for the Prisma methodology (prisma flowchart) for article selection (McKenzie JE, Bossuyt PM, et al., 2021). The diagram below illustrates the article selection process derived from the critical review of academic data sources, in three main stages: article identification, article selection and article inclusion.

Figure 1. Prisma flow chart

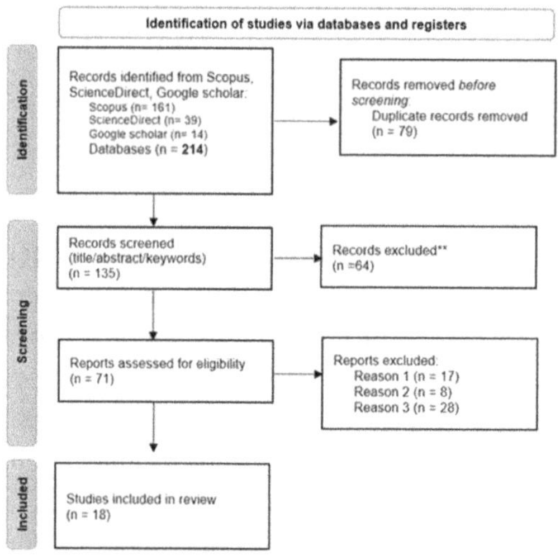

3. RESULTS AND DATABASE ANALYSIS

In order to carry out our analysis of the selected database by adapting to it the good practices outlined (Tursunbayeva et al., 2019), it is appropriate, as part of our systematic review, to study the trends of the publications included in our systematic review, according to continents, year of publication, and applied research methodology. The publication trends according to continent of publication in the figure below, show a high concentration of publications on artificial intelligence and work motivation in European countries (N=6; 33%), followed by Asian countries (N=4; 22%), while research in North America (N=3; 17%), the Middle East and Africa

(N=3; 17%) remains moderate and insufficient. The remainder of publications are attributed to Oceanic countries (Australia; N=2; 11%) with a remarkable scarcity of publications concerning the link between job motivation and the integration of AI. Based on the graph below, Europe accounts for the highest number of publications on the effect of the integration of artificial technologies on employee well-being in terms of work motivation, which can be explained by the importance attached to the subject of psychological and organizational development in an era of strong growth in artificial intelligence, and in different fields and professions. However, North American countries account for only 17% of publications, half as many as European countries. This percentage can probably be explained by the growing attention paid to the development of these new technologies (AI) with regard to their effect on the mental health of individuals.

Figure 2. Publications by continent

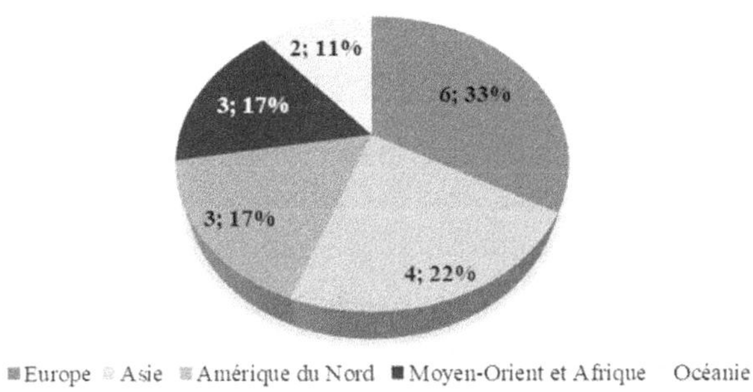

Furthermore, by diagnosing our database in terms of temporal consistency, we were able to observe a fluctuation in the number of publications by year of publication of the included articles over the predefined period (2020-2025). As figure shows, research on the link between artificial intelligence and work motivation increased exponentially between 2023-2024, with a peak in 2024 (N=11), demonstrating the growing importance of the subject of artificial intelligence and its effect on motivation at work, with a view to improving the process of integrating new artificial technologies into human resource management, while acting on the behavior and well-being of individuals. It's worth mentioning the considerable scarcity of research in this area between 2020-2023, which reflects the limited attention paid by researchers to organizational attitudes and behaviors in favor of integrating artificial intelligence into the organizational context (2020; N= 0), (2022; N= 3), (2023; N= 2). Based on this diagnosis, it appears that most of the work will take place in the 2022-2024 period, which can be explained by the rapid evolution of artificial intelligence tools in the field of human resources management. The emergence of artificial intelligence tools in human resources processes has prompted researchers and specialists in work psychology and the human and social sciences to align themselves with this growth from a motivational point of view. The concentration of research work on the theme of artificial intelligence and motivation at work during the above-mentioned period demonstrates the originality and topicality of our research problem, which can be the subject of confirmatory empirical analysis.

Figure 3. Year of publications

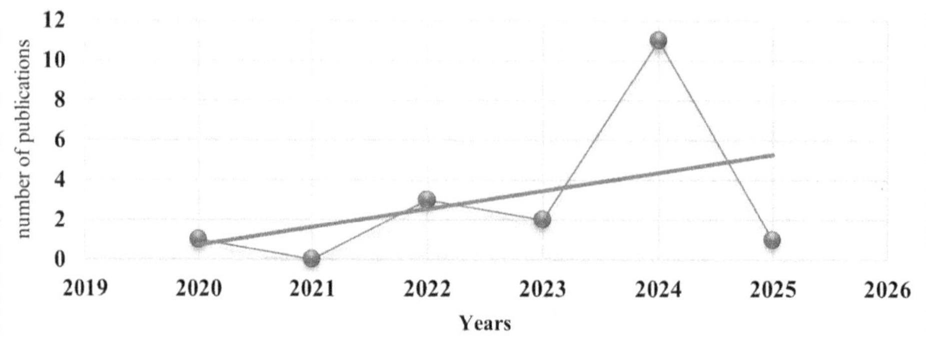

Analysis of the co-occurrence of keywords from the publications included in our final systematic review enables us to visualize the frequency of keywords, with their linking clusters. Figure below shows the visualization of key concepts extracted from the database of publications included in the systematic review analysis, generated by Vosviewer software. The diagram below illustrates the relationships and connections existing between the different keywords of the included publications dealing with artificial intelligence and work motivation. In this perspective, the nodes represent the keywords frequently used in the various articles in the database analyzed, and each node illustrates a set of links in the form of lines representing the frequency and strength of the keywords crossed between them.

Figure 4. Mapping of keyword co-occurrence

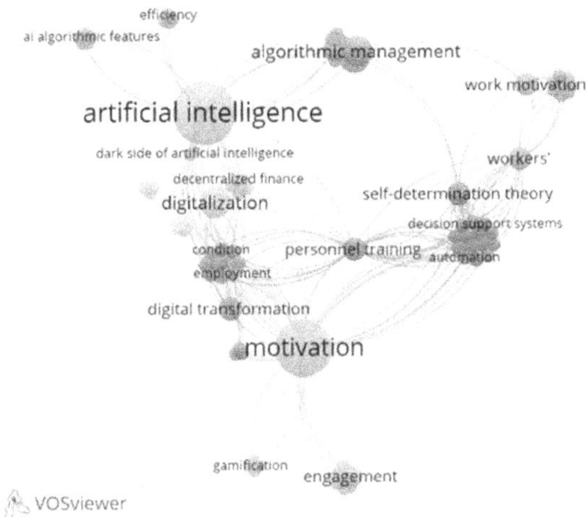

Source: Vosviewer

According to figure 4 above, the « artificial intelligence » cluster focuses on the concept of artificial intelligence, whose main keywords are « artificial intelligence », « algorithm », « algorithm management » and « digitization ». This tag cloud shows the strong and important link between these concepts in discussions on the new technology of artificial intelligence. The cluster illustrates the focus on the concept of « motivation», highlighting its close links with other concepts in other clusters, including « artificial intelligence », « algorithm », « digitalization », « self-determination theory ». Finally, these different clusters show the different concerns and close links between them, demonstrating the connections that exist when it comes to integrating artificial intelligence and individual motivation into the organizational environment.

4. DISCUSSION

The systematic literature review has shown the importance of the topic of work motivation in the age of artificial transition within organizations, and also in the context of human resource management processes. Over the past five years, many research studies have attempted to examine the effect of artificial intelligence technologies on organizational attitudes and behaviors, such as work motivation, organizational commitment and individual and collective performance. In particular, our research follows the systematic literature review approach, having highlighted the effect of artificial intelligence or artificial algorithms on employee motivation.

The results of the study show that the improvement of work motivation in the era of the introduction of artificial intelligence algorithms to the organizational environment depends on the indirect and significant effect of the work environment. For example, an organization whose work climate remains favorable for its employees can improve efficiency and employee commitment through favorable motivation (Dharmawan & Hartantono, 2024). Furthermore, the work of Dharmawan and Hartantono, (2024) conducted among 402 formal sector employees (DKI Jakarta province), and confirmed the positive correlation ($Cr= 0.71$, $t = 10.98$, $p < 0.001$) between artificial intelligence algorithms and work motivation. Thus, it is essential to underline that the importance placed on job requirements and resources within an organization for its employees, in the era of digital transformation (DT), has a significant impact on employee motivation, which in turn influences work engagement (Ye & Chen, 2024). Employees with a positive perception of performance appraisal have a positive effect on motivation (Collie et al., 2024). In addition, the integration of artificial intelligence into the organizational context increases employees' self-motivation, insofar as artificial intelligence algorithms help them to effectively achieve their goals, thus giving rise to a sense of internal motivation at work (Yakovenko et al., 2022). As a consequence, the integration of artificial intelligence algorithms in the workplace can help reinforce employees' need for autonomy, cited in self-determination theory (Deci & Ryan, 1985) as one of the psychological needs leading to improved motivation at work.

However, research carried out in the age of artificial intelligence has led to the development of a 4- step diagram of the employee life cycle: « needs - interests - incentives (motivations) – results » (Yakovenko et al., 2022). This schema is perfectly aligned with the principle of self-determination theory (SDT), which explains perfectly the link between the satisfaction of employee needs and positive results (performance, commitment, profitability), through the reinforcement of individual/collective, intrinsic/extrinsic or material/immaterial interests and incentives. Accordingly, the literature review on artificial intelligence tools in the field of human resources management, through advanced algorithms, has demonstrated an effective contribution to the personalization of employee needs through integrated databases. As a result, employees' needs can be met intelligently and individually, which in turn helps to improve motivation at work and achieve the desired results.

Nevertheless, some studies on the effect of artificial intelligence on organizational behavior, particularly work motivation, highlight the negative effect of introducing artificial intelligence technology into the organizational environment on employee motivation, leading to a reduction in employee focus (Hamarat et al., 2024). In addition to the positive effects of artificial intelligence at work, it is also likely to negatively affect positive work outcomes. In fact, artificial intelligence technology can increase the stress associated with technico-organizational change, employee dependency and skill requirements in the recruitment process, which in turn indirectly and negatively affects work motivation, and of course organizational effectiveness and commitment.

Furthermore, it should be noted that the stress of anticipating changes in the development of new technologies, such as artificial intelligence, in an organizational and managerial context, can in some cases contribute to a decrease in employee motivation (Collie et al., 2024). This leads to the conclusion that employee motivation in an organizational environment is subjective, and depends on individuals' perception of the integration of these new artificial technologies into their daily organizational lives. From another perspective, Mustafayev and colleagues (2024) conducted a study of 200 employees of 3 banks in Azerbaijan, on the effect of artificial intelligence on the work motivation of bank employees in Azerbaijan. The study showed a negative correlation between artificial intelligence update density and work motivation. As a result, it should be noted that AI-related change in the organizational environment is also likely to have a negative impact on work motivation, i.e. the increase in AI updates decreases work motivation. Overall, it can be noted that the level of motivation at work can differ from one environment to another, depending on various extrinsic or intrinsic factors, such as the specific characteristics of a community, the personality traits of individuals, or employees' resistance to change, citing for example the results of a study carried out among bank employees in Azerbaijan.

In addition, a number of authors have highlighted the impact of full and partial automation of decision-making on work motivation and organizational commitment. For this reason, an empirical analysis carried out on 102 participants from the manufacturing industry, approved that full automation of the decision-making process, without the integration of the human effect had a negative impact on employees' self-determined motivation, whereas during the partially automated process; partial integration of AI and human balance, work motivation was enhanced, in addition to organizational commitment (Passalacqua et al., 2024).

The integration of artificial intelligence in human resources management has a positive effect on employee motivation, as it helps them to perform assigned tasks efficiently thanks to the moderating effect of incentives or rewards, such as bonuses, recognition at work and the satisfaction of training and skills development needs in digital technology, including artificial intelligence (AL-Thabhawee, 2025). In the same context, the work of Qasem Almaraghi (2024) on the role of artificial intelligence in human resources management to improve work productivity and motivate employees, among 200 human resources management employees in Jordan, showed the positive effect of introducing artificial intelligence into HR processes, such as optimizing recruitment processes, objectivity and transparency in employee performance appraisals, improving the working environment and employee morale, thus enhancing the sense of motivation at work. Furthermore, in 2024, Edwards' work on the impact of automated human resource management processes on employee motivation revealed that organizations that integrate algorithmic human resource management systems based on artificial intelligence, experience higher levels of extrinsic motivation at work. Based on the above, organizations whose employees had a positive perception of the use of algorithmic systems in human resource management demonstrated higher levels of intrinsic motivation and lower levels of emotional exhaustion (Edwards et al., 2024). It is therefore worth noting that the integration of artificial systems into human resources management enhances both extrinsic and intrinsic motivation, without denying the considerable impact these systems have on employee behavior and well-being.

Dong et al., (2024) examined the comparison between AI-based and human-based management on participants' attitudes and behaviors, including performance, intrinsic motivation, perception of fairness and commitment. This study showed the significant similarity between AI-based management and human-based management on performance, intrinsic motivation, perception of fairness and commitment, In other words, the integration of artificial intelligence for human resource management can have the same results on fluctuations in employee motivation. On the basis of the above, the analysis carried out highlighted the considerable effect of artificial intelligence technologies on work motivation within an organizational environment. At the same time, it's important to highlight the importance of reinforcing individual well-being in the face of exponential artificial technological development. However, some authors have demonstrated the positive and significant effect of artificial intelligence on work motivation (Dharmawan & Hartantono, 2024 ; Ye & Chen, 2024 ; Collie et al., 2024 ; Yakovenko et al., 2022 ; AL-Thabhawee, 2025 ; Almaraghi, 2024 ; Edwards et al, 2024 ; Dong et al., 2024), including human resources management, while other authors have revealed the considerable negative impact of integrating these new artificial technologies into the organizational world (Dharmawan & Hartantono, 2024; Ye & Chen, 2024; Collie et al., 2024; Yakovenko et al., 2022). Briefly, the appended table summarizes the above-mentioned studies in our database, selected according to the systematic approach, with an overview of the results obtained and the means and approach used by the authors.

To conclude, analysis of our database has revealed a scarcity of research linking artificial intelligence to work motivation, although there has been an evolution in recent years, particularly since 2023. This paucity of research in this field highlighted the lack of attention paid to the effects of integrating artificial intelligence into the organizational context on well-being and organizational behaviors. The study also highlighted prospects for future research by integrating other variables such as personality traits, workload or working conditions. Without denying the originality and topicality of the present research problem in the field of work psychology and especially in the field of human resources management. From this, it remains important to encourage research into the attitudes and behaviors of individuals in the age of artificial intelligence, with a view to achieving coherence between the extreme development of new artificial technologies and the well-being of individuals. Finally, future research might try to understand to understand the relationship between technological change and the organizational attitudes of employees, or the determinants of improved or reinforced intrinsic motivation, in the era of the integration of artificial intelligence into the organizational environment.

CONCLUSION

In an environment where artificial intelligence technologies are evolving rapidly, organizations are faced with the real challenge of aligning the benefits of artificial intelligence technologies with the risks they bring. To do this, the organization needs to implement a set of efforts to reap the digital benefits, while improving employee well-being and motivation. Therefore, while integrating AI tools, the organization must maintain the principle of transparency of AI tools and facilitate the understanding of decisions made in the age of artificial intelligence, in order to avoid employee resistance to change and improve their well-being at work. Furthermore, the relationship between artificial intelligence technologies and individual well-being remains important to ensure the proper integration of these technologies into managerial practices and human resources management processes.

Our study aims to investigate the effect of artificial intelligence on work motivation, using a systematic literature review. A systematic literature review of selected articles has enabled us to identify publication trends by year and continent. To enrich our diagnosis, an analysis of the co-occurrence of keywords from the publications included in our final systematic review enabled us to visualize the frequency of keywords, with their linking clusters. analysis of the works selected from the database highlighted the positive and significant effect for certain authors of artificial intelligence on work motivation and desired outcomes for an organization such as organizational commitment, productivity and performance (Dharmawan & Hartantono, 2024; Ye & Chen, 2024; Collie et al., 2024; Yakovenko et al., 2022). On the other hand, other research has demonstrated the decline in work motivation in the era of artificial transition in an organizational environment (Mustafayev et al., 2024; Hamarat et al., 2024; Passalacqua et al., 2024).

On another front, some authors have tried to examine the link between the integration of artificial systems in the management of human resources processes and employee motivation. These works have implied the positive and considerable effect of artificial systems for the management of human resources, by reinforcing the extrinsic and intrinsic motivation of employees, without denying the considerable impact of these systems on the behavior and well-being of employees (AL-Thabhawee, 2025; Almaraghi, 2024; Edwards et al., 2024; Dong et al., 2024). As a result, it is evident that today's organizations are more inclined to adopt mechanisms to facilitate the introduction of artificial intelligence tools into the human resources management process, as well as to improve the trust established between man and machine in order to positively influence their motivation at work, and subsequently their individual performance.

Recommendations

The advent of artificial intelligence has seen a significant evolution in human resources management processes, with the aim of automating and improving talent and competency management, training, recruitment and performance appraisal processes. In order to make the current artificial transition a success at both organizational and individual levels, managers need to ensure compliance with ethical principles, and more specifically to control the use of artificial intelligence tools in human capital management practices in an ethical and regulatory manner.

The majority of work on artificial intelligence focuses on the effect of new technologies in mimicking human cognitive processes, rather than replacing them. For this reason, organizations need to help provide a supportive environment for employees in the AI implementation phase, by reinforcing and encouraging collaboration between employees and AI tools. The participative approach has amply demonstrated its impact on organizational and behavioral changes within a work environment. As a result, the involvement and adoption of a participative approach towards employees in the decision-making process for the design and use of artificial intelligence can contribute to the successful introduction of artificial intelligence tools into human resources management processes, and to maintaining a high level of motivation at work.

In brief, consideration of the above elements can help maintain a favorable environment in which the integration of artificial intelligence tools into human resource management promotes rather than reduces motivation at work. The ultimate goal is to implement new artificial technologies in collaboration with employees, and by ensuring a sense of satisfaction of the psychological needs that enable improved work motivation, in order to achieve positive outcomes such as organizational commitment and work performance.

Overall, we strongly recommend that human resources managers and organizational leaders pay attention to the motivational aspect of employees when faced with the integration and use of artificial intelligence tools in human resources mechanisms such as training, performance assessment and recruitment. Managers must therefore ensure alignment and balance between artificial transition and employee mental health, which in turn has a significant effect on desired outcomes.

Future Research Directions

The challenge for organizations is to maintain a balance between the integration of artificial technologies and desired organizational outcomes, in particular by optimizing the effect of this artificial transition on the organizational well-being of employees. The emergence of artificial intelligence tools in the field of human resources management offers many managerial and organizational benefits, but also raises questions and challenges of alignment between technological transition and human and motivational well-being at work.

Furthermore, scientific research into artificial intelligence in the context of human resource management cannot be limited exclusively to the opportunities it offers, but it would be wise for future research to focus on the mechanisms aimed at the success and alignment of the artificial transition of organizations with the well-being and professional fulfillment of employees. Our study focused on the effect of integrating artificial intelligence technologies on work motivation in the field of human resource management, in the light of a systematic literature review. For this reason, we suggest that future research examine this research issue using a quantitative or qualitative methodological approach for field confirmation.

Moreover, it is necessary to pursue research in this field, with particular emphasis on examining the impact of artificial intelligence on intrinsic and extrinsic motivation, in order to understand the in-depth effect of these technologies on the dimensions of work motivation. At the same time, the integration of certain endogenous variables, such as individual personality traits, or exogenous variables, such as workload, could constitute a new direction for researchers in the field of human resource management in this era marked by advances in artificial technology.

Finally, in the era of the growing emergence of artificial intelligence technologies, scientific research must focus on understanding the motivational dynamics of employees, with a view to enhancing commitment and organizational performance. It must also contribute to the generation of knowledge, in collaboration with practitioners in the field, on the policies and strategies to be deployed for the successful and effective integration of artificial intelligence tools into a work environment.

REFERENCES

AL-Thabhawee. (2025). Artificial intelligence and its role in human resources management. International Journal of Accounting, Management [IJAMESC]. *Economics and Social Sciences*, *3*(1), 1–20. DOI: 10.61990/ijamesc.v3i1.353

Allam, Y., Habachi, M., & Tabit, Y. (2024). Intelligence artificielle et la motivation RH: Revue théorique. International Journal of Accounting, Finance, Auditing. *Management and Economics*, *5*(12), 602–613. DOI: 10.5281/zenodo.14538222

Almaraghi, D. M. Q. (2024). Artificial intelligence and the future of human resource management: Data analysis and decision guidance to enhance work productivity and employee motivation. *Pakistan Journal of Life and Social Sciences*, *22*(2). Advance online publication. DOI: 10.57239/PJLSS-2024-22.2.00910

Chilunjika, A., Intauno, K., & Chilunjika, S.R. (2022). Artificial intelligence and public sector human resource management in South Africa: Opportunities, challenges and prospects. SA Journal of Human Resource Management, 20(0). . v20i0.1972DOI: <ALIGNMENT.qj></ALIGNMENT>10.4102/sajhrm

Collie, R. J., Martin, A. J., & Gasevic, D. (2024). Teachers' generative AI self-efficacy, valuing, and integration at work: Examining job resources and demands. *Computers and Education: Artificial Intelligence*, *7*(100333), 100333. Advance online publication. DOI: 10.1016/j.caeai.2024.100333

Deci, E. L., & Ryan, R. M. (1985). The general causality orientations scale: Self-determination in personality. *Journal of Research in Personality*, *19*(2), 109–134. DOI: 10.1016/0092-6566(85)90023-6

Dharmawan, A. P., & Hartantono, N., & Lasmy. (2024). Role of generative artificial intelligence and work environment on the motivation of workers. *3rd International Conference on Creative Communication and Innovative Technology (ICCIT)*, 1–5. DOI: 10.1109/ICCIT62134.2024.10701197

Dong, M., Bonnefon, J. F., & Rahwan, I. (2024). Toward human-centered AI management: Methodological challenges and future directions. *Technovation*, *131*(102953), 102953. Advance online publication. DOI: 10.1016/j.technovation.2024.102953

Edwards, M. R., Zubielevitch, E., Okimoto, T., Parker, S., & Anseel, F. (2024). Managerial control or feedback provision: How perceptions of algorithmic HR systems shape employee motivation, behavior, and well-being. *Human Resource Management*, *63*(4), 691–710. DOI: 10.1002/hrm.22218

Forest, J., & Mageau, G.A. (2008). La motivation au travail selon la théorie de l'autodétermination. Psychologie Québec, 25(5).

Gagné, M., Parent-Rocheleau, X., Bujold, A., Gaudet, M.-C., & Lirio, P. (2022). How algorithmic management influences worker motivation: A self-determination theory perspective. *Psychologie Canadienne, 63*(2), 247–260. DOI: 10.1037/cap0000324

Hamarat, H., Sahin, H., Koç Apuhan, A., & İnan, R. (2024). The dark side of artificial intelligence: Threats to tourism workers. *Worldwide Hospitality and Tourism Themes, 16*(2), 127–137. DOI: 10.1108/WHATT-03-2024-0061

Ikhide, J. E., Timur, A. T., & Ogunmokun, O. A. (2023). A balanced perspective on the affordance of a gamified HRM system for employees' creative performance. *Personnel Review, 52*(3), 631–648. DOI: 10.1108/PR-01-2021-0062

Lin, S. (2023). Based on the Two-factor Theory, The Influence of Artificial Intelligence on Employee Motivation Is Analyzed. *Frontiers in Business, Economics and Management, 11*(3), 91–94. DOI: 10.54097/fbem.v11i3.13194

Moustaid, E., & Moflih, Y. (2024). L'impact de l'introduction de l'intelligence artificielle sur le marché du travail. *Revue Française d'Economie et de Gestion, 5*(7), 249–271.

Mustafayev, M. (2024). The impact of artificial intelligence on the motivation of bank employees in Azerbaijan. In Lecture Notes in Networks and Systems. International Conference on Smart Environment and Green Technologies, 1252. Springer. DOI: 10.1007/978-3-031-81564-5_45

Nawaz, N., Arunachalam, H., Pathi, B. K., & Gajenderan, V. (2024). The adoption of artificial intelligence in human resources management practices. *International Journal of Information Management Data Insights, 4*(1), 100208. Advance online publication. DOI: 10.1016/j.jjimei.2023.100208

Oladipo, E. K., Adeyemo, S. F., Oluwasanya, G. J., Oyinloye, O. R., Oyeyiola, O. H., Akinrinmade, I. D., Elutade, O. A., Areo, D. O., Hamzat, I. O., Olakanmi, O. D., Ayanronbi, I. I., Akanmu, A. J., Ajekiigbe, F. O., Taiwo, M. O., Ogunfidodo, V. M., Adekunle, C. A., Adeleke, P. O., Olubunmi, D. A., Adeogun, P. A., & Nnaji, N. D. (2024). Impact and Challenges of Artificial Intelligence Integration in the African Health Sector: A Review. *Trends in Medical Research, 19*(1), 220–235. Advance online publication. DOI: 10.3923/tmr.2024.220.235

Parent-Rocheleau, X., & Parker, S. K. (2022). Algorithms as work designers: How algorithmic management influences the design of jobs. *Human Resource Management Review*, *32*(3), 100838. Advance online publication. DOI: 10.1016/j.hrmr.2021.100838

Passalacqua, M., Pellerin, R., Yahia, E., Magnani, F., Rosin, F., Joblot, L., & Léger, P.-M. (2024). Practice with less AI makes perfect: Partially automated AI during training leads to better worker motivation, engagement, and skill acquisition. *International Journal of Human-Computer Interaction*, *1*(21). Advance online publication. DOI: 10.1080/10447318.2024.2319914

Sadeghi, S. (2024). Employee well-being in the age of AI: Perceptions, concerns, behaviors, and outcomes. DOI: 10.48550/ARXIV.2412.04796

Vinichenko, M. V., Melnichuk, A. V., & Karácsony, P. (2020). Technologies of improving the university efficiency by using artificial intelligence: Motivational aspect. *Journal of Entrepreneurship and Sustainability Issues*, *7*(4), 2696–2714. DOI: 10.9770/jesi.2020.7.4(9)

Yakovenko, Y. Y., Bilyk, M. Y., & Oliinyk, Y. V. (2022). The transformative impact of the development of artificial intelligence on employment and work motivation in business in the conditions of the information economy. 2022 IEEE 4th International Conference on Modern Electrical and Energy System (MEES).

Yang, X., & Yan, S. (2024). Encourage or reject employee involvement: Value creation in Human Resource Management in the AI era-an evolutionary game analysis of enterprises and employees. *Behavioral Sciences (Basel, Switzerland)*, *14*(12), 1220. Advance online publication. DOI: 10.3390/bs14121220 PMID: 39767361

Ye, Y., & Chen, K.-H. (2024). Hospitality employees and digital transformation: The mediating roles of alienation and motivation. *International Journal of Hospitality Management*, *119*(103731), 103731. Advance online publication. DOI: 10.1016/j.ijhm.2024.103731

Yilmaz, R., & Karaoglan Yilmaz, F. G. (2023). The effect of generative artificial intelligence (AI)-based tool use on students' computational thinking skills, programming self-efficacy and motivation. *Computers and Education: Artificial Intelligence.*, *4*, 100147. Advance online publication. DOI: 10.1016/j.caeai.2023.100147

Zhou, Y., Wang, L., & Chen, W. (2023). The dark side of AI-enabled HRM on employees based on AI algorithmic features. *Journal of Organizational Change Management*, *36*(7), 1222–1241. DOI: 10.1108/JOCM-10-2022-0308

KEY TERMS AND DEFINITIONS

Artificial Intelligence: Artificial intelligence is an algorithmic technology designed to solve the most complex problems. It is defined as machines or robots capable of performing tasks that have already been carried out by human beings, and of analyzing large databases.

Motivation at Work: This is the feeling of pleasure that employees derive from accomplishing the tasks assigned to them, while at the same time ensuring efficiency and performance. An individual's motivation encompasses both intrinsic and extrinsic motivation. The latter can be stimulated by incentives and rewards.

Systematic Literature Review: A structured and rigorous literature review methodology, which aims to select the articles included in the systematic analysis or meta-analysis of a big database. This methodology is known by the use of the PRISMA 2020 Cheek List and PRISMA diagram.

Human Resources Management: Is the discipline of managing recruitment processes, performance evaluation and employee competency management. It aims to optimize human capital management processes and practices, with a view to guaranteeing commitment and performance in the workplace.

Work Performance: Refers to the performance of individuals in relation to their work, encompassing task performance and contextual performance within organizational environments.

Work Commitment: Is the positive attachment employees feel towards the organization. It can contribute to the smooth running of the organization in the short term, as well as to long-term performance in tasks and attitudes of organizational citizenship.

Système Algorithm RH: These are artificial intelligence-based systems designed to help HR managers streamline and optimize human resources processes, in employee performance appraisal, talent management and recruitment, as well as competency management.

APPENDIX

Table 1. Annex: summary bibliography of articles included in the systematic review

Authors	Year	Title	Published	Research objectives	Methodology	Sample	Findings
Collie, R. J., Martin, A. J., Gasevic, D.	2024	Teachers' generative AI self-efficacy, valuing, and integration at work: Examining job resources and demands	Computers and Education: Artificial Intelligence	Study the contextual factors influencing teachers' motivation and commitment to exploiting generative AI.	Quantitative	339 primary (56%) and secondary (39%) school teachers in Australia.	Perceived positive evaluation of AI had a positive effect on motivation, with a higher result for secondary school teachers in a teaching context. Stress associated with workplace changes due to the integration of new technologies reduced their motivation to integrate AI.
Dharmawan, A.P. & Hartantono, N.	2024	Role of Generative Artificial Intelligence and Work Environment on the Motivation of Workers	2024 3rd International Conference on Creative Communication and Innovative Technology, ICCIT 2024	Studies the impact of generative artificial intelligence (GAI) and the work environment on the motivation of formal sector workers in the province of DKI Jakarta.	Quantitative	402 formal sector employees in the province of DKI Jakarta	GAI is positively correlated with work motivation (regression coefficient = 0.71, $t = 10.98$, $p < 0.001$). the work environment has a significant indirect effect on the GAI-motivation relationship ($\beta = 0.55$, $p < 0.001$). Sophisticated AI technologies and a supportive organizational climate enable improved employee effectiveness and engagement.

continued on following page

Table 1. Continued

Authors	Year	Title	Published	Research objectives	Methodology	Sample	Findings
Yakovenko, Y.Y., Bilyk, M.Y., Oliinyk, Y.V.	2022	The Transformative Impact of the Development of Artificial Intelligence on Employment and Work Motivation in Business in the Conditions of the Information Economy	Proceedings of the 2022 IEEE 4th International Conference on Modern Electrical and Energy System, MEES 2022	Examine the effect of artificial intelligence on employee motivation, highlighting direct, indirect and non-monetary economic motivation methods and the main principles of motivation system development.	Qualitative	Innovative Ukrainian companies	As a result, the development of artificial intelligence in the work process makes employees less dependent on general management, which in turn increases self-motivation. In addition, AI algorithms help employees to achieve their goals more effectively, which can boost their internal motivation at work. The research constructs a diagram of the employee life cycle in the digital age: « needs - interests - incentives (motivations) – results ».
Hamarat, H., Sahin, H., Koç Apuhan, A.	2024	The dark side of artificial intelligence: threats to tourism workers	Worldwide Hospitality and Tourism Themes	Examine the negative effects of artificial intelligence on the future careers and work motivation of employees in the tourism sector.	Qualitative	Documentary analysis of 13 articles and two book chapters in the Science Direct and Web of Science databases.	the introduction of artificial intelligence in the tourism sector negatively affects work motivation and leads to a reduction in worker concentration. Thus, the unavailability of direct studies on the negative effects of artificial intelligence on employees in the tourism sector.

continued on following page

Table 1. Continued

Authors	Year	Title	Published	Research objectives	Methodology	Sample	Findings
Mustafayev, M., Mammadov, F.S., Aliev, R.A., Kacprzyk, J., Pedrycz, W.	2024	The Impact of Artificial Intelligence on the Motivation of Bank Employees in Azerbaijan	Lecture Notes in Networks and Systems & Springer Science and Business Media Deutschland GmbH	Study of the effect of artificial intelligence on the work motivation of bank employees in Azerbaijan	Quantitative	200 employees from 3 banks in Azerbaijan.	Negative correlation between AI update density and work motivation and income. Then, A positive correlation between AI update density and workload.
Yang, X., Yan, S.	2024	Encourage or Reject Employee Involvement: Value Creation in Human Resource Management in the AI Era—An Evolutionary Game Analysis of Enterprises and Employees	Behavioral Sciences	Study the contribution of artificial intelligence to HRM and to the co-creation of value in HRM. Thus, the construction of an evolutionary game model to explore strategic choices between companies and employees.	Qualitative	-	The results are focused on behaviors between companies and employees, where they showed the highest probability of 2.39 from the equilibrium point (cooperation, active) to that of the second equilibrium point (non-cooperation, passive).
Ye, Y., Chen, K.-H.	2024	Hospitality employees and digital transformation: The mediating roles of alienation and motivation	International Journal of Hospitality Management	Examine the influence of work characteristics on engagement through the employee's work status (alienation and motivation).	Quantitative	425 Taiwanese hotel and restaurant employees	The study showed that Work demands and work resources have a significant impact on employee alienation and motivation in the era of digital transformation (DT), which in turn influences work engagement.

continued on following page

Table 1. Continued

Authors	Year	Title	Published	Research objectives	Methodology	Sample	Findings
Passalacqua, M., Pellerin, R., Yahia, E., Magnani, F., Rosin, F., Joblot, L., Léger, P.-M.	2024	Practice With Less AI Makes Perfect: Partially Automated AI During Training Leads to Better Worker Motivation, Engagement, and Skill Acquisition	International Journal of Human-Computer Interaction	Examine how training workers using an AI system affected their motivation, engagement and skill acquisition.	Quantitative	102 employees in the manufacturing industry.	complete automation of decision selection had a negative impact on perceived autonomy, self-determined motivation, engagement in the behavioral task and skill acquisition during training. Conversely, partially (partial integration and balance of human) automated AI enhanced motivation and engagement.
Vinichenko, M.V., Melnichuk, A.V., Karácsony, P.	2020	Technologies of improving the university efficiency by using artificial intelligence: Motivational aspect	Entrepreneurship and Sustainability Issues	Identify the most appropriate technologies for improving university efficiency using motivational artificial intelligence (AI).	Quantitative	Stage a: 237 participants, Stage b: 456 peoples.	Introducing AI into university operations enhances the competitiveness of promising and innovative teachers and has a positive impact on universities' image, efficiency, academic reputation and citation index.
AL-Thabhawee, H.F.	2025	Artificial Intelligence and Its Role in Human Resources Management	International Journal of Accounting, Management, Economics and Social Sciences (IJAMESC)	Measuring the role of artificial intelligence in human resources management at Najaf International Airport.	Quantitative	120 employees at Najaf International Airport	Artificial intelligence influences the human resources management process, and the moderating effect of incentives or rewards (bonus, recognition) to motivate employees to use AI, as well as training and development of technological skills influence motivation to adopt AI in everyday tasks.

continued on following page

Table 1. Continued

Authors	Year	Title	Published	Research objectives	Methodology	Sample	Findings
Qasem Almaraghi, D.M	2024	Artificial Intelligence and the Future of Human Resource Management: Data Analysis and Decision Guidance to Enhance Work Productivity and Employee Motivation	Pakistan Journal of Life and Social Sciences (PJLSS)	Study the role of artificial intelligence in human resources management by examining its use in data analysis and decision-making to improve work productivity and motivate employees.	Quantitative	200 human resources management employees in Jordan	The positive effect of artificial intelligence on optimizing recruitment processes, objectivity of employee performance appraisals, improving the working environment and employee morale, which in turn enhances their motivation at work.

continued on following page

Table 1. Continued

Authors	Year	Title	Published	Research objectives	Methodology	Sample	Findings
Edwards, M.R., et al.	2024	Managerial control or feedback provision: How perceptions of algorithmic	Human Resource Management	Examine the impact of automated human resources management processes (automation of employee performance and decision-making) on employee motivation.	Quantitative	Study in three-wave (NT1=401; NT2=379; NT3=303)	Employees in organizations with algorithmic HRM systems experience higher levels of extrinsic motivation at work. Thus, employees with a positive perception of the use of algorithmic HRM systems showed higher levels of intrinsic motivation and lower levels of emotional exhaustion. The results highlighted the considerable impact of these systems on employee motivation, behavior and well-being.
Dong, M., Bonnefon, J.F., Rahwan, I.	2024	Toward human-centered AI management: Methodological challenges and future directions	Technovation	Examined a comparison of AI or human-based management on participants' attitudes and behaviors, including performance, intrinsic motivation, perception of fairness and commitment.	Quantitative	504 participants in Mturk.	The study showed that AI-based management was not significantly different from human-based management in terms of performance, intrinsic motivation, perception of fairness and commitment.

Chapter 3
AI-Assisted Management and Employee Well-being Review and Future Research Directions

Farah Asmaa
https://orcid.org/0000-0002-4884-6801
ENCG, Sultan Moulay Slimane University, Morocco

Yassine Bamalk
https://orcid.org/0009-0000-0176-1563
IAE, France

ABSTRACT

The adoption of artificial intelligence (AI) technologies in the workplace has generated both concerns and optimism among employees. In response, scholars have dedicated considerable attention to understand the mechanisms through which AI may affect employee will-being, producing a significant number of publications in recent years. This chapter aims to map the current state of knowledge and to propose future research directions. To this end, an analysis was conducted on 313 articles sourced from Scopus and Web of Science. The results identify two approaches that explain how AI can assist in improving employee well-being. The first approach considers AI as a tool available to managers, enabling them to continuously monitor well-being indicators and take the necessary actions. While, the second approach views AI as a catalyst for transformation in the way work is organized and carried out by employees. These changes are not without challenges, thus opening new research avenues.

DOI: 10.4018/979-8-3373-5499-6.ch003

1. INTRODUCTION

Artificial intelligence (AI) is attracting growing interest in the workplace, profoundly transforming working environments and conditions. AI can now replicate or improve many functions traditionally performed by humans, including decision-making, process optimization, and content creation (Agrawal et al., 2018). These technological developments are transforming not only tasks but also organizational structures and interpersonal dynamics at work.

At the same time, employee well-being has become a central concern in human resource management. Numerous studies have demonstrated its close link to outcomes such as organizational commitment (Orabi and Bentaleb, 2020), job satisfaction, retention, and overall performance (Van De Voorde et al., 2012). In this context, understanding the impact of emerging technologies such as AI on employee well-being has become increasingly important, especially as AI continues to influence both the content and context of work.

Changes in the workplace, particularly those brought about by automation and digitalization, have significant repercussions on employee well-being (Nazareno and Schiff, 2021). AI can affect well-being in several ways. First, by altering autonomy and decision-making power, second, by increasing or reducing mental load, and by influencing how employees are monitored or evaluated (Cramarenco et al., 2023; Gallie et al., 2017; Nazareno and Schiff, 2021). While some studies highlight the potential of AI to improve working conditions (by reducing repetitive tasks and improving health and safety), others raise concerns about job insecurity, increased surveillance, and a loss of meaning at work.

Studying the impacts of AI on employee well-being is therefore both timely and complex. Despite a growing number of publications on this topic, there is a lack of structured reviews that inventory the existing literature, identify research gaps, and highlight emerging themes. To our knowledge, a synthetic and systematic review specifically addressing current trends and future research directions is still lacking.

The objective of this paper is to provide a preliminary bibliometric review that can serve as a basis for researchers wishing to explore the relationship between AI and employee well-being. By analyzing the academic literature using standardized bibliometric methods (Aria and Cuccurullo, 2017), this chapter aims to identify dominant research streams, understudied areas, and emerging concepts that could inform future research.

Our results indicate that two main approaches dominate current research on AI and employee well-being. The first views AI as a tool to improve health, safety, and well-being at work, for example through assistive technologies or better data-driven decision-making. The second approach sees AI as a driver of fundamental transformations in the nature of work, raising questions of ethics, identity, and skills development. Both perspectives offer valuable insights, but they also reveal significant tensions and unanswered questions.

Overall, this study contributes to a better understanding of the link between AI and well-being in the research world. It also provides guidance for researchers seeking to study this topic on possible avenues. Indeed, further research is needed to better understand the conditions under which AI can contribute to well-being and to develop strategies to mitigate its potential risks and support employees in a changing world of work.

2. LITERATURE REVIEW

The scientific literature on well-being at work has developed in last years but it was not subject to consensus, and few researchers have been interested in its definition (Bernard et al., 2022). We will try in this section to explain this concept and link between well-being and IA.

2.1 Well-Being at Work

Several researchers have attempted to define the concept, First of Chatillon and Richard, (2015) articulates well-being at work into four main components: the meaning given to work (that the activity is useful, that we know what it is used for, etc.), the social link (with colleagues essentially), activity (mastering it, leading it well, etc.), and comfort (work environment and quality of life at work), while for *the American Psychological Association*, it is the result of six factors: balance of privacy - working life, employee involvement, health and safety, employee recognition and employee development, all linked together through communication.

For its part, the International Labour Organization links well-being to work by: *"all aspects of working life, the quality and safety of the work environment, how workers feel about their work, their work environment, the working climate and work organization*". Richard (2012), in turn considers it as "*a two-dimensional construct: an emotional or affective dimension related to pleasure and all the positive effects, and a cognitive dimension related to awareness of the meaning that work takes for the person*".

According to Fisher, (2014), researchers have distinguished between several aspects of the concept sometimes incoherently. Some researchers perceive well-being at work in subjective hedonic terms, « *hedonism*» refers to the satisfaction of our expectations in different spheres of our life, and to pleasant emotions felt (Berkman, 1971; Diener, 1984 ; Diener & *al.* 1985 ; Watson, & *al.*, 1988 ; Massé, & al., 1998; Warr, 1990; Achilles, 2003; Daniels, 2000; Diener, 2000 ; Keyes, 2006), others consider that «eudemonism» is the desire to fulfil oneself and to reach one's full potential (Kraut, 1979; Waterman, 1993; Ryff, & Keyes, 1995; Ryan, & Deci, 2001 ; Keyes, & Lopez, 2002; Deci & Ryan, 2008*)*. While other researchers have combined the two approaches and consider well-being at work as complementary (Biétry & Creusier, 2013; 2025; First of Chatillon and Richard, 2015).

This diversity of definitions highlights several dimensions of well-being at work (Bernard, 2019):

- ***Self-relationship***: sense of competence, efficiency, autonomy, self-confidence.
  -***Relationship with others***: working environment, relationship with his/her manager(s), with peers, with collaborators.
  -***Relationship to work***: working environment and conditions, content of the work, meaning given to work, balance between personal life and professional life.

2.2 Artificial Intelligence

Currently, artificial intelligence (AI) has become the catalyst for innovation, gradually integrating into several services. AI translates the ability of computers to reproduce certain aspects of human intelligence (Kaaria, 2024). The first use of the concept dates to 1955, by the American computer scientist J. McCarthy. He considers it as *"the science and engineering of making intelligent machine"* (Manning, 2020). However, since the 2010s, AI has seen surprising advances due to: deep learning, increasing data availability and the use of graphics processors (François et Aubernon, 2024).

Russell & Norvig (2016) defines artificial intelligence as a set of techniques that enable the execution of tasks by machines, such as perception and decision-making learning.

Shapiro (1992) proposes a broader definition of artificial intelligence as a field of science and engineering that deals with understanding through the computer, intelligent behavior and the creation of artificial systems that generate this behavior. In this dynamic definition, Julia (2019) recalls that it is no longer intelligence that characterizes AI systems, but rather their ability to recognize through machine learning.

Often in the aspheric of work three types of AI are distinguished:

Assisted AI: Refers to technology that enables employees to perform their tasks more efficiently or accurately. In this case, the machine is essentially a tool used by a human operator (Bobillier Chaumon & al., 2018).

Decision AI: It leverages the advanced computational capabilities of AI and machine learning algorithms to continuously integrate and process dynamic data volumes, allowing rapid adaptation to environmental changes. This analytical flexibility provides organizations with increased strategic agility, which is essential in an ever-changing economic and technological environment (Chanphati & Thosuwanchot, 2023). Nevertheless, this evolution raises fundamental questions about the autonomy of automated systems and human control, as well as the effect of these technologies on decision-making dynamics. (Alblowi, 2023).

Prescriptive AI: It has radically transformed analytical capabilities. AI offers the possibility to stimulate different scenarios, anticipate performance fluctuations or recommend strategic actions (Griguer & Lakhouil, 2023), through the analysis of big data integrating several variables.

2.3 Theoretical Framework for the Link Between Wellness at Work and Artificial Intelligence

The link between the two concepts can be analyzed by mobilizing several theoretical frameworks. The technology acceptance and adoption (TAM) model developed by Davis (1989) is one of the models used to explain this relationship. Based on three principles: a) Perceived utility of this technology reflects the feeling that it improves individual performance at work, b) Perceived ease of use: refers to easy use of this technology, and finally c) The attitude of individuals towards this technology indicates the individual reaction which is influenced by the two previous factors, so it is the key mediator of acceptance of the technology. Trenerry & al., (2021) point out that the integration of technology depends not only on its design but also on its acceptance and adoption by individuals.

The work of Backelr & al., (2004) on the model of employment requirements and resources can be used to analyze individuals' ability to adapt, or their difficulties or lack of resources to adapt, which can generate stress. Trenerry & al., (2021) used the Work Requirements and Resources model, showing the importance of certain resources in reducing the effect of various occupational requirements on burnout. The authors analyzed how stress factors such as overload and emotional pressures interfere with autonomy and performance. Although this interaction did not impact work efficiency, it was linked to increased burnout and cynicism among professionals (Bakker et al., 2005).

The technostress as described by pat Tarafdar (2010): *"Stress on users due to application multitasking, constant connectivity, information overload, frequent system upgrades and uncertainty, the continuous re-learning and occupational insecurities and technical problems associated with the use of ICTs."* According to this researcher, technostress creates a feeling of insecurity in relation to technologies, a decrease in confidence and comfort in general, which has a negative impact on the level of satisfaction at work of individuals.

Gaillard (1993) states that technostress and mental load refer to the relationship between environmental requirements and the availability of resources to perform tasks. According to the theories of mental load (cognitive-energetic theories), resources are distinguished by the information processing capacity and requests referring to the level of processing required to perform the task well. Whereas for stress theories, the definition of both demands and resources is much broader and more diverse. The requests refer not only to the task, but also to the requirements of the work environment, including physical, psychosocial and organizational aspects. In the case of technostress, we will talk about technological resources (Salanova & al., 2014) and protective factors of technostress (Ragu Nathan & al., 2008).

2.4 Impact of Artificial Intelligence on Well-Being at Work

After having briefly presented the two concepts, as well as the theoretical framework that can be mobilized to study the link between the two concepts. We will in this point focus on the impact of Artificial Intelligence on well-being at work. Three major impacts was founded in literature: digital competency development, obsolescence of skills and the impact on organizational culture and professional identity.

2.4.1 Digital Competency Development

Many researchers (Bobillier Chaumon & al., 2018; Hommel & Cohen, 2023; Lopez, 2017; Trenerry & al., 2021) have studied the importance of developing skills related to the digital world to support employees in facing and better adapting to the transformations brought about by digital technology, including AI. Cukier & al. (2023) explore digital skills and the skills gap in the Canadian context, Stressing the importance of developing skills to meet frequently changing requirements and the difficulties that threaten companies in filling vacancies. These authors emphasize the importance of categorizing jobs and defining digital skills frameworks (Cukier & al., 2023). Hommel and Cohen (2023) suggest addressing AI-related topics and education, to reduce the level of AI-related anxiety among students and prepare them to thrive and adapt in an ever-changing environment.

Mercier (2020) questioned the well-being of teachers at work during the pandemic in the context of distance education and stressed the importance of "*diversifying digital tools to promote digital skills development*" (p. 111). Lopez (2017) emphasizes the role of technology in improving employee well-being at work, while underlining the need to manage their effects and associated risks in an ethical manner, mainly related to the requirement to acquire new skills to remain competitive

In the same sense of idea, Bobillier Chaumon & al., (2018) examine the contribution of technologies to the favorable development of activity, autonomy and revitalization of the profession. These authors add that digital technologies can either facilitate or hinder professional tasks, affecting efficiency and time management. However, it is difficult for employees to perform their work effectively in such an environment if they are not adequately trained. Since they are constantly called upon in their function, at work and outside, they must develop skills in accessibility management to manage their availability and their visibility at work (Bobillier Chaumon & al., 2018).

2.4.2 Obsolescence of Skills and Well-Being

Employees may develop anxiety because of fear of losing their jobs because of not being able to meet new labor market demands and then being unable to master the tasks transformed by technology (Bobillier Chaumon & al., 2018). Job insecurity, according to Sverke et al., (2002) has adverse effects on employees' organizational attitudes, occupational attitudes, health, and even their relationship with the organization. This situation pushes employees to enter a continuous learning loop would be a way of reducing redundancies and promoting well-being, since it would generate Employees able to adapt to technological change (Vargas, 2017).

Even if this encourages the professional development of employees, it can generate for them an overload of work and continuous stress, thus affecting their well-being (Psyché & al., (2024). Indeed, Vargas (2017) points out that lifelong learning can transform the employee into a consumer of *nomadic training*. Faced with this situation, organizations are called upon to develop more and more self-organizing systems while ensuring the representation of self and its fulfillment needs at work (Valenduc & Vendramin, 2016).

Finally, the relationship between skills obsolescence and well-being at work is complex and multidimensional. Gicquel (2014) highlights the importance of digital governance skills for business decision-makers. Garcia & al., (2020) invite organizations to integrate new employees to deal with the obsolescence of skills, highlighting the value of having a diverse workforce can improve learning agility. For his part, Strootbants (2007) points out that the social construction of skills involves both capacity and recognition and allows to individualize progression and remuneration in the workplace.

2.4.3 Organizational Culture and Professional Identity

The increased integration of AI is pushing to broaden the analysis to new ways of thinking individually and collectively in the workplace. Labour relations have evolved towards a form of sociability privatization (Psyché & al., 2024).

In this sense, Vendramin (2007) proposes the concept of *cooperative nomadism* to describe the relationship to the collective in highly individualized universes, where work in copresence and at a distance propagates. Collective engagement becomes a compromise between the collective dimension and the individual's personal dimension at work (Osty, 2016). With the popularization of telework (digital-induced and AI-facilitated), the workspace is becoming virtual, changing how employees interact and perceive each other and the separation between work and personal life (Gillet and Tremblay, 2023; Rosanvallon, 2007; Tremblay and Mathieu, 2023). The individual at work is built at the crossroads of copresence and co-activity collectives, reflecting a broader conception of modes of integration into work.

Mouly (2022) explores the effect of AI on employee engagement and well-being at work. He says that digital solutions improve the efficiency, relationships and autonomy of employees, thus contributing to their satisfaction and recognition. Nevertheless, Tremblay & al., (2023), question the protection of privacy and the social impact of technological decisions.

3. METHODOLOGY

Consistent with the aim of this paper, the bibliometric analysis technique was employed. Bibliometry is defined by Aria et Cuccurullo (2017) as: "being a part of research evaluation methodology and the numerical analysis of the publications produced by individuals or institutions in a specific area in a specific region and the relations between these publications"

The initial step involved identifying the databases to be used for the document search, with Web of Science and Scopus being the options under consideration. The search document databases are peer-reviewed articles and proceeding papers that are written in English. Drawing on previous literature reviews (e.g., Pereira et al., 2023), we relied on publications from 1995 onwards, with the aim of including works that coincide with recent technological developments. The query strings used to find documents are: (TITLE-ABS-KEY ("Artificial Intelligence" OR "AI" OR "Chatbot" OR "Machine Learning" OR "ML" OR "Deep Learning") AND TITLE-ABS-KEY ("employee well-being" OR "employee wellbeing" OR "employee welfare" OR "employee wellness" OR "employee health" OR "employee happiness" OR "employee satisfaction")) AND PUBYEAR > 1994 AND PUBYEAR <

2025 AND (LIMIT-TO (DOCTYPE, “ar”) OR LIMIT-TO (DOCTYPE, “cp”) OR LIMIT-TO (DOCTYPE, “re”) OR LIMIT-TO (DOCTYPE, “cr”)) AND (LIMIT-TO (LANGUAGE, “English”)) on Scopus and (“Artificial Intelligence” OR “AI” OR “Chatbot” OR “Machine Learning” OR “ML” OR “Deep Learning” (All Fields) and “employee well-being” OR “employee wellbeing” OR “employee welfare” OR “employee wellness” OR “employee health” OR “employee happiness” OR “employee satisfaction” (All Fields) and 2024 or 2024 or 2023 or 2022 or 2021 or 2020 or 2019 or 2018 or 2017 or 2016 or 2015 or 2014 or 2013 or 2012 or 2011 or 2010 or 2008 or 2007 or 2006 or 2005 or 2004 or 2001 or 2000 or 1998 or 1995 (Publication Years) and Article or Proceeding Paper or Review Article (Document Types) and English (Languages)) on WoS.

Once the initial results are obtained (n= 377 papers), the selected database is exported as plain text and BibTeX formats from WoS and Scopus, respectively. Then, the Bibliometrix package as an RStudio tool is used to combine both databases into a single file and to remove any duplicate articles (fig. 1).

Figure 1. PRISMA diagram

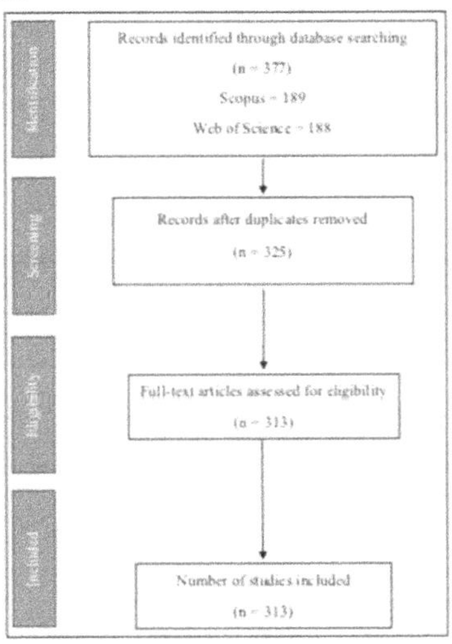

This filtering process led to the acquisition of 313 papers after harmonizing the results. The final articles were then imported into the Biblioshiny platform in order to carry out a more in-depth analysis of the data.

4. RESULTS

The results indicate that the database analyzed covers the period from 1995 to 2024. During this timeframe, a total of 313 documents were identified, from 213 different sources (Table 1).

Table 1. Summary of bibliographic information

Description	Results
MAIN INFORMATION ABOUT DATA	
Timespan	1995:2024
Sources (e.g., Journals)	213
Documents	313
Annual Growth Rate %	7,87
Document Average Age	4,16
Average citations per doc	10,6
References	9073
DOCUMENT CONTENTS	
Keywords Plus (ID)	1498
Author's Keywords (DE)	1153
AUTHORS	
Authors	1084
Authors of single-authored docs	22
AUTHORS COLLABORATION	
Single-authored docs	30
Co-Authors per Doc	4,13
International co-authorships %	16,29
DOCUMENT TYPES	
article	240
proceedings paper	73

The average growth rate based on this corpus is 7.87%. However, the real acceleration took place in 2019, which can be attributed to the deterioration in employee well-being due to the emergence of COVID-19 (Juchnowicz & Kinowska, 2021). This upward trend continues exponentially, with substantial increases every year (Fig. 2).

Figure 2. Annual scientific production

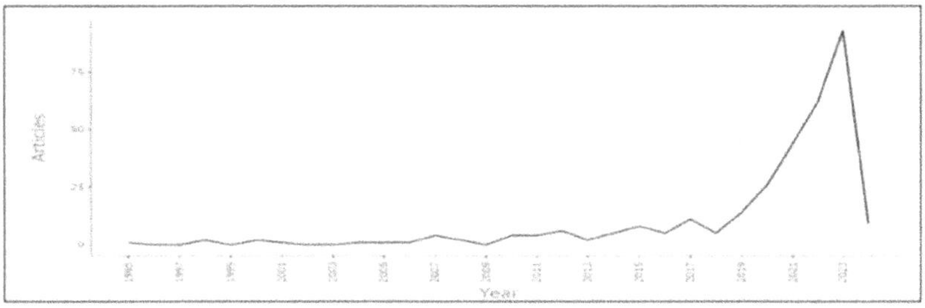

As far as the authors involved are concerned, considerable diversity is observed, with a total of 1084 individuals. Of these, 22 contributed as sole authors, highlighting the wealth of individual perspectives in the database. Author collaboration also stands out with an average of 4.13 co-authors per document, underlining an environment conducive to the exchange of ideas and intellectual cooperation. Notably, international collaboration accounts for 16.29% of collaborations, indicating a global dimension to knowledge creation within the database.

Document types analyses shows a predominance of articles, with a total number of 240. The significant presence of articles suggests an emphasis on conventional academic writing. Conference proceedings are also well represented, totalling 73 documents. These documents, generally from scientific or academic conferences, may contain original contributions, research results and discussions, enriching the database with perspectives from major scientific events.

Table 2 illustrates the main journals that received more citations on this analyzed database. The journal with the highest number in the field of well-being at work was "Journal of Applied Psychology" with 331 citations, followed by the "Journal of Occupational and Environmental Medicine" and the "Academy of Management Journal" with 118 and 114 citations, respectively.

Table 2. Sources with the largest number of citations

Sources	Articles
Journal of Applied Psychology	331
Mechanical Systems and Signal Processing	122
IEEE Transactions on Industrial Informatics	119
Journal of Occupational and Environmental Medicine	118
Academy of Management Journal	114
Journal of Organizational Behavior	98

continued on following page

Table 2. Continued

Sources	Articles
Journal of Management	81
IEEE Transactions on Industrial Electronics	72
IEEE Transactions on Instrumentation and Measurement	70
International Journal of Human Resource Management	70

The journals that received the highest number of citations regarding this topic were journals related to AI, with a focus on well-being at work, like "Mechanical Systems and Signal Processing" and "IEEE Transactions on Industrial Informatics" are also gradually gaining importance.

As seen in Table 3, Huo and Boxall hold the record for the highest number of cited articles, achieving an h-index of 7 and 6, respectively. The article titled "lean production and the well-being of the frontline manager: the job demands–resources model as a diagnostic tool in Chinese manufacturing" suggested that future researchers should explore solutions other than compensation to address the threat of role overload, an issue they identified during a qualitative study of well-being (Huo and Boxall, 2017).

Table 3. Author impact factor

Element	h_index	g_index	m_index	TC	NP	PY_start
HUO M	7	9	0,875	124	9	2017
BOXALL P	6	7	0,75	107	7	2017
CHEN J	4	5	0,8	127	5	2020
CHEN Z	4	5	1	100	5	2021
LI S	4	5	1,333	31	5	2022
ZHANG X	4	6	0,8	108	6	2020
DEJOY D	3	3	0,375	54	3	2017
FERREIRA A	3	4	0,231	114	4	2012
JIANG Z	3	3	0,6	22	3	2020
LI J	3	3	1	25	3	2022

Zhang is the author following Huo and Boxall. In 2020, Zhang and his colleagues synthesized existing literature on "Smart offices", which stand out for their extensive use of AI and IoT, while suggesting directions for future research.

Table 4 presents the scientific production per country.

Table 4. Scientific production and average number of citations of articles by countries

Country	Freq	TC	Average Article Citations
USA	196	635	13,20
CHINA	145	1075	13,10
INDIA	30	105	6,60
AUSTRALIA	23	366	30,50
UK	22	4	0,70
GERMANY	17	70	7,00
SAUDI ARABIA	17	31	5,20
PORTUGAL	15	121	20,20
CANADA	12	5	1,20
HUNGARY	12	5	1,20

The United States has emerged in first place in terms of the quantity of published articles, with a total of 196 on the subject. Nevertheless, it does not hold the top position in either the number of citations or the average quotes per article. CHINA is the second country with 145 publications. This country has a total of 1075 citations and an average of 13.10 citations per article. Australia has published 23 articles on the subject, taking the fourth place, yet it is the top country in terms of average citations received per article.

Table 5 presents the top 10 most frequently referenced articles, with their ranking determined by the number of citations they have received. Parker & Grote's publication was the most cited with a total of 155 citations. This paper proposed a central role for work design in understanding the impacts of digital technologies.

Table 5. Most cited articles

Paper	Total Citations	TC per Year
Automation, algorithms, and beyond: Why work design matters more than ever in a digital world (Parker & Grote, 2022).	155	51,67
Applications of unsupervised deep transfer learning to intelligent fault diagnosis: A survey and comparative study (Zhao et al., 2021).	151	45,25
A new deep transfer learning method for bearing fault diagnosis under different working conditions (Zhu et al., 2019).	145	29,00
Job stressors, job involvement and employee health: A test of identity theory (Frone et al., 1995).	118	3,93
Workplace well-being: The role of job crafting and autonomy support (Slemp et al., 2015).	101	10,10

continued on following page

Table 5. Continued

Paper	Total Citations	TC per Year
A new online detection approach for rolling bearing incipient fault via self-adaptive deep feature matching (Mao et al., 2019).	78	15,60
Employee churn prediction (Saradhi & Palshikar, 2011).	71	5,07
Distribution-invariant deep belief network for intelligent fault diagnosis of machines under new working conditions (Xing & Jia, 2020).	70	17,50
Sick at work: presenteeism among nurses in a Portuguese public hospital (Martinez & Ferreira, 2012).	70	5,38
iWorkSafe: towards healthy workplaces during COVID-19 with an intelligent pHealth App for industrial settings. (Kaiser et al., 2021).	67	16,75

The articles by Parker & Grote (2022) and Zhao et al. (2021) are the most frequently referenced in terms of annual citations, with 51,67 and 45,25 citations, respectively. Therefore, they can serve as crucial references for the investigation of the relationship between AI and employee well-being.

Figure 3 shows how the study of the relationship between AI and employee well-being has evolved and interest in publishing-related work has increased.

Figure 3. Annual spectroscopic analysis of publications

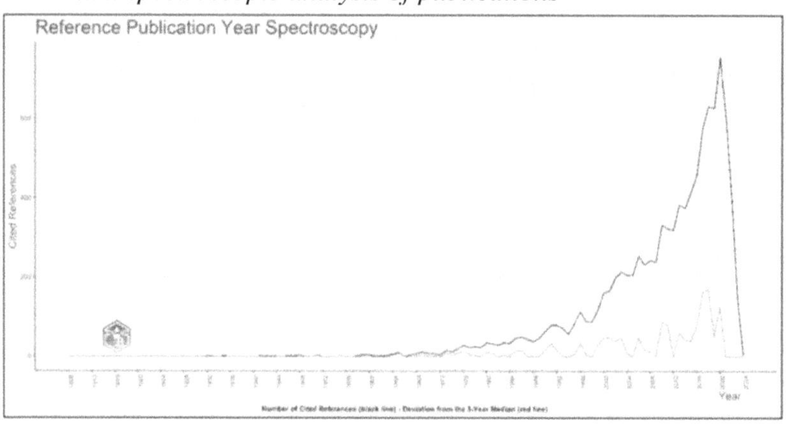

Spectroscopic analysis commences in 1995, marking the emergence of related publications. However, as shown in Fig. 3, a substantial rise in the related scientific production did not occur until 2020.

Figure 4. presents the co-occurrence analysis of the authors' keywords. The size of the nodes in the figure indicates the frequency of use of the keywords by the authors, while the colors indicate distinct keyword groups. Pink circles: with keywords representative of artificial intelligence, green circles are about employee well-being and blue circles are about machine learning.

Figure 4. The conceptual structure

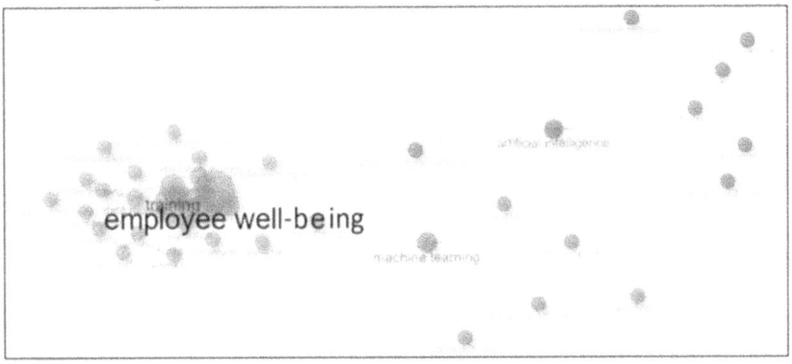

The initial cluster focuses on artificial intelligence, and the main keywords encompass artificial intelligence, industry 4.0, employee health, occupational health, employee engagement, etc. Articles on this topic mainly focus on how artificial intelligence could improve employee health, occupational health, employee engagement (Stamate et al., 2021; West et al., 2023). The second cluster prioritize employee well-being. Related papers primarily focus on what could improve employee welfare (Zhang et al., 2022; Zhang et al., 2023). The third clustering theme is machine learning. The papers in this theme predominantly discuss the use of machine learning in developing employee well-being, like his satisfaction (Raed et al., 2023).

Figure 5 showcases information regarding the authors' countries. The color assigned to each country corresponds to the number of national papers, and the thickness of the inter- country connections signifies the frequency of collaboration.

Figure 5. The rate of collaboration between countries based on authors' affiliations

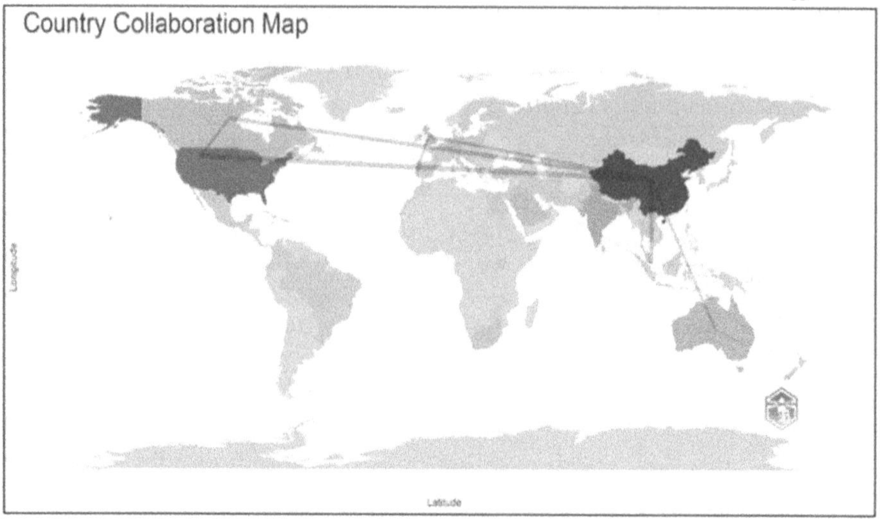

The USA and China are the darkest-shaded countries, suggesting that researchers from these nations have authored the most articles. The thickest link connecting the USA and China signifies a more frequent collaboration and communication between authors from both countries. In addition, China and both Singapore and Canada collaborate more frequently.

4. DISCUSSION

The aim of this paper was to have an overview of Artificial Intelligence (AI) in the field of well-being at work. The analyze shows that scientific production regarding the use of the AI by employees was increased since 2019, which can be attributed to the deterioration in employee well-being due to the advent or emergence of COVID-19.

The results indicate that the United States and China are the countries with the highest number of publications, followed by Australia.

Derived from the acquired results, the main journals regarding the use of AI for employee well-being are "Journal of Applied Psychology" and "IEEE Transactions on Industrial Informatics". The articles with the strongest impact are titled "Automation, algorithms, and beyond: Why work design matters more than ever in a digital world" and "Applications of unsupervised deep transfer learning to intelligent fault diagnosis: A survey and comparative study", which sought to insure efficient adoption of AI in favor of employee well-being.

In terms of scientific structure, two main approaches describe how AI can influence employee well-being. The first approach views AI as a tool for promoting occupational health and well-being, for example, by predicting potential risks or safety incidents in the workplace, analyzing the root cause of an incident, and facilitating decision-making (Howard, 2022). The second approach views AI as a catalyst for change in the nature of work, involving the automation of demanding job tasks (Nazareno and Schiff, 2021), while also contributing to occupational hazards for employees, including reduced autonomy and increased stress related to the fear of becoming obsolete if a job is fully automated (Howard 2022).

To manage the changing working conditions associated with AI, Cramarenco et al. (2023)

emphasized the importance of skills upgrading. It is essential for workers to be able to use and interact effectively with AI systems in all their applications, and for companies to foster effective human-machine collaboration.

In this regard, it seems important to emphasize that employees' inability to acquire new technological skills can create skills obsolescence and impact their employment opportunities (Cramarenco et al., 2023). It is therefore important to better understand the skills employees need to support them in this context of major technological change; this is an initial avenue of research emerging from this work. Others will be developed in the conclusion below.

5. CONCLUSION

This study aimed to provide an overview of the current state of research on the relationship between artificial intelligence (AI) and employee well-being, and to identify avenues for future research. Through a bibliometric analysis of 313 publications, two main approaches were identified: AI as a managerial tool for supporting employee well-being, and AI as a transformative force that changes work.

First, the approach positioning AI as a tool for well-being management highlights its potential to detect early signs of distress, support real-time monitoring, and enhance decision-making for health and safety. This aligns with a technocentric vision in which AI contributes to more proactive and personalized well-being strategies. The challenge lies in implementing these tools in ways that foster trust and transparency, rather than reinforcing control and anxiety.

Second, the perspective of AI as a driver of work transformation points to more systemic and structural impacts. AI reshapes job tasks, alters skill requirements, and influences professional identities. While it may reduce cognitive load and enhance productivity, it also brings about risks such as job insecurity, increased pressure for continuous upskilling, and the potential erosion of meaningful work. This duality refers to the job demands and resources model, which suggests that without adequate resources, technological demands can have a negative impact on well-being.

Rather than opposing these two views, this paper suggests that they should be understood as complementary. A comprehensive understanding of AI's impact on employee well-being must consider both the micro-level (individual experience and adoption) and the macro-level (organizational transformation and power dynamics).

The results also reveal several research gaps and opportunities for further exploration:

- Comparative studies across industries and cultural contexts to understand divergent effects.
- Longitudinal research to assess the consequences of AI on well-being, satisfaction at work, and professional identity.
- A deeper investigation of the acceptance and resistance dynamics surrounding AI implementation, using models such as TAM (Technology Acceptance Model).
- Exploration of how AI influences human-machine collaboration and team dynamics.
- Greater attention to inclusive skill development strategies, avoiding the marginalization of vulnerable employee groups in the digital transition.

Ultimately, while AI has the potential to enhance well-being at work, its integration must be approached with critical awareness of its organizational, ethical, and social implications. Future research should move beyond purely technological narratives and adopt interdisciplinary frameworks that center human values in the digital workplace. The findings in this chapter provide avenues for exploring these issues.

REFERENCES

Abord de Chatillon, E., & Richard, D. (2015). Du sens, du lien, de l'activité et de confort (SLAC): Proposition pour une modélisation des conditions du bien-être au travail. *Revue française de gestion, 41*(249), 53–71. https://doi.org/DOI: 10.3166/rfg.2015.00153

Achilles, C. M. (2003). The "why's" of class size: Student behavior in small classes. *Review of Educational Research, 73*(3), 321–368. DOI: 10.3102/00346543073003321

Agrawal, A., Gans, J., & Goldfarb, A. (2018). Prediction, judgment, and complexity: A theory of decision-making and artificial intelligence. *The economics of artificial intelligence. Agenda (Durban, South Africa)*, •••, 89–110.

Alblowi, K. (2023). A three-tiered analysis of the factors influencing the adoption of forensic accounting field in Saudi Arabia. *International Journal of Professional Business Review*, *8*(6), e02185. DOI: 10.26668/businessreview/2023.v8i6.2185

Aria, M., & Cuccurullo, C. (2017). bibliometrix: An R-tool for comprehensive science mapping analysis. *Journal of Informetrics*, *11*(4), 959–975. DOI: 10.1016/j.joi.2017.08.007

Bakker, A. B., Demerouti, E., & Euwema, M. C. (2005). Job resources buffer the impact of job demands on burnout. *Journal of Occupational Health Psychology*, *10*(2), 170–180. DOI: 10.1037/1076-8998.10.2.170 PMID: 15826226

Bakker, A. B., Demerouti, E., & Verbeke, W. (2004). Using the job demands–resources model to predict burnout and performance. *Human Resource Management*, *43*(1), 83–104. DOI: 10.1002/hrm.20004

Berkman, P. L. (1971). Measurement of mental health in a general population survey. *American Journal of Epidemiology*, *94*(2), 105–111. DOI: 10.1093/oxfordjournals.aje.a121301 PMID: 5568599

Bobillier Chaumon, M. E., Cuvillier, B., Sarnin, P., & Vacherand-Revel, J. (2018). Usage des TIC et évolutions des pratiques socioprofessionnelles des cadres: Quels repères pour le métier et quelles incidences sur la santé? *Pratiques Psychologiques*, *24*(4), 349–373. DOI: 10.1016/j.prps.2018.01.001

Chanphati, J., & Thosuwanchot, N. (2023). Strategic flexibility: A systematic review and future research directions. *Journal of Strategy and Management*, *16*(3), 470–491. DOI: 10.1108/JSMA-08-2022-0134

Cramarenco, R. E., Burcă-Voicu, M. I., & Dabija, D. C. (2023). The impact of artificial intelligence (AI) on employees' skills and well-being in global labor markets: A systematic review. *Oeconomia Copernicana*, *14*(3), 731–767. DOI: 10.24136/oc.2023.022

Cynthia, D. (2014). Fisher, Conceptualizing and measuring wellbeing at work, in: Peter Y. Chen, L. Cary, Cooper (Eds.), Work and Wellbeing: Wellbeing: A Complete Reference Guide Vol III, John Wiley & Sons. DOI: 10.1002/9781118539415.wbwell018

Daniels, K. (2000). Measures of five aspects of affective well-being at work. *Human Relations*, *53*(2), 275–294. DOI: 10.1177/a010564

Deci, E. L., & Ryan, R. M. (2008). Self-determination theory: A macrotheory of human motivation, development, and health. *Canadian Psychology*, *49*(3), 182–185. DOI: 10.1037/a0012801

Diener, E. (1984). Subjective well-being. *Psychological Bulletin*, *95*(3), 542–575. DOI: 10.1037/0033-2909.95.3.542 PMID: 6399758

Diener, E. (2000). Subjective well-being: The science of happiness and a proposal for a national index. *The American Psychologist*, *55*(1), 34–43. DOI: 10.1037/0003-066X.55.1.34 PMID: 11392863

Diener, E., Emmons, R. A., Larsen, R. J., & Griffin, S. (1985). The Satisfaction With Life Scale. *Journal of Personality Assessment*, *49*(1), 71–75. DOI: 10.1207/s15327752jpa4901_13 PMID: 16367493

Frone, M. R., Russell, M., & Cooper, M. L. (1995). Job stressors, job involvement and employee health: A test of identity theory. *Journal of Occupational and Organizational Psychology*, *68*(1), 1–11. DOI: 10.1111/j.2044-8325.1995.tb00684.x

Gaillard, A. W. K. (1993). Comparing the concepts of mental load and stress. *Ergonomics*, *36*(9), 991–1005. DOI: 10.1080/00140139308967972 PMID: 8404841

Gallie, D., Felstead, A., Green, F., & Inanc, H. (2017). The hidden face of job insecurity. *Work, Employment and Society*, *31*(1), 36–53. DOI: 10.1177/0950017015624399

Garfield, E. (2004). Historiographic mapping of knowledge domains literature. *Journal of Information Science*, *30*(2), 119–145. DOI: 10.1177/0165551504042802

Hommel, D., & Cohen, B. (2023). Reducing AI Anxiety Starts by Talking with Students | Faculty Focus. Teaching with Technology. https://www.facultyfocus.com/articles/teaching-with-technologyarticles/reducing-ai-anxiety-starts-by-talking-with-students/

Hommel, D., & Cohen, B. (2023). Reducing AI Anxiety Starts by Talking with Students | Faculty Focus. Teaching with Technology. https://www.facultyfocus.com/articles/teaching-with-technology-articles/reducing-ai-anxiety-starts-by-talking-with-students/

Howard, J. (2022). Algorithms and the future of work. *American Journal of Industrial Medicine*, *65*(12), 943–952. DOI: 10.1002/ajim.23429 PMID: 36128686

Huo, M. L., & Boxall, P. (2017). Lean production and the well-being of the front-line manager: The job demands–resources model as a diagnostic tool in Chinese manufacturing. *Asia Pacific Journal of Human Resources*, *55*(3), 280–297. DOI: 10.1111/1744-7941.12152

Jetha, A., Shamaee, A., Bonaccio, S., Gignac, M. A., Tucker, L. B., Tompa, E., Bültmann, U., Norman, C. D., Banks, C. G., & Smith, P. M. (2021). Fragmentation in the future of work: A horizon scan examining the impact of the changing nature of work on workers experiencing vulnerability. *American Journal of Industrial Medicine*, *64*(8), 649–666. DOI: 10.1002/ajim.23262 PMID: 34125433

Juchnowicz, M., & Kinowska, H. (2021). Employee well-being and digital work during the COVID-19 pandemic. *Information (Basel)*, *12*(8), 293. DOI: 10.3390/info12080293

Kaaria, A. (2024). Artificial Intelligence and Employee Well-Being: Balancing Technological Progressions with Human-Centric Workplace Strategies, a Research Agenda. *East African Journal of Information Technology*, *7*(1), 355–365. DOI: 10.37284/eajit.7.1.2281

Kaiser, M. S., Mahmud, M., Noor, M. B. T., Zenia, N. Z., Al Mamun, S., Mahmud, K. A., & Hussain, A. (2021). iWorkSafe: Towards healthy workplaces during COVID-19 with an intelligent pHealth App for industrial settings. *IEEE Access : Practical Innovations, Open Solutions*, *9*, 13814–13828. DOI: 10.1109/ACCESS.2021.3050193

Keyes, C. L. M. (2006). The subjective well-being of America's youth: Toward a comprehensive assessment. *Adolescent & Family Health*, *4*(1), 3–11.

Keyes, C. L. M., & Lopez, S. J. (2002). Toward a science of mental health: Positive directions in diagnosis and interventions. In Snyder, C. R., & Lopez, S. J. (Eds.), *Handbook of positive psychology* (pp. 45–59). Oxford University Press.

Kraut, R. E., & Johnston, R. E. (1979). Social and emotional messages of smiling: An ethological approach. *Journal of Personality and Social Psychology*, *37*(9), 1539–1553. DOI: 10.1037/0022-3514.37.9.1539

Manning C. (2020), *Artificial Intelligence Definitions*, Stanford University, Human-Centered Artificial Intelligence – HAI.

Mao, W., Chen, J., Liang, X., & Zhang, X. (2019). A new online detection approach for rolling bearing incipient fault via self-adaptive deep feature matching. *IEEE Transactions on Instrumentation and Measurement*, *69*(2), 443–456. DOI: 10.1109/TIM.2019.2903699

Martinez, L. F., & Ferreira, A. I. (2012). Sick at work: Presenteeism among nurses in a Portuguese public hospital. *Stress and Health*, *28*(4), 297–304. DOI: 10.1002/smi.1432 PMID: 22282226

Nazareno, L., & Schiff, D. S. (2021). The impact of automation and artificial intelligence on worker well-being. *Technology in Society*, *67*, 101679. DOI: 10.1016/j.techsoc.2021.101679

Orabi, M., & Bentaleb, C. (2020). Les pratiques de bien-être au travail dans les entreprises au Maroc: Enseignements d'une étude de cas. *Moroccan Journal of Quantitative and Qualitative Research*, *2*(1), 1–14.

Parker, S. K., & Grote, G. (2022). Automation, algorithms, and beyond: Why work design matters more than ever in a digital world. *Applied Psychology*, *71*(4), 1171–1204. DOI: 10.1111/apps.12241

Pereira, V., Hadjielias, E., Christofi, M., & Vrontis, D. (2023). A systematic literature review on the impact of artificial intelligence on workplace outcomes: A multi-process perspective. *Human Resource Management Review*, *33*(1), 100857. DOI: 10.1016/j.hrmr.2021.100857

Raed, H., Qawasmeh, E., Alserhan, A., Ahmad, H., Hammouri, Q., Halim, M., & Darawsheh, D. (2023). Utilizing business intelligence and digital transformation and leadership to enhance employee job satisfaction and business added value in greater Amman municipality. *International Journal of Data and Network Science*, *7*(3), 1077–1084. DOI: 10.5267/j.ijdns.2023.5.016

Ragu-Nathan, T. S., Tarafdar, M., Ragu-Nathan, B. S., & Tu, Q. (2008). The consequences of technostress for end users in organizations: Conceptual development and empirical validation. *Information Systems Research*, *19*(4), 417–433. DOI: 10.1287/isre.1070.0165

Russell, S. J., & Norvig, P. (2016). *Artificial Intelligence: A Modern Approach*. Pearson Education Limited.

Ryan, R. M., & Deci, E. L. (2001). On happiness and human potentials: A review of research on hedonic and eudaimonic well-being. *Annual Review of Psychology*, *52*(1), 141–166. DOI: 10.1146/annurev.psych.52.1.141 PMID: 11148302

Ryff, C. D., & Keyes, C. L. M. (1995). The structure of psychological well-being revisited. *Journal of Personality and Social Psychology*, *69*(4), 719–727. DOI: 10.1037/0022-3514.69.4.719 PMID: 7473027

Salanova, M., Llorens, S., & Ventura, M. (2014). Technostress: The Dark Side of Technologies. In Korunka, C., & Hoonakker, P. (Eds.), *The Impact of ICT on Quality of Working Life*. Springer., DOI: 10.1007/978-94-017-8854-0_6

Saradhi, V. V., & Palshikar, G. K. (2011). Employee churn *prediction. Expert Systems with Applications*, *38*(3), 1999–2006. DOI: 10.1016/j.eswa.2010.07.134

Schank, R. C. (1987). What is AI, anyway? *AI Magazine*, *8*(4), 59. DOI: 10.1609/aimag.v8i4.623

Slemp, G. R., Kern, M. L., & Vella-Brodrick, D. A. (2015). Workplace well-being: The role of job crafting and autonomy support. *Psychology of Well-Being*, *5*(1), 1–17. DOI: 10.1186/s13612-015-0034-y

Stamate, A. N., Sauvé, G., & Denis, P. L. (2021). The rise of the machines and how they impact workers' psychological health: An empirical study. *Human Behavior and Emerging Technologies*, *3*(5), 942–955. DOI: 10.1002/hbe2.315

Tarafdar, M., Tu, Q., Ragu-Nathan, B. S., & Ragu-Nathan, T. S. (2007). The impact of technostress on role stress and productivity. *Journal of Management Information Systems*, *24*(1), 301–328. DOI: 10.2753/MIS0742-1222240109

Trenerry, B., Chng, S., Wang, Y., Suhaila, Z. S., Lim, S. S., Lu, H. Y., & Oh, P. H. (2021). Preparing workplaces for digital transformation: An integrative review and framework of multi-level factors.[. *Frontiers in Psychology*, *12*, 620766. Advance online publication. https://philpapers.org. DOI: 10.3389/fpsyg.2021.620766 PMID: 33833714

Van De Voorde, K., Paauwe, J., & Van Veldhoven, M. (2012). Employee well-being and the HRM–organizational performance relationship: A review of quantitative studies. *International Journal of Management Reviews*, *14*(4), 391–407. DOI: 10.1111/j.1468-2370.2011.00322.x

Warr, P. (1990). The measurement of well-being and other aspects of mental health. *Journal of Occupational Psychology*, *63*(3), 193–210. DOI: 10.1111/j.2044-8325.1990.tb00521.x

Waterman, A. S. (1993). Two conceptions of happiness: Contrasts of personal expressiveness (eudaimonia) and hedonic enjoyment. *Journal of Personality and Social Psychology*, *64*(4), 678–691. DOI: 10.1037/0022-3514.64.4.678

Watson, D., Clark, L. A., & Tellegen, A. (1988). Development and validation of brief measures of positive and negative affect: The PANAS scales. *Journal of Personality and Social Psychology*, *54*(6), 1063–1070. DOI: 10.1037/0022-3514.54.6.1063 PMID: 3397865

West, A. B., Guo, Y. V., & Bucher, A. (2023). Leveraging behavioral science and artificial intelligence to support mental health in the workplace: A pilot study. *Frontiers in Psychiatry*, *14*, 14. DOI: 10.3389/fpsyt.2023.1219229 PMID: 37928926

Xing, S., Lei, Y., Wang, S., & Jia, F. (2020). Distribution-invariant deep belief network for intelligent fault diagnosis of machines under new working conditions. *IEEE Transactions on Industrial Electronics*, *68*(3), 2617–2625. DOI: 10.1109/TIE.2020.2972461

Zhang, X., Zheng, P., Peng, T., He, Q., Lee, C. K., & Tang, R. (2022). Promoting employee health in smart office: A survey. *Advanced Engineering Informatics*, *51*, 101518. DOI: 10.1016/j.aei.2021.101518

Zhang, X., Zheng, P., Peng, T., Li, D., Zhang, X., & Tang, R. (2023). Privacy-preserving activity recognition using multimodal sensors in smart office. *Future Generation Computer Systems*, *148*, 27–38. DOI: 10.1016/j.future.2023.05.023

Zhao, Z., Zhang, Q., Yu, X., Sun, C., Wang, S., Yan, R., & Chen, X. (2021). Applications of unsupervised deep transfer learning to intelligent fault diagnosis: A survey and comparative study. *IEEE Transactions on Instrumentation and Measurement*, *70*, 1–28. DOI: 10.1109/TIM.2021.3116309

Zhu, J., Chen, N., & Shen, C. (2019). A new deep transfer learning method for bearing fault diagnosis under different working conditions. *IEEE Sensors Journal*, *20*(15), 8394–8402. DOI: 10.1109/JSEN.2019.2936932

Chapter 4
Revolutionizing Workplace Well-being through Artificial Intelligence with the BIAT Model

Roquia Cherkaoui
https://orcid.org/0009-0001-6266-3948
Cadi Ayyad-University, Morocco

Salma Aarab
Cadi Ayyad University, Morocco

ABSTRACT

In a context of accelerated transformation of professional environments by AI, this research proposes an in-depth analysis. The analysis is of its effects on well-being at work. It uses a theoretical framework called the BIAT (Bien-être au travail et Intelligence Artificielle) model, which combines the PERMA model and information about how organizations work, especially how much job demands vary and how much decision-making latitude there is. Based on a hypothetical-deductive approach and a positivist epistemology, the study adopts a mixed methodology: a qualitative exploratory phase involving company directors and founders, and a quantitative confirmatory phase involving employees. The results show that PD and DL play a mediating role between AI use and the five components of well-being (positivity, commitment, relationships, meaning, fulfillment). Decision latitude has a particularly

DOI: 10.4018/979-8-3373-5499-6.ch004

notable mediating effect. The study makes empirical contributions. It also proposes operational avenues. These avenues are for the ethical and sustainable integration of AI in organizations.

INTRODUCTION

Artificial Intelligence (AI) is now emerging as a major factor in the transformation of work, overturning organizational practices, decision making processes, and human resource management dynamics. By redefining modes of production, communication and collaboration, it is profoundly changing the structure and content of work, as well as industrial relations.

While the contributions of AI in terms of performance, operational efficiency and innovation have been widely highlighted (Brynjolfsson & McAfee, 2014; Bhargava, 2021), its impact on employee well-being remains relatively unexplored in the socio-economic context of developing countries.

In Morocco, the digital transition is progressing with a growing adoption of AI solutions in various sectors, although the level of investment and technological maturity remains below that of several emerging economies. The recent creation of structures dedicated to AI, such as the Euromed School of Digital Engineering and AI in Fez (2019), testifies to an institutional desire to strengthen national capabilities in this field.

On the other hand, issues of well-being at work are particularly salient: according to a survey by the Observatoire Marocain du Bonheur (2014), only 46% of employees say they are satisfied with their professional situation, while 36% express a strong sense of dissatisfaction.

These results are confirmed by the same organization's 2017 study, which highlights the differences between business sectors and territories, as well as the main levers for improvement (remuneration, recognition, work atmosphere).

In an increasingly complex and demanding work environment, characterized by work intensification and continuous skill change, well being at work is becoming a central issue for organizational sustainability. It is no longer limited to material or hygienic aspects, but also includes psychological, social and emotional dimensions, such as engagement, meaning, professional relationships, positive emotions and a sense of accomplishment (Morin, 2008; Creusier, 2015; Barry, 2020; Nande & Commeiras, 2022).

Thus, the introduction of AI could affect these components of well-being by modifying the structural dimensions of work, in particular decision latitude (LD) and professional demands (PD).

Although there is growing interest in the links between digital technologies and occupational health, few works have proposed an integrative theoretical framework to analyze the specific effects of AI on well-being in a multidimensional approach. This is the background of the present study, with the development of the BIAT (Well-being and AI) conceptual model.

The central problem of this research can therefore be formulated as follows:

To what extent does the introduction of AI have an impact on well-being through the transformation of work structures?

This general question can be broken down into three research questions:

1. To what extent does the introduction of AI change how employees perceive professional demands and decision-making latitude?
2. Do the five dimensions of well-being at work - positivity, engagement, relationships, meaning, and accomplishment - change as a result of these structural changes?
3. In the relationship between AI use and well-being at work, is there a mediating effect of these structural dimensions of work?

To answer these questions, the present study empirically examines the nature of the relationships between AI use, structural dimensions of work, and well-being. It then tests an integrative model to better understand the dynamics at work in Morocco.

This research takes a positivist stance and uses a hypothesis-deductive approach. It combines an interdisciplinary literature review and a dual empirical approach (qualitative and quantitative).

It aims to contribute both to scientific knowledge about the impact of AI in the workplace and to managerial discussions about the conditions for a socially sustainable technological transition.

The chapter is organized as follows: The first section is devoted to the conceptual and theoretical framework of the research, presenting the definitions, models mobilized, and hypotheses formulated. The second section is a presentation of the methodology, with a detailed description of the data collection and analysis protocol. The third section presents the empirical results and discusses their implications for the BIAT model. Finally, the last section offers a general conclusion, highlighting the implications for management, the limitations of the study and the prospects for future research.

1. CONCEPTUAL FRAMEWORK AND THEORECAL APPROACHES

The theoretical framework is based on a number of key concepts. First, five specific constructs of well-being at work are examined: artificial intelligence and its main models. Two structural dimensions of work, professional demands (PD) and decision latitude (DL), are then analyzed.

1.1. Artificial Intelligence: Definitions and Models

AI has evolved from an abstract philosophical concept to a technological reality since its inception. This transformation has led to a progressive redefinition of the concept. This has given rise to a variety of theoretical and methodological approaches.

Kok et al (2009) and Poole & Mackworth (2010) present it as a set of technologies aimed at to mimic human cognitive processes or to carry out tasks autonomously. The ability to interact with the environment, recognize patterns, and optimize decisions is emphasized by Ferras-Hernández (2018). Russell & Norvig (2020) highlight the role of algorithms and data in improving performance, while Zhang et al. (2020) emphasize the importance of big data for prediction and decision making.

These contributions converge on a broader vision of AI: it goes beyond human imitation to become a tool for learning, adapting, and making autonomous decisions, marking a technological revolution that redefines the human-machine relationship.

In organizations, AI transforms work processes and raises questions of appropriation. These questions are analyzed through frameworks such as sociomateriality (Orlikowski, 2007) or the TAM model, which shed light on the interactions between digital technologies and organizational dynamics.

1.1.1 Sociomateriality Theory

The theory of sociomateriality, introduced into the field of information science by Wanda Orlikowski (2007: 143), defines it as "the involvement of the social and the material in the everyday life of organizations". This theory places materiality at the heart of organizational life, to be analyzed in the same way as social interactions, in contrast to conventional approaches that tend to separate these elements. organization.

Technological devices and organizational contexts evolve together. They transform each other and continually reorganize work patterns and structures (Orlikowski, 2007).

When applied to AI, this theory sheds light on the ways in which AI is transforming professional practices: automating tasks, redefining skills, and changing working relationships and modes of collaboration. AI is becoming an organizational actor in its own right, whose impact depends as much on its technical capabilities as on its integration into social practices.

Thus, its effectiveness depends not only on its technological performance, but also on how it gets appropriated and adopted by the actors involved.

1.1.2 Acceptance Model (TAM)

The Technology Acceptance Model (TAM), developed by Fred Davis (1989), aims to explain the factors that influence people's intention to adopt or reject a technology, especially information systems.

The model is based on two key factors: perceived usefulness and perceived ease of use, derived from Fishbein and Ajzen's (1975) theory of reasoned action.

Perceived usefulness refers to the probability a user attributes to performance improvement thanks to a system (Davis, 1989), while perceived ease of use corresponds to the degree of effort expected in using the system (Davis, 1989).

These two factors have an impact on attitude and intention towards the adoption of a technology. External variables that may modulate their effects depending on the context are also included in the model.

These two factors determine individuals attitudes toward and intentions to adopt a technology. They are modulated by external variables related to the technological and organizational context.

1.2 Well Being at Work: Definitions and Dimensions

The concept of well being in the workplace has seen significant evolution, broadening to encompass more intricate psychological and social facets. Initially viewed as the pursuit of personal happiness, well-being is now understood in terms of living conditions and the work environment.

As Warr (1999) explains, the term encompasses the entire employee experience, encompassing both physical and psychological aspects. Mick et al. (2011) view well being as a balance of physical, mental, and social health, which is essential to professional achievement. Some approaches emphasize its evolution across different stages of one's career.

Pollard and Davidson (2001), for instance, define well-being as successful performance based on physical, cognitive, and socio-emotional functions. Well being is also tied to social responsibility. It has been described by Dagenais-Desmarais (2010:167) as *"a positive subjective experience shaped by social and organizational* relationships". Biétry and Creusier (2013:34) define it as *"a psychological state linked to relations with others, oneself, time, and the physical environment*".

Poilpot-Rocaboy (2017) did a study. It highlights the emotional role of work activity in the perception of well-being. For Bachelard (2017) and Saboune (2022), it is not a reward, but rather a tool for organizing work. The overall quality of an employee's experience and functioning is defined by Zheng et al. (2015).

Within this framework, we will examine two key theories: the theory of basic psychological needs and the PERMA model.

1.2.1 Theory of Basic Psychological Needs

The Theory of Basic Psychological Needs (TBPF), derived from the Self determination Theory developed by Deci and Ryan (1985, 2000), identifies three universal needs essential to well-being: autonomy, competence, and social belonging.

The need for autonomy refers to the feeling of being at the origin of one's actions (Deci and Ryan, 1985, 2008; Ryan and Deci, 2017). It is not independence, but the ability to make self determined choices, even with external support (Deci, Koestner and Ryan, 1999; Ferrand et al., 2015). On the other hand, heteronomy, defined by external constraints, curtails this autonomy and erodes well-being.

The need for competence means that people need to feel like they can do well and reach their goals (Deci and Ryan, 1985; Ryan and Deci, 2002). Its satisfaction fosters motivation and commitment, while its frustration engenders doubt, feelings of failure, and demotivation (Ferrand et al., 2015).

Lastly, the desire to feel a sense of belonging and be accepted by others is a fundamental aspect of social integration (Ryan & Deci, 2001, 2002). Anxiety and malaise can result from a lack of recognition or isolation (Wall, 2009; Ryan and Deci, 2017).

Ryan and Deci (2000, 2002, 2017) argue that satisfying these three needs is essential to well being at work.

1.2.2 Perma Model

The model comprises five interconnected dimensions.

- **Positivity:** Seligman says that positive emotions like joy, gratitude, and hope can help you deal with stress and make you resilient. It was shown by Fredrickson (2001) that positivity broadens and enriches social interactions. The positive emotions it brings can help you feel better and be happier. Positivity can also help your body feel better, and increases resilience and prolongs life expectancy (Friedman, 2007).
- **Engagement:** In the organizational context, engagement is linked to the concept of "flow," where a state of intense concentration and accomplish-

ment is achieved by the individual who is absorbed in a stimulating task (Csikszentmihalyi, 1990). According to Donaldson et al (2020), engagement is essential to well-being. It promotes total involvement in daily tasks. It is also associated with better mental well-being (Bakker and Demerouti, 2008). A person who is committed has clear goals, controls their actions, and is deeply interested in their activities (Awofeso and Rabih, 2022).

- **Relationships:** In 2011, Seligman stated that interpersonal interactions are essential for providing emotional support and enhancing resilience in the workplace. Positive relationships have been shown to promote not only engagement and motivation, but also employee retention (Bakker and Demerouti, 2007). Bakker et al. (2008) demonstrate that strong relationships based on trust and communication improve stress management, enhance collective performance, and reduce burnout. These relationships are also sources of self-worth and appreciation. They contribute to high well-being (Goodman et al., 2018; Donaldson et al., 2020).
- **Meaning:** Seligman (2011) asserts that the concept of meaning in the workplace is understood as a contribution to a mission that transcends individual interests. Steger (2012) and Heintzelman and King (2016) point out that meaning gives direction and coherence to life. This improves self-esteem and resilience in the face of challenges. According to Heintzelman and King (2014), meaning at work is associated with better mental health and life satisfaction. In other words, having a sense of purpose can protect against burnout by motivating you to overcome daily demands.
- **Accomplishment:** Seligman's (2011) theory posits that accomplishment is associated with achieving meaningful goals, which in turn fosters motivation, self confidence, and resilience. Experiences of accomplishment reduce anxiety and depression. This improves mental health. According to El-Anzi (2005), Machell et al. (2015), and Villavicencio and Bernardo (2013), personal achievement improves self-esteem and resilience. Brunzell et al. (2016) show that these experiences recall past successes, which contributes to better management of stress and negative emotions.

1.3 Professional Demands and Decision- Latitude

In this context, some models have been made to understand how professional demands (PD) and decision latitude (DL) affect well-being at work. Two main models are the focus here: the Job Demands-Resources (JD-R) model and the Demand-Control model.

1.3.1 Requirements-Resources Model (JD-R)

Developed by Bakker and Demerouti (2007), the JD-R model enables us to analyze the effects of working conditions on employee health, well-being and performance, by distinguishing two key dimensions: PD and professional resources. These elements interact in distinct but interdependent processes, influencing experience at work.

PD refers to those aspects of work that place high demands on employees physically, cognitively or emotionally and which can adversely affect their well-being. According to Karasek (1979), this includes workload, task complexity or time constraints. In the same vein, Demerouti et al (2001:501): *"point out that these demands require sustained effort, likely to entail physiological or psychological costs, such as burnout*".

Conversely, job resources are those elements of work that facilitate the achievement of objectives, stimulate learning and support personal development (Demerouti et al., 2001). The interaction between demands and resources is central: resources act as a buffer, mitigating the negative impact of demands (Bakker and Demerouti, 2007).

Bakker et al (2003) differentiate between two processes: demands activate a tension process, while resources trigger a motivational process, influencing both employee well-being and performance (Demerouti et al., 2001).

In practice, this model is used to identify occupational risks, design targeted interventions, strengthen resources and promote an optimal balance between constraints and supports.

1.3.2 Demand-Control Model (JDC)

Karasek's (1979) Demand-Control Model (JDC) says that work stress comes from the mix of two things: how much control someone has over their work and how they act at work. DL has two parts. The first part is decision making authority. This means the ability to choose how to do one's tasks and to participate in decision making. The second part is intellectual discretion. This means the ability to develop one's skills. This means that it represents both a power of action and a lever for professional development.

Initiative, commitment, and innovation are all stimulated by a high level of DL (Ohly et al., 2006). The model says that a lot of work can make people feel good and get things done, but not having enough freedom can cause stress, frustration, and a feeling that you can't do anything. This can hurt your mental health.

The role of PD in regulating stress is significant., as pressure is converted into constructive energy by it (Karasek, 1979). High demands and low DL are particularly harmful, while high demands and high DL are beneficial in active situations.

1.4. Research Model: Concept and Hypotheses

The main aim of this research is to examine the interactions between AI and the structural dimensions of work. This includes PD and DL. The aim is also to examine their influence on well-being at work. It also aims to analyze and evaluate the impact of these interactions on the various components of well-being, such as engagement, interpersonal relationships, the meaning given to work, the sense of accomplishment, and positive emotions.

Figure 1. Research design

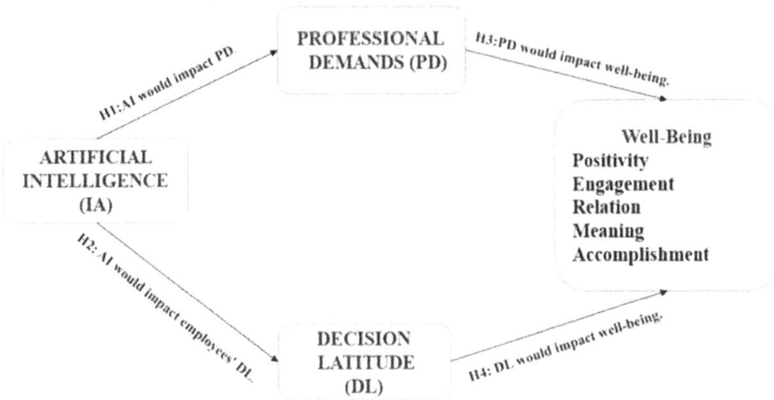

Sources: Authors

1.4.1 Hypotheses Relating to the Impact of AI on the Work Structure

Profound changes are being brought about by AI in PD. By automating repetitive tasks, it reduces the cognitive load and potentially improves productivity (Bostrom et Yudkowsky, 2014). However, this evolution comes with new demands. These demands include adaptation, upskilling, and reskilling. These are responses to changes in the labor market (Morandini et al., 2023).

AI is also changing the nature of remaining tasks and increasing the complexity of human-machine interactions. It helps people learn the skills needed to work well with these technologies (Xie et al., 2021; Parent-Rocheleau et Parker, 2021). The following hypothesis is formulated in light of the aforementioned work:

H1: Artificial intelligence would influence professional demands.

Concurrently, AI reconfigures the DL. By delegating routine tasks, it refocuses employees on high value added activities, thereby stimulating creativity, judgment, and initiative (Davenport et Kirby, 2016). It also offers easier access to information thanks to intelligent tools that promote faster decision-making (Lahrache et Bekkaoui, 2024). However, some automated systems can limit autonomy by imposing standardized choices (Davenport et Westerman, 2018; Barocas et al., 2024). Based on earlier work, we suggest the second hypothesis:

H2: Artificial intelligence would impact employees'decisions latitude.

1.4.2 Hypotheses Relating to the Impact of Structural Dimensions on Well-Being

In this study, we put forward two main hypotheses to examine the impact of PD and DL on various aspects of job satisfaction, drawing from the Job Demands-Resources Model (JDR) pioneered by Bakker and Demerouti (2001, 2007, 2014).

H3: Job demands influence well-being at work.
H4: Decision latitude would impact well-being at work.

To study these relationships in greater depth, secondary hypotheses have been developed. These studies look at how different people's well-being at work is affected by PD and DL.

Professional Demands, Decision Latitude and Positivity

A positive result between job demands and resources is key to reducing work related stress and generating positive emotions (Bakker & Demerouti, 2007). When demands are high but resources are sufficient, they can enhance motivation and strengthen positive perceptions of the professional environment (Galanakis & Tsitouri, 2022).

By enabling employees to organize their work autonomously, DL reinforces their sense of competence and mastery (Karasek et Theorell, 1990). This fosters positive emotions, such as satisfaction, optimism, and pride, contributing to an emotionally healthy environment (Bakker et Demerouti, 2007). It also facilitates emotional regulation, reducing the risk of burnout and fostering a cooperative work climate (Brotheridge et Grandey, 2002; Sonnentag, 2018).

In light of these findings, we propose two hypotheses:

H3.1: Professional demands would be associated with a variation in the level of positivity employees perceive in their work environment.
H4.1: Decision latitude would be linked to how positive employees feel at work.

Professional Demands, Decision Latitude, and Engagement

Engagement to work, conceptualized through the dimensions of vigor, dedication, and absorption (Schaufeli et Bakker, 2004), appears closely linked to the nature of PD. Those perceived as stimulating reinforce engagement. Those deemed excessive or constraining can lead to gradual disengagement (Bakker et Demerouti, 2017).

DL is also a determining factor. The connection between control over work and organizational engagement was established by Karasek and Theorell (1990). The ability to regulate effort is enhanced by autonomy, as confirmed by Schaufeli and Bakker (2004). Hakanen et al. (2021) show that it helps maintain employee engagement.

Furthermore, DL is a pivotal element of organizational engagement. Karasek and Theorell (1990) establish a link between control over work and organizational engagement. This relationship is confirmed by Schaufeli and Bakker (2004). They emphasize that autonomy enables better effort regulation. Employees' commitment is maintained by autonomy, according to Hakanen et al. (2021).

Finally, the perceived fairness of distributing autonomy, linked to procedural justice, reinforces commitment even under pressure (Colquitt et al., 2001).

Based on these findings, two hypotheses can be formulated:

> H3.2: Professional demands would affect employee level of engagement with their organization.
> H4.2: Decision latitude would affect employees commitment to their organization.

Professional Demands, Decision Latitude and Relationships

High PD, especially in the form of overload or continuous pressure, can have a negative impact on social interactions, impair interpersonal relations, and weaken team cohesion (Van Der Doef et Maes, 1999; African Scientific Journal, 2023). However, the presence of social resources such as support from colleagues or superiors plays a significant moderating role (Bakker et Demerouti, 2001).

DL also contributes to the quality of professional relations by offering greater flexibility in work organization and collective interactions (Gilbert de Terssac, 2012). When there's sufficient social support, it reduces the negative impacts of demands on mental health (Johnson et Hall, 1988) and enhances teamwork (Bakker et Demerouti, 2007; Douanla, Kenne et Yomgni, 2022).

This leads to the following two hypotheses:

> H3.3: Professional demands would affect the quality of interpersonal relations at work.

H4.3: Decision latitude would affect the quality of relationships at work.

Professional Demands, Decision Latitude, and Perception of Meaning

PD impact the perception of meaning at work, depending on whether they are perceived as development opportunities or as constraints incompatible with personal aspirations. Alignment with individual values strengthens the sense of purpose. A mismatch tends to reduce motivation and satisfaction (Bakker et Demerouti, 2017).

The opportunity to use one s skills and influence the content of one's work also promotes perceived meaning. This autonomy places a high value on the individual, strengthens commitment, and encourages personal investment (Douanla, Kenne et Yomgni, 2020). Vandenberghe et al. (2009) point out that decision latitude, by boosting satisfaction, helps reduce avoidance behaviors such as absenteeism.

These things make us think the following:

H3.4: Professional demands would impact how meaning is attributed to work
H4.4: Decision latitude would impact the perception of meaning attributed to work.

Professional Demands, Decision Latitude, and Accomplishment

The link between PD and a sense of accomplishment is based on the difference between factors that are seen as challenges, which make you perform better, learn more, and feel satisfied, and those that are seen as obstacles, like role ambiguity or organizational conflict, which make you less motivated (Cavanaugh et al., 2000).

LD, on the other coast, reinforces the sense of personal and professional accomplishment by enabling the individual to observe the concrete impact of his or her decisions on results. This empowerment feeds prosocial motivation. It also encourages an ethical commitment to action.

The following hypotheses are derived from these findings:

H3.5: Job demands would affect the perceived level of personal and professional accomplishment.
H4.5: Decision latitude would influence the level of perceived personal and professional accomplishment.

2. METHODOLOGY

This study uses a combined methodology consisting of a qualitative exploratory and a quantitative confirmatory phase. This methodological choice is justified by the need to study an area that is still little explored in the Moroccan context. As far as we know, this is the first study that examines AI's effects on occupational wellness through the PD and DL dimensions.

2.1 Exploratory Study

The exploratory phase of this research aims to capture the perceived impact of AI on the structural dimensions of work, namely PD and DL, as well as on the PERMA model's components of well-being. The aim is to identify the perceived mechanisms of influence and the specificities of the Moroccan organizational context in order to feed and refine the initial conceptual model.

2.1.1 Sample and Collection Method

The analysis of Table 1, which presents the characteristics of the qualitative purposive sample, highlights the diversity of the profiles of the interviewees, but also highlights the common characteristics. The sample consists of eight mostly male respondents (seven male/one female), with a relatively young average age between 23 and 39. All of them are in responsible positions in Moroccan organizations integrating Artificial Intelligence, especially in the field of AI. They are directors, managers, founders or consultants, which testifies to the strategic role of Artificial Intelligence in organizational decisions.

Academically, the participants have a high level of education, ranging from professional bachelor's degrees to Phds, with a predominance of business, marketing, management,

engineering and entrepreneurship backgrounds. This diversity enriches analyses of the impact of AI on organizational dynamics and well-being at work.

Lengths ranged from 10 months to seven years, providing both recent and established perspectives on evolving management practices in the digital context.

Finally, the variety of business sectors represented - agri-food, digital, marketing, events, real estate, import-export - ensures sectoral heterogeneity. This enriches the understanding of the impact of AI in professional environments with different organizational logics.

Table 1. Qualitative sample characteristics

Respondent	Gender	Age	Degree/Training	Occupied post	Seniority	Sector of activity
1	Woman	23 years	Master's in International Business	Export logistics manager	10 months	Agri-food
2	Man	24 years	Master's in Entrepreneurship	Manager	4 years	Marketing / Press
3	Man	28 years	Professional Bachelor's in Business Management	General Manager	4 years	Communication, production, event management
4	Man	33 years	Master's in Digital Marketing	Director	7 years	Digital marketing, SEO, website creation
5	Man	39 years	Computer engineer, Master's in Information Systems, Master's 2 student in entrepreneurship	Founder, Manager,Recruitment manager	6 years	Digital, digital marketing
6	Man	25 years	Bachelors in Organizational Management	Director	1 years 10 months	Digital services
7	Man	27 years	Master's in Marketing, Master's in Data Science, 3rd year PhD student	General Director	5 years	Real estate
8	Man	29 years	State Engineer in Food Industry and Safety	QHSE Consultant,Manager	4 years	Computer development, import/export, digital

Source: Authors

2.1.2 Data Collection and Progressing

The interviews lasted an average of 55 minutes. They were audio recorded with the consent of the participants and then transcribed in full to ensure accuracy. Theoretical saturation, a fundamental methodological criterion in qualitative research, was reached after eight interviews, justifying stopping collecting data.

Data analysis was conducted using NVivo 15 software. This software allowed for rigorous thematic coding of the verbatims, classification of the data into conceptual categories, and analytical triangulation to ensure the reliability of the results. This treatment facilitated identifying recurring perceptions regarding the impact of AI on transforming work and well-being in Moroccan organizations.

2.2 Confirmatory Study

This research, the quantitative confirmatory phase, aims to test a set of a priori hypotheses to statistically validate the relationships between AI integration, PD, DL, and job wellbeing. A structured questionnaire was developed using validated scales: Karasek's Job Content Questionnaire (JCQ) for the structural dimensions of work and Seligman's PERMA-Profiler scale to measure well-being. Responses were collected on a 5-point Likert scale.

The sample for the survey was 142 employees from organizations that have had AI implementation in their work processes. Data collection was done by sending the questionnaire to employees of companies that had participated in the semi-structured interviews. In order to broaden the sample, the questionnaire was also distributed on LinkedIn.

The sample is predominantly male and young. More than 85% of respondents are under 35 years of age. The level of education is high. More than 54% of the participants have a Bac+5 or higher.

In terms of occupational status, the majority of respondents are employees. A minority are self-employed. Finally, seniority in the use of AI remains limited: 92.3% report having used AI for less than three years. The data collected was analyzed using SmartPLS, a tool for assessing relationships between variables under study and testing model hypotheses.

2.2.1 Presentation of Research Model Variables

In the research model, special attention is paid to two fundamental variables: AI and working wellbeing. Each of these variables is measured by several constructs.

Well-being at work is addressed through five dimensions: Positivity, Engagement, Relationship, Meaning, and Accomplishment, measured through ten constructs, according to the items developed by Butler and Kern (2014).

As for AI, it is measured by four constructs, according to the items proposed by Buabeng-Andoh (2018) and Maryanto and Kaihatu (2021): speed of task completion, performance improvement, ease of use of AI tools, and access to learning support.

These two variables are analyzed through mediation variables in order to examine their impact. PD, measured by workload, task complexity, and concentration required, and DL, which includes freedom in organizing work, adapting AI tools, and speed of decision making, play a crucial role in this analysis, in line with Karasek (1985) constructs.

Table 2. Variables and constructs

LIBEL	MODALITIES	CODE	AUTHORS
AI **Exogenous variable**	Finish tasks faster. Improved performance with AI. AI tool ease of use. Easy access to learning materials.	IA1 IA2 IA3 IA4	Buabeng-Andoh (2018). Maryanto and Kaihatu (2021
PROFESSIONAL DEMANDS **Mediator variable**	Reduced workload. Increased task complexity. It requires a lot of focus.	EX1 EX2 EX3	Robert Karasek (1985) Bakker et Demerouti (2007)
DECISION LATITUDE. **Mediating variable:**	Freedom in work organization. Adjustment of AI tool functionalities. Fast, efficient decision-making is key.	LAT1 LAT2 LAT3	
POSITIVITY **Endogenous variable.**	Stress reduction with AI. Sense of control with AI.	POS1 POS2	
ENGAGEMENT **Endogenous variable:**	improved concentration with AI. Loss of sense of time with AI.	ENG1 ENG2	Butler et Kern en (2014)
RELATION **Endogenous variable**	Colleague support for AI integration. AI improves communication.	REL1 REL2	
MEANING **Endogenous variable**	Valuing work with AI. Contribution to significant AI projects.	SS1 SS2	
ACCOMPLISHMENT **Endogenous variable**	Fast progress towards goals. Easy attainment of objectives	ACC1 ACC2	

Source: Authors

2.2.2 Presentation of the Preliminary Conceptual Model

After identifying the observable variables associated with each latent variable, the analysis focused on the interaction relationships between these variables.The preliminary conceptual model of the research is graphically depicted using Smart-PLS software, as shown in figure 2.

Figure 2. Preliminary conceptual model of the research

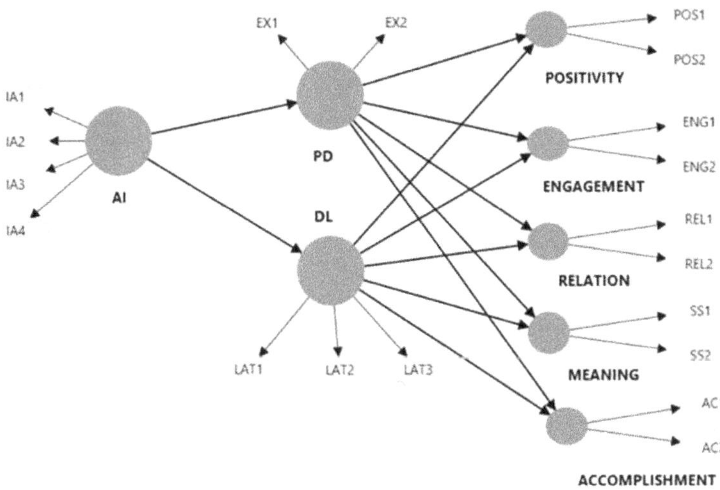

Source: Smart PLS results

This figure illustrates a reflective measurement model. The direction of causality is established from the latent variable to the observed variables. The model consists of 20 latent constructs.

Before embarking on the model refinement process, it is imperative to verify the adequacy of the sample size.

Following the recommendations of Hair et al. (2014), an a priori power analysis was conducted to determine the minimum sample size required to validate the PLS-SEM model. Considering a significance level of 5%, a power of 80%, an average effect ($f^2 = 0.15$), and a maximum of two predictors for an endogenous variable, the minimum required sample size is 68 observations. The sample used in this study (n = 142) far exceeds this threshold, ensuring sufficient robustness of the estimates.

3. RESULTS AND DISCUSSION

In an approach that articulates exploration and validation, this axis articulates the results of both qualitative and quantitative research, confronting them with the theoretical frameworks that have been mobilized.

Each subsection combines the presentation of results with their critical discussion. The aim is to bring empirical contributions into dialogue with theoretical references.

3.1 Results and Discussion of Exploratory Study

The thematic content analysis conducted with eight respondents allows the study of the integration of artificial intelligence in their work environment, with the aim of understanding the perceptions associated with this technology. This analysis examines the relationship between AI and well-being at work, identifying the main effects along several axes, namely:

3.1.1 AI in General (Axis 1)

AI plays a central role in the digital transformation of the organizations surveyed: All respondents describe it as: " *The set of technologies that facilitate the execution of tasks*". The first respondent highlights its role in the execution of daily tasks, while the second emphasizes its impact on *"reducing repetitive tasks, increasing sales, and optimizing processes*". AI aims to *"improve accuracy, speed and productivity*". According to respondent 5.

The tools used, such as ChatGPT Plus, DeepSeek, and Canva, have been integrated for several years, as mentioned by respondents 6 and 3. The impact on workload is perceived positively: respondent 4 notes that AI has allowed him to *"focus on high value-added tasks*", and The seventh respondent adds that: *"It has contributed to his skill development* ".

All agree with Haenlein and Kaplan (2019), who see AI as a means of facilitating tasks and improving productivity, and Makarius et al. (2020), who highlight its role in task optimization and decision making.The interviews confirm that AI enables automation, streamlining and time savings.It is perceived as a lever for efficiency, improves performance and is seen as a useful tool for managers and employees.

3.1.2 Perceived Effect of AI on PD (Axis 2)

The interviews show that the introduction of AI has changed professional requirements, shifting expectations towards more complex and higher value added tasks. The third respondent notes: *"The execution of tasks has become faster and more efficient*", citing examples such as *"inventory, drafting emails, and determining routes*".This reflects an increased demand for speed and precision.

Respondent 2 adds that *AI: "has allowed for a better distribution of tasks, each of us performs our tasks in a balanced manner* ".

One of the respondents mentions increased pressure, like respondent 5, who indicates that "decisions must be made more quickly with AI, which sometimes increases the pressure. "However, respondents 6 and 8 emphasize that *"AI reduces repetitive tasks and promotes analytical and creative missions*". Respondent 4 specifies that AI *"has reduced repetitive tasks and accelerated missions like data analysis* ". Respondent 8 also mentions that *"training has facilitated the adoption of AI, optimizing data analysis and report entry while developing skills*".

The introduction of AI has thus transformed PD by freeing up time for higher value-added tasks. This is in line with the work of Deming (2017) and Lebraty (2019), who see AI as a means of replacing simple tasks and freeing up time for strategic activities.The results also support Arntz, Gregory, and Zierahn (2016), who claim that AI fosters the development of creative and analytical capabilities. While Parker and Grote (2020) suggest that automation can increase workloads, the efficiencies are remarkable.

3.1.3 Perceived Effect of Ai on DI (Axis 3)

The interviews show that the use of AI has increased employees digital literacy. Respondent 1 explains: AI helps me make decisions quickly and correctly. Respondent 3 adds that: *"AI enhances autonomy by simplifying recurring tasks and reducing dependence on superiors, AI has strengthened employee autonomy by simplifying most tasks*". "Employees are increasingly dependent on AI recommendations", notes Respondent 4 *"This dependence is perceived positively, as it supports greater autonomy and efficiency* ".

The work of Brynjolfsson and McAfee (2014) shows that AI frees employees from repetitive tasks and increases their decision-making autonomy, although this leads to dependence on AI systems.Wilson and Daugherty (2018) emphasize that AI helps employees make complex decisions and increases their accountability.AI improves decision latitude by automating repetitive tasks and providing decision support tools, allowing employees to focus on higher-value tasks.This increased autonomy is perceived positively and increases employee efficiency.

3.1.4 Well-Being at Work (Axis 4)

The integration of AI into the work environment improves employees well-being by fostering a positive climate, reducing stress, and better organizing tasks. The second respondent notes a *"Decrease in stress since the introduction of AI* and an increase in satisfaction", which is consistent with Seligman's (2011) work on positive emotions and well being. Fredrickson (2001) argues that these emotions broaden thought processes and encourage constructive behavior. Respondent 3 adds that *"AI has contributed to better work organization, reducing pressure and providing comfort*". However, the fourth respondent emphasizes that: *"AI does not completely replace human interactions, which are essential to maintaining a good work environment*".

AI has increased employee engagement, with the first respondent noting: *"a positive change in employee engagement due to the reduction of repetitive tasks*", and the second respondent stating that*: "AI is perceived as a support tool. Everyone emphasizes that AI facilitates collaboration. It does so by centralizing information. It also automates exchanges. It gives meaning back to work.* ". According to the first respondent: *"AI has changed employees understanding of their work*". The second respondent adds: *"AI has changed employees understanding of their work: AI improves productivity and well being*". In terms of professional development, the third respondent states that: *"AI helps develop skills, and the fourth respondent notes that it improves access to information and collective performance*".

All respondents confirm that *"AI plays a key role in their work by reducing cognitive load, improving sharing and collaboration, and creating a calmer and more motivating work environment*". This is in line with the analysis of Jarrahi (2018), who considers AI as a support tool that reduces stress related to repetitive tasks. The results show that the integration of AI improves the well-being of employees by reducing stress, improving work organization, and promoting collaboration. It is perceived as a lever to increase performance, job satisfaction, autonomy, and strengthen a positive climate.

The following figure shows a word cloud illustrating employees' positive perceptions of how AI affects their wellbeing.

Figure 3. Thematic frequencies

Source: NVIVO results

3.2 Confirmatory Study Results and Discussion

In a confirmatory approach based on PLS structural equation modeling, the analysis begins with the evaluation of the measurement model, specifically through the criteria of reliability and validity. This preliminary step is essential before moving on to hypothesis testing and overall validation of the structural model.

3.2.1 Validation of the Research Measurement Model

Validation of the measurement model is essential to ensure the reliability and validity of the constructs used in this research. It involves evaluating the relationships between latent variables and their observed indicators by verifying convergent and discriminant validity, as well as the reliability of the measurements.

Table 3. Measurement model quality index

	Items	Facteur Loading	Alpha Cronbach	Fiabilité composite	AVE
AI	IA1 IA2 IA3 IA4	0.829 0.834 0.757 0.837	0.831	0.888	0.664
Professional Demands1	EX1 EX2	0.918 0.613	0.399	0.750	0.609
Decision Latitude	LAT1 LAT2 LAT3	0.874 0.838 0.808	0.792	0.878	0.706
Positive	POS1 POS2	0.855 0.877	0.668	0.857	0.750
Engagement	ENG1 ENG2	0.904 0.869	0.730	0.880	0.786
Relation	REL1 REL2	0.733 0.895	0.521	0.800	0.669
Meaning	SS1 SS2	0.899 0.905	0.771	0.897	0.814
Accomplishment	AC1 AC2	0.935 0.935	0.856	0.933	0.874

Source: Authors, based on smartpls results

The obtained results are evidence of the good specification of the measurement model for all the constructs under evaluation.

The observed factor loadings are mostly above 0.7, indicating a strong contribution of the items to the measurement of their respective dimensions. This reflects a satisfactory fit between the observed variables and the latent factors.

The Cronbach's alpha coefficients are mostly higher than the recommended threshold of 0.7, indicating an acceptable internal reliability, with the notable exception of the construct of professional demands, whose alpha of 0.399 indicates an insufficient internal consistency.

In the context of PLS-SEM modeling, it is widely accepted that composite reliability is a more appropriate measure of internal reliability than Cronbach's alpha. Unlike Cronbach's alpha, composite reliability takes into account individual factor loadings, making it more precise in the context of PLS-SEM, where models are often complex and indicators may have different weights.

In addition, the composite reliability values are all above 0.7, confirming satisfactory internal consistency of the various scales. Similarly, the Average Variance Extracted (AVE) is consistently above the threshold of 0.5, indicating good convergent validity of the constructs, meaning that the items share a sufficient proportion of variance with the factor they measure.

Furthermore, the AVE is a key indicator of convergent validity, and a value greater than 0.50 indicates that the majority of the variance of the indicators is well explained by the underlying latent variable (Fornell & Larcker, 1981).In this regard, Hair et al. (2021) specify that if the composite reliability is greater than 0.70 and the AVE exceeds 0.50, the variable can be considered reliable and valid, even if the Cronbach's alpha is less than 0.70.

Discriminant validity was assessed using two approaches commonly recommended in the literature: the first is based on Fornell and Larcker's (1981) criterion that the square root of the AVE of each construct must be greater than its correlations with the other constructs, indicating that each construct shares more variance with its own indicators than with those of another construct (Hair et al., 2022).

Table 4. Variable correlation (AVE root)

		AI	DL			PD		
	0.935							
AI	0.605							
DL	0.685							
ENGAGEMENT	0.634			0.887				
MEANING	0.703			0.712	0.902			
PD	0.485			0.596	0.488			
POSITIVITY	0.613			0.722	0.678		0.866	
RELATION	0.455			0.631	0.571		0.486	0.818

Source: Smart PLS results

The second approach is to examine cross-loadings, where the external loading of an indicator on its construct is expected to be greater than the sum of its loadings on the other constructs (Hair et al., 2022). The results of the analyses conducted in this study show that both of these criteria are met, confirming that the discriminant validity of the model is adequately established.

Table 5. Cross-loading index

	ACCOMPLISHMENT	ENGAGEMENT	PD	AI	DL	POSITIVITY	RELATION	MEANING
AC1	0.935	0.600	0.437	0.568	0.644	0.602	0.407	0.695
AC2	0.935	0.585	0.471	0.563	0.636	0.544	0.444	0.619
ENG1	0.619	0.904	0.554	0.684	0.768	0.723	0.535	0.726
ENG2	0.499	0.869	0.501	0.517	0.660	0.546	0.589	0.524
EX1	0.477	0.582	0.918	0.688	0.631	0.542	0.435	0.442
EX2	0.236	0.295	0.613	0.280	0.270	0.235	0.268	0.310
IA1	0.579	0.558	0.564	0.829	0.586	0.578	0.393	0.520
IA2	0.493	0.569	0.534	0.834	0.574	0.558	0.417	0.550
IA3	0.376	0.487	0.535	0.757	0.545	0.490	0.300	0.372
IA4	0.517	0.607	0.570	0.837	0.629	0.544	0.397	0.476
LAT1	0.598	0.756	0.517	0.620	0.874	0.615	0.619	0.576
LAT2	0.538	0.626	0.541	0.634	0.838	0.598	0.446	0.624
LAT3	0.587	0.651	0.520	0.554	0.808	0.728	0.526	0.616
POS1	0.485	0.578	0.466	0.546	0.638	0.855	0.384	0.523
POS2	0.574	0.670	0.467	0.607	0.695	0.877	0.456	0.647
REL1	0.195	0.430	0.328	0.303	0.393	0.282	0.733	0.293
REL2	0.498	0.586	0.424	0.439	0.614	0.484	0.895	0.594
SS1	0.625	0.644	0.468	0.581	0.636	0.583	0.501	0.899
SS2	0.644	0.641	0.413	0.484	0.662	0.639	0.529	0.905

Source: Smart PLS results

Overall, these results demonstrate the reliability and validity of the construction measures used for the assessment of AI and DL, as well as the different components of well-being at work, which have satisfactory psychometric qualities.

In the graph generated by the PLS software, the estimation of all the parameters of the constructs is shown.

Figure 4. Estimated measurement model under PLS

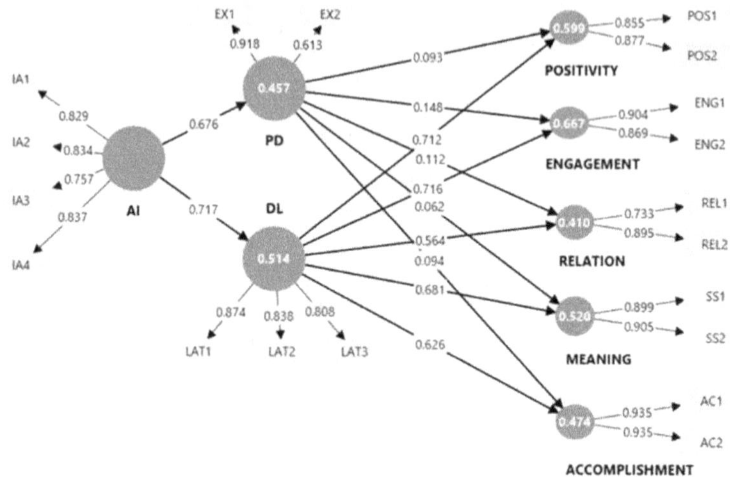

Source: Smart PLS results

3.2.2 Structural Model Evaluation

Once the reflective measurement model is evaluated, the analysis continues by examining the structural model to test the hypotheses and estimate the direct and indirect effects between AI (exogenous variable), the dimensions of workplace wellbeing (endogenous variables), and the mediators (PD and DL).

However, it is crucial to verify the absence of multicollinearity problems among the model variables before proceeding with the analysis.

Table 6. Variance inflation factor (VIF)

	VIF
AC1	2.271
AC2	2.271
ENG1	1.492
ENG2	1.492
EX1	1.066
EX2	1.066
IA1	2.308
IA2	2.403

continued on following page

Table 6. Continued

	VIF
IA3	1.678
IA4	2.000
LAT1	1.946
LAT2	1.789
LAT3	1.490
POS1	1.335
POS2	1.335
REL1	1.141
REL2	1.141
SS1	1.650
SS2	1.650

Source: Smart PLS results

The VIF values, which are all below 2.5 (ranging from 1.066 to 2.403), indicate the absence of significant multicollinearity. This guarantees reliable estimates of the regression coefficients and a good distinction between the independent variables, which strengthens the validity of the model.

Testing Research Hypotheses Using PLS Method

The hypotheses are tested by analyzing the statistical significance of the path coefficients estimated using the bootstrap method. In accordance with the recommendations of Hair et al. (2022), this significance is evaluated using t values, according to the classical thresholds: $t > 1.96$ ($p < 0.05$), $t > 2.57$ ($p < 0.01$), and $t > 3.29$ ($p < 0.001$).

The results presented, derived from the SmartPLS software, provide the estimated coefficients and associated p-values. This allows the statistical validity of the proposed relationships between the model variables to be assessed.

Table 7. Structural model hypothesis testing

	Échantillon original (O)	Moyenne de l'échantillon (M)	Écart-type (STDEV)	Statistiques T (|O/STDEV|)	Valeurs P
AI -> DL	0.717	0.719	0.046	15.687	0.000
AI -> PD	0.676	0.682	0.053	12.724	0.000
DL -> ACCOMPLISHMENT	0.626	0.622	0.080	7.849	0.000
DL -> ENGAGEMENT	0.716	0.714	0.058	12.271	0.000
DL -> MEANING	0.681	0.680	0.082	8.298	0.000
DL -> POSITIVITY	0.712	0.712	0.056	12.640	0.000
DL -> RELATION	0.564	0.570	0.079	7.132	0.000
PD -> ACCOMPLISHMENT	0.094	0.097	0.096	0.975	0.330
PD -> ENGAGEMENT	0.148	0.149	0.070	2.128	0.033
PD -> MEANING	0.062	0.061	0.097	0.638	0.524
PD -> POSITIVITY	0.093	0.094	0.069	1.350	0.177
PD -> RELATION	0.112	0.103	0.080	1.401	0.161

Source: Smart PLS results

In fact, seven relationships show a highly significant relationship at a threshold of less than 0.01, with Student's t-values well above 3.29. This is especially true for the relationships expressed by hypotheses: H4.1, H4.2, H4.3, H.4.4, and H4.5.

Moreover, with a Student's t-value significantly greater than 1.96, only one relationship, represented by hypothesis H3.2, shows a highly significant relationship at a threshold lower than 0.05.

On the other hand, hypotheses H3.1, H3.3, H3.4, and H3.5 are rejected as not significant.

Mediator Effect Test

At this level, we proceeded to test the indirect relationships, specifically the mediating effect of PD and DL between AI and the dimensions of well-being at work, in addition to the direct hypotheses initially formulated.

The following hypotheses were formulated as a result:

Table 8. Hypotheses

Hypothesis related to PD	Hypothesis related to DL
H3.a: Profession demands would mediate the link between artificial intelligence and positivity.	H4.a: Decision latitude would mediate the relationship between artificial intelligence and positivity.
H3.b: Professional demands would mediate the effect of artificial intelligence on engagement.	H4.b: The relationship between artificial intelligence and engagement would be mediated by decision latitude.
H3.c:Professional demands would mediate the relationships between artificial intelligence on relationship.	H4.C:Decision latitude would have a mediating effect on the relationships between artificial intelligence and interpersonal relationships.
H3.d: : Professional demands would act as a mediator in the relationship between artificial intelligence and meaning at work.	H4.d: Decision latitude would have a mediating effect on the relationship between artificial intelligence and the meaning of work.
H3.e: Professional demands would mediate the relationship between artificial intelligence and accomplishment.	H4.e: The relationship between artificial intelligence and accomplishment would be mediated by decision latitude.

To this end, the PLS approach, operationalized by the SMART PLS software, allows us to highlight the results related to indirect effects. These are presented in the table below:

Table 9. Mediation hypothesis test

	Échantillon original (O)	Moyenne de l'échantillon (M)	Écart-type (STDEV)	Statistiques T (|O/STDEV|)	Valeurs P
AI -> DL -> ENGAGEMENT	0.513	0.514	0.057	8.949	0.000
AI -> PD -> POSITIVITY	0.063	0.065	0.048	1.308	0.191
AI -> DL -> MEANING	0.488	0.489	0.071	6.879	0.000
AI -> PD -> RELATION	0.076	0.071	0.056	1.361	0.174
AI -> DL -> POSITIVITY	0.511	0.513	0.060	8.557	0.000
AI -> DL -> RELATION	0.404	0.410	0.063	6.424	0.000
AI -> PD -> ACCOMPLISHMENT	0.064	0.069	0.068	0.937	0.349
AI -> DL -> ACCOMPLISHMENT	0.449	0.448	0.070	6.371	0.000

continued on following page

Table 9. Continued

	Échantillon original (O)	Moyenne de l'échantillon (M)	Écart-type (STDEV)	Statistiques T (|O/STDEV|)	Valeurs P
AI -> PD -> ENGAGEMENT	0.100	0.102	0.050	2.011	0.044
AI -> PD -> MEANING	0.042	0.043	0.067	0.622	0.534

Source: Smart PLS results

Reading the results presented in Table 6, we can conclude that out of the ten indirect relationships tested, six relationships are validated: in fact, five relationships show a highly significant relationship at a threshold lower than 0.01, with Students t-values significantly higher than 3.29, especially regarding the relationships expressed by hypotheses H4.a, H4.b, H4.c, H4.d, H4.e. While hypothesis H3.b shows a highly significant relationship at a threshold lower than 0.05 with a t-value greater than 1.96, hypothesis H3.c shows a highly significant relationship at a threshold lower than 0.05 with a t-value greater than 1.96.

While H3.b shows a highly significant relationship at a threshold lower than 0.05 with a t-value greater than 1.96.

On the other hand, hypotheses H3.a, H3.c, H3.d, H3.e are rejected because they show no significance according to Hair et al (2022) usual t-thresholds (>1.96; >2.57; >3.29).

Structural Model Quality Assessment

It is appropriate to use the structural model quality assessment (Hair et al., 2022) to evaluate the model's ability to predict the target constructs.

For the coefficient of determination, Table 7 shows that DL has an R^2 of 0.514. This indicates a moderate relationship with AI. Similarly, PD has an R^2 of 0.457, also indicating a moderate relationship with AI. On the other hand, the variables Positivity, Involvement, Relationships, Meaning, and Accomplishment all have an R^2 between 0.33 and 0.67, indicating a moderate relationship with DL and PD.

There is a slight difference when we compare this with the adjusted coefficient of determination.

Table 10. Determination coefficient

	R-carré	R-carré ajusté
ACCOMPLISHMENT	0.474	0.466
DL	0.514	0.511
ENGAGEMENT	0.667	0.662
MEANING	0.520	0.513
PD	0.457	0.453
POSITIVITY	0.599	0.593
RELATION	0.410	0.401

Source: Smart PLS results

The results of the strength of the effect show that AI has a strong influence on PD ($f^2 = 1.058$) and LD ($f^2 = 0.842$). DL also shows a significant effect on four dimensions of well-being at work, with values above 0.35. The exception is interpersonal relations, where the effect remains moderate.

In contrast, PD has no significant effect on positivity, purpose, relationships, and accomplishment ($f^2 < 0.02$). It has only a weak effect on commitment ($f^2 = 0.040$).

Table 11. F^2 effect size

	carré f
AI -> DL	1.058
AI -> PD	0.842
DL -> ACCOMPLISHMENT	0.453
DL -> ENGAGEMENT	0.936
DL -> MEANING	0.588
DL -> POSITIVITY	0.769
DL -> RELATION	0.328
PD -> ACCOMPLISHMENT	0.010
PD -> ENGAGEMENT	0.040
PD -> MEANING	0.005
PD -> POSITIVITY	0.013
PD -> RELATION	0.013

Source: Smart PLS results

The Stone-Geisser Q^2 coefficient is a measure of the predictive ability of the model. As can be seen in Table 9, all of the variables have Q^2 values greater than 0, which indicates an acceptable level of predictive validity for all blocks of variables (Hair et al., 2022).

Table 12. Stone-Geisser coefficient (Q2)

	Q^2predict	EQM	EAM
ACCOMPLISHMENT	0.349	0.825	0.664
DL	0.508	0.716	0.587
ENGAGEMENT	0.455	0.750	0.592
MEANING	0.337	0.831	0.663
PD	0.445	0.757	0.596
POSITIVITY	0.429	0.772	0.623
RELATION	0.205	0.906	0.703

Source: Smart PLS results

The final indicator to consider is the SRMR. Generally, a value below 0.08 is considered the threshold of an acceptable model (Henseler et al., 2016; Hair et al., 2017). Our study estimated SRMR value is 0.07, suggesting that the data is of good quality.

However the SRMR is a useful indicator of model fit, researchers should not use it in isolation to accept or reject a model. They should consider a range of indicators, such as: R^2, Q^2, path coefficients, and effect sizes (Hair et al., 2021:216).

This result confirms a good degree of agreement between the empirical data and the conceptual model. Thus, the validity of the proposed mode is strengthened.

Figure 5. Structural model

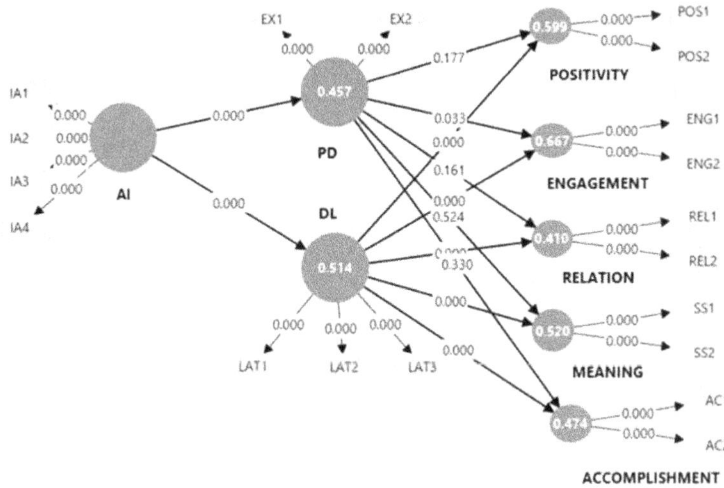

Source: Smart PLS results

3.2.3 Discussion of Results

Analysis of the results shows that integrating AI into the work environment is significantly associated with increasing DL ($\beta = 0.717$, $p < 0.001$) as well as intensifying PD ($\beta = 0.676$, $p < 0.001$).These results confirm hypotheses H1 and H2, indicating that AI has a significant impact on these two dimensions of work.

This observation is in line with the work of Brynjolfsson and McAfee (2014), who emphasize that AI tends to augment human capabilities rather than replace them, particularly enriching cognitive and decision-making tasks. Similarly, Autor (2015) highlights that automation changes the structure of jobs by promoting non-routine activities that require more judgment and autonomy. These results suggest that AI is not limited to streamlining processes, but also reshapes the contours of professional activity by enhancing individual agency.

With regard to the mechanisms linking technological changes to well-being at work, the results confirm the central role of DLit exerts a significant positive influence on all the dimensions of well-being studied: professional performance, commitment, meaning of work, positive emotions, and quality of interpersonal relationships ($p < 0.001$ for all).These results validate hypotheses H4.1 to H4.5, showing that AI indirectly affects these components through DL. Therefore, mediation hypotheses H4.a to H4.e are also confirmed.

This dynamic is perfectly in line with the demand-control model proposed by Karasek (1979), according to which a high degree of decision-making control mitigates the effects of work-related stress and enhances well-being. It is also supported by Deci and Ryan (2000) self-determination theory, which identifies autonomy as a fundamental psychological need.

In contrast, PD although enhanced by AI, have only a limited effect on well-being: only the relationships with commitment appear significant ($\beta = 0.148$, $p = 0.033$), while their relationships with achievement, meaning, positive emotions, and interpersonal relationships remain insignificant. Hypotheses H3.1, H3.3, H3.4, and H3.5 are therefore rejected.

This observation is consistent with Bakker and Demerouti's (2007) model of job demands and resources. According to this model, demands that are not compensated by adequate resources can have only a marginal or even negative effect on well-being indicators.

The PLS structural equation analysis reveals that only DL has a significant mediating role between AI and the dimensions of well-being at work, while PD only has an effect on engagement.

Five significant relationships were identified:

Employee engagement is strongly influenced by DL (71.6%) and to a lesser extent by PD (14.8%), suggesting that work engagement depends on both decision autonomy and a moderate level of task stimulation. Managers must therefore create a participative environment that promotes decision autonomy while providing engaging professional challenges.

On the other hand, for the other dimensions of well-being, namely positive emotions (71.2% explained by the DL), meaning of work (68.1% explained by the DL), accomplishment (62.6% explained by the DL), and quality of professional relationships (56.4% explained by the DL), the PD shows no significant effect. To improve the emotional, existential, and relational well-being of employees, managers should focus on expanding the scope of action, clarifying the purpose of work, and promoting accountability in professional interactions.

This lack of effect can be explained by the way the PD have been operationalized, namely the reduction of workload and task complexity. These indicators reflect structural constraints rather than sources of intrinsic engagement, but in a context where employees have a high degree of DL, these demands tend to lose their explanatory power, as employees then perceive workload and complexity as manageable challenges rather than stressors.

Autonomy acts as a protective moderator. It mitigates the effects of constraints and enhances perceptions of control and competence.

In addition, motivational, social, and existential factors are more important than quantitative variables related to work intensity or difficulty for the subjective components of well-being, such as meaning, positive emotions, or quality of relationships.

Only the dimension of engagement, which is more behavioral, seems to be partially activated by a certain level of demands. It serves as a source of stimulation and mobilization.

CONCLUSION

This chapter offers an original contribution to the analysis of the impact of AI on workplace well-being, using the BIAT (Workplace Well-being and AI) model, designed as an integrative framework that intersects organizational, human, technological and ethical dimensions. By articulating the contributions of the Job Demands-Resources (JD-R) model, the Karasek model (JDC) and the PERMA model, this research sheds light on the dynamics through which AI reconfigures work conditions and redefines employees' subjective experience.

Empirical results show that the introduction of AI in professional environments significantly changes the organization of work, increasing PD and decreasing DL, and that these two dimensions emerge as important mediators in the relationship between the use of AI and the components of job satisfaction. Perceived autonomy emerges as an essential lever for engagement and a sense of achievement, although its positive effect may be limited in cases of overload or badly regulated pressure.

Onc of thc main contributions of this study lies in the recognition of the structuring role of AI in the work experience, beyond its simple technological function. It thus calls for a rethinking of management practices in order to conceive AI as a lever for employee empowerment, provided that their autonomy is preserved, the constraints generated are contained, and an environment conducive to professional development is fostered.

At the theoretical and methodological level, this research highlights the central mediating mechanisms of freedom of choice and EP, thereby enriching the explanatory models of well-being in technological contexts. Carried out in the Moroccan context, it also provides a contextualized perspective that highlights cultural and organizational specificities that influence the perceived effects of AI. Furthermore, the development of the BIAT model represents a significant conceptual advance, as it brings together dimensions that are often treated separately in a single approach.

However, it is important to emphasize that this quantitative reading contrasts with the qualitative data obtained from interviews with directors and founders of companies that have integrated AI into their processes. These actors emphasize the structuring role of PD in creating a stimulating and motivating environment conducive to the development of well-being. The discrepancy between quantitative results and qualitative observations requires a nuanced interpretation that takes account of the nature of the tasks, the level of autonomy provided, and the organizational culture in which the work experience is embedded.

From a managerial perspective, the results invite a rethinking of AI integration along four priority orientations: first, strengthen decision making autonomy by considering AI as a tool for augmenting rather than substituting human capabilities; next, regulate PD by ensuring that it is accompanied by adequate resources such as training, support, and work reorganization; furthermore, restore meaning to work by embedding the use of AI in a shared vision of organizational goals. Finally, preserve human interactions by maintaining spaces for cooperation and exchange to ensure the quality of the organizational climate. Such human centered technology governance that balances performance, well-being, and social justice is a prerequisite for the successful integration of AI.

Despite its contributions, this study has certain limitations. The exclusive use of the PERMA model, while useful, does not encompass all dimensions of well-being, particularly those related to organizational justice or recognition. Moreover, the conceptual critiques directed at this model (overlaps, partial validity) can limit the scope of the results. Furthermore, certain aspects specific to AI, such as algorithmic transparency or user interfaces, have not been systematically taken into account, even though they strongly influence perceptions. The cross-sectional methodology also limits the robustness of causal inferences, and the organizational context under study makes the results difficult to generalize.

To address these limitations, several research avenues emerge: It would be appropriate to use longitudinal approaches to track the trajectories of AI's impact on the psychosocial dimensions of work over time.

It would also be relevant to refine the analyses by distinguishing types of AI according to their functionalities and degree of automation. A thorough exploration of ethical dimensions such as surveillance, algorithmic fairness, or privacy protection would help to better understand workers' attitudes. Finally, comparative studies in other cultural and sectoral contexts would help to test the robustness and transferability of the BIAT model.

REFERENCES

Arntz, M., Gregory, T., & Zierahn, U. (2016). The risk of automation for jobs in OECD countries: A comparative analysis.

Bachelard, O. (2017). Optimiser le bien-être au travail et la performance globale : Enjeux et perspectives. *Regards*, *51*(1), 169–179. DOI: 10.3917/regar.051.0169

Bakker, A. B., & Demerouti, E. (2017). Job demands–resources theory: Taking stock and looking forward. *Journal of Occupational Health Psychology*, *22*(3), 273–285. DOI: 10.1037/ocp0000056 PMID: 27732008

Ballesteros-Leiva, F., Poilpot-Rocaboy, G., & St-Onge, S. (2017). The relationship between life-domain interactions and the well-being of internationally mobile employees. *Personnel Review*, *46*(2), 237–254. DOI: 10.1108/PR-05-2015-0142

Boucher, K. B. (2023). Mécanismes expliquant l'effet longitudinal du climat de sécurité psychosocial sur l'engagement et l'épuisement chez les professionnels de l'enseignement et des soins de santé pendant la pandémie COVID-19 (Doctoral dissertation, Université Laval).

Brunzell, T., Stokes, H., & Waters, L. (2016). Trauma-informed positive education: Using positive psychology to strengthen vulnerable students. *Contemporary School Psychology*, *20*(1), 63–83. DOI: 10.1007/s40688-015-0070-x

Cavanaugh, M. A., Boswell, W. R., Roehling, M. V., & Boudreau, J. W. (2000). An empirical examination of self-reported work stress among US managers. *The Journal of Applied Psychology*, *85*(1), 65–74. DOI: 10.1037/0021-9010.85.1.65 PMID: 10740957

De Terssac, G. (2012). Autonomie et travail. Dictionnaire du travail, 47-53.

Demerouti, E. (2025). Job demands-resources and conservation of resources theories: How do they help to explain employee well-being and future job design? *Journal of Business Research*, *192*(C), 115296. DOI: 10.1016/j.jbusres.2025.115296

Demerouti, E., Bakker, A. B., & Halbesleben, J. R. (2015). Productive and counterproductive job crafting: A daily diary study. *Journal of Occupational Health Psychology*, *20*(4), 457–469. DOI: 10.1037/a0039002 PMID: 25798721

Deming, D. J. (2021). *The growing importance of decision-making on the job (No. w28733)*. National Bureau of Economic Research.

Demlehner, Q., & Laumer, S. (2020). Shall we use it or not? Explaining the adoption of artificial intelligence for car manufacturing purposes.

Donaldson, S. I., & Donaldson, S. I. (2020). The positive functioning at work scale: Psychometric assessment, validation, and measurement invariance. *Journal of Well-Being Assessment*, *4*(2), 181–215. DOI: 10.1007/s41543-020-00033-1

Douanla, J., Kenne, J. M. N., & Tawembe, N. P. Y. (2020). Latitude décisionnelle, implication et comportements de citoyenneté organisationnelle : Une mise en exergue des relations singulières en situation de sous-emploi. *Revue Française d'Economie et de Gestion*, *1*(6).

Goodman, L. A., Wilson, J. M., Helms, J. E., Greenstein, N., & Medzhitova, J. (2018). Becoming an advocate: Processes and outcomes of a relationship-centered advocacy training model. *The Counseling Psychologist*, *46*(2), 122–153. DOI: 10.1177/0011000018757168

Harju, L. K., Kaltiainen, J., & Hakanen, J. J. (2021). The double-edged sword of job crafting: The effects of job crafting on changes in job demands and employee well-being. *Human Resource Management*, *60*(6), 953–968. DOI: 10.1002/hrm.22054

Jarrahi, M. H. (2018). Artificial intelligence and the future of work: Human-AI symbiosis in organizationnal decision making. *Business Horizons*, *61*(4), 577–586. DOI: 10.1016/j.bushor.2018.03.007

Johnson, J. V., & Hall, E. M. (1988). Job strain, work place social support, and cardiovascular disease: A cross-sectional study of a random sample of the Swedish working population. *American Journal of Public Health*, *78*(10), 1336–1342. DOI: 10.2105/AJPH.78.10.1336 PMID: 3421392

Khaw, D., & Kern, M. (2014). A cross-cultural comparison of the PERMA model of well-being. *Undergraduate Journal of Psychology at Berkeley, University of California*, *8*(1), 10–23.

Kirby, J., & Davenport, T. (2016). The knowledge jobs most likely to be automated. *Harvard Business Review*, 1–2.

Lahrache, , RBekkaoui, , A. (2024). The impact of artificial intelligence on decision-making. *Revue Internationale des Sciences de Gestion*, *7*(3).

Lu, Y. (2019). Artificial intelligence : A survey on evolution, models, applications and future trends. *Journal of Management Analytics*, *6*(1), 1–29. DOI: 10.1080/23270012.2019.1570365

Moura, E. O. D., & Bispo, M. D. S. (2020). Sociomateriality: Theories, methodology, and practice. Canadian Journal of Administrative Sciences/Revue Canadienne des Sciences de l'Administration, 37(3), 350-365.

Mourad, K., & Salahddine, A. (2023). The acceptance of SAP by the employees of the Regional Agricultural Valuation Office of Souss Massa: TAM2. *American Scientific Journal*, *3*(16), 544–544.

Parker, S. K., & Grote, G. (2022). Automation, algorithms, and beyond: Why work design matters more than ever in a digital world. *Applied Psychology*, *71*(4), 1171–1204. DOI: 10.1111/apps.12241

Pinck, A. S., & Sonnentag, S. (2018). Leader mindfulness and employee well-being: The mediating role of transformational leadership. *Mindfulness*, *9*(3), 884–896. DOI: 10.1007/s12671-017-0828-5

Saboune, K. (2022). The deterioration of well-being at work in an EHPAD: An analysis based on the concept of the psychological contract and the job demands-resources model. @. *GRH*, *42*(1), 35–58. DOI: 10.3917/grh.042.0035

Schaufeli, W. B. (2017). Applying the Job Demands-Resources model: A 'how to'guide to measuring and tackling work engagement and burnout. *Organizational Dynamics*, *46*(2), 120–132. DOI: 10.1016/j.orgdyn.2017.04.008

Sonnentag, S. (2018). The recovery paradox: Portraying the complex interplay between job stressors, lack of recovery, and poor well-being. *Research in Organizational Behavior*, *38*, 169–185. DOI: 10.1016/j.riob.2018.11.002

Van der Doef, M., & Maes, S. (1999). The job demand-control (-support) model and psychological well-being: A review of 20 years of empirical research. *Work and Stress*, *13*(2), 87–114. DOI: 10.1080/026783799296084

Vandenberghe, C., Stordeur, S., & d'Hoore, W. (2009). Une analyse des effets de la latitude de décision, de l'épuisement émotionnel et de la satisfaction au travail sur l'absentéisme au sein des unités de soins infirmiers. *Le Travail Humain*, *72*(3), 209–228. DOI: 10.3917/th.723.0209

Vansteenkiste, M., Ryan, R. M., & Soenens, B. (2020). Basic psychological need theory: Advancements, critical themes, and future directions. *Motivation and Emotion*, *44*(1), 1–31. DOI: 10.1007/s11031-019-09818-1

Wang, W., Yin, H., & Huang, S. (2016). The missing links between emotional job demand and exhaustion and satisfaction: Testing a moderated mediation model. *Journal of Management & Organization*, *22*(1), 80–95. DOI: 10.1017/jmo.2015.21

Wilson, H. J., & Daugherty, P. R. (2018). Collaborative intelligence: Humans and AI are joining forces. *Harvard Business Review*, *96*(4), 114–123.

Zhang, R., Yang, Y., Fang, Q., Liu, Y., Zhu, X., Wang, M., & Su, L. (2020). Effect of indoors artificial lighting conditions on computer-based learning performance. *International Journal of Environmental Research and Public Health, 17*(7), 2537. DOI: 10.3390/ijerph17072537 PMID: 32276306

Zhou, W., Wang, C., Liu, Y., Zhang, W., & Chen, Z. (2017). A Research of Influence on HR Management of Robots Used in a Large Scale. *J. Nanjing Univ. Philos. Humanit. Soc. Sci*, *54*, 23–34.

ENDNOTE

1 After applying the PLS algorithm and performing several iterations, we eliminated one item below 0;6 from the professional requirements variable.

Chapter 5
The contribution of artificial intelligence to the entrepreneur's resilience

Hafsa Ouahi
https://orcid.org/0009-0003-1541-4708
Faculty of Legal, Economic and Social Sciences, Marrakesh, Morocco

Mohamed Bouikiker
Faculty of Legal, Economic and Social Sciences, Marrakesh, Morocco

Majda El Agy
Faculty of Legal, Economic and Social Sciences, Marrakesh, Morocco

ABSTRACT

The aim of this research is to explore how artificial intelligence strengthens the individual resilience of entrepreneurs. To achieve this, we undertook a literature review, drawing on social cognitive theory (Bandura, 1986), to analyze the links between artificial intelligence and entrepreneurial resilience. Next, an exploratory qualitative study was conducted with ten entrepreneurs operating in the ICT sector. The results show that artificial intelligence is a tool that enables entrepreneurs to be more innovative and productive. In addition, AI strengthens the individual resilience of entrepreneurs, optimizing time management and promoting more effective post-adversity learning. Additionally, the present research makes two major contributions. Theoretically, this research relates artificial intelligence to the individual resilience of entrepreneurs. From an empirical point of view, shedding light on how artificial intelligence enhances entrepreneurial resilience as an indispensable point on which

DOI: 10.4018/979-8-3373-5499-6.ch005

Moroccan entrepreneurial actors can draw, particularly in times of adversity.

1. INTRODUCTION

Given the frequency of entrepreneurial failures, resilience is of crucial importance for entrepreneurs, allowing them to recover from these setbacks and advance the entrepreneurial process (Yang & Danes, 2015). Indeed, this ability of entrepreneurs to respond positively and grow despite adversity provides them with several advantages, both economically and psychologically (Li et al., 2024).

Furthermore, through a review of the literature on entrepreneur's resilience, we found that its antecedents mainly focus on personal characteristics, such as confidence (Hayward et al., 2010), optimism (Duchek, 2018), learning (Lafuente et al., 2019) and experience (Yao et al., 2021), and environmental factors, namely collective intelligence (Mignenan, 2021) and co-founder support (Li et al., 2024). Despite these advances, scientific literature on entrepreneur's resilience reveals some dissatisfaction. The marginalization of the role of new technologies, namely artificial intelligence (AI), in building and developing a resilient posture is one of these shortcomings. To our knowledge, previous studies have addressed the role of digitalization or digital transformation in organizational resilience (Amghar et al., 2023; Gu et al., 2023; Nguyen et al., 2024), thus ignoring the importance of AI and the individual resilience of entrepreneurs.

According to the World Bank report published in 2024, the survival rate of Moroccan businesses after 5 years is estimated at 53%, and the official exit rate through deregistration is only 1.2%. Indeed, this survival rate places partial emphasis on the individual resilience of Moroccan entrepreneurs. In this sense, Jaldi (2022) and Benraoui et al., (2023) have argued that this resilience depends on several internal and external factors, such as AI.

Based on data from the Organization for Economic Co-operation and Development (OECD) (2023), the report of the United Nations Educational, Scientific and Cultural Organization (UNESCO, 2024) highlights a significant progression between 2020 and 2023 in the adoption of AI by Moroccan companies. This adoption concerns various sectors, particularly media, marketing, social platforms, and IT infrastructure. Therefore, the main objective of this research is to highlight the opportunities that AI offers to entrepreneurs in the technology sector, while analyzing how this innovative tool strengthens their resilience in the face of challenges encountered in their entrepreneurial activity. This need, both theoretical and empirical, leads us to seek answers to the following main question: **How does artificial intelligence strengthen the resilience of entrepreneurs?**

This general question is broken down into three sub-questions:

- What factors determine the adoption of artificial intelligence by Moroccan entrepreneurs?
- How do AI tools strengthen the individual resilience of Moroccan entrepreneurs after adversity?

To address this issue, this research will first rely on a literature review that synthesizes the main previous research and key concepts associated with entrepreneur's resilience and AI. An exploratory qualitative study is then required to deepen our knowledge of this question.

2. LITERATURE REVIEW

2.1. Entrepreneur's Resilience

With the emergence of the notion of "second-chance entrepreneurship," the individual resilience of entrepreneurs continues to occupy an important place in entrepreneurial literature (Bernard, 2008; Cusin, 2017; Branicki et al. 2018; Gentile & Mothe, 2022; Tanner et al.2022). Indeed, through a thorough review of the literature, it appears that there is currently no unanimously accepted definition. Several authors define this concept as a personality trait (Hayward et al. 2010; Ayala & Manzano, 2014; Ngah & Salleh, 2015), while others favor the notion of process, thus integrating the shock experienced as an essential dimension in the resilience process (Cope, 2011; Bernard & Barbosa, 2016; Bernard & Fayolle, 2016; Cusin, 2017; Gentile & Mothe, 2022).

The trait approach considers resilience as a unique personal quality or capacity that allows the entrepreneur to cope with a disruptive event and adapt to it in a positive manner (Duening, 2010; Bullough & Renko, 2013; Bullough et al., 2014). Among these qualities, Hayward et al. (2010) focused on trust, Ayala and Manzano (2014) drew attention to optimism, resourcefulness, tolerance for ambiguity, and robustness. Finally, Fatoki (2018) highlighted tenacity, ingenuity, optimism, communication skills, and the ability to manage impulses and strong emotions.

Then, adopting the same perspective, Fatoki (2018) asserts that the resilience of the entrepreneur is a personal characteristic that allows them to withstand and quickly overcome adversity, in order to continue their entrepreneurial activity in the best conditions.

In the same vein, Mignenan (2021) argued that resilience is not limited to the entrepreneur's ability to cope with adversity, but also encompasses their tenacity to persist and succeed, by identifying the opportunities offered by the crisis and profoundly transforming the business.

In contrast to the trait approach, the process perspective, as a nascent approach in entrepreneurship research, defines entrepreneur's resilience as a dynamic process, which unfolds in response to various contingencies and leads to positive adaptation (Bernard & Dubard Barbosa, 2016; Bernard & Fayolle, 2016; Cusin, 2017; Fisher et al., 2016; Gentile & Mothe, 2022; Yang & Danes, 2015). This non-linear process consists of several phases, describing the actual journey that the entrepreneur follows after a total entrepreneurial failure (Cusin, 2017) or entrepreneurial adversity (Gentile & Mothe, 2022). According to Tian and Fan (2014, p. 252), this represents "an unfortunate event or circumstance or a state of serious and persistent difficulty" that negatively affects entrepreneurial activity (Gentile & Mothe, 2022). These authors proposed that the concept of entrepreneurial adversity encompasses the various stressful situations that generate psychological, financial, and social costs for entrepreneurs, such as workload, loneliness, isolation, loss of markets, and financial difficulties.

Based on the work of Cope (2011) and Ucbasaran et al. (2013), Cusin (2017) suggests that this process consists of three stages: absorbing the emotional shock, understanding failure, and starting a new career. With this in mind, through research on how entrepreneur resilience is built, Gentile and Mothe (2022) asserted that the process of resilience after adversity is broken down into several phases, namely: acceptance, resistance, resolution, recovery, and personal development.

In the Moroccan context, this resilience has attracted growing interest among researchers in recent years (Bengrich et al., 2020; Yacoubi & Tourabi, 2021; Mouatif & El Agy, 2023; Mdarbi & Belkebir, 2024; Allal-Chérif et al., 2024). Indeed, the analysis of these works reveals that these authors follow the same logic as their foreign counterparts, by conceiving resilience either as a personality trait and an ability to resist and adapt to difficult situations (Bengrich et al., 2020; Yacoubi & Tourabi, 2021), or as an evolutionary process through which the entrepreneur develops knowledge, skills and abilities allowing him to progress despite adversity (Mouatif & El Agy, 2023).

Following the trait approach, Bengrich et al. (2020) consider the resilience of the entrepreneur as the ability to withstand a difficult or highly stressful situation. This ability to project oneself into the future represents a main component of the psychological capital of the entrepreneur, which has a positive and significant impact on the economic performance of companies operating in the city of Agadir (Idem, 2020). Furthermore, by studying how sustainable Esports entrepreneurs in emerging countries, including Morocco, seek to develop a sustainable economic activity, Allal-Chérif et al. (2024) assert that resilience is manifested among Moroccan entrepreneurs by boldness, resourcefulness, agility and the ability to do more with less in often difficult conditions. In the same vein, by developing a conceptual framework on the contribution of individual entrepreneur resilience to the organizational resilience of small and medium-sized enterprises (SMEs), Yacoubi and Tourabi (2021) highlight the importance of the ability to anticipate potential threats. In this sense, it is no longer simply a matter of managing crises once they occur, but of developing the mental capacities to anticipate them, cope effectively, and bounce back quickly.

However, by contextualizing entrepreneur's resilience in the Moroccan entrepreneurial context, Mouatif & El Agy (2023) stipulate that it takes the form of a dynamic and evolving process through which entrepreneurs acquire knowledge and skills that enable them to face an uncertain future with positivity, creativity, and optimism.

Table 1 below presents a comprehensive summary of different approaches to the concept of entrepreneur's resilience.

Table 1. Different approaches to the concept of entrepreneur's resilience

Approach	Authors	Definition
Resilience as a personality trait, quality, or emotional skill	**Hayward et al., (2010)**	Resilience is a positive quality associated with an entrepreneur's confidence and ability to bounce back and create new businesses after failure. The authors distinguish three types of resilience: emotional, social, and financial.
	Ayala & Manzano (2014)	Resilience is a quality of entrepreneurs. The authors distinguish three dimensions of resilience: optimism, resourcefulness, tolerance of ambiguity, and robustness.
	Fatoki (2018)	The resilience of the entrepreneur is a personal characteristic that allows him to withstand and quickly overcome adversity, in order to continue his entrepreneurial activity in the best conditions.
	Yacoubi & Tourabi (2021)	Resilience is defined as the entrepreneur's ability to anticipate potential threats, cope effectively with unexpected events, and adapt to changes in order to become stronger than before.
	Achir et al., (2024)	Resilience is the ability of entrepreneurial leaders to remain optimistic, trust their intuition, seize opportunities and overcome obstacles.

continued on following page

Table 1. Continued

Approach	Authors	Definition
Resilience as a dynamic and evolving process	**Bernard & Barbosa (2016)**	Resilience is defined as a dynamic process of absorbing a shock, of rebuilding oneself, and of producing meaning from the situation experienced, all through interactions with the environment as support and sustaining the dynamic itself.
	Cusin (2017)	Resilience is defined as a dynamic process involving interactions between the individual victim of a trauma, such as total entrepreneurial failure.
	Gentile & Mothe (2022)	Resilience is described as the mental trajectory taken by the entrepreneur to overcome a situation of adversity, particularly in relation to the phases of recovery and personal development following the adversity.
	Mouatif & El Agy (2023)	Resilience is defined as an evolutionary process during which the entrepreneur gradually develops knowledge, skills and competencies enabling him to face an uncertain future with positivity, creativity and optimism.

Source: Authors

Thus, despite its importance in describing and understanding the notion of resilience by giving a lot of weight to the time variable, the process perspective has some limitations. First, the resilience process can extend over variable periods (days, months, years) making it difficult to compare cases and trajectories. Second, it is sometimes difficult to distinguish the precise moment when resilience begins and stabilizes. This is why many researchers are also interested in resilience as a capacity, considered as a set of internal resources that can be mobilized in the face of adversity (Ayala & Manzano, 2014; Fatoki, 2018; Mdarbi & Belkebir, 2024). Following this logic, by placing our research in the trait perspective and following the example of Hayward et al. (2010) and Bengrich et al. (2020), we define resilience as "*the entrepreneur's ability to recover, adapt, bounce back, and even thrive after change or adversity affecting entrepreneurial activity*." This ability is strengthened through several external and technological factors, particularly AI, which today constitutes a promising ally for entrepreneurs facing uncertain environments (Shepherd & Majchrzak, 2022).

2.2. Artificial Intelligence

The Fourth Industrial Revolution marks an increased use of emerging technologies, such as artificial intelligence (Budhwar et al., 2022). Indeed, the application of these advanced technologies is transforming the way business is conducted nationally and internationally (Agarwal et al., 2017; Malik et al., 2022).

In the entrepreneurial context, AI has been the subject of several studies in recent years (Townsend & Hunt, 2019; Shepherd & Majchrzak, 2022; Budhwar et al., 2022; Jorzik et al., 2024). Indeed, a review of these studies reveals that there is no sufficiently comprehensive and valid definition of AI. The authors approach this notion based on the research subject and the available data.

According to Tambe et al. (2019, p. 16), artificial intelligence refers to "*a broad class of technologies that enable a computer to perform tasks that typically require human cognition, including adaptive decision-making*." These technologies enable the execution of several tasks such as learning, analysis, and problem-solving, by imitating human cognitive functions (Graham et al., 2020).

Along the same lines, in providing a brief history of artificial intelligence, Kaplan and Haenlein (2019) describe AI as "*a system's ability to correctly interpret external data, learn from it, and use this learning to achieve specific goals and tasks through flexible adaptation*" (p. 17).

Furthermore, focusing on the functional approach to AI, Feng et al. (2024) assert that AI is a set of tools, techniques, and algorithms designed to think like humans and mimic their actions. This observation was confirmed by Huy et al. (2023). These authors argued that AI is the most common way to process available information and anticipate data by integrating it into an algorithm, which then generates new test data.

In the same vein, Di Vaio et al. (2020) define AI as the ability of a computer system to collect external data, interpret it, and process it. Such a system acts intelligently, being able to perform tasks and continue to learn from this process, while demonstrating certain human behaviors, such as cognition.

Finally, through research on the contribution of AI to corporate sustainability performance, Jabbour et al. (2025) approach AI as "*a technological asset enabling the development of capabilities related to extracting information from data analysis*" (p. 3). These capabilities constitute the main source of competitive advantage for user companies (Idem, 2025). In Morocco, AI, like the resilience of the entrepreneur, has been the subject of several research studies, particularly in the field of entrepreneurship where its potential is attracting growing interest (Amghar et al., 2023; Benraoui et al., 2023; Mir & Barka, 2024; Znady & Bazi, 2025). In this sense, through research on crisis management in Morocco, Bentahar & Bouazzaoui (2022) present AI as a major technological advance, based on deep learning algorithms, making it possible to effectively optimize the tasks and production systems of companies. This new technology constitutes, according to the authors, a key element for the success of any economic project, especially in a constantly changing context where digital technology is increasingly playing an important role. This observation was subsequently confirmed through research on the opportunities offered by AI to entrepreneurs in terms of disruptive innovation, by Guetaya et al. (2024), who indicate that AI is one of the fields of computer science used to create systems capable of stimulating human intelligence. These intelligent systems enable entrepreneurs to increase their productivity while significantly reducing their operational costs (Idem, 2024).

For the purposes of this research, we define artificial intelligence as "*a field of computer science that aims to create systems capable of performing tasks normally requiring human intelligence*." This includes capabilities such as natural language understanding, image recognition, decision-making, and learning from data. From this perspective, to theoretically explain how AI strengthens entrepreneur resilience, we draw on Bandura's (1986) sociocognitive theory, which is based on the concept of triadic reciprocal determinism.

2.3. Artificial Intelligence and Entrepreneur's Resilience: Social Cognitive Theory (Bandura, 1986)

Social cognitive theory emerged in the 1980s. This theory has its origins in the work of Bandura (1986), particularly the book "*Social Foundations of Thought and Action: A Social Cognitive Theory*."

Through this theory, Bandura (1986) defends the idea of a triadic reciprocal determinism between three major sets of factors: personal factors, environmental factors, and individual behavior.

In fact, personal factors encompass beliefs, thoughts, expectations, and, in particular, the sense of self-efficacy. Environmental factors consist of the potential environment, common to all in a given situation, and the actual environment, shaped by individual behavior. Finally, regarding individual behavior, Bandura (1986) highlights the existence of a mutual influence between the environment and the individual. In this sense, Bandura (1986) argues that individuals make judgments and decisions based on these factors. These factors influence their perceptions and feelings, which in turn determine their actions.

In the context of artificial intelligence, several authors have suggested that social cognitive theory constitutes a relevant theoretical framework for analyzing this phenomenon (Ameen et al., 2022; Budhwar et al., 2022; Hu & Pan, 2023). In this sense, through quantitative research among Indian consumers who used online food services during the Covid-19 pandemic, Das and Ramalingam (2022) used this theory to study consumer satisfaction with these services, analyzing the influence of product involvement and consumer resilience on their reactions. In this same context, it is important to note that this theory has also been used to analyze the formation of behaviors related to the use of information technologies and their impacts. This allows us to better understand how technological artifacts, combined with personal factors, contribute to the definition of certain positive objectives (Hu et al., 2016).

According to Ameen et al. (2022), numerous studies have studied the various elements that affect the adoption of AI and the effects that follow this adoption. However, understanding the influence of personal factors, in conjunction with AI, on the behaviors of using this technology and their impact on individual performance, from a global perspective, remains limited (Lee et al., 2022). To address these gaps, this research draws on social cognitive theory (Bandura, 1986) to examine how entrepreneurs in the information and communication technology sector interact with AI based on their environment, thereby promoting positive resilience.

2.4. Implementing Artificial Intelligence: Between Opportunity and Threat?

In recent years, a growing debate has emerged in academic research around the question "*does AI represent an opportunity or a threat for entrepreneurs*?"

According to Shepherd and Majchrzak (2022), AI represents an undeniable opportunity for entrepreneurs as it allows them to capitalize on the emotion economy by analyzing and understanding the needs and behaviors of employees and consumers on a much deeper level. In fact, advanced solutions such as chatbots (Alexa and Siri) allow entrepreneurs to better interact with their customers, not only responding to requests for information, but also taking into account their emotions and emotional needs. These advanced solutions also offer the possibility of creating more personalized and empathetic experiences, thus strengthening customer relationships. Next, Guetaya et al. (2024) assert that AI is effective in the healthcare sector. For example, the use of AI-powered chatbots can provide 24/7 customer support, predictive analytics tools can help companies anticipate hardware failures or service outages, and virtual assistants can simplify complex processes for end users.

Furthermore, Huang and Rust (2018) argue that AI is effective in performing many mechanical tasks that are typically repetitive and require reliable performance. For example, in industrial research, Boeing used AI developed by Citrine Informatics to identify metal alloys suitable for mass 3D printing. By analyzing 10 million combinations from experimental data, technical books and handwritten notebooks, a discovery process that usually took several years could be reduced to a few days (Wired Chen, 2017, cited by OECD, 2024).

Along the same lines, McKinsey and Company (2018) argued that AI is transforming the business world, generating opportunities that create value for users. This observation was confirmed by Shepherd and Majchrzak (2022). These authors argued that AI is redistributing professional skills in the economy. This change, which mainly affects a few professions such as managers, plumbers, teachers, and caregivers, represents a business opportunity for entrepreneurs.

Following this logic, Chalmers et al. (2021) argued that AI is a lever for entrepreneurs, as it can support business creation processes in various ways. This assertion was supported, based on an exploratory study on entrepreneurial education in the AI era, by Vecchiarini and Somià (2023). These authors stipulate that the application of AI in the management of university student employment and entrepreneurship is of great value, as it helps understand the overall situation, update data in real time, provide personalized advice, reduce pressure, and improve employment efficiency. Finally, through quantitative research on the impact of digitalization on business resilience and employee resilience, Nguyen et al. (2024) stated that AI represents a significant opportunity for entrepreneurs. These authors specified that the adoption of AI-enabled technologies improves information sharing and service quality. Similarly, Bag et al. (2021) stated that these innovations extend to optimizing work processes and facilitating agile procurement strategies. This finding was supported by Döhring et al. (2021). These authors highlighted that automating processes through AI in the workplace promotes both productivity and business growth by optimizing speed to market, a crucial factor in competitive environments.

In the Moroccan context, the 2024 UNESCO AI Readiness Assessment Report indicates that, although Morocco has not yet unveiled an official national AI strategy, the country has a favorable environment for the development of a comprehensive AI vision. This is evident, according to the report, in the country's success in boosting its digital ecosystem, particularly with regard to connectivity, access to data, cybersecurity, and the protection of personal data.

In relation to the use of AI, OECD data assessing total venture capital investments in AI and by sector shows that there is a significant increase between 2020 and 2024. Indeed, according to UNESCO (2024) the sectors experiencing significant investment in Morocco are: health and biotechnologies, media, marketing and social platforms as well as IT infrastructures.

Furthermore, according to Znady & Bazi (2025), the favorable environment for the integration of AI, characterizing Morocco, opens the way to numerous opportunities for entrepreneurs. In this regard, Mirt and Barka (2024) stipulated that, technological solutions such as AI and virtual reality, offer new possibilities for innovations in the Moroccan entrepreneurial context. In fact, entrepreneurs can develop new products and services based on these technologies, which allows them to differentiate themselves in the market. For example, and in the context of the automotive industry, of which Morocco is one of the most prominent players in Africa, there are numerous applications of AI in autonomous cars. They mainly concern driving training through Machine Learning to teach the car how to behave in the event of an accident. AI is also used to verify the quality of automotive components as part of predictive maintenance, to understand the environment through sensor data, to analyze driver behavior, and for cybersecurity to monitor connectivity and prevent hacking attempts (UNESCO, 2024). Jaldi (2022), for his part, asserts that speech-to-text technology through "Machine Learning" allows companies to save time by eliminating the need for manual typing. They simply dictate the text and let the computer transcribe it into writing. However, while AI offers many opportunities for entrepreneurs, some authors believe it poses a threat to the economy in general and to entrepreneurs in particular (Zuboff, 2019; Kellogg et al., 2020; Kane et al., 2021). According to Kane et al. (2021), the use of AI can lead to a "dystopian" world where humans lose control over their lives. This loss of control could also affect entrepreneurs, who risk becoming overly dependent on automated systems, reducing their ability to make decisions and adapt flexibly to market changes. This finding was confirmed by Shepherd and Majchrzak (2022). These researchers argued that AI can reinforce increased surveillance and control, both at the management and employee levels, which can lead to a reduction in the autonomy of entrepreneurs in their own decision-making. In addition, the same authors specified that the use of AI could also lead to excessive standardization of entrepreneurial practices, thus limiting creativity and innovation, crucial elements for success in a competitive economic environment. Thus, while AI offers opportunities for efficiency and profitability, it also carries risks that, if poorly managed, could limit entrepreneurial freedom and the ability to evolve in the face of unforeseen challenges (Shepherd et al., 2022).

2.5. Artificial Intelligence and Entrepreneur's Resilience: What Contributions?

Previous research in entrepreneurship has focused extensively on exploring the determinants and factors influencing entrepreneurs' resilience after adversity (Hayward et al., 2010; Lafuente et al., 2019; Mignenan, 2021). In this regard, AI is among the elements that have received particular attention (Hu & Pan, 2023).

According to Chen et al. (2023), mastering AI enables entrepreneurs to strengthen their creative thinking, seize new opportunities, and improve their decision-making processes. This is achieved through real-time analysis of large volumes of data from multiple sources (market, customers, suppliers, personal networks, bankers). These data, often complex and unstructured, are transformed into usable information, which allows the entrepreneur to have a global and up-to-date vision of their environment (Benraoui et al., 2023). Furthermore, it is worth noting that AI offers entrepreneurs a multitude of proposals, alternative scenarios and global visions of the situation (Shepherd & Majchrzak, 2022). This in-depth understanding of the mechanisms specific to each situation is particularly important in decision-making, as it helps to mitigate the cognitive biases inherent in human reasoning. It is in this sense that these authors describe AI as a cognitive amplifier. Badhon et al. (2025), for their part, argue that another crucial advantage of AI lies in the transparency that these technologies offer in decision-making. Indeed, some AI tools integrate decision-making traceability systems, producing detailed reports of the steps that led to a given recommendation. This traceability strengthens the entrepreneur's confidence in the process, while helping to reduce cognitive biases and objectify decisions. For example, in agriculture, AI is fueling the precision revolution by enabling farmers to optimize crop management and improve yields. By collecting data on weather, soil, and crop conditions using IoT sensors, drones, and satellites, farmers can use machine learning algorithms to make informed decisions on irrigation management, fertilization, and pest control, thereby maximizing yields while minimizing environmental impact. Moreover, according to Korzynski et al. (2023), the effective use of AI allows entrepreneurs not only to innovate their products or services, but also to optimize their internal processes, anticipate market trends, and better understand their customers' needs. This enables them to make more informed and strategic decisions, thereby reducing risks and increasing their chances of thriving in an ever-changing economic environment (Shepherd & Majchrzak, 2022).

In the same perspective, it is interesting to mention that AI is capable of improving productivity and reducing production costs (Acemoglu & Restrepo, 2018). This optimization of costs and time allows entrepreneurs to be more flexible and productive, especially in times of uncertainty, which strengthens their resilience. For example, in the manufacturing sector, AI optimizes production processes and reduces costs by identifying inefficiencies and proposing improvements. By using Internet of Things sensors and real-time monitoring systems, manufacturers can collect data on equipment performance and production conditions, then use machine learning algorithms to optimize operations, thus improving productivity and profitability (Guetaya et al., 2024). Additionally, in conducting quantitative research on the impact of AI on entrepreneurs' individual resilience, Hu and Pan (2023) suggested that AI products can offer more powerful features and social interaction with users, which can also promote their resilience. Similarly, Hoffman and Novak (2018) stipulated that, unlike traditional computer systems, AI offers entrepreneurs several advantages, such as autonomy, adaptability, and self-learning. These skills allow entrepreneurs to adapt to new situations and learn from their experiences (Hu & Pan, 2023).

In the same vein, Budhwar et al. (2022) showed that AI can have a positive impact on productivity by helping entrepreneurs work more efficiently. Entrepreneurs can use AI to improve work-life balance, flexibility, autonomy, independence, and creativity, which in turn strengthens their resilience.

Furthermore, Lee et al. (2022) argue that AI enables entrepreneurs to develop responses and behaviors that help them manage external stressors, improve their mental health, and increase their personal resilience. Similarly, Kang and Shao (2023) found that AI interactivity has a positive effect on users' sense of psychological ownership, indicating that AI's sociability can strengthen entrepreneurs' resilience.

Next, according to Shepherd and Majchrzak (2022), AI can support entrepreneurs in creating new businesses. Indeed, exposure to the national and international market allows entrepreneurs to discover new technologies used in various contexts, thus broadening their vision and opportunities for innovation.

Along the same lines, Benraoui et al. (2023) mentioned that AI is a relevant solution to ensure the survival of entrepreneurs during the crisis. This innovative tool plays a key role in strengthening entrepreneurs' abilities to initiate digital marketing, online sales, automate information flows, and manage human resources, using algorithms considered excellent antidotes to crisis. This observation is rooted in Jaldi's (2022) comments, which indicate that chatbots and virtual assistants can qualify prospects, answer customer questions, and offer a personalized experience.

Furthermore, according to Shepherd (2015), emotions and cognition are two essential factors that impact entrepreneurs' decisions, particularly in times of adversity. Indeed, to mitigate the biases introduced by these factors, Huang et al. (2019) suggest that AI represents an effective way to improve the quality of decisions made by entrepreneurs during difficult times, thereby strengthening their resilience. However, despite their contribution to the general understanding of how AI strengthens entrepreneurs' resilience, the aforementioned research studies have several notable limitations. First, they do not explicitly or thoroughly explore the link between AI and the individual resilience of entrepreneurs, focusing instead on the organizational or technical effects of AI. Second, to our knowledge, even research conducted in the Moroccan context, such as that of Bentahar & Bouazzaoui (2022), Benraoui et al. (2023), Mir & Barka (2024), Guetaya et al. (2024), or Znady & Bazi (2025), focuses on the organizational resilience of businesses, thus neglecting the personal level of the entrepreneur as a central actor in the resilience process. This lack of individual-centered analysis leaves a scientific void that our research aims to fill, by exploring in a specific and contextualized manner how AI can become a lever for strengthening the personal resilience of Moroccan entrepreneurs in the face of the various adversities in their environment.

3. RESEARCH METHODOLOGY

3.1 Research Context

In this research, we have focused on very small and small enterprises. These structures are characterized by sales of less than 3 million dirhams and a workforce of less than 10 employees (SME Charter, 2002, cited by Sedjari et al., 2025). This choice is explained, firstly, by the importance of these units in the Moroccan economy. Indeed, the country's productive fabric is largely dominated by these structures. In 2021, Morocco had 370,000 formal enterprises, of which 78.8% were very small enterprises and 9.2% small enterprises (World Bank & Moroccan Observatory for Micro, Small and Medium Enterprises, 2024). Secondly, and given their resource constraints, very small businesses appear to be the main entities affected by this issue of artificial intelligence.

As a sector of activity, we have chosen the information and communication technology (ICT) sector. According to the Moroccan Office of Industrial and Commercial Property, the number of technology companies created in 2024 reached 2,733 (OMPIC, 2025). This number represents 4.01% of the companies created during the year (Idem, 2025). Indeed, given the importance of this sector to the country's economic development, this low rate reflects its multiple challenges, namely the rapid obsolescence of technologies, market fluctuations and frequently changing customer needs. This prevalence of challenges makes the sector a fertile ground for studying entrepreneur's resilience.

3.2 Data Collection and Analysis

The present research aims to understand how artificial intelligence contributes to the resilience of entrepreneurs operating in the ICT sector in the Marrakesh-Safi region. In fact, in order to achieve our ultimate goal, we will focus on the entrepreneur as a unit of analysis and source of data.

From a methodological point of view, we have opted for an exploratory qualitative approach that enables us to analyze in depth the contribution of AI to entrepreneur's resilience. Indeed, this approach is part of an interpretivist epistemological paradigm that aims to apprehend a social phenomenon from the point of view of the interviewees and interpret their perceptions, giving meaning to their behaviors (Thiétart, 2014). In terms of reasoning, our research follows an abductive approach, which involves going back and forth between theory and the field. Following this logic, we mobilized semi-structured interviews with 10 entrepreneurs operating in the ICT sector (Table 3). The first entrepreneur was selected according to Hlady

Rispal's (2015) selection criteria, presented in Table 2. The other entrepreneurs were then identified using the snowball sampling method.

Table 2. Entrepreneur selection criteria

Selection criteria	Selected criteria
Theoretical representativeness	Selection of suitable respondents to answer our questions on artificial intelligence and entrepreneur's resilience.
Variety	The entrepreneurs we interviewed are involved in a wide range of activities, enabling us to gather a variety of viewpoints.
Balance	It's a question of balancing the profiles and experience of the entrepreneurs.
Potential for discovery	We've chosen cases with interesting insights into AI and entrepreneur's resilience.

Source: Authors

These interviews, lasting between 30 minutes and 1h15 minutes, were conducted over a three-month period, face-to-face and remotely, using the ZOOM platform and Google Meet. We continued our research until we reached data saturation, that is, the point at which no new information was likely to enrich our analysis or reveal additional findings (Hlady Rispal, 2015).

Table 3. Sample characteristics

Interviewed entrepreneurs	Gender and age		Main activity	Date of creation	Legal form	Duration of the interview	Date of the interview
ENTR 1	M*	34 years	Application development and design	2019	SMLLC***	49 minutes	29/01/2025
ENTR 2	M	32 years	Digital marketing	2021	SMLLC	32 minutes	11/03/2025
ENTR 3	M	36 years	Development and commercialization of software and platforms	2015	SMLLC	38 minutes	7/03/2025
ENTR 4	M	55 years	The creation of IT solutions and products	2018	SMLLC	30 minutes	14/03/2025
ENTR 5	M	26 years	Digital marketing and web development	2023	SMLLC	40 minutes	25/01/2025

continued on following page

Table 3. Continued

Interviewed entrepreneurs	Gender and age		Main activity	Date of creation	Legal form	Duration of the interview	Date of the interview
ENTR 6	M	28 years	Application development for money transfer and payment	2022	SMLLC	44 minutes	23/01/2025
ENTR 7	F**	28 years	Creation of IT solutions and products	2023	SMLLC	35 minutes	14/03/2025
ENTR 8	M	25 years	Creation of IT solutions and products	2020	SMLLC	1h14 minutes	24/02/2025
ENTR 9	M	33 years	The development of IT solutions	2016	SMLLC	35 minutes	13/02/2025
ENTR 10	M	30 years	Creation of IT solutions and products	2018	SMLLC	40 minutes	15/03/2025

Source: Authors. M*: Male ; F**: Female ; SMLLC***: Single-Member Limited Liability Company

Having completed the interviews with the entrepreneurs, we proceeded to transcribe the voice recordings, which total 7 hours. This stage consists of a faithful production of what was said by the interviewee, resulting in 85 pages. To correct spelling and stylistic errors, we transcribed the text. This phase gave us an initial idea of the results we could expect.

In addition, given the limited number of interviews, a manual content analysis of the statements made by the entrepreneurs concerned was carried out in accordance with the protocol established by Miles and Huberman (2003). To this end, we began with a simple coding procedure, enabling each co-author to analyze the transcripts individually, and to present an initial coding by reconciling the literature with the selected results. Subsequently, we carried out a double coding, comparing the analysis of each co-author to identify the main elements to be retained and which will form the basis of our analysis. On this basis, we retained the following codes: the adoption of AI by entrepreneurs, entrepreneur's resilience after adversity and the contribution of AI to entrepreneur's resilience.

From an ethical point of view, entrepreneurs have been informed of the purpose of our research and the nature of the data that will be collected. Secondly, we obtained the consent of all the entrepreneurs before starting the interviews. Finally, we also took care to guarantee their anonymity and confidentiality, notably through the use of codes (ENTR 1, ENTR 2...).

4. RESEARCH RESULTS

4.1. The Adoption of AI by Entrepreneurs

Our question on the adoption of AI by entrepreneurs revealed that it represents an opportunity. This innovative tool enables entrepreneurs to increase their productivity, be more efficient and improve their creativity. This translates into the automation of several repetitive tasks such as automatically answering customer questions via WhatsApp or Facebook, sorting incoming applications, as well as generating factors and purchase orders. These automations enable entrepreneurs to save time and focus on higher value-added tasks, as indicated by the first respondent: *"AI is an advantage for me, because it enables us to be more productive, faster and more creative"* (Entrepreneur 1). This result was also confirmed by the ninth entrepreneur interviewed, who emphasized that AI enables entrepreneurs in the ICT sector to gain in speed and flexibility. According to him, a project that previously required a month's work can now be finalized in just ten days thanks to the integration of AI: *"For example, a project that previously required a month's work, today with AI I can finalize the project in 10 days"* (Entrepreneur 9).

In this sense, as asserted by the sixth respondent, this new technology does indeed play an important role in bringing customers and entrepreneurs closer together in the sense that it enables the latter to quickly identify and respond to different customer needs: *"In the money transfer and payments sector, AI can improve the way we operate and interact with our customers"* (Entrepreneur 6). This result was confirmed by the fourth interviewee, who explained that, although he is not an accounting expert, he manages to design a personalized, relevant and functional solution thanks to AI. The latter acts as a knowledge bridge between him and the accounting field, facilitating understanding of the customer's specific needs and strengthening collaboration between the two parties: *"For example, using AI trained on an accounting model enables us to get closer to the accountant's potential needs"* (Entrepreneur 4).

However, with rapidly changing market trends and technological advances, some entrepreneurs say AI poses a threat to entrepreneurial activity. With this in mind, the sixth interviewee points out that integrating AI represents a costly investment for entrepreneurs. Indeed, the latter must also acquire a specific set of skills in order to manage the impact of AI on their business as a whole: *"AI can also pose challenges, particularly in terms of integration costs, skills required and data protection"* (Entrepreneur 6). The second respondent, on the other hand, argues that AI could lead to the disappearance of certain products, such as landing pages, due to customers' ability to generate landing pages automatically via AI: *"Thanks to AI, the customer no longer needs us to generate landing pages"* (Entrepreneur 2).

When it comes to the skills needed to integrate AI, the research results underline the importance of having some technical skills and a basic background in the work field to be able to direct and optimize the benefits offered by AI. This is evident, of course, in the statements made by the third entrepreneur, who stipulates that: *"to benefit from a very efficient and productive AI, in my experience you first need to have a background and a foundation in the field of development"* (Entrepreneur 3). This observation was confirmed by the second respondent, who asserted that the integration of AI requires specific technical skills, particularly for entrepreneurs whose basic field is not IT: *"For an IT entrepreneur, the adoption of AI does not require any major additional skills, since he already has the necessary technical foundations. On the other hand, for a non-IT entrepreneur, training is essential in order to maximize the benefits offered by AI and take full advantage of it"* (Entrepreneur 2). Finally, the results also emphasize the importance of language skills to be able to effectively guide AI in the desired direction, ensuring precise and relevant interactions with the tool. This is reflected in the statements of the fourth respondent, who explains: *"To maximize the opportunities offered by AI you need to know how to communicate with it"* (Entrepreneur 4).

Furthermore, our question on support from the people around the entrepreneur in integrating AI shows that, unlike the immediate circle, which has no significant effect, the professional circle plays a key role in this process. In this sense, the fifth respondent suggests that support from the professional circle is manifested through experience-sharing practices and concrete recommendations for implementing effective AI systems: *"My professional circle encouraged me by sharing feedback and recommending suitable tools and solutions. Furthermore, colleagues and technology partners helped me implement AI systems into my processes"* (Entrepreneur 5). However, it is interesting to note that beyond the support from the circle, the results indicate that integrating AI is above all a matter of survival for entrepreneurs. The fourth interviewee explains: *"The decision to integrate AI is an obligation to ensure the survival of the company." In this case, the question of survival becomes first, before talking about support from loved ones or professionals"* (Entrepreneur 4). This observation was confirmed by the ninth respondent who states that the adoption of AI becomes essential to remain competitive and ensure the sustainability of the company: *"We are obliged to integrate it and follow the trend to remain competitive in the market"* (Entrepreneur 9). Finally, as for the AI solutions used by entrepreneurs, the results emphasize text generative tools (ChatGPT, Jasper AI, Notion AI, Grock, Perplexity, Qwen2.5), images (DALL-E, META AI), data and reasoning (Causal AI). In this sense, these tools are very effective, according to the respondents, on several fronts. In this regard, the third respondent draws attention to the effectiveness of these tools in converting languages, as well as correcting coding errors: *"AI tools allow us to convert language X to another, more comprehensive language... We also use these solutions to correct errors that exist in coding"* (Entrepreneur 3).

The ninth respondent, for his part, argues that these technologies are effective in content and image generation, as well as in strategic thinking: *"AI is useful in everything from content generation on LinkedIn, image generation, and strategic thinking"* (Entrepreneur 9). He defined AI as a set of intelligent assistants designed to facilitate various tasks for users, including entrepreneurs: *"As I said before, AI is a set of assistants. It has a thinking capacity that helps us formulate strategies"* (Entrepreneur 9).

Table 4 below presents a summary of the results related to the question of AI adoption. It highlights, in more detail, the AI tools used by entrepreneurs in the ICT sector, the factors facilitating this adoption, as well as the skills required for its integration. In addition, this table also presents the advantages offered by AI to Moroccan entrepreneurs, while highlighting the potential risks associated with its use.

Table 4. Facilitators, skills, benefits and risks related to the adoption of AI in the ICT sector in Morocco

	Facilitating factors	**Required skills**	**Benefits offered**	**Associated risks**
Adoption of AI	• Professional entourage.	• Technical skills • Background in the field of work • Language skills.	• Productivity • Creativity • Speed • Bringing the entrepreneur and customers closer together • Language Conversion • Content and image generation.	• Expencive investment • Disappearance of products • Data protection issue • Lack of skills necessary for integration.
AI tools used	• **Text generative tools:** ChatGPT, Jasper AI, Notion AI, Grock, Perplexity, Qwen2.5 ; • **Generative image tools:** DALL-E, META AI ; • **Generative data and reasoning tools:** Causal AI.			

Source: Authors

4.2. Entrepreneur's Resilience After Adversity

The results show that, among entrepreneurs in the information and communications technology sector, adversity is perceived as a difficult period marked by obstacles, challenges, and unfavorable conditions. These situations can be the source of various factors, as the tenth entrepreneur points out: *"Entrepreneurial adversity represents times when unforeseen challenges, such as customer loss, market saturation, or financial crises, test our ability to adapt and overcome obstacles"* (Entrepreneur 10). However, the first respondent states that adversity is an opportunity to strengthen the entrepreneur's resilience, learn from difficult situations, and increase the company's adaptability. *"Entrepreneurial adversity is not an end in itself, but rather a stage that builds character, vision, and resilience. Every challenge is an opportunity to learn, grow, and make the company stronger and more adaptable"* (Entrepreneur 1).

To cope with this adversity while developing resilience, the entrepreneurs interviewed emphasized the importance of agility and risk-taking, stressing the need to step outside one's comfort zone. *"Personally, I think you have to be resilient and agile above all else to venture out and take risks"* (Entrepreneur 8). They also highlighted the importance of effective communication to manage customer expectations, as well as the technical expertise needed to offer tailored solutions. *"Communication is very important because it allows us to understand customer needs and overcome difficult times"* (Entrepreneur 5). In addition, a clear vision, strong leadership, informed decision-making and good stress management are considered essential, as indicated by the fourth respondent: *"In terms of qualities, I first cite patience and stress management, as well as solid and very strong leadership"* (Entrepreneur 4).

During these times, entrepreneurs use several AI tools, including ChatGPT: *"During the period of stagnation, I can say that AI, particularly the ChatGPT tool, helped us launch another project to resolve the situation"* (Entrepreneur 5), intelligent chatbots: *"We integrated chatbots to manage part of our customer service. They quickly answer users' common questions, 24/7, while improving their experience"* (Entrepreneur 7), and Deep6, Grock, META AI, Perplexity, and Qwen2.5.

Figure 1 below provides a summary of the results relating to the theme of resilience after adversity. More specifically, it highlights the different forms of adversity encountered by entrepreneurs in the ICT sector, as well as the resources and levers mobilized to address them.

Figure 1. Resilience after adversity: challenges and resources mobilized

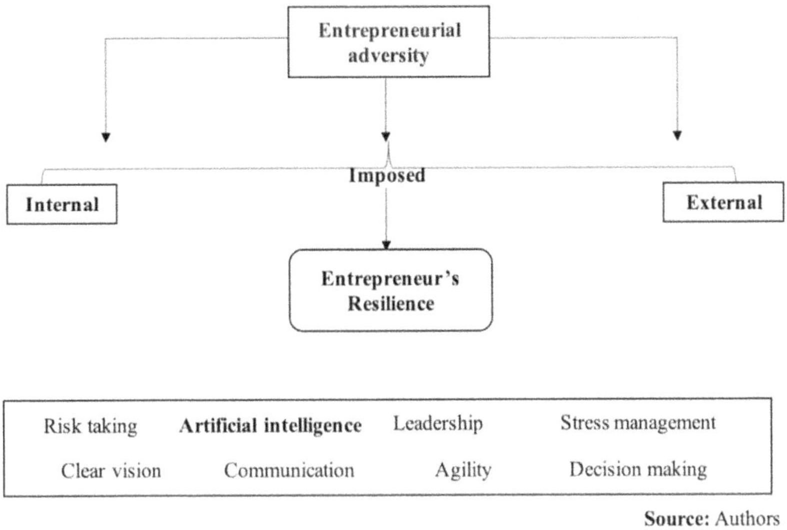

Source: Authors

According to Figure 1, entrepreneurial adversity, whether internal or external, requires entrepreneurs to demonstrate resilience. This resilience, conceived here as a capacity, does not manifest automatically but requires the mobilization of various resources. Among these, the results emphasize risk-taking, a clear vision, communication, leadership, agility, stress management, and decision-making. To these resources is now added an increasingly decisive lever: AI. Indeed, thanks to its analytical and decision-making capabilities, AI constitutes a powerful lever for strengthening entrepreneurs' resilience. This is precisely the point that the following section focuses on, examining how AI strengthens entrepreneurs' resilience after adversity.

4.3. The Contribution of AI to Entrepreneur's Resilience

Our results show that AI contributes to strengthening entrepreneurs' resilience on several levels. First of all, this tool gives these entrepreneurs the opportunity to be more creative by delegating repetitive tasks and focusing on those with high added value. *"AI allows me to focus on high added value tasks by automating repetitive processes, which leaves more room to innovate and think about strategic projects"* (Entrepreneur 9). In addition, the second respondent added that the ideas generated by AI allow them to have a global vision of the evolution of customer needs and to propose creative ideas to meet them. *"AI allows me to gain efficiency, better understand market expectations, and test ideas quickly, while freeing up mental space for more ambitious and creative projects. AI allows me to push the limits of creativity while reducing risks."*

Furthermore, it is worth noting that the research results indicate that the use of AI tools such as ChatGPT and Causal AI allows entrepreneurs to make quality decisions. Indeed, as the last speaker pointed out, the discussions initiated with ChatGPT offer entrepreneurs a wide range of possibilities and perspectives on a given situation. These different options can then be tested and analyzed by AI to identify the most relevant solution: *"When we analyze the data with AI in a more advanced way, it gives us several perspectives on the solution to unblock the situation"* (Entrepreneur 10). For example, the second interviewee points out that, as part of the launch of the *"Club.ma.pro"* project, an initiative aimed at the private sector aimed at encouraging companies to encourage their employees to practice a sporting activity, AI tools such as ChatGPT played an important role in the decision-making process. According to him, several decisions regarding the functionalities to be integrated were made based on suggestions, analyses and discussions conducted with AI. This helped to inform choices, guide the design of services and support more structured and relevant decision-making: *"To introduce functionalities into the Club.ma.pro platform, we discussed with AI, particularly ChatGPT. It helps us make decisions on the nature of the functionalities to integrate"* (Entrepreneur 2). This statement was supported by the ninth respondent who draws attention to the multiplicity of roles characterizing AI. This multiplicity plays an important role in decision-making in the sense that it allows entrepreneurs in the ICT sector to make effective decisions without having to master the underlying mechanisms of different situations. Then, as the same interviewee explains, the weight of AI in terms of strategic thinking is also important in the sense that it allows entrepreneurs to adapt their strategies and adjust their business models to better face different types of adversity: *"AI is a set of assistants. It has a capacity for reflection that helps us formulate and adjust our strategies after a shock"* (Entrepreneur 9).

Adding to this, and beyond creativity, AI also helps to optimize entrepreneurs' time, as indicated by the fifth interviewee: *"A good use of AI allows us to save a lot of time."* This optimal time management translates, according to the results, into two main aspects. On the one hand, AI allows entrepreneurs in the ICT sector to complete tasks in a reduced time, whereas they previously required a much longer duration. On the other hand, the interviewees argue that AI recommends a better organization of priorities according to the urgency and importance of the missions, thus strengthening the productivity and self-efficacy of these entrepreneurs: "*AI allows us to complete tasks in a very limited time, although these tasks previously required a longer duration*" (Entrepreneur 8), "*AI gives us alerts on important dates... It allows us to be up to date*" (Entrepreneur 6). However, unlike previous research, it is important to note that AI does not necessarily reduce working hours. Indeed, the time saved through optimal use of AI is reassigned to other tasks. "*When you save time, you try to dedicate it to other projects, you think about working more.*" (Entrepreneur 3). This observation was confirmed by the seventh respondent. According to him, the AI intervention has led to many changes, encouraging us to work more to cover daily expenses: "*AI changes a lot of things, which encourages us to multitask to cover the daily expenses*" (Entrepreneur 7).

In this regard, it is important to note that this reallocation does not directly affect work-life balance. According to the ninth respondent, this balance remains a personal issue on which AI has no impact: "*For me, the use of AI has no impact on work-life balance*" (Entrepreneur 10), "*Devoting time to family is another issue that has no relation to the use of AI*" (Entrepreneur 7).

After adversity, the entrepreneurs interviewed affirm that the use of AI is essential to be able to analyze past mistakes, better understand trends, and learn lessons for gradual improvement. "*AI allows me to transform adversity into learning opportunities. It helps me analyze past mistakes, simulate solutions, and obtain precise feedback on my actions. Thanks to AI, I can optimize my learning processes in a more targeted and efficient manner, which makes me more resilient.*" (Entrepreneur 10). The integration of AI into this learning process goes beyond simple error analysis; it improves entrepreneurs' self-efficacy and strengthens their confidence and ability to overcome future challenges. "*For me, using AI increases our confidence in performing different tasks and overcoming difficult moments*" (Entrepreneur 5). However, it is important to note that despite the massive use of AI by entrepreneurs in the information and communication technology sector, their confidence in this tool remains relative. In this regard, the seventh respondent points out that the effectiveness of AI relies on rigorous and continuous monitoring of the results it generates: "*Certainly, AI makes a lot of things easier for us, but we always have to check the reliability of the information generated.*" (Entrepreneur 7).

To conclude, our question about the role of AI in strengthening social ties revealed the lack of a direct link between the use of this technology and maintaining these ties. Indeed, the results indicate that entrepreneurs can build their own connections independently without resorting to AI: "*I don't think AI has an impact on social ties. You can develop and strengthen your social ties without AI*" (Entrepreneur 6).

Based on this analysis, we have presented a summary of all the results in Figure 2. More specifically, the following figure presents, first, the main elements related to the integration of AI: technical and linguistic skills, as well as support from professional circles. The same figure then highlights the personal aspects through which AI strengthens the entrepreneur's resilience: creativity, decision-making ability, self-efficacy, learning, and self-confidence. Finally, this synthetic view also exposes the barriers that hinder the construction and development of a resilient mindset such as: work overload, the absence of a work-family balance and the absence of social ties.

Figure 2. Main research results

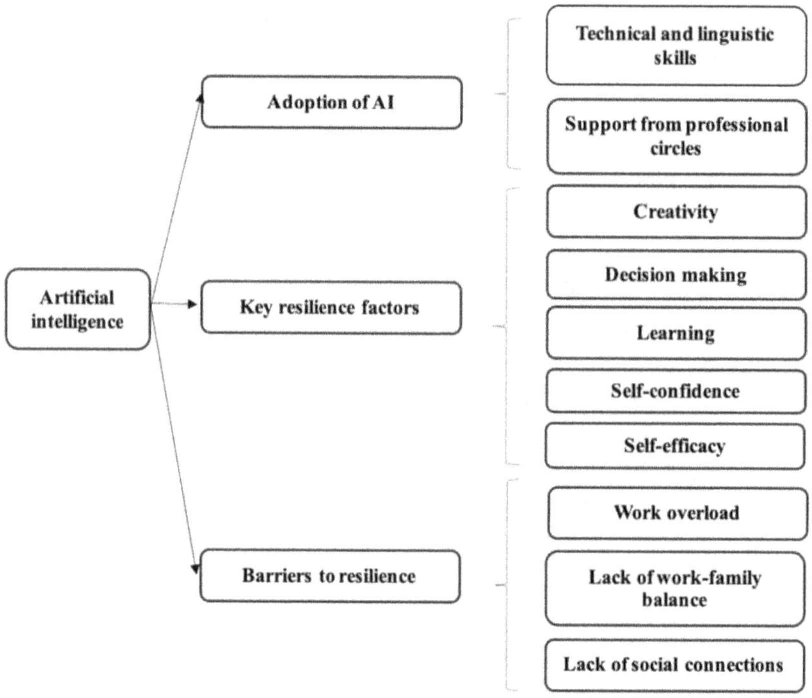

Source : Authors

5. DISCUSSION OF THE RESULTS

Entrepreneur's resilience in the face of adversity has received significant recent attention (Cusin, 2017; Chhatwani et al., 2022; Gentile & Mothe, 2022), but remains insufficient. Authors have studied the antecedents that strengthen this capacity, generally focusing on individual resources, such as optimism (Ayala & Manzano, 2014), self-efficacy (Emrizal et al., 2020), and self-confidence (Hayward et al., 2010), as well as environmental factors (Dimitriadis, 2021; Mignenan, 2022). Among the gaps in the literature regarding these antecedents, we highlight the role of information technology, particularly AI.

In this context, through this research, we seek to understand how AI fosters a resilient posture among entrepreneurs in the face of adversity. Using data from interviews conducted with entrepreneurs operating in the information and communication technology sector, we reveal the place of AI in the development of individual resilience among these entrepreneurs, obviously based on the theoretical foundations of Bandura's social cognitive theory (1986). Our results reveal three major themes; two themes relating to the benefits of adopting AI by these entrepreneurs and its contribution to their resilience. Another linked to understanding the resilience of these entrepreneurs after adversity.

5.1. AI Adoption by Entrepreneurs

The results of this topic reveal the importance of AI for business development and productivity improvement through tools that ensure speed and creativity. This result corroborates that of Döhring et al. (2021), where they stipulate that AI-powered process automation optimizes speed to market, which guarantees the growth and productivity of entrepreneurs, a crucial factor in ensuring a competitive advantage in the market. Furthermore, the speed of technological solutions, such as rapid software development, and the opportunities to generate innovative ideas allow entrepreneurs to achieve a certain differentiation in the market (Mirt & Barka, 2024). This speed strengthens the resilience of entrepreneurs by allowing them to align with market needs and stay up to date with its evolution.

According to the entrepreneurs interviewed, AI plays a catalytic role in customer relations. They emphasized that it enables closer contact with customers by more quickly identifying, understanding, and satisfying their needs. This was supported by Shepherd and Majchrzak (2022), who showed that AI represents a key opportunity for entrepreneurs. In this sense, it offers them the ability to harness the emotion economy by deeply analyzing the needs and behaviors of employees and consumers. Indeed, this understanding of customer needs allows them to optimize the customer experience, personalize customer interactions with greater empathy, and consequently strengthen customer relationships, increase customer loyalty, and ensure a competitive advantage in the market (Korzynski et al., 2023).

The integration of AI poses threats to entrepreneurial activity. According to interviewees' responses, with the rapid evolution of technologies and the development of markets, AI integration remains costly. In addition to the high investment costs, entrepreneurs are still in need of developing their skills in order to manage the impact of AI on the business and be able to manage its trends. Among the undesirable effects of AI we found the disappearance of certain services or products that are obsolete today with technological advances. The threats of AI for entrepreneurs and the economy have been demonstrated in the literature by some authors, such as (Zuboff, 2019; Kellogg et al., 2020; Kane et al., 2021). These researchers mentioned its negative impact on the autonomy of entrepreneurs and the ability to make decisions. This is explained by the fact that AI risks controlling the lives of human beings, in the sense that entrepreneurs can become too dependent on automated systems (Kane et al., 2021; Shepherd & Majchrzak, 2022). As an additional point, it is interesting to note that the risks associated with AI in terms of protecting and leaking sensitive data also limit its use. The reason why some entrepreneurs decide to entrust only optional tasks to these tools. This result originates from the comments made by Shepherd & Majchrzak (2022), who argued that the inability of AI to protect data limits its use. In addition, these authors formulate an approach called "Dark Side of AI" by which they expose the risks associated with the use of AI, such as the initiation of destructive entrepreneurial actions, risk of hacking strategic algorithms and high exposure to cyberattacks. Also confirming this idea, Chalmers et al. (2023) stipulate that the use of AI offers entrepreneurs easily accessible mechanisms for moral disengagement, by transferring responsibility to AI algorithms. Entrepreneurs added the importance of AI in ensuring the sustainability and survival of their businesses. It enables adaptation to intensifying competition and high customer demands, as well as innovation and resource optimization. Through task automation and speed of execution, AI simplifies work for entrepreneurs, performing tasks that require high performance (Huang & Rust, 2018).

Furthermore, it is worth mentioning that the results revealed the importance of professional social support in the integration of AI. By benefiting from the expertise and guidance of their professional entourage, entrepreneurs can receive relevant recommendations on AI usage and trends.

5.2. Entrepreneur's Resilience After Adversity

To understand resilience, it is first important to understand how the entrepreneurs interviewed perceive adversity. According to them, adversity is a difficult period characterized by challenges and obstacles related, for example, to a financial crisis or market saturation. This aligns with the definition proposed by Tian and Fan (2014) and Gentile and Mothe (2022), which defines it as a serious difficulty that negatively impacts the business. This situation has negative consequences for the entrepreneur, their social life, and their financial situation, testing their adaptability. However, some entrepreneurs argue that adversity represents an opportunity for learning and development, strengthening their resilience and the company's ability to adapt to the challenges of the entrepreneurial context. This research finding confirms the idea that the most determining factor is how an entrepreneur perceives adversity

(Mouatif & El Agy, 2023). This finding also highlights the importance of the failure intelligence phase (Cusin, 2017), during which the post-failure learning process begins, thus making it possible to identify opportunities offered by the new situation.

Entrepreneur's resilience has been addressed in the literature by various authors as a capacity (Hayward et al., 2010; Ayala & Manzano, 2014; Ngah & Salleh, 2015) or a process (Bernard & Fayolle, 2016; Cusin, 2017; Gentile & Mothe, 2022) that allows the entrepreneur to cope with adversity. Indeed, it is automatically linked to positive adaptation with the challenges and challenges related to the entrepreneurial context (Bullough & Renko, 2013; Bullough et al., 2014). By adopting a resilient posture, entrepreneurs can overcome adversity and continue their entrepreneurial activities (Fatoki, 2018). In the same vein, the definition we adopt in our research presents resilience as a capacity allowing the entrepreneur to bounce back from adversity that has negatively affected entrepreneurial activity. In this context, the entrepreneurs interviewed suggest that their resilience has allowed them to face the challenges they encountered during their entrepreneurial careers. Individual capacities such as stress management and patience promote this capacity. On the other hand, the entrepreneurs interviewed mentioned other elements that contributed to their adaptation to adversity, including agility, which promotes rapid adaptation to market developments, given rapid technological advances, as well as risk tolerance, given that new technologies introduce opportunities and innovations every day, and daring to invest in them promotes management and adaptation to challenges, thus gaining a competitive advantage. In addition, good customer relations are considered important to cope with adversity through good communication and mastery of technical tools. As already mentioned, AI promotes customer relations and the satisfaction of customer needs. Entrepreneurs have used AI to find solutions to the problems encountered. In the same context, Lee et al. (2022) showed that AI facilitates the development of responses for entrepreneurs that allow them to manage stressors. This is through the creative ideas it offers and the improvement of the decision-making process (Chen et al., 2023).

5.3. Contribution of AI to Entrepreneur's Resilience

The analysis of the results of this theme, which represents the core of our research, reveals that AI is also one of the antecedents that strengthens entrepreneurs' resilience in the face of adversity. Indeed, AI offers several advantages for entrepreneurs, which we discussed in the first theme. Among these advantages, we found the opportunity to be creative, and, according to entrepreneurs, being creative allows them to exploit tasks with greater added value. This observation was supported by Chen et al. (2023), who stipulate that mastering AI fosters innovation and creative thinking, which consequently contributes to their resilience during times of adversity. This asset allows entrepreneurs to anticipate market changes and meet customer needs. According to Shepherd and Majchrzak (2022), this minimizes risks and increases the chances of maintaining one's position in a constantly evolving economic market.

In fact, according to research findings, the use of AI-based tools enables entrepreneurs to make quality decisions. This result is theoretically explained by the fact that real-time analysis of big data and the transformation of this data into actionable information allows entrepreneurs to master different situations, enabling them to make quality decisions (Benraoui et al., 2023). This quality is manifested in particular by the transparency and traceability offered by the mitigation of cognitive biases inherent in human reasoning (Badhon et al., 2025).

Also, the results showed that AI contributes to the development and learning of entrepreneurs. According to the literature, this learning allows entrepreneurs to overcome these failures. The possibility of self-learning offered by AI (Hoffman & Novak, 2018) allows the entrepreneur to adapt better to challenging situations and learn from experiences (Hu & Pan, 2023). This learning is certainly important for the development of individual capabilities. This is explained by the fact that apart from detecting and analyzing errors, it strengthens self-efficacy and self-confidence, and consequently the ability to overcome future challenges. The importance of self-efficacy and self-confidence for strengthening resilience is well supported in the literature by highlighting the direct link between these aspects (Hayward et al., 2010; De Hoe & Janssen, 2018; Emrizal et al., 2020). This confirms the findings of social cognitive theory (Bandura, 1986), which emphasizes the interaction between personal factors such as self-confidence, self-efficacy, and resilience, and AI as an environmental factor.

In addition, since tasks are completed quickly and more efficiently thanks to this innovative technological tool, AI provides entrepreneurs with more free time, allowing them to devote themselves to other projects within their businesses. However, despite being effective in task execution (Budhwar et al., 2022), AI does not reduce entrepreneurs' workload. This is explained by the fact that entrepreneurs' desire to improve and develop themselves pushes them to exploit the time saved through the use of AI in other projects within their businesses. In fact, this result allows us to generalize the idea that advanced technologies, such as AI, often induce changes in employees' workload and responsibilities by introducing new automated processes. This forces them to adapt quickly and efficiently (Verhoef et al., 2021), which also applies to entrepreneurs operating in the ICT sector.

Furthermore, contrary to the findings of Santos et al. (2023), the research results affirm that the use of AI has no effect on work-life balance. This is explained by the fact that entrepreneurs in the ICT sector felt obliged to constantly use AI tools to remain competitive. This can lead to work overload and thus reduce time spent with family. From another perspective, it is relevant to mention that the fact that AI has no impact on work-life balance can be largely attributed to the predominantly male composition (9 out of 10 entrepreneurs surveyed). Indeed, this issue concerns women much more than men, who still struggle to find a balance between these two important spheres of life compared to their male counterparts (Sundaresan, 2014).

Moreover, no one can deny the importance of the social environment for the development of resilience in entrepreneurs (Bernard & Barbosa, 2016; Bernard & Fayolle, 2016; Cusin, 2017). The crucial role of social ties has already been supported by one of the founders of the concept of resilience, Cyrunlik (2002), who said that each individual who has experienced an adversity situation cannot regain their balance without external input. This possibility of building and maintaining ties is not influenced by AI. Indeed, this result calls into question the argument that AI products guarantee social interaction with users (Hu & Pan, 2023). This is explained by the fact that AI can in no way replace authentic and deep human interactions, which are essential for establishing and maintaining strong social ties. Furthermore, drawing on the theoretical postulates of social cognitive theory (Bandura, 1986), this research highlights the role of triadic reciprocal determinism in strengthening entrepreneurs' resilience. More specifically, AI, as an external factor integrated into the entrepreneur's environment, interacts with personal factors such as self-efficacy, learning, and self-confidence. This dynamic contributes to strengthening the entrepreneur's individual resilience.

Finally, to our knowledge, research on how AI strengthens entrepreneurs' individual resilience in other sectors remains scarce, if not nonexistent. This absence significantly limits the possibilities for cross-sector comparisons, making them difficult, if not impractical. However, based on the results of this research, we can suggest that the daily interaction between entrepreneurs and the technological tools generally characterizing the ICT sector facilitates the integration and use of AI. Furthermore, the high level of technical skills in coding and designing AI-based algorithms, which distinguishes entrepreneurs operating in the ICT sector, allows them to fully exploit the potential of this technology (Santos et al., 2023). In contrast, these skills are rarely present in other sectors of activity, which may partly explain the negative perception that some entrepreneurs have towards AI.

6. RESEARCH IMPLICATIONS, LIMITATIONS AND FUTURE DIRECTIONS

The main objective of the present research is to understand how AI strengthens the individual resilience of entrepreneurs in the ICT sector. From this perspective, this research makes important contributions on several levels.

On a theoretical level, this research relates AI to the individual resilience of ICT entrepreneurs. In this sense, the focus on the entrepreneur as the unit of analysis can also be seen as a contribution of this research, given that previous research generally focuses on the firm as a whole (Amghar et al., 2023; Bag et al., 2023; Benraoui et al., 2023; Gómez et al., 2024).

At managerial level, the research findings offer practical implications, highlighting the opportunities offered by AI, as well as its impact on entrepreneur's resilience after adversity. Firstly, entrepreneurs and managers need to recognize the importance of adopting AI and transforming business model capabilities and components. Second, this research has compiled a set of concrete examples of how AI-based tools can be used to build entrepreneur's resilience after adversity. This comprehensive framework describes in detail which AI tools can be a facilitator and a barrier to resilience. This is important insofar as entrepreneurs will take these elements into consideration for future scenarios for managing difficult times.

Furthermore, the elements retained from this research will help to identify the real needs of entrepreneurs in terms of resilience and support, which will enable the development of more targeted and effective public policies. Such policies could foster the development of an institutional framework conducive to innovation, the creation of solid businesses, and local economic dynamism. More specifically, shedding light on how AI strengthens entrepreneur's resilience is an indispensable point on which Moroccan entrepreneurial players, consultants, researchers, banking institutions and the government can draw to formulate and enrich new entrepreneurial promotion strategies, especially in uncertain environments.

In addition, it is worth pointing out that, although they represent a way of responding to all entrepreneurial adversities of an internal or external nature, the integration and implementation of new technologies such as AI require both skilled and digitally literate employees and managers, as well as significant investment in new technologies and technical capabilities to make the most of the advantages offered by these tools.

On a social level, by highlighting the resilience of entrepreneurs, this research contributes indirectly to job creation, reducing unemployment, and boosting the economy. It also fosters a resilient entrepreneurial culture, capable of adapting to change and taking advantage of different adversities, which benefits the community as a whole.

Despite its contributions, this research has certain limitations. In fact, although it is useful in terms of the reliability of the results, the concentration on a particular region, such as the Marrakech-Safi region, constitutes the main limitation of this research work. This concentration limits the generalizability of the results.

This limitation does, however, open the way to numerous research perspectives. In the future, it would be relevant to replicate this research in other regions of the Kingdom in order to compare results and identify regional specificities in terms of entrepreneur's resilience. Secondly, a comparative approach between northern and southern regions, or between urban and rural environments, would also enable a better understanding of the contribution of context on entrepreneurs' resilience capacities. Finally, we also propose to carry out a mixed study, while focusing on resilient entrepreneurs after a total entrepreneurial failure as a unit of analysis to understand how AI helps entrepreneurs overcome the grief and depression engendered by failure.

7. CONCLUSION

The present research follows on from work exploring the link between AI and entrepreneur's resilience (Chalmers et al., 2022; Hu and Pan, 2023; Ameen et al., 2024). More specifically, it aims to understand how AI strengthens the individual resilience of ICT entrepreneurs in the Marrakech-Safi region.

To this end, we presented the theoretical underpinnings relating to the notion of entrepreneur's resilience, as well as artificial intelligence. Next, we mobilized social cognitive theory (Bandura, 1986), followed by a theoretical synthesis of research work linking these two concepts, to provide a theoretical answer to our problem.

In addition, from a methodological point of view, we conducted an exploratory study based on semi-directive interviews with ten entrepreneurs operating in the ICT sector and located in the Marrakesh-Safi region. The data collected was then analyzed from a manual content analysis perspective, in line with the recommendations of Miles and Huberman (2003).

The results of this research confirm that AI represents an undeniable opportunity for entrepreneurs in the ICT sector. Indeed, the mastery of IT tools and the possession of a theoretical background specific to their field of activity enable them to fully and effectively exploit the advantages offered by AI. In this sense, it's worth pointing out that the adoption of AI by entrepreneurs in the ICT sector has today become an obligation to ensure their survival and maintain their competitiveness on both national and international markets.

In the same vein, the research results indicate that entrepreneurs in the ICT sector perceive entrepreneurial adversity as a difficult situation marked by ups and downs in entrepreneurial activity. In this sense, the same results show that personal qualities such as agility, risk-taking, communication and resilience are essential to pursue the entrepreneurial opportunity under the best conditions.

Furthermore, in relation to AI's contribution to the resilience of ICT entrepreneurs, the research results show that, through the advanced analyses and propositions it offers, AI constitutes an element that strengthens the decision-making capacity of ICT entrepreneurs. Next, the same results reveal that AI as a new technological tool offers these entrepreneurs the opportunity to be more creative and productive, by delegating repetitive tasks and focusing on those with high added value. Secondly, the same results affirm that AI enables entrepreneurs to optimize their time, allowing them to grant more time to their families. In addition, it's important to mention that the use of AI is essential, particularly in difficult times, so that mistakes can be analyzed and lessons learned to improve incrementally. Finally, contrary to previous studies, the present research shows that AI does not contribute to strengthening entrepreneurs' social ties.

REFERENCES

Acemoglu, D., & Restrepo, P. (2019). Artificial Intelligence, Automation, and Work. *The Economics of Artificial Intelligence*, 197–236. https://doi.org/DOI: 10.7208/chicago/9780226613475.003.0008

Achir, C., Rafili, M., Douari, A., & Idrissi, K. (2024). Les Nouveaux facteurs de la Résilience Organisationnelle dans l'Entrepreneuriat Marocain Contemporain. *Revue Française d'Economie et de Gestion, 5*, 101–122.

Agrawal, A., Gans, J., & Goldfarb, A. (2017). What to expect from artificial intelligence. *MIT Sloan Management Review, 58*(3), 23–26. DOI: 10.7551/mit-press/11645.003.0008

Allal-Chérif, O., Guaita-Martínez, J. M., & Montesinos Sansaloni, E. (2024). Sustainable esports entrepreneurs in emerging countries: Audacity, resourcefulness, innovation, transmission, and resilience in adversity. *Journal of Business Research*, 171(October 2023). https://doi.org/DOI: 10.1016/j.jbusres.2023.114382

Ameen, N., Tarba, S., Cheah, J. H., Xia, S., & Sharma, G. D. (2024). Coupling Artificial Intelligence Capability and Strategic Agility for Enhanced Product and Service Creativity. *British Journal of Management, 35*(4), 1916–1934. DOI: 10.1111/1467-8551.12797

Ameen, N., Tarhini, A., Reppel, A., & Anand, A. (2021). Customer experiences in the age of artificial intelligence. *Computers in Human Behavior, 114*, 106548. DOI: 10.1016/j.chb.2020.106548 PMID: 32905175

Amghar, N., Ait Lahcen, D., & Mrhari, A. (2023). La transformation digitale et la résilience des TPME en période de crises: Études de cas. *Alternatives Managériales Economiques,* E-ISSN: 2665-7511. 5(3), 381–401.

Ayala, J. C., & Manzano, G. (2014). The resilience of the entrepreneur. Influence on the success of the business. A longitudinal analysis. *Journal of Economic Psychology, 42*, 126–135. DOI: 10.1016/j.joep.2014.02.004

Badhon, B., Chakrabortty, R. K., Anavatti, S. G., & Vanhoucke, M. (2025). A Multi-Module Explainable Artificial Intelligence Framework for Project Risk Management: Enhancing Transparency in Decision-making. *Engineering Applications of Artificial Intelligence, 148*, 110427. DOI: 10.1016/j.engappai.2025.110427

Bag, S., Dhamija, P., Luthra, S., & Huisingh, D. (2023). How big data analytics can help manufacturing companies strengthen supply chain resilience in the context of the COVID-19 pandemic. *International Journal of Logistics Management, 34*(4), 1141–1164. DOI: 10.1108/IJLM-02-2021-0095

Bandura, A. (1986). The Explanatory and Predictive Scope of Self-Efficacy Theory. *Journal of Social and Clinical Psychology, 4*(3), 359–373. DOI: 10.1521/jscp.1986.4.3.359

Banque Mondiale et OMTPME. (2024). Libérer le potentiel du secteur privé marocain: une analyse de la dynamique des entreprises et de la productivité. Accessible via: https://omtpme.ma/nos-publications/#rapports_annuels

Bengrich, M., Abdelbaki, N., & Bribich, S. (2020). Capital psychologique et performance économique des entreprises marocaines: quel rôle modérateur du profil de l'entrepreneur? *Moroccan Journal of Entrepreneurship, Innovation and Management (MJEIM),* 5(1), 47–61. https://doi.org/DOI: 10.48396/IMIST.PRSM/mjeim-v5i1.20480

Benraoui, A., Es-skalli, K., & Lahmouchi, M. (2023). Le rôle de l'innovation technologique et l'intelligence artificielle dans le renforcement de la résilience des entreprises en période de crise. *Revue Française d'Economie et de Gestion, 4*(9), 1–18.

Bentahar, A., & Bouazzaoui, R. (2022). Entrepreneurship: A strategic choice for greater economic resilience and crisis management in Morocco. *Revue Française d'Economie et de Gestion, 3*(2), 122–140.

Bernard, M.-J. (2008). L'entrepreneuriat comme un processus de résilience. *Revue internationale de psychosociologie*, 32, 119-140. https://doi.org/DOI: 10.3917/rips.032.0119

Bernard, M.-J., & Dubard Barbosa, S. (2016). Résilience et entrepreneuriat: Une approche dynamique et biographique de l'acte d'entreprendre. *M@n@gement*, 19(2), 89. https://doi.org/DOI: 10.3917/mana.192.0089

Bernard, M.-J., & Fayolle, A. (2016). La résilience, une nouvelle approche de la dimension émotionnelle. *Entreprendre & Innover, n° 29*(2), 16–26. https://doi.org/DOI: 10.3917/entin.029.0016

Branicki, L. J., Sullivan-Taylor, B., & Livschitz, S. R. (2018). How entrepreneurial resilience generates resilient SMEs. *International Journal of Entrepreneurial Behaviour & Research, 24*(7), 1244–1263. DOI: 10.1108/IJEBR-11-2016-0396

Budhwar, P., Malik, A., De Silva, M. T. T., & Thevisuthan, P. (2022). Artificial intelligence–challenges and opportunities for international HRM: A review and research agenda. *International Journal of Human Resource Management*, *33*(6), 1065–1097. DOI: 10.1080/09585192.2022.2035161

Bullough, A., & Renko, M. (2013). Entrepreneurial resilience during challenging times. *Business Horizons*, *56*(3), 343–350. DOI: 10.1016/j.bushor.2013.01.001

Bullough, A., Renko, M., & Myatt, T. (2014). Danger zone entrepreneurs: The importance of resilience and self-efficacy for entrepreneurial intentions. *Entrepreneurship Theory and Practice*, *38*(3), 473–499. DOI: 10.1111/etap.12006

Chalmers, D., MacKenzie, N. G., & Carter, S. (2021). Artificial Intelligence and Entrepreneurship: Implications for Venture Creation in the Fourth Industrial Revolution. *Entrepreneurship Theory and Practice*, *45*(5), 1028–1053. DOI: 10.1177/1042258720934581

Chen, L., Ifenthaler, D., Yau, J. Y. K., & Sun, W. (2024). Artificial intelligence in entrepreneurship education: A scoping review. *Education + Training*, *66*(6), 589–608. DOI: 10.1108/ET-05-2023-0169

Chhatwani, M., Mishra, S. K., Varma, A., & Rai, H. (2022). Psychological resilience and business survival chances: A study of small firms in the USA during COVID-19. *Journal of Business Research*, *142*, 277–286. DOI: 10.1016/j.jbusres.2021.12.048

Cope, J. (2011). Entrepreneurial learning from failure: An interpretative phenomenological analysis. *Journal of Business Venturing*, *26*(6), 604–623. DOI: 10.1016/j.jbusvent.2010.06.002

Cusin, J. (2017). The Role of the Tutor in the Resilience of the Post-Bankruptcy Entrepreneur: The Case of the 60.000 Rebonds Association. *Revue de l'Entrepreneuriat*, *16*(2), 91–122. DOI: 10.3917/entre.162.0091

Cyrulnik, B. (2002). *Un merveilleux malheur*. Odile Jacob.

Das, M., & Ramalingam, M. (2022). What drives product involvement and satisfaction with OFDs amid COVID-19? *Journal of Retailing and Consumer Services*, *68*(June), 103063. DOI: 10.1016/j.jretconser.2022.103063

Di Vaio, A., Palladino, R., Hassan, R., & Escobar, O. (2020). Artificial intelligence and business models in the sustainable development goals perspective: A systematic literature review. *Journal of Business Research*, *121*(January), 283–314. DOI: 10.1016/j.jbusres.2020.08.019

Dimitriadis, S. (2021). Social capital and entrepreneur resilience: Entrepreneur performance during violent protests in Togo. *Strategic Management Journal*, *42*(11), 1993–2019. DOI: 10.1002/smj.3292

Döhring, B., Hristov, A., Maier, C., Roeger, W., & Thum-Thysen, A. (2021). COVID-19 acceleration in digitalisation, aggregate productivity growth and the functional income distribution. In *International Economics and Economic Policy* (Vol. 18, Issue 3). Springer Berlin Heidelberg. https://doi.org/DOI: 10.1007/s10368-021-00511-8

Duchek, S. (2018). Entrepreneurial resilience: A biographical analysis of successful entrepreneurs. *The International Entrepreneurship and Management Journal*, *14*(2), 429–455. DOI: 10.1007/s11365-017-0467-2

Duening, T. N. (2010). Five minds for the entrepreneurial future: Cognitive skills as the intellectual foundation for next generation entrepreneurship curricula. *The Journal of Entrepreneurship*, *19*(1), 1–22. DOI: 10.1177/097135570901900101

Emrizal, E., & Primadona, P. (2023). The Role Of Entrepreneurial Resilience And Entrepreneurial Self-Efficacy On Entrepreneurial Intention On Students In Padang City. *International Journal of Science. Technology & Management*, *4*(1), 80–84. DOI: 10.46729/ijstm.v4i1.752

Fatoki, O. (2018). The impact of entrepreneurial resilience on the success of small and medium enterprises in South Africa. *Sustainability (Basel)*, *10*(7), 2527. Advance online publication. DOI: 10.3390/su10072527

Feng, C., Ye, X., Li, J., & Yang, J. (2024). How does artificial intelligence affect the transformation of China's green economic growth? An analysis from internal-structure perspective. *Journal of Environmental Management*, *351*(November 2023), 119923. https://doi.org/DOI: 10.1016/j.jenvman.2023.119923

Fisher, R., Maritz, A., & Lobo, A. (2016). Does Individual Resilience affect Entrepreneurial Success? *Academy of Entrepreneurship Journal*, *22*(2), 39–53. DOI: 10.25916/sut.26409538

Gentile, C., & Mothe, C. (2022). La résilience de l'entrepreneur face à l'adversité: Une approche processuelle. *Revue de l'Entrepreneuriat*, *21*(4), 61–93. DOI: 10.3917/entre.pr.0045

Gómez, J., Krammer, S. M. S., Pérez-Aradros, B., & Salazar, I. (2024). Resilience to the pandemic: The role of female management, multi-unit structure, and business model innovation. *Journal of Business Research*, *172*, 114428. Advance online publication. DOI: 10.1016/j.jbusres.2023.114428

Graham, S. A., Lee, E. E., Jeste, D. V., Van Patten, R., Twamley, E. W., Nebeker, C., Yamada, Y., Kim, H. C., & Depp, C. A. (2020). Artificial intelligence approaches to predicting and detecting cognitive decline in older adults: A conceptual review. *Psychiatry Research*, *284*, 112732. DOI: 10.1016/j.psychres.2019.112732 PMID: 31978628

Gu, X., Chan, H. K., Thadani, D. R., Chan, F. K. S., & Peng, Y. (2023). The role of digital techniques in organisational resilience and performance of logistics firms in response to disruptive events: Flooding as an example. *International Journal of Production Economics*, *266*(July), 109033. DOI: 10.1016/j.ijpe.2023.109033

Guetaya, L., Addoumi, N., Bourgrine, K., & Douari, A. (2024). Innovations Disruptives : L'entrepreneuriat dans l'ère de l'Intelligence Artificielle. *Africain Scientifique Journal*, 03 (25), numéro, 273–295.

Haenlein, M., & Kaplan, A. (2019). A brief history of artificial intelligence: On the past, present, and future of artificial intelligence. *California Management Review*, *61*(4), 5–14. DOI: 10.1177/0008125619864925

Hayward, M. L. A., Forster, W. R., Sarasvathy, S. D., & Fredrickson, B. L. (2010). Beyond hubris: How highly confident entrepreneurs rebound to venture again. *Journal of Business Venturing*, *25*(6), 569–578. DOI: 10.1016/j.jbusvent.2009.03.002

Hlady Rispal, M. and Jouison-Laffitte, E. (2015). The Contribution of Qualitative Methods to the Development of the Field of Entrepreneurship. *Revue de l'Entrepreneuriat / Review of Entrepreneurship*. 14(1), 15-40. https://doi.org/DOI: 10.3917/entre.141.0015

Hoffman, D. L., & Novak, T. P. (2018). Consumer and object experience in the internet of things: An assemblage theory approach. *The Journal of Consumer Research*, *44*(6), 1178–1204. DOI: 10.1093/jcr/ucx105

Hu, M., Zhang, M., & Luo, N. (2016). Understanding participation on video sharing communities: The role of self-construal and community interactivity. *Computers in Human Behavior*, *62*, 105–115. DOI: 10.1016/j.chb.2016.03.077

Hu, Q., & Pan, Z. (2023). Can AI benefit individual resilience? The mediation roles of AI routinization and infusion. *Journal of Retailing and Consumer Services*, *73*, 103339. DOI: 10.1016/j.jretconser.2023.103339

Huang, M. H., Rust, R., & Maksimovic, V. (2019). The feeling economy: Managing in the next generation of AI (AI). *California Management Review*, *61*(4), 43–65. DOI: 10.1177/0008125619863436

Huang, M. H., & Rust, R. T. (2018). Artificial Intelligence in Service. *Journal of Service Research*, *21*(2), 155–172. DOI: 10.1177/1094670517752459

Huy, V., Nguyen, H., Vo-Thanh, T., Thinh, N. H. T., & Dung, T. T. T. (2023). Generative AI, Why, How, and Outcomes: A User Adoption Study. *AIS Transactions on Human-Computer Interaction*, *16*(1), 1–27. DOI: 10.17705/1thci.00198

Jabbour, A. B., Laguir, I., Stekelorum, R., & Gupta, S. (2025). The nexus of artificial intelligence and sustainability performance: Unveiling the impact of supply chain transparency and customer pressure on ethical conduct. *Journal of Environmental Management*, *379*(March), 124847. DOI: 10.1016/j.jenvman.2025.124847 PMID: 40054355

Jaldi, S. (2022). L' intelligence artificielle au Maroc : entre encadrement réglementaire et stratégie économique. Policy Brief, N°59/22.

Jorzik, P., Antonio, J. L., Kanbach, D. K., Kallmuenzer, A., & Kraus, S. (2024). Sowing the seeds for sustainability: A business model innovation perspective on artificial intelligence in green technology startups. *Technological Forecasting and Social Change*, *208*(August), 123653. DOI: 10.1016/j.techfore.2024.123653

Kane, G. C., Young, A. G., Majchrzak, A., & Ransbotham, S. (2021). Avoiding an oppressive future of machine learning: A design theory for emancipatory assistants. *Management Information Systems Quarterly*, *45*(1), 371–396. DOI: 10.25300/MISQ/2021/1578

Kang, W., & Shao, B. (2023). The impact of voice assistants' intelligent attributes on consumer well-being: Findings from PLS-SEM and fsQCA. *Journal of Retailing and Consumer Services, 70*(May 2022), 103130. https://doi.org/DOI: 10.1016/j.jretconser.2022.103130

Kellogg, K. C., Valentine, M., & Christin, A. (2020). Algorithms at work: the new contested terrain of control academy of management annals algorithms at work: the new contested terrain of control. *The Academy of Management Annals*, *14*(1), 366–410. DOI: 10.5465/annals.2018.0174

Korzynski, P., Mazurek, G., Krzypkowska, P., & Kurasinski, A. (2023). Artificial intelligence prompt engineering as a new digital competence: Analysis of generative AI technologies such as ChatGPT. *Entrepreneurial Business and Economics Review*, *11*(3), 25–37. DOI: 10.15678/EBER.2023.110302

Lafuente, E., Vaillant, Y., Vendrell-Herrero, F., & Gomes, E. (2019). Bouncing Back from Failure: Entrepreneurial Resilience and the Internationalisation of Subsequent Ventures Created by Serial Entrepreneurs. *Applied Psychology*, *68*(4), 658–694. DOI: 10.1111/apps.12175

Lee, I., Zhang, H., Moore, K., Zhou, X., Perret, B., Cheng, Y., Zheng, R., & Pu, G. (2022). AI Book Club: An Innovative Professional Development Model for AI Education. *SIGCSE 2022 - Proceedings of the 53rd ACM Technical Symposium on Computer Science Education, 1*, 202–208. https://doi.org/DOI: 10.1145/3478431.3499318

Li, X., Zhang, M., Liu, W., & Wang, Z. (2024). The impact of entrepreneurial co-founders' support on founders' entrepreneurial resilience in the high-tech industry: The roles of perceived digital technology and perceived failure-tolerant climate. *Technological Forecasting and Social Change*, *202*(March), 123320. DOI: 10.1016/j.techfore.2024.123320

Malik, A., De Silva, M. T. T., Budhwar, P., & Srikanth, N. R. (2021). Elevating talents' experience through innovative artificial intelligence-mediated knowledge sharing: Evidence from an IT-multinational enterprise. *Journal of International Management*, *27*(4), 100871. DOI: 10.1016/j.intman.2021.100871

Mckinsey, & Company. (2018). Notes From the Ai Frontier: Modeling the Impact of Ai on the World Economy. Modeling the Global Economic Impact of AI | McKinsey, September, 1–61. https://www.mckinsey.com/featured-insights/artificial-intelligence/notes-from-the-ai-frontier-modeling-the-impact-of-ai-on-the-world-economy

Mdarbi, S., & Belkebir, Z. (2024). La contribution de la littératie financière et de la résilience entrepreneuriale dans la survie des entreprises: Élaboration d'un cadre conceptuel. [REMAC]. *Revue de Management et Cultures*, *12*, 122–137.

Mignenan, V. (2021). Collective Intelligence and Entrepreneurial Resilience in the Context of Covid-19. *International Business Research*, *14*(9), 1. DOI: 10.5539/ibr.v14n9p1

Miles, M., & Huberman, (2003). Analyse des données qualitatives. Bruxelles: De Boeck Université.

Mir, J., & Barka, H. (2024). L ' entrepreneuriat digital au Maroc : Zoom sur les startups digitales de la région de l ' Oriental. *International Journal of Accounting, Finance, Auditing. Management and Economics*, *5*(1), 51–67. DOI: 10.5281/zenodo.10547363

Mouatif, M., & El Agy, M. (2023). Entrepreneur's resilience process and entrepreneurial rebound : A preliminary exploration of the Moroccan context. Innovative Space of Scientific Research Journals ISSN 2351-8014 69(2), 331–339.

Ngah, R., & Salleh, Z. (2015). Emotional Intelligence and Entrepreneurs' innovativeness towards Entrepreneurial Success: A Preliminary Study. *American Journal of Economics*, *2015*(2), 285–290. DOI: 10.5923/c.economics.201501.37

Nguyen, M., Malik, A., Sharma, P., Kingshott, R., & Gugnani, R. (2024). High involvement work system and organizational and employee resilience: Impact of digitalisation in crisis situations. *Technological Forecasting and Social Change*, *205*(June), 123510. DOI: 10.1016/j.techfore.2024.123510

OCDE. BCG & ING. (2024). The Adoption of Artificial Intelligence in Firms : New Evidence for policymaking. In OECD publishing. https://doi.org/https://doi.org/10.1787/f9ef33c3

Santoro, G., Bertoldi, B., Giachino, C., & Candelo, E. (2020). Exploring the relationship between entrepreneurial resilience and success: The moderating role of stakeholders' engagement. *Journal of Business Research*, *119*, 142–150. DOI: 10.1016/j.jbusres.2018.11.052

Sedjari, S., Essaadi, U. A., Kebdani, H. E. L., & Moutaqi, B. E. L. (2025). Renforcer l ' accompagnement entrepreneurial des TPE et auto- entrepreneurs pour intégrer l ' économie informelle au Maroc. *International Journal of Accounting, Finance, Auditing. Management and Economics*, *6*(2), 194–216. DOI: 10.5281/zenodo.14788100

Shepherd, D. (2015). Party on! A call for entrepreneurship research that is more interactive, activity based, cognitively hot, compassionate, and pro-social. *Journal of Business Venturing*, *30*(4), 489–507. DOI: 10.1016/j.jbusvent.2015.02.001

Shepherd, D. A., & Majchrzak, A. (2022). Machines augmenting entrepreneurs: Opportunities (and threats) at the Nexus of artificial intelligence and entrepreneurship. *Journal of Business Venturing*, *37*(4), 106227. Advance online publication. DOI: 10.1016/j.jbusvent.2022.106227

Shepherd, D. A., Osofero, M., & Wincent, J. (2022). A personal adversity model of justifying the costs of entrepreneurial action: The case of oil thieves in the Niger DELTA. *Journal of Business Venturing*, *37*(1), 106163. DOI: 10.1016/j.jbusvent.2021.106163

Sundaresan, S. (2014). Work-Life Balance – Implications for Working Women. Int. J. Sustain. Dev. 7 (7), 93–102. OIDA. *International Journal of Sustainable Development*, *7*(7), 93–102.

Tambe, P., Cappelli, P., & Yakubovich, V. (2019). Artificial Intelligence in Human Resources Management: Challenges and a Path Forward. SSRN *Electronic Journal, January 2018*. https://doi.org/DOI: 10.1177/0008125619867910

Tanner, S., Prayag, D. G., & Coelho Kuntz, D. J. (2022). Psychological capital, social capital and organizational resilience: A Herringbone Model perspective. *International Journal of Disaster Risk Reduction*, *78*(July), 103149. DOI: 10.1016/j.ijdrr.2022.103149

Thiétart, R.-A. (2014). Méthodes de Recherche. In *Management. 4ème Édition*. Dunod., DOI: 10.3917/dunod.thiet.2014.01

Tian, Y., & Fan, X. (2014). Adversity quotients, environmental variables and career adaptability in student nurses. *Journal of Vocational Behavior*, *85*(3), 251–257. DOI: 10.1016/j.jvb.2014.07.006

Townsend, D. M., & Hunt, R. A. (2019, January). Entrepreneurial action, creativity, & judgment in the age of artificial intelligence. *Journal of Business Venturing Insights*, *11*, e00126. DOI: 10.1016/j.jbvi.2019.e00126

Ucbasaran, D., Shepherd, D. A., Lockett, A., & Lyon, S. J. (2013). Life After Business Failure: The Process and Consequences of Business Failure for Entrepreneurs. *Journal of Management* (Vol. 39, Issue 1, pp. 163–202). https://doi.org/DOI: 10.1177/0149206312457823

UNESCO. (2024). *MAROC: Rapport d'évaluation de l'état de préparation à l'intelligence artificielle*. Place de Fontenoy.

Vecchiarini, M., & Somià, T. (2023). Redefining entrepreneurship education in the age of artificial intelligence: An explorative analysis. *International Journal of Management Education*, *21*(3), 1–11. DOI: 10.1016/j.ijme.2023.100879

Verhoef, P. C., Broekhuizen, T., Bart, Y., Bhattacharya, A., Dong, J. Q., Fabian, N., & Haenlein, M. (2021). Digital transformation: A multidisciplinary reflection and research agenda. *Journal of Business Research*, *122*, 889–901. DOI: 10.1016/j.jbusres.2019.09.022

Yacoubi, L., & Tourabi, A. (2021). Résilience psychologique de l'entrepreneur et résilience organisationnelle de la PME : élaboration d'un cadre conceptuel. *Alternatives Managériales et Economiques*. E-ISSN: 2665-7511 Vol 3, No 2, 2020-238

Yang, Y., & Danes, S. M. (2015). Resiliency and resilience process of trepreneurs in new venture creation. *Entrepreneurship Research Journal*, *5*(1), 1–30. DOI: 10.1515/erj-2013-0076

Yao, K., Li, X., & Liang, B. (2021). Failure learning and entrepreneurial resilience: The moderating role of firms' knowledge breadth and knowledge depth. *Journal of Knowledge Management, 25*(9), 2141–2160. DOI: 10.1108/JKM-10-2020-0772

Zuboff, S. (2019). *The Age of Surveillance Capitalism*. Profile Books Limited.

ADDITIONAL READING

Chae, B., & Goh, G. (2020). Digital entrepreneurs in artificial intelligence and data analytics: Who are they? *Journal of Open Innovation, 6*(3), 56. DOI: 10.3390/joitmc6030056

Csaszar, F. A., Ketkar, H., & Kim, H. (2024). Artificial intelligence and strategic decision-making: Evidence from entrepreneurs and investors. *Strategy Science, 9*(4), 322–345. DOI: 10.1287/stsc.2024.0190

Gupta, V., & Yang, H. (2024). Generative artificial intelligence (AI) technology adoption model for entrepreneurs: Case of ChatGPT. *Internet Reference Services Quarterly, 28*(2), 223–242. DOI: 10.1080/10875301.2023.2300114

Truong, Y., Schneckenberg, D., Battisti, M., & Jabbouri, R. (2023). Guest editorial: Artificial intelligence as an enabler for entrepreneurs: an integrative perspective and future research directions. *International Journal of Entrepreneurial Behaviour & Research, 29*(4), 801–815. DOI: 10.1108/IJEBR-04-2023-033

Upadhyay, N., Upadhyay, S., & Dwivedi, Y. K. (2022). Theorizing artificial intelligence acceptance and digital entrepreneurship model. *International Journal of Entrepreneurial Behaviour & Research, 28*(5), 1138–1166. DOI: 10.1108/IJEBR-01-2021-0052

KEY TERMS AND DEFINITIONS

Entrepreneur's Resilience: Reflects the skills and abilities an entrepreneur must possess, enabling them to overcome various challenges, bounce back from failure, and thrive in a disadvantageous and uncertain environment.

AI: Represents all the systems and technologies capable of simulating human intelligence, enabling entrepreneurs to make better decisions and save time and resources.

Entrepreneurial Self-Efficacy: Corresponds to an entrepreneur's belief in their personal and professional skills to achieve their goals and successfully complete their project.

Adversity: Includes all the difficult challenges, difficulties, and constraints that an entrepreneur faces on the path to realizing their project.

Entrepreneurial Creativity: Reflects the ability of entrepreneurs to propose new solutions to acquire new markets or cope with times of adversity.

Entrepreneurial Learning: Describes the process by which an entrepreneur acquires knowledge and strengthens their skills through exposure to their entrepreneurial environment throughout the development of their project.

Entrepreneurial Confidence: Corresponds to the entrepreneur's belief in their skills and abilities to succeed in their entrepreneurial project.

Chapter 6
Ethical Implications of Transparency in AI-Driven Marketing Strategies:
A Scoping Review

Yasmine Benimma
https://orcid.org/0009-0006-8856-2383
Sidi Mohammed Ben Abdellah University, Morocco

Amina Bennouna
Sidi Mohammed Ben Abdellah University, Morocco

ABSTRACT

This scoping review examines the ethical implications of AI in digital marketing strategies, focusing on personalization and customer experience optimization. As AI becomes increasingly integrated into marketing practices, concerns arise regarding privacy, transparency, and the ethical use of data. The study analyzes 144 academic sources to identify key themes, theoretical perspectives, and practical challenges at the intersection of AI ethics and marketing. Findings reveal four primary ethical tensions: the personalization-privacy paradox, algorithmic biases in customer segmentation, transparency deficits in automated decision-making, and accountability gaps in AI-driven marketing systems. The review proposes a framework for ethical AI marketing that balances business objectives with consumer rights protection, offering practical guidelines for implementing transparent and accountable AI systems in marketing contexts. This study contributes to ongoing discussions on responsible innovation in digital marketing and provides direction

DOI: 10.4018/979-8-3373-5499-6.ch006

for future research in this emerging field.

INTRODUCTION

Marketing has been profoundly transformed by artificial intelligence (AI), which has redefined business strategies and consumer engagement. Facilitated by sophisticated tools such as advanced customer segmentation, predictive analysis of purchasing behaviors, and real-time delivery of hyper-personalized content, this technological revolution has enabled companies to achieve unprecedented levels of precision and efficiency. These advances optimize marketing campaigns and change consumer expectations, who now expect personalized experiences tailored to their consumption habits and preferences.

However, the race for performance and profitability often obscures the complex ethical issues underlying these remarkable advances. Transparency is a central concern for legislators, consumer advocates, and society at large, as well as for marketing professionals faced with these challenges. In this context, transparency is not limited to simply disclosing data collection practices. It encompasses the entire algorithmic decision-making process, from the development of AI models to their implementation in real-world business contexts.

Information Asymmetries and Algorithmic Opacity

One of the major problems posed by AI in marketing lies in the growing information asymmetry between companies and consumers. While traditional marketing relied on relatively transparent and understandable mechanisms (market research or satisfaction surveys), AI systems often operate like black boxes, whose decisions are opaque, even to their own designers. Techniques such as deep learning or artificial neural networks generate extremely complex models capable of identifying subtle correlations in data, but whose internal logic remains difficult to interpret.

This opacity raises crucial questions: how can a consumer challenge a marketing decision targeting them if they don't understand the criteria used by the algorithm? How can informed consent be guaranteed when the profiling and personalization mechanisms are incomprehensible to a non-expert? These questions highlight a fundamental paradox: the more advanced AI systems become, the more likely they are to erode consumer trust, precisely because of their lack of transparency.

The Privacy Paradox: Personalization vs. Surveillance

The privacy paradox represents another major ethical dilemma. Consumers have a strong desire for personalized experiences, including optimized user interfaces, targeted promotional offers, and tailored product recommendations. However, this personalization relies on the accumulation of vast amounts of data, often implemented without the individual's knowledge or understanding of the consequences. Behavioral data (browsing history, social media interactions, geolocation), demographic data, and even psychographic data (preferences, values, opinions) are all being leveraged by AI technologies to generate profiles of unparalleled accuracy.

This situation poses an ethical dilemma: to what extent can organizations acquire and use data without infringing on privacy? The European General Data Protection Regulation (GDPR) aims to regulate these practices; however, gaps remain, particularly due to the constant evolution of surveillance techniques (third-party cookies, fingerprinting, facial recognition). Therefore, transparency is not only a legal requirement, but also a moral one, as it is necessary to protect the autonomy and dignity of consumers.

The Societal and Democratic Result of Marketing Algorithms

Beyond individual concerns, the application of AI in marketing has broader societal consequences. In addition to influencing purchasing decisions, algorithms also influence social norms, perceptions, and democratic processes. For example, targeted advertising systems can exacerbate stereotypes by associating specific products with specific genders or ethnicities, or by creating information silos, where consumers are exposed only to content that matches their cognitive biases.

To top it all off, some AI models trained on historical data can perpetuate systemic discrimination. Research has shown that dynamic pricing or ad-rating algorithms can perpetuate pre-existing inequalities by disadvantaging certain socioeconomic groups. These biases are rendered imperceptible in the absence of transparency, making it impossible to correct their harmful consequences.

A Regulatory Landscape in Full Evolution

Regulators around the world are beginning to address these obstacles. The European AI Act aims to regulate high-risk uses of AI, while the GDPR already imposes transparency and privacy-by-design obligations. In the United States, states such as

California have implemented comparable legislation (CPRA), and countries such as Canada and Australia are strengthening their legal systems.

However, regulation alone is not enough. Developing responsible and effective AI systems requires a multidisciplinary approach that integrates algorithmic ethics, consumer law, and behavioral science.

CONTEXT AND OBJECTIVES OF RESEARCH

The integration of artificial intelligence into marketing processes is not simply a technical improvement; it is a fundamental transformation in how companies perceive and interact with their customers. Modern marketing ecosystems frequently use machine learning algorithms for various activities, including emotion analysis, predictive customer assessment, automated content creation, and dynamic price optimization. These tools offer exceptional efficiency and capabilities; however, they also raise new ethical questions that are poorly suited to current marketing models.

The main challenge addressed by this analysis is the inherent conflict between ethical marketing and the operational requirements of artificial intelligence. Effective artificial intelligence systems require significant amounts of high-quality data and significant operational autonomy to optimize their algorithms. Ethical marketing, however, requires the protection of privacy, the defense of consumer autonomy, and the preservation of fair market policies. These criteria frequently appear to be incongruous, particularly in practice, due to the opaque nature of numerous AI decision- making procedures.

Our study goals mirror the complexity of this terrain. First, with special focus on how transparency shortcomings aggravate other ethical issues, we want to methodically identify and classify the main ethical dilemmas related with artificial intelligence-driven marketing. Second, we want to build a strong conceptual basis for examining these problems by synthesizing pertinent theoretical models from many fields. This covers combining ideas from computer science ethics, conventional commercial ethics, and developing AI governance structures.

Third, the study looks at how different markets' cultural and legal environments affect both the application and view of transparency. Under GDPR, the European Union's rights-based approach stands quite different from the more laissez-faire environment in the United States; China's state-centric model offers still another different framework. Global marketing operations that have to negotiate several countries at once depend on an awareness of these differences.

At last, and maybe most importantly, the study transcends problem identification to offer specific remedies and best practices. By means of study of real-world case studies and newly established industry standards, we generate pragmatic suggestions for applying transparent artificial intelligence systems that fulfill ethical requirements as well as commercial goals.

This pragmatic approach captures our view that ethical marketing is a source of long-term brand value and competitive advantage rather than only a compliance need.

The central research question guiding this review is: **How can businesses ethically integrate artificial intelligence into their digital marketing strategies while respecting user privacy and meeting regulatory and societal expectations?** This question reflects the complex interplay between technological capabilities, business objectives, and ethical responsibilities in contemporary marketing practice.

METHODOLOGY

Careful design of the methodological approach for this scoping study allowed the multidisciplinary character of the topic to be accommodated while preserving strict academic standards. We used a five-phase approach methodically mapping the conceptual terrain of artificial intelligence transparency in marketing using the framework developed by Arksey and O'Malley (2005).

The first phase consisted in thorough operationalizing and concept identification. Iterative reading of literature from both technical and social science fields helped develop key words including "algorithmic transparency," "explainable artificial intelligence," and "ethical personalizing." Given the essentially multidisciplinary character of the topic, this cross- pollination of vocabulary was absolutely vital.

We used a multi-channcl approach in our literature search to cover the whole range of pertinent points of view. Peer-reviewed research in marketing, computer science, and ethical journals came from academic databases. Industry sources shed light on new best practices and useful applications. Offering vital policy context were regulatory documents. From an initial pool of more than 200 possible sources, we narrowed down our choices to 144 papers that fit tight relevance and quality standards.

A mixed inductive-deductive coding system was applied for theme analysis. Originally developed naturally from the literature, initial codes were arranged under an iterative consensus process among the study team into higher-order topics. This method let us spot both predicted trends—like privacy issues—and unexpected revelations—like the growing attention on environmental effects of artificial intelligence systems.

Our conceptual framework evolved from combining these ideas into a logical system connecting stages of artificial intelligence development to fundamental ethical values. For researchers as well as for practitioners trying to put transparent

AI systems into use, the resulting matrix functions as both an analytical tool and a useful manual.

At last, our gap study went beyond merely pointing up unresolved issues to suggest certain areas of future study. This forward-thinking perspective is particularly beneficial in an area that is evolving at a rapid pace, such as artificial intelligence ethics, where the knowledge deficits of today may become the focus of regulation in the future.

Rhetorical Underpinnings

Using several theoretical traditions, each offering special insights to this intricate problem, the ethical study of artificial intelligence transparency in marketing benefits from Originating in Westin's (1967) foundational work, privacy theory offers the basic perspective of personal data as an expansion of individual sovereignty. From the most basic level, openness is important since consumers cannot truly exert control over their personal data without knowing how it is utilized.

Scholars like O'Neil (2016) and Noble (2018) have developed the idea of algorithmic responsibility, which expands this basis by looking at how opaque decision-making systems could support and magnify societal injustices. Their efforts show that openness is about preserving fair processes and stopping damage at society levels, not only about personal rights. This is especially pertinent for marketing uses because algorithmic decisions on creditworthiness, pricing, or product availability might have significant lifetime effects.

Ethical theories from moral philosophy present several angles on the reasons behind openness. Utilitarians assess transparency depending on its effects on general welfare and system outcomes: how disclosure policies influence these results? From a deontological standpoint, openness is seen as a moral obligation based on honesty and regard for individuals independent of results. Virtue ethics considers how openness practices reflect corporate principles and emphasizes the character and intentions of persons building and implementing AI systems.

Emerging theoretical ideas that try to operationalize philosophical ideas in technical systems are "value-sensitive design" (Senihji, 2023) and "participatory AI" (Leonard, 2024). These methods understand that openness cannot be thrown on as an afterthought but rather must be built into systems from their very beginning. They also underline the requirement of include many stakeholders in system design to guarantee that transparency methods really satisfy user needs rather than only satisfy legal minimums.

Given that it crosses usually compartmentalized fields, the theoretical synthesis offered in this paper is especially useful. Combining computer science, marketing, and ethical points of view helps us to have a more complete awareness of transparency that concurrently considers technical feasibility, corporate practicality, and moral obligations.

Principal Uses and Ethical Difficulties

The integration of artificial intelligence into many marketing initiatives raises numerous transparency concerns that require careful consideration. Personalized advertising systems, perhaps the most obvious AI tool in marketing, illustrate the tension between efficiency and ethical behavior. To optimize content distribution, contemporary recommendation engines analyze thousands of data points per user, building systems so complex that even their creators struggle to explain the selection of particular content. This opacity is ethically questionable due to the algorithms' ability to generate filters or regulate sensitive groups through micro-targeted messages.

Predictive analytics presents distinct but equally important challenges for customer relationship management. When algorithms rank consumers based on their creditworthiness, churn risk, or lifetime value, they make decisions that can have a significant impact on their economic prospects. In this context, the ethical imperative of transparency goes beyond simple disclosure to encompass the ability to understand and potentially challenge algorithmic decisions that affect life prospects. Current systems operate as enigmatic black boxes, with no possibility of appeal or rectification, and often fall short of this standard. Dynamic pricing systems pose an additional source of transparency concerns. While price discrimination is a traditional aspect of marketing, artificial intelligence systems are capable of applying it with unprecedented precision and scope. Ethical questions are heightened when pricing systems identify and exploit customer vulnerabilities, particularly those related to urgent demands or addictive tendencies. In this context, transparency requires not only disclosing potential price fluctuations but also openly communicating the factors that influence pricing decisions and ways to defend against abusive behavior.

Conversational artificial intelligence and virtual influencers pose new transparency challenges in human-AI interactions. As these systems increasingly replicate human behavior, they risk misleading users about the nature of their interactions. In addition to technical transparency, ethical responsibilities in this context encompass what might be called "experiential transparency," which involves ensuring that users can quickly discern whether they are interacting with a human or an algorithm, and recognizing the commercial nature of the interaction. Each of these applications illustrates how artificial intelligence is changing marketing strategies in complex ways given current ethical standards. The need for open methods that are not only technically adequate but also relevant to ordinary consumers operating in commercial environments where attention is restricted and power asymmetries prevail is present in all scenarios.

Comparative and Intercultural Perspectives

The application and perception of transparency in AI-powered marketing are heavily influenced by cultural and legal environments, posing major challenges for global businesses. The European Union's comprehensive approach, embodied by the GDPR and the AI Act, establishes strict standards for algorithmic transparency, grounded in the protection of fundamental rights. These regulations require not only transparent disclosure of data practices, but also meaningful explanations for automated decisions and robust safeguards against human intervention. The EU's concept embodies a cultural orientation that prioritizes individual privacy and institutional accountability, even if this can slow the pace of innovation.

Conversely, the United States maintains a more fragmented regulatory environment, favoring sector-specific regulations and voluntary standards. This approach results in significant gaps in transparency protections, despite its alignment with cultural values that prioritize market freedom and innovation. Many AI-powered marketing tools operate in regulatory gray areas and rely on lengthy service contracts that few consumers read or understand. The lack of federal guidance often leads to compliance complexity without ensuring optimal transparency, despite the strengthening of privacy safeguards by some states, such as California.

The Chinese strategy presents a third distinct paradigm, in which data governance serves state objectives, sometimes in conflict with consumer protection. The broader ecosystem prioritizes state access to data and algorithmic control, despite new regulations, such as the Personal Information Protection Act (PIPL), that establish minimum transparency standards. This poses unique challenges for implementing transparency, as disclosure may satisfy legal requirements without truly empowering consumers.

These regional variations have significant implications for global marketing operations. A transparency method designed for European compliance could be oversized for the US market, but insufficient for Chinese requirements. Furthermore, perceptions of technically identical transparency systems may vary from market to market due to cultural differences in privacy expectations. Japanese consumers may have different expectations than their Brazilian counterparts regarding data disclosure, even in the absence of legislative differences.

The following table summarizes the main transparency requirements in the main jurisdictions:

Table 1. Comparative analysis of transparency requirements across key jurisdictions

Region	Key Regulations	Transparency Focus	Enforcement Approach
EU	GDPR, AI Act	Explainability, rights	Strong, centralized
US	Sectoral laws	Disclosure, choice	Fragmented, complaint- driven
China	PIPL, DSL	State oversight	Variable, politically mediated
Canada	PIPEDA, AIDA	Accountability	Proactive, principles-based

Understanding these variations is crucial for developing transparency strategies that are both compliant and culturally resonant across global markets.

THE ETHICAL INTEGRATION OF AI IN DIGITAL MARKETING: COMPREHENSIVE AND IN-DEPTH CASE STUDIES

1. Carrefour and Google Cloud: Algorithmic Transparency as a Strategic Pillar

The collaboration between Google Cloud and Carrefour marks a significant milestone in the responsible integration of artificial intelligence technologies into digital marketing. This ambitious partnership, born in response to evolving consumer expectations regarding data protection and the growing requirements of the GDPR, has resulted in an operational model of rare sophistication. The Carrefour Group has established a charter for responsible artificial intelligence that not only meets legal obligations but also profoundly transforms the relationship between the brand and its customers. The result of eighteen months of research and development in collaboration with Google Cloud's technical teams, this fundamental document establishes unparalleled transparency standards for all customer interaction systems, including conversational chatbots, recommendation engines, and real-time personalization tools. The most remarkable innovation of this partnership lies in the creation of a revolutionary customer interface offering unparalleled granular control over personal data. Unlike traditional methods, which limited transparency to complex and rarely consulted privacy policies, Carrefour now offers its customers an interactive interface allowing them to:

- Understand precisely why each product is recommended to them ("This almond milk is suggested because you bought three lactose-free products last month and viewed five vegetarian recipes")
- Choose from six different levels of detail in the explanations provided, from a simplified version to an in-depth technical analysis of the algorithmic criteria.

- Determine with exceptional precision the retention period for each category of data, from purchase histories (configurable from 1 to 24 months) to browsing data (from 1 week to 6 months)
- Select their preferred communication channels from twelve distinct options, with the ability to set specific time slots for each type of notification.

This approach recognizes a fundamental principle: transparency must be as diverse as the clientele itself. A Parisian student passionate about technology will thus be able to access detailed technical explanations on how recommendation algorithms work, while a retired woman from Marseille will prefer a simplified visual summary accompanied by audio explanations. The results of this initiative, measured on a panel of 50,000 clients followed over eighteen months, are particularly eloquent: a 28% increase in the trust index, a 40% reduction in complaints related to personal data, and a 15% improvement in the conversion rate on personalized recommendations. This success has inspired several competitors, including Auchan and Fnac, who are now developing similar resolutions, thereby contributing to raising the ethical standards of the entire sector.

2. Flipkart in India: The Heavy Consequences of an Opaque Approach to Marketing AI

A notable example of the significant risks associated with the opaque and insufficiently regulated use of artificial intelligence algorithms in digital marketing is the unfortunate experience of Flipkart, the undisputed leader in e-commerce in India. This case, which gained widespread attention in 2022, was the result of an in-depth academic investigation that revealed the platform's use of a sophisticated dynamic pricing system. The consequences of this system were systematically detrimental to consumers in rural areas and lower socioeconomic groups. Researchers have even shown that the prices of strictly identical products can be increased by up to 15% for some users. This algorithmic discrimination is particularly pronounced for shoppers identified as residing in economically disadvantaged regions or who accessed the site via certain types of mobile devices associated with low incomes.

Flipkart is embroiled in a multifaceted crisis of exceptional proportions due to the complete lack of transparency regarding the criteria governing these price variations and the inability of consumers to understand the underlying mechanisms of these algorithmic decisions. Indian competition authorities quickly launched an in-depth investigation to determine whether these practices could be considered a form of algorithmic discrimination contrary to the principles of transparency and fairness. This investigation was preceded by threats of financial penalties of up to 10% of the company's annual turnover. The revelation of these practices sent a considerable shockwave through public opinion, leading to the launch of numerous boycott campaigns. Orchestrated by particularly active consumer associations, these campaigns were relayed with remarkable effectiveness on social media, where the hashtag #FlipkartDiscriminates went viral. In one week, Flipkart's market valuation plummeted by 12%, resulting in a multi-billion dollar loss in market capitalization and forcing the company's management to act quickly. The financial repercussions were immediate.

This crisis highlighted two major developments, specific to the Indian market but with implications for all modern digital economies. First, it demonstrated the remarkable progress made in digital literacy among the population, even in the country's least developed regions. Consumers are now able to recognize and denounce practices they consider discriminatory or abusive. Second, it illustrated the revolutionary effectiveness of digital activism mechanisms, with social media now offering citizens unprecedented means of action and collective mobilization, capable of forcing digital giants to change their practices in record time. Flipkart was forced to implement an ambitious recovery plan in the face of this entirely predictable storm. This strategy included the following key measures: publishing a white paper providing a comprehensive overview of the many factors influencing pricing on its platform, creating a real-time price simulator allowing users to understand the process by which the final amount offered to them is determined, and implementing an independent audit of its algorithms to identify and correct any potential bias. This case is a stark warning to all e-commerce players: in a world where consumers are increasingly informed and vigilant, algorithmic opacity is no longer a viable option and can lead to crises of trust in record time, with potentially devastating financial and reputational consequences.

3. Sephora: When Explainability Becomes a Competitive Advantage

With its Color IQ tool, Sephora has implemented an artificial intelligence policy that perfectly illustrates the ethical application of emerging technologies. The beauty giant has managed to transform a potential source of controversy into a powerful customer engagement tool, despite the delicate challenge of facial analysis, a technology often perceived as intrusive.The Color IQ system, which is currently in use at more than 2,500 points of sale worldwide, is based on a highly sophisticated technical architecture that integrates computer vision, machine learning, and conversational interfaces. This architecture is complemented by exemplary data protection protocols.

Sephora's primary innovation is its algorithmic explainability pedagogical approach. The Color IQ analysis procedure involves a minimum of eight steps of active transparency for a customer:

Pre-analysis explanation: A 3D animation details how the camera works and the types of data collected (shade, texture, imperfections) even before the scan begins.
Real-time visualization: The technical parameters and measurement points are displayed on the screen during the analysis, which utilizes a 12MP resolution and a light spectrum of 400- 700nm.
Interactive results: A dynamic color wheel provides a precise representation of the complexion's analysis, including confidence indicators for each parameter.
Explanation of recommendations: The detailed match note that accompanies each recommended product ("94%: matches your warm tone and medium intensity") is provided.
Evolutionary history: The consumer has the ability to observe the progression of their beauty profile over the past six months.
Data control: Options for the immediate deletion or retention of images and analyses with granularity.
Expert mode: Aesthetics professionals have access to technical metadata.
Secure export: Get a complete digital report on your smartphone.

This exceptional business performance is the result of radical transparency: the average basket increases by 20% for purchases guided by Color IQ, and 92% of consumers choose to save their beauty profile. The satisfaction rate of repeat users reaches 97%. Sephora has successfully set a new industry standard, demonstrating that explainable AI can not only meet regulatory requirements but also generate tangible business value. The group has since expanded this approach to other areas, including fragrance recommendation (Fragrance IQ) and hair analysis (Hair ID), thus solidifying its status as a pioneer of responsible innovation in the beauty sector.

4. Spotify: Reinventing Music Recommendation Without Compromising Privacy

The complete overhaul of Spotify's music recommendation system represents a significant step in the widespread adoption of privacy-by-design principles. Faced with growing criticism regarding the massive collection of user data and increasingly stringent requirements from European regulators, the music streaming leader undertook a fundamental transformation of its algorithmic infrastructure in 2020. This transformation involved the gradual abandonment of traditional methods of individual tracking in favor of a new approach called "privacy-preserving collaborative filtering."

This technological revolution is based on three complementary pillars:

1. The intelligent cultural grouping: Spotify has created a unique musical taxonomy grouping users' likes into 16 cultural macro-clusters—such as "Global K-Pop," "French Indie," or "Old School Hip-Hop"—which are further broken out into 256 subcategories. This system lets one precisely analyze preferences without calling for personal tracking.
2. Encrypted embeddings: Using completely encrypted 512-dimensional vectors under a hybrid cryptography system integrating parts of homomorphic encryption with AES-256, similarity between users is computed. This technique guarantees that even Spotify cannot access user raw listening data.
3. Advanced federated learning: Direct training of recommendation models on users' devices via a tailored TensorFlow Federated implementation. Only the average gradients (never the raw data) are aggregated on the central servers.

The performance of this new system, gradually deployed between 2021 and 2023, challenges preconceived notions: with 93% relevance in its recommendations (compared to 97% for the old system based on full tracking), it highlights how it is possible to reconcile algorithmic excellence with strict respect for privacy. A 40% decrease in server bandwidth, total eradication of data breaches—no instances recorded since deployment—and a 15% boost in engagement from privacy-conscious consumers are other noteworthy advantages. Now serving as a baseline for the whole streaming business, this performance brought Spotify many honors, including the Responsible Innovation Award from the European Commission in 2022.

5. L'Oréal Paris: Technological Excellence at the Service of Privacy

L'Oréal Paris's Colorsonic program not only sets new benchmarks in data protection but also marks a significant progress in the use of artificial intelligence technology to the cosmetic industry. Based on a very sophisticated "privacy by design" architecture created in partnership with cryptography experts from ENS and algorithmic ethics experts from CNRS, this high- tech hair diagnosis system is deployed in over 500 partner salons in France.

Colorsonic's technical approach stands out due to several major innovations:

Advanced edge processing: Direct on the specific device, the whole analysis process—high- resolution image capture (24MP), hair texture evaluation, needs diagnosis—is performed without any cloud-based raw data transmission. The system uses a custom SoC (System on Chip) equipped with an NPU (Neural Processing Unit) dedicated to processing computer vision algorithms.

Partial homomorphic encryption: For analyses requiring higher computational power (such as comparison with the L'Oréal product database), only highly transformed and encrypted metadata are transmitted via a Fully Homomorphic Encryption (FHE) protocol, allowing calculations on encrypted data. Even in the event of interception, this data is mathematically unusable.

Granular consent management: Customers have exceptional control over their data, being able to choose from seven different levels of sharing (from immediate deletion after analysis to anonymized integration in R&D studies) through an intuitive touch interface.

The results of this system, measured over two years of operation, confirm its success: no security incidents or GDPR non-compliance have been reported, 70% of customers choose to voluntarily share certain data for long-term tracking, and equipped salons record a 25% increase in sales of products recommended by the system. Above all, L'Oréal has succeeded in establishing a new ethical standard in an industry often criticized for its data collection practices, demonstrating that it is possible to reconcile cutting-edge technological innovation with absolute respect for privacy.

6. Airbnb: The Fight Against Algorithmic Bias as a Business Imperative

Proactively managing discrimination risks in recommendation systems is exemplified by Airbnb's algorithmic transparency policy, in effect since 2021. The platform redesigned its rating methodology by incorporating new technical advances and organizational techniques after numerous academic studies revealed racial and socioeconomic disparities in its home rating system.

Airbnb's new ethical approach is based on five complementary pillars:

1. Proactive elimination of sensitive variables: The system has now eliminated 27 potentially discriminatory characteristics, including host names, images, and overly specific geographic indicators.
2. Continuous auditing with IBM Fairness 360: Technical teams are quickly informed of any potential bias by an automated system that evaluates algorithmic decisions daily against 12 distinct fairness criteria. An automated system, IBM Fairness 360, evaluates algorithmic decisions daily based on 12 distinct fairness criteria, alerting technical teams to potential bias.
3. Differential Transparency: Today, hosts receive a "fairness score" that details the methodology used to calculate their ranking and offers specific suggestions for improving it without resorting to discriminatory methods.

4. The Independent Ethics Committee: This team, composed of external algorithmic and social science experts, is responsible for overseeing any substantial changes to the recommendation system. All substantial changes to the recommendation system are overseen by the independent ethics committee, composed of algorithmic and social science experts unaffiliated with the organization.
5. The Open Research Program: Airbnb regularly publishes articles providing a comprehensive overview of its methods and results, thus encouraging feedback and peer review. The results of this initiative are particularly encouraging: a 40% reduction in racial disparities in accommodation rankings (MIT 2023 study), an 18% increase in bookings in disadvantaged communities, and a significant improvement in the satisfaction of minority hosts. This case illustrates that a proactive approach to algorithmic ethics can improve a platform's social standing and generate tangible business benefits.

7. Nestlé: Reinventing Advertising Practices with Responsible AI Nestlé: Reinventing Advertising Practices with Responsible AI

Nestlé has implemented a groundbreaking artificial intelligence platform, the "Responsible Targeting Framework," to revolutionize its digital marketing campaigns. This advanced system represents a significant step forward from traditional digital marketing strategies, as it integrates ethical considerations into its decision-making processes. The technical key effectively integrates numerous highly advanced algorithmic layers working in perfect harmony. A first level of ethical control applies strict guidelines that automatically exclude sensitive demographic segments, such as children under 12 for certain product categories or vulnerable populations for potentially inappropriate offers. This function is based on a comprehensive contextual analysis including a minimum of 47 sociodemographic and behavioral criteria. The Augmented Transparency module, meanwhile, generates personalized and understandable explanations for each targeting decision. This allows marketing teams to precisely understand the reasons for the selection or exclusion of a specific demographic group. These comprehensive explanations, written in clear and simple language, are easily navigated and accessible via a simple interface that varies in detail. The self-limiting mechanism, a remarkable invention, actively prevents overexposure to advertising by dynamically adjusting the display frequency and calculating an "ad fatigue index" for each user in real time.

A rigorous set of control mechanisms, including a weekly algorithmic survey conducted by a multidisciplinary committee composed of data protection legal experts, experienced data scientists, and consumer representatives, completes this complex system. Marketing teams have the unique ability to activate an "algorithmic pause," allowing campaigns to be temporarily halted while conducting in-depth investigations in the event of unexpected behavior. This interface provides complete visibility into the system's decisions and is accessible in real time. The result: a 35% reduction in advertising targeting complaints, a 12% increase in advertising return on investment thanks to more relevant and better accepted targeting, and recognition of the Nestlé Award of Excellence in 2023 by the Alliance for Responsible Advertising for this innovative approach. These are all particularly significant concrete results.

8. Decathlon: Reinventing Physical Retail with Privacy-Respecting AI

Decathlon has fundamentally rethought the customer experience in its connected stores thanks to an embedded artificial intelligence solution that redefines the standards of ethical personalization in physical retail. This complex technical system, the result of three years of research and development in partnership with experts in algorithmic ethics, is based on an innovative architecture combining several cutting-edge technologies. Specifically created IoT sensors provide permanent anonymizing from the capturing phase and gather aggregated data on consumer flows. These gadgets, placed thoughtfully about the store, enable the study of consumer pathways and areas of interest without ever directly tracking the customers. The real technological achievement is the recommendation systems that run fully on edge computing—that is, directly on local processing units instead of in the cloud—so removing any chance of data leaking or abuse. Interactive screens placed close to the pertinent products show personalized recommendations in context, therefore providing useful advice without requiring any specific identity. Decathlon has instituted especially strict ethical policies including end-to-end encryption of biometric data when used for postural or gestural analyses, a "guest mode" option allowing for quick deactivation of any data collecting, and automatic deactivation following 20 minutes of inactivity to prevent any continuous passive data collecting. This project has remarkably improved commercial performance and customer experience: Equipped stores record a notable 22% increase in average basket size thanks more relevant and better-accepted suggestions; above all, the group can boast having received zero complaints from the CNIL since the initial deployment in 2021, an outstanding result for a technology that is intrinsically intrusive; 90% of customers report being "perfectly comfortable" with this discreet and respectful technology. This success illustrates that it is possible to reconcile advanced technological innovation with absolute respect for privacy, paving the way for a new generation of intelligent and ethical physical retail.

9. Michelin: The Excellence of Responsible Conversational AI
Michelin: The Excellence of Responsible Conversational AI

Michelin has revolutionized its customer service by developing a technical assistance chatbot that sets new standards in algorithmic ethics in the industrial sector. Deployed in 23 countries and accessible in 14 languages, this advanced conversational platform combines ethical and technical breakthroughs. Developed internally by Michelin's R&D teams, the "controlled veracity" mechanism uses a three-layer verification system: cross-referencing official technical sources, analyzing contextual coherence, and validating semantic similarity with certified knowledge bases, so drastically limiting hallucinations and other possible deviations of language models. Every interaction comes under a complete logbook that the client can access at any moment to provide complete openness on the reaction process. This record covers not only the technical sources used but also the background of exchanges, the degree of trust connected with every response element, and any system limits found. The source weighting system, particularly sophisticated, dynamically assigns credibility coefficients to each piece of information based on its origin (manufacturer data, field experience feedback, official technical documentation), its freshness, and its coherence with the overall available knowledge. Michelin has complemented these technical advancements with strong ethical guarantees, including an annual independent certification of the knowledge bases, a strict limitation on the topics that can be addressed (with automatic transfer to a human for out-of- scope questions), and an option to transfer to a human expert that is always clearly visible and accessible with one click. The operational performance of this system is impressive: 89% of requests are resolved without human intervention, the customer satisfaction rate reaches 94% according to post-interaction surveys, and the average processing time for technical requests is reduced by 40%. This success reveals that a rigorous approach to conversational AI can not only improve operational efficiency but also strengthen the trust of customers and partners, in a sector where technical precision is absolutely critical.

10. La Poste: Logistics Optimization through a Socially Responsible AI

The La Poste group has created an artificial intelligence platform that integrates traditional operational performance indicators with social and environmental parameters to optimize delivery routes through pioneering integration. These proprietary algorithms, which are the outcome of five years of research conducted in collaboration with the CNRS and the École des Mines, are founded on a multi-criteria modeling of uncommon complexity. The system evaluates a minimum of 78 unique parameters in five primary categories: costs and operational efficiency (distance traveled, delivery time, success rate), environmental footprint (CO_2 emissions, energy consumption, circularity), working conditions (hardship, work-life balance, exposure to risks), customer satisfaction (delivery windows, real-time tracking), and network resilience (redundancy, flexibility, adaptability). Rather than systematically prioritizing economic performance at the expense of other considerations, the genuine innovation is in the system's capacity to identify optima that concurrently satisfy these various dimensions. Postal workers have an exceptionally transparent interface that allows them to understand the optimization of their route. This interface allows them to visualize the various trade-offs made by the system between carbon footprint, distance traveled, and working time. This technical approach is accompanied by strong ethical commitments, such as a rigorous algorithmic limitation of daily working hours, enhanced protection of postal workers' data, and full human validation of proposals with extreme or unusual characteristics. This strategy offers numerous significant advantages while maintaining overall operational efficiency in line with the organization's objectives: a 23% improvement in working conditions indicators and a 15% reduction in CO_2 emissions from the distribution network. This case study demonstrates the ability to achieve a harmonious balance between economic efficiency, social responsibility, and environmental performance through a comprehensive and ethical approach to artificial intelligence in logistics.

11. Renault: Vehicle Configuration by a Contextual and Ethical AI

Renault's online vehicle configuration tool has been extensively redesigned, exceptionally illustrating the ethical integration of artificial intelligence within the automotive industry. Accessible in 18 European countries, this next-generation platform is based on this innovative technical architecture. The majority of recommendation calculations are performed client-side, rather than on central servers. AI algorithms analyze the customer's selections in real time to warn them of inconsistent combinations or suggest complementary configurations, while they explore the various options for customizing their vehicle. This procedure is executed locally in the customer's browser. This decentralized approach allows for the creation of configuration profiles that are both comprehensive and relevant, without requiring server-side data persistence, as each session is inherently anonymous and autonomous. The customer benefits from clear visual explanations highlighting the concrete benefits of each recommended option, such as long-term savings, comfort, and performance. Renault has implemented effective measures to prevent sensitive inferences, including prohibiting the system from inferring personal information from configuration choices. The data actually transmitted to Renault servers is strictly limited to the minimum information necessary to execute the order, in accordance with the customer's explicit consent. Inactive sessions are irrevocably deleted after a predetermined period, thanks to an automatic purge function. The results of this ethical approach are particularly convincing: an 18% increase in the configuration completion rate, a 30% reduction in abandonments during the process, and, above all, no reported data protection or compliance incidents since the launch of the new platform in 2022. Renault has thus demonstrated that a privacy-friendly approach can not only meet regulatory requirements but also significantly improve business performance and customer satisfaction in a highly competitive sector.

12. IKEA: The Multicultural Approach to Algorithmic Decoration

By directly integrating the principles of algorithmic inclusion into its recommendation engine, the IKEA group has transformed its interior design app. The Swedish multinational has implemented an artificial intelligence system capable of evaluating the cultural diversity of its proposals in real time, in response to criticism regarding the Eurocentrism of its automated suggestions. To prevent a user in Dubai from receiving the same suggestions as a customer in Paris, the algorithm automatically evaluates its results, fed by a database of 15,000 architectural styles classified according to their geographical origin and socio-historical context. This ensures a balanced exposure to global influences. True innovation is the "budget-aware recommendation" module. The system adapts its proposals to the financial reality of each neighborhood by discretely cross- referencing postal codes with local macroeconomic data, ensuring that sensitive personal information is never accumulated. The visual explanations, which are presented in the form of interactive heat maps, provide an groundbreaking level of transparency in the digital decoration sector by demonstrating the consequence of each element (dominant color, congestion, functionality) on the final score of the suggestion. Deployed in 12 countries, this system allowed IKEA to increase its conversions in suburban areas by 34% while reducing returns for "cultural mismatch" by 22%, demonstrating that an AI sensitive to local contexts can generate both inclusion and commercial performance.

13. Zalando: Algorithmic Transparency as an Industrial Standard

Zalando has undertaken a complete overhaul of its clothing recommendation system to make it a benchmark for algorithmic fairness in online fashion. The platform has developed "FairFit," a unique infrastructure combining continuous audit and enhanced explainability.

This system continuously scans 47 potential dimensions of bias, from the gender representation of premium brands to the ethnic diversity of the models presented. When an imbalance is detected (An overrepresentation of small sizes in the search results for "evening dress"), the algorithm automatically triggers a rebalancing while notifying the ethics team via a dedicated dashboard. Each product now displays an "Ethical Score" calculated based on 12 ESG criteria, including the carbon footprint of transportation, the social certifications of factories, and even the representativeness of the brand's advertising campaigns. But the most disruptive innovation lies in the "active feedback" mechanism: users can not only reject a suggestion but also specify exactly why (too expensive, inappropriate style, ethical issues) through a tree-structured interface that directly retrains the models. The results speak for themselves: 90% of identified biases are corrected within 72 hours, and brands with a high ethical score benefit from a 17% increase in their conversion rate, proving that transparency can become a major competitive advantage in fashion e-commerce.

14. Starbucks: Contextual Personalization Without Surveillance

Starbucks has completely reevaluated its personalized marketing roadmap by implementing an algorithmic architecture that emphasizes geographical and temporal context over individual monitoring. Their "Algorithmic Barista" analyzes a variety of non-personal data in real-time, including local weather conditions, pedestrian traffic around the store, emerging regional trends (identified through NLP embeddings analyzing Google Maps reviews), and even lunar cycles, which are statistically correlated with preferences for hot or cold beverages. The system generates recommendations based on this contextual matrix rather than on purchase history when a customer activates the app. It employs advanced clustering techniques to predict probable preferences without ever storing an individual profile. This logic is further advanced by the "Incognito Mode" option, which provides a variety of culturally adapted combinations that are arbitrary. This is a form of "responsible discovery" that is inspired by mechanisms of controlled serendipity. Despite the fact that this approach collects 60% less personal data than traditional systems, it maintains a relevance rate of 85% and has even increased new product trials by 12%. This suggests that consumers value both surprise and predictability when their privacy is respected. The performance challenges industry conventions.

15. Lego: The Conversational AI Certified "Child-Safe"

Lego developed "BuildBuddy," a chatbot that functions as both a creative assistant and an ethical guardian, in response to the unique challenges posed by the interaction between AI and young users. The technical architecture is constructed upon three layers of protection: a language model that is specifically trained to identify and rephrase inappropriate requests, voice recognition that is executed locally on the device (audio waveforms are converted to text prior to transmission), and a "algorithmic age" system that predicts the user's maturity in real-time based on their linguistic patterns. Parents are provided with a distinctive dashboard that displays aggregated metrics such as "time spent on castles vs. spaceships" or "trends in questions asked," rather than the raw conversations (which are safeguarded by end-to-end encryption). This feature enables educational monitoring without compromising privacy. The device has achieved COPPA certification in the United States, a first for a conversational AI. This resulted in a 40% increase in interaction time among 6- to 12-year-olds, illustrating that a fun and immersive experience can coexist with a rigorous ethical approach.

16. Vinted: Algorithmic Fairness in the Circular Economy

Vinted's "FairPrice AI" module has transformed its automated pricing system into an active instrument of economic justice. This system uses a multidimensional approach to evaluate each new listing, including the historical median price of comparable items in the seller's region, local purchasing power estimated from anonymized INSEE/Eurostat data, and account age (to protect newcomers from pricing errors). When an anomaly is detected, such as an abnormally high price in a modest neighborhood, the AI generates not a block, but a reasoned suggestion: "Your shirt is 28% higher than the average price in the 93rd arrondissement."Advice: 45€ would increase your chances of selling by 62%.

Discriminatory patterns, such as systematic price reductions for vendors from specific postal areas, are identified through a continuous audit of transactions in conjunction with this educational approach. The outcomes are tangible: a 35% decrease in unjustified pricing discrepancies and a 22% increase in seller satisfaction in rural areas, which demonstrate that AI can be a factor in promoting fairness in the collaborative economy.

Table 2. Summary of ethical AI cases in marketing

Company	Sector	Innovation Key	Ethical Mechanism	Results	Impact
Carrefour	Retail	Client data control dashboard 6 levels of algorithmic transparency	6 levels of algorithmic transparency	+28% trust, +15% conversion	New sector standard
Flipkart	E-commerce	Opaque dynamic pricing	No explanation for price variations	-12% valuation, boycott	Regulatory and reputational crises
Sephora	Beauty	Color IQ (explainable facial analysis)	8 steps of active transparency	+20% average basket, 97% satisfaction	Transformation of an intrusive technology into an asset
Spotify	Streaming	"Privacy-Preserving Collaborative Filtering"	Recommendations based on anonymized cultural clusters	93% relevance, -40% bandwidth	Proof that privacy and performance coexist
L'Oréal	Beauty	Hair diagnostic edge computing	7 levels of GDPR consent	+25% sales, 0 security incidents	Maximum protection of biometric data
Airbnb	Housing	Continuous bias audit (IBM Fairness 360)	Removal of 27 discriminatory variables	+18% bookings in disadvantaged neighborhoods	Reduction of 40% in racial disparities
Nestlé	Food	Industry "Responsible" advertising targeting	Filtering of sensitive audiences (children)	+12% ROI but partial opacity	Demonstration of the limits of selective ethics
Decathlon	Retail	Anonymous IoT sensors in-store	Guest mode with instant activation	+22% average basket, 0 complaints CNIL	Personalization without identification
Michelin	Industry	Triple-check technical chatbot	Consultable interaction log	94% customer satisfaction	Reduction of AI hallucinations
La Poste	Logistics	Multi-criteria optimization (78 parameters)	Algorithmic capping of working hours	-15% CO_2 emissions	Balance between performance, environment, and social conditions
Renault	Automobile	Vehicle configuration locally (browser)	Automatic data purge	+18% order completion	Privacy by Design
IKEA	Retail	Anti-Eurocentric Algorithm	Adaptation to local budgets via postal code	-22% product returns	Economic and cultural inclusion
Zalando	Fashion	"FairFit" (detection of 47 biases)	Visible ethical score by product	+17% conversion for ethical brands	Correction of 90% of biases within 72 hours
Starbucks	Restaurant	"Algorithmic Barista" (geo-temporal context)	Incognito Mode for random recommendations	85% relevance with -60% data	Personalization without individual tracking

continued on following page

Table 2. Continued

Company	Sector	Innovation Key	Ethical Mechanism	Results	Impact
Lego	Toys	Chatbot "BuildBuddy" (COPPA certified)	E2E encryption + aggregated parental metrics	+40% child engagement	Enhanced protection for minors
Vinted	E-commerce	"FairPrice AI" (geo-economic fairness)	Educational alerts on pricing	+22% satisfaction among rural sellers	Reduction of 35% in unjustified price discrepancies

Key Takeaways

1. Transparency=Trust=Performance
   - The Carrefour/Sephora cases demonstrate that explainability improves GDPR compliance and customer experience by 20% on average basket size.
2. Privacy by Design Payoff
   - Spotify and Renault demonstrate that relevance and data minimization can coexist (85–93%).
3. Combating bias = Competitive advantage
   - Equity is turned into a business lever by Airbnb (+18% bookings) and Zalando (+17% conversion).
4. Risky industries o o E-commerce:
   - Fairness (Vinted) versus pricing opacity (Flipkart)
   - Beauty: Managed intrusive technologies (L'Oréal/Sephora)

Table 3. Benchmark sectoral

Need	Best Example	Solution
Customer transparency	Carrefour	Granular data control
Privacy protection	Spotify	Anonymized cultural clusters
Anti-discrimination	Airbnb	Continuous bias audit
Protection of minors	Lego	Chatbot COPPA-certified
Economic fairness	Vinted	Prices adapted to local purchasing power

A MULTIDIMENSIONAL FRAMEWORK FOR TRANSPARENT AI IN MARKETING

Our comprehensive examination of theoretical perspectives, practical challenges, and real- world implementations has resulted in the development of a multidimensional system that aims to establish transparency in AI-driven marketing. This model acknowledges that transparency is not a static and distinctive attribute, but rather a dynamic and evolving commitment that encompasses technical, ethical, organizational, and societal dimensions.

Enriched with analyses and recommendations for companies that are interested in responsible AI, this is a comprehensive examination of each essential component.

1. Explainability: Beyond Technical Transparency

If explainable AI (XAI) has become a popular term in discussions regarding AI ethics, its application in marketing necessitates considerably more than mere superficial interpretability. Organizations must implement adaptive explainability, which involves the translation of algorithmic decisions into information that is comprehensible to a variety of stakeholders, including end users, regulators, and internal teams.

- Technical Explainability is the process of elucidating the workings of an AI model, including its inputs, processing logic, and outputs. Nevertheless, the model's architecture (decision trees, neural networks, etc.) alone is insufficient.
- Logical Explanation extends its scope by providing a rationale for the decision made by a system, such as the reason a customer was denied a promotional offer or received targeted advertising. This necessitates contextual reasoning that is consistent with user expectations.
- User-Centered Personalization allows individuals to adjust the level of detail in the explanations received. A tech-savvy user might desire granular insights, while an occasional consumer would prefer a simplified summary.

Emerging techniques like counterfactual explanations ("You saw this ad because you visited site X, but not Y") and interactive dashboards can enhance understanding. Furthermore, companies should explore real-time explanation interfaces, allowing users to query AI decisions on demand, rather than relying on static disclosures.

2. Dynamic Privacy Controls: Moving Beyond Compliance Policies Dynamic Privacy Controls: Moving Beyond Compliance Policies

Traditional privacy policies—long static documents hidden at the bottom of the page—are unsuitable for AI-driven marketing, where data usage is continuous and evolving. Instead, organizations should implement interactive and real-time controllable privacy interfaces, allowing:

- Consumers to dynamically modify their data access permissions (disabling facial recognition in ads without leaving the platform).
- To provide clear and immediate feedback on the effect of changes ("Disabling geolocation will limit personalized store recommendations").
- To use principles of intuitive design to make privacy settings accessible, avoiding legal jargon in favor of visual and interactive mechanisms.

Privacy slider could allow users to choose between maximum personalization (full data sharing) and minimal data collection (generic ads), with real-time examples of the consequences of each choice. Moreover, contextual notifications—such as explaining why the AI is requesting access to a new type of data—can build trust by reducing opacity.

3. Algorithmic Fairness: From Bias Detection to Systemic Accountability Algorithmic Fairness: From Bias Detection to Systemic Accountability

Transparency alone does not guarantee fairness. AI systems in marketing can perpetuate biases—whether in advertising targeting, credit scoring, or dynamic pricing—if they are not actively audited and corrected.

- Regular Bias Audits should evaluate models to detect demographic disparities (race, gender, age) using standardized fairness metrics (demographic parity, equality of opportunity, etc.).
- A Third-Party Certification may be necessary for high-risk applications (loan approvals or job advertisements), where independent auditors validate algorithmic fairness.
- Publishing the audit results, even in a synthetic form, demonstrates proactive responsibility. Some jurisdictions will require it (the European AI Act), but voluntary disclosure can strengthen brand trust.

Moreover, bias mitigation must be iterative—continuously refining the models as new biases emerge. If a job advertising platform disproportionately targets men for tech roles, the system should be retrained and monitored to correct this bias.

4. Cross-Cutting Ethical Governance Transversal Ethical Governance

A responsible AI cannot be confined to technical teams. A holistic governance structure integrates diverse perspectives to shape transparency practices:

- Ethics Committees should include lawyers, marketers, data scientists, representatives from civil society, and consumer advocates. Their role is to examine high-risk AI deployments and align them with ethical standards.
- A Chief Ethics Officer (CEO)—or a similar role—can anchor ethical considerations at the decision-making level, ensuring that transparency is prioritized alongside profitability.
- Whistleblower Protections should encourage employees to report unethical uses of AI without fear of retaliation, fostering internal accountability.

A multinational company could create regional ethics committees to adapt policies to local expectations, ensuring that global standards respect cultural sensitivities.

5. Environmental Transparency: The Hidden Impact of AI Environmental Transparency:

The carbon footprint of large AI models (GPT-4, generative advertising tools) is an often-overlooked ethical issue. Training a single model can emit as much CO_2 as five cars over their entire lifespan (Strubell et al., 2019). Marketing companies must:

- Disclose the Energy Consumption of their AIs in their CSR reports, detailing the resources required for client systems.
- Adopt Green AI Practices, such as eco-efficient algorithms (model pruning, quantization) or data centers powered by renewable energy.
- Offset Carbon Emissions by investing in environmental projects, aligning the use of AI with their sustainability goals.

Transparency here is not limited to internal tracking but includes customer disclosures—such as a "carbon label" on AI-generated advertisements, similar to nutritional labels.

6. Cultural Adaptation of Transparency Cultural Adaptation of Transparency Transparency is perceived differently across cultures. A universal approach might risk displeasing users or violating local norms.
    - Linguistic Localization is the foundation—translate the explanations into local languages.

- Cultural Relevance requires adapting what is disclosed and how. In individualistic societies (the United States), users prioritize data ownership and the freedom to deactivate.

In collectivist cultures (Japan), transparency could highlight how AI serves collective harmony.

- Trust Mechanisms vary—some cultures trust state-verified AIs (EU), while others prefer corporate self-regulation (United States).

A/B tests of transparency interfaces in different markets can reveal the most effective approaches.

7. Participatory Transparency: Involving Affected Communities Participatory Transparency: Involving the Affected Communities

Stakeholders should co-create transparency standards rather than passively endure them. Possible methods:

- User Advisory Councils—diverse consumers evaluating explanation tools.
- Public Consultation Periods—gathering feedback before the deployment of high-influence AI.
- Co-Design Workshops—collaborating with users to create useful transparency features. If a bank uses AI for loan applications, community forums with candidates could reveal gaps in explanations that are invisible to engineers.

8. Adaptive Transparency: Evolving with Technology and Society Adaptive Transparency: Evolving with Technology and Society

Transparency standards must be adaptable and evolve in accordance with technological advancements, such as new XAI techniques.

- Regulatory Changes (future laws on AI).
- Societal Expectations (the growing demand for digital rights).

Feedback cycles must be institutionalized by organizations, which must conduct regular user surveys, comply with regulations and draw on best practices to refine their approach.

CONCLUSION: TRANSPARENCY, AN ORGANIZATIONAL COMMITMENT

In this model, transparency isn't a simple checkbox; it's an ongoing, multifaceted effort that requires stakeholder engagement, governance, and technology investments. By applying these principles, companies can build trust, mitigate risk, and align AI-driven marketing with societal values, transforming transparency into a competitive advantage rather than a regulatory burden.

Conclusion and Strategic Vision: The Imperative of Ethical Transparency in AI-Driven Marketing

One of the most significant transformations in the history of commerce is the integration of artificial intelligence into marketing. This revolution is redefining how companies interact with consumers, optimize their campaigns, and generate growth. However, as this study shows, this transformation is not simply a technological or operational evolution; it is fundamentally ethical. Transparency, the foundation of trust, accountability, and sustainable competitive advantage in the digital age, serves as a boundary between AI's immense potential and its risks.

From Optional to Essential: Transparency as a Strategic Imperative

Transparency has evolved from an optional extra to a fundamental prerequisite for ethical and effective marketing. Once regulations such as the European AI Act or the California Privacy Act legally define this transparency, simply complying with these regulations is no longer sufficient. Consumer expectations are evolving at an even faster pace than the laws, demanding greater transparency, fairness, and control over the use of their data and the algorithmic decisions that influence them.

- Competitive differentiation: In crowded markets, brands that make transparency a value proposition rather than a regulatory burden will stand out. Companies that offer real-time explanations ("Why am I seeing this ad?") or dynamic consent tools, for example, will strengthen customer loyalty.
- Risk management: The financial and reputational repercussions of opaque AI systems are considerable. Data misuse, discriminatory targeting, or deceptive practices (dark patterns) can lead to penalties, consumer distrust, and permanent brand damage. These risks are mitigated through proactive transparency.

Establishing meaningful transparency is not simple – it requires systemic changes at multiple levels:

1. Technical Foundations: Technical Underpinnings:
    - Invest in Explainable AI (XAI) tools that balance accuracy and interpretability, utilizing techniques such as interactive interfaces or counterfactual explanations.
    - Create real-time disclosure systems that are customized to the specific requirements of users, such as explanations that can be adjusted based on their profiles.
2. Alignment of Organizations: Organizational Alignment: o Establish cross-functional ethics committees that include representatives from marketing, legal, data science, and civil society to supervise the deployment of AI.
    - Designate Chief Ethics Officers (or their equivalents) to ensure transparency at the topmost level of decision-making.
3. User-Centered Design: User-Centered Design:
    - Replace static privacy policies with interactive interfaces (preference sliders, contextual notifications) allowing users to control their data.
    - Conduct bias audits and publish summaries of the results to demonstrate commitment.

The Future of Ethical AI: Emerging Challenges and Research Directions

As AI progresses, the issues of transparency become more complex. Among the key challenges:

- Generative AI & Deepfakes: AI-generated content (synthetic influencers, hyper- personalized advertisements) requires clear labeling and traceability to avoid deception.
- Neuromarketing & Emotional AI: Technologies analyzing biometric data (eye movements, brain waves) raise questions about informed consent and psychological manipulation.
- Metaverse & Immersive Advertising: Virtual environments introduce new complexities, such as the disclosure of algorithms that shape experiences.

To address this, collaboration is crucial:

- Sector Partnerships: Professional groups (Partnership on AI) must develop voluntary standards for new technologies.

- Academic research: Interdisciplinary studies are imperative to explore the effectiveness of new disclosure methods and cultural perceptions of transparency.
- Regulatory innovation: To protect consumer rights, legislators must establish agile frameworks that adapt to technological advances.

Reinventing Marketing Ethics in the Algorithmic Era

Traditional marketing ethics, designed for human decision-making, are ill-suited to an era characterized by autonomous, opaque, and vast systems. A new paradigm must be established:

- Human values: Fairness, autonomy, and confidentiality.
- Technical realities: The potential and constraints of AI.
- Business pragmatism: Methods for reconciling profitability and transparency.

For example, algorithmic impact assessments could become as commonplace as financial assessments, evaluating not only return on investment but also societal implications.

The Trust Dividend: Transparency as a Sustainable Advantage

In a context of growing skepticism toward tech giants and brands, ethical transparency may prove to be the most advantageous distinction. Companies that implement it will:

- Build more meaningful relationships: Transparency fosters emotional trust, transforming customers into brand advocates.
- Foster innovation: Fairness and explainability constraints can serve as a catalyst for innovative results, such as privacy-preserving methods like federated learning.
- Influence industry standards: Pioneers will set benchmarks and influence regulation.

Final Perspective: The Way Forward

The opportunities are vast, despite the complexity of the path. The digital economy of the future will be driven by organizations that view transparency as an investment in trust, rather than an expense. They will not only circumvent the dangers of opaque AI but also identify new ways to generate value through authentic and fair interactions with their customers. Trust is the currency of commerce, a truth that endures as AI continues to redefine marketing. In the age of algorithms, transparency is its guarantee. Companies that understand this will thrive, not only as major players, but also as pioneers of a more ethical and sustainable digital future.

REFERENCES

Arksey, H., & O'Malley, L. (2005). Scoping studies: Towards a methodological framework. 'International Journal of Social Research Methodology, 8'(1), 19-32. DOI: 10.1080/1364557032000119616

Hosanagar, K. (2019). *A human's guide to machine intelligence.* Viking.

Noble, S. U. (2018). *Algorithms of oppression: How search engines reinforce racism.* NYU Press.

Binns, R. (2018). Fairness in machine learning: Lessons from political philosophy. '*Proceedings of the 2018 Conference on Fairness, Accountability, and Transparency*', 149-159.

Brodie, R. J., Ilic, A., Juric, B., & Hollebeck, L. D. (2011). Customer engagement: Conceptual domain, fundamental propositions, and implications for research. 'Journal of Service Research, 14' (3), 252-271. DOI: 10.1177/1094670511411703

Diakopoulos, N. (2015). Algorithmic accountability: Journalistic investigation of computational power structures. 'Digital Journalism, 3'(3), 398-415.

Senihji, M. (2023). *Ethical AI in marketing: Principles and practical implementation.* MIT Press.

Floridi, L. (2019). Establishing the rules for building trustworthy AI. 'Nature Machine Intelligence, 1'(6), 261-262.

Goodman, B., & Flaxman, S. (2017). European Union regulations on algorithmic decision-making and a "right to explanation". 'AI Magazine, 38'(3), 50-57.

Kietzmann, J., Paschen, J., & Treen, E. (2018). Artificial intelligence in advertising: How marketers can leverage artificial intelligence along the consumer journey. 'Journal of Advertising Research, 58'(3), 263-267.

Lemon, K. N., & Verhoef, P. C. (2016). Understanding customer experience throughout the customer journey. 'Journal of Marketing, 80' (6), 69-96. DOI: 10.1509/jm.15.0420

Leonard, T. (2024). Understanding and predicting customer preferences in retail using AI: A literature review. 'International Journal of Economic Studies and Management, 4' (1), 45-62. https://doi.org/DOI: 10.1111/ijesm.2024.4.issue-1

Maghraoui, O., & Belghith, A. (2019). Ethical challenges of AI-driven personalization in digital marketing. 'Journal of Business Ethics, 156' (4), 747-763. DOI: 10.1007/s10551-019-04193-w

Mansouri, S. (2018). The personalization-privacy paradox in AI marketing. 'Marketing Science, 37' (5), 733-751. DOI: 10.1287/mksc.2018.1115

Martin, K. (2018). Ethical implications and accountability of algorithms. 'Journal of Business Ethics, 160'(4), 835-850.

Munn, Z., Peters, M. D. J., Stern, C., Tufanaru, C., McArthur, A., & Aromataris, E. (2018). Systematic review or scoping review ? Guidance for authors when choosing between a systematic or scoping review approach. 'BMC Medical Research Methodology, 18' (1), 143. DOI: 10.1186/s12874-018-0611-x

Kotler, P., & Armstrong, G. (2017). *Principles of marketing* (17th ed.). Pearson Education.

Westin, A. F. (1967). *Privacy and freedom*. Atheneum Press.

Nissenbaum, H. (2010). *Privacy in context: Technology, policy, and the integrity of social life*. Stanford University Press.

Rust, R. T. (2020). The future of marketing. 'International Journal of Research in Marketing, 37'(1), 15-26.

Isaac, H. (2020). 'Stratégie et intelligence artificielle'. Enjeux numériques, 12. Paris- Dauphine University Press.

Taddeo, M., & Floridi, L. (2018). How AI can be a force for good. 'Science, 361'(6404), 751-752.

Zuboff, S. (2019). *The age of surveillance capitalism: The fight for a human future at the new frontier of power*. PublicAffairs.

O'Neil, C. (2016). *Weapons of math destruction: How big data increases inequality and threatens democracy*. Crown Publish.

Wedel, M., & Kannan, P. K. (2016). Marketing analytics for data-rich environments. 'Journal of Marketing, 80'(6), 97-121. DOI: 10.1509/jm.15.0413

Wirtz, J., & Zeithaml, V. (2018). AI and machine learning in customer service. 'Journal of Service Management, 29'(5), 907-931.

ADDITIONAL READING

Industry Reports Gartner. (2023). 'Market guide for AI in marketing'. Gartner Research.

Industry Reports:

Industry ReportsMcKinsey & Company. (2022). *The state of AI in 2022: Adoption and value creation*. McKinsey Analytics.

Industry ReportsPwC. (2023). *Responsible AI toolkit for marketers*. PricewaterhouseCoopers LLP.

Regulatory Documents European Union. (2016). General Data Protection Regulation (GDPR). [EU]. *Regulation, 2016*(679).

Regulatory Documents European Commission. (2021). Proposal for a regulation laying down harmonized rules on artificial intelligence (Artificial Intelligence Act). COM(2021) 206 final.

Chapter 7
The Authenticity of Influencers in the age of Artificial Intelligence – Effect on Moroccan Consumers' Behavior:
Dyadic Approach

Imane Margom
https://orcid.org/0000-0003-1368-8783
Sidi Mohamed Ben Abdellah University (Usmba) Fez, Morocco

Mohammed Ben Amar
Sidi Mohamed Ben Abdellah University (Usmba) Fez, Morocco

ABSTRACT

This research investigates the perceived authenticity of Instagram influencers and its impact on Moroccan consumers, focusing on the duality between human and AI-generated influencers. A dyadic qualitative approach was used, incorporating both influencers and consumers through semi-structured interviews, considering their cultural context. Results show that authenticity is a key factor for both groups. Influencers view it as vital for credibility and trust with followers, while consumers consider it fundamental in shaping their purchasing behavior, though paid collaborations can undermine perceived authenticity. The study also explores the rise of AI-generated influencers, known as virtual influencers (VI), suggesting that their lack of authenticity may limit their effectiveness in Moroccan influencer marketing. This research underscores the importance of human influence in marketing strat-

DOI: 10.4018/979-8-3373-5499-6.ch007

egies and highlights the tension between technological innovation and consumer demand for authenticity.

1. INTRODUCTION

In an ever-evolving digital landscape, influencer marketing has established itself as an essential strategic tool for brands. The perceived authenticity of influencers is now considered a key success factor due to its impact on source credibility, consumer trust, and purchasing behavior. However, the rise of virtual influencers (VIs) -AI-generated digital personas- raises questions about the central role of authenticity in influencer marketing and brings forth new challenges regarding their perceived effectiveness.

In this context, the present study explores the effect of human influencers' authenticity on Moroccan consumers' behavior, employing a qualitative approach that combines semi-structured interviews with both consumers and human influencers. Unlike human influencers, VIs, despite being integrated into the marketing strategies of major brands, lack personal experience and spontaneous emotions, which could limit their influence.

Thus, our study pursues a dual objective:

1. To explore the impact of human influencers' perceived authenticity on the attitudes and purchase intentions of Moroccan consumers.
2. To contrast these findings with the characteristics of virtual influencers, drawing on existing literature to assess their limitations and potential.

Accordingly, our research question is as follows:

Does an influencer's authenticity positively influence the attitudes and purchase intentions of Moroccan consumers, in contrast to virtual influencers?

To address this research question, the study adopts a qualitative approach aimed at understanding how consumers perceive the authenticity of human influencers and how it influences their behavior, through a dual perspective: that of influencers and Moroccan consumers. This approach enables us to analyze the dynamics of influence from both the content creators' and consumers' viewpoints, thereby enhancing the understanding of authenticity mechanisms in influencer marketing.

However, due to their digital nature, virtual influencers cannot be analyzed through the same methodological framework, as it is not possible to conduct direct interviews with them to explore their perception of authenticity. Consequently, we have opted for a comparative analysis based on existing literature, allowing us to critically assess the challenges associated with their emergence and the implications for influencer marketing strategies in Morocco and beyond.

2. LITERATURE REVIEW

2.1. Influencer Authenticity

The concept of authenticity dates back to ancient Greek philosophy, encapsulated in the maxim *"to thine own self be true"*, and has evolved through various philosophical movements. From the self-direction, reliability, and coherence theories of the 20th-century modernists to postmodernist reflections on the multifaceted nature of authenticity, the concept has undergone significant theoretical development (Luthans & Avolio, 2003).

Most psychological scholars have studied the lack of authentic behavior in individuals, often associating inauthenticity with deceptiveness, manipulation, and dishonesty. In contrast, authenticity is frequently described as a state of trustworthiness, reliability, and truthfulness (Luthans & Avolio, 2003).

2.1.1. Definitions of Authenticity

Authenticity has been conceptualized in multiple ways across disciplines. According to Heidegger (1962), authenticity is "a process of being true to oneself, of living in accordance with one's own being", while Erickson (1995) defines it as acting in alignment with one's values and principles.

Fine (2003) describes an authentic person as one who is "sincere, innocent, original, genuine, and unaffected". Similarly, Harter (2002) considers authenticity as "the ability to take ownership of one's personal experiences, including thoughts, emotions, needs, desires, preferences, or beliefs". An authentic individual, according to Harter, is someone who remains true to themselves, expressing their thoughts and feelings in alignment with their inner self.

Building on these perspectives, Kernis and Goldman (2006) argue that access to one's 'true self' or 'core self' is essential for authenticity in daily life. They identify four distinct yet interdependent components:

- Self-awareness
- Unbiased processing
- Behavior
- Relational orientation

Finally, Barrett-Lennard (1998) proposes a three-tiered model of authenticity, which comprises:

- **(a)** A person's primary experience
- **(b)** Symbolized awareness
- (c) External behaviors and communication

This model theoretically encapsulates the coherence between one's internal experiences, conscious perception, and external expressions, forming the foundation of authentic behavior.

These multiple definitions, though rich and insightful, are often presented in juxtaposition without a cohesive conceptual synthesis. To clarify this landscape, we propose a categorization of the most referenced models into three core dimensions: (1) self-knowledge and internal coherence, (2) emotional and behavioral transparency, and (3) contextual alignment with social norms. This framework provides a clearer understanding of how authenticity is perceived and interpreted in the field of influencer marketing.

2.1.2. Models of Authenticity

The first model of authenticity was introduced by Barrett-Lennard (1998), drawing inspiration from Rogers' (1961) client-centered psychology. This model conceptualizes authenticity through three key levels:

- A: An individual's primary experience
- B: Their symbolized awareness
- C: Their external behaviors and communication (Barrett-Lennard, 1998)

To achieve coherence across these levels, Barrett-Lennard (1998) proposes that an individual undergoes three distinct phases, illustrated in Figure 1:

1. **Self-alienation**
2. **Authentic living**
3. **Acceptance of external influences**

These three phases link the three levels A, B and C mentioned above, with the aim of re-establishing balance in the individual's life, both with himself and with those around him, in a coherent and consistent way (Barrett-Lennard, 1998).

Figure 1. Barrett-Lennard's (1998) Model of Authenticity

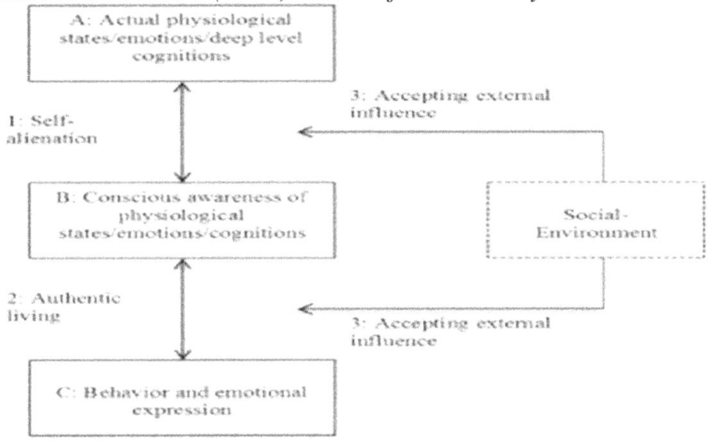

Source: *Barrett-Lennard, G. (1998)*

The second model is the "Authentic Leadership" framework proposed by Walumbwa et al. (2008), which consists of four key components, illustrated in Figure 2:

Figure 2. The "Authentic Leadership Model" by Walumbwa et al. (2008)

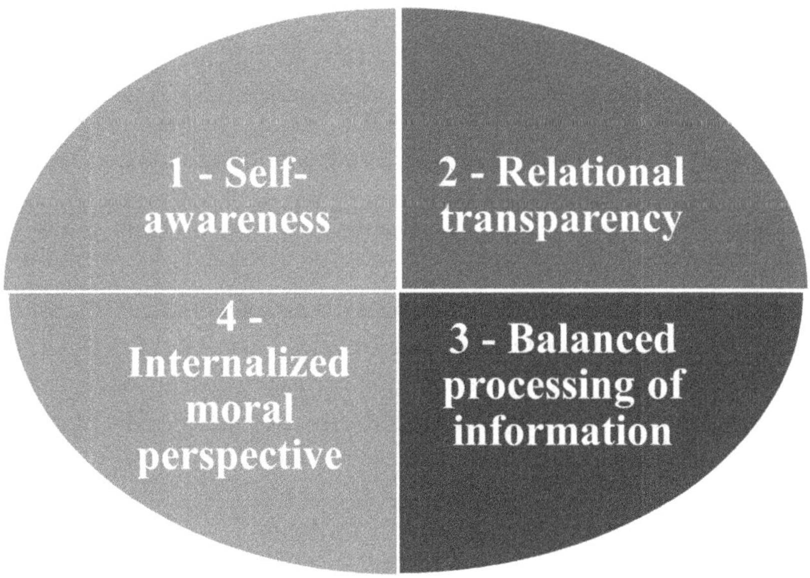

Source: *Adapted from Walumbwa et al. (2008)*

The authors state that the authentic leader brings together these four components to achieve the right balance, starting with the recognition of his values, emotions, identity and motivations, followed by the way he behaves with others, translated by his "authentic self" (Walumbwa et al., 2008). He or she must also balance information processing with the ability to carefully analyze all types of information in order to make the right decisions. And finally, the leader must self-regulate according to internal convictions and social norms.

In short, the authentic leader must be faithful to his or her beliefs and values, act in accordance with his or her convictions, respect those of others, and build relationships of trust based on transparency.

2.1.3. Definitions of an "Authentic Leader"

Authors Shamir and Eilam et al (2005) state that authentic leaders "can be differentiated from less authentic or inauthentic leaders by four interrelated characteristics:

1) The degree of integration of the leadership role into their self-concept
2) The level of clarity of their self-concept, and whether this clarity is centered around deeply held values and convictions
3) The extent to which their different goals are aligned
4) The level of congruence between their behaviours and their self-concept" (Shamir and Eilam et al., 2005).

Authors Ilies, Morgeson and Nahrgang (2005) believe that authentic leaders are "deeply aware of their values and beliefs, they are confident, authentic, reliable and trustworthy. Authentic leaders focus on building the strengths of their followers in order to expand their thinking and create a positive and engaging organizational framework".

And authors Walumbwa et al (2008) define the authentic leader as "a behavioral model that requires and promotes positive psychological capabilities and a positive ethical climate, to foster greater self-awareness, internalized moral perspective, balanced information processing and relational transparency that promotes the development of leaders and their collaborators".

2.1.4. The Influence of Influencer Authenticity on Consumer Behavior

The notion of authenticity has attracted the interest of several researchers in the fields of advertising, communication & marketing and public relations (Abidin, 2018; Argyris et al., 2020, Casaló et al., 2020; Munnukka et al., 2019; Stubb, 2018,

De Vries et al, 2012; Cotter, 2019). Brands are more likely to collaborate with influencers perceived as authentic and credible by their communities, in order to reduce resistance to the advertising message (De Vries et al, 2012). Moreover, social network users much prefer to draw inspiration from the authentic experiences of similar, ordinary people like today's influencers than from the fake, artificial illustrations of celebrities (Cotter, 2019). Through their truthful, real-life experiences, influencers create a sense of closeness, familiarity and intimacy thus sparking engagement with their followers (Cotter, 2019). What's more, authentic influencers often self-select the brands they will collaborate with, which are in line with their personal images, in order to maintain their authenticity and credibility as perceived by their followers (Abidin, 2018).

As a result, several researchers have stated that authenticity is one of the influencer characteristics that contributes most to the effectiveness of endorsement via influencer marketing (Argyris et al., 2020, Casaló et al., 2018; Munnukka et al., 2019; Stubb, 2018). Indeed, influencers have the power to convince consumers to buy the products and brands they endorse (Childers et al., 2018; Lou & Yuan, 2019), since they are considered authentic opinion leaders (Casaló, et al., 2018; Uzunoğlu & Kip, 2014). In sum, authenticity enhances message effectiveness through recipients' identification with the sender's message (Brown et al., 2003) and positively impacts brand attitude (Lim et al, 2017) and consumers' purchase intentions (Fritz, Schoenmueller, & Bruhn, 2017; Lim et al, 2017). In the scientific literature, there is unanimous agreement on the perceived authenticity of influencers, concerning their positive influence on consumer behavior (Torres et al, 2019; Lim et al, 2017).

A recently completed 2020 study, entitled "The ethics of authenticity: social media influencers and the production of sponsored content" by authors Wellman, Stoldt, Tully and Ekdale, examines the travel and tourism media industry. The results showed that influencers use the concept of authenticity as an ethical framework when producing sponsored content, and that authenticity is the key ethical principle in influencer marketing.

In 2020, the study "What makes followers loyal? The Role of Influencer Interactivity in Building Influencer Brand Value", by authors Sunghee Jun and Jisu Yi, looks at a mechanism for "how followers become loyal to social media influencers". Based on 282 social network users, they were asked to answer a survey based on their perceptions of an influencer they follow on social networks. The results showed that the influencer's authenticity positively influences consumers' brand behaviors.

A 2019 study entitled: "A call to authenticity: public responses to social media influencer endorsements in strategic communication" by authors Essi Pöyry, Matilde Pelkonen, Emma Naumanen, and Salla-Maaria Laaksonen, examines subscribers' attitudes and purchase intent using the concepts of celebrity endorsement and authenticity. Based on a sample of 592 Instagram followers who follow 45 celebrities, they were asked to respond to a survey on nine celebrity photos. The results show that perceived authenticity positively impacts consumer attitudes and purchase intentions.

2.1.5. Theoretical Foundations of Digital Influence

To further support our analysis of influence mechanisms in digital contexts, several interdisciplinary theoretical models prove relevant:

- *The Technology Acceptance Model (TAM)* (Davis, 1989) explains how perceived usefulness and ease of use influence users' acceptance of digital agents.
- *The Elaboration Likelihood Model (ELM)* (Petty & Cacioppo, 1986) differentiates between central and peripheral processing routes in persuasion, influenced by the perceived authenticity of the message source.
- *Source Credibility Theory* (Hovland et al.) highlights trustworthiness, expertise, and attractiveness as key dimensions in assessing the effectiveness of communicators.
    - *Parasocial Interaction Theory* (Horton & Wohl, 1956) offers insight into how audiences form one-sided yet emotionally engaging relationships with media figures, whether human or virtual.

2.2. Virtual Influencers: Innovation and the Authenticity Debate

The rise of virtual influencers (VIs) represents a significant advancement in digital marketing, providing brands with new opportunities to engage with consumers. Before examining their role and impact, it is essential to define what constitutes a virtual influencer.

Virtual influencers are digitally created artificial humans associated with internet fame, using software and algorithms to perform tasks similar to human influencers (Thomas & Fowler, 2021). They are computer-generated artificial characters with a strong social media presence and following (Zhang & Wei, 2021). Often referred to as computer-generated influencers (CGIs) or artificial intelligence influencers (AIIs), these digital personas are programmed to engage with audiences through social media interactions (Wibawa et al., 2022). Some are designed by individual programmers or entire media agencies, which frequently choose to remain anonymous (Stein et al., 2022).

These digital entities are meticulously crafted to replicate human influencers and are increasingly being integrated into the communication strategies of major corporations. However, despite their growing popularity, their ability to build consumer trust and effectively influence purchasing behavior remains a subject of debate, particularly due to the critical issue of perceived authenticity

2.2.1. Virtual Influencers and Their Impact on Consumers

Unlike human influencers, who establish their credibility through personal experiences and close connections with their audience, virtual influencers (VIs) lack cultural identity and real-life experiences. According to Cottrell (2023), the absence of an identifiable past or specific cultural background limits the effect of social similarity, a key factor in building consumer trust and engagement. This limitation raises concerns about their ability to influence purchase intentions, particularly in sectors where authenticity and identification are essential.

Research on the effectiveness of VIs presents mixed results. Some studies indicate that they can enhance brand image and awareness (Lou et al., 2023), while others highlight their inability to generate deep emotional engagement (Franke et al., 2023). For instance, Franke et al. (2023) found that consumers respond more favorably to VIs for technology-related products, but prefer human influencers when it comes to lifestyle, fashion, or social impact initiatives. These findings suggest that the effectiveness of VIs depends largely on the context and the type of product being promoted.

Despite these uncertainties, brands' interest in virtual influencers continues to grow. Multinational corporations such as KFC, LVMH, Mini, Netflix, Nike, and Samsung have already integrated these digital avatars into their marketing strategies (Baklanov, 2019). Some of the most well known VIs, including Lil Miquela, Shudu Gram, and Frost, have collaborated with luxury brands and technology companies, generating both admiration and skepticism regarding their true effectiveness in influencer marketing (Agrawal, 2022). In 2022, 75% of Generation Z consumers in the United States followed at least one virtual influencer on social media (Statista, 2023). This growing adoption suggests a shift in digital behavior, even though consumers remain more inclined to trust human influencers, especially in sectors where emotional connection and relational proximity are crucial.

In summary, virtual influencers represent a major innovation in digital marketing, but their impact on consumers remains a subject of debate. While their flexibility and complete content control appeal to brands, their lack of perceived authenticity and emotional engagement remains a barrier to widespread adoption, particularly for products where human connection is a key driver of persuasion and loyalty.

2.2.2. Technological Developments and the Integration of AI Influencers

The emergence of virtual influencers has been made possible by major advancements in artificial intelligence, particularly in areas such as natural language generation, voice recognition, 3D modeling, and natural language processing (Huang & Rust, 2018). These technologies now enable the creation of avatars capable of producing content autonomously and interacting with consumers on social media, thereby simulating a certain degree of authenticity.

Luxury and fashion brands were among the first industries to embrace virtual influencers, incorporating these digital avatars into their marketing strategies to appeal to a digital-savvy audience seeking innovation. Jhawar, Kumar, and Varshney (2023) highlight how luxury brands such as Chanel, Burberry, Dior, Prada, Versace, Marc Jacobs, and Louis Vuitton have increasingly integrated virtual influencers into their promotional campaigns, leveraging their futuristic appeal. One notable example is Balmain's launch of a campaign featuring virtual models like Margot, Shudu, and Zhi, reinforcing the brand's vision of blending technology with high fashion (Vogue Business, 2022).

In the cosmetics sector, virtual influencers are playing an increasingly central role in brand collaborations. Kim and Baek (2023) analyze how consumers perceive these influencers, focusing in particular on their authenticity and the "uncanny valley" effect, two factors that directly influence their effectiveness in marketing campaigns. A striking example is Fenty Beauty, which has teamed up with Shudu Gram, a digital model who has won over a large audience on social networks, reinforcing the brand's digital approach (Vogue Business, 2022).

In addition, Lil Miquela, one of the most famous virtual influencers, has made influencer marketing history by participating in prestigious events in the fashion world. Her digital presence was notably illustrated on Prada's social networks during Milan Fashion Week, demonstrating the ability of virtual influencers to mobilize audiences and influence consumer perception in the fashion industry (Fashion & Marketing Reports, 2021).

Recent advances in artificial intelligence, with techniques such as generative adversarial networks (GANs) (Goodfellow et al., 2020) and conversational models such as GPT-4, now make it possible to create avatars capable of generating personalized, emotionally simulated content, as well as natural language interactions. Despite these technical advances, some consumers still perceive these productions as mechanical and devoid of emotional depth, which limits their ability to establish a genuine relational bond.

2.2.3. Perceived Authenticity and Limitations of AI Influencers

Virtual influencers are becoming increasingly attractive to brands, not least because of the total control they offer over their image and the perfectly calibrated content they can disseminate. Nevertheless, the question of perceived authenticity remains central to the relationship with consumers, as it conditions trust and commitment. A number of studies point to the absence of real emotions and personal experiences in these digital avatars as a major hindrance to their acceptance by the public (Castelo et al., 2019). Conversely, human influencers inspire more trust because they are perceived as more spontaneous, expressive and creative.

Authenticity represents a fundamental lever in the way consumers evaluate and interact with influencers. When a message is deemed authentic, it elicits a stronger emotional connection, mitigating the perception of purely commercial intent (Ilicic & Webster, 2016; Kowalczyk & Pounders, 2016; Shoenberger et al., 2021). This dimension takes on particular importance in comparisons between human influencers and AI-powered virtual entities, which struggle to demonstrate spontaneity, personal narrative or embodied emotion.

This lack of emotional depth is regularly observed in various fields. For example, in the tourism sector, Tussyadiah et al (2020) have highlighted the limitations of AI-generated recommendations. Although users recognize the relevance and personalization of these suggestions, they are reticent about their emotional reliability, particularly in situations where subjective experience is decisive in decision-making. This doubt is accentuated by the way consumers receive such content: according to Ahn, Kim and Sung (2021), interactions with messages produced by artificial intelligence tend to create a psychological distance, thus diminishing their persuasive power. Unlike content created by humans, AI-generated content is often perceived as artificial and soulless, which undermines its impact.

Influencer marketing relies to a large extent on the influencer's ability to build lasting credibility with his or her audience. However, the work of Stein et al (2022) shows that virtual influencers are frequently perceived as mere advertising vectors, which limits their ability to exert a real and lasting influence on purchasing decisions. Their lack of real-life experience and emotional connection weakens the relationship of trust. Another determining factor in this relationship is the perceived similarity between the influencer and the members of his or her audience, often referred to as homophily. In this respect, Han & Balabanis (2024) and Stein et al. (2022) point out that consumers find it difficult to identify with virtual influencers, due to the lack of shared values, common experiences and concrete interactions. This lack of social resonance undermines their credibility and hampers their effectiveness as influencers.

2.2.4. Ethical Risks and Transparency Concerns

The fast growth of virtual influencers raises major ethical questions, notably about the transparency of practices, algorithmic manipulation and the explicit disclosure of the synthetic identity of these avatars. Mittelstadt et al (2016) point out that the opacity of algorithms and automated persuasion mechanisms call into question the fundamental principles of trust, free will and informed consent in digital interactions.

These issues become all the more sensitive in cultural contexts with a strong relational dimension, such as Morocco, where trust is largely based on the emotional presence and perceived sincerity of exchanges. The absence of authentic human characteristics in virtual influencers can therefore be perceived as a form of deception or symbolic manipulation. This perception represents a major obstacle for brands wishing to integrate these artificial figures into their communication strategy without compromising their ethical relationship with consumers.

3. RESEARCH PROPOSITION

This research aims to analyze the effect of the perceived authenticity of human influencers on the behavior of Moroccan consumers. Authenticity - nurtured by the expression of sincere emotions, accounts of personal experiences and lived interactions - is regularly highlighted in the literature as a central lever of consumer engagement with human influencers.

The methodology adopted is based on a series of semi-structured face-to-face interviews with both human influencers and Moroccan consumers. This dual point of view enables us to gain a better understanding of perceptions of authenticity, and to examine their effects on consumer attitudes and purchase intentions.

However, this approach cannot be transposed to virtual influencers (VIs), whose presence is exclusively digital and devoid of concrete human experience. While some research recognizes their effectiveness in targeted communication strategies, they lack key elements such as spontaneous emotion, a grounding in lived experience and relational depth - qualities essential to building trust and exerting lasting influence.

On this basis, the following hypothesis is formulated:

The perceived authenticity of a human influencer positively influences the attitudes and purchasing intentions of Moroccan consumers, unlike virtual influencers.

To test this hypothesis, an exploratory qualitative study was conducted using a double-case logic. Interviews were subjected to content and lexical analysis, supported by theoretical triangulation. The final objective is to identify perceived differences in authenticity between human and virtual influencers, and to examine how Moroccan cultural specificities influence these perceptions.

4. RESEARCH METHODOLOGY

In this study, we seek to explore the effect of human influencers' perceived authenticity on the behavior of Moroccan consumers, considering two perspectives: those of Moroccan influencers and consumers.

The approach adopted is resolutely qualitative, as it enables us to grasp the complexity of subjective perceptions, individual values and emotional connections - dimensions that are particularly important in the Moroccan context, where purchasing decisions are often based on bonds of trust, empathy and social proximity.

This methodological choice is based on semi-directive face-to-face interviews, in order to better understand the feelings and experiences of the Moroccan players involved. The qualitative nature of this approach enables us to gather rich, nuanced data, suited to exploring cultural phenomena rooted in the daily lives of Moroccan consumers.

By integrating this dual perspective, the study seeks to highlight the cultural specificities that influence perceptions of authenticity, and to understand how these perceptions shape attitudes and purchase intentions within the Moroccan context.

4.1. Research Protocols

- **Field Approach**

We employed a multiple case study approach, involving two distinct samples: one composed of 10 Moroccan consumers and the other of 10 Moroccan influencers. This dyadic approach aligns with a cross-perspective analysis and allows triangulation between discourses from both sides of the influence process.

- **Sample Selection**

Influencer Sample: The influencer sample was selected through netnographic analysis, examining a panel of 465 Moroccan influencer accounts on Instagram. The selection criteria included:

- Their partnerships with well-known brands,
- The quality of the content on their Instagram accounts,
- The regularity and relevance of their publications,
- Consumer engagement metrics, including comments, views, and likes, ensuring a genuine interaction between influencers and their communities.

Consumer Sample: Consumers were selected through direct interviews, based on:

- Their regular use of Instagram as their primary social network,
- A following of at least 10 influencers,
- A history of purchasing products or brands based on influencer recommendations,
- An age range of 20 to 65 years, ensuring significant generational and social diversity.

Choice of Research Field: Instagram

Instagram was chosen as the primary research field due to its central role in influencer marketing. Consumers spend more time on Instagram than on other similar sites, highlighting its importance in understanding the dynamics of influencer marketing (Sheldon & Bryant, 2016). Furthermore, Instagram has become the most used social network by influencers and the most downloaded globally, making it the ideal platform to analyze the phenomenon of influence through its numerous features (Statista, 2024).

In 2024, 71% of influencer marketing campaigns were conducted on Instagram, reinforcing its position as the leading platform in this domain (Independant.io, 2024). Moreover, 96% of marketers consider Instagram the most relevant social network for influencer partnerships, highlighting its effectiveness in reaching target audiences (Independant.io, 2024). This dominance can be attributed to Instagram's strong visual appeal, high engagement rates, and its continuous efforts to adapt to market trends. By offering new possibilities to enhance transparency and authenticity in influencer marketing, Instagram fosters greater consumer trust and encourages online purchases through influencer recommendations (Ki and Kim, 2019; Pramesthi and Astubi, 2018)

Instagram enables an "expressive use of the web" (Proulx, 2012) and is appreciated for its creativity and visual nature (Kim et al., 2017). Perceived as the "convergence of cultural forces" (Marwick, 2015), Instagram is also described as "the fastest-growing medium among mobile-sensitive users" (Abidin, 2015). Its posts function as "real-time billboards for eager and attentive eyes" (Abidin, 2014), further contributing to the honesty and transparency in influencer marketing.

Thus, Instagram, as a platform dominated by influencers, stands out as a key medium for this research, allowing for a deeper understanding of the perceived authenticity and the evolution of influencer marketing through its visual and human interactions.

- **Data Collection Tools**

Semi-structured interviews were conducted with both influencers and consumers. This format allowed for an in-depth exploration of participants' experiences and perceptions, providing rich, qualitative data.

- **Data Processing**

The collected data were transcribed sociologically, followed by lemmatization and coding of the interviews. This meticulous processing ensures that the data are well-prepared for subsequent analysis. Data were lemmatized, anonymized, and coded using sociological analysis principles. A lexicometric cleaning process was performed to prepare for software analysis.

- **Data Analysis**
  - A lexical analysis was conducted using Iramuteq software (version 0.7 alpha 2) to uncover recurring themes in the data.
  - Additionally, manual content analysis was employed to obtain a more nuanced understanding of participants' narratives and to identify key patterns and themes.
- **Discussion of Results**

Thematic findings were interpreted through theoretical triangulation, drawing from psychological (authenticity theories), sociological (parasocial interaction), and technological (AI ethics) frameworks. This integrative approach enhances the robustness of qualitative insights by validating them across disciplines. Results are presented comparatively, highlighting perceived strengths and limitations of human versus virtual influencers in a Moroccan context.

5. EMPIRICAL RESULTS

This section presents the results of our qualitative study, highlighting the cross-perceptions of Moroccan influencers and consumers.

First, we present the results of the lexical analysis carried out using Iramuteq software. This step provides an overview of the discourse collected, through a visual representation of the terms most frequently used by the participants. Analysis in the form of word clouds reveals the main lexical fields mobilized by Moroccan consumers and influencers, providing an initial overview of their experiences.

In a second stage, we deepen the analysis with a thematic reading of the content. The aim here is to uncover the deeper meaning of the discourse through a structured interpretation of what was said during the interviews. This analysis phase brings out points of convergence, as well as significant differences between the two groups interviewed, while taking into account the cultural nuances specific to the Moroccan context.

The results are presented using a two-stage comparative approach. We begin with a detailed examination of the testimonies of Moroccan influencers, highlighting elements linked to their perception of authenticity, their relationship with the public, and their role in building engagement. We will then analyze the discourses of Moroccan consumers, in order to better understand their expectations, their relationship to digital influence, and their sensitivity to perceived authenticity.

This double reading will enable us to shed light on our problematic from an enriched angle, anchored in lived, contextualized experiences.

5.1. Lexical Analysis

With the empirical data collection process completed, we proceeded with data analysis using Iramuteq software. To this end, we processed the full transcriptions of the interviews conducted during field research, dividing them into two main categories:

- The ten interviews conducted with the consumer sample
- The ten interviews conducted with the influencer sample

In order to gain a comprehensive understanding of our research problem by considering both key actors, we decided to present this lexical analysis as a comparative examination between the consumer corpus and the influencer corpus.

5.1.1. Word clouds: Consumers vs. Influencers

The word cloud provides a graphical representation of the most frequently occurring words in the interview transcripts. The font size and visibility of the words indicate their frequency and significance in the narratives of both consumers and influencers (figure 3).

Figure 3. Word cloud of consumers vs. word cloud of influencers

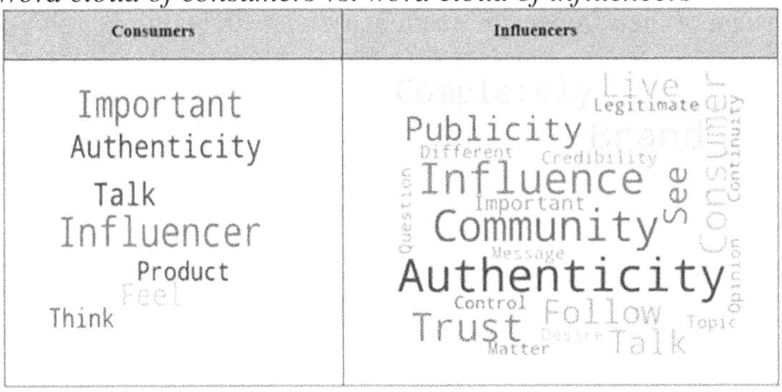

Source: *Output from Iramuteq*

- **Interpretation of the consumer word cloud**

The word **"Influencer"** dominates the consumer word cloud, followed by **"Important," "Feel,"** and **"Authenticity."** This suggests that consumers place significant emphasis on the role of influencers, particularly in terms of their authenticity and emotional connection.

The presence of **"Talk," "Feel,"** and **"Think"** further reinforces the idea that consumer engagement with influencers is driven by discourse, emotions, and cognitive evaluation. Additionally, the inclusion of **"Product"** highlights that consumers associate influencer authenticity not only with personal connection but also with product recommendations, emphasizing the importance of interaction, perceived credibility, and product endorsement in shaping consumer behavior.

- **Interpretation of the influencers' word cloud**

In the influencers' word cloud, the most dominant terms are **"Authenticity," "Influence," "Community," "Trust,"** and **"Consumer."** This suggests that influencers place authenticity at the core of their strategy, considering it a key factor in establishing a trust-based relationship with their community and consumers.

The presence of the words **"Influence"** and **"Community"** indicates that influencers perceive their role as being centered around engagement and audience connection, highlighting the importance of social interaction and a sense of belonging.

The term **"Trust"** also appears as a central element, reinforcing the idea that credibility and transparency are crucial factors in their influence. Additionally, words such as **"Follow," "Talk,"** and **"See"** emphasize the role of communication and exchange in fostering audience engagement.

Finally, the presence of terms like **"Brand"** and **"Publicity"** indicates that influencers are aware of their impact on brand marketing strategies, but also of the challenge of maintaining their authenticity while engaging in commercial collaborations.

To conclude, the common terms between the consumer and influencer word clouds include: **"Authenticity," "Important," and "Talk."**

This similarity suggests that both groups recognize authenticity as a key factor in influencer marketing. While consumers associate authenticity with trust and the influencer's ability to genuinely connect with their audience, influencers perceive it as an essential element for maintaining their credibility and fostering engagement.

5.2. Content Analysis

The content analysis will be conducted separately for each sample. By analyzing the feedback and opinions of each interviewed group, we aim to grasp individual perceptions, compare them within their respective groups, and ultimately extract clear and constructive conclusions.

To structure the content analysis, we organized the findings into three major thematic clusters based on the narratives of both influencers and consumers:

- Authenticity as a Strategic Asset for Human Influencers
- Consumers' Segmented Perception of Authenticity
- The Perceived Limitations of Virtual Influencers (VIs)

This thematic framework allows for a more focused interpretation of the qualitative data while highlighting both convergence and divergence in the viewpoints of the two participant groups.

To enhance the readability and structure of the content analysis, we will apply a naming code.

- For the influencer sample: Each influencer will be designated using a code, e.g., I-1 refers to Influencer No.1, and so forth. These references correspond to Appendix No.1, which summarizes all relevant information regarding the interviewed influencers.
- For the consumer sample: The same approach will be applied, where C-1 represents Consumer No.1, and so on, as detailed in Appendix No.2.

5.2.1 Analysis of Influencers' Perception of Authenticity

The ten interviewed influencers unanimously emphasized the importance of authenticity in influencer marketing, considering it one of the most fundamental criteria for their success. Below, we highlight key excerpts from their testimonials.

I-1 refers to the humanization of marketing, contrasting traditional media formats such as magazines and billboards with today's influencer marketing, which is centered around real people who share their lived experiences with products. According to her, authenticity plays a crucial role, as influencers have the freedom to refuse brand collaborations, select partnerships that align with their identity, and openly share their real-time product experiences. She firmly states:

"Yes, exactly! That's why people today turn more towards influencers rather than other types of advertising. Because, actually, we are not like a magazine page—you can't just rent us to spread a message however brands want. No, brands come to us, and we have the freedom to decide whether or not to collaborate with them. It depends on whether the brand aligns with who we are as individuals, whether we believe in it, whether we would actually use it, and whether we find it interesting for our followers. That's what's great—we are not like a billboard where any brand can just pay us for an ad." (I-1).

She further asserts that an influencer's authenticity is the key to their success:

"The only reason we continue to exist as influencers is that we've already proven ourselves. You can't last long in this field if you're fake or if you accept just any brand or collaboration. If we truly want to sustain ourselves, if we want to be real and successful, we have to be authentic. And yes, clearly, if people see that we are authentic, they will trust us more and more over time. That, in turn, becomes our strength—it helps us build loyalty among our followers, and that's what matters." (I-1).

Finally, she highlights a major difference between traditional media and influencer marketing, pointing out that influencers engage in real interactions with their followers, allowing them to better understand their audience's needs and desires:

"It's truly a real exchange between us and our followers. We also take their opinions into account to continue communicating in ways that meet their needs and desires." (I-1).

I-2 briefly underscores that authenticity and credibility are the cornerstones of influencer marketing success, stating:

"Authenticity and credibility are the key elements to success in influencer marketing. Nothing else matters more." (I-2).

I-3 agrees with I-2 and clarifies:

"Yes, authenticity is always linked to credibility in some way... Today, we can distinguish between influencers who are genuinely authentic and those who promote products just for compensation. That's my opinion." (I-3).

I-4 states that a lack of authenticity harms an influencer's legitimacy and creates doubt within their community:

"Yes, being authentic is essential for me. If people detect that someone is fake, it completely destroys the trust that followers have in them. So, no matter the product or cause you are defending, it won't be legitimate. The key is to be authentic, to be yourself, and not to change." (I-4).

I-5, in turn, links authenticity to credibility and highlights the importance of this criterion by denouncing the unethical behavior of certain influencers and their excessive pursuit of profit. He adds that influence is about identifying with a person, not just an advertising panel. Finally, he emphasizes that while Moroccan consumers are curious about influencer authenticity, they are also capable of distinguishing between genuine and deceptive behaviors:

"Yes, madam, of course, credibility and authenticity play a huge role. That's why, if you ever meet influencers, tell them that if they want to last in this industry, they should be less greedy. I'm not talking about ambition but about greed. If influencers start rushing and promoting just anything, it loses all meaning. Influence is about identification with a person. When we see an ad on television, it's just a commercial—we either like it or not, and then we move on. But when it's a person endorsing a product, people start wondering: Do they truly believe in it? Do they use it? Do they embody its values? That's the real question. And let me tell you, Moroccan consumers are not naive; they listen to feedback from people on Instagram." (I-5).

I-6 emphasizes that authenticity is already fundamental and that consumers strongly perceive it:

"Yes, honestly, it's very important. Consumers demand it, they see it, they feel it—it's something you can strongly sense. Being authentic is indispensable." (I-6).

I-7 emphasizes that authenticity is crucial, as it fosters a genuine connection with followers, allowing them to identify with influencers and trust them when they perceive sincerity:

"Yes, it's extremely important! People identify with us, and they trust us when they see that we are truly sincere and authentic. If they feel that we are real, that we are not just promoting products for the sake of it, they are much more likely to engage with us and take our recommendations seriously." (I-7).

I-8 agrees with I-1 and I-4, stating that authenticity leads to trust, explaining:

"Yes, absolutely! I am certain that when an authentic person shares something -whether it's paid or unpaid- it has an impact on people because they trust them." (I-8).

I-9 strongly asserts that authenticity is essential, referencing their own experience with positive feedback from brands on their perceived trustworthiness:

"Authenticity is important in my opinion. For some people, maybe not as much—it's a complex issue. But personally, I think so. I receive messages from brands that tell me, 'You have a community that really trusts you.' And when you hear things like that, it feels good. It means I'm not just doing anything random it's completely legitimate... But in general, yes, authenticity is important." (I-9).

I-10 aligns with I-2, I-3, and I-5, reinforcing the idea that authenticity is closely linked to credibility:

"Absolutely, and it ties back to credibility. Authenticity, for me, is part of credibility. Because when you're credible, in a way, you are authentic, you're not going to lie to people. To me, it all connects. So, of course, when someone is authentic, you can see that they are real, that it's not just a façade. I think consumers or followers are more likely to trust and return to these people. For example, I feel like some people follow X or Y for daily content, but they will really listen to Z, A, B, or C for recommendations. So yes, authenticity and credibility directly influence consumer behavior, positively or negatively." (I-10).

We observe that the interviewed influencers place significant importance on authenticity, considering it a cornerstone of their influence and success in the digital space. For these influencers, authenticity goes beyond just maintaining an image; it is seen as an essential part of the humanization of marketing. This marks a clear shift from traditional forms of advertising, such as magazines and billboards, to a more personal and relatable approach, where real people share their lived experiences in rcal-timc.

By focusing on authentic content, influencers distinguish themselves from conventional advertising methods, creating a unique value proposition for brands. The importance of direct communication and active engagement with their followers is particularly emphasized, as it allows them to build meaningful connections with their audience. Influencers highlight that this two-way interaction fosters a deeper understanding of their followers' needs and preferences, which enables them to create content that resonates with their audience on a personal level.

Moreover, authenticity is frequently associated with credibility, as these influencers stress that consumers are more likely to relate to real individuals rather than corporate advertisements or product placements. This shift towards human-centric marketing reinforces the notion that influencers, through their authentic self-presentation, build stronger, trust-based relationships with their communities. The ability of influencers to be perceived as genuine and transparent leads to increased consumer trust, which, in turn, enhances their capacity to shape attitudes and drive purchasing decisions. This trust, established through authenticity, is a crucial factor in their ongoing influence over consumer behavior.

Additionally, many influencers agree that remaining authentic is key to their long-term success in the industry. As one influencer noted, being authentic helps to maintain the loyalty of their followers, as consumers can easily detect when influencers are not being genuine or are simply promoting products for financial gain. This transparency, or lack thereof, is quickly identified by followers, which can either strengthen or undermine the influencer's credibility.

In conclusion, authenticity is more than just a buzzword for the influencers interviewed. It is a critical strategic asset that forms the foundation of their personal brand and their influence over consumer behavior. By embracing authenticity, they not only foster a stronger emotional connection with their followers but also build credibility and trust, essential components for sustaining their impact in the highly competitive field of influencer marketing.

5.2.2 Analysis of Consumer Perceptions of Authenticity

The majority of consumers emphasize the importance of influencer authenticity in shaping their behavior but specify that its impact remains conditional on certain factors.

C-1 and C-10 express disappointment regarding the rarity of authenticity, arguing that most influencers lose their authenticity as they gain popularity:

"Absolutely! Unfortunately, we don't see much authenticity in our Moroccan influencers or even others. It's really a shame. I think they are more authentic at the beginning of their journey, but as they gain more followers, it fades. Very few influencers have managed to retain their authenticity." (C-1)

"Oh yes, it's essential! But unfortunately, I don't think it's a quality we still find in influencers these days." (C-10)

C-2, on the other hand, states that authenticity does not influence his purchasing decisions, as he considers himself rational and bases his choices on technical product evaluations and their relevance to his interests:

"No, not really. I rely on technical tests for high-end equipment within my field of interest." (C-2).

C-3 questions the very notion of influencer authenticity, arguing that a paid collaboration inherently compromises sincerity:

"An influencer, the moment they are paid to promote a brand, is no longer authentic. No, because what you're talking about is very rare. And when it happens, it's usually in cases of dissatisfaction—like an influencer buying a product from a brand they don't have a partnership with and then having a bad experience. That's mostly what I see on Instagram. An influencer who isn't affiliated with a brand will likely have a negative experience with it. Personally, I don't base my brand choices on the bad experiences of X or Y." (C-3).

C-4, however, associates authenticity with sincerity and trust, stating that when an influencer builds a strong relationship of trust with their followers, their recommendations carry greater influence:

"Naturally, when we talk about sincerity, it's linked to trust. When an influencer successfully establishes that bond of trust with their followers, of course, we are more likely to believe them when they recommend something." (C-4).

C-5 acknowledges the overall importance of authenticity in influencer marketing but clarifies that it does not personally influence his purchasing behavior. While he appreciates the sincerity and transparency that authenticity can bring, he remains largely independent in his decision-making process:

"More or less, I do appreciate this aspect, but it doesn't really influence me. Of course, authenticity is valuable, and I understand why it matters to many people. But personally, I don't let it dictate my choices—I rely more on my own research and preferences rather than trusting an influencer simply because they appear authentic." (C-5).

C-6 makes the connection between the number of collaborations and the degree of authenticity of the influencer, believing that an influencer who recommends multiple brands, especially competing brands, reflects a discredited image and loses authenticity. On the other hand, an influencer who limits their collaborations to a few brands is seen as more genuine and authentic, which can lead to a purchase action from the consumer:

"Yes, I think authenticity is important because today, we see influencers who share just about anything. One day they promote one brand, and the next day, a competing brand. You can clearly feel it's just pure advertising. I much prefer an influencer who talks about three products a year and presents them very well. Even if we go out and buy the product, our opinion aligns with the influencer's. Authenticity is key; we need to feel it in order to trust the recommendations of an influencer." (C-6).

C-7, C-8, and C-9 agree on the importance of authenticity in influencers, emphasizing the need for influencers to stay true to themselves and avoid being consumed by money and pure advertising.

"Yes, staying true to oneself and not falling into the trap of money and pure advertising is really important. When an influencer is genuine, it makes their recommendations feel more trustworthy." (C-7)

"It's very important. You can tell when someone speaks from knowledge and experience, not just pushing a product. That authenticity makes their words more convincing." (C-8)

"Yes, it's important. You can feel it when someone is being real. It's noticeable in the way they talk, and it makes you trust them more." (C-9)

Despite some divergences in opinions, particularly concerning the paradox between paid recommendations and perceived authenticity, the majority of consumers emphasize the importance of authenticity as a decisive factor in influencer marketing. They argue that when an influencer remains true to their values and doesn't let financial incentives drive their decisions, their credibility is significantly strengthened. This credibility, in turn, enhances the power and effectiveness of their recommendations. Consumers often feel that when influencers present themselves authentically, they are more trustworthy, and this trust directly influences their attitudes and purchasing decisions.

However, the concept of authenticity becomes more complex when paid partnerships are involved. Several consumers believe that once an influencer is paid to promote a product, their authenticity is compromised. This view stems from the idea that any collaboration motivated by money diminishes the influencer's sincerity, making their recommendations less genuine in the eyes of the audience. As a result, some consumers question the legitimacy of influencers who engage in multiple paid partnerships, especially when promoting competing brands. These behaviors can create a sense of inconsistency, further distancing the influencer from being perceived as truly authentic.

Interestingly, some consumers highlight that authenticity is not merely about the absence of paid collaborations but also about the consistency and transparency of an influencer's actions. Influencers who limit their partnerships to a select number of brands are seen as more credible and trustworthy. This selective approach aligns with their personal values, reinforcing the sense of authenticity. In contrast, those who indiscriminately promote numerous brands, regardless of relevance, are viewed as engaging in mere advertising, which undermines their authenticity.

The overwhelming consensus is that authenticity is not just a desirable trait but a fundamental aspect of an influencer's ability to connect with their audience. Consumers are more likely to trust influencers who remain consistent in their message, avoid overly commercial content, and maintain transparency in their engagements. This trust leads to greater consumer confidence, which, in turn, influences purchasing behavior. Authenticity, therefore, remains a cornerstone of effective influencer marketing, particularly in contexts where trust and personal connection are paramount.

6. DISCUSSION OF THE RESULTS

Through our qualitative study, we aimed to answer the following research question: **Does the authenticity of an influencer positively affect the attitudes and purchase intentions of Moroccan consumers, as opposed to virtual influencers?** To address this question, we conducted a lexical analysis and content analysis on the two study samples. Utilizing the Iramuteq software for an overall view and performing an in-depth interpretation through manual content analysis, a confrontation between the two main actors in influencer marketing is essential. This confrontation allows us to cover the full landscape of influence, considering both the sender (the influencer) and the receiver (the consumer). The results will be examined in light of existing theories to support our qualitative insights and, where applicable, highlight divergences relative to our problem in the Moroccan context, in comparison with the literature.

In this approach, we employed the theoretical triangulation method, relying on the literature review presented earlier, which highlights several disciplinary perspectives. This methodology allows us to confront, analyze, and interpret our research findings with greater rigor and clarity.

6.1. Influencer Authenticity: A Key Lever in Influencer Marketing

The results of our qualitative study demonstrate that perceived authenticity is a fundamental criterion for both human influencers and Moroccan consumers. Both groups acknowledge its impact on attitudes and purchase intentions, thus confirming its central role in the effectiveness of influencer marketing.

6.1.1. Authenticity: The Pillar of Credibility and Trust

The influencers interviewed unanimously emphasize that authenticity is an essential condition for maintaining their credibility. They primarily define it as staying true to oneself, without artifice, in order to preserve the trust of their audience. This perception aligns with the work of Brown et al. (2008), who suggest that authenticity enhances the effectiveness of the message by fostering consumer identification with the communicator.

In this context, influencers argue that influencer marketing has humanized advertising. Unlike traditional media such as magazines or billboards, the influencer is a real person who shares their lived experiences, preferences, and personal stories. This experiential and relational dimension contributes to strengthening consumer engagement.

However, this characteristic is absent in virtual influencers. As highlighted by Castelo et al. (2019), consumers are often less inclined to trust AI-generated content, believing it lacks real-life experience and authenticity. While human influencers capitalize on their personal experience and spontaneity, virtual influencers are algorithmic creations incapable of genuinely experiencing a product or service.

6.1.2. Authenticity and Leadership of Influence: A Double-Edged Sword

The analysis of the interviews also reveals that authenticity is not solely based on perceived sincerity but also on the strategic decisions made by influencers. By drawing on Walumbwa et al.'s (2008) authentic leadership model, several practices are highlighted by the influencers interviewed:

- **Self-awareness**: Some refuse collaborations that do not align with their values.
- **Balanced information processing**: They select partnerships based on how well they align with their image and principles.
- **Relational transparency**: They share their experiences in real-time with their community.
- **Internalized moral perspective**: They prioritize brands they genuinely use and believe in.

However, a challenge arises: authenticity can be weakened by the proliferation of sponsored collaborations. Some consumers feel that an influencer who promotes too many brands or competing products loses credibility. This observation aligns with Zickmund's (2007) reflection, which suggests that authenticity is a process of staying true to oneself and one's values.

In this context, virtual influencers present a new challenge. As noted by Tussyadiah et al. (2020), although their recommendations are precise and personalized, they tend to provoke increased skepticism, especially in sectors where emotion and lived experience are key criteria. In other words, relational transparency and staying true to values, which are crucial among human influencers, are nearly nonexistent in virtual influencers, who remain purely commercial entities controlled by brands.

6.1.3. Consumers and Their Perception of Authenticity: a Behavioral Segmentation

The Moroccan consumers interviewed confirmed that authenticity plays a decisive role in their perception of influencers, although its impact varies across individuals.

To interpret these differences in consumer behavior, we can refer to the Elaboration Likelihood Model (ELM), which provides a useful framework.

1. **Consumers advocating authenticity as a key influencing factor**
    - o They believe that an authentic influencer is one who stays true to themselves and avoids falling into a purely commercial mindset.

- They are influenced by influencers who limit their collaborations and select their partnerships in a discriminatory manner.
- They are more likely to purchase a product promoted by an influencer perceived as sincere and credible.

2. **Consumers skeptical about influencer authenticity**
   - They consider authenticity to be a rare concept, with some influencers accepting any type of collaboration for financial reasons.
   - They question the sincerity of sponsored recommendations, believing that any paid collaboration compromises the influencer's objectivity.
3. **Rational and pragmatic consumers**
   - They do not rely on influencers but rather assess the product independently, focusing on its technical features and price-value ratio.
   - They take a more cognitive and analytical approach in their purchasing decisions.

These differences in perception align with the Elaboration Likelihood Model (ELM) by Petty and Cacioppo (1986). Some consumers adopt a central route, analyzing the arguments presented in the advertisement based on the product's attributes. Others prefer a peripheral route, where indicators such as credibility, authenticity, and the emotion generated by the message play a more significant role (Lien, 2001).

6.2. Comparison with Virtual Influencers: A Lack of Emotional Connection

The results of our survey reveal a clear gap between the expectations of Moroccan consumers and the characteristics of virtual influencers (VIs) as described in the literature. As purely digital entities, VIs come up against structural limitations when it comes to meeting the emotional and relational needs of a public in search of authenticity.

This contrast is reinforced by the contributions of Source Credibility Theory, according to which persuasiveness rests on two key dimensions: perceived competence and trustworthiness. While human influencers benefit from their affective proximity and the anchoring of their discourse in concrete experience, VIs, on the other hand, struggle to embody these attributes, particularly in cultural contexts such as Morocco, where human relationships and trust play a central role.

6.2.1. Lack of Real-Life Experience and Relational Transparency

Unlike human influencers, who draw on their personal backgrounds and relational sincerity to establish a connection with their audience, VIs have no real-life experience to share. As Castelo et al. (2019) point out, their algorithmic nature deprives them of any subjectivity or history of their own, which are essential elements in the construction of perceived authenticity. As a result, the emotional relationship with consumers remains superficial, if not non-existent, severely limiting their potential for engagement.

6.2.2. Lack of Perceived Authenticity and Credibility

One of the main brakes on the effectiveness of virtual influencers is a perceived lack of authenticity and credibility. As Petty and Cacioppo (1986) point out, some consumers process influencer messages via the "peripheral route", relying on elements such as perceived authenticity and trustworthiness. Yet these elements are often absent in VIs, perceived more as marketing tools than authentic personalities (Stein et al., 2022). This perception greatly impairs their ability to generate lasting influence, as they generate less trust due to their lack of real personal commitment.

What's more, unlike human influencers capable of expressing spontaneous emotions and creating a form of affective closeness with their community, VIs are unable to interact authentically or adapt their communication in an emotionally responsive way. Their artificial nature diminishes their persuasive power, as consumers seek relationships based on sincerity and personal identification (Han & Balabanis, 2024). This inability to establish a lasting bond of trust limits attachment to these digital entities, which struggle to establish relationships comparable to those that human influencers can forge (Franke et al., 2023).

6.3. The Importance of Interpersonal Relationships in the Moroccan Context

In a Moroccan context, where interpersonal relationships play an essential role in building trust (Balambo, 2014; Chibi, 2021), human influencers have a clear advantage. Moroccan consumers attach particular importance to emotional closeness and authenticity in their social interactions. They place more trust in people who are perceived as close to them, able to understand their expectations and respond empathetically. Virtual influencers, as artificial entities, are unable to satisfy these fundamental emotional needs.

These cultural preferences are fully in line with Hofstede's theoretical framework of cultural dimensions. According to Hofstede (2001), Morocco has high scores for collectivism and uncertainty avoidance. In this type of society, loyalty, group membership and trust in personal relationships are structuring values. As a result, the credibility of a message depends closely on the perceived sincerity and proximity of the person communicating it. Human influencers, by sharing their lived experiences and expressing their emotions, meet these cultural expectations. VIs, on the other hand, suffer from a lack of spontaneity and personal narrative, making them less able to establish relational links in an environment where human warmth is an essential vector of trust.

Ultimately, while virtual influencers offer undeniable technological advantages - not least in terms of image control and brand consistency - their lack of authenticity, emotional connection and human relationships severely limits their effectiveness in cultural contexts such as Morocco. Moroccan consumers, attached to human relationships and authenticity, turn more naturally to human influencers, capable of generating sincere and engaging emotional bonds.

6.4. Discussion Closing

The results of our study highlight the central role played by the perceived authenticity of human influencers in shaping the attitudes and purchasing intentions of Moroccan consumers. This authenticity is embodied in several key dimensions: lived experience, personal commitment, relational transparency, as well as the ability to create a sincere emotional bond with their community. These elements are all levers that reinforce consumer confidence and significantly influence their decisions.

In particular, the ability of human influencers to share personal stories and interact in real time with their followers helps build the credibility and perceived closeness essential to the effectiveness of their influence. Virtual influencers, on the other hand, have significant limitations, due to their lack of spontaneity, authentic emotion and grounding in reality. Although their use in digital marketing strategies is growing, their ability to generate trust and genuine buy-in remains limited. Their artificial character, often perceived as purely fabricated, makes it difficult to establish a deep emotional bond with audiences.

So, while human and virtual influencers can coexist in the digital ecosystem, perceived authenticity is a decisive differentiating factor. In cultural contexts such as Morocco, where human proximity and interpersonal relationships are fundamental to building trust, human influencers retain a clear advantage. For brands wishing to establish a sincere and lasting relationship with their audience, it therefore seems crucial to partner with influencer profiles whose values, stories and emotional anchoring resonate with consumers' deepest expectations.

7. CONCLUSION

The results of this study confirm the central role of perceived authenticity in influencer marketing, particularly within the Moroccan context. Our interviews reveal that consumers value human influencers for their transparency, lived experience, and ability to create an emotional connection, all of which enhance their credibility and influence on purchase intention.

In contrast, when compared to virtual influencers (VIs), several major differences emerge:

- Emotion and lived experience, which are key elements of perceived authenticity, are absent in VIs, limiting their ability to foster trust.
- The relational model of influencer marketing relies on consumer identification with influencers. However, VIs, as artificial entities, struggle to generate this connection.
- In the Moroccan context, where interpersonal relationships play a crucial role in building trust, VIs are likely to encounter greater resistance.

7.1. Theoretical and Methodological Contributions

This research enriches existing work on influence marketing and perceived authenticity, highlighting the decisive role of lived experience and relational transparency in the construction of consumer perceptions. By analyzing the specificities of the Moroccan context, it contributes to refining the understanding of authenticity in cultural environments still little explored by mainstream literature.

Theoretically, the study takes an interdisciplinary approach, crossing frameworks from psychology (parasocial interaction theory), communication (ELM model, source credibility theory), and culture (Hofstede's dimensions, 2001). This integration enables us to better contextualize the mechanisms of reception and identification with influence in non-Western societies, where social norms, relational expectations and emotional dynamics differ significantly.

In addition, this research initiates a reflection on the limits of virtual influencers, showing that their effectiveness remains conditional on contexts where trust, emotional proximity and personal identification are central to consumers' decision-making processes.

From a methodological point of view, this study stands out for its qualitative approach. The use of individual semi-structured interviews enabled us to gather rich, nuanced data rooted in the participants' own experiences. This immersive approach enabled a detailed reading of motivations, feelings and mechanisms of influence, which are difficult to access using standardized quantitative methods. In this way, the protocol adopted contributes to strengthening the methodological tools that can be mobilized in influence marketing studies, particularly in complex cultural contexts.

7.2. Managerial Implications

This study offers several actionable insights for marketers and brands seeking to refine their influence strategies:

- Collaborations should focus on human influencers who are perceived as genuinely authentic, particularly those whose content reflects real-life experiences and demonstrates sincere engagement with their communities.
- The use of virtual influencers should be considered strategically, especially in industries where innovation and brand aesthetics are more critical than emotional or relational depth—such as fashion, technology, or design.
- Content strategies should prioritize human-centered storytelling, fostering interaction through emotionally engaging, transparent narratives that resonate with the values and lifestyles of target audiences.
- Finally, brands should prepare for the emergence of hybrid formats, where virtual influencers are enriched with human-like traits that simulate authenticity. When culturally tailored and communicated with transparency, this approach can offer a balance between the scalability and consistency of virtual personas and the emotional resonance expected by consumers.

7.3. Study Limitations and Research Perspectives

Although this study provides valuable insights into the authenticity of human influencers and their comparison with virtual influencers (VIs), it presents several limitations:

- The lack of interviews with specialists involved in the creation of virtual influencers limits our understanding of strategies that could enhance their perceived authenticity.
- Additionally, while the sample size is consistent with the objectives of qualitative research, which aims to provide in-depth insights rather than generalizable results, it is important to note that this may limit the broader applica-

bility of the findings to the entire Moroccan population. Future studies could consider using a mixed-methods approach to enrich the findings by combining qualitative depth with quantitative breadth, which could strengthen both internal and external validity.
- Social desirability bias and social façade bias are inherent limitations of the study. These biases could have influenced participants to give responses they believed to be socially acceptable or expected, rather than providing a completely genuine response. This is particularly relevant in the context of influencers, as they may be more likely to present themselves in a favorable light.

7.4. Future Research Directions

To further deepen this reflection, several research avenues can be explored:

- Exploring how consumers perceive the authenticity of virtual influencers across different industries (e.g., fashion, technology, gaming, wellness), particularly in relation to the emotional expectations specific to each sector.
- Conducting cross-cultural quantitative studies to compare the impact of human and virtual influencers on purchase intention in both collectivist and individualist societies, using cultural dimensions frameworks.
- Analyzing the storytelling and personalization strategies employed by virtual influencers to compensate for their lack of lived experience, with a focus on emotional AI and algorithm-driven narratives.
- Interviewing designers, marketers, and creative agencies behind VIs to gain deeper insights into the ethical, technological, and strategic challenges of developing AI personas.
- Developing a managerial decision-making matrix to help brands determine when to favor human, virtual, or hybrid influencers, based on campaign goals, sector-specific expectations, and cultural trust factors.

In conclusion, this study emphasizes the importance of perceived authenticity in influencer marketing and the challenges posed by the emergence of virtual influencers. As VIs continue to evolve, it is crucial to better understand the conditions under which they can coexist with human influencers and align with consumer expectations in terms of authenticity, emotional connection, and trust.

REFERENCES

Abidin, C. (2014). # IntagLam: Instagram as a repository of taste, a burgeoning marketplace, a war of eyeballs. *Mobile media making in an age of smartphones*, 119-128.

Abidin, C. (2015). Intimités communicatives: influenceurs et interconnexion perçue. *Ada: A Journal of Gender, New Media, &. Technology*, (8), 1–16.

Abidin, C. (2018). *Internet celebrity: Understanding fame online*. Emerald Group Publishing. DOI: 10.1108/9781787560765

Agarwal, A. (2022). *The birth, the pull & the rise of virtual influencers*. Social Samosa. https://www.socialsamosa.com/2022/05/the-birth-the-pull-the-rise-of-virtual-influencers/

Ahn, J., Kim, J., & Sung, Y. (2021). AI-powered recommendations: The roles of perceived similarity and psychological distance on persuasion. *International Journal of Advertising*, *40*(8), 1366–1384. DOI: 10.1080/02650487.2021.1982529

Argyris, Y. A., Wang, Z., Kim, Y., & Yin, Z. (2020). Les effets de la congruence visuelle sur l'augmentation de l'engagement des consommateurs à la marque: Une enquête empirique sur le marketing d'influence sur Instagram à l'aide d'algorithmes d'apprentissage profond pour la classification automatique des images. *Computers in Human Behavior, 112*, 106443. DOI: 10.1016/j.chb.2020.106443

Astuti, B., & Putri, A. P. (2018). Analysis on the effect of Instagram use on consumer purchase intensity. *Review of Integrative Business and Economics Research*, *7*(2), 24–38.

Baklanov, N. (2019). *The top Instagram virtual influencers in 2019*. HypeAuditor. https://hypeauditor.com/blog/the-top-instagram-virtual-influencers-in-2019/

Balambo, M. A. (2014). Hofstede's model revisited: An application for measuring the Moroccan national culture. *International Journal of Business Quantitative Economics and Applied Management Research*, *1*(3), 7–20.

Barrett-Lennard, G. T. (1998). Carl Rogers' Helping System: Journey & Substance. *Sage (Atlanta, Ga.)*.

Brown, D., & Hayes, N. (2008). *Marketing d'influence*. Routledge. DOI: 10.4324/9780080557700

Casaló, L. V., Flavián, C., & Ibáñez-Sánchez, S. (2020). Influenceurs sur Instagram: Antécédents et conséquences du leadership d'opinion. *Journal of Business Research, 117*, 510–519. DOI: 10.1016/j.jbusres.2018.07.005

Castelo, N., Bos, M. W., & Lehmann, D. R. (2019). Task-dependent algorithm aversion. *JMR, Journal of Marketing Research, 56*(5), 809–825. DOI: 10.1177/0022243719851788

Chibi, M. (2021). Collectivism and individualism as cultural aspects in Arabic/English argumentative writing by Moroccan students. *International Journal of English Literature and Social Sciences, 6*(4), 60–69. DOI: 10.22161/ijels.64.10

Childers, C. C., Lemon, L. L., & Hoy, M. G. (2018). # Sponsored# Ad: Agency perspective on influencer marketing campaigns. *Journal of Current Issues and Research in Advertising, 40*(3), 258–274. DOI: 10.1080/10641734.2018.1521113

Cotter, K. (2019). Playing the visibility game: How digital influencers and algorithms negotiate influence on Instagram. *New Media & Society, 21*(4), 895–913. DOI: 10.1177/1461444818815684

Cottrell, N. **(2023).** *Virtual influencers: Homophily and its impact on consumer purchase intention.* ResearchGate. https://www.researchgate.net/publication/371126113_Virtual_Influencers_Homophily_and_its_Impact_on_Consumer_Purchase_Intention

Davis, F. D. (1989). Perceived usefulness, perceived ease of use, and user acceptance of information technology. *Management Information Systems Quarterly, 13*(3), 319–340. DOI: 10.2307/249008

De Vries, L., Gensler, S., & Leeflang, P. S. (2012). Popularity of brand posts on brand fan pages: An investigation of the effects of social media marketing. *Journal of Interactive Marketing, 26*(2), 83–91. DOI: 10.1016/j.intmar.2012.01.003

Eilam, G., & Shamir, B. (2005). "What's your story?" A life-stories approach to authentic leadership development. *The Leadership Quarterly, 16*(3), 395–417. DOI: 10.1016/j.leaqua.2005.03.005

Fashion & Marketing Reports. **(2021).** *Lil Miquela takes over Prada's Instagram during Milan Fashion Week.* https://www.voguebusiness.com/technology/what-influencer-marketing-looks-like-in-the-metaverse

Fine, G. A. (2003). Crafting authenticity: The validation of identity in self-taught art. *Theory and Society, 32*(2), 153–180. DOI: 10.1023/A:1023943503531

Franke, C., Groeppel-Klein, A., & Müller, K. (2023). Consumers' responses to virtual influencers as advertising endorsers: Novel and effective or uncanny and deceiving? *Journal of Advertising*, *52*(4), 523–539. DOI: 10.1080/00913367.2022.2154721

Fritz, K., Schoenmueller, V., & Bruhn, M. (2017). Authenticity in branding–exploring antecedents and consequences of brand authenticity. *European Journal of Marketing*, *51*(2), 324–348. DOI: 10.1108/EJM-10-2014-0633

Goodfellow, I., Pouget-Abadie, J., Mirza, M., Xu, B., Warde-Farley, D., Ozair, S., Courville, A., & Bengio, Y. (2014). Generative adversarial nets. *Advances in Neural Information Processing Systems*, •••, 27.

Han, J., & Balabanis, G. (2024). Meta-analysis of social media influencer impact: Key antecedents and theoretical foundations. *Psychology and Marketing*, *41*(2), 394–426. https://doi.org/xxxxx. DOI: 10.1002/mar.21927

Harter, S. (2002). Authenticité. In Snyder, C. R., & Lopez, S. J. (Eds.), *Handbook of positive psychology* (pp. 382–394). Oxford University Press.

Heidegger, M. (1962). *L'être et le temps*. SCM Press.

Hofstede, G. (2001). *Culture's consequences: Comparing values, behaviors, institutions and organizations across nations* (2nd ed.). Sage Publications.

Horton, D., & Wohl, R. R. (1956). Mass communication and parasocial interaction: Observations on intimacy at a distance. *Psychiatry*, *19*(3), 215–229. DOI: 10.1080/00332747.1956.11023049 PMID: 13359569

Hovland, C. I., Janis, I. L., & Kelley, H. H. (1953). *Communication and persuasion: Psychological studies of opinion change*. Yale University Press.

Huang, M.-H., & Rust, R. T. (2018). Artificial intelligence in service. *Journal of Service Research*, *21*(2), 155–172. DOI: 10.1177/1094670517752459

Ilicic, J., & Webster, C. M. (2016). Being true to oneself: Investigating celebrity brand authenticity. *Psychology and Marketing*, *33*(6), 410–420. DOI: 10.1002/mar.20887

Ilies, R., Morgeson, F. P., & Nahrgang, J. D. (2005). Authentic leadership and eudaemonic well-being: Understanding leader–follower outcomes. *The Leadership Quarterly*, *16*(3), 373–394. DOI: 10.1016/j.leaqua.2005.03.002

Independant.io. **(2024).** 25 statistiques & 5 tendances sur le marketing d'influence. *Independant.io*. https://independant.io/statistiques-marketing-influence/

Jhawar, A., Kumar, P., & Varshney, S. (2023). The emergence of virtual influencers: A shift in the influencer marketing paradigm. *Young Consumers*, *24*(4), 468–484. DOI: 10.1108/YC-05-2022-1529

Jun, S., & Yi, J. (2020). What makes followers loyal? The role of influencer interactivity in building influencer brand equity. *Journal of Product and Brand Management*, *29*(6), 803–814. DOI: 10.1108/JPBM-02-2019-2280

Kernis, M. H., & Goldman, B. M. (2006). Une conceptualisation multidimensionnelle de l'authenticité: Théorie et recherche. *Advances in Experimental Social Psychology*, *38*, 283–357. DOI: 10.1016/S0065-2601(06)38006-9

Ki, C. W. C., & Kim, Y. K. (2019). Le mécanisme par lequel les influenceurs des médias sociaux persuadent les consommateurs: Le rôle du désir des consommateurs d'imiter. *Psychology and Marketing*, *36*(10), 905–922. DOI: 10.1002/mar.21244

Kim, J. J.,Phua, J. et Jin, S. V. (2017). Utilisations et gratifications des sites de réseautage social pour rapprocher et lier le capital social: une comparaison de Facebook, Twitter, Instagram et Snapchat. *Les ordinateurs dans le comportement humain, 72*, 115-122.

Kim, M., & Baek, T. H. (2023). Are virtual influencers friends or foes? Uncovering the perceived creepiness and authenticity of virtual influencers in social media marketing in the United States. *International Journal of Human-Computer Interaction*, •••, 1–14. DOI: 10.1080/10447318.2023.2175575

Kowalczyk, C. M., & Pounders, K. R. (2016). Transforming celebrities through social media: The role of authenticity and emotional attachment. *Journal of Product and Brand Management*, *25*(4), 345–356. DOI: 10.1108/JPBM-09-2015-0969

Lien, N.-H. (2001). Elaboration likelihood model in consumer research: A review. *Actes du National Science Council, Part C: Humanities and Social Sciences*, *11*(4), 301–310.

Lim, X.-J., Radzol, A., Cheah, J.-H., & Wong, M. (2017). The impact of Social Media Influencers on Purchase Intention and the Mediation Effect of Customer Attitude. *Asian Journal of Business Research*, *7*(2), 19–36. DOI: 10.14707/ajbr.170035

Lou, C., Kiew, S. T. J., Chen, T., Lee, T. Y. M., Ong, J. E. C., & Phua, Z. (2023). Authentically fake? How consumers respond to the influence of virtual influencers. *Journal of Advertising*, *52*(4), 540–557. DOI: 10.1080/00913367.2022.2149641

Lou, C., & Yuan, S. (2019). Influencer marketing: How message value and credibility affect consumer trust of branded content on social media. *Journal of Interactive Advertising*, *19*(1), 58–73. DOI: 10.1080/15252019.2018.1533501

Luthans, F., & Avolio, B. J. (2003). Authentic leadership development. *Positive organizational scholarship, 241*(258), 1-26.

Marabelli, M., Newell, S., & Handunge, V. (2021). The lifecycle of algorithmic decision-making systems: Organizational choices and ethical challenges. *The Journal of Strategic Information Systems, 30*(3), 101683. Advance online publication. DOI: 10.1016/j.jsis.2021.101683

Marwick, A. E. (2015). Instafame: selfies de luxe dans l'économie de l'attention. *Culture publique, 27*(1 (75)), 137-160.

Mittelstadt, B. D., Allo, P., Taddeo, M., Wachter, S., & Floridi, L. (2016). The ethics of algorithms: Mapping the debate. *Big Data & Society, 3*(2), 1–21. DOI: 10.1177/2053951716679679

Munnukka, J., Maity, D., Reinikainen, H., & Luoma-aho, V. (2019). "Thanks for watching". The effectiveness of YouTube vlog endorsements. *Computers in Human Behavior, 93*, 226–234. DOI: 10.1016/j.chb.2018.12.014

Newell, S., & Marabelli, M. (2015). Strategic opportunities (and challenges) of algorithmic decision-making: A call for action on the long-term societal effects of 'datification. *The Journal of Strategic Information Systems, 24*(1), 3–14. DOI: 10.1016/j.jsis.2015.02.001

Open, A. I. (2023). *GPT-4 technical report*. https://openai.com/research/gpt-4

Petty, R. E., Cacioppo, J. T., Petty, R. E., & Cacioppo, J. T. (1986). *The elaboration likelihood model of persuasion*. Springer New York.

Pöyry, E., Pelkonen, M., Naumanen, E., & Laaksonen, S. (2019). Un appel à l'authenticité: réponses du public aux endossements des influenceurs des médias sociaux dans la communication stratégique. *Revue internationale de communication stratégique, 13*, 336 - 351.

Proulx, S., Millette, M., & Heaton, L. (2012). *Médias sociaux: enjeux pour la communication*. Puq.

Rogers, C. R. (1961). *Sur le fait de devenir une personne: le point de vue d'un thérapeute sur la psychothérapie*. Constable.

Sheldon, P., & Bryant, K. (2016). Instagram: Motives for its use and relationship with narcissism and contextual age. *Computers in Human Behavior, 58*, 89–97. DOI: 10.1016/j.chb.2015.12.059

Shoenberger, H., Kim, E., & Sun, Y. (2021). Advertising during COVID-19: Exploring perceived brand message authenticity and potential psychological reactance. *Journal of Advertising*, *50*(3), 253–261. DOI: 10.1080/00913367.2021.1927914

Statista. (2023, January 6). Virtual influencers—Statistics & facts. Statista. Retrieved from https://www.statista.com/topics/9805/virtual-influencers/#topicOverview

Statista. (2024). Instagram - Statistics & Facts. Available at: https://www.statista.com/topics/1882/instagram/#topicOverview (Accessed February 27, 2025).

Stein, J., Barton, K., & Pennington, J. (2022). Virtual influencers: More human than humans? *Journal of Digital and Social Media Marketing*, *10*(1), 15–26.

Stein, J.-P., Breves, P. L., & Anders, N. (2022). Parasocial interactions with real and virtual influencers: The role of perceived similarity and human-likeness. *New Media & Society*, *26*(6), 3433–3453. DOI: 10.1177/14614448221102900

Stubb, C. (2018). Story versus info: Tracking blog readers' online viewing time of sponsored blog posts based on content-specific elements. *Computers in Human Behavior*, *82*, 54–62. DOI: 10.1016/j.chb.2018.01.001

Thomas, V. L., & Fowler, K. (2021). Close encounters of the AI kind: Use of AI influencers as brand endorsers. *Journal of Advertising*, *50*(1), 11–25. DOI: 10.1080/00913367.2020.1810595

Torres, P., Augusto, M., & Matos, M. (2019). Antecedents and outcomes of digital influencer endorsement: An exploratory study. *Psychology and Marketing*, *36*(12), 1267–1276. DOI: 10.1002/mar.21274

Tussyadiah, I., Li, S., & Miller, G. (2020). Privacy protection in tourism: Where we are and where we should be heading for. *Journal of Travel Research*, *59*(7), 1223–1234. DOI: 10.1177/0047287519883030

Uzunoğlu, E., & Kip, S. M. (2014). Brand communication through digital influencers: Leveraging blogger engagement. *International Journal of Information Management*, *34*(5), 592–602. DOI: 10.1016/j.ijinfomgt.2014.04.007

Vogue Business. (2022). *Balmain's virtual army*. https://www.voguebusiness.com/fashion/balmains-virtual-army

Vogue Business. (2022). *Shudu Gram collaborates with Fenty Beauty*. https://www.voguebusiness.com/beauty/shudu-gram-collaborates-with-fenty-beauty

Walumbwa, F. O., Avolio, B. J., Gardner, W. L., Wernsing, T. S., & Peterson, S. J. (2008). Authentic leadership: Development and validation of a theory-based measure. *Journal of Management*, *34*(1), 89–126. DOI: 10.1177/0149206307308913

Wellman, M. L., Stoldt, R., Tully, M., & Ekdale, B. (2020). Ethics of authenticity: Social media influencers and the production of sponsored content. *Journal of Media Ethics, 35*(2), 68–82. DOI: 10.1080/23736992.2020.1736078

Wibawa, R. C., Pratiwi, C. P., Wahyono, E., Hidayat, D., & Adiasari, W. (2022). Virtual Influencers: Is The Persona Trustworthy? [JAMIKA]. *Jurnal Manajemen Informatika, 12*(1), 51–62. DOI: 10.34010/jamika.v12i1.6706

Zhang, L., & Wei, W. (2021). Influencer Marketing: A Comparison of Traditional Celebrity, Social Media Influencer, and AI Influencer Endorsement. *Boston University Business Horizons, 4*(3), 58–68.

Zickmund, S. (2007). Deliberation, phronesis, and authenticity: Heidegger's early conception of rhetoric. *Philosophy & Rhetoric, 40*(4), 406–415. DOI: 10.2307/25655289

APPENDIX

Table 1. Influencer sample

Influencer	Age	Gender	Marital status	Level of education	Thematic on Instagram	Most used social network	Number of followers	Number of collaborations with brands
1	30	female	Married	Bac+5	Sport and healthy nutrition	Instagram	445 000	several
2	36	female	Married	Bac+5	Life style	Instagram and tik tok	485 000	several
3	39	female	Married	Bac+2	Fashion and clothing	Instagram	210 000	several
4	37	female	Divorced	Bac+3	Life style	Instagram	547 000	several
5	Not specified	male	married	Bac+5	Sport and Entrepreneurship	Instagram et twitter	212 000	several
6	34	female	Married	Bac+3	Healthy diet	Instagram	27 600	several
7	Not specified	female	Married	Bac+5	Fashion	Instagram	151 000	several
8	31	female	Married	Bac+3	Life style	Instagram	202 000	several
9	Not specified	Couple (one man and one woman)	Married	Bac +5	Storytellers and tavels	Instagram	108 000	several
10	30	female	Married	Bac+5	Fashion and music in festival	Instagram	73 400	several

Source: Personal elaboration

Table 2. Consumer sample

Consumer	Gender	Age	Marital status	Level of education	Profession	Number of influencers followed on Instagram	Number of purchases recommended by influencers on Instagram
female	female	34	married	Bac+5	Manager of an international sport franchise	50	20
2	male	39	married	Bac+5	Executive in computer science	20	5
3	female	35	married	Bac+5	Customer Service Manager	20	3
4	female	32	married	Bac+5	Responsible for monitoring strategic projects in the banking sector	12	1/mouth
5	female	26	single	Bac+5	Quality Engineer	18	10
6	female	36	married	Bac+5	Director of project management	100	3
7	male	64	married	Bac+4	retired	23	5
8	female	27	single	Bac+2	salesperson	300	5
9	female	24	single	Bac+2	salesperson	500	3
10	female	61	married	Bac+3	retired	20	3

Source: Personal elaboration

Chapter 8
A Bayesian Network Framework for AI-Driven Risk Mitigation

Wissem Ennouri
https://orcid.org/0000-0003-3329-0393
Sfax University, Tunisia

ABSTRACT

This chapter examines the critical challenge of uncertainty in risk management, a persistent issue for organizations operating in dynamic and complex environments. It explores the strategic integration of Artificial Intelligence (AI) with risk management processes, focusing on Bayesian Networks (BNs) as a robust analytical framework. BNs enable probabilistic modeling of risk factor dependencies, providing a systematic approach to anticipate, assess, and mitigate threats before they escalate. By combining AI's predictive capabilities with BNs' structured reasoning, organizations can enhance decision-making resilience and agility. The chapter establishes a triangular relationship between uncertainty, AI-driven solutions, and BN models, demonstrating their collective contribution to robust risk mitigation.

INTRODUCTION

One of the most important issues facing organizations today is managing uncertainty in settings that are becoming more complicated and dynamic. This chapter examines this issue. Instead of adopting a traditional strategy, it emphasizes a tactical viewpoint that incorporates artificial intelligence (AI) into risk management procedures. Bayesian Networks (BNs), a powerful analytical tool that may depict probabilistic correlations between various risk indicators, are given special attention.

DOI: 10.4018/979-8-3373-5499-6.ch008

Organizations may predict risks, assess their possible impact, and take preventive steps before problems worsen thanks to BNs' special capacity to capture interdependencies among unknown variables. Organizations may increase their resilience and make better, faster decisions in the face of uncertainty by fusing the structured reasoning provided by Bayesian models with the predictive power of artificial intelligence. The chapter explores the triangle relationship between Bayesian modeling, AI-based solutions, and uncertainty in an effort to clarify how these elements cooperate to promote a more successful risk reduction approach. We'll talk about key ideas that are necessary to comprehend and apply AI-enhanced risk management. A more thorough understanding of contemporary risk management techniques is provided by the chapter's consideration of organizational and cultural elements that affect the adoption of such technology.

SECTION 1: THE REALITY OF UNCERTAINTY IN RISK MANAGEMENT

Uncertainty is a persistent and difficult reality in the intricate world of risk management that exists today. It affects almost every industry, from financial systems to healthcare and supply chains, making it challenging for businesses to make confident plans. Unlike well-defined hazards that can be evaluated with unambiguous probabilities, uncertainty often occurs when there's not enough data, when the environment changes rapidly, or when numerous unpredictable elements combine at once. Consider the financial markets. A combination of geopolitical developments, inflation patterns, and fluctuating investor attitude influence their volatility, all of which are subject to sudden changes. Similar to this, natural disasters, abrupt changes in legislation, or public health emergencies like pandemics can upset the delicate equilibrium of global supply networks. These actual cases demonstrate how crucial it is for businesses to implement adaptable, data-driven risk management techniques. Conventional, rule-based systems are insufficient nowadays. A more flexible strategy that can react to ambiguity as it arises is required.

1.1 How can We Understand the Complexity of Uncertainty?

There are numerous ways that uncertainty manifests itself. We must comprehend its various forms in order to effectively address it. The majority of analysts divide uncertainty into three primary groups:

- Events like manufacturing equipment failure are examples of aleatory (Statistical) uncertainty, which has its roots in innate unpredictability.

Probability distributions can frequently be used to model such uncertainties, offering a statistical basis for analysis (Liang et al., 2024; Li and Montomoli, 2024).

- Insufficient information leads to epistemic uncertainty. It complicates future prediction. Cybersecurity is a prime example. Cyberattacks are always evolving, and it's difficult to predict when or how they will occur (Simwanda et al., 2025; Motti et al., 2022).
- Human choices lead to behavioral unpredictability. For example, stock values in financial markets might vary in unanticipated ways due to investor moods and emotional reactions (Wu et al., 2024).

Businesses risk making bad choices, wasting money, or losing their competitive edge if they disregard these many forms of uncertainty.

1.2 What are the Costs of Uncertainty in Decision-Making?

Beyond operational challenges, uncertainty has serious negative implications on an organization's finances, reputation, and strategy if it is not equipped to handle its consequences.

1.2.1 The Impact of Supply Chain Disruptions

The vulnerability of global supply systems was starkly revealed by the COVID-19 pandemic (Longo et al., 2023). Companies around the world faced spiraling delays, raw material shortages, and rising costs when Chinese manufacturing hubs closed. According to McKinsey, supply chain interruptions cost companies more than 4 trillion USD in losses in 2020 alone (Alessandria et al., 2023). One notable example is the automobile sector, when titans like Ford and General Motors were forced to halt production due to a scarcity of semiconductors, costing them billions of dollars in lost income as they tried to fulfill market demand (Mohammad et al., 2022).

1.2.2 Data and Cybersecurity Issues

Cyber dangers are a growing source of uncertainty in a world that is becoming more digitally connected (Arisian et al., 2025). Organizations safeguarding vast repositories of sensitive data are prime targets for cybercriminals. The 2017 Equifax breach, which compromised the personal details of 147 million individuals, illustrates this peril, costing the company 1.4 billion USD in fines, legal settlements, and security upgrades (Moore, 2017). This uncertainty is amplified by three factors:

- The unpredictable motives of attackers, ranging from financial gain to espionage or activism.
- The relentless evolution of hacking techniques, outpacing traditional defenses.
- The interconnectedness of digital networks, where a single vulnerability can jeopardize an entire system.

1.2.3 Regulatory and Compliance Risks

The regulatory environment is perpetually shifting as governments respond to pressing issues like environmental sustainability, financial oversight, and data privacy. These changes introduce uncertainty, compelling businesses to adapt swiftly. The European Union's General Data Protection Regulation (GDPR[1]), for instance, enforces rigorous data privacy standards, with non-compliance penalties reaching up to 4% of global revenue. Similarly, energy sector firms must continually realign their strategies to comply with evolving emissions regulations, influencing long-term planning and investment.

1.3 Why Traditional Risk Management Approaches Fall Short

Despite the pervasive nature of uncertainty, many organizations cling to traditional risk management methods—often deterministic and rule-based—that prove inadequate in today's dynamic contexts, where conditions shift rapidly and interact unpredictably (Ennouri, 2021).

1.3.1 The limitations of Static Risk Models

Conventional risk assessment techniques frequently rely on fixed probabilities, failing to reflect the fluid nature of modern risks. For example:

- Logistics operations assess weather-related risks using historical climate data, yet climate change renders these patterns increasingly obsolete.
- Economic models based on stable GDP growth and inflation rates were blindsided by the unprecedented disruptions of the COVID-19 crisis.

The 2008 financial crisis offers a stark lesson in these shortcomings (Zhang, 2025). Many institutions leaned on Value-at-Risk (VaR) models presuming market stability; when markets crashed, these models vastly underestimated losses, fueling a devastating financial collapse (Thiele, 2019).

1.3.2 The Impact of Incomplete and Biased Data

The quality of the underlying data determines how successful risk models are, but companies frequently struggle with skewed or incomplete datasets. AI systems that have been trained on incomplete patient records run the danger of making inaccurate diagnoses or administering poor therapies in the healthcare industry (Yadav et al., 2025). Cybersecurity models based on historical attack patterns are vulnerable to new hacking techniques. Adding to these problems, decision-makers often struggle to understand the results of intricate statistical models, which erodes confidence in automated evaluations.

1.4 The New Concept: AI and Bayesian Networks

Given the shortcomings of conventional techniques, a more adaptable and data-driven strategy is essential. BNs and AI offer strong answers to this problem. A probabilistic framework provided by BNs continuously updates risk probabilities in response to new information.

Decision-makers can better understand complex risk linkages thanks to improved interpretability, which maps interdependence among risk factors and clarifies their interactions. A manufacturing organization evaluating production delay risks, for example, could use a BN to analyze supplier reliability based on past performance, weather-related logistics impacts, and changes in market demand that impact inventory. The network provides a more accurate and responsive risk profile by instantly modifying its probability in response to new information, such as updated weather forecasts or supplier updates.

1.5 Integration with Well-Known Frameworks for Risk Management

Understanding how the AI-driven BN framework presented in this chapter complements and improves upon established risk management standards, such as the Committee of Sponsoring Organizations (COSO) and the International Organization for Standardization's (ISO) 31000 risk management standard, is crucial to fully appreciating its value. These frameworks offer fundamental ideas for methodically and openly managing risks, and our approach's theoretical underpinnings and practical applicability are strengthened when they are integrated.

By highlighting the significance of internal controls, risk assessment, and fraud detection and prevention, the COSO framework aims to integrate risk management with organizational strategy and performance. This is enhanced by the BN framework, which provides a dynamic, data-driven approach to risk assessment. It overcomes the drawbacks of static models by using probabilistic modeling to provide real-time adjustments to risk probabilities as new data becomes available. By offering more precision and adaptability, this capacity strengthens COSO's focus on risk identification and analysis, supporting internal controls and enabling proactive risk mitigation—two essential components of constructing organizational resilience.

Similar to this, ISO 31000 creates a well recognized standard for structured, transparent, and credible risk management, with its fundamental ideas focused on stakeholder participation, continuous improvement, and systematic processes. These ideas are inherently consistent with the BN method. A key component of ISO 31000, its graphical structure makes complex risk assessments understandable to stakeholders and encourages openness by explicitly mapping risk interdependencies. Furthermore, the standard's emphasis on iterative improvement is supported by the framework's ability to integrate expert knowledge and adjust to new data, guaranteeing that risk management procedures continue to be sensitive to changing uncertainties.

Through the integration of AI-powered BNs with COSO and ISO 31000, the framework enhances current procedures without displacing them. It gives businesses a sophisticated yet transparent tool to enhance risk assessments, make better decisions, and guarantee adherence to standard-based tactics. By fusing cutting-edge technology with conventional risk management, this integration provides a comprehensive strategy for handling uncertainty in complicated settings.

1.5 Solutions

Even while uncertainty is still a problem, it can be solved with creative tools. A transparent, probabilistic approach to mapping risk interconnections is offered by Bayesian networks; for instance, they can be used to evaluate flood probabilities by connecting rainfall to river levels (Pearl, 1988). AI enhances this by analyzing enormous datasets to find trends, such new cyberthreats, while maintaining outputs' clarity. When combined, they get around the drawbacks of conventional methods. But problems still exist: AI needs close supervision to reduce biases in training sets, and Bayesian networks depend on high-quality data (Zhang and Meng, 2024). These tools, however, turn uncertainty from a liability into a chance for resilient, well-informed decision-making. The following part will examine how AI transparency supports this change, laying the groundwork for a more thorough analysis of these solutions.

SECTION 2: TRANSPARENCY IS ESSENTIAL TO AI-DRIVEN RISK MANAGEMENT

Transparency becomes a key component of trust, responsibility, and moral behavior as businesses use AI for risk management more and more. Although AI is unmatched in its capacity to analyze large datasets and spot danger trends (Waltersdorfer and Sabou, 2025), its frequent opacity—often referred to as a "black box"—raises questions regarding interpretability and fairness (Marcus and Teuwen, 2024). By enabling decision-makers to comprehend AI outputs, guaranteeing adherence to laws such as the EU's AI Act and GDPR, and reducing biases that can result in unfair outcomes (e.g., in hiring or lending, Xiong and Kim, 2025), transparency tackles these problems.

For instance, the 2008 financial crisis highlighted the dangers of opaque models, where untraceable risk assessments in mortgage-backed securities fueled systemic collapse. Transparent AI, conversely, fosters trust—studies show a 40% increase in physician confidence when AI diagnostics explain their logic (Choi Li et al., 2025)—and meets rising regulatory demands (e.g., fines up to 30 million EURO for non-compliance). Explainable AI (XAI) techniques, such as SHAP and LIME, enhance this clarity by revealing decision drivers, while BNs naturally provide it through graphical, probabilistic structures (explored further in Section 3). Transparency thus transforms AI from a mysterious tool into a reliable, defensible asset, setting the stage for its integration with risk management frameworks.

Thus, transparency serves dual purposes in AI-driven risk management:

- Empowering decision-makers to comprehend and validate AI-generated insights.
- Ensuring fairness, ethics, and compliance with regulatory standards.

2.1 Why Transparency is Essential in AI-Driven Risk Management

Transparency is important to the effective integration of AI into risk management. Its absence undermines confidence, accountability, and fairness, while its presence fosters adoption and ethical practice (Park and Yoon, 2024).

2.1.1 Building Trust and Enhancing AI Adoption

Trust is pivotal to the widespread acceptance of AI in risk management. When decision-making processes remain hidden, organizations hesitate to rely fully on AI recommendations. Research consistently shows that transparent AI systems—

those that clarify their reasoning—inspire greater user confidence and encourage actionable responses.

In healthcare, for example, AI tools designed to diagnose conditions and drug discovery, and patient monitoring disease often face skepticism from physicians unless their logic is verifiable (Choi Li et al., 2025). A 2022 Harvard Medical School[2] study revealed that doctors were 40% more likely to trust AI recommendations when accompanied by clear explanations. Similarly, in finance, banks leverage AI to evaluate creditworthiness and flag fraud (Nallakaruppan et al., 2024). An opaque denial of a loan risks alienating customers and inviting legal scrutiny, whereas a transparent explanation—such as citing a high debt-to-income ratio—enhances acceptance by both clients and regulators.

2.1.2 Ensuring Accountability and Regulatory Compliance

Globally, governments are intensifying demands for AI transparency, especially in sectors impacting human rights, financial stability, and public safety. Key regulations underscore this priority:

- The European Union's AI Act[3]: Mandates explainability and auditability for AI in critical applications.
- The General Data Protection Regulation[4] (GDPR): Requires explanations for AI decisions in areas like hiring and credit scoring.
- The U.S. SEC AI Guidelines[5]: Obliges financial institutions to disclose how AI trading algorithms assess risks.

Non-compliance carries steep consequences. In Europe for example the non-compliance with AI practices imposes fines up to 30 million EURO or 6% of the company's worldwide annual turnover, whichever is higher, which raises a primordial notion relating to the use of AI which is transparency.

2.1.3 Resolving Prejudice and Ethical Issues in AI Models

AI bias, which results from faulty data or algorithms, is still a major problem (Kekez et al., 2025). Such biases may continue unnoticed in the absence of openness, leading to biased results. Notable examples include predictive policing models that reinforce racial profiling, lending algorithms that unfairly penalize minority borrowers, and automated recruiting tools that disadvantage female candidates because of biased training data (Xiong and Kim, 2025). Organizations can detect and address these problems with the help of transparent systems, which encourage moral and just decision-making (Hao et al., 2024).

2.2 Explainable AI's Function in Risk Management

Explainable AI (XAI) has become a key remedy for AI's opacity, making decision-making procedures understandable and accessible.

2.2.1 Explainable AI: What is it?

XAI includes methods that provide understandable, concise justifications for AI judgments. XAI bridges the gap between complicated algorithms and human users by ensuring judgments are traceable and intelligible, in contrast to black-box models that provide results without context.

The significance of Explainable AI (XAI) is emphasized in a number of publications. For example, Biswas et al. (2024) used XAI techniques to balance investments in cyber insurance with IT security measures for businesses. Financial companies can create useful cyber insurance products with the aid of their methodology.

Similarly, with their XAI-based model, Niu et al. (2024) improved healthcare decision-making. This algorithm demonstrated efficacy in predicting illness risks by extracting longitudinal data from electronic health records. Furthermore, it was successful in producing comprehensible proof to back up its hypotheses.

2.2.2 Techniques to Improve AI Transparency

There are a number of strategies to increase AI transparency, including:

- Feature Importance Analysis: Highlights key variables driving decisions (e.g., predictive process monitoring) (Mehdiyev et al., 2025).
- Decision Trees and Rule-Based Models: Describe rational processes leading to conclusions (e.g., decision home energy management systems and model predictive control) (Ruddick et al., 2024).
- The novel method known as Local Interpretable Model-Agnostic Explanations (LIME) functions as a model-agnostic XAI algorithm. According to Ul Hassan et al. (2025), the phrase "model-agnostic" refers to the fact that LIME may be used to explain the inner workings of different machine learning (ML) and deep learning (DL) algorithms, irrespective of their particular complexity or features.
- An improved methodology called SHapley Additive exPlanations (SHAP) was created to standardize and enhance model interpretability across various deep learning (DL) and machine learning (ML) models. Its primary objective is to provide a thorough and consistent framework for elucidating complex

models so that practitioners and academics may better comprehend and have confidence in their forecasts (Ul Hassan et al., 2025).

2.2.3 Real-World Applications of XAI in Risk Management

XAI is transforming risk mitigation across industries. Financial institutions use SHAP to justify fraud flags, healthcare providers employ LIME to explain high-risk patient classifications, and cybersecurity teams apply feature importance analysis to reduce false positives in threat detection. By enhancing interpretability, XAI strengthens trust, compliance, and accuracy (Biswas et al., 2024), (Nikiforidis et al., 2024)).

2.3 How Bayesian Networks Provide a Transparent AI Framework

BNs stand out as a powerful, transparent approach to AI-driven risk management.

2.3.1 Why Bayesian Networks are Naturally Transparent

Unlike deep learning's intricate neural networks, BNs use graphical structures and conditional probabilities to depict relationships among risk factors. Nodes represent variables, and edges indicate dependencies, offering a visual, intuitive framework. This transparency distinguishes BNs from opaque alternatives by enabling decision-makers to track the relationships between risks and how they affect results.

2.3.2 Black-Box AI Models Versus Bayesian Networks

Artificial intelligence systems with opaque or difficult-to-understand internal workings are referred to as "black-box" AI models. These models, which are frequently built using sophisticated statistical techniques or deep learning, produce predictions or judgments without offering clear justification. Because of this, users and even engineers could find it difficult to comprehend how certain inputs result in particular outputs. Concerns are raised by black-box AI's lack of interpretability in crucial fields like healthcare, banking, and law, where justice and accountability are crucial (Wahlström et al., 2024). To increase openness and confidence in AI-driven decision-making, researchers have underlined the necessity of explainable AI (XAI) (Setzu et al., 2021).

Table 1. BN vs. Black-Box

Feature	Bayesian Networks	Black-Box AI Models
Transparency	High – Clear probabilities and relationships	Low – Obscure decision processes
Explainability	Intuitive cause-and-effect reasoning	Limited, often needing extra tools
Flexibility	Dynamically adapts to new data	Typically requires retraining

By combining interpretability and predictive power, BNs guarantee that risk evaluations are reliable and responsible.

2.4 Solutions

In AI-driven risk management, transparency is essential, especially when making critical choices like allocating resources or assessing threats. In legal contexts, opaque AI runs the danger of bias and unfairness; transparent models, on the other hand, make predictions more clear and allow for well-informed, defendable acts. By revealing biases, this transparency not only reduces ethical hazards but also enables AI to comply with legal requirements, strengthening organizational resilience. Transparency, which eliminates doubt, builds confidence, and strengthens accountability, ultimately characterizes AI's value in risk management.

SECTION 3: BAYESIAN NETWORKS FOR RISK MANAGEMENT

The process of risk management is complex and involves assessing a number of interrelated and unpredictable elements that influence choices. The intricacy of these relationships is frequently difficult for traditional risk management approaches to capture. By offering a transparent and organized framework, BNs fill this need (Ennouri, 2021). According to Ying et al. (2024), a BN is a probabilistic graphical model that uses a Directed Acyclic Graph (DAG) to show how variables relate to one another. Conditional probability, or the likelihood of an event occurring given the occurrence of another event, is another crucial component (Vagnoli and Remenyte-Prescott, 2022). The Bayes Theorem, which is formulated as follows (1), is the foundation of BN.

$$P(A/B) = \frac{P(B/A)P(A)}{P(B)}$$ (1) (Leray, 2006)

Where:
P (A B): Probability of event *A* given *B*.
P (B A): Probability of event *B* given *A*.

$P(A)$: Prior probability of A.

$P(B)$: Marginal probability of B.

And the joint probability distribution of all variables defined as:

$$P(X_1, X_2, \dots, X_n) = \prod_{i=1}^{n} P(X_i \backslash Parents\ (X_i))\ (2)\ \text{(Leary, 2006)}$$

Where *Parents (Xi)* represents the set of variables directly influencing *Xi*.

The BNs power stems from three core strengths:

- Modeling uncertainty through probability theory, rather than relying on fixed, deterministic outcomes.
- Clarifying cause-and-effect relationships, making the dependencies driving risk explicit.
- Adapting dynamically by updating probabilities as new information emerges.

This combination of transparency and flexibility makes BNs a valuable tool for AI-supported risk assessment and mitigation.

3.1 Understanding Bayesian Networks in Risk Management

By providing a straightforward approach to examining uncertainty and interdependence, BNs are excellent in managing the complexities of risk. BNs offer a reliable solution in contrast to traditional methods, which could simplify or obfuscate these dynamics (Juliani and Maciel, 2024). Their capacity to combine visual aids and probabilistic reasoning guarantees that decision-makers can comprehend and have faith in the risk assessment procedure. Belief networks (BNs) are probabilistic graphical models that are used to describe and reason about knowledge in an organized manner. They are composed of a directed acyclic graph (DAG), in which variables are represented by nodes and causal or probabilistic connections between those variables are indicated by edges. BNs are a useful tool in risk management because of their structure, which enables them to simulate complicated systems and successfully manage uncertainty. BNs offer a methodical approach to risk identification, assessment, and mitigation by leveraging their capacity to handle interdependencies across various risk components. Transportation, cybersecurity, and emerging technologies are just a few of the areas where BNs are used in risk management. By showcasing their capacity to represent intricate operational hazards, Zhou and Yuen (2024) proved the effectiveness of BNs in organizational sustainability risk management for container shipping businesses. In a similar vein, d'Ambrosio et al. (2023) improved cybersecurity tactics by introducing Bayesian threat graph networks to include insider threats into risk management frameworks.

Mouti et al. (2022) highlighted the adaptability of BNs in high-stakes situations by proposing an advanced attack detection framework based on probabilistic BNs for managing cyber risks. In addition to traditional risk management, BNs have been used in innovative domains like 6G-IoT networks. Ibrahim et al. (2024) optimized resource allocation in next-generation communication systems by combining AI-driven scheduling with a Bayesian game-theoretic method. Additionally, Bakhtiari et al. (2025) provided insights into risk transmission and mitigation across complex systems by modeling multi-hazard hazards and resilience in interconnected vital infrastructures using dynamic BNs. These illustrations show how adaptable and reliable BNs are at handling a variety of uncertainties in various industries. Their combination with AI can further improve risk management's decision-making, transparency, and prediction accuracy, as this chapter will demonstrate.

3.2 Essential Elements of Bayesian Systems

Three essential components of BNs, each specifically designed to represent supply chain risks.

3.2.1 The Nodes

Nodes stand for supply chain risk variables, which are random variables that affect hazards. They may be:

- Discrete: Risk levels are categorized as “Low”, “Medium”, or “High”.
- Continuous: Quantitative metrics include likelihood percentages, inventory levels, and delivery lead times.

  A BN applied to a supply chain, for example, might include the following nodes:
- Supplier reliability (High, Medium, Low)
- Transportation delays (in days)
- Demand fluctuations (0% to 100%)

These nodes form the foundation for explicitly modeling risk factors.

3.2.2 The Directed Edges

The conditional dependencies (for example in supply chain risks) are indicated by directed edges connecting nodes. An edge from *A* to *B* indicates that *A* determines the probability of *B*. A BN can model a variety of cause-and-effect interactions in a supply chain setting. It might illustrate, for example, how weather (*A*) affects transportation delays (*B*), which in turn impact supply shortages (*C*). By evaluating the relationships between these occurrences, this kind of probabilistic modeling offers important insights into possible hazards and supply chain interruptions. BNs help better decision-making for operational planning and risk mitigation by quantifying these relationships.

Figure 1. BN example

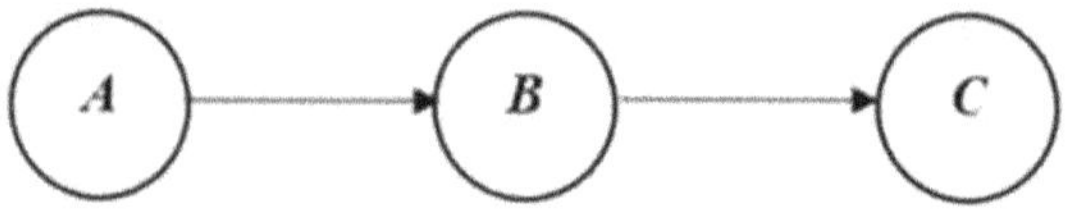

One way to express this relationship is:

P(*C**A*, *B*)

The such structure can provides for managers an interpretable way of risk propagation within the system.

3.2.3 The Conditional Probability Tables (CPTs)

Every node has a CPT that measures the variation in its probability according to its parent nodes. For instance, parent nodes like supplier reliability (High, Medium, Low) and transport method (Air, Sea, Land) could provide a CPT for delivery punctuality in a BN evaluating the risk of late deliveries (Table 2).

Figure 2. BN for late delivery

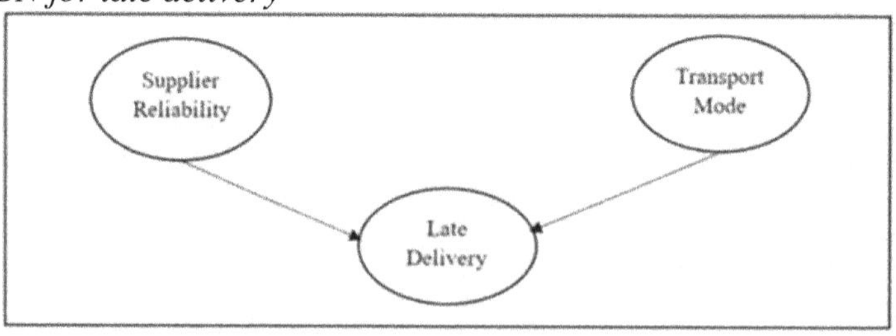

Table 2. Example of CPTs

Supplier reliability	Transport mode	Probability of late delivery
High	Air	5%
High	Sea	15%
Low	Air	20%
Low	Sea	40%

A supply from an uncertain source via sea transit has a far higher chance of being delayed, as this table demonstrates. BNs remove the uncertainty that is sometimes inherent in opaque AI models by clearly and quantitatively conveying the risks.

3.3 How the Bayesian Networks Improve the Risk Management's Transparency

As explained in section 2, BNs set themselves apart from conventional AI models by providing intrinsic transparency. In contrast to the opaque methods of deep learning, BNs explicitly map risk factor correlations using graphical structures called nodes and edges (Juliani and Maciel, 2024). In supply chain management, for instance, a BN might quantify these dependencies (e.g., 40% delay risk with low supplier reliability) by linking weather conditions to transportation delays using conditional probability tables.

3.3.1 A Comparison of Conventional AI Models in Supply Chains with Bayesian Networks

The BNs directly map correlations between risk factors, in contrast to deep learning systems that frequently hide their core methods. This difference is brought to light via a comparison:

Table 3. BNs vs. Deep Learning

Feature	Bayesian Networks	Deep learning / Opaque AI
Interpretability	High – Transparent causal relationships	Low – Opaque processes
Probabilistic Reasoning	Clearly defined distributions	Based on hidden layers and weights
Data Requirements	Effective with limited data	Requires large datasets
Decision Transparency	Fully explainable	Often lacks readable insights

It is important to take into account other conventional risk management frameworks like decision trees and fuzzy logic in addition to the comparison with opaque AI models. Because of their visual clarity and simplicity, decision trees are seen as useful tools for making decisions in the face of uncertainty. However, in situations when there are many interconnected variables, their usefulness is diminished because the tree structure may become jumbled and challenging to understand. On the other hand, fuzzy logic is skilled at handling vague or unclear data by utilizing fuzzy sets, which can be useful in qualitative risk evaluations. However, it is devoid of the explicit probabilistic framework that BNs offer, which is necessary for calculating risk probabilities and revising them in light of new information. BNs provide a distinct benefit in the context of AI-driven risk reduction, where machine learning integration with transparent and interpretable models is essential. Their graphical representation guarantees that the decision-making process stays intelligible and defendable to stakeholders, while their probabilistic character facilitates the effective integration of AI techniques like automated structure learning and parameter optimization. This comparative viewpoint emphasizes why BNs were chosen as the study's underlying framework because they support the dual goals of using AI to improve risk insights and preserving the openness required for efficient risk management. This openness lessens the need for further XAI tools and facilitates decision-making in areas that need explanation, including stakeholder communication or regulatory compliance (see section 2). In section 3.4, its real-world uses are described.

3.4 Some Examples of Bayesian Networks in Risk Management

This section focuses on a few examples of BNs in providing transparent and practical supply chain risk management solutions.

3.4.1 The Case of Risk Management in Supply Chain Operations

a. The context

By examining variables including weather, supplier dependability, transit delays, and inventory levels, a company aims to evaluate order fulfillment risks. To model these relationships and forecast the possibility of successful or delayed order fulfillment, a Bayesian Network is utilized.

b. Step 1: The definition of the variables and their relationships

The following dependencies and variables will be used to determine of the BN's structure:

- Weather conditions (W): Affects transportation delays.
- Supplier reliability (S): Affects delivery timeliness.
- Inventory levels (I): Affects order fulfillment.
- Transportation delays (T): Affects delivery timeliness.
- Delivery timeliness (D): Affects order fulfillment.
- Order fulfillment (O): The final outcome to be predicted.

The following relationships will used to represent the BN:

- W → T (weather conditions influence transportation delays).
- S → D (supplier reliability influences delivery timeliness).
- T → D (transportation delays influence delivery timeliness).
- D → O (delivery timeliness influences order fulfillment).
- I → O (inventory levels influence order fulfillment).

c. Second step: the collect information and estimate probabilities

For each variable's conditional probabilities are estimated using historical data. For example:

- For Weather conditions (W):
  If: P (W = “Bad weather”) = 0.3
  Then: P (W = “Good weather”) = 0.7
- For Transportation delays (T):
  If: W = “Bad weather”, so, P (T = “Delayed”) = 0.8
  If W = “Good weather”, so, P (T = “Delayed”) = 0.1
- For Supplier reliability (S):
  P (S = “Reliable”) = 0.9
  P (S = “Unreliable”) = 0.1
- Delivery timeliness (D):
  If S = “Reliable” and T = “No delay”, P (D = “On time”) = 0.95
  If S = “Unreliable” or T = “Delayed”, P (D = “On time”) = 0.5
- Order fulfillment (O):
  If D = “On time” and I = “Sufficient”, P (O = “Successful”) = 0.98
  If D = “Delayed” or I = “Insufficient”, P (O = “Successful”) = 0.6

d. Step 3: build the Bayesian Network

The BN was constructed using *Graphviz*, a widely-used open-source software for graph visualization, allowing us to create the following network representation.

Figure 3. BN for order fulfillment prediction

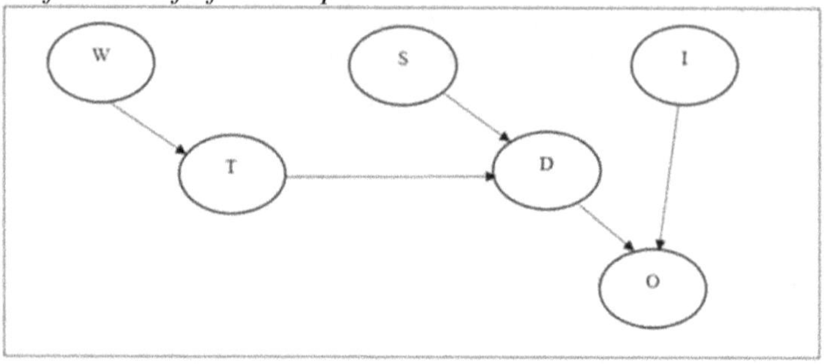

e. Step 4: Perform inference

The BN enables the calculation of probabilities for specific scenarios based on observed data. For example:

- Scenario 1: Bad weather conditions

If W = "Bad weather", what is the probability of successful order fulfillment (O = "Successful")? The network takes inventory levels, supplier dependability, and transportation delays into account when calculating P (O = "Successful" \ W = "Bad weather").

- Scenario 2: Unreliable supplier

What is the probability of a delayed order fulfillment (O = "Delayed") if S = "Unreliable"? The network integrates other factors to calculate P (O = "Delayed" \ S = "Unreliable").

f. Step 5: Make informed decisions

The inference's findings enable the company to reduce risks by making data-driven decisions. For instance, the business can diversify its supply base or increase reserves if a supplier is unreliable, or it can set up alternate modes of transportation if inclement weather is forecast.

To summarize, a BN offers a probabilistic framework for modeling intricate correlations between variables and forecasting hazards. It assists managers in foreseeing any problems and taking proactive measures to improve the dependability of the supply chain.

3.4.2 The Bayesian Network for AI-driven Cybersecurity Risk Detection

a. Context

The goal of a financial institution is to identify and stop cyberattacks that target consumer transactions. In order to forecast the likelihood of fraudulent transactions, the organization models the correlations between a number of variables, including login location, transaction amount, time of day, and suspicious activity, using a BN.

b. First step: The Definition of the variables and their relationships

For this case, the BN will structure by the following variables and dependencies:

- Login location (L): The geographic location from which a user logs in. This influences the probability of fraud.
- Transaction amount (A): The monetary value of the transaction. This influences the probability of fraud.
- Time of day (T): The time at which the transaction occurs. This influences the likelihood of suspicious activity.
- Suspicious activity (S): A binary variable indicating whether the activity is flagged as suspicious.
- Fraud probability (F): The final outcome to be predicted, representing the likelihood of a fraudulent transaction.

The relationships are represented as directed edges, for example:

- L → F (login location influences fraud probability).
- A → F (transaction amount influences fraud probability).
- T → S (time of day influences suspicious activity).
- S → F (suspicious activity influences fraud probability).

c. Step 2: Collect data and define probabilities

Historical data is used to estimate conditional probabilities for each variable. For instance:

- Login location (L):
  P (L = "Unusual location") = 0.1
  P (L = "Usual location") = 0.9
- Transaction amount (A):
  P (A = "High amount") = 0.2
  P (A = "Normal amount") = 0.8
- Time of day (T):
  P (T = "Unusual time") = 0.3
  P (T = "Normal Time") = 0.7
- Suspicious activity (S):
  If T = "Unusual time", P (S = "Yes") = 0.6
  If T = "Normal time", P (S = "Yes") = 0.1
- Fraud probability (F):
  If L = "Unusual location" or A = "High Amount" or S = "Yes", P (F = "High") = 0.9
  Otherwise, P (F = "High") = 0.05

d. Step 3: Build the Bayesian Network

The BN was constructed using *Graphviz*, a widely-used open-source software for graph visualization, allowing us to create the following network representation.

Figure 4. BN for fraud detection

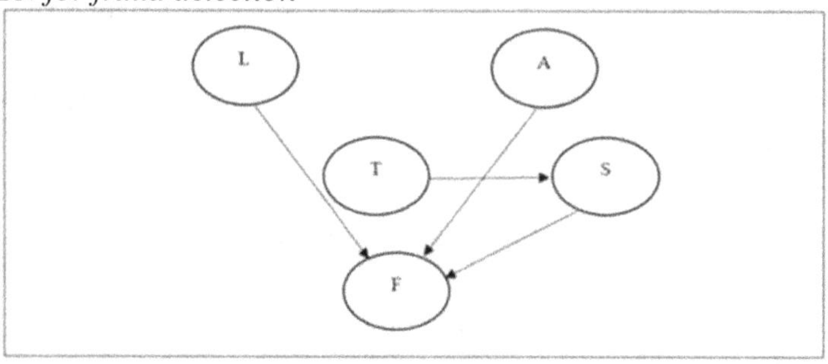

e. Step 4: Perform inference

The BN enables the calculation of probabilities for specific scenarios based on observed data. For example:

- Scenario 1: Unusual login location and high transaction amount

What is the likelihood of fraud (F = "High") if L = "Unusual location" and A = "High amount"? The network calculates P (F = "High" \ L = "Unusual location," A = "High amount") by taking into account how these characteristics affect the likelihood of fraud.

- Scenario 2: Unusual time of day

What is the likelihood of fraud if T = "Unusual time" (F = "High")? The network integrates the influence of suspicious activity (S) and other variables to calculate P (F = "High" \ T = "Unusual time").

f. Step 5: Make informed decisions

The financial institution can take proactive steps to prevent fraud thanks to the inference's findings. For instance:

- If the fraud probability is high due to an unusual login location or high transaction amount, the institution can trigger additional authentication steps or block the transaction temporarily for review.
- If suspicious activity is detected due to an unusual time of day, the institution can flag the account for further monitoring.

We may conclude from this example that BN offers a probabilistic framework for modeling intricate correlations between variables and forecasting cybersecurity threats. Through pattern analysis and data-driven decision-making, it assists financial institutions in identifying and stopping fraudulent transactions.

3.5 The Bayesian Networks' Potential for AI-Driven Risk Reduction

The BNs are always changing, using cutting-edge AI technologies to improve risk assessment in real time and automate decision-making. A number of new developments underscore the growing significance of BNs in this field as the need for clear and intelligent risk mitigation solutions increases.

The emergence of mixed AI-Bayesian models is one important development. These models combine the interpretability and probabilistic reasoning of BNs with the benefits of deep learning, which is particularly good at recognizing patterns. This combination enables companies to take use of AI's predictive capabilities while preserving their capacity to defend and explain choices, which is crucial in sectors like cybersecurity, healthcare, and finance.

The use of Dynamic Bayesian Networks (DBNs) is another interesting trend. DBNs are intended to reflect the way hazards change over time, in contrast to typical BNs, which model static relationships. Applications where risks are dynamic and alter in reaction to outside influences, such supply chain management, fraud detection, and financial forecasting, benefit greatly from this feature.

Moreover, the use of BNs is changing due to developments in automated Bayesian inference systems. These AI-enhanced systems can manage streaming data in real-time, allowing businesses to identify and address issues as they arise. In fast-paced settings like cybersecurity, where threats must be recognized and eliminated immediately to avoid serious damage, this real-time capability is extremely important.

The BNs are positioned to be crucial as companies place a greater emphasis on openness, flexibility, and ethics in their AI solutions. They are essential for developing clever, dependable, and morally sound risk reduction techniques because of their capacity to offer unambiguous, probabilistic insights into complicated systems. By guaranteeing that risk evaluations are precise and comprehensible, BNs will improve decision-making in the future and promote confidence in AI-driven systems.

3.6 Solutions

Although BNs provide a strong framework for evaluating risk, they have limitations. Careful planning and the availability of reliable, high-quality data are critical to their efficacy. Complex real-world situations can occasionally be oversimplified by structural assumptions, such as conditional independence between variables. Furthermore, incomplete or sparse data can produce inaccurate probability estimates, which compromises the model's accuracy. AI fills this gap by increasing and supplementing BNs' capabilities. AI overcomes these constraints by combining data-driven insights and sophisticated learning strategies, allowing for more accurate and flexible risk evaluations. Notwithstanding these difficulties, BNs continue to be a fundamental component of interpretable and transparent modeling, offering a strong and unambiguous base. The combination of BNs and AI promises to further develop this clarity, providing more accurate risk assessment while maintaining the capacity to defend and explain choices. We will examine how AI improves this framework in the following section, making sure that risk mitigation is not only clever but also based on knowing the "why" behind each choice.

SECTION 4: ENHANCING RISK INSIGHTS WITH AI AND BAYESIAN NETWORKS

4.1 How AI and Bayesian Networks can Operate Together?

Historically, risk assessment has relied on expert opinion and statistical models. These approaches, however, frequently fall short in addressing the complex and dynamic character of modern hazards. A revolutionary answer is provided by the combination of AI and BNs, which enables businesses to create risk management systems that are more precise, flexible, and open. A robust probabilistic framework for simulating hazards and their interdependencies is offered by BNs. AI strengthens this foundation by utilizing cutting-edge computational methods to increase responsiveness and prediction accuracy. In particular, AI helps by:

- Extracting subtle patterns from vast datasets that traditional approaches might overlook.
- Refining probability estimates and dynamically updating risk factors as conditions evolve.
- Automating risk detection and facilitating scenario simulations for strategic planning.

The synergy between AI and BNs revolutionizes risk assessment by combining predictive power with structured reasoning. AI improves BNs by deep learning parameter optimization (e.g., predictive maintenance, Zohuri et al., 2022), automating structure learning (e.g., supply chain risk mapping, Ennouri, 2021), and improving probability estimates (e.g., real-time fraud detection modifications). These improvements ensure that insights are still interpretable by building upon the transparent foundation of BNs.

4.2 How AI Improves Risk Analysis Using Bayesian Networks

Through a number of technological developments that are covered in the ensuing subsections, AI enhances the capabilities of BNs.

4.2.1 Bayesian Network Probability Estimate by AI

Expert inputs or static historical data are used to populate CPTs in conventional BNs. Such static inputs, however, become obsolete in contexts that are changing quickly. By allowing for dynamic updates to probability estimations, AI overcomes this constraint. It accomplishes this by:

- Refinement of probability values using real-time data stream analysis. In order to fill a major void in the real-time assessment of collision damage implications for risk assessment, Zhang et al. (2025) develop a revolutionary deep learning-based approach. Their study presents a hybrid deep learning model that combines the best features of sophisticated deep learning architectures and hyperparameter optimization strategies. In particular, the system enables the efficient regression of complex temporal data by integrating Transformer models with Long Short-Term Memory (LSTM) networks. This creative method offers a solid answer for real-time risk management applications in addition to improving the accuracy of damage assessment.
- Using large datasets and machine learning to extract probability distributions. In addition to increasing the accuracy of collapse resistance forecasts, using machine learning to derive probability distributions from massive datasets offers important new information about risk assessment (Guo et al., 2025).
- A revolutionary step in risk assessment and mitigation is the discovery of new risk patterns that were not previously taken into consideration. It is feasible to find subtle, previously missed correlations and patterns in complex datasets by utilizing sophisticated analytical approaches like machine learning and data mining. These trends frequently highlight latent weaknesses or changing dangers that conventional approaches might overlook.

In order to understand this idea, we will analyze the example of improving bank fraud detection. Think about a financial organization that uses a BN to evaluate fraud risk based on factors like customer spending patterns (constant, inconsistent), geolocation (domestic, foreign), and transaction quantity (low, medium, high). The BN has historically relied on preset probability. By tracking real-time transaction data, identifying abnormalities (such as odd spending spikes), and modifying fraud probabilities appropriately, artificial intelligence improves this approach. Furthermore, AI improves detection accuracy while maintaining the transparency of the BN's decision-making process by detecting latent correlations, such as connecting a customer's device ID to previous fraud instances.

4.2.2 Automatic Structure Learning Using Machine Learning

Manually creating a BN's structure is a laborious process that requires a great deal of domain knowledge and is frequently constrained by human bias or oversight. AI uses machine learning to automate the structure learning process in order to overcome this difficulty. Three main processes are involved in this approach: identifying risk factor correlations from historical data, improving forecasting accuracy by optimizing the BN structure, and exposing risk dependencies that were previously unknown. A lot of historical data can be analyzed by machine learning algorithms to find complex connections and linkages between risk factors. These algorithms' examination of this data allows them to find patterns that manual analysis would miss. Machine learning, for instance, can identify the long-term interactions between factors like market volatility, credit scores, and economic indicators in financial risk assessment. Proactive risk management and better decision-making are made possible by this skill, which provides an improved understanding of the underlying dynamics causing risks. The structure of the BN can be improved and refined by machine learning if correlations between risk factors have been found. In order to more accurately depict the actual dependencies between variables, the network's nodes and edges are adjusted during this optimization phase. To make sure the BN structure matches the data, methods like score based or constraint-based learning are frequently used. The predictive accuracy of the model is greatly increased by refining the BN, enabling more accurate forecasts and more intelligent risk mitigation techniques.

Finding hidden or previously unknown relationships between risk factors is one of machine learning's best features in BN structure learning. Conventional approaches frequently depend on preconceived notions about connections, which can ignore important but subtle interactions. However, machine learning has the ability to independently examine the data and uncover these hidden relationships. Organizations can create more reliable risk models and carry out focused interventions to address previously unanticipated threats by exposing these hidden links. Take supply risk assessment as an example to better understand this idea. Machine learning may evaluate past disruption data in supply chain management to create a BN that models risk, including transportation problems and supplier delays. This automation guarantees that the BN reflects the most important risk correlations and lessens the need for manual design (Ennouri, 2021).

4.2.3 Bayesian Parameter Optimization with Deep Learning

By optimizing probability distributions, deep learning greatly expands the capabilities of BNs, increasing their adaptability and responsiveness to intricate, real-world data. This is achieved using a number of sophisticated methods:

- Managing unstructured data: According to Zohuri et al. (2022), deep learning models are capable of converting unstructured data—like text or images—into probabilistic inputs that BNs can easily include. This enhances the network's analytical scope by enabling the integration of various data kinds.
- According to Wu (2024), employing recurrent neural networks (RNNs): RNNs work especially well with sequential data, allowing the BN to dynamically update probabilities in response to changing trends over time. This is particularly helpful in situations where data patterns are constantly changing, such as time-series analysis.
- Using variational Bayesian techniques: Even in high-dimensional environments, these techniques offer an effective means of estimating complex probability distributions (Hong et al., 2025). Deep learning guarantees that the BN maintains high accuracy while remaining computationally tractable by approximating complex distributions.

Consider the manufacturing example of predictive maintenance to further understand this idea. Think about a manufacturing plant that employs a BN to forecast equipment problems by analyzing sensor data, including temperature and vibration readings. Real-time sensor data is analyzed by deep learning models, which then transform it into dynamic probability distributions that are supplied to the BN. Through this integration, proactive maintenance scheduling is made possible by the system's increased ability to anticipate possible faults. The factory may thereby optimize resource allocation, drastically cut down on unscheduled downtime, and improve overall operational efficiency. Combining deep learning and BNs allows for more intelligent and data-driven decision-making across a range of applications in addition to increasing the accuracy of predictive models.

4.3 The AI-Driven Risk Simulation and Scenario Testing

AI expands the value of BNs by facilitating advanced scenario testing and risk simulation, building on these technological advancements. Organizations may proactively anticipate and prepare for possible hazards by using this capability. While the BN determines the odds of different outcomes, AI creates a variety of realistic risk scenarios, such as market declines, cyberattacks, or natural disasters. The best mitigation strategy can then be identified by decision-makers by simulating various reaction tactics.

Consider a logistics company that wants to model supply chain risks, for example. The business assesses the possible effects of supplier delays brought on by severe weather conditions. The algorithm analyzes patterns in meteorological data using AI to forecast a 40% increase in delay risk. After that, this data is entered into a BN, which models several mitigation techniques like expanding inventory levels or diversifying sources. The integrated AI-BN system determines the best course of action to reduce interruptions by doing thousands of simulations. With the help of this strategy, the business may move from a reactive to a proactive risk management framework, increasing operational effectiveness and resilience in the face of uncertainty.

4.4 AI and Bayesian Networks in Supply Risk Mitigation

We present, in this section, a case study of Globe International Business (GIB), a Tunisian company looking to reduce supply chain risks, to demonstrate the real-world use of AI and BNs.

a. Problem statement

For raw materials, GIB depends on a global supply chain, which exposes it to risks including natural disasters, supplier delays, and quality issues. Historically, these uncertainties have raised costs and caused production disruptions. To guarantee business continuity, the organization wants to put in place a strong risk management system.

b. AI-BN Model for supply risk

GIB develops a BN to model its supply chain risks, incorporating the following key nodes:

- Supplier reliability (SR): Assessed using historical data on delivery performance and quality metrics.
- Geopolitical stability (GS): Evaluated based on political and economic conditions in supplier regions.
- Weather conditions (WC): Monitored through meteorological forecasts affecting transportation.
- Quality control (QC): Tracked via defect rates and supplier quality processes.
- Demand fluctuations (DF): Forecasted using market trends and sales data.

The BN captures probabilistic dependencies among these factors, enabling the company to quantify the likelihood of disruptions (The BN was constructed using *Graphviz*).

Figure 5. BN for supply chain disruption

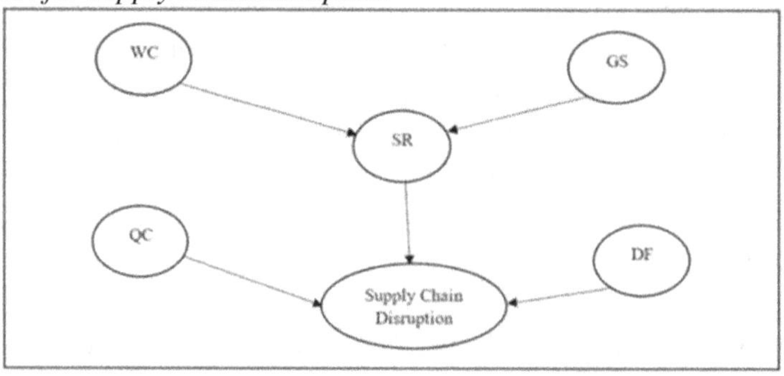

c. AI enhancements

AI is integrated to enhance the BN's functionality:

- Real-time data integration: AI algorithms process data from multisource be enabled to provide real-time estimation of the system health state for up-to-date risk evaluation and operation situational awareness (Ahmed et al., 2025).
- Predictive analytics: Machine learning models analyze historical and current supplier data to predict performance and potential disruptions. Indeed, the adoption and integration of AI technologies are boosting the production of data that can be collected, analyzed, and exploited for decision-making through big data analytics (Basile et al., 2024).
- Automated structure optimization: AI refines the BN structure by identifying the most significant risk factors and their interrelationships from large datasets.
- Dynamic probability updates: The BN's CPTs are updated in real time as new data emerges, ensuring the model reflects current conditions.

d. Results

The AI-enhanced BN delivers several benefits:

- Proactive risk management: Early alerts enable GIB Corporation to preempt disruptions, such as by sourcing alternative suppliers.
- Enhanced decision-making: Scenario simulations allow managers to evaluate strategies, such as increasing inventory for critical components, based on their projected impact (Yang et al.,2024).

Operational efficiency: By minimizing disruptions, the company reduces costs and maintains production schedules more effectively.

This case study illustrates how supply chain risk management is transformed into a proactive, data-driven process through the integration of AI and BNs, improving resilience in a complex global context (see Ennouri, 2021 for further details).

4.5 Bayesian Networks and Artificial Intelligence's Role in Risk Mitigation

The combination of AI and BNs offers a revolutionary approach to contemporary risk management, as this section demonstrates. This potent combination improves structural modeling through sophisticated machine learning approaches, optimizes parameters using deep learning methods, and strengthens risk identification through AI-driven probability estimates. Additionally, by supporting thorough scenario testing and simulation, it facilitates proactive decision-making. In the future, BNs will continue to be a vital component of risk mitigation plans as AI technologies advance. They will be crucial in tackling increasingly difficult decision-making problems in a variety of fields because of their exceptional capacity to blend accu racy and interpretability.

SECTION 5: USING SCENARIO TESTING TO INCORPORATE RESILIENCE INTO DECISION-MAKING

5.1 The Role That Resilience Plays in Risk Mitigation

Organizations face an extensive variety of risks in today's unstable and unpredictable world, from supply chain disruptions to cyber threats and economic downturns. These ever-changing issues are frequently not adequately addressed by traditional risk management techniques, which place an emphasis on avoidance and mitigation. Businesses must include resilience into their decision-making procedures in order to adapt, bounce back, and prosper in the face of such unpredictability. In risk management, resilience describes an organization's ability to:

- Anticipate potential threats before they emerge.
- Absorb shocks to limit disruptions when risks materialize.
- Adapt efficiently to maintain business continuity.

A vital tool for achieving this resilience is scenario testing, which empowers organizations to explore "what-if" scenarios, evaluate potential outcomes, and strengthen their risk mitigation strategies. Scenario testing becomes a solid, data-driven method of managing uncertainty when AI and BNs are added.

5.2 How Scenario Testing Contributes to Resilience

5.2.1 Describe the Scenario Testing Process

A method of risk analysis that focuses forward, scenario testing models various scenarios and evaluates how they might affect organizational operations. It gives decision-makers the tools they need to:

- Simulate risk events, such as cyberattacks, financial crises, or supply chain breakdowns.
- Analyze how risks interact and escalate using Bayesian inference.
- Evaluate the effectiveness of mitigation strategies before crises unfold.

Unlike static models, scenario testing offers a flexible framework that adapts to shifting circumstances, making it an essential component of resilience-focused risk management.

5.2.2 The Weaknesses of Conventional Risk Models

Conventional risk models lack the flexibility for managing unanticipated interruptions since they are frequently based on past data and fixed assumptions. During the COVID-19 pandemic, a notable example emerged, as numerous companies depended on static supply chain models that were unable to support:

- Global lockdowns and trade restrictions.
- Sudden and unprecedented demand shifts.
- Unexpected supplier failures.

Consequently, these organizations faced severe operational challenges and financial setbacks. A more flexible option that allows for readiness for a wide range of possible hazards is scenario testing, which is improved by AI and BNs.

5.3 Bayesian Networks Driven by AI for Scenario Testing

5.3.1 How Scenario Analysis is Improved by Bayesian Networks

A BN is a graphical model that maps the associations between risk factors and determines the probabilities of various outcomes, as was previously discussed in this chapter. It is perfect for scenario testing because of its advantages:

- Explicit modeling: It makes the causal relationships between hazards more clear.
- Quantification of uncertainty: It records probabilistic relationships between variables.
- Dynamic updates: As new information becomes available, it instantly modifies the probabilities.

To estimate P (Loan Default \ Economic downturn, Unemployment rate, Interest rate changes), for example, a financial institution evaluating credit risk may utilize a BN. The BN quickly recalculates default probability in the event of an increase in unemployment, facilitating better-informed risk management.

5.3.2 How Artificial Intelligence Might Improve Bayesian Scenario Testing

Artificial Intelligence amplifies BNs by:

- Analyzing vast datasets to identify early risk indicators.
- Generating diverse risk scenarios based on historical patterns and current trends.
- Automating probability updates to minimize human bias and enhance precision.

Together, AI and BNs enable organizations to simulate complex risk landscapes with greater accuracy and adaptability.

5.4 Real-World Uses for Scenario Testing Augmented by AI

5.4.1 Supply Chain Disruptions: A Case Study

Problem: In an era of geopolitical tensions, a Tunisian multinational retail company wants to assess the risks of supplier failure. (In this case *Graphviz* tool was used to build the BN).

BN model:

- Supplier reliability (S) → Delivery delays (D).
- Port congestion (P) → Increased shipping costs (C).
- Geopolitical risk (G) → Supplier reliability (S).

Figure 6. BN for supplier risk

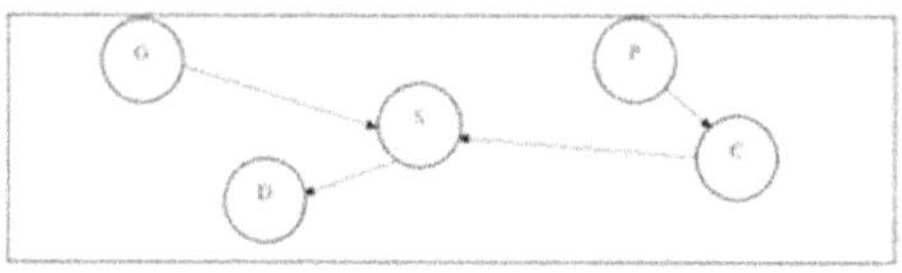

Scenario simulation: To assess the effect of geopolitical instability on supplier reliability, a scenario simulation is run out using *GeNIe*, a BN modeling tool created by *BayesFusion*. The baseline scenario shows consistent supply chain operations with a comparatively low likelihood of supplier failure at 5% under typical circumstances. But in the event of a geopolitical crisis, rising political and economic tensions seriously upset supplier networks, causing more uncertainty and logistical difficulties. Consequently, the probability of supplier failure increases to 35%, underscoring the significant influence of external geopolitical factors on the resilience of supply chains. This analysis underscores the importance of proactive risk management strategies to mitigate disruptions in volatile environments.

Mitigation approach: A diversification strategy is used to improve supply chain resilience and reduce the risks related to supplier breakdowns. The business reduces its reliance on any one source by sourcing parts and materials from several vendors in several geographical areas, which lowers its susceptibility to geopolitical changes. Greater flexibility and adaptability are ensured by this strategy, which permits operations to proceed even in the event that one provider is impacted. Consequently, supply chain stability is greatly increased as the likelihood of supplier failure drops from 35% to 12%. This proactive approach improves the organization's resilience to outside shocks and protects business continuity.

5.4.2 Cybersecurity Risk: AI-Powered Attack Simulations

Problem: By utilizing a BN to model important contributing elements, a financial institution aims to assess its vulnerability to malware infections. The probabilistic relationships between important variables influencing cybersecurity risks are captured by the model. In particular, the phishing success rate (P) is strongly impacted by employee cyber awareness (E), since greater awareness lowers the probability of successful phishing attempts. Furthermore, the efficacy of attack mitigation (M) is influenced by IT security measures (I), guaranteeing that strong security protocols improve the organization's capacity to thwart phishing attacks. Finally, the frequency of phishing attempts (A) is determined by the hacker activity level (H), which reflects the severity of external threats. The organization can measure its vulnerability to phishing threats and put targeted security measures in place by examining these interdependencies.

Scenario simulation: Using *GeNIe*, a tool for creating probabilistic models to examine how various activities affect phishing risk, a scenario simulation is carried out. To evaluate the effect of AI-based interventions on phishing risk reduction, a scenario simulation is run. Low employee knowledge results in a 30% phishing success rate in the absence of AI intervention, indicating a serious vulnerability to cyber risks. AI-driven training programs, on the other hand, give staff members individualized, flexible instruction on identifying and thwarting phishing attacks. The usefulness of AI-based education in enhancing cybersecurity resilience is demonstrated by the considerable reduction in the phishing success rate to 10% brought about by this improved training. These results highlight how important AI is to raising awareness and reducing the effectiveness of phishing attempts inside the organization.

Mitigation strategy: A real-time AI threat detection system is used as an advanced mitigation method to further improve cybersecurity resilience. This technology proactively detects phishing attempts before they reach employees, continuously monitors network activity, and looks for unusual patterns. The AI system can dynamically adjust to new threats by utilizing machine learning algorithms and anomaly detection, which greatly lowers the probability that phishing assaults will be successful. The phishing success rate therefore falls to less than 5%, indicating how well real-time AI-driven threat identification works to reduce cybersecurity risks and improve the company's general level of security.

5.5 The Future of Scenario Testing

By increasing the dynamic, predictive, and analytical nature of scenario testing, AI-driven BNs are revolutionizing resilience planning. This section emphasizes that:

- Scenario testing prepares organizations for diverse risk scenarios.
- AI enhances BNs by refining probability estimates and scenario creation.
- Practical examples demonstrate risk reductions of significant percentage.

As businesses increasingly embrace advanced AI-driven frameworks, BNs will remain central to resilience-focused decision-making, equipping organizations to navigate an uncertain future with confidence.

SECTION 6: IMPLEMENTING AI-DRIVEN RISK MITIGATION

Depending on the resilience-tested knowledge obtained from AI-enhanced BNs, this part provides a thorough how-to for using this cutting-edge architecture in practical settings. The theoretical robustness and clarity created in previous phases are converted into workable solutions throughout the implementation step. These strategies give businesses the ability to anticipate possible hazards as well as to endure and come back from failures. This procedure, which is guided by the transparency principle, skillfully combines technological complexity with real-world, quantifiable impact.

6.1 The Integration With Current Systems

Integrating AI-BN solutions into current operational workflows is a crucial first step in implementing AI-driven risk mitigation into practice. Take, for example, a real-time dashboard that tracks supply chain risks and is updated dynamically by AI in response to outside events like supplier delays or weather interruptions (Saad et al., 2024). Real-time actionability and accuracy of risk projections are guaranteed by this integration. Training is just as important. Teams must possess the abilities to interpret and respond to the AI-BN framework's outputs. For instance, if the system indicates that there is a 75% chance of a cyber breach, it should also include detailed information about the contributing elements, such as odd login habits or software flaws. Staff members may react quickly and confidently without questioning the rationale of the model thanks to this degree of openness, whether that means rerouting shipments, patching systems, or taking other precautionary actions. Maintaining the system's agility also requires regular updates, which enable the AI to improve risk probabilities in response to new information (Bakhtiari et al., 2025).

6.2 How Transparency Affects Deployment

The effectiveness of transparency is critical to the real-world implementation of AI-BNs. For instance, a resilience-tested BN may identify ventilator shortages as a major risk factor and forecast a 70% chance of an infectious disease outbreak in a healthcare environment. With this knowledge, hospital administrators may successfully defend preventative actions to boards and authorities, such hoarding medical supplies. Their trust is based on the model's transparency and the ability to follow its logic (Larson et al., 2024). This transparency reaches beyond decisions made inside. Decisions supported by transparent, verifiable data are more likely to be accepted by stakeholders, such as staff members, auditors, and outside partners. This promotes system trust in addition to adhering to ethical and legal requirements. To anticipate and lessen cyberattacks, for example, a cybersecurity company may implement a transparent AI-BN framework. Both internal teams and external auditors would be able to see the framework's efficacy and defensibility, guaranteeing broad acceptance and confidence.

6.3 The Three Keys: Observation, Assessment, And Adjustment

AI-driven risk mitigation requires constant observation and adjustment to remain effective. The accuracy of the AI-BN forecasts should be evaluated by routine audits. For instance, was the supply chain disruption from the previous quarter correctly predicted by the system? If not, the model ought to be modified in light of actual occurrences or scenario results (Zhou and Yuen, 2024).

Suppose a situation where a flood risk projection exaggerated the impact because of factors that were not taken into account, such recent infrastructure improvements. In these situations, the model should be adjusted to take these variables into consideration, guaranteeing that its forecasts stay precise and applicable. By incorporating resilience into the organization's fundamental functions, this continual evaluation and adaption process guarantees that the AI-BN architecture develops in parallel with new threats.

6.4 Developing Organizational Resilience

Finally, the application of AI-BNs turns the framework into a strong barrier against uncertainty by converting predicted insights into workable plans. Organizations may confidently handle unforeseen issues by incorporating AI-BNs into workflows, emphasizing openness, and committing to continual development. This strategy ensures long-term sustainability and profitability by improving risk reduction and cultivating a resilient culture. AI-enhanced BNs become more than just a predictive tool through this methodical deployment approach; they develop into a dynamic, adaptable system that enables businesses to prosper in a continually changing risk environment.

SECTION 7: CHALLENGES AND FUTURE DIRECTIONS

As this chapter illustrates, the combination of AI with BNs provides a revolutionary method of risk mitigation. To achieve its full potential, however, there are a number of obstacles that must be overcome for its long-term success and practical implementation. These challenges—data quality, model complexity, scalability, and ethical considerations—are thoroughly examined in this section, along with workable answers and future approaches. By addressing these problems, the AI-BN framework can develop into a more reliable, flexible, and reliable instrument for risk management in a variety of fields.

7.1 The Current Challenges in Risk Mitigation

7.1.1 Quality and Reliability of Data

The quality of input data determines how effective BNs are, because organizations usually deal with noisy, biased, or incomplete datasets (Mouti et al., 2022). A supply chain BN that uses out-of-date supplier performance indicators, for instance, can overstate or underestimate interruption risks, which could result in less-than-ideal choices. In cybersecurity, models that struggle to adjust to new hacking strategies are an example of how inadequate attack data can reduce the accuracy of threat detection (Arisian et al., 2025). Furthermore, unfairness and trust can be undermined by biased data, such as medical records that are skewed toward particular populations (Yadav et al., 2025). Real-time applications, where data streams need to be continuously evaluated, exacerbate these problems.

7.1.2 The Compromise Between Complexity and Clarity

The complexity of BNs can make them difficult to interpret when they grow to simulate complex risk scenarios, such as multi-hazard risks in critical infrastructure (Bakhtiari et al., 2025) (Nikiforidis et al., 2024). Despite effectively capturing interdependencies, a BN with dozens of nodes and edges may be too complex for decision-makers without technical knowledge. This conflict is seen in supply chain management, where intricate models that relate demand variations, weather, and geopolitics (section 4.4) run the risk of becoming unfeasible for practical use. Finding a balance between transparency and predictive capability is still difficult, especially in high-stakes industries like healthcare or finance where clarity is essential.

7.1.3 Performance and Transparency

Although it can occasionally conflict with quickly optimization, transparency is a fundamental component of successful risk control. For instance, a model's predicted accuracy may be lowered if it is simplified to make it easier to understand (Waltersdorfer and Sabou, 2025). Organizations can use explainable AI (XAI) methods, like SHAP (SHapley Additive exPlanations), which offer insights into how particular variables affect predictions, to overcome this difficulty. By preserving transparency without compromising functionality, these tools guarantee that models continue to be precise and intelligible.

7.1.4 Flexibility and Calculation Requirements

flexibility is a problem for AI-enhanced BNs because to their high computational complexity, particularly for real-time applications. As discussed in section 3.5, dynamic BNs put a strain on computational resources in large-scale systems such as 6G-IoT networks or global supply chains since they necessitate regular changes to probability tables as new data becomes available (Ibrahim et al., 2024). Small businesses may find it difficult to adopt these frameworks because they lack access to sophisticated infrastructure. These demands are further increased by including deep learning for parameter optimization (section 4.2.3), which calls for expensive hardware or cloud solutions. Adoption of AI-BN is further complicated by organizational and regulatory considerations in addition to computational demands.

7.1.5 Difficulties with Regulations

Regulations governing the use of AI and BNs in risk management are becoming stricter, especially in countries that place a high value on responsible and moral technology use. AI systems must meet strict restrictions set by frameworks like the General Data Protection Regulation[6] (GDPR) and the European Union's AI Act[7], particularly in high-stakes industries like vital infrastructure, healthcare, and finance. According to Waltersdorfer and Sabou (2025), these standards require explainability and human oversight in automated decision-making processes, as well as transparency, justice, and responsibility. Because of their intrinsic transparency, BNs provide a clear advantage in this regulatory environment. In contrary to opaque AI models, BNs use probabilistic reasoning and a graphical layout that make it easy for enterprises to map risk elements and their interdependencies. This interpretability complies with regulations like GDPR's chapter 3, section 4, and article 22, which ensures people have the right to know why automated systems made certain judgments. For example, a BN utilized in credit risk assessment can provide a traceable rationale for regulatory evaluation by directly linking variables such as income levels and repayment history to default probabilities. Similar to this, BNs' conditional probability tables, which can be examined to guarantee adherence to accuracy and fairness standards, complement the AI Act's emphasis on auditability.

However, there are substantial obstacles in the way of attaining complete regulatory compliance. By putting strong data governance procedures in place, organizations may make sure that BNs handle data protection issues like those mentioned in GDPR. Another crucial issue is bias prevention; a BN may generate misleading risk evaluations and violate regulatory equality requirements if it is trained on unbalanced datasets, such as those that overrepresent particular demographic groups. Furthermore, regulatory frameworks must be continuously adjusted due to their dynamic nature. Organizations must upgrade their AI-BN systems to be compliant with changing legislation, which requires resources and experience. The intricacy of regulations highlights the necessity of proactive approaches to incorporate legal considerations into the development and implementation of AI-driven risk management systems, guaranteeing their legal and efficient adoption.

7.1.6 Human and Organizational Issues with AI-Driven Risk Management

Along with technological and legal challenges, there are major organizational and human limitations to the use of AI-driven BNs in risk management. There is a strong opposition to change, especially in industries that depend on conventional risk assessment techniques, where workers may view AI as a danger to their job security or human knowledge. For example, because probabilistic BN outputs are complicated, risk managers accustomed to deterministic models may mistrust them, which could result in underutilization. AI is a disruptive force that is frequently resisted by hierarchical or risk-averse organizational structures, but innovation-driven cultures are more adaptable. The operational gaps, including a lack of technical infrastructure or experience, make this resistance worse, especially in businesses with limited resources. Acceptance and trust are essential on a human level. Uncertain AI decision-making or previous technology setbacks can breed mistrust, and cognitive biases like confirmation bias might skew users' interpretations of AI insights, calling for solutions that make the underlying reasoning more clear. Adoption is made more difficult by ethical issues since opaque AI runs the risk of enhancing past biases, as shown by discriminatory lending algorithm results (Xiong and Kim, 2025). A multidimensional strategy is needed to address these issues: stakeholder engagement to match tools with organizational objectives and promote ownership; transparent design and bias-mitigating algorithms to reduce bias; and education and training to demystify AI-BNs and create competence. While proactive change management, such as employee involvement and measurable success indicators (e.g., lower incident rates), can allay concerns about displacement, leadership must promote AI adoption by clearly communicating its advantages, such as increased accuracy and resilience. The key to overcome these obstacles is to view organizational and human capability as fundamental rather than optional. Organizations can effectively manage the interplay between these challenges and technical-regulatory demands by fostering trust, investing in workforce upskilling, and integrating ethical rigor. For instance, cultures that prioritize data integrity enhance AI reliability, while ethical practices simplify compliance. Only then will AI-BNs be able to turn risk management into a strategic, proactive role.

7.2 The New Solutions

7.2.1 Improved the Database

Organizations can use sophisticated data management systems that incorporate real-time collecting, validation, and purification to lessen problems with data quality. For example, in supply chains, IoT sensors can offer real-time shipping data, and AI-powered anomaly detection can highlight discrepancies (Saad et al., 2024). As shown in cybersecurity applications, methods such as federated learning, in which models are trained on decentralized datasets, can likewise improve data diversity while addressing privacy issues (Arisian et al., 2025). By ensuring that BNs run on dependable, current inputs, these pipelines improve prediction accuracy.

7.2.2 Simplified Bayesian Networks

Modular designs and automated scaling can simplify BNs without compromising their strength. In a supply chain BN, for example, separating supplier reliability from transportation hazards is an example of how modular BNs divide complicated networks into smaller, interconnected sub-models (section 3.4.1). As demonstrated in structure learning advancements (section 4.2.2), automated pruning, driven by machine learning, removes superfluous nodes and edges. These methods support the transparency objectives listed in section 2 by preserving predictive power while improving the digestibility of outputs.

7.2.3 Using Edge Computing for Flexibility

By processing data closer to its source, edge computing presents a viable solution to computational limitations. In a cybersecurity context (section 3.4.2), edge devices could perform initial BN inference on transaction data, reducing latency and server load. Combined with cloud-based AI for periodic updates, this hybrid approach balances scalability and real-time responsiveness. Research into lightweight BN algorithms, optimized for low-resource environments, further supports broader adoption (Zhou and Yuen, 2024).

7.2.4 Ethical AI Frameworks

Mitigating ethical risks requires embedding fairness and accountability into AI-BN design. Techniques like SHAP and LIME (section 2.2.2) can expose biases in risk predictions, enabling corrective actions such as reweighting datasets. Establishing clear accountability protocols—e.g., logging model decisions for audits—aligns with regulatory demands (Larson et al., 2024). In healthcare, hybrid human-AI workflows, where clinicians validate BN outputs, can reduce error risks, fostering trust and ethical compliance (Choi Li et al., 2025).

7.3 Future Directions for AI-Enhanced Risk Mitigation

7.3.1 Quantum Computing and AI-BN Fusion

Quantum computing promises to revolutionize AI-BN frameworks by exponentially accelerating inference and optimization tasks (Bar and Karakose, 2025). For instance, quantum algorithms could solve large-scale CPTs in seconds, enabling real-time risk analysis for complex systems like financial markets or climate models. Early applications in drug discovery (Satheeskumar, 2024) suggest potential for risk-related fields, where rapid scenario testing (section 5) could predict cascading failures with unprecedented precision. While still nascent, this fusion could redefine the scalability and accuracy of risk mitigation.

7.3.2 AI-Powered Natural Language Explanations

Building on transparency's pivotal role (section 2), future BNs could leverage natural language processing to generate intuitive explanations of risk predictions. For example, a BN that evaluates flood risk, for instance, may produce the following output: "High rainfall raises river levels by 60%, increasing flood probability to 85%." Such clarity, facilitated by models such as transformers (Zhang et al.,

2025), improves adoption among stakeholders who are not experts by bridging the gap between technical outputs and decision-makers. This is in line with section 6's realistic deployment objectives.

7.3.3 Ability to React to Changing Threats

To stay ahead of dynamic risks—e.g., climate change or geopolitical shifts—AI-BNs must incorporate continuous learning. As demonstrated in predictive maintenance (section 4.2.3), reinforcement learning may be used to improve BN structures in response to actual results. In order to provide resilience, supply chains may need to modify their probability in response to emerging trade rules (section 5). When combined with streaming data analytics, adaptive BNs have the potential to anticipate new dangers and change risk management from a reactive to a proactive discipline (Ahmed et al., 2025).

7.3.4 Standardization Across Domains

Standardized AI-BN frameworks are necessary due to the variety of risk management applications (such as supply chains, cybersecurity, and healthcare). To expedite deployment, future initiatives could provide open-source templates that incorporate the best practices from sections 3.6. Knowledge graph-inspired collaborative systems might exchange BN structures and datasets across industries, spurring innovation and guaranteeing uniformity in tackling universal issues like data ethics and quality (Waltersdorfer and Sabou, 2025).

7.5.4 A Simple Way to be Continued

Although data dependability, complexity, flexibility, and ethics are major obstacles to AI-enhanced BNs, they can be overcome with focused advancements. While quantum computing, NLP explanations, adaptive learning, and standards map out a revolutionary future, improved data pipelines, optimized models, edge computing, and ethical frameworks offer instant fixes. By expanding upon the useful applications (parts 3.4, 4.4) and resilience tactics (section 5), these developments guarantee that AI-BNs continue to be both innovative and reliable. The development of this framework will rely on two agreements: utilizing technology advancements and placing a high priority on transparency, as dangers increase in scope and interconnectedness. AI-BNs can enable enterprises to not only reduce risks but also take advantage of opportunities in an unpredictable environment by tackling present constraints and embracing future potential. Their position as an element of resilient, intelligent decision-making in a world growing more complex is cemented by moving forward.

CONCLUSION

This chapter has demonstrated how AI-enhanced BNs can successfully convert uncertainty into a framework for transparent and organized decision-making. We developed a method that puts clarity first by methodically identifying risks and implementing focused solutions, allowing businesses to transform uncertain threats into useful insights. In addition to improving risk mitigation, this paradigm encourages well-informed decision-making in a variety of fields. Transparency will remain the foundation of successful risk management in the future. New developments, such natural language explanations driven by AI, have the potential to improve decision-making even more. These developments will make complex models easier for stakeholders to understand by offering more concise, understandable explanations for risk assessments and mitigation techniques. To preserve confidence and guarantee the framework's scalability and flexibility across a range of industries, issues like data bias and automation resistance must be proactively addressed.

Beyond just decreasing risk, the combination of AI and BNs opens up new possibilities. Organizations may successfully negotiate complexity by utilizing this strong combination, transforming perceived weaknesses into strategic advantages. This method not only increases resilience but also helps decision-makers survive in an environment of uncertainty.

REFERENCES

Ahmed, I., Croci, A., Antonello, F., & Zio, E. (2025). Integration of artificial intelligence within an advanced filtering framework for real-time system state estimation and risk prediction with application to a nuclear microreactor. *Nuclear Engineering and Technology*, *57*(5), 103353. DOI: 10.1016/j.net.2024.103353

Alessandria, G., Yar Khan, S., Khederlarian, A., Mix, C., & Ruhl, K. J. (2023). The aggregate effects of global and local supply chain disruptions: 2020–2022. *Journal of International Economics*, *146*, 103788. DOI: 10.1016/j.jinteco.2023.103788

Arisian, S., Halat, K., Hafezalkotob, A., & Maskey, R. (2025). Coopetitive Resilience: Integrating Cyber Threat Intelligence Platforms in Critical Supply Chains. *Transportation Research Part E, Logistics and Transportation Review*, *197*, 104043. DOI: 10.1016/j.tre.2025.104043

Bakhtiari, S., Najafi, M. R., Goda, K., & Peerhossaini, H. (2025). A dynamic Bayesian network approach to characterize multi-hazard risks and resilience in interconnected critical infrastructures. *Reliability Engineering & System Safety*, *257*, 110815. Advance online publication. DOI: 10.1016/j.ress.2025.110815

Bar, N. F., & Karakose, M. (2025). An approach for automated generation of quantum computing models using deep learning. *Ain Shams Engineering Journal*, *16*(4), 103327. DOI: 10.1016/j.asej.2025.103327

Basile, L. J., Carbonara, N., Panniello, U., & Pellegrino, R. (2024). The role of big data analytics in improving the quality of healthcare services in the Italian context: The mediating role of risk management. *Technovation*, *133*, 103010. DOI: 10.1016/j.technovation.2024.103010

Biswas, B., Mukhopadhyay, A., Kumar, A., & Delen, D. (2024). A hybrid framework using explainable AI (XAI) in cyber-risk management for defence and recovery against phishing attacks. *Decision Support Systems*, *177*, 114102. DOI: 10.1016/j.dss.2023.114102

Choi Li, A. K., Rauf, I. A., & Keshavjee, K. (2025). Knowledge is not all you need for comfort in use of AI in healthcare. *Public Health*, *238*, 254–259. DOI: 10.1016/j.puhe.2024.11.019 PMID: 39700868

D'Ambrosio, N., Perrone, G., & Romano, S. P. (2023). Including insider threats into risk management through Bayesian threat graph networks. *Computers & Security*, *133*, 103410. DOI: 10.1016/j.cose.2023.103410

Ennouri, W. (2021). Développement d'un modèle de gestion des risques dans la chaîne logistique basé sur les réseaux bayésiens. Thèse de doctorat spécialité Sciences de gestion: Logistique et Production, Faculté des Sciences Economiques et de Gestion-Sfax, Tunisie.

Guo, Y., Yang, B., Alqawzai, S., Chen, K., & Kong, D. (2025). Machine learning-based and interpretable models for predicting the resistance and probability of progressive collapse of steel frame-composite floor structures. *Engineering Structures*, *332*, 120089. DOI: 10.1016/j.engstruct.2025.120089

Hao, X., Demir, E., & Eyers, D. (2024). Exploring collaborative decision-making: A quasi-experimental study of human and Generative AI interaction. *Technology in Society*, *78*, 102662. DOI: 10.1016/j.techsoc.2024.102662

Hong, F., Wei, P., Bi, S., & Beer, M. (2025). Efficient variational Bayesian model updating by Bayesian active learning. *Mechanical Systems and Signal Processing*, *224*, 112113. DOI: 10.1016/j.ymssp.2024.112113

Ibrahim, A. M. A., Chen, Z., Eljailany, H. A., Yu, G., Ipaye, A. A., Abouda, K. A., & Idress, W. M. (2024). Advancing 6G-IoT networks: Willow catkin packet transmission scheduling with AI and Bayesian game-theoretic approach-based resource allocation. *Internet of Things : Engineering Cyber Physical Human Systems*, *25*, 101119. DOI: 10.1016/j.iot.2024.101119

Juliani, F., & Maciel, C. D. (2024). Bayesian networks supporting management practices: A multifaceted perspective based on the literature. *International Journal of Information Management Data Insights*, *4*(1), 100231. DOI: 10.1016/j.jjimei.2024.100231

Kekez, I., Lauwaert, L., & Ređep, N. B. (2025). Is artificial intelligence (AI) research biased and conceptually vague? A systematic review of research on bias and discrimination in the context of using AI in human resource management. *Technology in Society*, *81*, 102818. DOI: 10.1016/j.techsoc.2025.102818

Larson, D. B., Doo, F. X., Allen, B.Jr, Mongan, J., Flanders, A. E., & Wald, C. (2024). Proceedings from the 2022 ACR-RSNA workshop on safety, effectiveness, reliability, and transparency in AI. *Journal of the American College of Radiology*, *21*(7), 1119–1129. DOI: 10.1016/j.jacr.2024.01.024 PMID: 38354844

Leray, P. (2006) 'Réseaux bayésiens: apprentissage et diagnostic de systèmes complexes. Modélisation et simulation', *Université de Rouen*. FFTEL-00485862.

Li, Z., & Montomoli, M. (2024). Aleatory uncertainty quantification based on multi-fidelity deep neural networks. *Reliability Engineering & System Safety*, *245*, 109975. DOI: 10.1016/j.ress.2024.109975

Liang, T., Wang, F., Wang, S., Li, K., Ma, X., & Mo, X. (2024). Towards unified aleatory and epistemic uncertainty quantification for machinery health prognostic through sequential heteroscedastic Gaussian process regression. Advanced Engineering Informatics Volume 62. *Advanced Engineering Informatics*, *102719*, 102719. Advance online publication. DOI: 10.1016/j.aei.2024.102719

Longo, F., Mirabelli, G., Padovano, A., & Solina, V. (2023). The Digital Supply Chain Twin paradigm for enhancing resilience and sustainability against COVID-like crises. *Procedia Computer Science*, *217*, 1940–1947. DOI: 10.1016/j.procs.2022.12.394 PMID: 36687282

Marcus, E., & Teuwen, J. (2024). Artificial intelligence and explanation: How, why, and when to explain black boxes. *European Journal of Radiology*, *173*, 111393. DOI: 10.1016/j.ejrad.2024.111393 PMID: 38417186

Mehdiyev, N., Majlatow, M., & Fettke, P. (2025). Integrating permutation feature importance with conformal prediction for robust Explainable Artificial Intelligence in predictive process monitoring. *Engineering Applications of Artificial Intelligence*, *149*, 110363. DOI: 10.1016/j.engappai.2025.110363

Mohammad, W., Elomri, A., & Kerbache, L. (2022). The Global Semiconductor Chip Shortage: Causes, Implications, and Potential Remedies. *IFAC-PapersOnLine*, *55*(10), 476–483. DOI: 10.1016/j.ifacol.2022.09.439

Moore, T. (2017). On the harms arising from the Equifax data breach of 2017. *International Journal of Critical Infrastructure Protection*, *19*, 47–48. DOI: 10.1016/j.ijcip.2017.10.004

Mouti, S., Shukla, S. K., Althubiti, S. A., Ahmed, M. A., Alenezi, F., & Arumugam, M. (2022). Cyber security risk management with attack detection frameworks using multi-connect variational auto-encoder with probabilistic Bayesian networks. *Computers & Electrical Engineering*, *103*, 108308. DOI: 10.1016/j.compeleceng.2022.108308

Nallakaruppan, K., Balusamy, B., Lawanya Shri, M., Malathi, V., & Bhattacharyya, S. (2024). An Explainable AI framework for credit evaluation and analysis. *Applied Soft Computing*, *153*, 111307. DOI: 10.1016/j.asoc.2024.111307

Nikiforidis, K., Kyrtsoglou, A., Vafeiadis, T., Kotsiopoulos, T., Nizamis, A., Ioannidis, D., & Sarigiannidis, P. (2024). Enhancing transparency and trust in AI-powered manufacturing: A survey of explainable AI (XAI) applications in smart manufacturing in the era of industry 4.0/5.0. *ICT Express*. Advance online publication. DOI: 10.1016/j.icte.2024.12.001

Niu, S., Yin, Q., Ma, J., Song, Y., Xu, Y., Bai, L., Pan, W., & Yang, X. (2024). Enhancing healthcare decision support through explainable AI models for risk prediction. *Decision Support Systems*, *181*, 114228. DOI: 10.1016/j.dss.2024.114228

Park, K., & Yoon, H. Y. (2024). Beyond the code: The impact of AI algorithm transparency signaling on user trust and relational satisfaction. *Public Relations Review*, *50*(5), 102507. DOI: 10.1016/j.pubrev.2024.102507

Ruddick, J., Ceusters, G., Van Kriekinge, G., Genov, E., De Cauwer, C., Coosemans, T., & Messagie, M. (2024). Real-world validation of safe reinforcement learning, model predictive control and decision tree-based home energy management systems. *Energy and AI*, *18*, 100448. DOI: 10.1016/j.egyai.2024.100448

Saad, S. M., Ubeywarna, D., & Zhang, H. (2024). Supply network risk mitigation—Industry 4.0 approach. *Procedia Computer Science*, *232*, 3206–3215. DOI: 10.1016/j.procs.2024.02.136

Satheeskumar, R. (2024). Enhancing drug discovery with AI: Predictive modeling of pharmacokinetics using graph neural networks and ensemble learning. Intelligent Pharmacy. Advance online publication. DOI: 10.1016/j.ipha.2024.11.002

Setzu, M., Guidotti, R., Monreale, A., Turini, F., Pedreschi, D., & Giannotti, F. (2021). GLocalX - From Local to Global Explanations of Black Box AI Models. *Artificial Intelligence*, *294*, 103457. DOI: 10.1016/j.artint.2021.103457

Simwanda, L., Ikotun, B. D., Ilunga, F. M., & Onyari, E. K. (2025). Epistemic uncertainties in torque capacity prediction models for circular CFDST members. *Journal of Constructional Steel Research*, *226*, 109299. DOI: 10.1016/j.jcsr.2024.109299

Thiele, S. (2019). Detecting underestimates of risk in VaR models. *Journal of Banking & Finance*, *101*, 12–20. DOI: 10.1016/j.jbankfin.2019.01.018

Ul Hassan, S., Abdulkadir, S. J., Zahid, M. S. M., & Al-Selwi, S. M. (2025). Local interpretable model-agnostic explanation approach for medical imaging analysis: A systematic literature review. *Computers in Biology and Medicine*, *185*, 109569. DOI: 10.1016/j.compbiomed.2024.109569 PMID: 39705792

Vagnoli, M., & Remenyte-Prescott, R. (2022). Updating conditional probabilities of Bayesian belief networks by merging expert knowledge and system monitoring data. *Automation in Construction*, *140*, 104366. DOI: 10.1016/j.autcon.2022.104366

Wahlström, M., Tammentie, B., Salonen, T. T., & Karvonen, A. (2024). AI and the transformation of industrial work: Hybrid intelligence vs double-black box effect. *Applied Ergonomics*, *118*, 104271. DOI: 10.1016/j.apergo.2024.104271 PMID: 38579495

Waltersdorfer, L., & Sabou, M. (2025). Leveraging knowledge graphs for AI system auditing and transparency. *Journal of Web Semantics*, *84*, 100849. DOI: 10.1016/j.websem.2024.100849

Wu, D., Zhang, T., Zhang, J., Lv, H., Yue, C., & Fu, M. (2024). Sensitivity analysis and multiobjective optimization for rural house retrofitting considering construction and occupant behavior uncertainty: A case study of Jiaxian, China. *Applied Energy*, *360*, 122835. DOI: 10.1016/j.apenergy.2024.122835

Wu, Y. (2024, June 30). Enterprise financial sharing and risk identification model combining recurrent neural networks with transformer model supported by blockchain. *Heliyon*, *10*(12), e32639. DOI: 10.1016/j.heliyon.2024.e32639 PMID: 38988581

Xiong, Y., & Kim, J. K. (2025). Who wants to be hired by AI? How message frames and AI transparency impact individuals' attitudes and behaviors toward companies using AI in hiring. *Computers in Human Behavior: Artificial Humans*, *3*, 100120. DOI: 10.1016/j.chbah.2025.100120

Yadav, N., Kumar, R., Pandey, D. (2025). 12 - Impact of artificial intelligence bias in medical systems. Revolutionizing Medical Systems using Artificial Intelligence, A Breakthrough in Healthcare, 227-243. DOI: 10.1016/B978-0-443-32862-6.00012-2

Yang, S., Demichela, M., Geng, J., Wang, L., & Ling, Z. (2024). A data-driven Bayesian network of management and organizational factors for human reliability analysis in the process industry. *Heliyon*, *10*(15), e35048. DOI: 10.1016/j.heliyon.2024.e35048 PMID: 39166060

Ying, X., Lu, A., Cai, Q., & Lu, J. (2024). Bayesian network modeling applied to food risks: Data from General Administration of Customs of China as an example. *Applied Food Research*, *4*(2), 100565. DOI: 10.1016/j.afres.2024.100565

Yuan, Y., Chaffart, D., Wu, T., & Zhu, J. (2024). Transparency: The Missing Link to Boosting AI Transformations in Chemical Engineering. *Engineering (Beijing)*, *39*, 45–60. DOI: 10.1016/j.eng.2023.11.024

Zhang, C., & Meng, Y. (2024). Bayesian deep learning: An enhanced AI framework for legal reasoning alignment. *Computer Law & Security Review*, *55*, 106073. DOI: 10.1016/j.clsr.2024.106073

Zhang, M., Wang, H., Conti, F., Manderbacka, T., Remes, H., & Hirdaris, S. (2025). A hybrid deep learning method for the real-time prediction of collision damage consequences in operational conditions. *Engineering Applications of Artificial Intelligence*, *145*, 110158. DOI: 10.1016/j.engappai.2025.110158

Zhang, W. (2025). Bank liquidity supply and corporate investment during the 2008–2009 financial crisis. *The North American Journal of Economics and Finance*, *76*, 102371. DOI: 10.1016/j.najef.2025.102371

Zhou, Y., & Yuen, K. F. (2024). A Bayesian network model for container shipping companies' organisational sustainability risk management. *Transportation Research Part D, Transport and Environment*, *126*, 103999. DOI: 10.1016/j.trd.2023.103999

Zohuri, B., Mossavar-Rahmani, F., & Behgounia, F. (2022). Chapter 4 - Structured and unstructured data processing. Knowledge is Power in Four Dimensions: Models to Forecast Future Paradigm With Artificial Intelligence Integration in Energy and Other Use Cases, Pages 87-119. DOI: 10.1016/B978-0-323-95112-8.00004-0

ENDNOTES

1 https://gdpr-info.eu/

2 https://hms.harvard.edu/

3 https://artificialintelligenceact.eu/

4 https://gdpr-info.eu/

5 https://www.sec.gov/ai

6 Rules relating to the protection of natural persons with regard to the processing of personal data and rules relating to the free movement of personal data (General Data Protection Regulation (GDPR) – Legal Text)

7 EU AI Act: first regulation on artificial intelligence (https://www.europarl.europa.eu)

Chapter 9

Transparent AI for car Price Prediction Balancing Accuracy and Interpretability

Abdelhafid Ayaou
https://orcid.org/0009-0000-6272-4547
Higher School of Technology of Nador, Morocco

Fouad El Otmani
https://orcid.org/0000-0003-4433-4558
Higher School of Technology of Nador, Morocco

Mohamed Atounti
Higher School of Technology of Nador, Morocco

ABSTRACT

This study introduces an artificial intelligence system which predicts used car prices in Morocco to overcome the weaknesses of conventional valuation techniques that produce subjective and inconsistent results. The evaluation of multiple machine learning models resulted in CatBoost being chosen as the most effective model for prediction purposes. The final model reached an R^2 score of 91.35% after processing a web-scraped dataset from local automotive platforms through extensive preprocessing and hyperparameter tuning. The application of SHapley Additive exPlanations (SHAP) ensured model transparency. The system operates through a web-based interface which provides instant price forecasts together with analytical explanations and automated systems for monitoring data shifts and market adjustments. The study shows that combining advanced prediction capabilities with transparent

DOI: 10.4018/979-8-3373-5499-6.ch009

models and ongoing monitoring systems enhances fairness, accountability, and user trust in AI-based pricing systems for emerging markets like Morocco.

1. INTRODUCTION

The accurate pricing of used cars remains difficult in Morocco because traditional valuation methods are subjective and vehicle conditions and market demand vary widely. The research develops a machine learning pricing system which addresses the Moroccan used car market requirements. The model received training from the CatBoost algorithm using data extracted from local online automotive platforms while undergoing advanced preprocessing and hyperparameter optimization. The web application presents the final system which uses SHapley Additive exPlanations (SHAP) to provide transparent predictions that show users how mileage and registration year and transmission affect price estimates.

The automotive industry functions as a vital economic sector which drives technological advancement and international trade activities. In Morocco, it is also important and the automotive sector has grown, reaching $11 billion in automotive exports in 2022 (Morocco World News, 2023). Industrial development is also coupled with the development of the used car market which gives customers more options for used cars than new cars. However, this is because used car pricing is not as straightforward as that of new cars.

Whereas new cars are fairly easy to price, used car prices depend on a number of variables, including mileage, year of first registration, type of fuel, brand, transmission, and market trends. Many conventional approaches to pricing are subjective, based on the expertise of an individual, a dealership, or simple rule-based heuristics. Buyers may pay more than they should for the vehicles, and sellers may leave money on the table for their assets, resulting in financial losses. This is because there is a need to use data in the pricing process in order to increase the precision of the prices and to achieve equity, transparency and effectiveness of the market for all participants.

Machine learning represents a suitable technique for used car pricing prediction since it analyzes numerous samples to identify nonlinear relationships between variables better than traditional statistical methods (Taylor, Brown, & Adams, 2019). The research develops a standard used car pricing prediction system for the Moroccan market through a purpose-built dataset obtained from online marketplaces by web scraping methods. The vehicle dataset included make, model, year of registration, mileage, fuel type, transmission, and price as its main attributes.

The evaluation of machine learning algorithms for prediction showed CatBoost, LightGBM, and XGBoost to be the most effective. The optimal algorithm was identified as CatBoost through extensive hyperparameter tuning and optimization which produced an R^2 of 91.35% and an RMSE of 27,568.31 indicating its effectiveness for used car price prediction. The model received implementation into a web-based application which allows users to submit vehicle details to receive immediate price estimates. The system includes price comparison tools along with market trend analysis to assist buyers and sellers in making well-informed choices.

The predictive accuracy of the model was essential while maintaining interpretability to guarantee pricing recommendations receive proper understanding. This research implements SHAP to analyze the used car price prediction model to understand how different features interact during prediction generation while also gaining insight into the model's decision-making process. The model needs to be interpretable because it serves as a requirement for developing user trust alongside practical implementation.

A data drift and market change detection system was implemented to prevent the model's accuracy from deteriorating with time. The model remains updatable through monitoring tools which allows it to adapt to changing price trends for increased long-term relevance.

The research provides a detailed description of how the model was developed. The research starts with a literature review that includes a review of car price prediction studies and an identification of research gaps. The methodology section outlines the process of data collection and preparation together with machine learning model development. The result and discussion section evaluates ML model performance through a comparison of their results while discussing hyperparameter tuning and residual analysis and model interpretability and monitoring techniques. The study concludes by discussing the model's real world applications while suggesting improvements that include real-time pricing and larger dataset size and an adaptive learning model for market trend changes.

2. REVIEW OF LITERATURE

2.1. Used Car Price Prediction: The Conventional Approach and the Statistical Learning Approach

The used car pricing system functions as an active system which multiple elements affect including different vehicle characteristics and technical details. The conventional pricing methods through expert appraisals and dealership valuations and rule-based assessments prove inaccurate and subjective because they fail to track market dynamics according to Zhang et al. (2018).

Machine learning operates as a data-based system which employs learning algorithms to study data patterns for future trend prediction. ML algorithms demonstrate superior flexibility compared to statistical regression models because they can detect non-linear relationships and identify complex patterns which standard models miss (Kumar et al., 2020).

2.2. Car Price Prediction Using Machine Learning Algorithms

The following ML models have been applied to car price prediction and are discussed in this study:

- **Linear Regression and Polynomial Regression:** Although these models are popular because of their simplicity, they have a drawback of being inefficient in the presence of non-linear relationships and are poor in high dimensional spaces (Brown, 2019).
- **Decision Trees and Random Forests:** Decision trees divide the data into different classes based on the features while random forests improve the prediction accuracy by using many decision trees and avoid overfitting (Breiman, 2001).
- **Gradient Boosting Algorithms:** Some of the boosting algorithms include XGBoost, LightGBM, and CatBoost which learn from residual errors by building up successive models. Of all the algorithms discussed, CatBoost has been shown to work very well with categorical data and is a good choice for used car price estimation (Prokhorenkova et al., 2018).
- **Support Vector Machines (SVM):** SVMs use kernel functions to form the relationships between the variables but are costly to compute and are not extendable for large datasets (Cortes & Vapnik, 1995).
- **Deep Learning Models:** Prices have been predicted using neural networks like CNN for image-based analysis and RNN for time series forecasting but they require large amount of data and high computational power (LeCun et al., 2015).

Among these approaches, gradient boosting models, especially CatBoost have been found to outperform traditional methods in used car price prediction. Because of their capability to learn the objective function, manage categorical variables, and create interactions between features, these models are most suitable for application in the real world.

2.3. Challenges in Machine Learning-Based Price Prediction

In recent studies, the following challenges have been identified in the implementation of ML in price prediction models:

- **Data Quality and Availability:** In emerging markets like Morocco, there are limited datasets on used car pricing, which means that data was scraped from the web and a lot of data cleaning was done to deal with incomplete and incorrect data.
- **Feature Engineering:** It is crucial to encode categorical features such as the type of transmission and fuel in numerical form. Target encoding and boosting based encoding are commonly used to improve the model's predictive capacity.
- **Market Dynamics:** Pre-owned car prices keep changing with the economic conditions, customer needs, and government policies. Since ML models are not updated in real time, they may become outdated, which requires active tracking and retraining of the models.
- **Model Interpretability:** Although the boosting models achieve high accuracy, the black box nature of the models is a major drawback. SHAP (Shapley Additive Explained) values are used to explain how each feature affects the price prediction, thus increasing the credibility of the model (Lundberg & Lee, 2017).
- **Deployment and Scalability:** For the models to be used in production, they have to be able to provide real time inference, be scalable and be integrated into the dealership and online platforms and also to satisfy the privacy and security requirements.

These challenges should be met to create a accurate, efficient and easily explainable machine learning based car price prediction model.

2.4. Research Gaps and Contributions of This Study

The present study was conducted in Morocco, an emerging economy; hence, there is limited research on ML-based pricing models in this market. Previous research has mainly focused on the accuracy of the models with little concern to the monitoring of the models, interpretability and the ability to update the models in real time. The contributions of this study include:

- Creation of a new dataset through data extraction to ensure that the data collected is relevant to the Moroccan market.

- Assessment of a number of techniques for the purpose of establishing that CatBoost is the most accurate in making the predictions ($R^2 = 91.35\%$).
- Integration of model monitoring mechanisms to detect data drift, for the purpose of ensuring that the models are accurate in the long run.
- Applicability of SHAP for the purpose of making the features influence on the pricing decision easily understandable.

In order to close these research gaps, this study offers a practical solution for used car price estimation based on historical data as well as future recommendations for price changes.

2.5. Broader Context of Price Prediction and Interpretability

The use of machine learning for vehicle price prediction in Moroccan local markets has grown, while most research studies have focused on worldwide applications. Lin et al. (2021) analyzed the Chinese automotive market through XGBoost and obtained a 20% enhancement in forecasting precision compared to traditional dealership-based methods. Javed et al. (2022) studied used car price forecasting in South Asia and demonstrated how integrating regional, brand-specific, and economic data decreased the occurrence of pricing bias.

Research and practice in American and European mature markets concentrate on prediction accuracy together with the importance of pricing fairness and model interpretability. The LIME framework proposed by Ribeiro et al. (2016), along with SHAP, allows users to generate transparent and explainable outputs from sophisticated ML models. These tools enhance user trust while maintaining regulatory compliance and expanding AI-powered pricing system acceptance.

Algorithmic models trained with biased or incomplete datasets, according to Corbett-Davies et al. (2018), will amplify existing historical inequalities. The pricing process affects consumer financing, insurance underwriting, and resale value assessments. However, most studies addressing transparency and interpretability in Western and Asian contexts fail to consider the problems faced by African markets.

This research contributes to filling this knowledge gap through the implementation of interpretable ML methods in the Moroccan used car market while addressing data constraints, model transparency, and fairness through SHAP. Recent advancements in SHAP theory work toward developing better explanations, which are necessary for ethical AI pricing system deployments (Sundararajan & Najmi, 2020). Zhang and Ahmed (2022) present step-by-step procedures for using SHAP to enhance pricing fairness while providing guidance on merging model transparency with ethical AI standards.

SHAP functions both as an interpretability tool and as a means of implementing AI transparency principles aligned with ethical AI guidelines from the European Commission (2020) and IEEE (2019). SHAP enables output feature attribution in a human-readable format, thus supporting auditability and user trust — fundamental components of responsible AI.

2.6. Industry Trends in the Used Car Market

The used car industry experiences fast transformation because of digitalization alongside changes in consumer behavior and technological advancements. The market has shifted toward online platforms Moteur.ma, Avito and wandaloo which now dominate the industry instead of traditional dealership-first models. The platforms have accelerated the need for automated pricing tools to ensure consistent, data-driven valuations.

The increasing digitalization of vehicle transactions in Morocco forces private sellers and dealerships to implement transparent pricing systems because of rising market demands. Companies worldwide use machine learning and artificial intelligence to improve market efficiency and build trust through transparent pricing engines. The transition to algorithmic pricing demonstrates why researchers need to develop scalable interpretable models like CatBoost combined with SHAP as shown in this research.

3. METHODOLOGY

This section describes how a machine learning model was developed to predict the prices of used cars in Morocco. The methodology consists of four main phases: In the first phase, data was collected; in the second phase, the data was cleaned and prepared for modeling; in the third phase, the machine learning experiments were conducted; and in the last phase, the final model was deployed in a web application. Each stage is important for guaranteeing the validity, precision, and usability of the predictive system. As shown in **Figure 1**, an overview of the entire methodology pipeline is presented.

Figure 1. Overview of the entire pipeline of the methodology

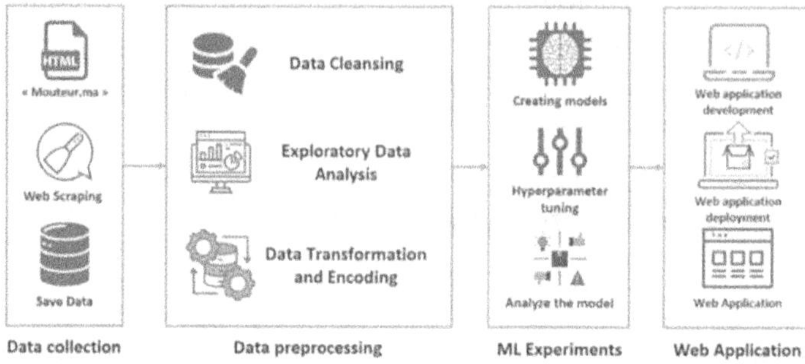

The first stage of the methodology is Data Collection, where all the data was gathered from a Moroccan online marketplace that deals with used cars. As there was no readily available dataset specific to the region, a web scraper was used to gather information on car make, model, year, mileage, fuel type, and price. This raw data forms the basis of the next step.

Then, the Data Preprocessing stage focuses on the propagation of the data collected in its raw form to a form that is suitable for application in machine learning. This includes data cleaning to deal with missing or incomplete data, data preparation to reveal underlying patterns through EDA, and feature encoding to work with categorical features. These preprocessing steps make sure that the data is in the correct form for effective modeling.

The third stage of the process is Machine Learning Experiments, in which a large number of algorithms are chosen, trained, and compared. The best-performing model was optimized using advanced hyperparameter tuning techniques. The R^2 and RMSE score were used as performance metrics to choose the best model.

Last, in the Deployment stage, the best predictive model is integrated into a web application. This application allows users to input vehicle details and receive accurate value estimates, along with interpretability functionality that clearly explains how individual features influence the predicted price. Additionally, the deployment process entails model monitoring to ensure continued accuracy as market conditions change.

The following subsections explain in detail each stage of the methodology, starting with data collection.

3.1. Data Collection

The first step toward building a predictive model for used car prices involved building a dataset which accurately represents the used car market in Morocco. This paper explains the data source and web scraping method for data collection and presents some preliminary results. Additional verification steps were implemented to enhance both the quality and the breadth of the collected data.

3.1.1. Data Source and Collection Methodology

The data set for this study was collected from www.moteur.ma which operates as one of Morocco's leading websites for used car transactions. The dataset contains vital attributes including brand, model, year, mileage, transmission, fuel type and vehicle feature to develop an accurate predictive model.

The data collection process utilized *BeautifulSoup* as a Python library for web scraping purposes. Web scraping refers to the method of extracting data in structured formats from websites through HTML document parsing (Mitchell, 2015). The scraping process followed these essential steps:

- **Target Pages:** All the URLs of the car advertisements on the platform were systematically identified.
- **HTTP Requests:** The scraper made HTTP GET requests to the platform and requested the advertisement pages as a user would.
- **Parsing HTML Content:** After downloading the HTML documents, we used *BeautifulSoup* to parse through the HTML and gather structured information from the HTML tags.
- **Data Storage:** The data was extracted and stored in a CSV file and then preprocessed and analyzed further.
- **Verification and Quality Checks:** To ensure that the data was complete, the data was checked for errors and omissions before moving to the preprocessing stage.

The dataset was compiled from the scrape included both numerical and categorical features relevant to predictive modelling. Ethical considerations were observed in the scraping process, such that the process was conducted within the context of the platform's terms of service and data privacy policies.

3.1.2. Ethical and Legal Aspects of Web Scraping

Web scraping involves extracting data from websites using automated tools. While technically feasible, it must be performed responsibly and ethically. For this study, the scraping process complied with the publicly available content of the www .moteur.ma platform, which is widely used in Morocco for listing used cars.

Only publicly listed, non-personal data such as make, model, price, fuel type, and mileage were collected. No user accounts, private messages, or identifiable personal information were accessed. The scraping was rate-limited to avoid burdening the website's servers and aligned with general data ethics best practices.

Furthermore, researchers recommend adherence to website terms of service and national data privacy regulations (Mitchell, 2015). While Moroccan data laws are still evolving, this study followed a responsible scraping approach consistent with global research practices (Munzert et al., 2015). Future work should consider the integration of APIs or formal data partnerships for enhanced compliance.

3.1.3. Description of the Dataset

The dataset developed for this study includes 32,333 used car listings, which give a comprehensive and accurate picture of the used car market in Morocco. Each record contains information about the vehicle's specs, ownership, and market factors. Some of the fields included are brand, model, registration year, mileage, transmission, fuel type, tax horsepower, customs clearance, and final sale price. Other factors like first-use, guarantee, import, and available features were also obtained to enhance the price prediction model.

In Table 1 below, an overview of the dataset's variables is given in relation to the model training and evaluation.

Table 1. The description of the dataset features

Feature Name	Description
name	Full name of the car, including brand and model
mileage	Total mileage traveled by the car (in kilometers)
year_reg	Year of the car's registration
trans_type	Transmission type (manual or automatic)
fuel_type	Fuel type used by the car (e.g., diesel, gasoline)
date	Date the advertisement was posted on the platform
tax_horsepower	Administrative engine power unit

continued on following page

Table 1. Continued

Feature Name	Description
doors	Number of doors on the car
first_hand	Indicates if the car was purchased directly from the original owner
customized	Indicates if the car has been customized (e.g., tuning)
customs_cleared	Indicates if the car has been customs-cleared
under_warranty	Indicates if the car is still under warranty
import_new	Indicates if the car was imported in new condition
color	The car's color
body_type	Type of car body (e.g., SUV, sedan, hatchback)
options	List of available car options (e.g., airbags, GPS)
price	Selling price of the car in Moroccan Dirhams (Dhs)

The data was gathered from French-language sources, which means that categorical variables such as *fuel_type*, *trans_type*, *body_type*, and *color* are in French. This linguistic feature is in line with the usual practice in Moroccan car listings and should therefore be taken into account when analyzing the data.

3.2. Data Preprocessing

The preprocessing phase is important to ensure that the dataset is ready and appropriate for application to machine learning models. As such, since used car pricing is rather complex and ambiguous, appropriate preprocessing is vital for data quality, accuracy of model predictions, and biases avoidance. The main steps are data cleaning, handling missing values, outliers' detection and handling, categorical variables encoding, and feature scaling and transformation.

3.2.1. Data Cleaning

Data cleaning is an important step in data preparation to ensure that the data is error-free, consistent and has no redundancies. The process entails addressing formatting problems, missing data handling, data redundancy or duplication and feature scaling to improve the interpretability of the models.

The first major problem in the dataset was the form of the data. Some features like the *mileage* and *price* had characters like commas and spaces which are not numerical and therefore could not be easily processed numerically. All such characters were removed and the values were all converted to numeric data type to ensure that all the records were in the same format.

To improve feature granularity the *name* column which had both brand and model information combined in it was split into two columns *brand* and *model.* This transformation enabled a more fine-grained analysis and a clearer distinction between different kinds of vehicles based on the type of vehicle.

This was another important challenge in the handling of missing values. Different approaches were used according to the type of the feature:

- **Mileage:** Missing values were imputed using the mean within each *year_reg* category to make the estimation as realistic as much as possible.
- **Tax Horsepower and Doors:** Since these attributes are more product related, missing values were replaced by the mean value for each *brand* and *model.*
- **Body Type, Transmission Type and Options:** The mean of the most frequent value in each *brand* and *model* was used for imputation. If there were still missing values, then the overall frequency of values in the dataset was used.
- **Color:** The missing values in the *color* feature were replaced by the most frequent *color* in the dataset.

We detected duplicate records and deleted them to avoid violating the integrity of the dataset. In all, 78 duplicate entries were detected and erased to avoid having redundant data that may compromise the predictive models. First, some unneeded features were erased to make the dataset easier to use. The *date* column which kept the information about the date of the advertisement was not considered to be helpful for the price prediction and therefore was removed to avoid increasing the number of features and reducing the computation time.

These are some of the comprehensive cleaning steps that have been taken on the dataset to ensure that the data is accurate, consistent and reliable for further analysis and modeling.

3.2.2. Exploratory Data Analysis

Exploratory Data Analysis (EDA) is an important step in the realization of the dataset's structure, patterns, outliers and relationships between variables. This phase guarantees that the dataset is ready for machine learning model building by giving information about the distributions, correlations and categorical relationships.

3.2.2.1. Outlier Detection and Treatment

Outliers can cause significant distortion of model predictions, especially for numerical features like mileage and price where extreme values were seen. These anomalies can be identified and managed using the Interquartile Range (IQR) method, for which the following calculation was made:

$$IQR = Q3 - Q1$$

where **Q1** and **Q3** represent the first and third quartiles, respectively. The lower and upper bounds for acceptable values are computed as:

$$Lower\ Bound = Q1 - 1.5 \times IQR$$

$$Upper\ Bound = Q3 + 1.5 \times IQR$$

Any values more or less than these bounds were considered outliers. The initial distribution of numerical features is shown in **Figure 2** where it is clear that there are extreme values in all numerical features. If these outliers are not removed they have the potential to skew model training.

Figure 2. Initial distributions and boxplots of numerical features before outlier removal

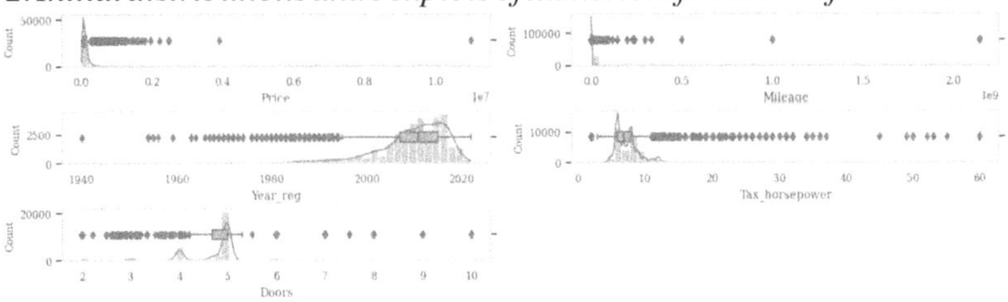

To reduce their effect a quantile capping approach was used which restricts the extreme values to be within the 5th and 95th percentiles. However, after a detailed investigation, only *mileage* and *price* were corrected because these values were not normal distributed. **Figure 3** shows the refined distributions of mileage and price after performing outlier treatment to see the effect of capping on the feature distribution.

Figure 3. Refined distributions and boxplots of mileage and price after outlier removal

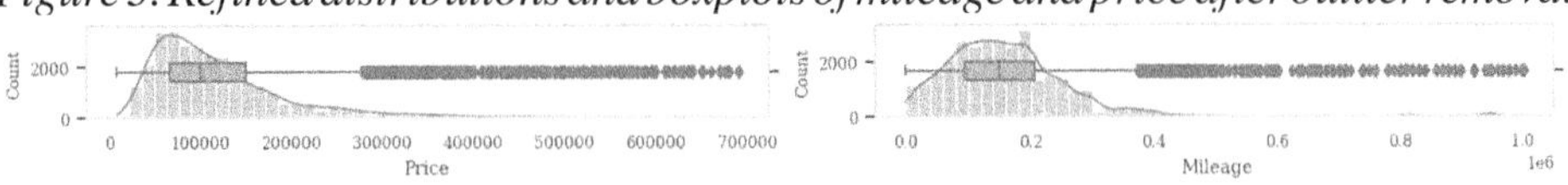

3.2.2.2. Correlation Analysis and Feature Relationships

In order to understand the relationship between the numerical features and the target variable, the Pearson correlation coefficient was used. This metric quantifies the linear correlation between two variables, each of which is continuous, and returns a value that lies between **−1** and **1**, such that:

$$r = \frac{\sum (X_i - \bar{X})(Y_i - \bar{Y})}{\sqrt{\sum (X_i - \bar{X})^2 \sum (Y_i - \bar{Y})^2}}$$

where X and Y represent two numerical variables, and $\bar{X}$ and $\bar{Y}$ are their respective means. The magnitude of r corresponds to the strength of the relationship, and its sign to the direction of the correlation.

The correlation heatmap of numerical features is depicted in **Figure 4**, which helps to visualize these relationships and show how different features affect price.

Figure 4. Correlation heatmap of numerical features

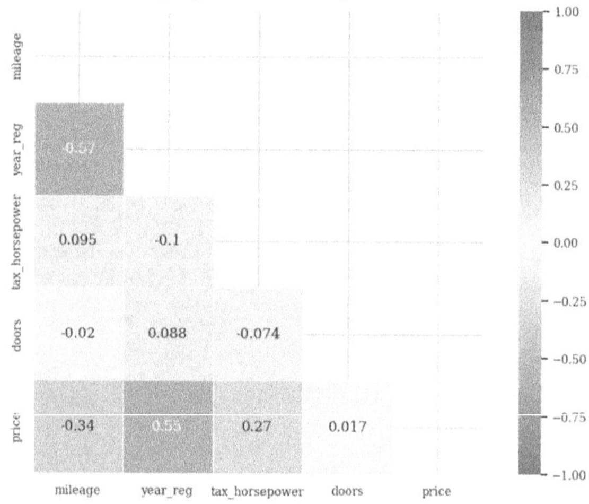

From the correlation analysis, the following were revealed:

- ***year_reg*** (*r = 0.55*): A very high positive correlation with price, thus confirming that new cars are more expensive than the old ones.
- ***mileage*** (*r = -0.34*): This is a moderately high negative correlation with price which means that cars with high mileage are worth less than cars with low mileage.

- ***tax_horsepower*** (*r = 0.27*): This is a moderate positive correlation which means that higher powered cars are more expensive.
- ***doors*** (*r = 0.017*): This correlation is almost zero with price, which means that the doors feature has a negligible impact on the valuation of a car.

Although correlation does not mean causation, these findings reveal important predictors of price. Features with weak or no correlation, for example, doors were considered unessential for the price prediction and were eliminated from the analysis to improve the model accuracy.

3.2.2.3. Analysis of Categorical Features

Understanding the distribution of categorical variables can give some ideas about the composition of the dataset and their importance in the context of predictive modelling. Looking at their frequency also helps to determine the appropriate encoding techniques and to check how they affect the price prediction.

Figure 5. Distribution of low-cardinality categorical variables

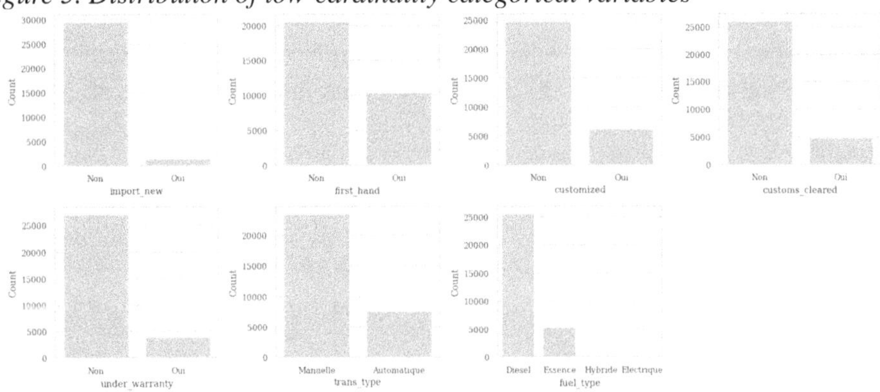

Figure 5 shows the frequency of low cardinality categorical variables in the dataset. The analysis shows that manual transmission cars are most preferred in the market, and this is due to factors such as affordability and low maintenance costs. Likewise, diesel cars are the most dominant type of car in the dataset, as far as consumers are concerned, they are the most preferred because of issues on fuel economy and ownership costs. On the other hand, hybrid and electric cars are almost non-existent, and are therefore represented by a very low percentage of the dataset. Because of their infrequent occurrence, these records were excluded in order to preserve the data for equilibrium and to prevent compromising the stability of the predictive modelling process. Moreover, a large number of the cars are not first-hand,

indicating a strong second-hand market. Very few cars are still under warranty which may affect the price and purchase confidence. Import and customize cars are also not very common which means that most of the cars are locally bought and serviced. From these categorical distributions it is possible to gain a basic understanding of the structure of the dataset and the directions of the preprocessing procedures such as categorical encoding and feature selection. The results of this analysis are used to improve the way that categorical variables are handled in the machine learning models and to achieve a proper balance in the representation of market practices.

These categorical trends reveal cultural patterns in Moroccan vehicle use. The dominant preference for manual transmission vehicles suggests a market accustomed to cost-effective and repairable options, which aligns with broader economic behaviors in the region. Similarly, the high prevalence of diesel vehicles reflects fuel price sensitivity, particularly for drivers covering long distances or in rural areas. These observed preferences reinforce the importance of aligning machine learning models with local usage norms and consumer expectations.

3.2.2.4. Relationship Between Categorical Features and Price

To compare price distributions across categories, boxplots were used to analyze how categorical features affect vehicle pricing. **Figure 6** shows the relationship between price and key categorical variables and how they help set the value of a vehicle.

Figure 6. Boxplots of categorical features vs. price

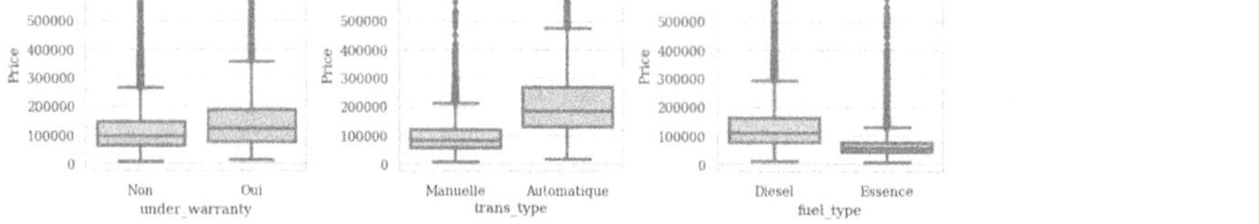

Categorical variables reveal some important patterns in pricing. Imported vehicles *(import_new)* are more expensive than domestic vehicles because of their limited availability and better quality. In the same manner, vehicles with a history of one ownership *(first_hand)* have more expensive price distributions than vehicles with more owners, consistent with the preference for a known vehicle history with minimal wear.

The effect of warranty (*under_warranty*) is also material: cars that are still under warranty have a clear price premium. This is because consumers regard warranties as a way of protecting themselves against the costs of repairs, thereby increasing the vehicle's attractiveness. There is a clear influence of transmission type (*trans_type*) on the price, with automatic transmission cars being priced higher than manual transmission cars, which is in line with the market perception that automatic cars are better than manual cars. It is important to note that the analysis of fuel type (*fuel_type*) does not support the initial hypothesis that electric vehicles are more expensive than vehicles fueled by gasoline. Rather, the data shows that diesel vehicles have higher price distributions than gasoline vehicles. This is because diesel cars are very popular in the Moroccan market due to their high fuel efficiency and lower running costs. Customization (*customized*) seems to have a negligible effect on price; the prices are fairly equally distributed between the customized and non-customized vehicles. This may indicate that while modifications might improve appearance or performance, they do not necessarily result in a higher resale value. These results are useful in understanding the impact of categorical variables on pricing patterns and thus inform the next steps of feature selection and model training.

3.2.3. Data Splitting

After the data has been prepared and analyzed, the dataset was randomly split (20% testing, 80% training). The training set was employed for model development including hyperparameter tuning and cross-validation. The final model's performance was evaluated on unseen data using the testing set to do this, to ensure reliability and generality. **Figure 7** presents the price distributions for both the training and testing sets. The equivalence in the distributions confirms that the two subsets are a fair representation of the full dataset as they are mutually inclusive.

Figure 7. Price distribution in training and testing sets

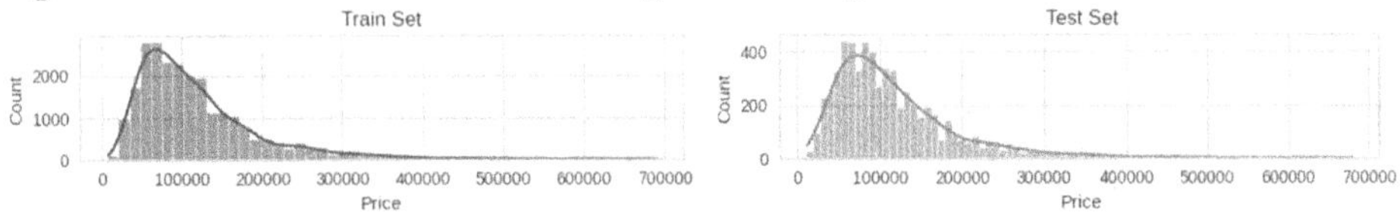

3.2.4. Encoding of Categorical Variables

Using Categorical Features in Machine Learning Models requires that they be represented numerically. This ensures that algorithms can actually use and understand categorical information, and that categorical relationships are maintained. Because of the type of the dataset, several encoding techniques were used as a function of the cardinality of the categorical variables and their type.

3.2.4.1. One-Hot Encoding for Low-Cardinality Features

For categorical variables with a limited number of unique values, one-hot encoding (OHE) was used. This method encodes each category into a binary feature; a value of 1 means that the category is present, and 0 means it is not. It is particularly effective for nominal variables that have no inherent order (Bishop, 2006). To maintain interpretability while not injecting ordinal relationships, this approach was used to encode variables such as *trans_type* and *fuel_type* in the dataset. However, OHE adds dimensionality to the dataset, which is reasonable for low category number cases.

3.2.4.2. Multi-Label Binarization for Multi-Valued Features

Some categorical features, like *options*, have their values stored as a list of multiple values per entry, describing different vehicle features, like GPS, airbags, leather seats. Because these attributes are not easily encoded into a one-hot encoding framework, multi-label binarization was used instead. This technique creates separate binary columns for each unique option, helping the dataset capture the presence or absence of certain car features without forcing artificial hierarchies (Pedregosa et al., 2011). Multi-label encoding helps maintain vehicle attributes in a structured manner such that models can tell one car from another by their extra features.

3.2.4.3. Leave-One-Out Target Encoding for High-Cardinality Features

High Cardinality categorical variables like *brand* and *model* are a problem because of the many categories that are present. Using one hot encoding to encode these variables would create many features thus increasing memory requirement and the risk of overfitting. Instead, leave one out target encoding was used where each category is replaced by the mean target value (*price*) found excluding the particular instance. This technique maintains the meaningful relationships between the categorical variables and the target variable with no increase in dimensionality (Micci-Barreca, 2001).

The encoding is performed using the following formula:

$$c_i = \frac{\sum_{j \neq i} t_j}{n - 1 + R}$$

where:

- c_i is the encoded value for the *i*-th record,
- t_j represents the target value (*price*) for the *j*-th record,
- n is the number of records with the same category,
- R is a regularization factor used to prevent overfitting, especially for rare categories.

To avoid leakage, leave one out encoding should be done within the context of cross validation such that encoding transformations are learned from training data and not applied to validation or test data. This encoding technique is especially useful for tree-based models that can exploit the encoded values without the need for any further transformations. Also, this method does not bring additional high dimensional complexity compared to one-hot encoding and thus is computationally efficient and retains the categorical feature predictive capability.

3.2.5. Feature Scaling and Transformation

Before feeding the dataset into a variety of machine learning models, feature scaling and transformation were performed. This work compares various kinds of machine learning models such as distance-based methods, regression techniques, gradient based algorithms and tree learning algorithms. It was necessary to preprocess the data in order to achieve numerical stability and to make the data compatible with all methods.

Feature scaling is the process of scaling numerical variables to a similar range of values to avoid having features with very large or very small magnitudes influencing the model. On the other hand, transformation methods are used to deal with skewness in the feature distributions since skewness affects the stability of the model performance, especially for models that are developed under the assumption of normal distribution of the data.

3.2.5.1. Feature Scaling: Z-Score Standardization

Certain machine learning models, particularly distance-based models (e.g., K-Nearest Neighbors, Support Vector Regression) and gradient-based optimization methods (e.g., Ridge Regression, Elastic Net), require standardized feature scales for accurate similarity measurements and numerical stability. To achieve this, Z-score standardization was applied to all numerical features, following the standard formula:

$$X' = \frac{X - \mu}{\sigma}$$

where:

- X' is the standardized feature value
- X is the original feature value
- μ is the mean of the feature
- σ is the standard deviation of the feature

This transformation ensures that all standardized features have a mean of 0 and a standard deviation of 1 (Kuiper, 2008). Standardization is particularly important for models relying on gradient descent optimization, such as Support Vector Machines (SVM) and Ridge Regression, where feature scaling significantly impacts the convergence of optimization processes.

While tree-based models (e.g., Random Forest, Gradient Boosting) are generally robust to variations in scale, standardization was applied across all models to maintain consistency and ensure comparability in performance evaluations.

3.2.5.2. Feature Transformation: Yeo-Johnson

All numerical features had different levels of skewness, which can affect many models that were developed under the assumption of normally distributed input data. To this end, the Yeo-Johnson transformation was used. Logarithmic and Box-Cox transformations are restricted to positive values only, but Yeo-Johnson is not (Yeo & Johnson, 2000). It is defined as:

$$X' = \begin{cases} \frac{(X+1)^{\lambda} - 1}{\lambda}, \text{ if } \lambda \neq 0, X \geq 0 \\ \log(X+1), \text{ if } \lambda = 0, X \geq 0 \\ -\frac{(-X+1)^{2-\lambda} - 1}{2-\lambda}, \text{ if } \lambda \neq 2, X < 0 \\ -\log(-X+1), \text{ if } \lambda = 2, X < 0 \end{cases}$$

where λ is automatically optimized to minimize skewness and achieve a more normal distribution.

Applying this transformation helped improve modeling accuracy. It enhanced stability during optimization for gradient-based models and enabled balanced splits in tree-based models, leading to better performance and improved interpretability.

3.3. Machine Learning Experiments

The preprocessed dataset was used to train machine learning models for car price prediction. The following section describes the model selection, the evaluation methodology, the techniques for making the models interpretable, and the strategies for monitoring them in order to obtain robust and reliable predictions.

3.3.1. Model Selection and Evaluation

The modeling process required investigation of various machine learning algorithms from basic to complex levels. The training models included linear regression-based methods together with tree algorithms and distance based learning and gradient boosting. The selection of models occurred because they could handle specific data challenges such as feature interactions and non-linear relationships and numerical issues.

The AutoML framework **PyCaret** performed model comparison and hyperparameter tuning according to Ali et al. (2020). The automation of preprocessing and hyperparameter tuning and performance comparison through this framework resulted in efficient and consistent results. The models became more robust through cross validation which reduced the chance of overfitting. The data was divided into five parts during each iteration where the model trained on four parts while validating on the last part. The performance metrics from all iterations were averaged to produce unbiased results (Stone, 1974). The evaluation metric RMSE measured the price prediction errors while penalizing large discrepancies. The R^2 Score evaluated the model's ability to explain price variations by determining its percentage of explained variation. The evaluation metrics provided essential information about model predictive accuracy.

3.3.2. Model Interpretation Using SHAP

The credibility and clarity of predictive models for price estimation depends heavily on understanding the decisions made by the model. Tree-based and gradient boosting models achieve high predictive accuracy but remain black box models because they do not show the steps that lead to specific predictions.

SHapley Additive exPlanations (SHAP) served as a model-agnostic interpretability tool to address this problem. Lundberg and Lee (2017) developed SHAP which uses cooperative game theory to determine fair shares for game participants through Shapley values. The machine learning approach of SHAP enables the assignment of importance values to features which explain their role in model predictions.

The mathematical representation of the SHAP values is as follows:

$$\phi_i = \sum_{S \subseteq F \setminus \{i\}} \frac{|S|!(|F| - |S| - 1)!}{|F|!} [f(S \cup \{i\}) - f(S)]$$

where:

- ϕ_i is the SHAP value for feature i
- F is the full set of features
- S represents a subset of features excluding i
- $f(S)$ is the model's prediction using only features in subset S
- The factorial terms ensure fair attribution by averaging over all possible feature orderings

SHAP enables both global and local interpretation of model predictions which helps users understand which features impact the model's output. The global SHAP analysis helps users understand feature importance throughout all predictions to identify which features drive model output results. Local SHAP explanations help users understand the specific impact of each feature on model output predictions for individual instances.

SHAP stands out as the preferred choice because it maintains theoretical feature importance properties and its sums have meaningful interpretations. SHAP serves as a universal explanation tool which works with tree-based models as well as linear models and neural networks. The versatility of SHAP has made it a popular choice for explaining numerous machine learning models. This study uses SHAP to explain our model through both global analysis which reveals feature importance and local analysis which explains individual predictions. The method enables straightforward understanding of the model's pricing decisions while allowing domain experts to validate the model's accuracy based on their available knowledge.

3.3.3. Model Monitoring

A surveillance framework was established to guarantee the predictive model's long-term reliability and accuracy. Machine learning models face two types of drift problems: data drift which occurs when input feature statistical distributions change over time and concept drift which emerges from market trends and economic shifts and consumer preference changes (Lu et al., 2018). The model becomes both inaccurate and unreliable when such drifts occur without proper monitoring.

The framework tracks distribution changes through statistical measures including the Kolmogorov-Smirnov (KS) test and Population Stability Index (PSI) (Grath & Buskirk, 2019). The metrics enable automated drift detection through their ability to detect training data versus new input differences.

Evidently AI (2021) was integrated into the monitoring pipeline to generate real-time data drift reports for automated process execution. The system evaluates drift by comparing historical training data with new incoming data using specialized statistical metrics. The automated retraining pipeline operates to adapt to changing data distributions which maintains model accuracy and market relevance.

3.4. Web Application Integration

For the accessibility and usability of the car price prediction model, a web application was developed and deployed. This application offers an interface to perform price forecast, data analysis, model explanation, and drift analysis to make the machine learning findings easily available to the business and consumers in the automotive sector in Morocco. The architecture and deployment methodology are detailed in **Figure 8**.

Figure 8. Web application deployment workflow

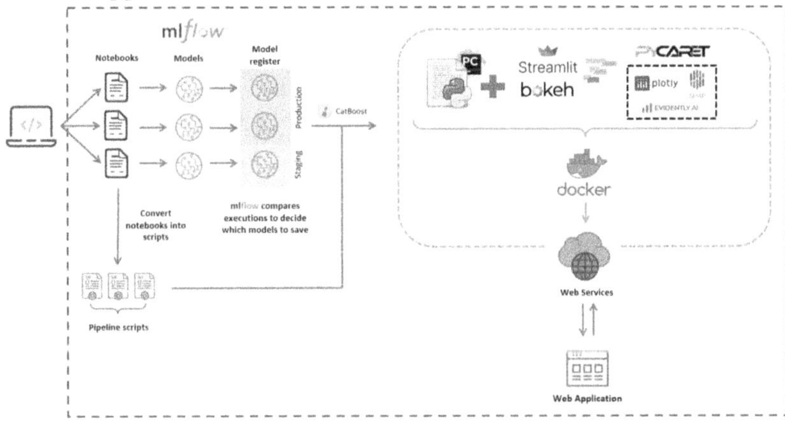

3.4.1. Methodology and Tools for Development

The web application was developed using a modular architecture to make the deployment and scaling up easy. The pipeline comprises several key components:

- **Model Management and Deployment:** The best performing model identified is saved and backed up, and the model version is controlled using MLflow (Zaharia et al., 2018). The application makes the model available for real-time inference through a user-friendly interface.

- **Web Interface:** Using Streamlit (Treuille et al., 2019), smooth interaction is provided to the predictive model without having to write a lot of back-end code. It has real-time data input and visualization.
- **Visualization and Interpretation:** The data exploration is very interactive and is achieved through Plotly (Plotly Technologies Inc., 2015) and Bokeh (Bokeh Development Team, 2018) for the creation of the graphs, while the model interpretability is boosted by SHAP for understanding the effects of the features on the price prediction.
- **Model Monitoring:** Data drift and market changes are continuously monitored by Evidently AI (Evidently AI, 2021) and it sends alerts for when it is time to retrain the model.
- **Deployment and Scalability:** The whole application is packed into containers using Docker (Merkel, 2014) for stable deployment across all the environments and cloud-readiness.

3.4.2. Web Application functionalities

There are multiple interactive components of the web application enabling users to explore the dataset, delve into detailed data insights, obtain car price predictions, examine the interpretability of these predictions, and monitor the model's behavior over time. An overview of the application's interface is presented in **Figure 9**.

Figure 9. Web application interfaces

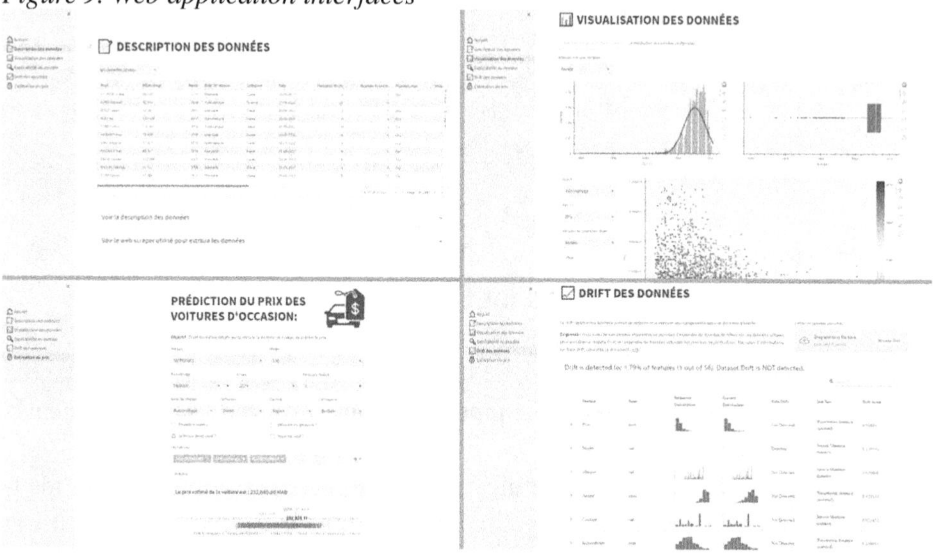

1. **Data Exploration:** The user is able to work with the data and examine some of the variables like brand, model, year, mileage, fuel type, transmission type, and price. Further transparency is achieved through the description of the method used in scraping data from the web.
2. **Data Visualization:** There is a separate module that enables the user to create histograms, scatter plots, and density plots to analyze the distribution of car prices and other vehicle features. This assists in the identification of price patterns and relationships between the characteristics of the car.
3. **Car Price Prediction and Interpretation:** It is a categorical model that classifies the input vehicle specifications and comes up with an estimated price of the vehicle. The SHAP feature importance analysis is also integrated to increase the understandability of the model and thereby the factors that affect the price prediction.
4. **Model Monitoring and Drift Detection:** Evidently AI keeps a close eye on the input data distributions and reports any large changes that may be detrimental to the model's performance. When drift occurs, the user is notified of possible market changes that may necessitate a retraining of the model.

4. RESULTS AND DISCUSSION

The following section presents machine learning experiment results to evaluate model performance in used car price prediction. Standard regression evaluation metrics are used to analyze the results and gain insights into the accuracy, reliability, and real-world applicability of the model. The section also presents analyses for model interpretability and monitoring to achieve transparency and to ensure accuracy over time is maintained.

4.1. Evaluation Metrics

The evaluation of model performance required the use of two standard regression metrics which included **Root Mean Square Error** and **R^2 score**. The two metrics provide distinct yet connected perspectives about model predictive accuracy and explanatory power which together provide a complete assessment of model quality.

4.1.1. Root Mean Square Error (RMSE)

RMSE measures the average prediction error by giving more importance to the larger differences between actual and predicted values. It is most applicable in regression models for detecting the influence of outliers. The RMSE is calculated as follows:

$$RMSE = \sqrt{\frac{1}{n}\sum_{i=1}^{n}(y_i - \bar{y}_i)^2}$$

where:

- y_i is the actual car price
- $\bar{y}_i$ is the predicted car price
- n is the total number of predictions

The RMSE is also expressed in the same unit as the target variable, Moroccan Dirhams, which gives a clear understanding of the average prediction error. Lower RMSE means better accuracy meaning it makes smaller errors in estimating the prices of cars.

4.1.2. Coefficient of Determination (R^2 Score)

The R^2 Score measures the proportion of variance in car prices explained by the model. It ranges from **0** to **1**:

- The result indicates that the model is able to predict most of the price changes when the R^2 value is close to 1.
- A value close to 0 shows that the model is not very good at making predictions.

The formula for R^2 is given by:

$$R^2 = 1 - \frac{\sum_{i=1}^{n}(y_i - \bar{y}_i)^2}{\sum_{i=1}^{n}(y_i - \bar{y})^2}$$

where:

- $\bar{y}$ is the mean of actual prices.

A high R^2 value means that the model has a good understanding of the pricing pattern, which makes the model easier to interpret. The importance of and interpretation of metrics

4.2. Model Performance Evaluation

To assess the predictive accuracy of various machine learning models, 5-fold cross-validation (Stone, 1974) was used to increase robustness and reduce overfitting. As shown in **Table 2**, the results highlight the comparative performance of different algorithms in predicting used car prices.

Table 2. Comparative performance of machine learning models

Model	RMSE	R^2 Score
CatBoost Regressor	**28,793.32**	**0.9057**
XGBoost Regressor	30,565.39	0.8937
LightGBM Regressor	30,803.79	0.8920
Extra Trees Regressor	31,830.80	0.8847
Random Forest Regressor	34,282.35	0.8662
Gradient Boosting Regressor	36,259.02	0.8504
Ridge Regression	39,935.70	0.8185
Bayesian Ridge	39,980.02	0.8181
Support Vector Regression (SVR)	41,864.71	0.8006
Decision Tree Regressor	44,725.89	0.7722
AdaBoost Regressor	52,437.04	0.6873
Linear Regression	59,422.65	0.6441
k-Nearest Neighbors (kNN)	59,422.65	0.5982
Lasso Regression	97,090.73	0.0720
Elastic Net	97,090.73	0.0720

It can be seen that boosting-based models outperformed traditional regression techniques significantly. Among them, CatBoost had the highest predictive accuracy with **RMSE** of **28,793.32** and **R^2 score** of **0.9057**, which means it explains about **90.57%** of the variance in used car prices.

Other boosting algorithms, such as XGBoost and LightGBM, also produced good results, which supported their efficiency in handling structured data once again. On the other hand, traditional regression models, Linear Regression, Ridge Regression, and Lasso Regression, had significantly higher errors, which supports the argument that these models are inadequate for capturing the complexity of the relationships in the dataset. In light of these results, the hyperparameters of the top three models, CatBoost, XGBoost, and LightGBM, were tuned to improve their performance even further.

4.3. Hyperparameter Optimization with Optuna

It is very important to tune hyperparameters of the machine learning models. Default parameter values are almost never optimal, and thus, there is a need to tune them to enhance the generalization. In order to do this, an automated optimization process was conducted using **Optuna**: a Bayesian optimization framework (Akiba et al., 2019).

Traditional methods like grid search, on the other hand, work by evaluating all the possible parameter combinations, which is a time-consuming process especially when the search space is large. **Optuna**, however, works by dynamically refining its search space based on the previous evaluations which reduces the computational cost while at the same time improving the convergence to the optimal parameters.

4.3.1. Hyperparameter Search Space and Optimization Strategy

The tuning process was performed on the key hyperparameters that control the tree complexity, learning efficiency, and regularization. **Table 3** below details the search space for each model for the critical parameters that affect predictive performance.

Table 3. Hyperparameter search space for CatBoost, XGBoost, and LightGBM

Model	Hyperparameter	Range
CatBoost	*iterations*	100 - 5000
	learning_rate	0.001 - 0.1
	depth	4 - 12
	l2_leaf_reg	2 - 10
	random_strength	0 - 10
XGBoost	*alpha*	0 - 1000
	min_child_weight	0 - 120
	subsample	0.5 - 1
	eta	0.1 - 0.5
	num_round	1 - 4000

continued on following page

Table 3. Continued

Model	Hyperparameter	Range
LightGBM	*learning_rate*	0.001 – 0.01
	num_leaves	0 - 100
	feature_fraction	0.1 - 100
	bagging_fraction	0.1 - 100
	bagging_freq	0 - 10
	max_depth	15 - 100
	min_data_in_leaf	10 - 200

The models were fine-tuned using 1000 trials and 5-fold cross validation to ensure robust performance estimation. The final optimized configurations were evaluated and the results are presented in **Table 4**.

Table 4. Performance of optimized models

Model	Optimized RMSE	Optimized R^2 Score
CatBoost	**27,568.31**	**0.9135**
XGBoost	28,125.78	0.9098
LightGBM	28,689.43	0.9052

The results show that hyperparameter tuning indeed enhanced model accuracy, decreasing RMSE and increasing R^2 scores. The optimized CatBoost model had the best performance with **RMSE** of **27,568.31** and **R^2 score** of **0.9135**. These enhancements highlight the importance of automated hyperparameter tuning for enhancing predictive capabilities.

4.4. Analysis of Residual and Learning Curve

The evaluation of machine learning model performance depends on more than just RMSE and R^2 value statistics. The behavior of a model becomes clearer through residual analysis and learning curves which help identify bias, variance problems and generalization capacity (James et al., 2013).

4.4.1. Residual Analysis

The analysis of residuals examines the quantities of errors which represent the differences between observed and forecasted values to verify that the model does not display any noticeable bias (Bishop, 2006).

The residual plot for the best model CatBoost Regressor in this study appears as **Figure 10**.

Key findings from residual analysis:

- **Symmetrical Residual Distribution:** This means that the model does not overestimate or underestimate the prices of cars and the residuals are equally distributed around zero.
- **Controlled Error Spread:** The majority of residual values lie within the reasonable range, which supports the accuracy of the estimates.
- **Constant Generalization Capability:** The training R^2 of 0.975 and the test R^2 of 0.909 show that the model is able to generalize well to the data that has not been seen before.

Figure 10. Residual distribution for CatBoost

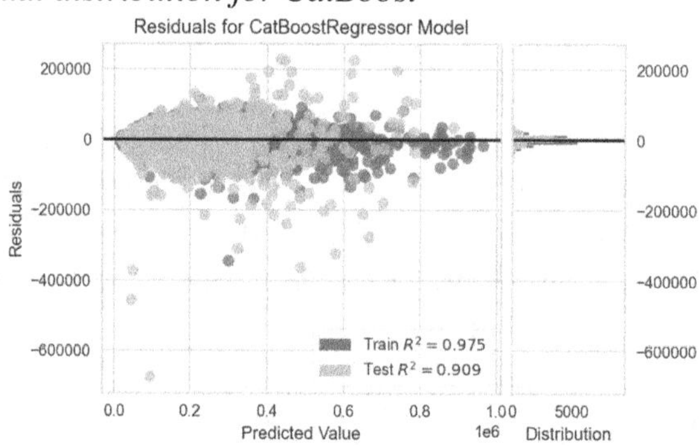

4.4.2. Learning Curve Analysis

Learning curves are useful for identifying whether the model is suffering from underfitting (lack of training) or overfitting (overemphasizing the training data at the expense of generalization). Monitoring the shifts in training and validation metrics is helpful in understanding the model behavior (Goodfellow et al., 2016).

The **Figure 11** depicts the learning curve of the CatBoost Regressor which shows how the performance of the model changes with increasing number of examples.

Key insights from the learning curve:

- **Sustainable Training Performance:** The model retains a high training accuracy, which indicates proper training.
- **Validation with Cross-Check:** The validation error decreases gradually, which indicates that more training data is beneficial for the generalization of the model.
- **Average Bias-Variance Tradeoff:** The graph of the training and validation scores indicates that the model does not overfit, thus supporting its reliability (Raschka, 2018)).

Figure 11. Learning curve for CatBoost

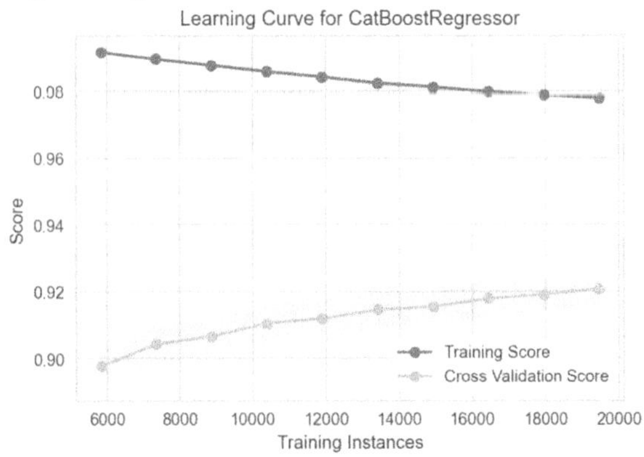

4.5. Model Interpretability Using SHAP

Majority of the used machine learning models include CatBoost, XGBoost, and LightGBM to name a few that offer high predictive accuracy but present a problem of explaining the thought process employed in arriving at particular price predictions.

This is because; while traditional linear regression models are easy to interpret due to the direct coefficient based explanation, these ensemble models capture feature interactions in a comprehensive manner to pose a challenge to interpretability. However, in the case of car price estimation it is important to know why a particular price was predicted to make the model more credible and understandable.

For the purpose of the above, SHapley Additive exPlanations (SHAP) was chosen as an interpretability framework. SHAP is a game theoretic interpretation that uses Shapley values to quantify the feature contribution to the model output. It offers two types of explanations: feature importance that shows the overall impact of the variables on the model's output and feature values that explain how each variable influenced the price of a given instance.

4.5.1. Global Feature Importance Analysis

In addition to the individual predictions, SHAP helps in identifying the most important factors that determine the prices of used cars across the entire dataset. The SHAP summary plot in **Figure 12** gives a ranked overview of feature importance.

Figure 12. SHAP summary plot of feature importance

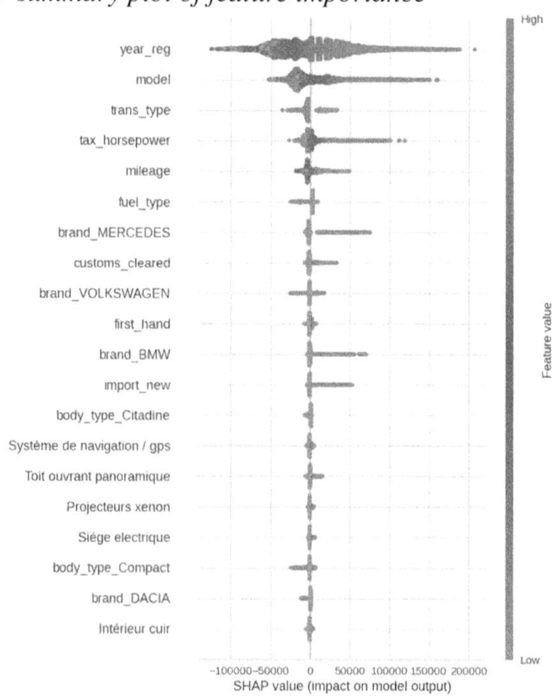

The analysis shows that *year_reg* is the most important feature, which is consistent with the previous analyses that stated that newer cars are more expensive. A higher value for *year_reg* has a positive effect on price since new cars are more desirable. The model variable is also highly influential in the price prediction process. Because this categorical feature was target encoded, its effect speaks to aggregated price trends for particular models, not to a direct numerical comparison. This transformation allows the model to use the brand effects efficiently.

The *trans_type* is another crucial determinant. Vehicles with automatic (*trans_type*=0) are more expensive than those with manual (*trans_type*=1) cars, which is consistent with market preferences. Similarly, *fuel_type* influences the price difference between gasoline (*fuel_type*=0) cars and diesel (*fuel_type*=1) cars. Other important factors are *mileage*, which has a negative effect on price, as well as several other features that are shown in **Figure 12**.

4.5.2. SHAP-Based Individual Prediction Analysis

It is imperative to grasp the notion of individual price forecasts so as to prevent any form of opacity. The SHAP force plot in **Figure 13** shows how different features affect the price of a particular prediction.

Figure 13. SHAP force plot for an individual prediction

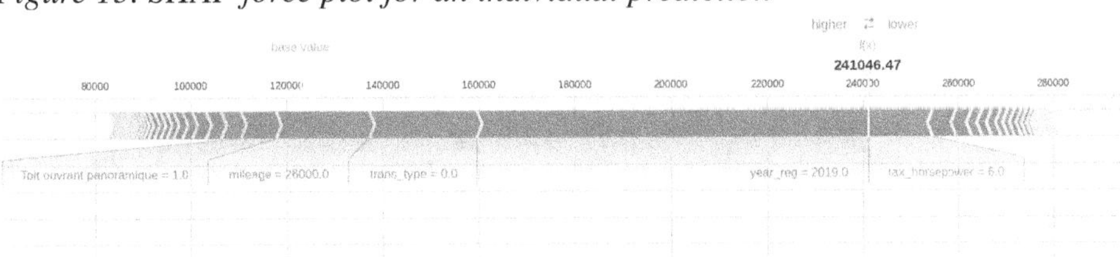

For a particular car listing, there are several key features that influence the estimated price of the car. One of the factors is the *mileage*; a car with lower mileage will have a higher price as used cars with low mileage are more desirable. It also has a positive contribution by being automatic, i.e., *trans_type=0* as people tend to prefer automatic cars owing to their ease of use.

Furthermore, there are some features which are options and they increase the price of the vehicle. In this particular example, panoramic sunroof *(Toit ouvrant panoramique=1)* is also seen as an added advantage and hence a preferred luxury feature.

On the other hand, a low value of fiscal horsepower *(tax_horsepower = 6)* is detrimental to the price. This means that cars with low tax horsepower are considered to be less powerful and, therefore, less interesting to buyers who are interested in performance. The model does a good job of encoding these pricing trends to ensure that its predictions are as close as possible to the actual market facts.

4.6. Comparison with Traditional Pricing Approaches

In the Moroccan market, car price estimation is traditionally performed using rule-based valuation systems, dealership experience, or expert opinion. While common, these approaches often lack consistency, transparency, and adaptability. Their reliance on human judgment also introduces subjectivity and bias.

In this study, CatBoost was employed with SHAP interpretability as its ML model which provides substantial advancements. The system uses data to generate objective prices and shows how specific features (e.g. mileage, fuel type) affect the prediction. The evaluation of traditional appraisal methods against rule-based pricing and machine learning approaches appears in **Table 5**.

Table 5. Used car price estimation methods comparison

Feature	Traditional Appraisal	Rule-Based System	ML-Based Model
Accuracy	Low to Medium	Medium	High
Transparency	Low	Low	High (via SHAP)
Bias Risk	High (human error)	Medium	Lower (auditable)
Scalability	Low	Medium	High
Update Flexibility	Low	Low	High (retrainable)

The evaluation demonstrates how contemporary ML models resolve fundamental problems that exist in traditional pricing systems. The combination of performance capabilities with explainability features in these models creates a deployable ethical framework for real-world applications.

The research by Zhang et al. (2018) has shown that manual and rule-based pricing methods have several limitations. The interpretability of ML models using SHAP has been demonstrated in recent AI transparency studies (Ribeiro et al., 2016; Lundberg & Lee, 2017).

4.7. Ethical Challenges in AI-Based Pricing

Machine learning models achieve better accuracy and scalability but generate ethical problems which affect consumer prices. One key issue is fairness. The model will maintain and strengthen existing biases from historical data when the training data contains systematic undervaluation of older vehicles and imported or less common vehicles thus producing unfair pricing recommendations.

Complex algorithms create another major problem because they lack transparency in their operations. Users who do not have SHAP tools will remain unable to understand the basis behind predicted prices. Users develop distrust when AI systems fail to provide clear explanations especially during crucial decisions about vehicle acquisitions or financing. AI systems need interpretable and traceable predictions to build trust and maintain accountability throughout their operations.

The research tackles these risks through SHAP implementation for both global and local explainability and proposes continuous prediction monitoring for bias detection and data drift assessment. AI pricing systems need ethical implementation which combines performance maintenance with user explanation transparency and fairness guarantees.

5. CONCLUSION

The research demonstrates that machine learning methods can effectively determine used car prices in the Moroccan market. The data set required division for machine learning algorithm analysis and cleaning and analysis purposes. CatBoost was chosen from the predictions as the best performing algorithm. The analysis also identified some important factors, such as the year of registration, mileage and transmission type, as the major factors that determine prices of vehicles. The model robustness was also enhanced through a detailed hyperparameter optimization and a very strong performance evaluation.

Besides predictive accuracy, interpretability was also emphasized to enhance the transparency of the model. To explain both global and individual feature importance, SHAP was used and the results showed very clearly that some attributes like car age, transmission type, and some brand attributes are very important in determining the price. The SHAP values of the model help in the understanding of the model in real-world applications like online marketplaces, car dealerships, and financial institutions.

While the model had a very high level of prediction precision, some constraints were noticed. Some prediction errors may be due to data collection biases because the prices are from postings of individual cars, and this may not be the same as the market prices. Therefore, the differences between the actual and predicted values could be that the model is actually capturing the real relationships between the characteristics of the cars and the actual market prices that are reasonable to expect, rather than the model being inaccurate.

From the practical viewpoint, full automation of the end-to-end workflow from data preparation, feature engineering, model training, and monitoring should make it possible to update the model regularly, and the model should be able to update itself to the market changes. The reliability and validity of the model can be ensured through the use of continuous learning methods. Also, the examination of other advanced models may lead to some additional understanding of the market mechanisms and consumer behavior.

In general, this research has great benefits to buyers, sellers, and automotive executives, specifically because of the use of advanced modeling strategies, the interpretability analysis, and the real-time web application. The improvement of the model in the automotive market in terms of precision, flexibility, and efficiency will be significantly enhanced by the continued expansion of the dataset, automated workflow, and advanced modeling techniques.

In future iterations of this work, the integration of emerging technologies could significantly enhance the adaptability and trustworthiness of the model. Blockchain can provide immutable records of vehicle ownership, service history, and accident data, offering a secure foundation for pricing. AI-powered negotiation systems may also personalize buyer-seller interactions by adapting price offers in real-time. Additionally, IoT-connected vehicles can supply live data on usage patterns, helping the model produce even more dynamic and accurate price recommendations. These innovations represent promising paths toward a fully intelligent, transparent, and automated vehicle pricing ecosystem.

REFERENCES

Ali, M., Arora, A., & Kapoor, A. (2020). PyCaret: An open-source, low-code machine learning library. *Journal of Machine Learning Research, 21*(245), 1–6.

Bishop, C. M. (2006). *Pattern recognition and machine learning*. Springer.

Breiman, L. (2001). Random forests. *Machine Learning, 45*(1), 5–32. DOI: 10.1023/A:1010933404324

Brown, T. (2019). *An introduction to polynomial regression*. https://www.datascience.com/blog/introduction-to-polynomial-regression

Corbett-Davies, S., Pierson, E., Feller, A., Goel, S., & Huq, A. (2018). Algorithmic decision making and the cost of fairness. *Proceedings of the ACM SIGKDD*, 797–806.

Cortes, C., & Vapnik, V. (1995). Support-vector networks. *Machine Learning, 20*(3), 273–297. DOI: 10.1007/BF00994018

European Commission. (2020). *Ethics guidelines for trustworthy AI*. High-Level Expert Group on AI. https://ec.europa.eu/newsroom/dae/document.cfm?doc_id=60419

Goodfellow, I., Bengio, Y., & Courville, A. (2016). *Deep learning*. MIT Press.

Grath, R., & Buskirk, P. (2019). Monitoring and detecting drift in predictive models: An industry perspective. *Journal of Data Science and Analytics, 7*(3), 112–129. DOI: 10.1016/j.jdsan.2019.03.005

IEEE. (2019). *Ethically aligned design: A vision for prioritizing human well-being with autonomous and intelligent systems* (1st ed.). https://ethicsinaction.ieee.org/

James, G., Witten, D., Hastie, T., & Tibshirani, R. (2013). *An introduction to statistical learning: With applications in R* (Vol. 103). Springer., DOI: 10.1007/978-1-4614-7138-7

Javed, A., Hussain, S., & Ali, M. (2022). Machine learning in automotive pricing: A case study from South Asia. *Applied Artificial Intelligence, 36*(1), 1–17.

Kumar, S., & Ashok, V. (2020). A comparative study on machine learning models for price prediction. *International Journal of Artificial Intelligence & Applications, 11*(2), 45–53. DOI: 10.5121/ijaia.2020.11204

LeCun, Y., Bengio, Y., & Hinton, G. (2015). Deep learning. *Nature, 521*(7553), 436–444. DOI: 10.1038/nature14539 PMID: 26017442

Lin, W., Zhang, H., & Xu, J. (2021). Predictive pricing of second-hand vehicles using XGBoost in emerging markets. *Journal of Intelligent Systems, 30*(2), 205–220.

Lundberg, S. M., & Lee, S. I. (2017). A unified approach to interpreting model predictions. *Advances in Neural Information Processing Systems, 30*, 4765–4774. DOI: 10.48550/arXiv.1705.07874

Merkel, D. (2014). Docker: Lightweight Linux containers for consistent development and deployment. *Linux Journal, 2014*(239), 2.

Mitchell, R. (2015). *Web scraping with Python: Collecting more data from the modern web*. O'Reilly Media.

Morocco World News. (2023, August). Automotive industry exports in Morocco soar to $11 billion in 2022. *Morocco World News*. https://www.moroccoworldnews.com/2023/08/357041/automotive-industry-exports-in-morocco-soar-to-11-billion-in-2022

Munzert, S., Rubba, C., Meißner, P., & Nyhuis, D. (2015). *Automated data collection with R: A practical guide to web scraping and text mining*. Wiley.

Pedregosa, F., Varoquaux, G., Gramfort, A., Michel, V., Thirion, B., Grisel, O., & Duchesnay, E. (2011). Scikit-learn: Machine learning in Python. *Journal of Machine Learning Research, 12*, 2825–2830.

Prokhorenkova, L., Gusev, G., Vorobev, A., Dorogush, A. V., & Gulin, A. (2018). CatBoost: Unbiased boosting with categorical features. *Advances in Neural Information Processing Systems, 31*, 6638–6648. https://proceedings.neurips.cc/paper/2018/hash/14491b756b449614c919e6a0a8682cd3-Abstract.html

Raschka, S. (2018). *Python machine learning: Machine learning and deep learning with Python, scikit-learn, and TensorFlow 2*. Packt Publishing.

Ribeiro, M. T., Singh, S., & Guestrin, C. (2016). "Why should I trust you?" Explaining the predictions of any classifier. In *Proceedings of the 22nd ACM SIGKDD International Conference on Knowledge Discovery and Data Mining* (pp. 1135–1144). ACM.

Stone, M. (1974). Cross-validation: A review. *Mathematical Modeling and Statistical Computation, 36*, 111–133.

Sundararajan, M., & Najmi, A. (2020). The many Shapley values for model explanation. *Proceedings of the 37th International Conference on Machine Learning (ICML 2020)*. https://proceedings.mlr.press/v119/sundararajan20a.html

Taylor, R., Brown, P., & Adams, S. (2019). Vehicle price prediction system using machine learning techniques. *International Journal of Advanced Computer Science and Applications, 10*(4), 123–130. https://www.researchgate.net/publication/317608326_Vehicle_Price_Prediction_System_using_Machine_Learning_Techniques

Zaharia, M., Xin, R., Wendell, P., Das, T., Armbrust, M., Dave, A., & Ghodsi, A. (2018). MLflow: A platform for managing the machine learning lifecycle. In *Proceedings of the 27th International Conference on Machine Learning (ICML).*

Zhang, T., & Ahmed, S. (2022). Fair pricing through explainable machine learning. *AI & Society, 37*(2), 456–470. DOI: 10.1007/s00146-021-01232-4

Zhang, Y. (2018). *A used car price evaluation model based on neural network* [Master's thesis, Tianjin University].

KEY TERMS AND DEFINITIONS

CatBoost: A gradient boosting algorithm that handles categorical data efficiently and is known for its high accuracy and performance on structured datasets.

Cross-Validation (CV): A model evaluation method that divides the data into subsets in order to ensure that the model will perform well on data that it has not seen before.

Data Drift: This is a phenomenon where there is a change in the statistical properties of the input data as it is collected over time, which may cause model degradation.

Feature Engineering: The conversion of raw data into relevant input variables that will enhance the model accuracy.

Hyperparameter Tuning: The process of optimizing a machine learning model by changing parameters that are defined before training the model to enhance its performance.

Machine Learning (ML): A branch of artificial intelligence (AI) that lets computers learn from data and make predictions or decisions without being explicitly programmed.

Regression Analysis: A statistical method used in predictive modeling to examine the relationship between a dependent variable (target) and one or more independent variables (features).

SHAP (Shapley Additive Explanations): A model interpretability technique that uses Shapley values to quantify how each feature contributes to the model's decision when making a prediction.

Web Scraping: The process of extracting data from websites using automated tools to create datasets for analysis.

Yeo-Johnson Transformation: A method used to improve the normality of numerical features. Unlike log or Box-Cox transformations, it can be applied to both positive and negative values.

Chapter 10
The Artificial Intelligence Revolution and The Moroccan Stock Market's Efficiency:
GPT3 Versus GPT4

Youness Ait Oummou
https://orcid.org/0000-0002-7423-1325
Cadi Ayyad University, Morocco

Driss Omerani
Cadi Ayyad University, Morocco

ABSTRACT

The present chapter examines the effect of artificial intelligence (AI), particularly the ChatGPT-3 and ChatGPT-4 models, on the efficiency of the Moroccan stock market. The chapter is founded upon an empirical approach mobilizing quantile regression analysis. Through this empirical approach, the chapter explores the contribution of AI tools to market efficiency, thereby offering a novel perspective on the Adaptive Market Hypothesis (AMH). The findings of the study reveal a varied effect of AI on the efficiency of the Moroccan stock market, accompanied by noteworthy observations and discernible distinctions between the two models examined. This chapter is intended to stimulate further reflection on the effect of artificial intelligence (AI) on financial markets and the potential for technological advancement in this domain to enhance overall market efficiency.

DOI: 10.4018/979-8-3373-5499-6.ch010

INTRODUCTION

Since the onset of the Industrial Revolution, technological progress has served as the primary catalyst for economic and social transformation, resulting in substantial changes in living conditions and the production of goods and services. In the contemporary economic landscape, characterized by profound complexity, organizations are compelled to address challenges necessitating a capacity for adaptation and continuous innovation. From an evolutionary perspective, Nelson & Winter (1982) conceptualize companies as organisms evolving within an economic ecosystem, motivated by the incessant pursuit of innovative methods to increase profits.

In a global context of liberalization, organizations are obliged to identify optimal financing solutions, notably through the use of financial markets, in particular stock markets. The validity of this assertion depends on the presence of an efficient market that can direct investors' funds toward the most profitable investment opportunities. In this regard, Fama (1965, 1970) conceptualizes an efficient market as an environment in which the prices of financial instruments reflect all available information. This state of affairs emerges as a consequence of a sufficient number of rational actors seeking to predict the future path of prices. However, as Herbert Simon's (1957, 1982) principle of bounded rationality asserts, human decision-making is not necessarily rational. Rather, it is limited by cognitive capacities, the stock of available information, and the temporal requirements of information management. This principle led to the emergence of the behaviorist movement, which postulates that markets frequently deviate from the ideal state of efficiency. Conversely, Andrew Lo (2004, 2005, 2017) employs an evolutionary perspective analogous to that of Nelson & Winter (1982), proposing that markets do not function as either completely efficient or completely inefficient systems, but rather demonstrate adaptability between these two extreme states. In this theoretical framework, market participants make adaptive decisions based on their respective feedbacks, and the formulated strategy is maintained as long as it is profitable. However, when the strategy becomes unprofitable, innovation becomes imperative to ensure the survival of invested capital.

In this particular context, the advent of Artificial Intelligence has fostered innovation that facilitates the automation of data analysis tasks and the formulation of creative recommendations. This, in turn, enables actors to adapt to different changes, thereby helping to improve decision-making processes at both the individual and institutional levels. The information processing theory (Wickens & Carswell, 2021) asserts that Artificial Intelligence (AI) enables the information processing of large amounts of data while noticing patterns that humans often miss in their decision-making (De Bruijn et al., 2022). Artificial Intelligence (AI) uses machine learning algorithms and other similar technologies to improve this, by taking human limitations into account (Podina & Caculidis-Tudor, 2023). The use of artificial intelligence tools has the ability to create new, sustainable results because they are quick and have accurate decision-making (Ali et al., 2024). The emergence of Artificial Intelligence is thus an invention that is likely going to change stock markets in a big way, affecting investors, professionals as well as companies offering securities. Changes in technology are causing a radical change in how we obtain information and make decisions. Artificial Intelligence systems, such as the linguistic model ChatGPT, which has quickly become popular since its inception in 2022, are already being extensively used for price forecasting, trend identification, and risk analysis. Such tools can improve market conditions and therefore move you to the ideal state of efficiency.

Despite the growing interest of researchers in artificial intelligence (AI), the existing literature reveals significant gaps.

With the exception of Almeida & Gonçalves (2024), who explicitly investigate the evolution of the degree of efficiency of cryptocurrency markets after the introduction of ChatGPT, no study, whether focused on developed or emerging markets, has directly investigated the effect of the advent of ChatGPT on market efficiency.

Furthermore, extant literature in both developed and emerging contexts predominantly emphasizes the predictive capacities of Large Language Models (LLMs), neglecting to formally evaluate their effect on market efficiency dynamics (see, e.g., Misra & Chaurasia, 2020; Ifleh & El Kabbouri, 2021; Mohanty et al., 2021; Chhajer et al., 2022; Oukhouya & El Himdi, 2023; Lin & Marques, 2024).

Furthermore, studies that examine the effect of the advent of AI tools on less developed financial markets, such as the Moroccan stock market, are scarce, despite their pertinence for analyzing the role of advanced technologies in enhancing efficiency in contexts characterized by various constraints (e.g., liquidity, number of listed companies, market size, etc.).

Moreover, novel artificial intelligence technologies, notably ChatGPT developed by Openai, are garnering mounting interest within the Moroccan context. A survey administered by the Boston Consulting Group between August and September of 2023 in 21 countries revealed that Morocco is the second country worldwide in terms of utilization of the artificial intelligence tool ChatGPT (Boston Consulting Group, 2024).

In light of the aforementioned limitations in the extant literature, this chapter seeks to address the following research question:

To what extent does the advent of artificial intelligence, notably through the ChatGPT-3 and ChatGPT-4 tools, affect the efficiency of the Moroccan stock market?

The study places particular emphasis on the Moroccan market due to its distinctive characteristics as a less developed market, where the adoption of advanced technologies such as Artificial Intelligence (AI) by market participants holds the potential to substantially enhance efficiency.

Therefore, the aim of this chapter is to analyze the effect of the ChatGPT-3 and 4 technological tools on the dynamics of Moroccan market efficiency. For this reason, the rest of this chapter is structured into four sections. Section 2 explores the theoretical framework for the evolution of financial market Efficiency in the light of the Adaptive Market Hypothesis (AMH), focusing on the role of innovation in terms of Artificial Intelligence technologies. Section 3 describes the materials and methods used to analyze our data, shedding light on the Adjusted market inefficiency magnitude (AMIM) measure and quantile regression methodology. Section 4 presents and discusses the main empirical results of our study. Finally, the last section concludes the chapter.

LITERATURE REVIEW: ARTIFICIAL INTELLIGENCE AND THE DYNAMICS OF FINANCIAL MARKET EFFICIENCY

The Adaptive Market Hypothesis: An Evolutionary Perspective on Market Efficiency and Adaptation

For many years, the Efficient Market Hypothesis (EMH) formulated by Fama (1965, 1970) was the predominant paradigm in finance. This hypothesis postulates that financial asset prices incorporate all relevant and available market information. This ideal condition of financial market efficiency is simply the result of the existence of a sufficient number of rational investors, who are in permanent competition to predict the future trajectory of financial instrument prices. This competitive dynamic automatically implies the exploitation of all information resources, and their mobilization in the decision-making process, which guarantees their incorporation into the purchase and sale prices of financial instruments. Consequently, in the context of efficient markets, prices instantly reflect the consensual and aggregated valuation of all market participants, based on all available information.

In a later work, Fama (1970) defined three key conditions for efficient price adjustment in financial markets. These conditions, central to market efficiency, determine the mechanisms by which the information is reflected in prices:

Absence of transaction costs: To ensure efficient price adjustment, the buying and selling of securities must not be constrained by costs (for example; commissions, taxes, etc.), which could slow down arbitrage, and therefore delay the process of incorporating information and adjusting prices.

Free access to information for all participants: All market participants must have unrestricted access to all information, including financial data, listed company reports and macroeconomic indicators. This condition of transparency prevents any kind of information asymmetry, which can restrict the process of market efficiency.

Rational consensus on the implications of information: Market participants must share a common collective understanding of the impact of relevant available information on the valuation of financial instruments. Without this condition, divergent points of view would lead to excessive volatility, which could be detrimental to the balancing of market prices.

In this context, D'Avolio et al. (2001) have articulated four fundamental conditions that are necessary for the proper functioning of financial markets;

Availability of information: The first condition is the availability of information to all participants, who must have access to all data. If this condition is not met, and information is insufficient to value financial instruments accurately, rational investors will no longer choose to invest their funds in the stock market, but will be interested in placing these funds in risk-free assets or low-yield bank accounts. Conversely, if investors are rational and have all the relevant information at their disposal, they will incorporate the new information into their decision-making in order to maximize their returns. In this case, the decisions taken by these actors have a direct influence on the prices of the securities in question, through the mechanisms of supply and demand. In the absence of information, markets risk stagnating, as only professional investors and specialists with access to information will be able to make optimal decisions.

Investor atomicity: The second condition is investor atomicity, which implies a large number of small investors who cannot influence share prices on their own. In this case, there is no single participant with the power to distort the trajectory of prices. This situation also protects the market from any systemic risk, by ensuring good risk diversification.

Protection of market participants: The third condition is the protection of market participants. Even in the presence of information shared by all parties, financial markets can stagnate if investor protection is not guaranteed. Legislation and regulation must protect all actors, which will help to build confidence in the market and, consequently, stimulate liquidity.

Market liquidity: The fourth condition is liquidity. Investors often take into account the size of the market and the volume of transactions, as well as the possibility of trading on the secondary market, when deciding to acquire securities. As a result, liquidity appears to be an essential factor, complementing the aforementioned conditions. Investors are more inclined to animate the market by opening positions in securities, especially when choices and opportunities are numerous and transaction costs are low.

Although the aforementioned conditions are fundamental principles for the proper functioning of financial markets, in reality they are often imperfectly met. Far from a totally efficient market, major financial institutions and central banks exert a significant influence on prices, calling into question the atomicity hypothesis. Similarly, investor protection and liquidity, especially in the context of less developed markets, remain widely debated. In the same perspective, the key principle of actor rationality assumed in the case of efficient markets has been the subject of wide-academic debate, more specifically among proponents of the behavioral school of thought.

This school of thought stipulates those financial markets are far from being qualified as efficient, and that economic agents are not at all totally rational. The roots of this school of thought go back to the principle of bounded rationality introduced by Simon (1957, 1982). According to this principle, the decision-making process for human beings is not necessarily rational, but this process is often limited by several factors such as cognitive abilities, time and the informational resources needed to make optimal decisions.

In this approach, Andrew Lo (2004, 2005, 2017) starts from an evolutionary perspective, proposing that financial markets are neither totally efficient nor completely inefficient, but they do have one universal characteristic; “Adaptation”.

In this context, investors and different market participants make decisions that adapt to different levels of market ecology. This process of learning from past mistakes ensures the refinement of decision-making skills over time, leading to optimal outcomes. A profitable strategy is maintained until it is demonstrated to be ineffective, at which point innovation intervenes to identify and implement new strategies.

As posited by Lo (2017, p. 188), the catalyst for market dynamics is survival, with these dynamics emerging solely from competition, innovation, and adaptation.

Artificial Intelligence (AI): an Innovative Technology

Innovation is a concept with a long history, founded on two main pillars: the originality and practical usefulness of the new idea introduced (Godin, 2015; Granstrand & Holgersson, 2020; Opesemowo, 2025). The originality of the innovation, in this context, is not confined to a mere invention, but rather signifies a departure from prevailing paradigms, whether in an incremental or revolutionary manner. Conversely, practical utility signifies the implementation of innovation in the tangible realm, transcending theoretical abstraction to address specific, demonstrable needs that enhance people's quality of life.

Technological innovation, in this regard, can be conceptualized as a cumulative process of knowledge and practice, the evolution of which can be associated with the transformation, diffusion, and progressive dynamics of a given technology (Christensen, 2015; Lee & Lee, 2013).

In the context of Artificial Intelligence (AI), novelty can manifest itself in the creation or development of new algorithms, or a paradigm change in the methodologies applied in problem-solving processes. On the other hand, the usefulness of this field can be measured by the impact of Artificial Intelligence, which can be attributed to the growth in adoption of these new technologies in various industrial, health and economic fields. So, the technological innovation of Artificial Intelligence (AI) tools represents a dynamic evolutionary process similar to the idea of creative destruction in Schumpeter's (1942) sense, where the progress of Artificial Intelligence (AI) tools presents a revolution that systematically disrupts and reconstructs not only the technological environment, but also the landscape of various sectors.

In this regard, artificial intelligence was first introduced in 1955 as a concept defined as the ability of machines to think and perform tasks that mimic human behavior (McCarthy et al., 2006; Kaplan & Haenlein, 2019; Gama & Magistretti, 2025). According to Marwala (2009, 2014; Marwala & Hurwitz, 2017), artificial intelligence can be defined to mean computational paradigm which codifies high-level cognitive and organizational capabilities, normally identified biological and physical systems, to solve problems autonomously. Kaplan and Haenlein, 2019 give a shorter definition of AI. According to this definition, systems with artificial intelligence can accurately interpret incoming data, learn from it, and then use it to perform specific tasks that require adaptive responses.

The advancement of the Artificial intelligence technology is largely due to the rapid advancement in machine learning and deep learning as well as the explosion in available data volumes. Consequently, machines can perform tasks as complex as interpreting natural language, recognizing images and making autonomous decisions (Brynjolfsson & McAfee, 2014; Jordan & Mitchell, 2015; Guler et al.,2024). At present, artificial intelligence (AI) definitely positions itself as a central transformational lever in all fields, especially in the economic and financial ones. It involves streamlining operational processes and systems, optimizing strategies, and reinforcing decision-making precision. The benefits of this brings about significant economic and strategic advantages according to a research paper by Kshetri et al. 2023.

Recently, the Revolution in Artificial Intelligence is especially evident in the appearance of large-scale language models like OpenAI's ChatGPT versions, most famously GPT3 and GPT4. These models, based on deep learning architectures, tend to market themselves as super algorithms poised to automate natural language and complex problem-solving innovations (Brown et al., 2020; Bouschery et al., 2023; Lund et al., 2023). Tools of this nature have been put to use in a plethora of ways, including the creation of conversational agents suited for dialogue in specific settings, as well as the automatic generation of novel text (Kshetri et al., 2023; Radford et al., 2019; Guler et al., 2024; Siddik et al., 2025). Such advances suggest that this revolution in Artificial Intelligence (AI) goes beyond algorithmic capabilities, but rather seeks to blur the line between machine and human potential, raising a multitude of possibilities for years to come. Once OpenAI launched GPT-4 in 2023, most analysts considered it a minor enhancement from its predecessor GPT-3. In reality, this advancement stemmed from a technological development that is quietly transformative. Contrary to the marketing fanfare that accompanied the previous versions, GPT-4 was released without any details on the model's architecture or scale. OpenAI has opted for secrecy, for reasons of security and the ever-increasing competition in this field. Despite the absence of a formal reveal, it is clear that significant progress has been made.

The size of the contextual window: GPT-4 is generally ten times larger than GPT-3, with an estimated 1,700 billion parameters compared with 175 billion for GPT-4 (Koubaa, 2023 This substantial increase in the number of parameters enables GPT-4 to achieve an unprecedented degree of contextual understanding. Whereas GPT-3 can process long texts (8192 tokens), GPT-4 easily analyzes them without losing the thread - thanks to a contextual memory extended to 32,768 tokens (the equivalent of 50 pages). A crucial advance for data analysts and investors working on multi-page company reports.

Multimodality: For the first time, a GPT model can see the world, with the ability to process images. This new version (ChatGPT-4) represents a revolution in this respect, in that it is now possible to analyze graphs to summarize trends, detect price deviations and so more.

Security: GPT-4 marks a turning point in risk management. With RBRM (Rule-Based Reward Models), OpenAI has integrated "automatic rules" to block dangerous or illegal responses. Unlike the old version (GPT-3), which could sometimes provide instructions that didn't comply with predefined regulations, GPT-4 categorically denies them due to RBRM.

In this respect, Table 1 presents a comparative analysis of the performance of ChatGPT-3 and ChatGPT-4, two tools that have undergone significant advances. Despite the fact that the two languages share many common features, as evidenced by their use of a single transformer architectural model, even though at different scales (See; Brown et al., 2020; Ouyang et al., 2022; Koubaa, 2023).

Table 1. Performance comparison; GPT-3 vs GPT-4

EXAM	GPT-4 (PERCENTILE)	GPT-3 (PERCENTILE)
ADVANCED PLACEMENT (AP) MICROECONOMICS	5 (82nd-100th)	4 (60th-82nd)
AP MACROECONOMICS	5 (84th-100th)	2 (33rd-48th)
SCHOLASTIC ASSESSMENT TEST (SAT) MATH	700/800 (89th)	590/800 (70th)
GRADUATE RECORD EXAMINATION (GRE) QUANTITATIVE	163/170 (80th)	147/170 (25th)

Source: OpenAI (2023)

In terms of performance, the GPT-4 has been shown to outperform the GPT-3 in economics and mathematics, as evidenced by its outstanding results on standardized exams. Specifically, it achieves the highest possible scores (5/5) on the AP Macroeconomics (percentile 84-100) and Microeconomics (percentile 82-100) exams, clearly outperforming the GPT-3, which fails the Macroeconomics exam (percentile 33-48). In mathematics, GPT-4 demonstrates a marked superiority in the SAT Math (700/800, 89th percentile) and GRE Quantitative (163/170, 80th percentile) exams, significantly outperforming GPT-3.5, which reaches the 70th and 25th percentiles in these assessments. This superiority can be attributed to its enhanced ability to process complex concepts and solve multi-step problems, even in the absence of visual ability. The GPT-4's improved contextual memory (32k tokens vs. 8k for the GPT-3) and more rigorous reasoning capabilities make it a reference tool of interest in many fields, including academia and demanding professional domains.

Artificial Intelligence at the Service of Market Efficiency: Towards a Systemic Revolution

The advent of sophisticated algorithms has led to the emergence of artificial intelligence (AI) as a pivotal catalyst for radical transformations in the financial market environment. This is achieved by facilitating search, analysis and exploitation of big data, allowing market prices to integrate this information at low cost.

According to the Adaptive Market Hypothesis, financial market participants are neither totally rational nor entirely irrational, but their behavior is adaptive in nature, with decisions that are satisfactory in Simon's sense in relation to their previous experiences (Lo, 2017). In the context of crises or shifting market ecologies, investors generally need time to apprehend the context and act objectively, which can give rise to heuristics, and consequently biased decisions. In this respect, Artificial Intelligence tools can intervene at this level, attenuating certain cognitive biases by providing objective analyses even in turbulent situations. Except that these tools can also reproduce or amplify these biases, especially if their algorithms are trained on biased historical data, or if databases are very limited, which can reinforce existing behavioral patterns rather than correct them.

The literature on adaptive markets recognizes that financial markets are environments where investment strategies evolve in response to market conditions. Artificial intelligence tools can accelerate this evolution, enabling the rapid identification of inefficiencies and the adaptation of innovative investment strategies to new contexts.

In this way, Artificial Intelligence (AI) can access and strategically use massive data to influence informational dynamics and limit informational asymmetries (Hadjitchoneva, 2020). The advent of artificial intelligence (AI) has made it possible to analyze massive amounts of data in real time, making it easier to identify invisible correlations, anticipate risks, and refine decision-making processes. This ability to transform information overload into actionable knowledge significantly reduces uncertainty at both the macro (market fluctuations, regulatory changes) and micro (cost management, resource allocation) levels.

From the same angle, the use of Artificial Intelligence (AI) tools in risk management appears to be gaining attention in the financial industry (Bussmann et al., 2021; Hemphill and Kelley, 2021; Larkin et al., 2022; Milojević & Redzepagic, 2021; Morgan et al., 2023; Weber et al., 2024; Kismawadi et al., 2024). Because of technological developments, decision making in risk management can now be AI powered. This is achieved by exploiting massive volumes of data, mobilizing advanced algorithms capable of guaranteeing objective decisions when it comes to quantifying different risks.

Artificial Intelligence therefore represents a major area of high added value for the financial industry, particularly in financial data analysis, decision-making and risk management.

In this regard, the advent of sophisticated linguistic models, such as ChatGPT, has elicited a marked increase of interest in the empirical literature, particularly with regard to their capacity to forecast stock market returns. Nevertheless, there is a paucity of studies that have explicitly examined their influence on market efficiency. Recent research has centered on the capacity of these models to process and interpret financial information, a prerequisite for extracting signals that can be utilized in investment decision-making.

Lopez-Lira & Tang's (2023) study, based on US stock market news headlines between October 2021 and December 2023, demonstrated that ChatGPT-4 is able to make significant predictions regarding daily returns, particularly for small-cap stocks, and in response to negative news, by reducing arbitrage opportunities. In a different context, Almeida & Gonçalves (2024) examined the effects of AI on crypto-currency markets, particularly after the launch of ChatGPT-3. Using the AMIM index and quantile analyses, the study highlights an improvement in crypto-currency efficiency associated with artificial intelligence. This translates into improved liquidity and more stable returns after the advent of ChatGPT.

Ma et al. (2024) analyzes the Chinese market in particular and emphasizes the impact language models have. In their research, Ma et al. (2024) shows that analyzing news headlines with ChatGPT-3.5 is far better than the Bag-of-Words (BoW) approach in predicting the weekly risk premium. ChatGPT and DeepSeek's predictive capability is examined by Chen et al. (2025) for not just the stock market return (S&P500) but also US macroeconomic factors, using Wall Street Journal headlines from 1996 to 2022. Chen et al. show that ChatGPT has the upper hand in predicting market trends and DeepSeek appears to be the underdog. This implies that it is important to point out that not every assessment appears to be constructive. Xie et al. (2023) take a zero-shot stance on evaluating the multimodal stock market prediction capabilities of ChatGPT using price data and tweets as input data. This method is known as zero-shot learning, where one uses a model without any domain-specific fine-tuning—in this case, ChatGPT. Although there is ample interest in this method and in the capability of ChatGPT-3 to leverage social information, Xie et al. (2023)'s results suggest that the approach is outclassed by simpler models like LSTM or Transformers.

Finally, Saggu & Ante (2023) assess the impact ChatGPT3 has had on AI related crypto assets. Using a synthetic control approach as well as attention metrics (Google search volume and financial news coverage), they show that there was a marked increase in the returns on these assets from November 2022.

This increase is primarily attributed to heightened attention from retail investors, indicating that AI can influence not only fundamentals but also market behaviors via attentional channels.

In summary, recent literature highlights the potential of artificial intelligence as a catalyst for the ideal state of market efficiency. This is achieved by enabling prices to instantly reflect all available information, thus rectifying information asymmetries and price adjustment costs. The capacity of sophisticated algorithms to assimilate not only economic data into analyses but also unstructured data (e.g., weather, social networks, images) has the potential to anticipate various environmental, social, and economic trends. Concurrently, Artificial Intelligence (AI) could contribute to the trend towards the representative agent concept, in which investors anonymously share predictive data with Artificial Intelligence (AI) tools, creating consensus on data interpretation objectively and without revealing strategic secrets. This revolution suggests stimulating markets to channel resources towards the most productive activities, while limiting the transaction costs associated with acquiring and processing information.

MATERIAL AND METHODS

Adjusted Market Inefficiency Magnitude (AMIM)

To model the dynamics of the Moroccan stock market's efficiency, we mobilize the recent measurement proposed by Le Tran & Leirvik (2019): Adjusted Market Inefficiency Magnitude. This measure has been widely used in the financial literature to analyze the behavior of financial market efficiency in different economic scenarios (see, for example, Le Tran & Leirvik, 2019; Mokni et al., 2020; Okoroafor & Leirvik, 2022; Almeida & Gonçalves, 2024; Bock & Geissel, 2024; Wei et al., 2024).

The approach proposed by Le Tran & Leirvik's (2019) is based on the pragmatic interpretation of Fama's (1970) Efficient Market Hypothesis, which implies that past returns cannot be used to forecast future stock market returns.

In the context of our study, assuming the Efficient Market Hypothesis (EMH) of Fama (1965, 1970), the βi coefficients associated to the autoregressive terms $AR(p)$ are expected to be significantly null.

$$AR_{(p)} : R_t = \beta_0 + \sum_{i=1}^{p} \beta_i R_{t-i} + \varepsilon_t \tag{1}$$

Contrary to the approach adopted by Lo (2004) which takes into account only the first AR term, Le Tran & Leirvik (2019) argue that the efficiency condition may be doubted as the number of non-zero AR parameters increases. A common approach to compute AMIM is to use Cholesky decomposition with the objective of establishing a consistent comparison of the estimated coefficients $\widehat{\beta}_i$.

This standardization step is necessary to avoid any biases related to the size of the coefficients $\widehat{\beta}_i$ and their different levels of correlation.

It can therefore be concluded that the standardized coefficient vector, which is assumed to follow a normal distribution, is implemented in the Market Inefficiency Magnitude (MIM) calculation as follows:

$$MIM_t = \frac{\sum_{i=1}^{p} \left| \widehat{\beta}_{i,i}^{standard} \right|}{1 + \sum_{i=1}^{p} \left| \widehat{\beta}_{i,i}^{standard} \right|} \tag{2}$$

This measure which is defined as the aggregation of the absolute values of the standardized coefficients, is normalized by oscillating within the interval [0, 1]. Using absolute values eliminates the sign effect of the coefficients, allowing to focus exclusively on violations of the Efficient Market Hypothesis. A value of MIM_t close to 0 indicates that the market is efficient, a situation where past returns have no impact on future trajectories. Conversely, a value approaching 1 signifies market inefficiency, where past returns exert a substantial influence on the future trajectory of those returns.

Despite the fact that MIM_t measures market efficiency, the number of lags in equation (1) can lead to an overestimation of inefficiency due to the high number of lags in the estimated model. To address this limitation, Le Tran & Leirvik (2019) propose an adjusted measure that corrects the overestimation by subtracting a threshold R_{CI} from the MIM_t and normalizing the value as follows:

$$AMIM_t = \frac{MIM_t - R_{CI}}{1 - R_{CI}} \quad (3)$$

In this case, if the measure $AMIM_t \leq 0$, it can be deduced that the measure $AMIM_t$ lies within the 95% confidence interval calculated under the efficient hypothesis. Consequently, the market is deemed efficient. Conversely, if the measure $AMIM_t > 0$, this signifies that the measure $AMIM_t$ surpasses the critical threshold R_{CI}, as determined by Monte Carlo simulations. This finding suggests market inefficiency, indicating that past returns significantly influence future returns.

To quantify the evolution of Moroccan stock market efficiency, we implement the methodology of one-year rolling windows (That is to say, precisely 250 days) to calculate the $AMIM_t$ measures, in accordance with the recommendations of Le Tran & Leirvik (2019, 2020).

Data and Econometric Methodology

The present study is rooted in a post-positivist epistemology, which places significant emphasis on empirical observation and the validation of hypotheses through quantitative data analysis. The reasoning adopted is of a hypothetico-deductive nature, in which the hypotheses are formulated on the basis of existing literature, then tested using empirical verification based on real data, specifically the closing prices of the MASI (Moroccan All Shares Index) covering the period from January 03, 2022 to January 02, 2025.

These closing prices are transformed into logarithmic returns to calculate the AMIM (Adjusted Market Inefficiency Magnitude) indicator. Subsequently, a quantile regression modeling approach is implemented to examine the contribution of Artificial Intelligence to the efficiency of the Moroccan stock market. Specifically, the study evaluates the effect of GPT-3 and GPT-4 on AMIM, while considering other factors that may influence the dynamics of Moroccan stock market efficiency.

This is made possible by adopting a quantile regression approach, which is particularly suited to analyzing the effect of Artificial Intelligence (AI) on the efficiency (low quantiles) and inefficiency (high quantiles) of the Moroccan stock market.

The following is the general specification of our quantile regression (QR) model:

$$Q(AMIM_t)(r) = \beta_0(r) + \sum_{j=1}^{4}\sum_{i=1}^{q}\beta_{1,i,j}(r).\ Controle_j + \sum_{j}^{2}\sum_{i=1}^{q}\beta_{2,i}(r).\ AI_j \tag{4}$$

Therefore, $Q(AMIM_t)(r)$ denotes the value relative to the AMIM quantile (r) at time t.

The term $Controle_j$ is employed to denote the control variable j, which is presumed to exert an influence on the AMIM level.

The proxy variable j, representing artificial intelligence, is denoted as AI_j.

In consideration of the aforementioned factors, this study aims to ascertain the effect of Artificial Intelligence (AI) instruments on the efficiency of the Moroccan stock market. To this end, control variables derived from extant literature are incorporated into the analysis. Specifically, in our case, the trajectory of global financial markets is represented by index returns (***RMCI_World***), which can also serve as a proxy for investors, even in the case of the Moroccan stock market (see, for example, Bena et al., 2017; Li et al., 2024; & Omerani & Oummou, 2023). Furthermore, uncertainty is measured by market volatility (**Volatility**), calculated using the logarithmic returns of the MASI index squared (see, for example, Corsi, 2009, and Mokni et al., 2024), and market liquidity (**Liquidity**), which remains a conventional predictor of stock market development, expressed as the percentage of trading volume to market capitalization ratio (Mokni et al., 2024). The MONIA (**MONIA**) index is also employed to represent monetary and financial policy in Morocco, by reflecting the average overnight interbank rate. This index is closely linked to the monetary policy decisions taken by the Moroccan central bank (Banque AL-Maghreb) and is also introduced with control variables.

Finally, the focal variable of interest in this study, artificial intelligence, is represented by proxy variables; which are ChatGPT3 (GPT3) and ChatGPT4 (GPT4). These variables are measured by dummy variables, which take the value 1 after the tool is launched (in our case, GPT3 and GPT4) and 0 otherwise. Consequently, the utilization of the Market Inefficiency Magnitude (AMIM) as a target variable furnishes a robust metric for quantifying the evolution of Moroccan stock market efficiency over time.

The final complete model of our study is expressed as follows:

$$Q(AMIM_t)(r) = \beta_0(r) + \sum_{i=1}^{q}\beta_{1,i}(r).\,RMCI\_World + \sum_{i=1}^{q}\beta_{2,i}(r).\,Volatility + \sum_{i=1}^{q}\beta_{3,i}(r).\,Liquidity + \sum_{i=1}^{q}\beta_{4,i}(r).\,MONIA + \sum_{i=1}^{q}\beta_{5,i}(r).\,GPT3 + \sum_{i=1}^{q}\beta_{6,i}(r).\,GPT4 \quad (5)$$

The regression model is employed to evaluate the effect of artificial intelligence (AI), particularly through the utilization of GPT-3 and GPT-4 tools, on the efficiency of the Moroccan stock market. The coefficients, denoted by $\beta_i(r)$, are estimated relative to the quantile r.This methodological approach is well fitted to analyzing the effect of the emergence of Artificial Intelligence tools (GPT3 and GPT4) on the efficiency and inefficiency dynamics of the Moroccan stock market.

In light of these considerations, the main objective of the present research is to examine the effect of the emergence of Artificial Intelligence tools (AI_i) on the efficiency of the Moroccan stock market, as quantified by AMIM. Where; $AI_i = \{$ **GPT3, GPT4** $\}$.

Then the following hypotheses will be tested through our empirical investigation:

H$_0$: The advent of Artificial Intelligence tools (AI_i) exerts no effect on the efficiency of the Moroccan stock market.
H$_1$: The advent of AI_i artificial intelligence tools, significantly affects the efficiency of the Moroccan stock market.
H$_{1a}$: The advent of AI_i tools exert a positive effect on the efficiency of the Moroccan stock market.

The adoption of advanced artificial intelligence tools could simplify the acquisition of information and facilitate the interpretation of economic and financial data, reducing information asymmetries, especially for retail investors.

H$_{1b}$: The advent of AI_i tools exert a negative effect on the efficiency of the Moroccan stock market.

Conversely, if Artificial Intelligence tools are used extensively, uncritically, or with limited capabilities, they have the potential to become a source of misinformation or misinterpretation. In this particular instance, Artificial Intelligence is likely to exert an influence that is more likely to result in the inefficiency of the stock market rather than its efficiency.

Table 2. Description of variables and data sources

Variable	Definition	Source	Mean	Standard Deviation	Max	Min
AMIM	Adjusted Market Inefficiency Magnitude (AMI) - calculated from logarithmic return data for the MASI stock market index.	Investing.com	0,093154	0,234341	0,772559	-0,22054
RMCI_World	Morgan Stanley Capital International World Index logarithmic returns	Investing.com	0,011971	0,956441	4,928013	-3,72844
Volatility	Market volatility calculated from logarithmic returns of the MASI index	Investing.com	0,300909	1,285895	0	24,53368
Liquidity	The liquidity of the market is measured in accordance with the trading volume and the total market capitalization	Casablanca Stock Market	0,045709	0,119134	1,633129	0,000902
MONIA	Moroccan Overnight Index Average	Bank AL-MAGHRIB	0,023961	0,006245	0,03018	0,01366

Artificial Intelligence (AI) variables are modeled using dummy variables, which take the value 1 from the official launch date of each version, and 0 otherwise.
GPT-3: From November 30, 2022 (Introducing ChatGPT | OpenAI).
GPT-4: From March 14, 2023 (GPT-4 | OpenAI).
Source: Authors calculations

RESULTS AND DISCUSSION

Evolution of the Moroccan Stock Market Efficiency

In order to assess the evolution of the complex dynamics of efficiency and inefficiency in the Moroccan stock market, we used equation (3) to determine the daily Market Inefficiency Magnitude (AMIM). This is based on the daily returns of the main Moroccan stock market index, “MASI,” implementing the moving window approach with a size of one year (250 business days).

The results obtained were then represented graphically in figure n.1, which highlights a remarkable evolution in the efficiency of the Moroccan stock market (measured by the MASI) in several distinct cycles. These phases are closely linked to changes in the global market environment, as well as the gradual advent of new technological tools on the international scene, notably artificial intelligence technologies. These technologies, which at first sight may be disruptive to the market, may generate externalities that may affect market dynamics.

Figure 1. Evolution of the Moroccan stock market's adjusted market inefficiency magnitude (AMIM)

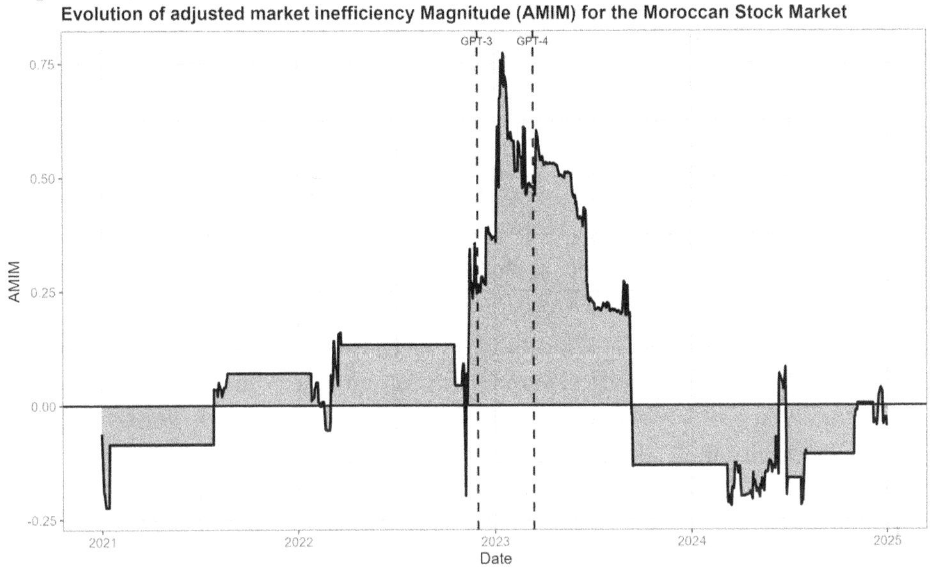

Source: Authors, using R software

At the inception of the study period, particularly in the initial half of 2021, the Moroccan stock market exhibited a modest degree of inefficiency, characterized by negative Market Inefficiency Magnitude (AMIM) values or those approaching zero. This finding suggests a period of relative stability, during which price adjustment mechanisms enable the market to function with increasing efficiency.

However, beginning in the latter half of 2021, a marked deterioration in the market's efficiency became evident, as evidenced by the systematic increase in AMIM values. This period corresponds with the release of ChatGPT-3, a significant technological advancement, to the general public on November 30, 2023, developed by the company OpenAI. Rather than resulting in an instant improvement in the Moroccan stock market's efficiency, this innovation (GPT-3) seems to have further worsened market inefficiency to a certain degree. In addition, Figure 1 shows that the AMIM values are maximized after such a technology is introduced indicating that there was considerable turbulence during that time period which could be blamed on a number of different reasons.

The introduction of new technological devices like chatbots can create lack of symmetry of information among some participants in the market. The early adopters of new technologies are able to set the pace on how the information is used which gives them an edge over those without access. This, therefore, leads to inefficiencies in the formation of the market price by using all relevant information which gives latecomers to the information which harms those using the info to update. While information and prices do need to capture all relevant pieces of information, their orderly sequencing takes time. At the same time, some of the new technology need the early users to go through a learning and adapting phase in accordance with the Adaptive Market Hypothesis (AMH).

Additionally, the inefficiency of the Moroccan stock market can be due to speculative actions, particularly from actors overemphasizing the usefulness of several technological tools. By encouraging overcomplex and over-ambitious accentuated trading, this had led to inefficiency of the Moroccan stock market. It is possible to interpret both these extreme inefficiencies as consequences of the process of available information which the AI technology provides not being properly exploited by the market. The very recent launch of ChatGPT-4 on 14 March 2023 marks the beginning of a paradigm shift towards efficiency of the Moroccan stock market. Unlike the launch of ChatGPT-3's ChatGPT-3, this new phase is defied by some form of temporary inefficiency followed by a decline in AMIM's values.

A multitude of factors are attributed to these fluctuations in the Moroccan stock market' efficiency. In particular, experience from launching version 3 of the ChatGPT tool seems to have helped market participants with responding to new technologies in a more rational manner. Moreover, it has been shown in version 4 that previous versions' inadequacies can be dealt with and enhanced. Despite this decline, these results implies that AMIM displayed a positive result over a five-month period, indicating a persistent pattern of inefficiency in the Moroccan stock market. This suggests that, while introducing new technological innovations may reduce market inefficiencies, it does not guarantee a quick transition to the ideal state of market efficiency.

Finally, as illustrated in Figure 1, subsequent phases of inefficiency are characterized by a non-persistent behavior in the context of the Moroccan stock market. Notably, AMIM recorded systematically negative results for the first time since the initial phase of our study

This development signifies an emerging trend toward enhanced efficiency in the Moroccan stock market. This suggests that the market has finally benefited from the new changes brought about by technological innovations, with ChatGPT-4 in particular acting as a positive externality, boosting the informational efficiency of the Moroccan stock market. While AMIM exhibited modestly favorable outcomes in certain periods, the prevailing market trend signifies an enhancement in efficiency, indicative of the market's adaptation to evolving circumstances.

ChatGPT and the Moroccan Stock Market Efficiency: Quantile Regression Model

Our graphical analysis of the Moroccan stock market's efficiency (with AMIM) reveals the potential value of econometric verification using quantile regression in empirically testing the impact of the launch of GPT-3 and GPT-4 on this evolution.

From this perspective, it is imperative to ascertain the stationarity of the variables employed prior to any econometric modeling, particularly in the context of time series. Failure to respect this property, in the presence of unit roots, can lead to spurious regression. The presence of such spurious regression can result in statistically significant outcomes that, in reality, do not accurately reflect genuine economic relationships. Consequently, the Augmented Dickey-Fuller (ADF) test is employed to ascertain the stationarity of the variables in our study (see Table 3).

Table 3. Results of the Augmented Dicky Fuller (ADF) Test

Variable/ model	P-value of ADF-Test			Decision
	With drift and trend	With drift and no trend	No drift and no trend	
AMIM	0.508	0.427	0.091	Unite Root
dAMIM	0.01	0.01	0.01	Stationary
R_MSCIW	0.01	0.01	0.01	Stationary
MONIA	0.965	0.519	0.798	Unite Root
dMONIA	0.01	0.01	0.01	Stationary
Volatility	0.01	0.01	0.01	Stationary
Liquidity	0.01	0.01	0.01	Stationary

Source: Authors, using R software

The results of the ADF test indicate that the variables R_MSCIW, Volatility, and Liquidity are stationary in level, as evidenced by the significant p-values (below the 5% critical threshold) for the three specifications of the ADF test (M3: model with constant and trend, M2: model with constant, M1: model without constant or trend). These findings suggest that the statistical properties of the three series under consideration are stable over time.

The AMIM and MONIA variables, however, exhibited a unit root, irrespective of the ADF test specification (M3, M2, M1). This finding indicates that the series are not stationary at level, and therefore their statistical moments are time-varying. Consequently, the utilization of these variables at a fixed level would lead to lower estimates. To circumvent the potential for spurious regression, we advocate for the utilization of their first differences, designated as dAMIM and dMONIA, which have been proven to be stationary, as evidenced by their ADF test p-values falling below the 5% critical threshold.

Consequently, these transformed variables can be employed to estimate our econometric model. However, it is imperative to acknowledge that their economic interpretation undergoes a transformation, as they now embody the daily variation of the AMIM and MONIA indices, as opposed to their absolute levels.

Table 4. Quantile regression model estimation results

Quantile (*r*)	0,1	0,35	0,6	0,85	0,9
Coefficient	**Estimation [T-value] (P-value)**	**Estimation [T-value] (P-value)**	**Estimation [T-value] (P-value)**	**Estimation [T-value] (P-value)**	**Estimation [T-value] (P-value)**
Intercept	-0,00175 [-0,51764] (0,60486)	0,00000 [0,00000] (1,00000)	0,00000 [0,00000] (1,00000)	0,00000 [0,00032] (0,99974)	0,00448 [1,20333] (0,22923)
Volatility	-0,01301 [-0,83155] (0,40593)	0,00000 [0,00000] (1,00000)	0,00000 [0,00000] (1,00000)	0,00596 [1,23182] (0,21841)	0,00688 [0,41465] (0,67852)
Liquidity	0,00354 [0,07801] (0,93784)	0,00000 [0,00000] (1,00000)	0,00000 [0,00000] (1,00000)	0,00000 [-0,00003] (0,99997)	-0,00144 [-0,02725] (0,97827)
RMSCIW	0,00030 [0,26394] (0,79190)	0,00000 [0,00000] (1,00000)	0,00000 [0,00000] (1,00000)	0,00000 [0,00032] (0,99974)	0,00119 [0,72395] (0,46932)
dMONIA	0,39195 [0,21283] (0,83152)	0,00000 [0,00000] (1,00000)	0,00000 [0,00000] (1,00000)	-0,00084 [-0,00067] (0,99946)	-0,68264 [-0,29772] (0,76600)
GPT-3	**-0,02166 [-7,34914] (0,00000)**	**-0,00508 [-2,12071] (0,03428)**	0,00107 [0,52731] (0,59813)	**0,01517 [3,25435] (0,00119)**	0,01622 [0,59856] (0,54965)
GPT-4	**0,01899 [7,54422] (0,00000)**	**0,00508 [2,12071] (0,03428)**	-0,00107 [-0,52746] (0,59803)	**-0,01363 [-3,04766] (0,00239)**	-0,01690 [-0,63461] (0,52588)

Source: Authors, using R software

As illustrated in Table 4, the results of our model estimation are presented in relation to the different quantiles. The low quantiles, specifically r = 0.1 and r = 0.35, correspond to periods of higher level of market efficiency (especially in the extreme case of r = 0.1). These periods are indicative of a general trend characterized by market efficiency, where AMIM varies downwards, meaning that dAMIM is systematically negative or close to zero. In this context, we find that the coefficients associated with the constant and the market volatility variable are negative, implying that they favor the inefficiency of the Moroccan stock market, except that their impacts are not statistically significant. While the impact of the remaining control variables, namely Liquidity, RMSCIW, and dMONIA, also lacks statistical significance, their estimated coefficients demonstrate positive signs that favor market efficiency. While the impact of these variables on market efficiency is not statistically significant within the context of the Moroccan stock market, these results align with existing literature. Specifically, it has been documented that as market volatility increases, the price formation process tends to deviate from an ideal state of efficiency. Conversely, a high level of market liquidity has been shown to enhance efficiency (see Al-Yahyaee et al., 2020; Mokni et al., 2024).

Despite the absence of statistical significance in our control variables (Volatility, Liquidity, RMSCIW, and dMONIA), their incorporation enables the mitigation of potential bias and the isolation of the net effect of the variables of interest pertaining to artificial intelligence, which has been demonstrated to be significant at the 1% level (for both levels; r = 0.1 and r = 0.35). The findings indicate that GPT-3 exerts a negative influence on variation in AMIM, while GPT-4 demonstrates a positive effect on AMIM.

With regard to the quantile r = 0.6, which represents the transition phase of the market from the ideal state of efficiency to inefficiency, neither the control variables nor those of interest are statistically significant. These findings underscore the adaptive nature of the market, particularly during periods of transition when market trajectory is ambiguous and is not influenced by the conventional determinants examined.

In the same context, particularly in the case of the extreme inefficiency situation (r = 0.9), the findings suggest that GPT-3 exerts a positive influence on the variation of AMIM in this instance. Conversely, GPT-4 demonstrates a negative effect of AMIM in the aforementioned situation. This finding confirms that of the extreme efficiency situation, where GPT-3 also favored inefficiency, while GPT-4 significantly favored the efficiency of the Moroccan stock market.

As demonstrated in Figure n.2, the estimated coefficients of the GPT-3 variable are systematically negative in the market efficiency phase ($r \leq 0.5$), while the signs remain systematically positive in periods of inefficiency ($r > 0.5$). In contrast, the second IA proxy variable, GPT-4, exhibited systematically positive values during periods of stock market efficiency ($r \leq 0.5$), with a structural change in signs displaying systematically negative values in the inefficiency regime ($r > 0.5$).

The observed discrepancy in the effect of the two versions of ChatGPT, GPT-3 and GPT-4, on the efficiency of the Moroccan stock market can be primarily attributed to the advancement in training data and analytical capabilities of the latter version. Specifically, GPT-3 (trained on data up to 2021) exhibits a limitation in its capabilities, while GPT-4 (trained up to 2023) demonstrates a marked enhancement in its capacity to understand, analyze, and process information, thereby signifying a notable advancement in its sophistication.

Figure 2. The effect of GPT-3 versus GPT-4 on the Moroccan stock market's adjusted market inefficiency magnitude (AMIM)

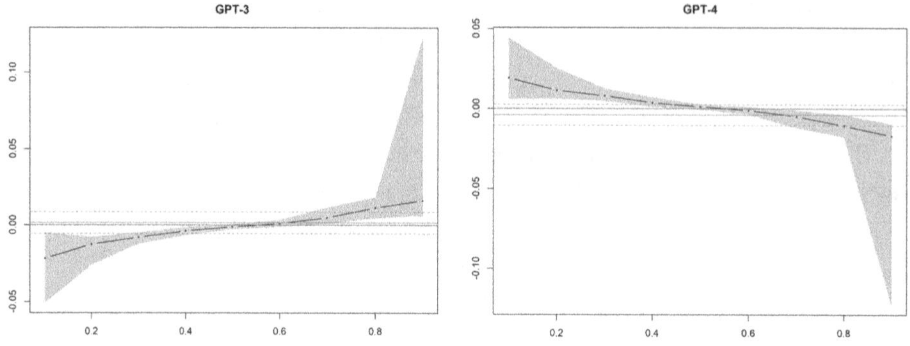

Source: *Authors, using R software*

The divergent effects on the evolution of Moroccan stock market efficiency are not random, but rather the result of contextual updating of Artificial Intelligence (AI) technologies.

The controversial effects come from the fact that GPT-4 is a massive improvement from GPT-3. It shows a better contextual understanding, consistency of responses, and the ability to precisely handle complex queries.

The upgrade to the model's version enables it to handle more information as well as introduce more precise decision-making directions. Thanks to this enhancement, the time required to analyze large volumes of information is significantly reduced, helping to reduce asymmetries, very particularly for less informed and less experienced investors, thus increasing stock market's efficiency.

In this context, GPT-3's lack of reasoning ability is likely to worsen existing biases, giving rise to more market inefficiency through approximate or ill-contextualized analyses. Consequently, this will cause a shift away from the ideal state of efficiency, leading to further promotion of irrational behavior. This finding suggests a decline in market efficiency following the launch of ChatGPT-3, as evidenced by the negative effect of the dummy variable (GPT-3) on the lower extreme values of the AMIM index (indicative of a decrease in efficiency levels) and a positive effect on its upper extreme values (suggestive of an intensification of inefficiency phases).

Thus, this result is consistent with Xie et al. (2023) who exhibited the functional limitation of this old version (GPT-3). Given that the Moroccan stock market is considered to have moderate liquidity and that the overwhelming majority of investors are non-professional individuals, these limitations seem to have harmed efficiency rather than improve it. We can deduct from these developments that there may be an excessively confident embrace of a ChatGPT-3 like innovation that doesn't contemplate its limitations, leading to stronger biased decisions than better information allocations than in developed contexts (see Almeida & Gonçalves, 2024; Ma et al., 2024).

On the contrary, the introduction of ChatGPT-4 illustrates a reversal trend, with a gradual improvement in the overall efficiency of the Moroccan stock market. This upgraded model has stronger analytical capability, which appears to have sustained better incorporation of market information – as are also observed by Lopez-Lira & Tang (2023) in developed markets. The new ChatGPT version has shown a favorable dynamic. Where the dummy-variable ChatGPT-4 has a positive effect on the minimum of the AMIM index extreme values. This highlights a rise in efficiency cumulatively. Further, oppositely, this dummy variable has a negative effect on the maximum AMIM index extreme values. This shows a fall in inefficiency phases cumulatively. This divergence in terms of effect between these two versions of ChatGPT serves to confirm the theoretical framework of the Adaptive Market Hypothesis (Lo, 2004, 2005, 2017). The Moroccan market has been noted as an ecosystem that is active and flexible. New technologies of Artificial Intelligence had different effects depending factors such as their complexity, the level of maturity, and the learning effect of the market actors. While ChatGPT-3, due to its shortcomings, may have served to deepen prevailing biases, ChatGPT-4 seems to have triggered a cumulative learning phenomenon that allows for more effective command of technological innovations in investment innovation.

This suggests that the effect of these technological changes is greatly moderated by their complexity as well as, and perhaps more importantly, the ability of local actors to strategically and rationally implement them. The relationship between market ecology and technology externalities is rich and complex, and particularly insightful at the micro level. Such insights are fundamental towards understanding the processes of implementing and adjusting frameworks of Artificial Intelligence in dynamic financial systems.

CONCLUSION

This chapter aimed to analyze the effect of the artificial intelligence (AI) technological revolution on the efficiency of the Moroccan stock market. More specifically, the study examined how the launch of ChatGPT 3 and ChatGPT 4 affected the efficiency of daily returns on the main Moroccan stock market index, MASI, between 03/01/2022 and 02/01/2025.

In this purpose, our research examined the determinants of the efficiency of the Moroccan stock market, measured by the Adjusted Market Inefficiency Magnitude (AMIM). In order to accomplish this objective, an evolutionary dynamics analysis of the market's efficiency was conducted over time, leading to the identification of discrete regimes of stability and efficiency. The dynamics of AMIM were examined both before and after the implementation of ChatGPT versions 3 and 4 by the company OpenAI.

This preliminary step of our analysis confirmed the presence of different levels and regimes of efficiency in the Moroccan stock market, which motivated the adoption of quantile regression modeling. This was done to capture the non-linear effects of the various determinants mobilized, including the IA proxy variables (namely GPT3 and GPT4), for different quantile levels 0.1, 0.35, 0.6, 0.85, and 0.9.

In addition to our variables of interest (GPT3 and GPT4), which are modeled using the dummy variable methodology, control variables extracted from the literature (R_MSCIW, MONIA, Volatility and Liquidity) have been implemented in our quartile regression model. While these variables were deemed insignificant in our approach, they enabled us to isolate and control the effect of GPT3 and GPT4 technologies on the efficiency dynamics of the Moroccan stock market.

The empirical results of our study demonstrate that the effect of our Artificial Intelligence (AI) proxy variables of interest varies significantly across quantiles, with the effects of the different tools studied (GPT3 and GPT4) on the Moroccan stock market exhibiting contradictory signs. Furthermore, the findings indicate substantial heterogeneity in the effect of the variables associated with ChatGPT3 and ChatGPT4 on the efficiency of the market under study, across various regimes. In light of the noted limitations of GPT3, which, instead of enhancing the efficiency (quantiles 0.1 and 0.35) of the market, appeared to favor inefficiency (quantiles 0.85 and 0.9), a contrasting outcome was observed, which was substantiated across all statistical models. Conversely, the GPT4 version demonstrated a positive effect on the efficiency of the Moroccan stock market, exhibiting a statistically significant effect on AMIM at the 0.1 and 0.35 quantiles. Concurrently, this version (GPT4), which has been developed in comparison to GPT3, exhibited a negative effect that was statistically significant on AMIM at the 0.85 and 0.9 quantile levels. As a result, a notable reduction in terms of inefficiency of the Moroccan stock market during extreme situations. These results are aligned with the principles of the Adaptive Market Hypothesis (Lo, 2004, 2005, 2017), which posits that markets oscillate between efficient and inefficient states as they adapt to the dynamics of the market environment. Contrary to the static vision of the market efficiency condition as defined by Fama (1965, 1970, 2014), the results suggest that the Moroccan stock market's efficiency presents a dynamic behavior rather than constant. The stock market's continuous interactions with its environment give rise to its dynamic nature, which is driven by competitive forces and the learning effect of market participants. In this context, international technological advancements, such as those in Artificial Intelligence, have the potential to influence financial markets. This phenomenon is illustrated by the emergence of sophisticated tools like the latest GPT version, which has the capacity to improve decision-making processes for a variety of individuals and organizations around the world. It offers promising avenues for the evolution and improvement of underdeveloped financial markets, particularly through the positive externalities generated by these new artificial intelligence technologies.

In practical terms, this research has several implications for various actors in the Moroccan market. The adverse effects of ChatGPT-3 exemplify the potential repercussions of relying too heavily on AI tools. This reliance can lead to biased collective decisions and compromise market efficiency, a phenomenon that is particularly evident in emergent contexts. These findings points to the necessity of adopting technological solutions in a more prudent and deliberate manner. Therefore, investors should systematically consider the limitations of language models and invest in advanced versions like ChatGPT-4, which has been shown to positively effect efficiency. The Capital Markets Authority (AMMC) is pivotal to financial markets in the Moroccan context. Then they should implement financial education programs that focus specifically on the limitations of AI tools. They must also establish transparency mechanisms regarding the use of AI tools in financial markets.

Moreover, the findings of our research underscore the necessity of implementing adaptive regulations in accordance with diverse market regimes. In periods of stable global market conditions, regulatory authorities should prioritize the reinforcement of transparency mechanisms. This can be achieved by mitigating information asymmetries through the utilization of advanced technological tools, thereby promoting efficiency. Conversely, in periods of market inefficiency, the implementation of targeted measures to mitigate excessive speculation is expected to stabilize the market, particularly during times of crisis. Mutual funds and individual investors, for their part, may find the "adjusted magnitude of market inefficiency" (AMIM) measure useful as a key indicator, allowing them to anticipate systemic risks and adjust their portfolios accordingly by adopting adaptive investment strategies.

However, it is imperative to acknowledge the limitations of this study. While the AMIM has demonstrated its utility in measuring the dynamics of market efficiency, a systematic comparison with other indicators, such as the Variance Ratio, the Hurst Exponent and TV-AR model, would contribute to the refinement of conclusions. Additionally, the present analysis does not directly address the actual adoption of these tools by Moroccan investors. This gap could be addressed through the implementation of field surveys. In conclusion, the absence of a direct application of these tools in a quantitative study on multimodal data (local news and market prices) limits our understanding of the precise mechanisms by which LLMs influence the market.

These limitations, however, give rise to a number of promising avenues for future research. A direct approach would be to establish a benchmark comparing the AMIM with other traditional efficiency measures in the Moroccan context. Concurrently, an in-depth behavioral study would provide a more comprehensive understanding of the adoption of AI tools by different types of local investors. Methodologically, the application of recent multimodal approaches to Moroccan data would represent significant progress. Consequently, extending this research to other emerging markets in the region would facilitate the identification of effects that are unique to the Moroccan context, thereby distinguishing them from more general regional trends.

Finally, this research contributes to a more profound understanding of the efficiency of less developed stock markets and calls for the exploration of alternative perspectives. The findings of this study demonstrate that financial market dynamics emerge from a complex interplay between institutional reforms, player behavior, and technological progress. The Moroccan market, characterized by the differential externality effect of AI tools such as ChatGPT, exemplifies this interdependence. This finding provides a foundation for subsequent research, focusing on the effect of multiple factors, including technological innovation, on the development of emerging markets. Such a comprehensive approach is imperative for formulating suitable financial policies and robust investment strategies in a rapidly evolving environment.

REFERENCES

Al-Yahyaee, K. H., Mensi, W., & Yoon, S. M. (2018). Efficiency, multifractality, and the long-memory property of the Bitcoin market: A comparative analysis with stock, currency, and gold markets. *Finance Research Letters*, *27*, 228–234. DOI: 10.1016/j.frl.2018.03.017

Ali, M., Khan, T. I., Khattak, M. N., & Şener, İ. (2024). Synergizing AI and business: Maximizing innovation, creativity, decision precision, and operational efficiency in high-tech enterprises. *Journal of Open Innovation*, *10*(3), 100352. DOI: 10.1016/j.joitmc.2024.100352

Almeida, J., & Gonçalves, T. C. (2024). The AI Revolution: Are Crypto Markets More Efficient after ChatGPT 3? *Finance Research Letters*, *66*, 105608. DOI: 10.1016/j.frl.2024.105608

Bena, J., Ferreira, M. A., Matos, P., & Pires, P. (2017). Are foreign investors locusts? The long-term effects of foreign institutional ownership. *Journal of Financial Economics*, *126*(1), 122–146. DOI: 10.1016/j.jfineco.2017.07.005

Bock, J., & Geissel, S. (2024). Evolution of stock market efficiency in Europe: Evidence from measuring periods of inefficiency. *Finance Research Letters*, *62*, 105129. DOI: 10.1016/j.frl.2024.105129

Boston Consulting Group. (2024, April 24). Consumers Know More About AI Than Business Leaders Think. https://www.bcg.com/publications/2024/consumers-know-more-about-ai-than-businesses-think

Bouschery, S. G., Blazevic, V., & Piller, F. T. (2023). Augmenting human innovation teams with artificial intelligence: Exploring transformer-based language models. *Journal of Product Innovation Management*, *40*(2), 139–153. DOI: 10.1111/jpim.12656

Brown, T., Mann, B., Ryder, N., Subbiah, M., Kaplan, J. D., Dhariwal, P., & Amodei, D. (2020). Language models are few-shot learners. *Advances in Neural Information Processing Systems*, *33*, 1877–1901.

Brynjolfsson, E., & McAfee, A. (2014). *The second machine age: Work, progress, and prosperity in a time of brilliant technologies*. WW Norton & company.

Bussmann, N., Giudici, P., Marinelli, D., & Papenbrock, J. (2021). Explainable machine learning in credit risk management. *Computational Economics*, *57*(1), 203–216. DOI: 10.1007/s10614-020-10042-0

Chen, J., Tang, G., Zhou, G., & Zhu, W. (2025). ChatGPT and Deepseek: Can They Predict the Stock Market and Macroeconomy? arXiv preprint arXiv:2502.10008.

Chhajer, P., Shah, M., & Kshirsagar, A. (2022). The applications of artificial neural networks, support vector machines, and long–short term memory for stock market prediction. *Decision Analytics Journal*, *2*, 100015. DOI: 10.1016/j.dajour.2021.100015

Christensen, C. M. (2015). *The innovator's dilemma: when new technologies cause great firms to fail.* Harvard Business Review Press.

Corsi, F. (2009). A simple approximate long-memory model of realized volatility. *Journal of Financial Econometrics*, *7*(2), 174–196. DOI: 10.1093/jjfinec/nbp001

D'avolio, G., Gildor, E., & Shleifer, A. (2001). Technology, information production, and market efficiency. Information Production, and Market Efficiency (September 2001).

De Bruijn, H., Warnier, M., & Janssen, M. (2022). The perils and pitfalls of explainable AI: Strategies for explaining algorithmic decision-making. *Government Information Quarterly*, *39*(2), 101666. DOI: 10.1016/j.giq.2021.101666

Fama, E. F. (1965). Random walks in stock market prices. *Financial Analysts Journal*, *51*(1), 75–80. DOI: 10.2469/faj.v51.n1.1861

Fama, E. F. (1970). Efficient capital markets. *The Journal of Finance*, *25*(2), 383–417. DOI: 10.2307/2325486

Fama, E. F. (2014). Two pillars of asset pricing. *The American Economic Review*, *104*(6), 1467–1485. DOI: 10.1257/aer.104.6.1467

Gama, F., & Magistretti, S. (2025). Artificial intelligence in innovation management: A review of innovation capabilities and a taxonomy of AI applications. *Journal of Product Innovation Management*, *42*(1), 76–111. DOI: 10.1111/jpim.12698

Godin, B. (2015). *Innovation contested: The idea of innovation over the centuries.* Routledge. DOI: 10.4324/9781315855608

Granstrand, O., & Holgersson, M. (2020). Innovation ecosystems: A conceptual review and a new definition. *Technovation*, *90*, 102098. DOI: 10.1016/j.technovation.2019.102098

Guler, N., Kirshner, S. N., & Vidgen, R. (2024). A literature review of artificial intelligence research in business and management using machine learning and ChatGPT. *Data and Information Management*, *8*(3), 100076. DOI: 10.1016/j.dim.2024.100076

Hadjitchoneva, J. (2020). L'intelligence artificielle au service de la prise de décisions plus efficace. Pour une recherche économique efficace, 149.

Hemphill, T. A., & Kelley, K. J. (2021). Artificial intelligence and the fifth phase of political risk management: An application to regulatory expropriation. *Thunderbird International Business Review*, *63*(5), 585–595. DOI: 10.1002/tie.22222

Ifleh, A., & El Kabbouri, M. (2021, December). Prediction of moroccan stock price based on machine learning algorithms. In *International Conference on Intelligent Systems Design and Applications* (pp. 735-741). Cham: Springer International Publishing.

Jordan, M. I., & Mitchell, T. M. (2015). Machine learning: Trends, perspectives, and prospects. *Science*, *349*(6245), 255–260. DOI: 10.1126/science.aaa8415 PMID: 26185243

Kaplan, A., & Haenlein, M. (2019). Siri, Siri, in my hand: Who's the fairest in the land? On the interpretations, illustrations, and implications of artificial intelligence. *Business Horizons*, *62*(1), 15–25. DOI: 10.1016/j.bushor.2018.08.004

Kismawadi, E. R., Aditchere, J., & Libeesh, P. C. (2024). Integration of Artificial Intelligence Technology in Islamic Financial Risk Management for Sustainable Development. In *Applications of Block Chain technology and Artificial Intelligence: Lead-ins in Banking, Finance, and Capital Market* (pp. 53–71). Springer International Publishing. DOI: 10.1007/978-3-031-47324-1_4

Koubaa, A. (2023). GPT-4 vs. GPT-3.5: A concise showdown. *Preprints. org*, 2023030422.

Kshetri, N., & Hughes, L. (2023). "So what if ChatGPT wrote it?" Multidisciplinary perspectives on opportunities, challenges and implications of generative conversational AI for research, practice and policy. *International Journal of Information Management*, *71*, 102642. DOI: 10.1016/j.ijinfomgt.2023.102642

Larkin, C., Drummond Otten, C., & Árvai, J. (2022). Paging Dr. JARVIS! Will people accept advice from artificial intelligence for consequential risk management decisions? *Journal of Risk Research*, *25*(4), 407–422. DOI: 10.1080/13669877.2021.1958047

Le Tran, V., & Leirvik, T. (2019). A simple but powerful measure of market efficiency. *Finance Research Letters*, *29*, 141–151. DOI: 10.1016/j.frl.2019.03.004

Le Tran, V., & Leirvik, T. (2020). Efficiency in the markets of crypto-currencies. *Finance Research Letters*, *35*, 101382. DOI: 10.1016/j.frl.2019.101382

Lee, K., & Lee, S. (2013). Patterns of technological innovation and evolution in the energy sector: A patent-based approach. *Energy Policy*, *59*, 415–432. DOI: 10.1016/j.enpol.2013.03.054

Li, B., Sun, Q., & Wei, Z. (2024). Implicit barriers, market integration and asset prices: Evidence from the inclusion of china a-shares in msci global indices. *Journal of International Financial Markets, Institutions and Money*, *93*, 101998. DOI: 10.1016/j.intfin.2024.101998

Lin, C. Y., & Marques, J. A. L. (2024). Stock market prediction using artificial intelligence: A systematic review of systematic reviews. *Social Sciences & Humanities Open*, *9*, 100864. DOI: 10.1016/j.ssaho.2024.100864

Lo, A. (2017). *Adaptive markets: Financial evolution at the speed of thought*. Princeton University Press.

Lo, A. W. (2004). The adaptive markets hypothesis: Market efficiency from an evolutionary perspective. *Journal of Portfolio Management*, *30*(5), 15–29. DOI: 10.3905/jpm.2004.442611

Lo, A. W. (2005). Reconciling efficient markets with behavioral finance: The adaptive markets hypothesis. *The Journal of Investment Consulting*, *7*(2), 21–44.

Lopez-Lira, A., & Tang, Y. (2023). Can chatgpt forecast stock price movements? return predictability and large language models. arXiv preprint arXiv:2304.07619.

Lund, B. D., Wang, T., Mannuru, N. R., Nie, B., Shimray, S., & Wang, Z. (2023). ChatGPT and a new academic reality: Artificial Intelligence-written research papers and the ethics of the large language models in scholarly publishing. *Journal of the Association for Information Science and Technology*, *74*(5), 570–581. DOI: 10.1002/asi.24750

Ma, F., Lyu, Z., & Li, H. (2024). Can ChatGPT predict Chinese equity premiums? *Finance Research Letters*, *65*, 105631. DOI: 10.1016/j.frl.2024.105631

Marwala, T. (Ed.). (2009). *Computational intelligence for missing data imputation, estimation, and management: Knowledge optimization techniques: Knowledge optimization techniques*. IGI Global.

Marwala, T. (2014). *Artificial intelligence techniques for rational decision making*. Springer. DOI: 10.1007/978-3-319-11424-8

Marwala, T., & Hurwitz, E. (2017). *Artificial intelligence and economic theory: Skynet in the market* (Vol. 1). Springer International Publishing.

McCarthy, J., Minsky, M. L., Rochester, N., & Shannon, C. E. (2006). A proposal for the dartmouth summer research project on artificial intelligence, august 31, 1955. *AI Magazine*, *27*(4), 12–12.

Milojević, N., & Redzepagic, S. (2021). Prospects of artificial intelligence and machine learning application in banking risk management. *Journal of Central Banking Theory and Practice*, *10*(3), 41–57. DOI: 10.2478/jcbtp-2021-0023

Misra, P., & Chaurasia, S. (2020). Data-driven trend forecasting in stock market using machine learning techniques. [JITR]. *Journal of Information Technology Research*, *13*(1), 130–149. DOI: 10.4018/JITR.2020010109

Mohanty, D. K., Parida, A. K., & Khuntia, S. S. (2021). Financial market prediction under deep learning framework using auto encoder and kernel extreme learning machine. *Applied Soft Computing*, *99*, 106898. DOI: 10.1016/j.asoc.2020.106898

Mokni, K., El Montasser, G., Ajmi, A. N., & Bouri, E. (2024). On the efficiency and its drivers in the cryptocurrency market: The case of Bitcoin and Ethereum. *Financial Innovation*, *10*(1), 39. DOI: 10.1186/s40854-023-00566-3

Morgan, T. R., Roath, A. S., & Richey, R. G. (2023). How risk, transparency, and knowledge influence the adaptability and flexibility dimensions of the responsiveness view. *Journal of Business Research*, *158*, 113641. DOI: 10.1016/j.jbusres.2022.113641

Nelson, R. R., & Winter, S. G. (1982). An Evolutionary Theory of Economic Change (Cambridge, Massachusetts and London, Belknap Press of Harvard University Press). Vol.

Okoroafor, U. C., & Leirvik, T. (2022). Time varying market efficiency in the Brent and WTI crude market. *Finance Research Letters*, *45*, 102191. DOI: 10.1016/j.frl.2021.102191

Omerani, D., & Oummou, Y. A. (2023). The effect of the Russian-Ukrainian Conflict on the main frontier Markets: An Event Study Approach. International Journal of Financial Studies. *Economics and Management*, *2*(2), 42–54.

Open, A. I. (2023). GPT-4 Technical Report. https://arxiv.org/pdf/2303.08774

Opesemowo, O. A. G. (2025). Artificial Intelligence in Mathematics Education: The Pros and Cons. In *Encyclopedia of Information Science and Technology, Sixth Edition* (pp. 1-18). IGI Global.

Oukhouya, H., & El Himdi, K. (2023, April). Comparing machine learning methods—svr, xgboost, lstm, and mlp—for forecasting the moroccan stock market. In Computer Sciences & Mathematics Forum (Vol. 7, No. 1, p. 39). MDPI.

Ouyang, L., Wu, J., Jiang, X., Almeida, D., Wainwright, C., Mishkin, P., & Lowe, R. (2022). Training language models to follow instructions with human feedback. *Advances in Neural Information Processing Systems*, *35*, 27730–27744.

Podina, I. R., & Caculidis-Tudor, D. (2023). Increasing Well-Being and Mental Health Through Cutting-Edge Technology and Artificial Intelligence. In *Brain, Decision Making and Mental Health* (pp. 347–364). Springer International Publishing. DOI: 10.1007/978-3-031-15959-6_17

Radford, A., Wu, J., Child, R., Luan, D., Amodei, D., & Sutskever, I. (2019). Language models are unsupervised multitask learners. OpenAI blog, 1(8), 9.

Ransbotham, S., Kiron, D., Gerbert, P., & Reeves, M. (2017). Reshaping business with artificial intelligence: Closing the gap between ambition and action. *MIT Sloan Management Review*, *59*(1).

Saggu, A., & Ante, L. (2023). The influence of ChatGPT on artificial intelligence related crypto assets: Evidence from a synthetic control analysis. *Finance Research Letters*, *55*, 103993. DOI: 10.1016/j.frl.2023.103993

Schumpeter, J. A. (1942). Capitalism, Socialism, and Democracy. *University of Illinois at Urbana-Champaign's Academy for Entrepreneurial Leadership Historical Research Reference in Entrepreneurship.*

Siddik, A. B., Li, Y., Du, A. M., & Migliavacca, M. (2025). Fueling financial development: The crucial role of generative AI financing across nations. *Finance Research Letters*, *72*, 106519. DOI: 10.1016/j.frl.2024.106519

Simon, H. (1957). A Behavioral Model of Rational Choice. Models of Man, Social and Rational: Mathematical Essays on Rational Human Behavior in a Social Setting/Wiley.

Simon, H. (1982). *Models of bounded rationality* (Vol. 3).

Weber, P., Carl, K. V., & Hinz, O. (2024). Applications of explainable artificial intelligence in finance—A systematic review of finance, information systems, and computer science literature. *Management Review Quarterly*, *74*(2), 867–907. DOI: 10.1007/s11301-023-00320-0

Wei, Y., Hu, R., Zhang, J., & Wang, Q. (2024). Does the carbon market signal the market efficiency of clean and dirty cryptocurrencies? An analysis of quantile directional dependence. *Finance Research Letters*, *67*, 105913. DOI: 10.1016/j.frl.2024.105913

Wickens, C. D., & Carswell, C. M. (2021). Information processing. Handbook of human factors and ergonomics, 114-158.

Xie, Q., Han, W., Lai, Y., Peng, M., & Huang, J. (2023). The wall street neophyte: A zero-shot analysis of chatgpt over multimodal stock movement prediction challenges. arXiv preprint arXiv:2304.05351.

ADDITIONAL READING

Abdedaime, M., Hazman, C., Qafas, A., Ibourk, A., & Guezzaz, A. (2025). AI and Impact Assessment of Public Policy: Case of New Town Program in Morocco. In *Advanced Computation Solutions for Energy Efficiency* (pp. 275-286). IGI Global Scientific Publishing.

Baliga, S., Murthy, H. K., Sadhale, A., & Upadhyaya, D. (2024). Advanced Applications of Generative AI and Natural Language Processing Models: Advancing Capabilities Safely in an Uncertain World. In A. Obaid, B. Bhushan, M. S., & S. Rajest (Eds.), Advanced Applications of Generative AI and Natural Language Processing Models (pp. 69-86). IGI Global Scientific Publishing. DOI: 10.4018/979-8-3693-0502-7.ch004

Bhuyan, B. P., & Singh, T. P. (2022). Artificial intelligence in financial portfolio management. In *Revolutionizing Business Practices Through Artificial Intelligence and Data-Rich Environments* (pp. 108–139). IGI Global Scientific Publishing. DOI: 10.4018/978-1-6684-4950-9.ch007

Elhissoufi, M., & Alla, L. (2024). Artificial Intelligence in Costumer Acquisition: A Bibliometric Study. In AI and data engineering solutions for effective marketing (pp. 1-22). IGI Global Scientific Publishing. DOI: 10.4018/979-8-3693-3172-9.ch001

Gadre-Patwardhan, S., Katdare, V. V., & Joshi, M. R. (2016). A review of artificially intelligent applications in the financial domain. *Artificial Intelligence in Financial Markets: Cutting Edge Applications for Risk Management, Portfolio Optimization and Economics*, 3-44.

Li, M. (2025). The impact of ChatGPT on teaching and learning in higher education: challenges, opportunities, and future scope. *Encyclopedia of Information Science and Technology, Sixth Edition*, 1-20.

Mupaikwa, E. (2025). The application of artificial intelligence and machine learning in academic libraries. In *Encyclopedia of Information Science and Technology* (6th ed., pp. 1–18). IGI Global Scientific Publishing.

Pandey, M. K., & Upadhyay, J. (2024). Overview of ChatGPT Model Architecture. In A. Obaid, B. Bhushan, M. S., & S. Rajest (Eds.), Advanced Applications of Generative AI and Natural Language Processing Models (pp. 87-107). IGI Global Scientific Publishing. DOI: 10.4018/979-8-3693-0502-7.ch005

Sadati, A., Gramlich, D., & Walker, T. (2024). Artificial Intelligence, Finance, and Sustainability: An Overview. Artificial Intelligence, Finance, and Sustainability: Economic, Ecological, and Ethical Implications, 3-16.

Shafik, W. (2024). Introduction to ChatGPT. In *Advanced applications of generative AI and natural language processing models* (pp. 1–25). IGI Global.

KEY TERMS AND DEFINITIONS

AMH (Adaptive Market Hypothesis): A theory which suggests that the efficiency of financial markets is dynamic and its evolution depends on factors that include competition, innovation and the learning effect of market participants.

AMIM (Adjusted Market Inefficiency Magnitude): An indicator for quantifying the efficiency of financial markets, taking into account the dynamic evolution of historical prices and their impact on their future trajectory.

Artificial Intelligence (AI): A computer science discipline that aims to develop systems capable of simulating human intelligence, so that they can perform tasks independently and autonomously.

Market Efficiency: The ideal situation in financial markets, where asset prices reflect all relevant information, enabling resources to be channeled into the most productive investments.

Quantile Regression: An econometric method for estimating the effect of explanatory variables on different quantiles of the distribution of a dependent variable, providing an in-depth analysis of the time series studied.

Positive Externality: A beneficial effect of an economic activity that benefits external parties without them having to pay the cost directly. For example, the development of Artificial Intelligence (AI) can improve market efficiency in an indirect way, benefiting all stakeholders.

Stock Market: physical or virtual space for the exchange of financial instruments such as stocks and bonds, playing a key role in the allocation of resources and the financing of the economy.

Chapter 11
Privacy Concerns and Ethical Considerations in Integrating AI into Tax Control Processes:
A Systematic Literature Review

Hicham Chanqaoui
https://orcid.org/0009-0002-7076-3874
Faculty of Legal, Economic, and Social Sciences, Cadi Ayyad University, Morocco

Abdelouahab El Boukhari
https://orcid.org/0009-0009-7894-8989
Faculty of Legal, Economic, and Social Sciences, Cadi Ayyad University, Morocco

Doha Sahraoui
https://orcid.org/0000-0002-7994-237X
Faculty of Legal, Economic, and Social Sciences, Cadi Ayyad University, Morocco

ABSTRACT

This chapter presents a systematic literature review (SLR) on the privacy concerns and ethical considerations arising from the integration of artificial intelligence (AI) into tax control processes. Using the PRISMA methodology, 91 peer-reviewed studies published between 2014 and 2024 were analyzed to explore the opportunities and risks associated with AI adoption in tax administration. The review identifies three core ethical themes: accountability and explainability, data protection and

DOI: 10.4018/979-8-3373-5499-6.ch011

privacy, and fairness and non-discrimination. Findings reveal widespread concerns regarding the opacity of AI decision-making, data misuse, and algorithmic bias, which may undermine taxpayer trust and procedural justice. The chapter offers policy recommendations and emphasizes the importance of human oversight, legal compliance, and fairness audits to ensure responsible AI deployment. This research provides valuable insights for policymakers, tax authorities, and scholars seeking to balance technological innovation with ethical governance in the evolving landscape of digital taxation.

INTRODUCTION

Tax systems are evolving in ways that were not predictable a decade ago. Artificial intelligence (AI) is no longer a speculative tool in this space; it is embedded in how tax administrations make decisions, manage risks, and interact with taxpayers. What used to be the job of human auditors and administrators is increasingly supported, and sometimes replaced, by expert systems, machine learning models, and automated data analysis (Rahayu, 2021). Various kinds of AI are now at play: process automation that manages repetitive tasks, cognitive insights that extract patterns from large datasets, and cognitive engagement tools that simulate human-like interactions. These systems draw from big data, processed at high speeds, to offer predictions and decisions that would be difficult for any human to make on their own (Bentley, 2019). Algorithms have shown a huge potential in anticipating fraud, detecting anomalies and assessing risk based on past data (Bevacqua, 2020; Martín López, 2022). This shift is technical and structural with legal and ethical questions multiplying. However, AI systems appear to function as *"black boxes."* That makes it harder for taxpayers to understand decisions, challenge outcomes, or trace accountability (Daly, 2024; Górski et al., 2024). Bias is a constant concern; it is not just algorithmic noise, but something that can lead to harmful outcomes if ignored. Discriminatory patterns might not always be visible, but they linger in training data, assumptions, and design (Martín López, 2022).

In jurisdictions where tax authorities are bound by duties to give reasons and act within legal authorizations, explainability becomes more than a feature, it becomes a requirement. Even Explainable AI (XAI) offers one response; these tools aim to bridge the gap between how a machine *"thinks"* and how a human can understand that thinking process. However, many XAI models have been created, but some still fail to meet legal expectations or give a false sense of clarity (Bevacqua, 2020; Martín López, 2022). So, transparency is not an option, especially when public sector decisions carry consequences for rights.

The Rule of Law comes up a lot in this systematic literature review (SLR). Not just as a principle to be safeguarded, but as a framework under stress. AI might help enforce laws more consistently. Alternatively, it might sidestep them. Some worry that opaque systems can undermine accountability, predictability, or equality before the law (Daly, 2024).

Tax authorities are clearly interested in using AI to improve compliance, detect evasion, and reduce costs (Palomino Guerrero, 2022). In some places, tools like natural language processing and predictive models are already embedded in audit procedures and risk assessment systems (Malashin et al., 2024a; Rahayu, 2021). Others are still exploring pilot programs or developing regulatory frameworks to keep up with the technology (Bevacqua, 2020; Puspita et al., 2024).

Real-world applications show tension. On one hand, AI is helping tax authorities build risk profiles, streamline inspections, and uncover hidden fraud using neural networks and classification techniques (Gomes & Balaniuk, 2024; Murorunkwere et al., 2023). On the other hand, these systems rely on data that may already carry historical bias or overlook underreported behaviors (Martín López, 2022).

Machine learning's opacity, especially in neural networks, poses another hurdle. If decision-makers can’t interpret predictions, trust breaks down (Bou Reslan & Jabbour Al Maalouf, 2024; Malashin et al., 2024b). Confidence tuning and rejection classes are proposed fixes, letting systems pause when uncertain, instead of guessing wrong (Malashin et al., 2024a). This issue presents a series of unresolved tensions with significant consequences. Between innovation and legality, automation and trust, what machines can do and what taxpayers expect them not to do, there’s a space, which is unresolved, complex, and filled with real consequences. This is where this SLR sits.

This chapter explores the different aspects of the ethical and privacy implications of AI integration in the tax control process. The SLR globally covers 91 peer-reviewed studies published between 2014 and 2024 using the PRISMA methodology. This systematic review ensures transparency and rigor in identifying, selecting, and analyzing literature across jurisdictions and disciplines. The review focuses on ethical challenges that have arisen in AI-enabled tax administration. Examples include accountability and explainability, data protection and privacy, as well as fairness and non-discrimination. The analysis is based on two main pillars: a bibliometric assessment, which maps patterns in references, keywords, and geographic distribution, and a thematic synthesis, which investigates the ethical concerns. The discussion section of this review highlights gaps in regulations, technical limitations, and existing doubts in the public sector, while the conclusion summarizes the key findings, limitations of the study, and finally, it offers practical recommendations for policymakers working in this rapidly evolving field.

METHODOLOGY

The Review Protocol (PRISMA)

This study aims to investigate the privacy concerns and ethical considerations when applying AI tools to tax control processes. In order to analyze the data available on the topic, we used a systematic literature review methodology, following the PRISMA (Preferred Reporting Items for Systematic Reviews and Meta-Analyses) method. The time span used for this literature review is 10 years ranging from 2014 up to 2024. The resources used are peer-reviewed articles and book chapters published in this period and obtained from the Scopus, Web of Science, and Cairn databases. The ten-year period allows us to include the most relevant and up-to-date papers and illustrates the evolution and progression of AI. The flow diagram below (Figure 1) represents the information flow during the different stages of this systematic review.

Figure 1. The PRISMA diagram

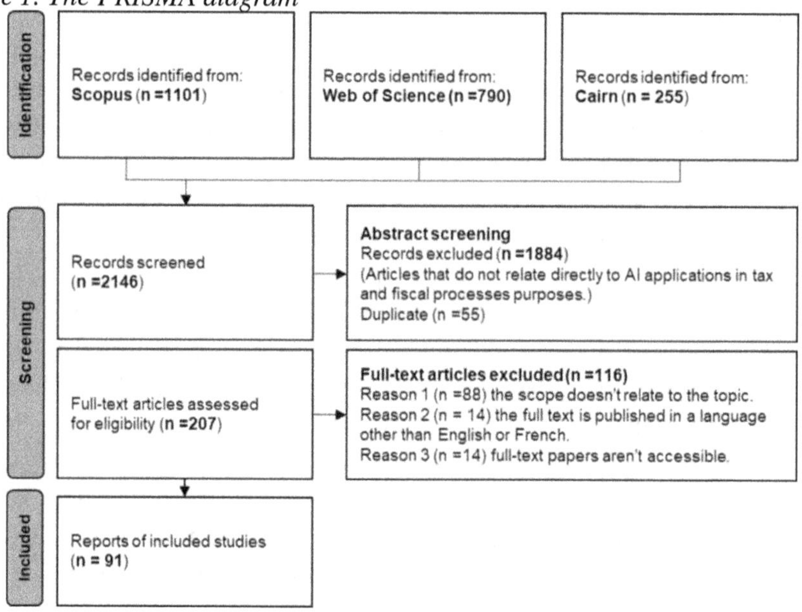

Systematic Searching Strategies

The systematic article search strategy was delineated through three primary phases: identification, screening, and eligibility. Subsequently, the collected data underwent rigorous processing and analysis to ensure the integrity and quality of the study's content.

Identification

Keywords for Search. During this step, a Boolean search strategy was used to query the databases. This made it easier to find relevant articles by using titles, abstracts, and keywords related to artificial intelligence, taxation, fiscal control, tax administration, and taxpayers. Table 1 shows the mobilized keywords in the research process.

Table 1. The Search Keywords

Language	Keywords
English	*"Artificial Intelligence", "AI", "Machine Learning", "Deep Learning", "Intelligent Systems", "Algorithmic Decision-Making", "Autonomous Systems", "Predictive Analytics", "Natural Language Processing", "data analytics", "Tax Control", "Fiscal Control", "Tax Compliance", "Tax Enforcement", "Tax Regulation", "Tax Practices", "Tax Audit*", "Fraud Detection", "Tax Governance", taxpayer*, "Tax Administration", "Tax Authority*".*
French	*"Intelligence Artificielle", "IA", "Apprentissage Automatique", "Apprentissage Profond", "Systèmes Intelligents", "Prise de Décision Algorithmique", "Systèmes Autonomes", "Analyse Prédictive", "Traitement du Langage Naturel", "Analyse de Données", "Contrôle Fiscal", "Conformité Fiscale", "Evasion Fiscale", "Détection de la Fraude"*

Screening

We evaluated and screened 2146 articles based on their abstract, title, and keywords. Besides, we excluded articles and book chapters that did not directly relate to AI applications in tax processes. Additionally, we sourced articles written in English and French, published between 2014 and 2024. Articles and book chapters did not meet the criteria were excluded (see Table 2). After the process had been carried out, a total of 207 articles were selected as relevant papers based on abstract screening, and ninety-one papers were included in the stage of full-text screening.

Table 2. Inclusion and exclusion criteria

Criteria	Timeline	Document type	Language	Content
Inclusion	2014 to 2024	Articles and book chapters.	English and French	Articles related directly to AI applications in tax and fiscal processes.
Exclusion	<2014	Other than articles and book chapters.	Other languages	Articles that do not explicitly pertain to the application of AI in tax control.

Eligibility

The eligibility process selected articles and book chapters that focus on the application of AI in tax administration to improve tax compliance, detect fraud, and enhance operational efficiency within fiscal systems. Any studies that were not related to the application of AI in tax administrations for control purposes were excluded. We have done an in-depth reading to ensure the accuracy of the study content. We extracted any studies that met the criteria. As a result, a standardized data extraction template was developed to collect relevant information, including introduction, objective of the study, context, application of AI, challenges/obstacles of AI adoption, implications for the tax administration, ethical considerations, concerns of taxpayers, theoretical framework, methodology, data collection method, data analysis, results and discussion, and conclusion.

Data Extraction and Analysis

This study began with a bibliometric analysis of ninety-one peer-reviewed articles and book chapters retrieved from Scopus, Web of Science, and Cairn databases. It is spanning publications from 2014 to 2024. A PRISMA flow diagram was used to guide the selection and screening process. We used VOSviewer software to detect patterns, trends, and connections in the literature. The goal was to examine citation networks, co-authorship clusters, influential publications, and research hotspots. This quantitative approach contributed to mapping the intellectual structure of the field. In addition, we identified the key contributors and emerging areas of focus.

We conducted a thematic analysis to qualitatively synthesize the full-text content of the selected studies after the bibliometric phase. Thematic analysis is particularly suited for identifying recurring patterns and conceptual categories across diverse research outputs. This method enabled us to extract and categorize themes related to the integration of artificial intelligence in tax administration. We used the available data to infer themes. That gave us a nuanced picture of how the different concepts of our study are interacted in different situations. However, the combination of bibliometric and content analysis thus provided insights into the current landscape of AI in tax control at macro-level and micro-level overview.

RESULTS

Background of the Selected Articles

Out of the ninety-one selected studies, the geographical distribution reveals a diverse range of research contexts. Six studies were conducted in Italy and the United States; five in Indonesia, four in China, the United Kingdom, France, and Australia; three in Rwanda, Germany, and international or European Union contexts; two in Chile, Egypt, Ukraine, Morocco, Estonia, South Korea, Latvia, Russia, Saudi Arabia, and Finland. The remaining studies were carried out in individual countries such as Romania, Jordan, Canada, Vietnam, Spain, Colombia, Greece, Armenia, Iran, Cyprus, Argentina, Japan, Botswana, Hungary, Lebanon, Peru, Belgium, Tunisia, Yemen, Ecuador, and the Netherlands, as well as in cross-national contexts such as *"Netherlands & United States," "Morocco & France," "European Countries," "Indonesia & Malaysia," "Latin America," "Malta & United Kingdom,"* and *"Morocco & USA."*

The map (Figure 2) reflects various countries' converging concerns over integrating AI into tax administration. Advanced nations like the U.S., China, and the UK are leading innovation. On the other hand, Italy, Indonesia, and Tunisia, which are facing high levels of evasion, view AI as a critical enforcement tool. The ethical use, privacy, and legal compliance were emphasized in digitally mature states such as Finland, Estonia, and Belgium. Meanwhile, the adaptation of AI to modernize governance has been a priority in reform-driven economies like Saudi Arabia, Egypt, and Morocco. In addition, the focus on behavioral insights and voluntary compliance been a concern for countries like Latvia and Rwanda

Figure 2. Global distribution of studies on AI in tax administration included in the SLR.

In terms of publication years, the distribution shows a growing scholarly interest over time. Two articles were published in 2014, one in 2016, one in 2017, four in 2018, four in 2019, and eleven in 2020. The upward trend continued with eight publications in 2021, nine in 2022, and a notable increase to nineteen in 2023 and thirty-one in 2024. This trend illustrates the escalating relevance of AI in tax administration, especially in the post-2020 era of digital transformation, highlighting increased attention to automation, fraud detection, and ethical considerations in the public sector.

Bibliometric Analysis

Most Frequent Sources

Table 3 presents the five most frequently cited sources in the reviewed literature. With five articles each, IEEE Access and the eJournal of Tax Research both appear most frequently. However, they differ significantly in their academic impact: IEEE Access has a high H-index of 242 and 124 citations, indicating broader academic influence and recognition. With a relevant focus on tax-specific research, the eJournal of Tax Research has an H-index of 12 and 38 citations.

Expert Systems with Applications stands out with the highest H-index (271), appearing twice, with strong reputation in AI and applied systems. It is followed by the Journal of Economic Behavior & Organization (H-index 136), Future Internet (H-index 60), with a high number of citations (108), we observed that this data represents a balance between high-impact generalist journals in technology and more specialized tax-focused journals

Table 3. Top five most frequent sources

Sources	f	H-index	no. of citations
IEEE Access	5	242	124
eJournal of Tax Research	5	12	38
Expert Systems with Applications	2	271	60
Journal of Economic Behavior & Organization	2	136	74
Future Internet	2	60	108

Co-Citation Analysis

The examination of the intellectual structure within a specific domain requires visualizing and interpreting co-citation networks as mentioned in Figure 3, which includes three clusters based on the relationships among articles.

Figure 3. Co-citation analysis

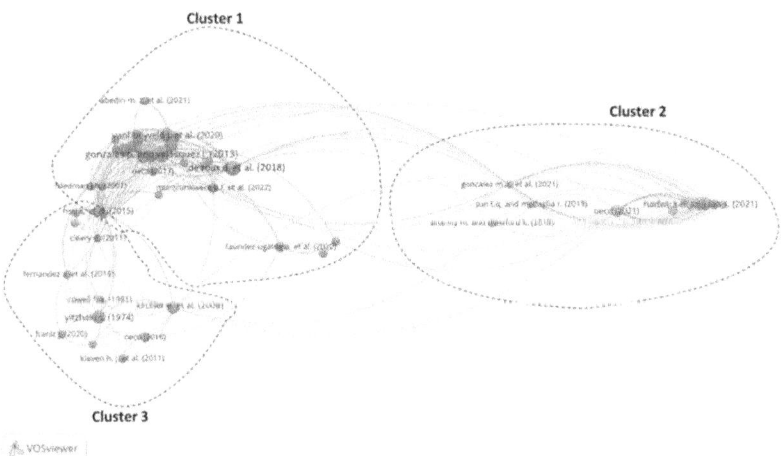

The core focus of the first cluster in the source material carries a predominant concern with the use of the different types of analytical and computational methods for identifying tax issues, especially those related to tax evasion and fraud and, also, managing these problems. A significant area involves leveraging data mining and machine learning techniques, including supervised and unsupervised algorithms such as neural networks, support vector machines, clustering, and anomaly detection, to identify suspicious patterns and behaviors in financial and transactional data. For instance, Castellón González & Velásquez (2013) examined the use of data mining methods to detect taxpayers who submit false invoices based on official data obtained from the Chilean Internal Revenue Service. Through this cluster of authors, social network analysis was widely discussed as an instrument to study connections among taxpayers. Graph-based models were also very deployed to discern evasion patterns. There are quite few papers that describe this subject in the area of tax administration and its technological impact. They also illustrate and analyze the use of third-party data, as well as tools to improve compliance and manage tax debt. The situation is exemplified by the report from the Organisation for Economic Co-operation and Development, which reveals that one outcome of the implementation of advanced technologies and data analytics by tax authorities is the reduction of the operating costs as well as the improvement of the community (OECD, 2017). Finally, some of the challenges such as the interpretability of the methods, the legal framework for the use of the data by the tax authorities, and the taxpayers' rights are also among the issues addressed in this cluster.

Cluster two consists primarily of OECD reports that were published over the period from 2019 to 2022. They are the ones that undertake a comparative study of tax administration in different countries, with the aspect of the digitalization impact, technologies, like AI, and recent occurrences such as the COVID-19 pandemic, as the focal point of the research. Hence, a report from the OECD in 2021 (OECD, 2021) highlighted how digital transformation and the initial steps taken during the COVID-19 era affected tax administrations. In other words, the researchers of these texts also take an evaluative stance on the application of advanced algorithms in the public sector, which include tax governance and the issue of transparency and the respect of the fundamental rights. For example, Raz (1979) depicts the rule of law from a purely negative perspective of freedom and dignity while Sun & Medaglia (2019) provide a global perspective of the adoption through the example of the Chinese healthcare sector.

In Cluster three, scholars are focusing on the economic and psychological domains of tax evasion and compliance, by testing models. A great example is the case where Kleven et al. (2011) provided an analysis of the Allingham & Sandmo (1972) model, according to which individuals take into account expected utility to make their income declaration, bearing in mind that the penalty for non-compliance with the tax payment is a likelihood. Moreover, writers in this category were dealing with the role of trust in public authorities, power effectiveness, social norms, and moral equity. For instance, Kirchler et al. (2008) suggest that a service and client approach facilitates a synergetic environment that can enhance both the power and trust in public authorities. Discrimination in the age of algorithms and the potential for algorithms to both reveal and perpetuate biases are also addressed by authors within this cluster.

Keywords Analysis

Figure 4 presents the keyword network, which is divided into three main clusters. Each cluster pulls the conversation in a different direction. The first cluster is about machine learning, fraud detection, predictive models, and neural networks. It focuses on the conception and design aspects where the technology engineers and data scientists test theories and build algorithms that aim to detect fraud. It is more interconnected with technical methods such as anomaly detection, support vector machines, and genetic algorithms.

The second cluster is about artificial intelligence, tax administration, privacy, trust, and ethics. This cluster reflects an institutional and even philosophical aspect of the subject. In this cluster, some critical questions are raised, such as: How far should we go? What do people lose when decision-making gets outsourced to code and algorithms? Furthermore, domains such as governance, blockchain, and compliance might seem like the processes that can harness the tools developed in cluster one. The term ethics is closely linked to trust and privacy, reflecting the importance of taking into consideration these concerns while implementing artificial intelligence in tax administration. The taxpayer term also belongs to this cluster, and it is closely linked to compliance and tax administration, which reflects how literature frames the human side of this AI-tax equation. Being near compliance and tax administration shows that most studies are viewing taxpayers in terms of whether they obey the rules and discussing how to get them to do so. The size of the node provides information about the role of this actor in this process. The taxpayer is just a variable to which rules and decisions are applied rather than being involved in the decision-making process.

The third cluster is about taxation, tax evasion, tax compliance, social norms, behavior, and social networks, indicating the role of behavior. This is where behavioral theories attempt to understand why people and organizations seek tax evasion and avoidance. The aim is not only to detect these practices but to provide an explanation for these behaviors. The term taxation is shown in the middle of Figure 4 close to machine learning (cluster 1) and artificial intelligence (cluster 2), indicating that despite the different angles, the aim of the discussion is the same: the optimization of taxation processes through advanced technology. When compared to the other clusters, three main questions arise: On the one hand, can we build intelligent systems? On the other hand, should we? And most importantly, in between, how would people behave when faced with these systems?

Figure 4. Keywords analysis

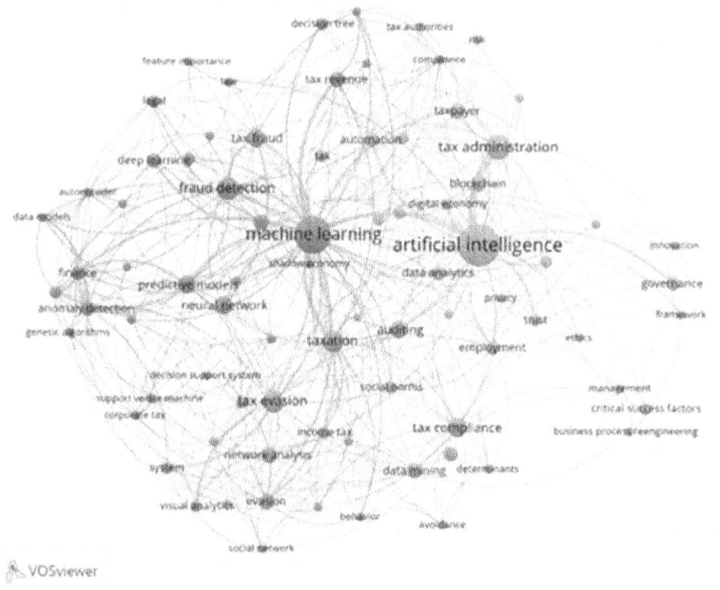

Ethical Considerations

The thematic analysis of our SLR combines data from published articles and book chapters. It investigates the privacy issues and moral concerns related to the use of AI in the tax control process. Findings are organized under three major categories: (1) *"accountability & explainability"*, (2) *"data protection & privacy"*, and (3) *"fairness & non-discrimination"* derived from the literature.

Accountability & Explainability

Need for Explainability & Transparency of AI Decisions in Tax Administration

The need for transparency and explainability in AI-driven decisions becomes a critical element in reshaping administrations' processes. In this context, with the huge potential of AI in fraud detection, non-compliance prediction, and audit optimization, studies reveal issues related to the opacity of algorithmic logic. That raises substantial concerns among taxpayers and tax administrations. The interpretation of AI-driven tax assessments becomes difficult for taxpayers and auditors (Pang &

Hua, 2024). The AI decision in tax audit must comply within a legal framework. The existence of explainable AI models may lack mechanisms for legal justification (Kuźniacki et al., 2022). In consequence, the AI-generated audit decisions must be characterized by being explainable and justifiable in legal terms (Caron, 2021). The transparency in tax enforcement needs more tools such as SHAP analysis in order to bring justification for AI-driven risk classification and ensure its interpretability (Shi et al., 2023). The *"black boxes,"* of AI model may have limited insight about how outcomes are determined. This lack of explainability impacts the taxpayers trust and reduces the ability of tax authorities' to justify audit decisions and risk classification (Alsadhan, 2023; Tagliaferri et al., 2020). Explainability is more than a technical feature; it becomes a legal and ethical imperative. According to jurisdictions subject to the General Data Protection Regulation (GDPR), individuals have the right to know how automated decisions are made and how they affect them.

One of the dilemmas the IT community faces, was showcased, in the Australian *"Pintarich v Deputy Commissioner of Taxation"* case, where the Australian Taxation Office (ATO) sent a letter created by the computer that, among other things, wrongfully treated General Interest Charges (GIC) (Woellner, 2020). After the ATO canceled the letter, a lawsuit surfaced thereby also exposing the issue of AI-generated decisions' transparency and fairness in taxation.

That humans lose faith in AI when the decisions are regarded as capricious, or perplexing is one of the realities that explain why public skepticism towards AI is on a rising trend. In an international study of AI use in public fraud detection, the fact that there is a low level of trust in the public was indicated as a significant enabler of adoption (Tan et al., 2023). Here, interpretability also gets to the heart of the algorithmic audit selection. The ensembles are a common practice not only in Tunisia but also in another country like Saudi Arabia, where the government uses these models in automobile insurance claims in the Kingdom to automatize the work. Nowadays, we know that systems categorize the taxpayers into different levels of risk. If such methods used in the selection are not clear, it will create room for the association of the allocation with the concepts of discrimination and injustice which was a problem during the time of the study (Kamoun et al., 2024).

In response, research shows bringing applicability frameworks to an AI system's design stage is a solution that endorses fairness, develops trust, and implements procedural integrity. As shown by the stage of the tax administration in Figure 5, the implications of the loss of explainability are ethical matters and they are intensifying.

Figure 5. Transparent VS Black-Box AI systems in tax administration

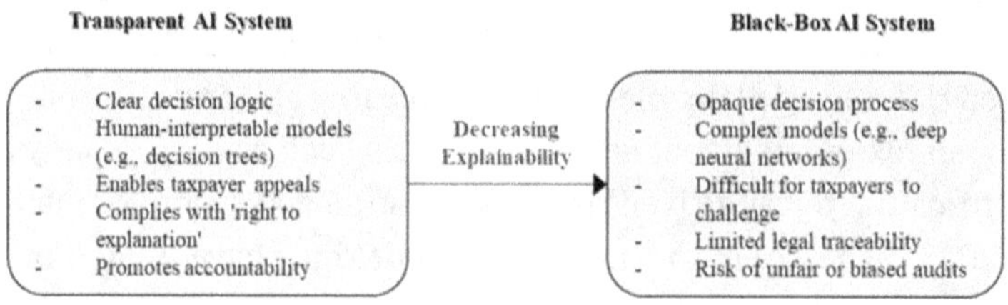

Need for Accountability of AI Decisions in Tax Administration

While it has always been important, as tax authorities increasingly turn to AI for tasks such as fraud detection, debt projection, and audit selection, upholding responsibility becomes more of critical importance. It lays down a coherent structure of technical and legal liability in cases where AI systems make mistakes, wrongly classify taxpayers, or bias the system. Multiple papers emphasize the current tensions between automatic decision-making and institutional responsibility.

In Italy a lack of standardized and clear audit selection procedures causes difficulty in the efforts to establish responsibility for AI-driven decisions (Tagliaferri et al., 2020). The adoption of an intricate algorithm like deep learning or using gradient boosting which is not easily interpretable is one of the problems that occur in relation to who is accountable for the design, the management of the system, or the institutions that employ such tools.

The approval of AI in public fraud detection has been outlined as a multi-faceted issue in the context of Belgium. It was highlighted in an interpretive structural model that "*trust*" and "*data governance*" are two most important aspects of the successful introduction of AI in the public sector according to Tan et al. (2023) study. One of the findings of the research is that poor accountability measures in the organizations may result in the loss of input (displeasure) and the public confidence crisis, mainly when AI errors lead to wrong taxpayer classification outcomes.

One of the most crucial things in keeping responsibility is differentiating between decision support and decision making. In Finland, AI is currently just being used to support human tax officers in the detection of insights and behavioral patterns, and not for making the final decision (Koivula et al., 2024). This system of workability will give rise to human responsibility, as a result of legal safeguards that curtail AI's self-governance in crucial areas like taxation.

The same worries about accountability that are so pressing in Europe are also felt elsewhere. For example, Saudi Arabia and Ecuador are dealing with the same issue on a daily basis. These countries use very intricate AI models to perform actions such as scoring taxpayers or predicting debt (Ordóñez-Placencia et al., 2024). Despite this shortcoming, it significantly improves efficiency by replacing the collectivism and time-consuming work which traditional organizations such as banks used to undertake. There is a missing opportunity here, as digital institutions can explain and clarify discrepancies without any commitment from staff members and sometimes bring to mind that the isolation is not complete.

One of the aspects where accountability is directly linked to fairness. In Tunisia and Yemen, research has been brought to fore that some unsuccessful situations with AI models may cause the company to face a severe disadvantage in audits or litigation with the tax department, while the taxpayers are still in full compliance (Kamoun et al., 2024; Shujaaddeen et al., 2024). From another perspective, the lack of an operational agency responsible for such drawbacks might damage the process of trust-making in public tax organizations and destroy the legitimacy of digital tax transformation.

Human Oversight in AI-Based Taxation

Relying on AI in the context of tax administration involves the observance of the primary factor, which is human intervention, especially when the machine learning models are getting more complicated and independent. Making human judgment a part of the AI decision-making process is the most essential issue that will promote fairness, protect the rights of taxpayers, and ensure the democratic accountability of society. By using AI in decision-making tax administrations remain the support of the democratic regime i.e., the institutional legitimacy and procedural justice, are ensured. Tax administrations should also take into account that it is important to have some human involvement in decision making with AI in order to fully engender legitimacy and procedural justice (Aoki et al., 2024).

Automation as a negative phenomenon is visible in the criticism of the *OECD's, Tax Administration 3.0* procedure, which in addition to automating taxes and digital compliance, also auto-recommends firing human tax officials further to audits and enforcement activities (Peeters, 2024). The thing that comes up frequently when talking about the justifications for keeping human supervision, is the occurrence of misclassification. A frequent point in the tax payers' opinions is that they are afraid of the lack of transparency, fairness and the ability to contradict the decisions of AI in the auditing sector resulting from these and similar problems that confirming the need to make decisions for which sufficient resources are accountable and understandable (Bentley, 2019).

Forbidding AI systems to make autonomous decisions about tax issues is a specific rule in the Finnish legislation (Koivula et al., 2024). The Finnish Tax Administration through the aid of AI models only uncovers knowledge and then the models, in turn, are the ones that guide the human officials in the decision-making process.

This model corroborates the current trend or best practices regarding regulation and technology that involves a combination of technology and human ethics.

Furthermore, the challenges of AI to handle intricate or situation-specific tax matters are demonstrated through the example of AI chatbots. Studies showed that chatbots can handle basic questions pretty well, but it seems that they often struggle when tax issues are quite complex and that really need a human's understanding and judgment.

Legal Oversight in AI-Assisted Taxation

The automated tax systems must ensure the respect of data protection laws that maintain people's rights. The potential of AI in figuring out taxpayers' profiles, choosing audits, and spotting fraud, requires laws that keep everything fair, clear, and respectful. In this context, the use of AI in tax requires a governmental commitment to follow rules in such a context (Munjeyi & Schutte, 2024).

AI-driven VAT tracking becomes one of the concerns that lead to much government oversight (Kleanthous & Chatzis, 2019). There is many worries about how the digital tax reporting and automated fraud detection might infringe folks' freedoms (Mosteanu, 2020). The gaps in regulations and the absence of specific tax laws for AI may represent a challenge to use this technology responsibly (Saragih et al., 2023). Lack of expertise can lead taxpayers to wonder about data safety.

Most common legal issues are how AI in taxation can react with data protection laws such as the GDPR. In this context, experts stress the need to balance AI tax enforcement with basic rights within EU regulations, such as *"privacy"* and the *"right to explanation"* under Article 22 of the GDPR (Fidelangeli & Galli, 2021). This means that people have the right to challenge decision made by automated system without human intervention.

As an example, Finland's approach showed how legal rules could shape AI use in tax collection. Here, AI is considered as a risk and a mechanism that makes the law stronger by improving how things are done (Daly, 2024).

In other contexts, especially in Germany, the Netherlands, Slovakia, and the UK, the rules about AI in taxation vary a lot. Some countries have a stricter law than others. The research revealed that weak and unclear regulations could make the use of AI safely harder.

The use of AI in tax law brings up many legal questions such as how AI can determine who should pay taxes without complicating things when trying to detect fraud, what counts as taxable income, and how tax law could be applied for digital services that cross borders (Fidelangeli & Galli, 2021). The ongoing discussions in Europe about the Digital Services Tax and the OECD's ideas on value creation show that legal systems need to evolve to handle new types of online taxes while making sure everyone pays their fair share willingly.

Data Protection & Privacy

Data Protection in AI-Driven Taxation

Tax authorities give great interest in handling sensitive taxpayer information by using new technology to catch fraud and stay compliant. Agencies need to be effective in order to respect their legal and ethical responsibilities, and to protect personal and financial data. Recent studies showed that the training data process could contain personal information. That raises many concerns about unauthorized access and misuse.

Pérez López et al. (2019) mention that AI systems in tax administration must follow strict privacy laws. For instance, the GDPR in Europe built to make sure that personal data is handled clearly, kept safe, and only used with proper consent (Lukianykhina et al., 2024). For instance, when tax authorities analyze taxpayer info with AI, they have to take steps to prevent any unauthorized access or misuse (Pérez López et al., 2019).

The blockchain technology used for managing VAT in Europe by tracking of transactions. However, there are many worries about the ethical considerations related to the use of taxpayer's information and privacy concerns. Even with the use of coding or masking methods, this technology still, represents a security space for data (Gaie & Mueck, 2022).

In Latvia, AI used to influence taxpayers' behavior. The approach relied on wage declaration data to classify taxpayers. It revealed many questions about the process of selecting data and how to keep it safe during automated communications (Saulitis & Chapkovski, 2024). The study showed the importance of using less taxpayers' data and the need for transparency. Also, making sure that people give informed consent when dealing with taxpayer information in AI tools.

Privacy Risks in Process Optimization

The use of AI systems in tax administrations improves efficiency, accuracy in audit and cost. However, when AI model deals with a huge amount of data can lead to privacy issues. If Tax authorities rely on detailed data that may influence taxpayer privacy and step into surveillance territory if we don't have adequate protections.

When it comes to the use of machine learning in taxes, it typically involves sensitive taxpayer information, so a robust security system is essential to keep this data safe and prevent any misuse (Schächtele, 2023). Furthermore, while real-time monitoring can help improve compliance, it can make companies uncomfortable with constant oversight, which they may perceive as intrusive (Vozár & Bán, 2024).

In Egypt, the Tax Authority applied AI-powered Business Process Reengineering (BPR) to improve efficiency and reduce costs. Privacy became a big concern. Nowadays, People are still wondering about taxpayers' right and fairness because of the unclear vision of the AI system. Even with all the positive side of such system, the privacy still need more attention and concern (Bayomy et al., 2024). However, Tax officials are conscious about how the evolution of AI affects both taxpayer and company data. That shows how important it is to have clear rules about data use with time.

For instance, a system was created to predict corporate tax issues by using over two million records (Siimon & Lukason, 2021). The outcomes of the model succeeded to predict tax problems by studying the financial behaviors of small to medium businesses. At the same time, it raised questions about consent, especially when taxpayer independence was touched by surveillance.

A recent study looked at how different tax agencies handle digital tech and privacy, and it appears that many of them are ahead when it comes to digital tools, but not so much with privacy rules (Strauss et al., 2020). The study noted that if AI tax systems are used efficiently and ignore the aspect of privacy from the beginning, it might become a surveillance tool. So, transparency and protections are essential to stop people from pushing back and to ensure people's trust in tax agencies.

Lack of Transparency in AI-Driven Tax Data Collection

The revelation of the ascertained and valid operation of AI at all data collections and also at the stage of its use in tax administration is vital for winning the society's trust in the good and legal performance of artificial intelligence. It is doubtful if one can say that such an explanation is sufficient, but many studies show that the lack of transparency in the methods, scope, and justification for AI-controlled tax data collection leads to a situation where they are questions about the fairness and equity of the taxpayers, and they do not know about it or do not consent. People are worried about taxpayers' rights, fairness, and whether they have enough information, especially since things are not very clear.

The taxpayers' lack of trust in using artificial intelligence for detection of fraud is the main factor that causes their dissatisfaction, which increases even more with the shadowiness of the decision-making process in the examination phase. This is amplified, in particular: (a) by the incomprehensibility and lack of clarity of both the grounds and the criteria of people's choice for detailed examination and (b) in the case when the audit phase is carried out without humans (Kieslich et al., 2022). Such obscurity might be the catalyst for a major erosion of confidence not only in the impartiality and accountability of the mechanisms of automatic enforcement but also in the whole system of taxes if there is a heavy impact of the issue, such as audits.

In the case of developing economies, as AI takes over financial and tax activities, there are also implementation difficulties that come up. According to a study in Lebanon, the author's survey of 454 certified accountants showed that the application of AI cut short the fraud detection time, eased the tax filing process, enhanced data quality, but still wrestled with some political hurdles, as Lebanon faced that time, resources scarcity, and inadequate digital infrastructure (Chávez-Díaz et al., 2024). Such research on AI in accounting and tax services confirms the revolutionary nature of AI and at the same time verifies the existence of institutional barriers to its adoption.

AI was used in Latvia in a controlled and carefully designed business experiment aimed at freeing businesses that did not pay the required wage taxes, by identifying them, and a subset of them receiving warnings to comply (Saulitis & Chapkovski, 2024). However, the absence of transparency concerning the business entities that were targeted for the intervention led to a feeling of uncertainty and mistrust. The management of various business enterprises posed misgiving about the fairness of the targeting process and expressed dissatisfaction with the lack of explanation provided for their inclusion in the campaign.

These results underline the significant role that communicating in a clear, truthful, and understandable manner play in AI-based tax oversight. If not employed, those well-planned tools may turn out to be of no benefit, as having their work uprooted by people who are not satisfied and the worry about the overdue process can be of a great power.

Fairness & Non Discrimination

Bias Prevention in AI Decision-Making

Operating practices in taxation administration need to focus primarily on the concept of justice, particularly if artificial intelligence becomes an essential part of the process. Decision-making that is done by systems trained by relevant past data can lead to unjustified biases which in turn initiate the perpetuation of biases of that kind, thus resulting in negative audit practices, different profiling of taxpayers, and inconsistent handling in terms of socio-economic, regional, or demographic aspects. Avoidance of such biases requires not only conscious design but also thorough testing, bias detection, and ethical monitoring being made a part of the process.

AI systems are in charge of keeping neutrality without any discrimination towards people's age, race, status, and the like, due to the fact that such platforms should outline all the variants which can be met with regarding the matching and enforcement policies and practice (Alrjoub et al., 2023). Equally, it is fair both that AI systems developed according to the ethical principles not to only decide on the issue of fairness, in particular, related to taxpayers' categorization and profiling projects but also that they stay away from algorithmic bias and provide a detailed communication throughout the process to the users (Ourdani et al., 2024). The use of the hierarchical attention mechanism, which shows the selected data as more critical while it as the base data is biased just to be removed, can be unfair to justice. Authors stress that there should be clear explanation techniques and fairness audits, to reduce the risk of disproportionate targeting of specific groups.

The modelling of arrears in the area of tax in Estonia shines a brighter light on the topic of fairness. The firm-level tax data form the basis for the study that predicts tax payment risk, and it uses these historical data to the exclusion of all other factors for payment risk evaluation (Siimon & Lukason, 2021). Despite the fact that the present case can enhance the administrative efficiency, the reliance solely on past debts as the biggest signal of the payment risk of the future may close the door for the emergence of companies remaining outside the reach of taxes, and at the same time, it may be a signal of widened social rifts. The projection of future success comes at the expense of the future failure of others and results in the greater segregation of those living on the edge of the society. The research does not refrain from suggesting that the use of human judgment alongside IT may be the viable option to maintain a balance between ethicality and accuracy in forecasting.

A very similar model was worked on in Russia, in that a hybrid approach combining genetic algorithms and clustering methods was utilized to detect anomalies in the data derived from point-of-sale (PoS) terminals (Malashin et al., 2024b). The performance of the model was fully consistent with the authors' expectations, and it revealed that the majority of the misuse patterns were also made by them (false positives). Nevertheless, the researchers realized that although the model was efficient in identifying suspicious behaviors, there was a likelihood of false positives and so expert validation of flagged cases was necessary to avoid unjust audits of complaint businesses.

All of these used cases clearly demonstrate the importance of human rights and transparency in all AI system phases of tax administration and the system ensures that the use of technology does not violate ethical principles.

Need for Fairness

In order to conclude and to reach the correct outcome with the use of AI in tax administration, we also need to look after another principle namely to ensure fairness and equality to all taxpayers and using unbiased and non-discriminatory methods. AI may help lower inefficiency, however, at the core of each operation, it is necessary to incorporate the fairness which should be thought of before the outset, and not just the afterthought. Moving to the automated decision-making in taxing is harder to do, whilst maintaining the fairness and accuracy of such decisions (Bevacqua, 2020).

As one of the top priority issues, AI systems have to guarantee precise performance besides the fact that the citizens see the enforcement of their tax-paying duties as just and equitable (Ingrams et al., 2022). Fair AI-powered tax enforcements are those that do not generate *"false positives,"* treat the citizens in a fair and efficient way, and provide them with the opportunity for appeal (Borrotti et al., 2023). All these necessities call for proper legal and regulatory frameworks which are consistent with data protection laws, for example, the GDPR, and at the same time protect principles of fairness and accountability (Kieslich et al., 2022).

In a research carried out among business companies located in Latvia, AI-powered communication strategies involving both threatening and persuasive messages were put to the test as to their effectiveness in increasing the declaration of wages used in tax compliance (Saulitis & Chapkovski, 2024). While it showed a positive result in the short run compliance, the businesses taking part questioned the fairness of the whole process and in particular the selection process. The participators questioned the selection process by reflecting on the basis of their chosen status, and more importantly, they re-evaluated the possibility of other comparable firms getting the same treatment. The investigations substantiate the requirement for the regulations based on the approachability and intelligibility of the selection facilities in AI-assistance taxpayer transactions.

In Egypt, a Business Process Reengineering (BPR) project which had as its goal an improvement in the efficiency of the tax office faced challenges of fairness as well. While the implementation of AI tools was used to make the operations more efficient, concerns appeared around the question of whether the automation was affecting too much certain groups of the tax payers (Bayomy et al., 2024). The authors state in their work that fairness can be achieved in these situations if transparent governance practices are followed by human decision makers and the new reengineered processes.

Finland is a prime example of the humane application of AI in the field of tax administration. The AI system is national, and it is designed for tax claim processing aid. The AI system was developed not to make decisions directly; instead, it was given the only function of decision support (Koivula et al., 2024). The Finnish Tax Administration disallows AI tools to play a decisive role in conflicts, especially in ambiguous or borderline cases, for the sake of fairness, the rule of law, and human judgment.

Finally, the Fidelangeli & Galli (2021) legal model referred to in the article has fairness as a legal requirement in the process of digital taxation. They posit that AI tools that are used to determine what is there to be taxed or who is to be taxed must not create discriminatory burdens or *"digital loopholes."* Proactive tax legislation is suggested by their work so as to anticipate AI's systemic implications and to guarantee fair tax allocation among digital economies.

Risk of Discriminatory Targeting of Taxpayers

AI enforcement of tax laws on the basis of poorly designed or insufficiently supervised algorithm models may be used which can lead to either the confirmation of the existing biases or the fomenting of new forms of discriminatory targeting. This matter becomes more serious if the training data are affected by the same disparities in the audit patterns, enforcement steps or the behavior of the taxpayers who are filing. Without effective measures to protect them, certain groups of taxpayers, by location, area of activity, size, or socio-economic status, might suffer an undue share of the scrutiny.

If AI systems are not properly tested, they might incorrectly label law-abiding taxpayers as criminals and this may lead to unnecessary audits and tarnishing of the taxpayer's image (Murorunkwere et al., 2022). A study of racial inequalities in the application of U.S. tax audits showed that even when race-blind process audit algorithms are used, Black taxpayers are still audited at much higher rates than non-Black taxpayers, and the range may vary from 2.9 to 4.7, mainly because of how the IRS runs the Earned Income Tax Credit (EITC) (Elzayn et al., 2023). The research paper utilized a partial identification method based on Bayesian Improved First Name and Surname Geocoding (BIFSG) to uncover the disparities in the audit results related to race.

Predictive analytics have been an object of research as a way to make the audit targeting more efficient, however, if the same analytics are used without the proper checks and balances, they can also be the source of some risks. One particular piece of research was an actual comparison of random audit tactics with AI-risk models, where the latter was a full-fledged agent-based model incorporating a minimum amount of behavioral economics (Hashimzade et al., 2016). Despite the fact that such a model as the one mentioned above enhances the speed and efficacy of audits, the gathering of data from different types of sources, such as register records, transaction records, and VAT returns can lead to the misinterpretation of legal network patterns as illegal ones, especially for small and informal economic units. The authors strongly posit that the confirmation of the pattern's validity by an expert is crucial to miss lawsuits.

In Ecuador, the application of deep learning algorithms has led to the generation of early warnings about tax debt, which has been adopted by authorities to act preemptively in the enforcement process (Ordóñez-Placencia et al., 2024). The use of the model also had the potential of classifying taxpayers in such a way that whole segments, like micro-enterprises, became high-risk cases without actually distinguishing between structural financial pressures and tax evasion. The mentioned mistakes could bring about the unfairness that would arise from the over-penalization of the weaker taxpayers and thus they would lead to the failure of the legislation enforcement.

These results show that the use of fairness audit, the availability of transparency features, and the input of humans in the development and deployment of AI models in the collection of tax are very important, and their absence may later become a systemic bias and lead to unequal treatment of taxpayer groups. Table 4 gives a comparison of ethical dilemmas in the process of AI integration in tax administration in some countries, showing the link between the issues' nature and socio-legal context, as well as technical applications. The findings provide an understanding of the ethical challenges in both common and location-specific terms and their relationship with the successful implementation and the management of AI in tax systems.

This table compares the ethical problems that prevail in the rich countries (e.g., Finland, Belgium, and Estonia) and countries in the developing stage (e.g., Egypt, Tunisia, and Ecuador). There lies the benefit, however, of examining the relationship between regulatory grip, technological access, and oversight potential of the AI administration over the taxation when comparing countries of different economic well-being.

Table 4. Cross-national analysis of ethical issues

Country	Ethical Considerations	Justification
Italy	Transparency, Audit Bias, Data Privacy	Use of black-box models (e.g., Gradient Boosting) in audit selection raises explainability and fairness concerns.
Yemen	Fairness, Misclassification Risk, Privacy	Hybrid NN model may misclassify taxpayers; lack of transparency impacts taxpayer trust.
Tunisia	Bias in ML Models, Audit Transparency	Audit models flagged VAT-related bias; interpretability is critical for enforcement acceptance.
Ecuador	Data Protection, Fair Enforcement	DeepSurv used for risk prediction raises questions about fair targeting and explanation of decisions.
Saudi Arabia	Black-box AI, Over-Surveillance	Multi-module fraud detection system risks taxpayer over-surveillance without transparency.
Estonia	Risk of Misclassification, Fairness	Tax arrears model may unfairly classify SMEs; fairness is essential in risk profiling.
Egypt	Change Resistance, Transparency, CRM Trust	BPR-driven process change met resistance; fairness and trust-building in automated processes were emphasized.
China	Surveillance Concerns, Black-box AI	GNN-based fraud detection enables deep profiling, raising privacy and surveillance concerns.
Russia	False Positives, Audit Fairness	Anomaly detection flagged legitimate entities; fairness and false positives were key risks.
Latvia	Trust in Nudges, Data Protection	Behavioral nudges raised questions about taxpayer manipulation and data usage transparency.

continued on following page

Table 4. Continued

Country	Ethical Considerations	Justification
Belgium	AI Accountability, Legal Constraints	Interviews revealed lack of trust in AI-driven classification; legal constraints prevent full automation.
Finland	Human Oversight, GDPR Compliance	AI used only for support (not decision-making) due to legal barriers; emphasis on explainability and GDPR.

Integrating Ethical Frameworks for AI Implementation in Tax Control

Policy Recommendations for Ethical AI Deployment

In the world of the literature AI systems must ensure the transparency in any tax-related decision-making process in order to maintain certain degree of accountability. Apart from that, it is a matter of fact that the new AI methods like Gradient Boosting and Hybrid Neural Networks have a very good performance in the detection of tax evasion and fraud (Shujaaddeen et al., 2024; Tagliaferri et al., 2020), but the *"black box"* phenomenon is a big question and challenge whether people's trust in automatic audit results will be maintained or undermined. Various studies propose conducting fairness audits and algorithmic impact assessments to prevent errors in AI systems before they are put into practically any application in the tax management department (Alsadhan, 2023; Didimo et al., 2018). The implementation of ethical principles of the design in AI from the very beginning can mark the path for responsible deployment. For example, to support the responsible adoption of AI in fraudulent public detection systems in Belgium, a reliable model has been offered for ethical AI governance with elements concerning trust, interoperability, data governance, and regulatory compliance (Tan et al., 2023).

Furthermore, within the dimension of the European Union, a VAT tracing system reliant on the blockchain technology and the privacy-by-design technique, which fully embraces GDPR requirements, will not only secure the privacy of the tax information but also accomplish the purpose of the taxpayer's identity being held in confidence (Gaie & Mueck, 2022). The model illustrates the manner by which the confidentiality requirement is satisfied and exhibits how the technical resources can work with the legal aspects to fulfill privacy and data security in e-tax.

It is also proposed that human supervision is obligatory in AI-driven processes in all legal systems. The experience of tax agencies in both Finland and Saudi Arabia points to the usage of AI systems as mere decision-support tools as the most ethical, which also attests to the high ethicality of the cases (Koivula et al., 2024). Through this procedure, the task of maintaining the ethical boundaries is completed while, in addition, the analytic capabilities of AI are kept.

The literature lays the emphasis on the fact that ethical principles need to be multiplied by the dimensions of technology, law, and human beings. It is encouraged that tax authorities are involved in the creation of a well-structured ethical system that is based on a set of principles from AI ethics in order to make sure that AI promulgation maintains democracy and responds to data protection rights as well as social equity goals (Kamoun et al., 2024; Ordóñez-Placencia et al., 2024).

Role of Policymakers in Ensuring Compliance with Privacy Laws

Policymakers who are situated at the intersection between regulation and innovation are those people who guide AI integration in taxation to ensure that the systems are privacy and data protection law compliant.

The application of AI to evaluate sensitive taxpayer information has various legal and ethical concerns like those related to data security, consent, and the possibility of mass surveillance. The challenges call for the development of policies where the starting point is the creating of rules governing the legal clarity, transparency, and defending individual rights.

Various studies reveal that a policy gap hinders the use of AI technologies in taxation without the requisite legal framework regulation. For instance, it was argued that the absence of AI-specific tax legislation in Tunisia and Estonia was a major stumbling block to the lawful and ethical execution of the new technology (Kamoun et al., 2024; Siimon & Lukason, 2021). These examples underscore the need to stipulate the AI standards that are explicitly regulating the latter's participation in audit selections, taxpayer classification, and debt enforcement.

Moreover, it is imperative for policymakers to also fortify the mechanisms for oversight so as to ensure that they are accountable. Specifically, in Belgium, the trustworthy governance model has been suggested where those responsible for policy make sure that AI systems are auditable, interoperable, and with no doubts about GDPR compliance (Tan et al., 2023). Such measures as the creation of bodies to control AI performance, algorithmic output audit, and the guarantee of procedural fairness in the automatic settlement of taxes are also part of this scope.

Another point is that there is a growing need for international cooperation in order to achieve no incongruity in the rules and prevent an unfair advantage from resulting from it. The uneven distribution of AI in different areas will hamper tax official's global compliance (Strauss et al., 2020). Aligned measures like the existence of data-sharing agreements between countries and the development of joint AI ethics frameworks that would oversee the policy cannot just speed up the process of ethical AI deployment but also maintain the legal consistency and accountability.

However, the commitment of the lawmakers to influence the public discourse of the country is at the same level of importance. As per the studies from Latvia and Finland, the general sentiment of taxpayer trust in AI-based tax systems looks positive, if the authorities give a clear message on the matters of AI's part in the enforcement process, and are open about the steps taken to safeguard taxpayer data (Koivula et al., 2024; Saulitis & Chapkovski, 2024). Full openness of AI usage coupled with effective privacy laws not only encourages compliance in tax payment among taxpayers but also helps to build trust.

Synthesis of Thematic Patterns and Ethical Dimensions

Table 5 presents the thematic framework that emerged from our systematic literature review, highlighting the key ethical dimensions associated with the integration of AI into tax control processes. This framework synthesizes the patterns across the ninety-one selected studies and encapsulates the most recurrent and significant concerns under three major themes: *"Accountability & Explainability," "Data Protection & Privacy,"* and *"Fairness & Non-Discrimination."*

The theme of *"Accountability & Explainability"* emerged as the most frequently discussed ethical category, with a remarkable concentration on the *"Need for Explainability & Transparency of AI Decisions in Tax Administration"* (n = 84). This result showed how scholars and practitioners worry about the lack of transparency of AI systems in taxation filed. With this huge influence of AI system in the domains of risk assessment and audit selection, the necessity of unveiling the decision-making process becomes very important in order to guarantee legal compliance, trust of the taxpayer, and procedural justice.

Two topic lists: *"Legal Oversight in AI-Assisted Taxation"* (n=25) and *"Need for Accountability"* (n=20) specifically highlight the importance of having clear rules and responsibilities to deal with errors or prejudices. Additionally, the issue of *"Human Oversight in AI-Based Taxation"* (n=10) is the one that stresses most that it is necessary to balance the decision-making by adding the human factor although technology is heavily involved.

The second emerging theme, *"Data Protection & Privacy,"* mirrors society's deep concerns regarding the misuse of sensitive taxpayer data in intelligent technology-driven environments. The sub-theme *"Data Protection in AI-Driven Taxation"* (n = 57) manifestly stands for the principle of the researchers' overwhelming support to the idea of AI only being used in compliance with data privacy laws such as the GDPR. By collaborating with AI, organizations benefit in their operations area, but a threat to the safety of the data, which is not owned by unauthorized persons such as through data misuse, and lacking consent acquisition mechanisms are the aspects that the studies address. The lower frequency with which *"Privacy Risks in*

Process Optimization" (n = 10) and the *"Lack of Transparency in AI-Driven Tax Data Collection"* (n = 4) are mentioned highlights the risk of privacy intrusion that is often neglected and, thus, becomes an issue as the pursuit of process efficiency takes place without it being ethically sound.

The subject of *"Fairness & Non-Discrimination"* is derived from a quickly expanding area of research dealing with the risk of bias and inequity in algorithmic tax enforcement. The problem of *"Bias Prevention in AI Decision-Making"* (n=50) was detected as a crucial one, and numerous studies witnessed the readiness of AI systems for utilizing either old or incomplete data that might lead to unjust decision-making of certain groups. The risk of the citizens' tax discrimination (n=40) was introduced as another component of the ethical dimension of profiling using algorithms, and the *"Welcoming of Equitableness"* (n=9) was introduced as normative demands for an equable procedure and legal protection. As units of information, they allude to the pressing demand for the practice of fairness audits, algorithmic impact assessments, and uninterrupted human control.

Table 5 serves as a ready-made instrument that allows to address the ethical problems occurred in tax organizations, to identify their scope, and their causal factors, and to help find the answers to those questions. Therefore, the analytical model of this thematic synthesis not only covers all the major discourse areas much in the same fashion that it guides the further discovery of issues gaps but also informs and sets a basis for the future ethical reviews, policy making, and governing of AI in the public sector.

Table 5. Themes of ethical considerations of AI-driven tax control

Themes	Subthemes	Frequency
Accountability & Explainability	Human Oversight in AI-Based Taxation	10
	Legal Oversight in AI-Assisted Taxation	25
	Need for Accountability of AI Decisions in Tax Administration	20
	Need for Explainability & Transparency of AI Decisions in Tax Administration	84
Data Protection & Privacy	Data Protection in AI-Driven Taxation	57
	Lack of Transparency in AI-Driven Tax Data Collection	4
	Privacy Risks in Process Optimization	10
Fairness & Non-Discrimination	Bias Prevention in AI Decision-Making	50
	Need for fairness	9
	Risk of Discriminatory Targeting of Taxpayers	40

DISCUSSION

Artificial intelligence makes it possible to do tasks that a human cannot or would take much longer to perform and, at the same time, it can also provide such basic services as including fraud prevention and enforcement optimization. Nonetheless, AI systems' efficiency does not go unchallenged, and the issue might be inadequate transparency and security of algorithms. For instance, it has been reported that eighty-four studies considered the concept of explainability to be crucial in AI decision-making, thus representing the common finding of the academy that the *"black box"* character of a large number of models is counter to trust and transparency. As seen in reports from Italy and Saudi Arabia, the mere use of gradient boosting and deep learning models, lacking however the presence of clear explanation mechanisms, has been the main driver of the rise of the publics' skepticism and creation of legal ambiguities (Tagliaferri et al., 2020).

The necessity of stringent data protections in AI-driven taxation was also outlined in fifty-seven articles. The primary issue of concern was the illegal acquisition of sensitive data of taxpayers, its misuse and lack of confidentiality which arose from regions like Egypt and Latvia where AI techniques were used in behavioral nudging or process optimization without clear governance protocols (Bayomy et al., 2024; Saulitis & Chapkovski, 2024). The cases suggest that legal safeguards and the consent of users should accompany technological progress.

The topic of fairness and non-discrimination was also revealed as an extremely important ethical frontier. Fifty documents presented various sides of the racial and gender bias problem. It was mainly about cases where AI could entrench the existing gaps in audit targeting and taxpayer classification. For example, Estonia and Russia faced similar issues with AI tools which, for all their productivity, were at the same time, capable of wrong firm classification arising from biased historical data or incorrect clustering techniques (Malashin et al., 2024a; Siimon & Lukason, 2021). These discoveries proliferate the significance of fairness audits and continual monitoring as tools of preventing unfair treatment.

Theoretical Implications

Theoretically, this article may be a lead for getting a detailed understanding of how AI is disrupting fundamental aspects of public law, administrative ethics, and digital governance. Beyond that, it follows the evolution of algorithmic accountability discussion which is a range of responsibilities towards the technical engineers, the institutional, and the policy-making levels.

What is especially important in the first place is that the review is making a significant contribution to AI governance by the means of procedural justice as well as the rule of law. Argumentation, e.g., relating AI governance to GDPR and precedent (e.g., Pintarich v Deputy Commissioner of Taxation) shows up-rooting legal norms in favor of the AI-biased procedure. The authors refer to the analogous results obtainable from explainable AI; the necessity of the government's decision-making for legally and ethically justifiable AI applications is emphasized further.

Additionally, this study brings the behavior tax compliance theories, like, for example, the *"slippery slope framework"*, into action by indicating changes in trust and power that are brought about not only by the behavior of the organization but also by the perceived fairness and transparency of AI tools. Hence, AI is represented as a machine for technological assistance and at the same time as a social and technical entity affecting taxpayers' actions and institutional legitimacy as well.

Practical Implications

The results of tax administration are highly meaningful in the sense of now. To facilitate the understanding of the AI systems, it is indispensable both from a moral and pragmatic point of view. The next result with Verifiability as a general principle in AI is based on previous work where the method was re-implemented for this purpose. Finland and Belgium's human-in-the-loop models, as good examples, are considered the ones that balance technology with ethical responsibility (Koivula et al., 2024; Tan et al., 2023).

It is also necessary for companies to have an infrastructure in place that will support the data governance tasks related to GDPR compliance. These should also include procedures through which the amount of data, consent from data subjects, and processing can be secured. Especially, this makes sense in terms of AI which is used in the detection of fraud and in debt recovery.

The review also points the importance of fair-by-design approach in AI systems. Moreover, decision-makers and tax officials need to be prepared and fight possible bias in a pro-active way through regular audits, validation techniques, and transparent decision-making protocols. For the confirmation, *"raceblind"* systems which was the subject of the U.S. research on the wrongful conducts (Elzayn et al., 2023) were proven to produce biased targeting, thus, the phenomenon showed that it is necessary not to analyze the mere inputs but also the outcomes without any preconceived idea.

Finally, an international framework is really important. Observing AI adoption and legal infrastructure in various countries, it becomes evident that there is a need for common ethical standards and regulations. This sort of cooperation will not only allow us to solve problems such as cross-border digital taxes but will also ensure that taxpayer rights are globally recognized in AI age.

CONCLUSION

This SLR discusses tax control procedures globally, mainly with a focus on AI integration within. The examination of ninety-one selected papers, the majority of which were case studies, indicated high agreement of academics in regard to the prominent ethical themes of *"Accountability & Explainability," "Data Protection & Privacy,"* and *"Fairness & Non-Discrimination."* Eighty-four occurrences mentioned the issue that an AI system will be required, through design, to explain its outcomes and to make the AI process transparent to human beings with easy language. The studies across different regions revealed the nature of the black-box AI model that influences how taxpayers' distrust and delegitimize the tax administration. That seems clear in situations where a decision's reasons are not transparently traceable during the audit or fraud detection phase (Pang & Hua, 2024).

Furthermore, *"Data protection and privacy"* became the most relevant ethical aspect. Moreover, 50% of the studies highlighted that it is crucial to make the use of AI compatible with the national and international data protection legislation like the GDPR. Some situations, like those in Egypt, Estonia, and Latvia, revealed conflicts between operational efficiency and personal data privacy, particularly when AI devices analyzed detailed information about tax payers (Ahmed Bayomy et al., 2021; Siimon & Lukason, 2021).

The reports on concepts like *"fairness and bias prevention"* were all encompassing. Apart from the references to the sub-topics being over ninety, it was also noticed that most of the studies exposed the numerous areas where AI models may have taken over or amplified social biases present in the training data. The following two instances are great examples for this: a target group in the U.S. for an audit and predictive tools in Ecuador and Tunisia, which altogether depicted the danger of the perpetuation of socio-economic and racial disparities while pretending to be objective in the decision-making process (Elzayn et al., 2023; Kamoun et al., 2024).

On the whole, the use of AI can mean that the fight against fraud, increased efficiency as well as compliance are all facilitated quite evidently. However, that is not the only change as the results constantly remind the value that is placed on moral ethics in design, legal control, and the involvement of humans.

This review offers policymakers with several practical measures. Initially, fairness audits must definitely be included in AI system deployment along with algorithmic impact assessments as a precondition in tax administration. Such instruments can easily spot and address prejudice before it reaches taxpayer outcomes. Next, AI models designed in an explainable way including those that are in agreement with legal frameworks such as the GDPR are helpful in three ways. They improve transparency, increase the likelihood that decisions will be challenged and ensure that judgments are made public. Last, the requirement of human oversight for all high-stakes decisions not only ensures accountability but also prevents procedural justice from violation. Finally, national tax authorities should coordinate with international partners to establish harmonized ethical standards and regulatory frameworks, ensuring consistency across borders and reducing legal ambiguity. These measures will help governments build trust and ensure that the integration of AI into taxation systems remains both effective and ethically grounded.

Limitations of the Review

This review provides a comprehensive synthesis of literature from 2014 to 2024. Even with the importance of the relevant papers written in English and French, we must mention many limitations related to linguistic and regional bias due to not taking into consideration relevant studies published in other languages.

In addition, thematic coding may represent a certain degree of subjectivity. Even with the rigorous screening process of the PRISMA protocol, consistency of thematic categorization may be affected. Challenges in theme consolidation included maintaining inter-coder reliability and managing the complexity of interdisciplinary literature (law, AI, economics, public administration).

However, in the bibliometric analysis, we were confined to three major databases: Scopus, Web of Science, and Cairn. Even with their relevance, we have excluded pertinent grey literature, institutional reports, and government documents. These papers may contribute to shaping AI implementation in practice.

This SLR's findings are temporally bound to the selected period (2014–2024). However, the technological and legal developments in AI and tax policy rapidly evolve, bringing out more insights. In consequence, reviews and updates are necessary to maintain relevance.

Future Research Directions

In Future research, taxpayer behavior, administrative efficiency, and ethical outcomes should by delved into comparative case studies in order to assess the real-world impact of AI tools. Empirically, explainability should be evaluated to reveal its influence in public trust and audit outcomes. Over time, the evolving effectiveness of fairness audits and accountability mechanisms should be explored through longitudinal studies.

Interdisciplinary inquiries are essential for designing effective AI systems that lawful and socially acceptable. This should be intersected with integration of legal scholarship, behavioral economics, and computer science. Moreover, taxpayer perspectives on AI-driven enforcement should be a main concern to investigate among vulnerable groups in order to ensure inclusive policy design.

Lastly, given the rapid pace of AI innovation, continuous monitoring and adaptive governance models should be developed. Policymakers and researchers must collaborate to co-create ethical standards and legal instruments that keep pace with technological change and transnational tax enforcement challenges.

REFERENCES

Ahmed Bayomy, N., & Khedr, E., A., & Abd-Elmegid, L. A. (. (2021). Adaptive model to support business process reengineering. *PeerJ. Computer Science*, *7*, e505. DOI: 10.7717/peerj-cs.505 PMID: 33987460

Allingham, M. G., & Sandmo, A. (1972). Income tax evasion: A theoretical analysis. *Journal of Public Economics*, *1*(3-4), 323–338. DOI: 10.1016/0047-2727(72)90010-2

Alrjoub, A. M. S., Al-Qudah, L. A. M., Al-Othman, L. N., Bataineh, A., Aburisheh, K. E., & Alkarabsheh, F. (2023). Information Technology and its Role in Improving the Quality of Financial Control due to Corona Pandemic: The Jordanian Income Tax as A Case Study. *International Journal of Professional Business Review*, *8*(4), e01568. DOI: 10.26668/businessreview/2023.v8i4.1568

Alsadhan, N. (2023). A Multi-Module Machine Learning Approach to Detect Tax Fraud. *Computer Systems Science and Engineering*, *46*(1), 241–253. DOI: 10.32604/csse.2023.033375

Aoki, N., Tatsumi, T., Naruse, G., & Maeda, K. (2024). Explainable AI for government: Does the type of explanation matter to the accuracy, fairness, and trustworthiness of an algorithmic decision as perceived by those who are affected? *Government Information Quarterly*, *41*(4), 101965. DOI: 10.1016/j.giq.2024.101965

Bayomy, N. A., Khedr, A. E., & Abd-Elmegid, L. A. (2024). A configurable mining approach for enhancing the business processes' performance. *Knowledge and Information Systems*, *66*(4), 2537–2560. DOI: 10.1007/s10115-023-02011-4

Bentley, D. (2019). Timeless principles of taxpayer protection: How they adapt to digital disruption. *eJournal of Tax Research.*

Bevacqua, J. (2020). Tax authority immunity in a digital tax administration world. *eJournal of Tax Research, 18*(2), 402–440.

Borrotti, M., Rabasco, M., & Santoro, A. (2023). Using accounting information to predict aggressive tax location decisions by European groups. *Economic Systems*, *47*(3), 101090. DOI: 10.1016/j.ecosys.2023.101090

Bou Reslan, F., & Jabbour Al Maalouf, N. (2024). Assessing the Transformative Impact of AI Adoption on Efficiency, Fraud Detection, and Skill Dynamics in Accounting Practices. *Journal of Risk and Financial Management*, *17*(12), 577. DOI: 10.3390/jrfm17120577

Caron, É. (2021). Le Big Data fiscal: Quelles conséquences pour le contrôle fiscal et les contribuables? *Gestion & Finances Publiques*, *6*(6), 77–83. DOI: 10.3166/gfp.2021.6.013

Castellón González, P., & Velásquez, J. D. (2013). Characterization and detection of taxpayers with false invoices using data mining techniques. *Expert Systems with Applications*, *40*(5), 1427–1436. DOI: 10.1016/j.eswa.2012.08.051

Chávez-Díaz, J. M., Aquiño-Perales, L., De-Velazco-Borda, J. L., Villagómez-Chinchay, J. A., & Flores-Sotelo, W. S. (2024). Artificial intelligence in accounting and auditing: Bibliometric analysis in Scopus 2020-2023. *Indonesian Journal of Electrical Engineering and Computer Science*, *36*(2), 1319. DOI: 10.11591/ijeecs.v36.i2.pp1319-1328

Daly, S. (2024). Artificial intelligence, the Rule of Law and public administration: The case of taxation. *The Cambridge Law Journal*, *83*(3), 437–464. DOI: 10.1017/S0008197324000448

Didimo, W., Giamminonni, L., Liotta, G., Montecchiani, F., & Pagliuca, D. (2018). A visual analytics system to support tax evasion discovery. *Decision Support Systems*, *110*, 71–83. DOI: 10.1016/j.dss.2018.03.008

Elzayn, H., Smith, E., Hertz, T., Guage, C., Ramesh, A., Fisher, R., Ho, D. E., & Goldin, J. (2023). Measuring and Mitigating Racial Disparities in Tax Audits. *The Quarterly Journal of Economics*, *140*(1), 113–163. DOI: 10.1093/qje/qjae027

Fidelangeli, A., & Galli, F. (2021). Artificial intelligence and tax law: Perspective and challenges. *CERIDAP, 4*. DOI: 10.13130/2723-9195/2021-4-27

Gaie, C., & Mueck, M. (2022). A hybrid blockchain proposal to improve value added tax recovery. *International Journal of Internet Technology and Secured Transactions*, *12*(1), 27. DOI: 10.1504/IJITST.2022.119668

Gomes, G. S. L., & Balaniuk, R. (2024). Identifying tax evasion in shell companies and fraudulent credits of Brazil's state value-added tax (ICMS). *Revista de Administração Pública*, *58*(4), e2023-0303. Advance online publication. DOI: 10.1590/0034-761220230303x

Górski, Ł., Kuźniacki, B., Almada, M., Tyliński, K., Calvo, M., Asnaghi, P. M., Almada, L., Iñiguez, H., Rubianes, F., Pera, O., & Nigrelli, J. I. (2024). Exploring explainable AI in the tax domain. *Artificial Intelligence and Law*, •••, 1–29. DOI: 10.1007/s10506-024-09395-w

Hashimzade, N., Myles, G. D., & Rablen, M. D. (2016). Predictive analytics and the targeting of audits. *Journal of Economic Behavior & Organization, 124*, 130–145. DOI: 10.1016/j.jebo.2015.11.009

Ingrams, A., Kaufmann, W., & Jacobs, D. (2022). In AI we trust? Citizen perceptions of AI in government decision making. *Policy and Internet, 14*(2), 390–409. DOI: 10.1002/poi3.276

Kamoun, A., Boujelbane, R., & Boujelben, S. (2024). A prediction model to detect non-compliant taxpayers using a supervised machine learning approach: Evidence from Tunisia. *Journal of Business Analytics, 8*(2), 116–133. DOI: 10.1080/2573234X.2024.2438195

Kieslich, K., Keller, B., & Starke, C. (2022). Artificial intelligence ethics by design. Evaluating public perception on the importance of ethical design principles of artificial intelligence. *Big Data & Society, 9*(1), 20539517221092956. Advance online publication. DOI: 10.1177/20539517221092956

Kirchler, E., Hoelzl, E., & Wahl, I. (2008). Enforced versus voluntary tax compliance: The "slippery slope" framework. *Journal of Economic Psychology, 29*(2), 210–225. DOI: 10.1016/j.joep.2007.05.004

Kleanthous, C., & Chatzis, S. (2019). Gated Mixture Variational Autoencoders for Value Added Tax audit case selection. *Knowledge-Based Systems, 188*, 105048. DOI: 10.1016/j.knosys.2019.105048

Kleven, H. J., Knudsen, M. B., Kreiner, C. T., Pedersen, S., & Saez, E. (2011). Unwilling or Unable to Cheat? Evidence From a Tax Audit Experiment in Denmark. *Econometrica, 79*(3), 651–692. DOI: 10.3982/ECTA9113

Koivula, K., Shamsuzzoha, A., & Shamsuzzaman, M. (2024). Application of artificial intelligence as a knowledge creation instrument in tax procedures. *Engineering Applications of Artificial Intelligence, 133*, 108417. DOI: 10.1016/j.engappai.2024.108417

Kuźniacki, B., Almada, M., Tyliński, K., Górski, L., Winogradska, B., & Zeldenrust, R. (2022). Towards eXplainable artificial intelligence (XAI) in tax law: The need for a minimum legal standard. *World Tax Journal, 14*(4). Advance online publication. DOI: 10.59403/2yhh9pa

Lukianykhina, O., Suprunenko, S., Slavkova, A., Skorba, O., & Zavrazhnyi, K. (2024). Digital Innovations in the Fiscal Policy of Ukraine: Promoting Sustainable Economic Development. *International Journal of Economics and Financial Issues, 14*(4), 77–86. DOI: 10.32479/ijefi.16202

Malashin, I. P., Masich, I. S., Tynchenko, V. S., Gantimurov, A. P., Nelyub, V. A., & Borodulin, A. S. (2024a). Confidence-Aware Rejection Class Minimization in Indirect Tax Audit Classification. *IEEE Access : Practical Innovations, Open Solutions*, *•••*, 1–1. DOI: 10.1109/ACCESS.2024.3519333

Malashin, I. P., Masich, I. S., Tynchenko, V. S., Gantimurov, A. P., Nelyub, V. A., Borodulin, A. S., Tokarev, S. I., & Vasilev, D. I. (2024b). Anomaly Detection in Restaurant Receipts Data. *IEEE Access : Practical Innovations, Open Solutions*, *12*, 145590–145607. DOI: 10.1109/ACCESS.2024.3471081

Martín López, J. (2022). INTELIGENCIA ARTIFICIAL, SESGOS Y NO DISCRIMINACIÓN EN EL ÁMBITO DE LA INSPECCIÓN TRIBUTARIA. *Revista Crónica Tributaria*, *182*(1), 51–89. DOI: 10.47092/CT.22.1.2

Mosteanu, N. R. (2020). Digital Systems and New Challenges of Financial Management – FinTech, XBRL, Blockchain and Cryptocurrencies. *Quality - Access to Success*, *21*(174).

Munjeyi, E., & Schutte, D. (2024). Examining the critical success factors influencing the diffusion of AI in tax administration in Botswana. *Cogent Social Sciences*, *10*(1), 2419537. DOI: 10.1080/23311886.2024.2419537

Murorunkwere, B. F., Haughton, D., Nzabanita, J., Kipkogei, F., & Kabano, I. (2023). Predicting tax fraud using supervised machine learning approach. *African Journal of Science, Technology, Innovation and Development*, *15*(6), 731–742. DOI: 10.1080/20421338.2023.2187930

Murorunkwere, B. F., Tuyishimire, O., Haughton, D., & Nzabanita, J. (2022). Fraud Detection Using Neural Networks: A Case Study of Income Tax. *Future Internet*, *14*(6), 168. DOI: 10.3390/fi14060168

OECD. (2017). *Tax Administration 2017: Comparative Information on OECD and Other Advanced and Emerging Economies*. OECD., DOI: 10.1787/tax_admin-2017-

OECD. (2021). *Tax Administration 2021: Comparative Information on OECD and other Advanced and Emerging Economies*. OECD., DOI: 10.1787/cef472b9-

Ordóñez-Placencia, J., Hallo, M., & Luján-Mora, S. (2024). A data mining model to predict the debts with risk of non-payment in tax administration. *International Journal of Information and Decision Sciences*. DOI: 10.1504/IJIDS.2024.140186

Ourdani, N., Aknin, N., & Chrayah, M. (2024). Towards a new approach to maximize tax collection using machine learning algorithms. *IAES International Journal of Artificial Intelligence*, *13*(1), 737. Advance online publication. DOI: 10.11591/ijai.v13.i1.pp737-746

Palomino Guerrero, M. (2022). Inteligencia artificial: Un mecanismo para frenar la evasión fiscal sin vulnerar los derechos del contribuyente. *Cuestiones Constitucionales*, *46*, 213–236. DOI: 10.22201/iij.24484881e.2022.46.17053

Pang, S., & Hua, G. (2024). How does digital tax administration affect R&D manipulation? Evidence from dual machine learning. *Technological Forecasting and Social Change*, *208*(123691), 123691. DOI: 10.1016/j.techfore.2024.123691

Peeters, B. (2024). Editorial: European law restrictions on tax authorities' use of artificial intelligence systems: Reflections on some recent developments. *EC Tax Review*, *33*(2), 54–57. DOI: 10.54648/ECTA2024006

Pérez López, C., Delgado Rodríguez, M. J., & De Lucas Santos, S. (2019). Tax Fraud Detection through Neural Networks: An Application Using a Sample of Personal Income Taxpayers. *Future Internet*, *11*(4), 86. DOI: 10.3390/fi11040086

Puspita, A. F., Palil, M. R. B., Puspaningrum, A., & Suman, A. (2024). Taxing artificial intelligence: Value impacts and governance in the tax sector (study in Indonesia and Malaysia). *Pakistan Journal of Life and Social Sciences*, *22*(1). Advance online publication. DOI: 10.57239/PJLSS-2024-22.1.00343

Rahayu, S. K. (2021). Utilization of artificial intelligence in tax audit in Indonesia. *Management and Accounting Review (MAR)*, *20*(3). https://ir.uitm.edu.my/id/eprint/61675/

Raz, J. (1979). *The authority of law: Essays on law and morality*. Oxford University Press., DOI: 10.1093/acprof:oso/9780198253457.001.0001

Saragih, A. H., Reyhani, Q., Setyowati, M. S., & Hendrawan, A. (2023). The potential of an artificial intelligence (AI) application for the tax administration system's modernization: The case of Indonesia. *Artificial Intelligence and Law*, *31*(3), 491–514. DOI: 10.1007/s10506-022-09321-y

Saulitis, A., & Chapkovski, P. (2024). Appealing, threatening or nudging? Assessing various communication strategies to promote tax compliance. *Public Choice*. Advance online publication. DOI: 10.1007/s11127-024-01194-w

Schächtele, S. (2023). Tax Responses at Low Taxable Incomes: Evidence from Germany*. *Fiscal Studies*, *41*(2), 411–439. DOI: 10.1111/1475-5890.12220

Shi, B., Dong, B., Xu, Y., Wang, J., Wang, Y., & Zheng, Q. (2023). An edge feature aware heterogeneous graph neural network model to support tax evasion detection. *Expert Systems with Applications*, *213*, 118903. DOI: 10.1016/j.eswa.2022.118903

Shujaaddeen, A., Ba-Alwi, F. M., & Al-Gaphari, G. (2024). A New Machine Learning Model for Detecting levels of Tax Evasion Based on Hybrid Neural Network. *International Journal of Intelligent Systems and Applications in Engineering, 2147–6799214.*

Siimon, Õ. R., & Lukason, O. (2021). A Decision Support System for Corporate Tax Arrears Prediction. *Sustainability (Basel), 13*(15), 8363. DOI: 10.3390/su13158363

Strauss, H., Fawcett, T., & Schutte, D. (2020). An evaluation of the digital response of tax authorities to optimise tax administration within the digitalised economy. *eJournal of Tax Research.*

Sun, T. Q., & Medaglia, R. (2019). Mapping the challenges of Artificial Intelligence in the public sector: Evidence from public healthcare. *Government Information Quarterly, 36*(2), 368–383. DOI: 10.1016/j.giq.2018.09.008

Tagliaferri, G., Scacciatelli, D., & Loro, P. A. D. (2020). VAT tax gap prediction: A 2-steps Gradient Boosting approach. *Statistical Methods & Applications, 32*(1), 237–270. DOI: 10.1007/s10260-022-00643-4

Tan, E., Petit Jean, M., Simonofski, A., Tombal, T., Kleizen, B., Sabbe, M., Bechoux, L., & Willem, P. (2023). Artificial intelligence and algorithmic decisions in fraud detection: An interpretive structural model. *Data & Policy, 5*, e25. DOI: 10.1017/dap.2023.22

Vozár, A., & Bán, E. (2024). Digitalisation, digital transformation – In the practice of the National Tax and Customs Office. *Public Finance Quarterly, 70*(1), 85–109. DOI: 10.35551/PFQ_2024_1_5

Woellner, R. (2020). It Is a Bad Look. *eJournal of Tax Research, 18*(2), 508–530.

Chapter 12

Artificial Intelligence effect on Renovation of Managerial Practices through Organizational Transformation of Health Care Sector in Horn of Africa

Wako Jio
https://orcid.org/0009-0003-6192-459X
Bule Hora University, Ethiopia

Shashi Kant
https://orcid.org/0000-0003-4722-5736
Bule Hora University, Ethiopia

Hirut Assegid
https://orcid.org/0009-0003-6192-459X
Bule Hora University, Ethiopia

ABSTRACT

This chapter investigates the radical changes Artificial Intelligence (AI) creates for healthcare managers in the Horn of Africa through its support of organizational transformation. Healthcare professionals totaling 385 participants completed surveys to investigate AI technology effects on managerial choices and workplace efficiency

DOI: 10.4018/979-8-3373-5499-6.ch012

and healthcare service quality standards. The study applied the Kaiser-Meyer-Olkin (KMO) measure to verify that the collected data displayed satisfactory sampling adequacy for a thorough analysis. The results from Confirmatory Factor Analysis (CFA) established substantial links that AI integration establishes with enhanced organizational managerial practices. The AMOS software generated results from the Structural Equation Modeling (SEM) method which proved AI boosts operational performance while it helps healthcare bodies develop innovative adaptable approaches. The analyzed data proves that artificial intelligence tools boost data-led decisions and operational efficiency as well as healthcare service quality.

INTRODUCTION

Global healthcare systems recognize the considerable importance of Artificial Intelligence integration because this technology can transform how managers operate and how organizations function (Manickam et al., 2022). Healthcare systems across the world use Artificial Intelligence as their fundamental tool to achieve operational optimization and better decision making processes along with individualized patient care (Aung et al., 2021). The concept of AI developed during the mid-twentieth century before transforming into practical applications that transform several industrial sectors including healthcare (Esmaeilzadeh, 2024. Modern healthcare management has experienced significant advancement through machine learning and automated systems and analytics which enable better proactive healthcare strategies (Al Kuwaiti et al., 2023). Research evidence presents continued documentation of AI benefits for healthcare which demonstrates its applications in predictive modeling and operational improvement and better patient interaction (Tak et al., 2025). Research findings show that deploying AI solutions results in advanced diagnosis accuracy combined with shorter waiting times and personalized therapeutic approaches (Aung et al., 2021). AI technology success has yet to overcome multiple operational obstacles. The adoption of artificial intelligence technologies in healthcare faces barriers from insufficient hardware systems and unpredicted opposition from medical staff alongside data protection matters (Manickam et al., 2022).

Research continues to lack substantial knowledge about how AI transforms managerial operations specifically within the Horn of Africa and other low-resource environments (Aung et al., 2021). Researchers typically pay little attention to the distinct economic and social and cultural obstacles that healthcare facilities encounter in this geographic area (Tak et al., 2025). The intention of this research is to bridge current comprehension shortfalls through an extensive healthcare management organizational transformation analysis that targets AI benefits for the Horn of Africa region (Chouaibi et al., 2022). This research aims to provide light on the ways in which AI may be used to address regional issues. ***"How does the integration of AI influence managerial practices and organizational transformation in the healthcare sector of the Horn of Africa?"*** By doing this, it hopes to give future academic—***"How does the integration of AI influence managerial practices and organizational transformation in the healthcare sector of the Horn of Africa?"***—this study seeks to illuminate the pathways through which AI can be harnessed to overcome local challenges. In doing so, it aims to provide actionable insights for future researchers and policymakers, guiding them in implementing AI strategies that resonate with the distinct needs of healthcare systems in this region. The findings will not only contribute to the academic discourse but will also inform practical applications, ultimately enhancing healthcare delivery in the Horn of Africa.ics and policymakers useful information that will help them use AI techniques that are sensitive to the unique requirements of healthcare systems in this area. The results will improve healthcare service in the Horn of Africa by informing practical applications as well as adding to the scholarly conversation.

BACKGROUND OF THE STUDY

The Horn of Africa healthcare system has several obstacles, including disease loads, insufficient infrastructure and little finances (Al Kuwaiti et al., 2023). These challenges are made worse by economic constraints, political instability, and a lack of competent labor. In response to these challenges, more and more individuals are interested in using artificial intelligence (AI) to enhance management and deliver healthcare (Manickam et al., 2022). But in this case, there are a number of actual barriers to AI adoption that restrict its potential advantages (Tak et al., 2025). One of the most well-known theme studies is the application of AI to diagnostic tools in Ethiopia. Healthcare practitioners frequently lack the technological infrastructure required to take use of AI's potential, but they may promise to increase the precision of their identification in the identification of illnesses like TB and malaria (Aung et al., 2021). For instance, due to inadequate internet connectivity, the pilot program in Ethiopia had significant difficulties while trying to diagnose illnesses in remote clinics. Thus, the anticipated advantages of prompt and precise diagnosis were not entirely negated, underscoring the necessity of comprehensive training initiatives and support systems (Al Kuwaiti et al., 2023).

Another example is found in Kenya, where city hospitals have developed an AI platform to speed up patient treatment and cut down on wait times (Tak et al., 2025). Medical personnel resisted installation despite the platform's potential to improve operational efficiency because they questioned the dependability of AI systems in comparison to more conventional methods (Aung et al., 2021). The implementation process was made much more challenging by this reluctance. This results from ignorance of AI technology and anxiety over losing one's career (Esmaeilzadeh, 2024). Furthermore, concerns about data protection and ethics significantly impede the adoption of AI. It is challenging to create a comprehensive AI solution that necessitates integrated datasets in many African health situations since patient data is frequently contained in scattered systems. According to research, when AI technology is used without robust data management systems, it might result in patient distrust and confidentiality issues (Al Kuwaiti et al., 2023). The challenges with implementing AI in African health systems are brought to light by these theme studies. They demonstrate that while AI has the ability to completely transform management practices, its successful use necessitates resolving infrastructure issues, encouraging a culture of acceptability among doctors, and guaranteeing the handling of ethical data. By carefully examining these problems, this study aims to provide a complete understanding of the challenges associated with integrating AI and provide potential solutions, paving the way for effective organizational transformation in hospital management (Aung et al., 2021).

STATEMENT OF THE PROBLEM

The environment of integrating artificial intelligence (AI) into business operations is complicated, with both opportunities and challenges (Manickam et al., 2022). The smooth integration of AI technology to enhance management procedures and spur significant organizational change is a desirable condition for a company (Chouaibi et al., 2022). However, there are gaps and conflicting findings in the literature that make it difficult to put this ideal into practice. The successful use of AI is being thwarted by several organizations (Aung et al., 2021). As a result, performance and transformational impact are not convincingly demonstrated. Although some studies point to promising outcomes, others point to barriers including reluctance to adapt, a lack of requisite expertise, and inadequate infrastructure, establishing a link between AI and poor certainty management techniques (Al Kuwaiti et al., 2023). In order to comprehend the methods via which AI impacts OT and RMP, a gap in theory is also maintained. The mediating function of organizational procedures and culture is frequently overlooked by current models. The achievements of IA integration may be significantly impacted by this (Esmaeilzadeh, 2024). Additionally, little is known about the adoption of AI and the industry-specific elements that might influence the impacts of sectoral variability. Due to contextual characteristics including industry kind, regional location, and organizational size, investigators were unable to affect the results of AI deployment (Aung et al., 2021).

As enterprises struggle to coordinate their AI initiatives with huge corporations, the true issues are evident (Esmaeilzadeh, 2024). The absence of a well-defined structure for implementing AI frequently results in disjointed endeavors that fail to yield the anticipated advantages (Misra et al., 2023). Additionally, ethical issues related to algorithmic bias and data exploitation are still complex and unrelated to the process of ethical integration (Al Kuwaiti et al., 2023). By offering a thorough examination of the connection between AI and RMP, this work aims to close these gaps. This study adds to a more comprehensive noun that illustrates the intricacy of integrating AI after examining the intermediary roles of organizational procedures and culture (Esmaeilzadeh, 2024). The significance of contextual elements will also be emphasized, providing insight into how various businesses might modify their approaches to effectively utilize AI. Identifying practical issues and providing effective recommendations, this study directs future researchers and politicians to create a reliable framework for the implementation of artificial intelligence. Ultimately, the purpose of this study is to pave the way for a more informed understanding of the possibilities of converting AI.

THEORETICAL FOUNDATION

Technology Acceptance Model (TAM): Users adopt technology through the widely applied Technology Acceptance Model (TAM). Davis (1989) established TAM which demonstrates that people base their technology adoption decisions on their perceived ease of use and usefulness (Utami, 2021). This model provides healthcare professionals with an explanation regarding their reactions to AI tools in medical settings. Healthcare practitioners will adopt AI when they view it as a user-friendly instrument which delivers better patient results. In healthcare facilities the Technology Acceptance Model provides an essential framework to assess the elements that promote or prevent AI technology implementation (Utami, 2021).

Diffusion of Innovations (DOI): The Diffusion of Innovations theory which Rogers (1962) developed studies the process and reasons behind technology and concept propagation with speed analysis (Call & Herber, 2022). The adoption process relies on communication pathways and social networks together with innovation-based perceptions according to this theory. Healthcare organizations along with their wider ecosystem can use DOI to understand the spread of AI technology throughout their networks. Knowledge about the adoption stages from beginning to completion enables researchers to uncover obstructing and supporting elements for AI implementation in healthcare specifically for the Horn of Africa facing infrastructure challenges with cultural impacts on innovation spread (Call & Herber, 2022).

Resource-Based View (RBV): The Resource-Based View (RBV) focuses on the internal resources and capabilities of an organization as key determinants of competitive advantage (Sharma et al., 2022). Organizations that effectively utilize distinctive resources including human capital and technology and organizational culture will normally achieve better performance results. Healthcare institutions can apply the Resource-Based View to evaluate their use of AI as a strategic resource which enhances managerial functions and service delivery. Healthcare leaders can develop performance-enhancing resource-oriented strategies for innovation and transformation by applying this theory to understand their organizational capabilities for implementing AI (Sharma et al., 2022).

Socio-Technical Systems Theory (STST): Socio-technological Systems Theory (STST) says that companies should think about both social and technological factors because they all operate together as a whole. The Australasian Health Publishing Company Limited (AMPC) employs this idea to show that for technology to work, social and technological components must be in sync. For AI to be successful in healthcare, it needs modern technology and operational cultures that support its usage. It also has to train personnel well and get stakeholders involved. STST builds a whole analytical framework to look at the problems with deploying AI in healthcare by targeting understanding the factors in the workplace that affect how people embrace new technologies (Zhang et al., 2023).

The ***Technology Acceptance Model (TAM)*** is the main theoretical lens for this investigation. The study's goals concerning how healthcare professionals see AI technology are based on TAM's conceptual framework, which focuses on views of ease of use and utility. The study looks at these perspectives to find things that make it easier or harder to use AI in management, which will help create effective ways to put it into reality. Utami, 2021 .

The Technology Acceptance Model (TAM), Diffusion of Innovations (DOI), Resource-Based View (RBV), and Socio-Technical Systems Theory (STST) are all good ways to look at how artificial intelligence (AI) is being used in healthcare in the Horn of Africa. Each of these concepts gives a thoughtful look at how AI may change how businesses are run and how they do business. The “Technology Acceptance Model (TAM)” says that perceived ease of use as well as imagined usefulness are two major elements that affect whether or not people utilize technology. Healthcare staff are more likely to adopt AI solutions if they think they are easy to use and would help them provide better care for patients. For artificial intelligence to be effectively integrated into management processes, it needs to be acceptable. This is because it changes how healthcare workers utilize AI in their daily work, which leads to better decisions and more accurate service delivery. The “Diffusion of Innovations (DOI)" concept focuses on how new technology propagate inside businesses. Some of the main things that are causing this spread are how much better AI is than current approaches, how well it works with existing systems, and how hard it is to put into practice. Healthcare practitioners would be able to make good strategies to help AI adoption in the Horn of Africa if they understood these factors. This would make sure that everyone involved in the process is kept up to date on new developments and that everyone is included. This is especially important in a nation where traditional ways of doing things might not want to change.

The "Resource-Based View (RBV)" says that businesses should use certain resources to be ahead of their competitors. In healthcare, AI might be considered as an essential asset that boosts operational capacity and improves patient outcomes. By aligning AI technology with the strategic goals of healthcare firms, managers may create an environment that encourages new ideas and change. This alignment is important to make sure that investments in AI really pay off by making services faster and better. Finally, "Socio-technological Systems Theory (STST)" focuses on how social and technology parts of a business work together. To successfully use artificial intelligence in healthcare, you need more than just good technological infrastructure; you also need a positive social environment. This means teaching healthcare professionals how to use new technology and making sure that changes are made appropriately so that staff are ready to use it.

DEFINITION AND ORIGIN OF TERMS

Artificial Intelligence (AI): The technology of Artificial Intelligence (AI) allows machines especially computer systems to imitate human-intelligences through their operations (Manickam et al., 2022). The process of artificial intelligence involves three main components which consist of information acquisition and rule development for usage and decision-making based on those rules along with automatic adjustment of processes. Artificial Intelligence gained its name in when researchers first employed the term during the Dartmouth Conference which launched the academic study of AI. The advancement of artificial intelligence technology has been extensive throughout decades as it developed various applications spanning from natural language processing to robotic systems and machine learning and deep learning systems (Manickam et al., 2022).

Healthcare Managerial Practices: Healthcare managerial practices consist of administrative strategies which combine organizational processes with administrative activities to organize healthcare services (Kawaguchi et al., 2022). The achievement of healthcare goals requires planning along with organizing while staffing resources under careful direction through controlling and leadership functions. The medical field adopted the traditional management theory definition of "managerial practices" to handle the distinct service quality requirements within its complicated structure (Kawaguchi et al., 2022).

Organizational Transformation: The modification of fundamental aspects associated with organizational culture including practices and structures along with performance enhancement serves as Organizational transformation (Chouaibi et al., 2022). This idea derives from beliefs about how to manage change while still acknowledging the need for organizations to grow. Organizations need to adapt in response to challenges from within as well as outside. Healthcare has to make big changes to how it works since emerging technologies like AI change how services are managed as well as delivered (Chouaibi et al., 2022).

Horn of Africa: There are five countries in the Horn of Africa: Ethiopia, Somalia, Djibouti, as well as Eritrea (Cavalerie et al., 2021). The shape of East Africa makes a horn-like shape that is called the "Horn of Africa." There are many different cultures and languages in this area, which has big social and economic problems like poverty, wars, and health disparities. It is important to understand the effects of healthcare AI in the Horn of Africa because they affect how to provide solutions that meet the demands of each community (McIntyre et al., 2023).

EMPIRICAL LITERATURE REVIEW

Artificial Intelligence and Renovation of Managerial Practices

Researchers have thoroughly looked at how artificial intelligence (AI) may be used in health care and found that it has the potential to change how management works in a number of situations (Manickam et al., 2022). A lot of research shows that AI technologies make decisions better, operations more efficient, and patient care better (Tak et al., 2025). For instance, research on Djibouti suggests that AI-based data analytics may assist healthcare administrators find patterns and trends in patient data, which can help them make better choices faster (Aung et al., 2021). The AI system in this study was able to forecast patient outcomes based on past data in a very impressive way. This helped healthcare leaders better use their resources and offer better services. Also, there is a lot of evidence that AI may help make operations more efficient (Al Kuwaiti et al., 2023). The study shows that applying AI, such automating robotic operations and teaching computers, may make healthcare organizations' administrative work a lot easier (Manickam et al., 2022). For instance, research on Somalia reveals that AI systems may automate processes that happen over and over again, such scheduling and billing meetings, releasing managers, and more, so that people can focus on strategic goals (Esmaeilzadeh, 2024).

This operational optimization not only increases productivity, but also increases employee satisfaction by reducing burnout associated with secular tasks. From the point of care in patient care, AI has shown its promise to personalize treatment plans and improve interactions with patients. This study investigated the use of AI in patient-based patient development (Al Kuwaiti et al., 2023). This led to the best health-related outcomes and increased patient satisfaction. By using artificial intelligence tools, health managers can facilitate the patient's approach, ensuring the adaptation of departure for individual needs and preferences (Aung et al., 2021). Nevertheless, empirical literature also emphasizes several problems associated with the implementation of AI in the practice of health care management. Resistance to change among healthcare workers is a recurring subject (Kawaguchi et al., 2022). Research shows that medical staffs are often skeptical of AI technology, due to poor ideas about accuracy and reliability. Such resistance may impede the adoption of AI, emphasizing the need for comprehensive training and changes in changes to the assistance of adoption (Al Kuwaiti et al., 2023).

H1: Artificial Intelligence and the renovation of managerial practices having empirical association.

Artificial Intelligence and Organizational Transformation

Artificial intelligence combines with organizational transformation to create significant interest since organizations face rapid development needs (Manickam et al., 2022). One of the exceptional subjects of the literature is the role of AI in improving operational efficiency. Studies show that artificial intelligence technologics, such as machine training and automation of robotic processes, allow organizations to automate routine tasks and optimize work processes (Al Kuwaiti et al., 2023). For example, in case of Djibouti City research shows that companies using AI control analytics have been shown to be observed by significant improvements in process efficiency. This allows resources to be directed towards strategic and innovation initiatives (Aung et al., 2021). In addition to operational improvements, AI has a significant impact on the organization's culture and employee engagement (Tak et al., 2025). The studies that include stress that AI contributes to a decision -based decision -based decision -making and encourage employees to use AI systems information in their daily activities (Esmaeilzadeh, 2024). This change not only improves the quality of decisions made at all organizational levels, but also allows employees to actively participate in the transformation process. Nevertheless, the literature also emphasizes the importance of changes in changes to eliminate the potential resistance of staff. Studies show that a successful organizational transformation requires a clear vision, effective communication and employee participation in order to overcome skepticism compared to AI technologies (Chouaibi et al., 2022). Furthermore, AI changes organizational structure and promotes a more flexible and flexible framework. This study shows that organizations implementing artificial intelligence technology tend to smooth out the hierarchy and promote intermittent cooperation (Manickam et al., 2022). This structural transformation is consistent with the broader trend in digital transformations where organizations need to be skilled and adapted to the prosperity of a competitive environment (Aung et al., 2021).

The benefits of AI in organizational transformation are well documented, but the empirical literature also highlights the problems facing organizations during this process (Chouaibi et al., 2022). Ethical issues regarding data confidentiality and algorithm bias have arisen as serious issues. Research highlights that if AI systems are not thoroughly controlled, they can perpetuate existing biases, leading to unfair appeal in the decision process (Esmaeilzadeh, 2024). As a result, organizations need to implement principles and trustworthy ethical management frameworks to ensure the responsible use of value-responsible AI (Al Kuwaiti et al., 2023).

H2: There is a significant empirical association between Artificial Intelligence and Organizational Transformation.

Organizational Transformation and Renovation of Managerial Practices

The relationship between organizational transformation and management practice reform was the focus of empirical research, particularly when organizations sailed through the complexities of modern commercial environments (Chouaibi et al., 2022). An organizational transformation refers to the complete changes an organization undergoes to improve performance, adapt to market dynamics, and improves competitiveness. Concurrently, the renovation of managerial practices involves the evolution of strategies, structures, and processes that guide how organizations operate and make decisions (Kawaguchi et al., 2022). The empirical literature highlights several key themes in this relationship, illustrating how transformative initiatives can lead to significant changes in managerial practices. One common tamp is the impact of technical outcomes on management practices (Tak et al., 2025). Research shows that digital transformation initiatives are forced by organizations to rethink their management approaches, often leading to more flexible and responsive practices. For example, In case of Eritrea research shows that organizations that use the advanced data analysis and artificial intelligence tools extend their decision -making opportunities, allowing managers to base their strategies on real -time data, and not only intuition (Manickam et al., 2022). The study has shown that companies that covered digital tools have experienced improvements in operational efficiency and employee participation, emphasizing the transformative capacity of technology in the evolution of management practices. Another important aspect of this relationship is the role of leadership in change management. Empirical research, such as research, emphasizes the importance of effective leadership in environmental development that drives change. Leadership approaches emphasizing innovation creation together with teamwork and open communication produce positive outcomes for organizational transformations (Chouaibi et al., 2022). Recent studies demonstrate transformational leadership stands as one of the essential elements for driving employees towards accepting organizational adjustments and new managerial systems. This leadership method fosters a learning environment for continuous development since transformational change requires such continuous improvement practices (Kawaguchi et al., 2022).

Moreover, the literature highlights the importance of aligning organizational culture with transformation efforts. This study highlights that culture has a significant impact on the way management practices are perceived and accepted in organizations (Kawaguchi et al., 2022). For change to be successful, organizations must develop a culture that supports change, encourages experience and value employee contributions. Empirical data show that organizations with strong adaptive crops are likely to successfully implement new management practices and achieve the desired transformation results (Chouaibi et al., 2022). For example, in case of Ethiopia, Somalia region research shows that thematic research on transformed healthcare organizations shows that promoting a culture of collaboration and innovation leads to improved patient care and operational efficiency. However, the literature also determines the problems that organizations are faced with in the transformation process (Tak et al., 2025). Resistance to changes is a conventional barrier, as employees may not decide in order to abandon the established practice. Research notes that successful transformations require not only a clear vision and strategy, but also effective ways to manage changes to mitigate resistance. Ensuring employee attractiveness and appropriate training at the start of the transformation process can contribute to a more gentle transition and improve the adoption of new management practices (Kawaguchi et al., 2022). In addition, empirical literature highlights the need for continuous evaluation and feedback mechanisms during transformation initiatives (Esmaeilzadeh, 2024). Studies indicate that organizations that implement iterative processes to monitor and refine their managerial practices succeed more in carrying out a lasting transformation (Kawaguchi et al., 2022).

H3: Organizational Transformation and Renovation of Managerial Practices having a significant empirical association.

Artificial Intelligence, Renovation of Managerial Practices and Organizational Transformation Mediation

The relationship between artificial intelligence (AI), fixing management practices, and changing organizations has become an important area of empirical study. This research shows how management practices may aid with changing an organization (Manickam et al., 2022). The rising body of research shows that it not only improves managerial procedures, but also sparks larger changes in the company (Kawaguchi et al., 2022). This review looks at real-world evidence that helps explain these connections and the ways they can be mediated. According to research, AI has a big effect on management practices since it gives managers tools to make better decisions, use resources more efficiently, and run their businesses more smoothly (Al Kuwaiti et al., 2023). For instance, research on the Djibouti Gobolad Region suggests that this study illustrates how AI regulate analytics may assist managers handle large volumes of data, which can lead to better strategic decisions (Aung et al., 2021). This chance lets businesses swiftly respond to changes in the market and the wants of customers, and it also lets them modify how they operate their businesses to better meet their goals (Kawaguchi et al., 2022). Also, real-world study shows that companies that use IA technology say they have greater flexibility in their decision-making, which helps create a culture of critical responsiveness that is necessary for effective change (Al Kuwaiti et al., 2023).

As proven, fixing management procedures can affect the link between using AI and making changes in a company (Aung et al., 2021). Recent research shows that transformational leadership is one of the most important things that may help workers embrace changes in the business and new management methods. This kind of leadership encourages people to keep learning and growing since transformational change needs people to keep getting better (Tak et al., 2021). But study reveals that there might be difficulties that come up during this middle step. Resistance to change is still a big problem since workers may be worried about how AI will affect their jobs and duties (Aung et al., 2021). Studies reveal that companies should focus on change management tactics that help employees and improve how people feel about AI technology. Training and creating an atmosphere of trust can assist reduce opposition and make it easier for managers to make changes (Al Kuwaiti et al., 2023). Also, ethical issues related to using AI might make this partnership more difficult. The study shows that AI systems need to fix problems with bias and privacy, because these concerns might make workers less confident and less likely to work together (Tak et al., 2021). To keep a culture that values innovation and cooperation going, which helps organizations change in a good way, it is necessary to employ AI responsibly and ethically (Aung et al., 2021).

H4: Artificial Intelligence, the renovation of managerial practices, and organizational transformation mediation having a significant empirical association

CONCEPTUAL FRAMEWORK

The conceptual framework was based on the literature that was looked at. H1 showed the directway. H4 is the result of multiplying H2 and H3, which is shown by the indirect path.

Figure 1. Conceptual framework

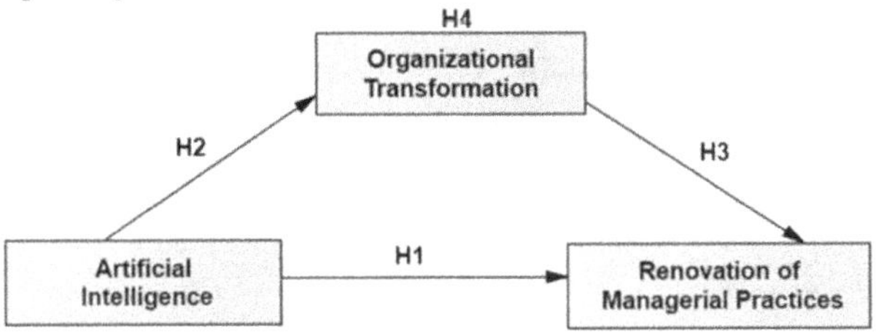

RESEARCH METHODOLOGY

The study employed a quantitative research strategy to look into the link among artificial intelligence (AI), fixing management practices, and changing organizations (Ghanad, 2023). We chose the number of participants of the sample of 385 respondents from various health care organizations in Africa, which ensured a diversified idea of the implementation and influence of AI technology. Data collection was facilitated through a structured questionnaire that incorporates validated scales derived from the relevant literature. This method made it possible to study the concept in a structured way (Ghanad, 2023).

Sample and Method

From various African healthcare institutions, 385 respondents provide a strong basis for study. This amount of data usually has adequate statistical power to find important relationships and apply the results to the wider group of healthcare professionals. Picking people from diverse firms makes sure that the sample is fair and includes a range of views and experiences. A sample size of 385 is a good and acceptable choice for looking at developments in healthcare across Africa since it gives consistent results and decreases the chance of making statistical errors.

Method of Analyze Data

We used the Bartlett spherical test and the Kaiser-Meyer-Olkin (KMO) measurements at the same time to see if the data could be used for factorial analysis. The KMO values showed that the sample was quite valid, which means that the data is good for the exploratory factor analysis (EFA) (Tak et al., 2025). We did an EFA to find out what the main structure of the construction was and to make the measurements clearer. The findings of the EFA led to the extraction of many variables that encompassed features of AI, management techniques, and organizational transformation. Then, these elements were utilized to build measurement models that were tested by modeling structural equations (SEMs) with AMOS software. SEM has helped us look at complicated connections between factors and come up with suggestions for the direct and indirect impacts that are shown in the suggested model (Tak et al., 2025).

Scale Development

A thorough examination of the relevant literature led to the creation of the scale for this investigation. This is a good representation of how artificial intelligence, management techniques, and organizational change work, as shown in earlier studies (Tanujaya et al., 2022). The first step in this approach was to read a lot of research to find out what scales and variables had already been found. The Davis Technology Acceptance Model, for instance, uses scales to quantify how easy it is to utilize perceived utilities as well as AI technologies. On the other hand, elements connected to management practices come from organizational behavior as well as change management. Each part of the scale was carefully designed to make sure it is clear and relevant to the healthcare sector. The first survey project has a number of parts in each design that make it possible to accurately measure each variable. After making the first scale (Tanujaya et al., 2022), pilot testing were done with a small group of people to find out whether there were any difficulties with the wording or lack of clarity. Feedback from pilot tests was used to make the scale even clearer and more reliable. Upon completion, the scale consisted of well-defined elements of each design that covered aspects such as decision-making, adaptability of management practices, and the perceptual effects of AI on the extent of organizational change. Each element is measured on a Likert scale (Tanujaya et al., 2022).

DATA ANALYSIS

Table 1. KMO and Bartlett's Test

Kaiser-Meyer-Olkin Measure of Sampling Adequacy.		**.850**
Bartlett's Test of Sphericity	Approx. Chi-Square	1419.738
	Df	91
	Sig.	.000

Source: Authors

Tablc 1 shows thc validity mcasurcmcnts. Thc KMO rcsult valuc is 0.850, indicating the validity of advanced sampling. KMO values above 0.70 are generally considered acceptable, whereas values near 1.0 indicate excellent sampling validity. This result suggests that data collected from a sample of 385 respondents are suitable for conducting Exploratory Factor Analysis (EFA) because it shows adequate correlations between the variables. Bartlett's spherical test also confirms the relevance of the data for factorial analysis, giving an approximate value of 1419,738 Chi squares with 91 degrees of freedom and a level of meaning of 0 000.

Table 2. Total variance explained

Component	**Initial Eigenvalues**			**Extraction Sums of Squared Loadings**			**Rotation Sums of Squared Loadings**		
	Total	**% of Variance**	**Cumulative %**	**Total**	**% of Variance**	**Cumulative %**	**Total**	**% of Variance**	**Cumulative %**
1	4.51	32.235	32.235	4.51	32.235	32.235	3.00	21.451	21.451
2	1.37	9.787	42.022	1.37	9.787	42.022	2.16	15.491	36.942
3	1.27	9.087	51.110	1.27	9.087	51.110	1.98	14.168	51.110

Source: Authors

Table 2 defines the general variance. The initial eigenvalues indicate that the first component explains a significant portion of the variance, with a total eigenvalue of 4.51, accounting for 32.235% of the total variance. This suggests that the first component captures important underlying factors in the dataset. The cumulative rate after the first component is also notable, reaching 32.235%. This indicates that this single factor contributes significantly to the overall variability in the data. Continuing the component, the eigenvalues for the second and third components are 1.37 and 1.27 respectively, explaining 9.787% and 9.087% of the variance. Together, these three components constitute a cumulative variance of 51.110%. This suggests that they together represent an important part of the fundamental structure of the data.

Note that the remaining components demonstrate their own values below 1.0. This generally indicates that there is little explanation for variance, raising the idea that the first three components are the most important. After rotation, the general dispersion explained by the first three components remains agreed, and the first component is 21.451%, and the second and third - 15.491%and 14.168%, respectively, to total dispersion. This rotation process helps to carry out a clearer interpretation of the factors by maximizing the dispersion explained by each component.

Table 3. Covariances

Covariance			Approximation	S.E.	C.R.	P	Hy.
Organizational Transformation	<-->	Artificial Intelligence	.242	.021	8.231	***	H2
Organizational Transformation	<-->	Renovation of Managerial Practices	.303	.032	7.692	***	**H3**
Artificial Intelligence	<-->	Renovation of Managerial Practices	.254	.24	7.831	***	**H1**

Source: Authors

Table 3 shows covariance estimates. The covariance between Organizational Transformation and Artificial Intelligence is reported at 0.242, with a standard error (S.E.) of 0.021 and a critical ratio (C.R.) of 8.231. The statistical significance is marked with asterisks (***), indicating a highly significant relationship. This powerful positive co-change suggests that increased implementation of AI and the level of organizational change technology highlight the role of AI as a driver of organizational change. Similarly, the incorporation between organizational transformation and rehabilitation of management practices is S.E. and measured at C.R. 7.692. It also presents an important positive link, assuming that improved management practices are closely related to successful efforts to transform the organization. Important conversations indicate that organizations focusing on rehabilitation of management practices are more likely to experience the consequences of major transformations. Finally, S.E. 0.024 and C.R. 7.831, this significant positive simultaneous suggests that adoption of AI technology is associated with improved management practices. This suggests that organizations using AI can improve management strategies and contribute to a culture of innovation and adaptation.

Table 4. Validity concern

	CR	AVE	MSV	MaxR(H)	AI	OT	RMP
AI	0.732	0.643	0.219	0.852	**0.654**		
OT	0.758	0.657	0.132	0.763	0.171	**0.665**	
RMP	0.793	0.603	0.274	0.797	0.383	0.193	**0.684**

Note: AI= Artificial Intelligence; OT= Organizational Transformation; RMP= Renovation of Managerial Practices

Source: Authors

Table 4 provides a survey of reliability The CR for each construct indicates a satisfactory level of internal consistency, with AI of 0.732, OT of 0.758, and RMP of 0.793. In general, CR values above 0.70 are considered acceptable, suggesting that items within each configuration reliably measure the intended concept. The AVE reflects good convergence validity, with an AVE score of 0.643 for AI, 0.657 for OT and 0.603 for RMP. AVE values above 0.50 are desirable as it means that a significant proportion of the observed variable variance is explained by the potential construct. The values presented indicate that each structure properly captures the planned variance. The MSV that measures the maximum correlation between structures is 0.219 for AI, 0.132 for OT, and 0.274 for RMP. These relatively low values include good discriminant reliability. This indicates that the structures are very different from each other. Finally, the additional reliability indicator, the MAXR(H), is 0.852 for AI, 0.763 for OT, and 0.797 for RMP, which supports measurement scale reliability.

Figure 2. Structural equation model

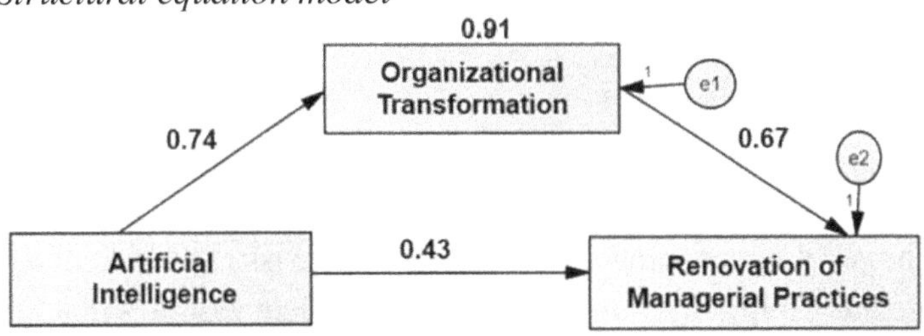

Table 5. Model fitness

Sig.	Chi-Sq	RMR	Fitness Goodness	Fitness Confirmatory	TLI	RMSEA
0.004	1.954	.036	0.930	0.912	0.911	.028

Source: Authors

Table 5 shows the model fit indicators. The level of meaning (sig.) is reported at 0.004. The values and associated meanings of Chi-Quadrate 1.954 indicate that the model is suitable for the data. Low values are generally preferred, but the level of meaning gives us confidence that the model does not deviate significantly from the observed data. The mean square residue (RMR) was recorded at 0.036, indicating good compliance. RMR values below 0.05 are generally considered acceptable. This suggests that the bodies are small and the model accurately represents the data. The Fitness Kindness Index (GFI) is reported to 0.930, as values above 0.90 are considered to represent well-adjusted models. This means a high level of adjustment quality. Similarly, the Check Adjustment Index (CFI) is 0.912, which also supports model validity. Values above 0.90 for CFI indicate that the proposed model provides good fit for the data. The TLI was also reported at 0.911, improving the completion of a great model. Values above 0.90 imply an acceptable correspondence between the hypothetical model and the observed data. Finally, the root error (RMSEA) for the approximate is seen at 0.028. This indicates that it is well below the generally accepted threshold of 0.05, indicating its proximity. RMSEA values below 0.05 suggest that the model fits well into the population covariance matrix.

Table 6. Regression examination

Relative			Approx.	S.E.	C.R.	P	Ass.
Organizational Transformation	<---	Artificial Intelligence	.864	.143	7.583	***	H2
Renovation of Managerial Practices	<---	Organizational Transformation	.328	.131	2.853	***	H3
Renovation of Managerial Practices	<---	Artificial Intelligence	.957	.192	7.958	***	H1

Source: Authors

Table 6 shows the results of regression. The regression coefficient for the relationship between AI and OT is reported as 0.864, with an S.E. of 0.143 and a C.R. of 7.583. The level of meaning is marked with asterisks (***), indicating a very significant relationship. This strong positive coefficient assumes that higher levels of AI are associated with a significant improvement in organizational transformation, confirming the hypothesis (H2), which AI positively affects from. The second studied relationship between OT and RMP, which has a coefficient of 0.328, S.E. From 0.131, and C.R. 2.853, also significant in p.

Table 7. Mediating effect

	Worth	Path Influence
Artificial Intelligence → Renovation of Managerial Practices	.43	Direct influence stated
Artificial Intelligence → Organizational Transformation → Renovation of Managerial Practices	.74*.67=.48	Indirect Influence Ensued
	.91	Partial mediation

Source: Authors

Table 7 illustrates the mediating role. The direct influence of AI on RMP is quantified at 0.43, indicating that AI has a significant and direct effect on the renovation of managerial practices. This direct relationship underscores the capacity of AI to enhance managerial strategies independently, reflecting its immediate impact on organizational practices. On the contrary, the indirect effect of AI on RMP via OT is calculated by multiplying the path: OT (0.74) of AI and RMP (0.67) of OT, leading to an indirect effect of 0.48. This suggests that an important part of the impact of AI on RMP is mediated by OT. This shows that AI is contributing to change in organizational transformation. Considering the general effect of AI on RMP combined with both direct and indirect effects, the general effect is reported to be 0.91. This comprehensive look highlights the important role AI plays in the formation of RMPs directly and indirectly via OT. The term "partial mediation" implies that organizational change is an essential mediator among AI and RMP, but that RMP's AI stays the same. This conclusion shows how important it is to use both direct and indirect ways to learn how AI can influence how managers do their jobs.

DISCUSSION

The study's results show that artificial intelligence (AI) is very important for encouraging organizational transformation (OT) and making management practices (RMP) better. The substantial positive relationships between these traits show that AI may help organizations evolve. The high covariance values suggest that businesses that employ AI technology are likely to go through big changes that will make it simpler for them to improve their management skills. Because of this dependency, businesses should view AI as a strategic tool that might change the way they run their operations and their management, not merely as a new piece of technology. Also, the link among AI and RMP is only partly mediated by OT, according to the mediation study. This research emphasizes how crucial organizational structures and procedures are to converting AI capabilities into useful management improvements. It implies that businesses need to concentrate on creating a transformation-friendly atmosphere in addition to using AI technology. Chapter outcomes are similar with previous studies like Esmaeilzadeh (2024), Tak et al., (2025), Al Kuwaiti et al., 2023). Also was founded on base RBV, DOI and TAM theories. Leaders may optimize AI's benefits and create more efficient management techniques that meet the needs of contemporary company by giving organizational transformation top priority. The study highlights the necessity of a comprehensive strategy to AI integration, with consequences for practitioners and policymakers. Companies should fund training and development initiatives that provide management the know-how to use AI efficiently. Additionally, encouraging an innovative and flexible culture might increase the possibility that organizational changes will be effective.

Table 7 shows how organizational transformation mediates the relationship between artificial intelligence (AI) and the renovation of managerial practices in the healthcare sector of the Horn of Africa. AI's direct effect on the renovation of management practices is measured at 0.43, suggesting a favorable but modest influence. This implies that artificial intelligence adoption may affect how healthcare managers run their organizations directly by means of work automation, better decision assistance, and more thorough data analysis. But the indirect impact is far more significant, mediated by organizational change. From artificial intelligence to organizational change, the road has a .74 impact; from organizational transformation to the restoration of management methods, the following path exhibits a 0.67 effect. This indirect route totals .48 when compounded, exceeding the direct impact of artificial intelligence by itself. This emphasizes that the most important shifts in management practices take place when AI installation is combined with more general organizational changes, like reorganization of processes, redefinition of responsibilities, and promotion of an innovative culture. 0.91 shows partial mediation by total impact including direct and indirect factors. Although artificial intelligence directly affects changing management practices, most of its effect is seen via the organizational change it sets off. This partial mediation implies that AI's efficacy in changing management practices is increased when it is included within a flexible and supportive organizational structure. Healthcare companies in the Horn of Africa should therefore give equal priority to not only AI use but also the related organizational transformations required to fully maximize its possibilities.

CONCLUSION

In conclusion, this study emphasizes how important artificial intelligence (AI) is to improving Renovation of Managerial Practices (RMP) and supporting Organizational Transformation (OT). The important direct and indirect effects of AI on RMP, which are mediated by OT, highlight the need for enterprises to employ AI strategically. As enterprises progressively negotiate the complexity of a fast developing business landscape, adopting AI not only as a technology innovation but as a complete transformation agent is vital. Chapter outcomes are similar with previous studies like Tak et al., (2025), Esmaeilzadeh (2024), Al Kuwaiti et al., 2023). Also was founded on base RBV, DOI and TAM theories. According to the findings, effective AI integration calls for not just financial investment in technology but also a dedication to promoting organizational transformation and enhancing management skills. Also, the information gained from this study gives managers and executives a basic understanding of how to use AI to improve management processes. By recognizing how these parts are connected, organizations can more effectively collaborate their strategy to make the most of AI. This will lead to both innovative practices as well as operational efficiency. The discussion of technology-driven workplace change should be further enhanced by future research initiatives that examine the long-term effects of AI on organizational culture and practices across several industries. All things considered, this research adds to the continuing discussion over the revolutionary possibilities of AI by providing a road map for businesses looking to prosper in a world that is becoming more and more digital. The limitations of cross-sector comparative research may highlight best practices and contextual factors that support successful AI integration. Long-term studies that look at the effects of AI over an extended period may also help us understand how long organizational changes brought about by AI could last.

MANAGERIAL IMPLICATIONS

The conclusion of this study is the key management impact that helps management's artificial intelligence (AI) transforms the organization and improves management techniques. In the beginning, leaders need to see them as strategic resources that can influence how an organization works and how it is set up, not just as technical tools. This point of view shows how important it is to have a full training program that teaches staff how to use AI correctly and encourages them to take a preventative approach to using AI. The study also talks about how crucial it is for businesses to establish a culture that is both innovative and adaptable. To successfully use AI and get the most out of its effects on organizational transformation (OT), leaders should make an atmosphere that supports change and fosters experimentation a top priority. By aligning business values with AI capabilities, leaders can make certain that transformation efforts are based on culture as well as technology. Also, managers should work on improving the processes and structures of the business to get the most out of AI. This is shown by the fact that AI can fix partial mediation and leadership practices (RMP). This includes looking at present processes again, establishing procedures for change management that will help people work together better, and helping people adjust to new methods of working. Finally, managers should take part in regular evaluations and input channels to see how well AI projects are doing and how they are changing management practices. Leaders may understand that AI can help management and company performance in the long run by being aware of how demand for the firm and its personnel changes. In light of this, these effects give managers a guide for negotiating AI integration issues and making big changes in their enterprises.

PRACTICAL IMPLICATIONS

The study's conclusions offer a variety of implications that businesses might utilize to try to successfully deploy artificial intelligence (AI). An organization should make it a top priority to create a clear AI strategy that helps them reach their global business goals. This involves setting a clear goal for using AI, including making operations more efficient, enhancing decision-making processes, or changing the way businesses engage with customers. Organizations can better judge how well AI initiatives are doing and set clear targets to make sure that resources are used wisely. Companies should also pay for training and development programs that teach staff how to use AI instruments and technologies. Giving staff hands-on training will assist you learn how to use AI in your regular job. This makes you more creative and better at what you do. Also, making it possible for groups to share ideas and best practices on how to utilize AI in a cooperative way helps the business as a whole get better at leveraging these technologies. Organizations should also make it a point to build a supportive infrastructure are provided that makes it simpler to use AI in their present processes. This might mean making sure that the data is of high quality, making sure that the IT infrastructure is up to date, and making sure that data management practices are solid. Companies can reduce any problems that come up during implementation and get the most out of AI by building a strong foundation. It's also important to keep iterating and evaluating. Companies need to set up feedback loops so they can see how AI changes how they operate and run their businesses. This iterative technique allows organizations to make modifications that keep artificial intelligence systems in line with evolving business needs.

THEORETICAL IMPLICATIONS

The study's findings add to our theoretical understanding of how Organizational Transformation (OT), Renovation of Managerial Practices (RMP), as well as Artificial Intelligence (AI) work together. The study adds to the corpus of research on technology adoption as well as organizational change by showing with real-world data how these two areas are connected. The study supports views that focus on how technology is altering the way organizations work and how managers do their jobs by verifying the premise that AI is a catalyst for change. Also, finding Organizational Transformation as a partial intermediary in the relationship between AI and RMP helps us understand better how technological advantages might lead to real-world management benefits. This mediating role means that the way AI is utilized in an organization and the environment it is employed in have a big effect on the results of AI, which are not only direct. This shows how important it is for businesses to focus on their own processes while still adopting new technologies. This is in line with and expands on existing notions about how organizations work and how to handle change. In addition to the technological parts, it means that theories of technology integration should also look at the culture, structure, and management styles of the business that determine how well these integrations work. This broader perspective enables future research to look at the multiple effects of AI in different types of organizations and how different factors may work together to affect outcomes.

RECOMMENDATIONS

Based on what this study found, there are a number of ways that businesses may utilize Artificial Intelligence (AI) to enhance their management and help their organizations change. This strategy should clearly state the aims of adopting AI and make sure that it takes into consideration the organization's strengths and weaknesses. By defining clear goals, businesses may better judge how well their AI initiatives are doing and make better use of their resources. Businesses should also set up an infrastructure that makes it easy to add AI to their present operations. Part of this is putting money into good IT systems as well as making sure that data governance processes are top-notch. Companies may make their AI initiatives work better and avoid problems by doing this. Companies should also create a culture of continuous improvement and set up regular feedback channels in order to see how AI affects managerial approaches and overall performance. This iterative process can help businesses modify their AI strategy as their needs change and they get new data in real time. Last but not least, departments need to work together for AI to work well. Encouraging teams from various departments to share best practices and observations might help everyone in the firm see AI's role more clearly. This would drive everyone to work together to reach big goals.

FUTURE DIRECTIONS

Future research on the links among artificial intelligence (AI), organizational transformation (OT), as well as renovation of management practices (RMP) should focus on a few key areas to gain more information and make it more useful in the real world. One interesting area of research is looking at how AI integration affects company culture as well as employee engagement over time. Learning about how AI affects communication, cooperation, and decision-making will help you comprehend the bigger picture of how adopting new technology affects people. Investigators ought to think about how the unique features of each industry affect how AI as well as organizational reform work together. distinct fields may provide distinct chances and challenges for employing AI, which might change how companies run their organizations. Comparative studies in different fields may show how to effectively use AI and what factors are important for its successful integration. Long-term research that look at how AI's effects alter over time could also help us understand how long-lasting the changes that AI makes to organizations can be. These sorts of studies could look at how companies change their goals and ways of doing things in response to new technologies and changes in the market. Lastly, looking at how leadership affects AI-driven transformation is another important field of research. By understanding how different leadership styles impact the adoption and fruitful use of AI, organizations may create effective leadership strategies that help them reach their transformation goals.

REFERENCES

Al Kuwaiti, A., Nazer, K., Al-Reedy, A., Al-Shehri, S., Al-Muhanna, A., Subbarayalu, A. V., Al Muhanna, D., & Al-Muhanna, F. A. (2023). A review of the role of artificial intelligence in healthcare. *Journal of Personalized Medicine*, *13*(6), 951. DOI: 10.3390/jpm13060951 PMID: 37373940

Aung, Y. Y. M., Wong, D. C. S., & Ting, D. S. W. (2021). The promise of artificial intelligence: A review of the opportunities and challenges of artificial intelligence in healthcare. *British Medical Bulletin*, *139*(1), 4–15. DOI: 10.1093/bmb/ldab016 PMID: 34405854

Call, D. R., & Herber, D. R. (2022). Applicability of the diffusion of innovation theory to accelerate model-based systems engineering adoption. *Systems Engineering*, *25*(6), 574–583. DOI: 10.1002/sys.21638

Cavalerie, L., Wardeh, M., Lebrasseur, O., Nanyingi, M., McIntyre, K. M., Kaba, M., Asrat, D., Christley, R., Pinchbeck, G., Baylis, M., & Mor, S. M. (2021). One hundred years of zoonoses research in the Horn of Africa: A scoping review. *PLoS Neglected Tropical Diseases*, *15*(7), e0009607. DOI: 10.1371/journal.pntd.0009607 PMID: 34270551

Chouaibi, S., Festa, G., Quaglia, R., & Rossi, M. (2022). The risky impact of digital transformation on organizational performance–evidence from Tunisia. *Technological Forecasting and Social Change*, *178*, 121571. DOI: 10.1016/j.techfore.2022.121571

Esmaeilzadeh, P. (2024). Challenges and strategies for wide-scale artificial intelligence (AI) deployment in healthcare practices: A perspective for healthcare organizations. *Artificial Intelligence in Medicine*, *151*, 102861. DOI: 10.1016/j.artmed.2024.102861 PMID: 38555850

Ghanad, A. (2023). An overview of quantitative research methods. *International Journal of Multidisciplinary Research and Analysis*, *6*(08), 3794–3803. DOI: 10.47191/ijmra/v6-i8-52

Kawaguchi, T., Tsutsumi, T., Nakano, D., & Torimura, T. (2022). MAFLD: Renovation of clinical practice and disease awareness of fatty liver. *Hepatology Research*, *52*(5), 422–432. DOI: 10.1111/hepr.13706 PMID: 34472683

Manickam, P., Mariappan, S. A., Murugesan, S. M., Hansda, S., Kaushik, A., Shinde, R., & Thipperudraswamy, S. P. (2022). Artificial intelligence (AI) and internet of medical things (IoMT) assisted biomedical systems for intelligent healthcare. *Biosensors (Basel)*, *12*(8), 562. DOI: 10.3390/bios12080562 PMID: 35892459

McIntyre, K. M., Cooper, M., & Baylis, M. (2023). Capacity for One Health research in the Horn of Africa. *One Health*, *16*, 100549. DOI: 10.1016/j.onehlt.2023.100549 PMID: 37363254

Misra, S. K., Sharma, S. K., Gupta, S., & Das, S. (2023). A framework to overcome challenges to the adoption of artificial intelligence in Indian Government Organizations. *Technological Forecasting and Social Change*, *194*, 122721. DOI: 10.1016/j.techfore.2023.122721

Sharma, M., Alkatheeri, H., Jabeen, F., & Sehrawat, R. (2022). Impact of COVID-19 pandemic on perishable food supply chain management: A contingent Resource-Based View (RBV) perspective. *International Journal of Logistics Management*, *33*(3), 796–817. DOI: 10.1108/IJLM-02-2021-0131

Tak, C. C., Zulnaidi, H., & Eu, L. K. (2025). Factors influencing the attitude of undergraduate students towards mathematical reasoning: An approach using AMOS-structural equation modelling. *Infinity Journal*, *14*(1), 109–124. DOI: 10.22460/infinity.v14i1.p109-124

Tanujaya, B., Prahmana, R. C. I., & Mumu, J. (2022). Likert scale in social sciences research: Problems and difficulties. *FWU Journal of Social Sciences*, *16*(4), 89–101.

Utami, T. L. W. (2021). Technology adoption on online learning during Covid-19 pandemic: Implementation of technology acceptance model (TAM). *Diponegoro International Journal of Business*, *4*(1), 8–19. DOI: 10.14710/dijb.4.1.2021.8-19

Zhang, X., Nutakor, F., Minlah, M. K., & Li, J. (2023). Can digital transformation drive green transformation in manufacturing companies?—Based on socio-technical systems theory perspective. *Sustainability (Basel)*, *15*(3), 2840. DOI: 10.3390/su15032840

KEY TERMS AND DEFINITIONS

Artificial Intelligence (AI): Artificial Intelligence (AI) is a branch of computer science that creates algorithms to do mental tasks that people used to do. AI systems can do things because they can grasp issues, learn how to do things, and communicate and perceive natural language.

Organizational Transformation (OT): This is a big change that impacts the organization's structure and methods, as well as its culture and strategic goals, in order to improve performance, comply with market rules, or become more competitive.

Renovation of Managerial Practices (RMP): Is the strategic process of changing how managers do things so they can better meet the needs of the industry and keep up with new technologies in order to improve the performance of the firm.

Mediation: Works as a statistical technique that needs a third variable, called a mediator, to connect a variable that is independent to a dependent one. Organizational Transformation connects the relationship among AI technology and the changes that need to be made to management practices.

Data Governance: Is the set of rules and procedures that companies use to keep their data safe and of high quality. These rules and procedures assist organizations manage the resources associated with data while still following the law.

Cultural Adaptability: An organization demonstrates cultural adaptability by modifying its operations through both internal and external elements to implement new technology and practices without endangering staff involvement and motivation.

Cross-Functional Collaboration: Unites workers from varied departments who share their expertise to achieve organizational targets together while integrating multiple viewpoints toward complicated issue resolution.

Compilation of References

Abidin, C. (2014). # IntagLam: Instagram as a repository of taste, a burgeoning marketplace, a war of eyeballs. *Mobile media making in an age of smartphones*, 119-128.

Abidin, C. (2015). Intimités communicatives: influenceurs et interconnexion perçue. *Ada: A Journal of Gender, New Media, &. Technology*, (8), 1–16.

Abidin, C. (2018). *Internet celebrity: Understanding fame online*. Emerald Group Publishing. DOI: 10.1108/9781787560765

Abord de Chatillon, E., & Richard, D. (2015). Du sens, du lien, de l'activité et de confort (SLAC): Proposition pour une modélisation des conditions du bien-être au travail. *Revue française de gestion, 41*(249), 53–71. https://doi.org/DOI: 10.3166/rfg.2015.00153

Acemoglu, D., & Restrepo, P. (2019). Artificial Intelligence, Automation, and Work. *The Economics of Artificial Intelligence*, 197–236. https://doi.org/DOI: 10.7208/chicago/9780226613475.003.0008

Achilles, C. M. (2003). The "why's" of class size: Student behavior in small classes. *Review of Educational Research, 73*(3), 321–368. DOI: 10.3102/00346543073003321

Achir, C., Rafili, M., Douari, A., & Idrissi, K. (2024). Les Nouveaux facteurs de la Résilience Organisationnelle dans l'Entrepreneuriat Marocain Contemporain. *Revue Française d'Economie et de Gestion, 5*, 101–122.

Agarwal, A. (2022). *The birth, the pull & the rise of virtual influencers*. Social Samosa. https://www.socialsamosa.com/2022/05/the-birth-the-pull-the-rise-of-virtual-influencers/

Agrawal, A., Gans, J., & Goldfarb, A. (2017). What to expect from artificial intelligence. *MIT Sloan Management Review, 58*(3), 23–26. DOI: 10.7551/mit-press/11645.003.0008

Agrawal, A., Gans, J., & Goldfarb, A. (2018). Prediction, judgment, and complexity: A theory of decision-making and artificial intelligence. *The economics of artificial intelligence. Agenda (Durban, South Africa), •••*, 89–110.

Ahmed Bayomy, N., & Khedr, E., A., & Abd-Elmegid, L. A. (. (2021). Adaptive model to support business process reengineering. *PeerJ. Computer Science, 7*, e505. DOI: 10.7717/peerj-cs.505 PMID: 33987460

Ahmed, I., Croci, A., Antonello, F., & Zio, E. (2025). Integration of artificial intelligence within an advanced filtering framework for real-time system state estimation and risk prediction with application to a nuclear microreactor. *Nuclear Engineering and Technology, 57*(5), 103353. DOI: 10.1016/j.net.2024.103353

Ahn, J., Kim, J., & Sung, Y. (2021). AI-powered recommendations: The roles of perceived similarity and psychological distance on persuasion. *International Journal of Advertising, 40*(8), 1366–1384. DOI: 10.1080/02650487.2021.1982529

Al Kuwaiti, A., Nazer, K., Al-Reedy, A., Al-Shehri, S., Al-Muhanna, A., Subbarayalu, A. V., Al Muhanna, D., & Al-Muhanna, F. A. (2023). A review of the role of artificial intelligence in healthcare. *Journal of Personalized Medicine, 13*(6), 951. DOI: 10.3390/jpm13060951 PMID: 37373940

Alblowi, K. (2023). A three-tiered analysis of the factors influencing the adoption of forensic accounting field in Saudi Arabia. *International Journal of Professional Business Review, 8*(6), e02185. DOI: 10.26668/businessreview/2023.v8i6.2185

Alessandria, G., Yar Khan, S., Khederlarian, A., Mix, C., & Ruhl, K. J. (2023). The aggregate effects of global and local supply chain disruptions: 2020–2022. *Journal of International Economics, 146*, 103788. DOI: 10.1016/j.jinteco.2023.103788

Ali, M., Arora, A., & Kapoor, A. (2020). PyCaret: An open-source, low-code machine learning library. *Journal of Machine Learning Research, 21*(245), 1–6.

Ali, M., Khan, T. I., Khattak, M. N., & Şener, İ. (2024). Synergizing AI and business: Maximizing innovation, creativity, decision precision, and operational efficiency in high-tech enterprises. *Journal of Open Innovation, 10*(3), 100352. DOI: 10.1016/j.joitmc.2024.100352

Allal-Chérif, O., Guaita-Martínez, J. M., & Montesinos Sansaloni, E. (2024). Sustainable esports entrepreneurs in emerging countries: Audacity, resourcefulness, innovation, transmission, and resilience in adversity. *Journal of Business Research*, 171(October 2023). https://doi.org/DOI: 10.1016/j.jbusres.2023.114382

Allam, Y., Habachi, M., & Tabit, Y. (2024). Intelligence artificielle et la motivation RH: Revue théorique. International Journal of Accounting, Finance, Auditing. *Management and Economics*, *5*(12), 602–613. DOI: 10.5281/zenodo.14538222

Allingham, M. G., & Sandmo, A. (1972). Income tax evasion: A theoretical analysis. *Journal of Public Economics*, *1*(3-4), 323–338. DOI: 10.1016/0047-2727(72)90010-2

Almaraghi, D. M. Q. (2024). Artificial intelligence and the future of human resource management: Data analysis and decision guidance to enhance work productivity and employee motivation. *Pakistan Journal of Life and Social Sciences*, *22*(2). Advance online publication. DOI: 10.57239/PJLSS-2024-22.2.00910

Almeida, J., & Gonçalves, T. C. (2024). The AI Revolution: Are Crypto Markets More Efficient after ChatGPT 3? *Finance Research Letters*, *66*, 105608. DOI: 10.1016/j.frl.2024.105608

Alrjoub, A. M. S., Al-Qudah, L. A. M., Al-Othman, L. N., Bataineh, A., Aburisheh, K. E., & Alkarabsheh, F. (2023). Information Technology and its Role in Improving the Quality of Financial Control due to Corona Pandemic: The Jordanian Income Tax as A Case Study. *International Journal of Professional Business Review*, *8*(4), e01568. DOI: 10.26668/businessreview/2023.v8i4.1568

Alsadhan, N. (2023). A Multi-Module Machine Learning Approach to Detect Tax Fraud. *Computer Systems Science and Engineering*, *46*(1), 241–253. DOI: 10.32604/csse.2023.033375

AL-Thabhawee. (2025). Artificial intelligence and its role in human resources management. International Journal of Accounting, Management [IJAMESC]. *Economics and Social Sciences*, *3*(1), 1–20. DOI: 10.61990/ijamesc.v3i1.353

Altrock, S., Mention, A.-L., & Aas, T. H. (2023). Being Human in the Digitally Enabled Workplace: Insights From the Robo-Advice Literature, in IEEE Transactions on Engineering Management, vol. 71, pp. 7876-7891, 2024, Doi: DOI: 10.1109/TEM.2023.3291820

Al-Yahyaee, K. H., Mensi, W., & Yoon, S. M. (2018). Efficiency, multifractality, and the long-memory property of the Bitcoin market: A comparative analysis with stock, currency, and gold markets. *Finance Research Letters*, *27*, 228–234. DOI: 10.1016/j.frl.2018.03.017

Ameen, N., Tarba, S., Cheah, J. H., Xia, S., & Sharma, G. D. (2024). Coupling Artificial Intelligence Capability and Strategic Agility for Enhanced Product and Service Creativity. *British Journal of Management*, *35*(4), 1916–1934. DOI: 10.1111/1467-8551.12797

Ameen, N., Tarhini, A., Reppel, A., & Anand, A. (2021). Customer experiences in the age of artificial intelligence. *Computers in Human Behavior, 114*, 106548. DOI: 10.1016/j.chb.2020.106548 PMID: 32905175

Amghar, N., Ait Lahcen, D., & Mrhari, A. (2023). La transformation digitale et la résilience des TPME en période de crises: Études de cas. *Alternatives Managériales Economiques,* E-ISSN: 2665-7511. 5(3), 381–401.

Aoki, N., Tatsumi, T., Naruse, G., & Maeda, K. (2024). Explainable AI for government: Does the type of explanation matter to the accuracy, fairness, and trustworthiness of an algorithmic decision as perceived by those who are affected? *Government Information Quarterly*, *41*(4), 101965. DOI: 10.1016/j.giq.2024.101965

Argyris, Y. A., Wang, Z., Kim, Y., & Yin, Z. (2020). Les effets de la congruence visuelle sur l'augmentation de l'engagement des consommateurs à la marque: Une enquête empirique sur le marketing d'influence sur Instagram à l'aide d'algorithmes d'apprentissage profond pour la classification automatique des images. *Computers in Human Behavior*, *112*, 106443. DOI: 10.1016/j.chb.2020.106443

Aria, M., & Cuccurullo, C. (2017). bibliometrix: An R-tool for comprehensive science mapping analysis. *Journal of Informetrics*, *11*(4), 959–975. DOI: 10.1016/j.joi.2017.08.007

Arisian, S., Halat, K., Hafezalkotob, A., & Maskey, R. (2025). Coopetitive Resilience: Integrating Cyber Threat Intelligence Platforms in Critical Supply Chains. *Transportation Research Part E, Logistics and Transportation Review*, *197*, 104043. DOI: 10.1016/j.tre.2025.104043

Arksey, H., & O'Malley, L. (2005). Scoping studies: Towards a methodological framework. 'International Journal of Social Research Methodology, 8'(1), 19-32. DOI: 10.1080/1364557032000119616

Arntz, M., Gregory, T., & Zierahn, U. (2016). The risk of automation for jobs in OECD countries: A comparative analysis.

Ashal, N., & Morshed, A. (2024). Transforming Procurement in the Arab Gulf: Integrating AI, Blockchain, and BI Tools for Enhanced Efficiency and Strategic Decision-Making Journal of Logistics. *Informatics and Service Science*, *11*(9), 266–279. DOI: 10.33168/JLISS.2024.0917

Astuti, B., & Putri, A. P. (2018). Analysis on the effect of Instagram use on consumer purchase intensity. *Review of Integrative Business and Economics Research*, *7*(2), 24–38.

Aung, Y. Y. M., Wong, D. C. S., & Ting, D. S. W. (2021). The promise of artificial intelligence: A review of the opportunities and challenges of artificial intelligence in healthcare. *British Medical Bulletin*, *139*(1), 4–15. DOI: 10.1093/bmb/ldab016 PMID: 34405854

Ayala, J. C., & Manzano, G. (2014). The resilience of the entrepreneur. Influence on the success of the business. A longitudinal analysis. *Journal of Economic Psychology*, *42*, 126–135. DOI: 10.1016/j.joep.2014.02.004

Bachelard, O. (2017). Optimiser le bien-être au travail et la performance globale : Enjeux et perspectives. *Regards*, *51*(1), 169–179. DOI: 10.3917/regar.051.0169

Badhon, B., Chakrabortty, R. K., Anavatti, S. G., & Vanhoucke, M. (2025). A Multi-Module Explainable Artificial Intelligence Framework for Project Risk Management: Enhancing Transparency in Decision-making. *Engineering Applications of Artificial Intelligence*, *148*, 110427. DOI: 10.1016/j.engappai.2025.110427

Bag, S., Dhamija, P., Luthra, S., & Huisingh, D. (2023). How big data analytics can help manufacturing companies strengthen supply chain resilience in the context of the COVID-19 pandemic. *International Journal of Logistics Management*, *34*(4), 1141–1164. DOI: 10.1108/IJLM-02-2021-0095

Bakhtiari, S., Najafi, M. R., Goda, K., & Peerhossaini, H. (2025). A dynamic Bayesian network approach to characterize multi-hazard risks and resilience in interconnected critical infrastructures. *Reliability Engineering & System Safety*, *257*, 110815. Advance online publication. DOI: 10.1016/j.ress.2025.110815

Bakker, A. B., & Demerouti, E. (2017). Job demands–resources theory: Taking stock and looking forward. *Journal of Occupational Health Psychology*, *22*(3), 273–285. DOI: 10.1037/ocp0000056 PMID: 27732008

Bakker, A. B., Demerouti, E., & Euwema, M. C. (2005). Job resources buffer the impact of job demands on burnout. *Journal of Occupational Health Psychology*, *10*(2), 170–180. DOI: 10.1037/1076-8998.10.2.170 PMID: 15826226

Bakker, A. B., Demerouti, E., & Verbeke, W. (2004). Using the job demands–resources model to predict burnout and performance. *Human Resource Management*, *43*(1), 83–104. DOI: 10.1002/hrm.20004

Baklanov, N. (2019). *The top Instagram virtual influencers in 2019*. HypeAuditor. https://hypeauditor.com/blog/the-top-instagram-virtual-influencers-in-2019/

Balambo, M. A. (2014). Hofstede's model revisited: An application for measuring the Moroccan national culture. *International Journal of Business Quantitative Economics and Applied Management Research*, *1*(3), 7–20.

Ballesteros-Leiva, F., Poilpot-Rocaboy, G., & St-Onge, S. (2017). The relationship between life-domain interactions and the well-being of internationally mobile employees. *Personnel Review*, *46*(2), 237–254. DOI: 10.1108/PR-05-2015-0142

Bandura, A. (1986). The Explanatory and Predictive Scope of Self-Efficacy Theory. *Journal of Social and Clinical Psychology*, *4*(3), 359–373. DOI: 10.1521/jscp.1986.4.3.359

Banque Mondiale et OMTPME. (2024). Libérer le potentiel du secteur privé marocain: une analyse de la dynamique des entreprises et de la productivité. Accessible via: https://omtpme.ma/nos-publications/#rapports_annuels

Bar, N. F., & Karakose, M. (2025). An approach for automated generation of quantum computing models using deep learning. *Ain Shams Engineering Journal*, *16*(4), 103327. DOI: 10.1016/j.asej.2025.103327

Barrett-Lennard, G. T. (1998). Carl Rogers′ Helping System: Journey & Substance. *Sage (Atlanta, Ga.)*.

Basile, L. J., Carbonara, N., Panniello, U., & Pellegrino, R. (2024). The role of big data analytics in improving the quality of healthcare services in the Italian context: The mediating role of risk management. *Technovation*, *133*, 103010. DOI: 10.1016/j.technovation.2024.103010

Bayomy, N. A., Khedr, A. E., & Abd-Elmegid, L. A. (2024). A configurable mining approach for enhancing the business processes' performance. *Knowledge and Information Systems*, *66*(4), 2537–2560. DOI: 10.1007/s10115-023-02011-4

Bena, J., Ferreira, M. A., Matos, P., & Pires, P. (2017). Are foreign investors locusts? The long-term effects of foreign institutional ownership. *Journal of Financial Economics*, *126*(1), 122–146. DOI: 10.1016/j.jfineco.2017.07.005

Bengrich, M., Abdelbaki, N., & Bribich, S. (2020). Capital psychologique et performance économique des entreprises marocaines: quel rôle modérateur du profil de l'entrepreneur? *Moroccan Journal of Entrepreneurship, Innovation and Management (MJEIM)*, 5(1), 47–61. https://doi.org/DOI: 10.48396/IMIST.PRSM/mjeim-v5i1.20480

Benraoui, A., Es-skalli, K., & Lahmouchi, M. (2023). Le rôle de l'innovation technologique et l'intelligence artificielle dans le renforcement de la résilience des entreprises en période de crise. *Revue Française d'Economie et de Gestion*, *4*(9), 1–18.

Bentahar, A., & Bouazzaoui, R. (2022). Entrepreneurship: A strategic choice for greater economic resilience and crisis management in Morocco. *Revue Française d'Economie et de Gestion*, *3*(2), 122–140.

Bentley, D. (2019). Timeless principles of taxpayer protection: How they adapt to digital disruption. *eJournal of Tax Research.*

Berkman, P. L. (1971). Measurement of mental health in a general population survey. *American Journal of Epidemiology*, *94*(2), 105–111. DOI: 10.1093/oxfordjournals.aje.a121301 PMID: 5568599

Bernard, M.-J. (2008). L'entrepreneuriat comme un processus de résilience. *Revue internationale de psychosociologie*, 32, 119-140. https://doi.org/DOI: 10.3917/rips.032.0119

Bernard, M.-J., & Dubard Barbosa, S. (2016). Résilience et entrepreneuriat: Une approche dynamique et biographique de l'acte d'entreprendre. *M@n@gement*, 19(2), 89. https://doi.org/DOI: 10.3917/mana.192.0089

Bernard, M.-J., & Fayolle, A. (2016). La résilience, une nouvelle approche de la dimension émotionnelle. *Entreprendre & Innover, n° 29*(2), 16–26. https://doi.org/DOI: 10.3917/entin.029.0016

Bevacqua, J. (2020). Tax authority immunity in a digital tax administration world. *eJournal of Tax Research, 18*(2), 402–440.

Bibi, M., Ajaz, M. A., Akaak, A. S., Noureen, S., & Alghizzawi, M. (2024). How the family business hotels of Europe are reshaping business models with AI and big data. In *Strategies and Approaches of Corporate Social Responsibility and Governance*. IGI Global.

Binns, R. (2018). Fairness in machine learning: Lessons from political philosophy. '*Proceedings of the 2018 Conference on Fairness, Accountability, and Transparency*', 149-159.

Bishop, C. M. (2006). *Pattern recognition and machine learning*. Springer.

Biswas, B., Mukhopadhyay, A., Kumar, A., & Delen, D. (2024). A hybrid framework using explainable AI (XAI) in cyber-risk management for defence and recovery against phishing attacks. *Decision Support Systems*, *177*, 114102. DOI: 10.1016/j.dss.2023.114102

Bobillier Chaumon, M. E., Cuvillier, B., Sarnin, P., & Vacherand-Revel, J. (2018). Usage des TIC et évolutions des pratiques socioprofessionnelles des cadres: Quels repères pour le métier et quelles incidences sur la santé? *Pratiques Psychologiques*, *24*(4), 349–373. DOI: 10.1016/j.prps.2018.01.001

Bock, J., & Geissel, S. (2024). Evolution of stock market efficiency in Europe: Evidence from measuring periods of inefficiency. *Finance Research Letters*, *62*, 105129. DOI: 10.1016/j.frl.2024.105129

Bohari, A., Wider, W., Udang, L. N., Jiang, L., & Tang, Y. (2024). Transformational leadership's role in shaping Education 4.0 within higher education. Journal of Infrastructure. *Policy and Development*, *8*(8), 4900. Advance online publication. DOI: 10.24294/jipd.v8i8.4900

Borrotti, M., Rabasco, M., & Santoro, A. (2023). Using accounting information to predict aggressive tax location decisions by European groups. *Economic Systems*, *47*(3), 101090. DOI: 10.1016/j.ecosys.2023.101090

Boston Consulting Group. (2024, April 24). Consumers Know More About AI Than Business Leaders Think. https://www.bcg.com/publications/2024/consumers-know-more-about-ai-than-businesses-think

Bou Reslan, F., & Jabbour Al Maalouf, N. (2024). Assessing the Transformative Impact of AI Adoption on Efficiency, Fraud Detection, and Skill Dynamics in Accounting Practices. *Journal of Risk and Financial Management*, *17*(12), 577. DOI: 10.3390/jrfm17120577

Boucher, K. B. (2023). Mécanismes expliquant l'effet longitudinal du climat de sécurité psychosocial sur l'engagement et l'épuisement chez les professionnels de l'enseignement et des soins de santé pendant la pandémie COVID-19 (Doctoral dissertation, Université Laval).

Bouschery, S. G., Blazevic, V., & Piller, F. T. (2023). Augmenting human innovation teams with artificial intelligence: Exploring transformer-based language models. *Journal of Product Innovation Management*, *40*(2), 139–153. DOI: 10.1111/jpim.12656

Branicki, L. J., Sullivan-Taylor, B., & Livschitz, S. R. (2018). How entrepreneurial resilience generates resilient SMEs. *International Journal of Entrepreneurial Behaviour & Research*, *24*(7), 1244–1263. DOI: 10.1108/IJEBR-11-2016-0396

Breiman, L. (2001). Random forests. *Machine Learning*, *45*(1), 5–32. DOI: 10.1023/A:1010933404324

Brodie, R. J., Ilic, A., Juric, B., & Hollebeck, L. D. (2011). Customer engagement: Conceptual domain, fundamental propositions, and implications for research. 'Journal of Service Research, 14' (3), 252-271. DOI: 10.1177/1094670511411703

Broo, D. G., & Schooling, J. (2023). Digital twins in infrastructure: Definitions, current practices, challenges and strategies. *International Journal of Construction Management*, *23*(4), 1–16. DOI: 10.1080/15623599.2021.1966980

Brown, T. (2019). *An introduction to polynomial regression*. https://www.datascience.com/blog/introduction-to-polynomial-regression

Brown, D., & Hayes, N. (2008). *Marketing d'influence*. Routledge. DOI: 10.4324/9780080557700

Brown, T., Mann, B., Ryder, N., Subbiah, M., Kaplan, J. D., Dhariwal, P., & Amodei, D. (2020). Language models are few-shot learners. *Advances in Neural Information Processing Systems*, *33*, 1877–1901.

Brunzell, T., Stokes, H., & Waters, L. (2016). Trauma-informed positive education: Using positive psychology to strengthen vulnerable students. *Contemporary School Psychology*, *20*(1), 63–83. DOI: 10.1007/s40688-015-0070-x

Brynjolfsson, E., & McAfee, A. (2014). *The second machine age: Work, progress, and prosperity in a time of brilliant technologies*. WW Norton & company.

Budhwar, P., Malik, A., De Silva, M. T. T., & Thevisuthan, P. (2022). Artificial intelligence–challenges and opportunities for international HRM: A review and research agenda. *International Journal of Human Resource Management*, *33*(6), 1065–1097. DOI: 10.1080/09585192.2022.2035161

Buhalis, D., Efthymiou, L., Uzunboylu, N., & Thrassou, A. (2024). Charting the progress of technology adoption in tourism and hospitality in the era of industry 4.0. *EuroMed Journal of Business*, *19*(1), 1–20. DOI: 10.1108/EMJB-11-2023-0310

Bullough, A., & Renko, M. (2013). Entrepreneurial resilience during challenging times. *Business Horizons*, *56*(3), 343–350. DOI: 10.1016/j.bushor.2013.01.001

Bullough, A., Renko, M., & Myatt, T. (2014). Danger zone entrepreneurs: The importance of resilience and self-efficacy for entrepreneurial intentions. *Entrepreneurship Theory and Practice*, *38*(3), 473–499. DOI: 10.1111/etap.12006

Bussmann, N., Giudici, P., Marinelli, D., & Papenbrock, J. (2021). Explainable machine learning in credit risk management. *Computational Economics*, *57*(1), 203–216. DOI: 10.1007/s10614-020-10042-0

Call, D. R., & Herber, D. R. (2022). Applicability of the diffusion of innovation theory to accelerate model-based systems engineering adoption. *Systems Engineering*, *25*(6), 574–583. DOI: 10.1002/sys.21638

Caron, É. (2021). Le Big Data fiscal: Quelles conséquences pour le contrôle fiscal et les contribuables? *Gestion & Finances Publiques*, *6*(6), 77–83. DOI: 10.3166/gfp.2021.6.013

Casaló, L. V., Flavián, C., & Ibáñez-Sánchez, S. (2020). Influenceurs sur Instagram: Antécédents et conséquences du leadership d'opinion. *Journal of Business Research, 117*, 510–519. DOI: 10.1016/j.jbusres.2018.07.005

Castellón González, P., & Velásquez, J. D. (2013). Characterization and detection of taxpayers with false invoices using data mining techniques. *Expert Systems with Applications, 40*(5), 1427–1436. DOI: 10.1016/j.eswa.2012.08.051

Castelo, N., Bos, M. W., & Lehmann, D. R. (2019). Task-dependent algorithm aversion. *JMR, Journal of Marketing Research, 56*(5), 809–825. DOI: 10.1177/0022243719851788

Cavalerie, L., Wardeh, M., Lebrasseur, O., Nanyingi, M., McIntyre, K. M., Kaba, M., Asrat, D., Christley, R., Pinchbeck, G., Baylis, M., & Mor, S. M. (2021). One hundred years of zoonoses research in the Horn of Africa: A scoping review. *PLoS Neglected Tropical Diseases, 15*(7), e0009607. DOI: 10.1371/journal.pntd.0009607 PMID: 34270551

Cavanaugh, M. A., Boswell, W. R., Roehling, M. V., & Boudreau, J. W. (2000). An empirical examination of self-reported work stress among US managers. *The Journal of Applied Psychology, 85*(1), 65–74. DOI: 10.1037/0021-9010.85.1.65 PMID: 10740957

Chalmers, D., MacKenzie, N. G., & Carter, S. (2021). Artificial Intelligence and Entrepreneurship: Implications for Venture Creation in the Fourth Industrial Revolution. *Entrepreneurship Theory and Practice, 45*(5), 1028–1053. DOI: 10.1177/1042258720934581

Chanphati, J., & Thosuwanchot, N. (2023). Strategic flexibility: A systematic review and future research directions. *Journal of Strategy and Management, 16*(3), 470–491. DOI: 10.1108/JSMA-08-2022-0134

Chávez-Díaz, J. M., Aquiño-Perales, L., De-Velazco-Borda, J. L., Villagómez-Chinchay, J. A., & Flores-Sotelo, W. S. (2024). Artificial intelligence in accounting and auditing: Bibliometric analysis in Scopus 2020-2023. *Indonesian Journal of Electrical Engineering and Computer Science, 36*(2), 1319. DOI: 10.11591/ijeecs.v36.i2.pp1319-1328

Chen, J., Tang, G., Zhou, G., & Zhu, W. (2025). ChatGPT and Deepseek: Can They Predict the Stock Market and Macroeconomy? arXiv preprint arXiv:2502.10008.

Chen, L., Ifenthaler, D., Yau, J. Y. K., & Sun, W. (2024). Artificial intelligence in entrepreneurship education: A scoping review. *Education + Training, 66*(6), 589–608. DOI: 10.1108/ET-05-2023-0169

Chhajer, P., Shah, M., & Kshirsagar, A. (2022). The applications of artificial neural networks, support vector machines, and long–short term memory for stock market prediction. *Decision Analytics Journal, 2*, 100015. DOI: 10.1016/j.dajour.2021.100015

Chhatwani, M., Mishra, S. K., Varma, A., & Rai, H. (2022). Psychological resilience and business survival chances: A study of small firms in the USA during COVID-19. *Journal of Business Research, 142*, 277–286. DOI: 10.1016/j.jbusres.2021.12.048

Chibi, M. (2021). Collectivism and individualism as cultural aspects in Arabic/English argumentative writing by Moroccan students. *International Journal of English Literature and Social Sciences, 6*(4), 60–69. DOI: 10.22161/ijels.64.10

Childers, C. C., Lemon, L. L., & Hoy, M. G. (2018). # Sponsored# Ad: Agency perspective on influencer marketing campaigns. *Journal of Current Issues and Research in Advertising, 40*(3), 258–274. DOI: 10.1080/10641734.2018.1521113

Chilunjika, A., Intauno, K., & Chilunjika, S.R. (2022). Artificial intelligence and public sector human resource management in South Africa: Opportunities, challenges and prospects. SA Journal of Human Resource Management, 20(0). . v20i0.1972DOI: <ALIGNMENT.qj></ALIGNMENT>10.4102/sajhrm

Choi Li, A. K., Rauf, I. A., & Keshavjee, K. (2025). Knowledge is not all you need for comfort in use of AI in healthcare. *Public Health, 238*, 254–259. DOI: 10.1016/j.puhe.2024.11.019 PMID: 39700868

Chouaibi, S., Festa, G., Quaglia, R., & Rossi, M. (2022). The risky impact of digital transformation on organizational performance–evidence from Tunisia. *Technological Forecasting and Social Change, 178*, 121571. DOI: 10.1016/j.techfore.2022.121571

Christensen, C. M. (2015). *The innovator's dilemma: when new technologies cause great firms to fail*. Harvard Business Review Press.

Ciruela-Lorenzo, A. M., Del-Aguila-Obra, A. R., Padilla-Meléndez, A., & Fernández-Portal, M. (2020). Digitalization of agri-cooperatives in the smart agriculture context: Proposal of a digital diagnosis tool. *Sustainability (Basel), 15*(12), 9999. Advance online publication. DOI: 10.3390/su12041325

Collie, R. J., Martin, A. J., & Gasevic, D. (2024). Teachers' generative AI self-efficacy, valuing, and integration at work: Examining job resources and demands. *Computers and Education: Artificial Intelligence, 7*(100333), 100333. Advance online publication. DOI: 10.1016/j.caeai.2024.100333

Cope, J. (2011). Entrepreneurial learning from failure: An interpretative phenomenological analysis. *Journal of Business Venturing, 26*(6), 604–623. DOI: 10.1016/j.jbusvent.2010.06.002

Corbett-Davies, S., Pierson, E., Feller, A., Goel, S., & Huq, A. (2018). Algorithmic decision making and the cost of fairness. *Proceedings of the ACM SIGKDD*, 797–806.

Corsi, F. (2009). A simple approximate long-memory model of realized volatility. *Journal of Financial Econometrics, 7*(2), 174–196. DOI: 10.1093/jjfinec/nbp001

Cortes, C., & Vapnik, V. (1995). Support-vector networks. *Machine Learning, 20*(3), 273–297. DOI: 10.1007/BF00994018

Cotter, K. (2019). Playing the visibility game: How digital influencers and algorithms negotiate influence on Instagram. *New Media & Society, 21*(4), 895–913. DOI: 10.1177/1461444818815684

Cottrell, N. **(2023).** *Virtual influencers: Homophily and its impact on consumer purchase intention*. ResearchGate. https://www.researchgate.net/publication/371126113_Virtual_Influencers_Homophily_and_its_Impact_on_Consumer_Purchase_Intention

Cramarenco, R. E., Burcă-Voicu, M. I., & Dabija, D. C. (2023). The impact of artificial intelligence (AI) on employees' skills and well-being in global labor markets: A systematic review. *Oeconomia Copernicana, 14*(3), 731–767. DOI: 10.24136/oc.2023.022

Cusin, J. (2017). The Role of the Tutor in the Resilience of the Post-Bankruptcy Entrepreneur: The Case of the 60.000 Rebonds Association. *Revue de l'Entrepreneuriat, 16*(2), 91–122. DOI: 10.3917/entre.162.0091

Cynthia, D. (2014). Fisher, Conceptualizing and measuring wellbeing at work, in: Peter Y. Chen, L. Cary, Cooper (Eds.), Work and Wellbeing: Wellbeing: A Complete Reference Guide Vol III, John Wiley & Sons. DOI: 10.1002/9781118539415.wbwell018

Cyrulnik, B. (2002). *Un merveilleux malheur*. Odile Jacob.

D'Ambrosio, N., Perrone, G., & Romano, S. P. (2023). Including insider threats into risk management through Bayesian threat graph networks. *Computers & Security, 133*, 103410. DOI: 10.1016/j.cose.2023.103410

Daly, S. (2024). Artificial intelligence, the Rule of Law and public administration: The case of taxation. *The Cambridge Law Journal, 83*(3), 437–464. DOI: 10.1017/S0008197324000448

Daniels, K. (2000). Measures of five aspects of affective well-being at work. *Human Relations, 53*(2), 275–294. DOI: 10.1177/a010564

Das, M., & Ramalingam, M. (2022). What drives product involvement and satisfaction with OFDs amid COVID-19? *Journal of Retailing and Consumer Services*, *68*(June), 103063. DOI: 10.1016/j.jretconser.2022.103063

Davis, F. D. (1989). Perceived usefulness, perceived ease of use, and user acceptance of information technology. *Management Information Systems Quarterly*, *13*(3), 319–340. DOI: 10.2307/249008

D'avolio, G., Gildor, E., & Shleifer, A. (2001). Technology, information production, and market efficiency. Information Production, and Market Efficiency (September 2001).

De Bruijn, H., Warnier, M., & Janssen, M. (2022). The perils and pitfalls of explainable AI: Strategies for explaining algorithmic decision-making. *Government Information Quarterly*, *39*(2), 101666. DOI: 10.1016/j.giq.2021.101666

De Terssac, G. (2012). Autonomie et travail. Dictionnaire du travail, 47-53.

De Vries, L., Gensler, S., & Leeflang, P. S. (2012). Popularity of brand posts on brand fan pages: An investigation of the effects of social media marketing. *Journal of Interactive Marketing*, *26*(2), 83–91. DOI: 10.1016/j.intmar.2012.01.003

Deci, E. L., & Ryan, R. M. (1985). The general causality orientations scale: Self-determination in personality. *Journal of Research in Personality*, *19*(2), 109–134. DOI: 10.1016/0092-6566(85)90023-6

Deci, E. L., & Ryan, R. M. (2008). Self-determination theory: A macrotheory of human motivation, development, and health. *Canadian Psychology*, *49*(3), 182–185. DOI: 10.1037/a0012801

Demerouti, E. (2025). Job demands-resources and conservation of resources theories: How do they help to explain employee well-being and future job design? *Journal of Business Research*, *192*(C), 115296. DOI: 10.1016/j.jbusres.2025.115296

Demerouti, E., Bakker, A. B., & Halbesleben, J. R. (2015). Productive and counterproductive job crafting: A daily diary study. *Journal of Occupational Health Psychology*, *20*(4), 457–469. DOI: 10.1037/a0039002 PMID: 25798721

Deming, D. J. (2021). *The growing importance of decision-making on the job (No. w28733)*. National Bureau of Economic Research.

Demlehner, Q., & Laumer, S. (2020). Shall we use it or not? Explaining the adoption of artificial intelligence for car manufacturing purposes.

Dharmawan, A. P., & Hartantono, N., & Lasmy. (2024). Role of generative artificial intelligence and work environment on the motivation of workers. *3rd International Conference on Creative Communication and Innovative Technology (ICCIT)*, 1–5. DOI: 10.1109/ICCIT62134.2024.10701197

Di Vaio, A., Palladino, R., Hassan, R., & Escobar, O. (2020). Artificial intelligence and business models in the sustainable development goals perspective: A systematic literature review. *Journal of Business Research, 121*(January), 283–314. DOI: 10.1016/j.jbusres.2020.08.019

Diakopoulos, N. (2015). Algorithmic accountability: Journalistic investigation of computational power structures. 'Digital Journalism, 3'(3), 398-415.

Díaz-Arancibia, J., Hochstetter-Diez, J., Bustamante-Mora, A., Sepúlveda-Cuevas, S., Albayay, I., & Arango-López, J. (2024). Bustamante- Mora, A.; Sepúlveda-Cuevas, S.; Albayay, I.; Arango-López, J. (2024). Navigating Digital Transformation and Technology Adoption: A Literature Review from Small and Medium-Sized Enterprises in Developing Countries. *Sustainability (Basel), 16*(14), 5946. DOI: 10.3390/su16145946

Didimo, W., Giamminonni, L., Liotta, G., Montecchiani, F., & Pagliuca, D. (2018). A visual analytics system to support tax evasion discovery. *Decision Support Systems, 110*, 71–83. DOI: 10.1016/j.dss.2018.03.008

Diener, E. (1984). Subjective well-being. *Psychological Bulletin, 95*(3), 542–575. DOI: 10.1037/0033-2909.95.3.542 PMID: 6399758

Diener, E. (2000). Subjective well-being: The science of happiness and a proposal for a national index. *The American Psychologist, 55*(1), 34–43. DOI: 10.1037/0003-066X.55.1.34 PMID: 11392863

Diener, E., Emmons, R. A., Larsen, R. J., & Griffin, S. (1985). The Satisfaction With Life Scale. *Journal of Personality Assessment, 49*(1), 71–75. DOI: 10.1207/s15327752jpa4901_13 PMID: 16367493

Dimitriadis, S. (2021). Social capital and entrepreneur resilience: Entrepreneur performance during violent protests in Togo. *Strategic Management Journal, 42*(11), 1993–2019. DOI: 10.1002/smj.3292

Djatmiko, G. H., Sinaga, O., & Pawirosumarto, S. (2025). Digital Transformation and Social Inclusion in Public Services: A Qualitative Analysis of E-Government Adoption for Marginalized Communities in Sustainable Governance. *Sustainability (Basel), 17*(7), 2908. DOI: 10.3390/su17072908

Döhring, B., Hristov, A., Maier, C., Roeger, W., & Thum-Thysen, A. (2021). COVID-19 acceleration in digitalisation, aggregate productivity growth and the functional income distribution. In *International Economics and Economic Policy* (Vol. 18, Issue 3). Springer Berlin Heidelberg. https://doi.org/DOI: 10.1007/s10368-021-00511-8

Donaldson, S. I., & Donaldson, S. I. (2020). The positive functioning at work scale: Psychometric assessment, validation, and measurement invariance. *Journal of Well-Being Assessment*, *4*(2), 181–215. DOI: 10.1007/s41543-020-00033-1

Dong, M., Bonnefon, J. F., & Rahwan, I. (2024). Toward human-centered AI management: Methodological challenges and future directions. *Technovation*, *131*(102953), 102953. Advance online publication. DOI: 10.1016/j.technovation.2024.102953

Douanla, J., Kenne, J. M. N., & Tawembe, N. P. Y. (2020). Latitude décisionnelle, implication et comportements de citoyenneté organisationnelle : Une mise en exergue des relations singulières en situation de sous-emploi. *Revue Française d'Economie et de Gestion*, *1*(6).

Duchek, S. (2018). Entrepreneurial resilience: A biographical analysis of successful entrepreneurs. *The International Entrepreneurship and Management Journal*, *14*(2), 429–455. DOI: 10.1007/s11365-017-0467-2

Duening, T. N. (2010). Five minds for the entrepreneurial future: Cognitive skills as the intellectual foundation for next generation entrepreneurship curricula. *The Journal of Entrepreneurship*, *19*(1), 1–22. DOI: 10.1177/097135570901900101

Edwards, M. R., Zubielevitch, E., Okimoto, T., Parker, S., & Anseel, F. (2024). Managerial control or feedback provision: How perceptions of algorithmic HR systems shape employee motivation, behavior, and well-being. *Human Resource Management*, *63*(4), 691–710. DOI: 10.1002/hrm.22218

Eilam, G., & Shamir, B. (2005). "What's your story?" A life-stories approach to authentic leadership development. *The Leadership Quarterly*, *16*(3), 395–417. DOI: 10.1016/j.leaqua.2005.03.005

Elzayn, H., Smith, E., Hertz, T., Guage, C., Ramesh, A., Fisher, R., Ho, D. E., & Goldin, J. (2023). Measuring and Mitigating Racial Disparities in Tax Audits. *The Quarterly Journal of Economics*, *140*(1), 113–163. DOI: 10.1093/qje/qjae027

Emrizal, E., & Primadona, P. (2023). The Role Of Entrepreneurial Resilience And Entrepreneurial Self-Efficacy On Entrepreneurial Intention On Students In Padang City. *International Journal of Science. Technology & Management*, *4*(1), 80–84. DOI: 10.46729/ijstm.v4i1.752

Ennouri, W. (2021). Développement d'un modèle de gestion des risques dans la chaîne logistique basé sur les réseaux bayésiens. Thèse de doctorat spécialité Sciences de gestion: Logistique et Production, Faculté des Sciences Economiques et de Gestion-Sfax, Tunisie.

Esmaeilzadeh, P. (2024). Challenges and strategies for wide-scale artificial intelligence (AI) deployment in healthcare practices: A perspective for healthcare organizations. *Artificial Intelligence in Medicine*, *151*, 102861. DOI: 10.1016/j.artmed.2024.102861 PMID: 38555850

European Commission. (2020). *Ethics guidelines for trustworthy AI*. High-Level Expert Group on AI. https://ec.europa.eu/newsroom/dae/document.cfm?doc_id=60419

Fama, E. F. (1965). Random walks in stock market prices. *Financial Analysts Journal*, *51*(1), 75–80. DOI: 10.2469/faj.v51.n1.1861

Fama, E. F. (1970). Efficient capital markets. *The Journal of Finance*, *25*(2), 383–417. DOI: 10.2307/2325486

Fama, E. F. (2014). Two pillars of asset pricing. *The American Economic Review*, *104*(6), 1467–1485. DOI: 10.1257/aer.104.6.1467

Fashion & Marketing Reports. **(2021).** *Lil Miquela takes over Prada's Instagram during Milan Fashion Week.* https://www.voguebusiness.com/technology/what-influencer-marketing-looks-like-in-the-metaverse

Fatoki, O. (2018). The impact of entrepreneurial resilience on the success of small and medium enterprises in South Africa. *Sustainability (Basel)*, *10*(7), 2527. Advance online publication. DOI: 10.3390/su10072527

Feng, C., Ye, X., Li, J., & Yang, J. (2024). How does artificial intelligence affect the transformation of China's green economic growth? An analysis from internal-structure perspective. *Journal of Environmental Management, 351*(November 2023), 119923. https://doi.org/DOI: 10.1016/j.jenvman.2023.119923

Fidelangeli, A., & Galli, F. (2021). Artificial intelligence and tax law: Perspective and challenges. *CERIDAP, 4*. DOI: 10.13130/2723-9195/2021-4-27

Fine, G. A. (2003). Crafting authenticity: The validation of identity in self-taught art. *Theory and Society*, *32*(2), 153–180. DOI: 10.1023/A:1023943503531

Fisher, R., Maritz, A., & Lobo, A. (2016). Does Individual Resilience affect Entrepreneurial Success? *Academy of Entrepreneurship Journal*, *22*(2), 39–53. DOI: 10.25916/sut.26409538

Floridi, L. (2019). Establishing the rules for building trustworthy AI. 'Nature Machine Intelligence, 1'(6), 261-262.

Forcina, A., Silvestri, L., De Felice, F., & Falcone, D. (2024). Exploring Industry 4.0 technologies to improve industrial resilience: A sociotechnical perspective. *Safety Science, 169*, 106351. Advance online publication. DOI: 10.1016/j.ssci.2023.106351

Forest, J., & Mageau, G.A. (2008). La motivation au travail selon la théorie de l'autodétermination. Psychologie Québec, 25(5).

Franke, C., Groeppel-Klein, A., & Müller, K. (2023). Consumers' responses to virtual influencers as advertising endorsers: Novel and effective or uncanny and deceiving? *Journal of Advertising, 52*(4), 523–539. DOI: 10.1080/00913367.2022.2154721

Fritz, K., Schoenmueller, V., & Bruhn, M. (2017). Authenticity in branding–exploring antecedents and consequences of brand authenticity. *European Journal of Marketing, 51*(2), 324–348. DOI: 10.1108/EJM-10-2014-0633

Frone, M. R., Russell, M., & Cooper, M. L. (1995). Job stressors, job involvement and employee health: A test of identity theory. *Journal of Occupational and Organizational Psychology, 68*(1), 1–11. DOI: 10.1111/j.2044-8325.1995.tb00684.x

Gagné, M., Parent-Rocheleau, X., Bujold, A., Gaudet, M.-C., & Lirio, P. (2022). How algorithmic management influences worker motivation: A self-determination theory perspective. *Psychologie Canadienne, 63*(2), 247–260. DOI: 10.1037/cap0000324

Gaie, C., & Mueck, M. (2022). A hybrid blockchain proposal to improve value added tax recovery. *International Journal of Internet Technology and Secured Transactions, 12*(1), 27. DOI: 10.1504/IJITST.2022.119668

Gaillard, A. W. K. (1993). Comparing the concepts of mental load and stress. *Ergonomics, 36*(9), 991–1005. DOI: 10.1080/00140139308967972 PMID: 8404841

Gallie, D., Felstead, A., Green, F., & Inanc, H. (2017). The hidden face of job insecurity. *Work, Employment and Society, 31*(1), 36–53. DOI: 10.1177/0950017015624399

Gama, F., & Magistretti, S. (2025). Artificial intelligence in innovation management: A review of innovation capabilities and a taxonomy of AI applications. *Journal of Product Innovation Management, 42*(1), 76–111. DOI: 10.1111/jpim.12698

Garfield, E. (2004). Historiographic mapping of knowledge domains literature. *Journal of Information Science, 30*(2), 119–145. DOI: 10.1177/0165551504042802

Gentile, C., & Mothe, C. (2022). La résilience de l'entrepreneur face à l'adversité: Une approche processuelle. *Revue de l'Entrepreneuriat, 21*(4), 61–93. DOI: 10.3917/entre.pr.0045

Ghanad, A. (2023). An overview of quantitative research methods. *International Journal of Multidisciplinary Research and Analysis, 6*(08), 3794–3803. DOI: 10.47191/ijmra/v6-i8-52

Godin, B. (2015). *Innovation contested: The idea of innovation over the centuries.* Routledge. DOI: 10.4324/9781315855608

Gomes, G. S. L., & Balaniuk, R. (2024). Identifying tax evasion in shell companies and fraudulent credits of Brazil's state value-added tax (ICMS). *Revista de Administração Pública, 58*(4), e2023-0303. Advance online publication. DOI: 10.1590/0034-761220230303x

Gómez, J., Krammer, S. M. S., Pérez-Aradros, B., & Salazar, I. (2024). Resilience to the pandemic: The role of female management, multi-unit structure, and business model innovation. *Journal of Business Research, 172*, 114428. Advance online publication. DOI: 10.1016/j.jbusres.2023.114428

Goodfellow, I., Bengio, Y., & Courville, A. (2016). *Deep learning.* MIT Press.

Goodfellow, I., Pouget-Abadie, J., Mirza, M., Xu, B., Warde-Farley, D., Ozair, S., Courville, A., & Bengio, Y. (2014). Generative adversarial nets. *Advances in Neural Information Processing Systems*, •••, 27.

Goodman, B., & Flaxman, S. (2017). European Union regulations on algorithmic decision-making and a "right to explanation". 'AI Magazine, 38'(3), 50-57.

Goodman, L. A., Wilson, J. M., Helms, J. E., Greenstein, N., & Medzhitova, J. (2018). Becoming an advocate: Processes and outcomes of a relationship-centered advocacy training model. *The Counseling Psychologist, 46*(2), 122–153. DOI: 10.1177/0011000018757168

Górski, Ł., Kuźniacki, B., Almada, M., Tyliński, K., Calvo, M., Asnaghi, P. M., Almada, L., Iñiguez, H., Rubianes, F., Pera, O., & Nigrelli, J. I. (2024). Exploring explainable AI in the tax domain. *Artificial Intelligence and Law*, •••, 1–29. DOI: 10.1007/s10506-024-09395-w

Graham, S. A., Lee, E. E., Jeste, D. V., Van Patten, R., Twamley, E. W., Nebeker, C., Yamada, Y., Kim, H. C., & Depp, C. A. (2020). Artificial intelligence approaches to predicting and detecting cognitive decline in older adults: A conceptual review. *Psychiatry Research, 284*, 112732. DOI: 10.1016/j.psychres.2019.112732 PMID: 31978628

Granstrand, O., & Holgersson, M. (2020). Innovation ecosystems: A conceptual review and a new definition. *Technovation, 90*, 102098. DOI: 10.1016/j.technovation.2019.102098

Grath, R., & Buskirk, P. (2019). Monitoring and detecting drift in predictive models: An industry perspective. *Journal of Data Science and Analytics*, *7*(3), 112–129. DOI: 10.1016/j.jdsan.2019.03.005

Guetaya, L., Addoumi, N., Bourgrine, K., & Douari, A. (2024). Innovations Disruptives : L'entrepreneuriat dans l'ère de l'Intelligence Artificielle. *Africain Scientifique Journal*, 03 (25), numéro, 273–295.

Guler, N., Kirshner, S. N., & Vidgen, R. (2024). A literature review of artificial intelligence research in business and management using machine learning and ChatGPT. *Data and Information Management*, *8*(3), 100076. DOI: 10.1016/j.dim.2024.100076

Guo, Y., Yang, B., Alqawzai, S., Chen, K., & Kong, D. (2025). Machine learning-based and interpretable models for predicting the resistance and probability of progressive collapse of steel frame-composite floor structures. *Engineering Structures*, *332*, 120089. DOI: 10.1016/j.engstruct.2025.120089

Gu, X., Chan, H. K., Thadani, D. R., Chan, F. K. S., & Peng, Y. (2023). The role of digital techniques in organisational resilience and performance of logistics firms in response to disruptive events: Flooding as an example. *International Journal of Production Economics*, *266*(July), 109033. DOI: 10.1016/j.ijpe.2023.109033

Hadjitchoneva, J. (2020). L'intelligence artificielle au service de la prise de décisions plus efficace. Pour une recherche économique efficace, 149.

Haenlein, M., & Kaplan, A. (2019). A brief history of artificial intelligence: On the past, present, and future of artificial intelligence. *California Management Review*, *61*(4), 5–14. DOI: 10.1177/0008125619864925

Hamarat, H., Sahin, H., Koç Apuhan, A., & Inan, R. (2024). The dark side of artificial intelligence: Threats to tourism workers. *Worldwide Hospitality and Tourism Themes*, *16*(2), 127–137. DOI: 10.1108/WHATT-03-2024-0061

Han, J., & Balabanis, G. (2024). Meta-analysis of social media influencer impact: Key antecedents and theoretical foundations. *Psychology and Marketing*, *41*(2), 394–426. https://doi.org/xxxxx. DOI: 10.1002/mar.21927

Hao, X., Demir, E., & Eyers, D. (2024). Exploring collaborative decision-making: A quasi-experimental study of human and Generative AI interaction. *Technology in Society*, *78*, 102662. DOI: 10.1016/j.techsoc.2024.102662

Harju, L. K., Kaltiainen, J., & Hakanen, J. J. (2021). The double-edged sword of job crafting: The effects of job crafting on changes in job demands and employee well-being. *Human Resource Management*, *60*(6), 953–968. DOI: 10.1002/hrm.22054

Harwood, S., & Eaves, S. (2020). Conceptualising technology, its development and future: The six genres of technology. *Technological Forecasting and Social Change*, *160*, 120174. DOI: 10.1016/j.techfore.2020.120174 PMID: 32904525

Hashimzade, N., Myles, G. D., & Rablen, M. D. (2016). Predictive analytics and the targeting of audits. *Journal of Economic Behavior & Organization*, *124*, 130–145. DOI: 10.1016/j.jebo.2015.11.009

Hayward, M. L. A., Forster, W. R., Sarasvathy, S. D., & Fredrickson, B. L. (2010). Beyond hubris: How highly confident entrepreneurs rebound to venture again. *Journal of Business Venturing*, *25*(6), 569–578. DOI: 10.1016/j.jbusvent.2009.03.002

Heidegger, M. (1962). *L'être et le temps*. SCM Press.

Hemphill, T. A., & Kelley, K. J. (2021). Artificial intelligence and the fifth phase of political risk management: An application to regulatory expropriation. *Thunderbird International Business Review*, *63*(5), 585–595. DOI: 10.1002/tie.22222

Hlady Rispal, M. and Jouison-Laffitte, E. (2015). The Contribution of Qualitative Methods to the Development of the Field of Entrepreneurship. *Revue de l'Entrepreneuriat / Review of Entrepreneurship*. 14(1), 15-40. https://doi.org/DOI: 10.3917/entre.141.0015

Hoffman, D. L., & Novak, T. P. (2018). Consumer and object experience in the internet of things: An assemblage theory approach. *The Journal of Consumer Research*, *44*(6), 1178–1204. DOI: 10.1093/jcr/ucx105

Hofstede, G. (2001). *Culture's consequences: Comparing values, behaviors, institutions and organizations across nations* (2nd ed.). Sage Publications.

Hommel, D., & Cohen, B. (2023). Reducing AI Anxiety Starts by Talking with Students | Faculty Focus. Teaching with Technology. https://www.facultyfocus.com/articles/teaching-with-technologyarticles/reducing-ai-anxiety-starts-by-talking-with-students/

Hommel, D., & Cohen, B. (2023). Reducing AI Anxiety Starts by Talking with Students | Faculty Focus. Teaching with Technology. https://www.facultyfocus.com/articles/teaching-with-technology-articles/reducing-ai-anxiety-starts-by-talking-with-students/

Hong, F., Wei, P., Bi, S., & Beer, M. (2025). Efficient variational Bayesian model updating by Bayesian active learning. *Mechanical Systems and Signal Processing*, *224*, 112113. DOI: 10.1016/j.ymssp.2024.112113

Horton, D., & Wohl, R. R. (1956). Mass communication and parasocial interaction: Observations on intimacy at a distance. *Psychiatry*, *19*(3), 215–229. DOI: 10.1080/00332747.1956.11023049 PMID: 13359569

Hosanagar, K. (2019). *A human's guide to machine intelligence*. Viking.

Hovland, C. I., Janis, I. L., & Kelley, H. H. (1953). *Communication and persuasion: Psychological studies of opinion change*. Yale University Press.

Howard, J. (2022). Algorithms and the future of work. *American Journal of Industrial Medicine*, *65*(12), 943–952. DOI: 10.1002/ajim.23429 PMID: 36128686

Huang, M. H., & Rust, R. T. (2018). Artificial Intelligence in Service. *Journal of Service Research*, *21*(2), 155–172. DOI: 10.1177/1094670517752459

Huang, M. H., Rust, R., & Maksimovic, V. (2019). The feeling economy: Managing in the next generation of AI (AI). *California Management Review*, *61*(4), 43–65. DOI: 10.1177/0008125619863436

Hu, M., Zhang, M., & Luo, N. (2016). Understanding participation on video sharing communities: The role of self-construal and community interactivity. *Computers in Human Behavior*, *62*, 105–115. DOI: 10.1016/j.chb.2016.03.077

Huo, M. L., & Boxall, P. (2017). Lean production and the well-being of the frontline manager: The job demands–resources model as a diagnostic tool in Chinese manufacturing. *Asia Pacific Journal of Human Resources*, *55*(3), 280–297. DOI: 10.1111/1744-7941.12152

Hu, Q., & Pan, Z. (2023). Can AI benefit individual resilience? The mediation roles of AI routinization and infusion. *Journal of Retailing and Consumer Services*, *73*, 103339. DOI: 10.1016/j.jretconser.2023.103339

Huy, V., Nguyen, H., Vo-Thanh, T., Thinh, N. H. T., & Dung, T. T. T. (2023). Generative AI, Why, How, and Outcomes: A User Adoption Study. *AIS Transactions on Human-Computer Interaction*, *16*(1), 1–27. DOI: 10.17705/1thci.00198

Ibrahim, A. M. A., Chen, Z., Eljailany, H. A., Yu, G., Ipaye, A. A., Abouda, K. A., & Idress, W. M. (2024). Advancing 6G-IoT networks: Willow catkin packet transmission scheduling with AI and Bayesian game-theoretic approach-based resource allocation. *Internet of Things : Engineering Cyber Physical Human Systems*, *25*, 101119. DOI: 10.1016/j.iot.2024.101119

IEEE. (2019). *Ethically aligned design: A vision for prioritizing human well-being with autonomous and intelligent systems* (1st ed.). https://ethicsinaction.ieee.org/

Ifleh, A., & El Kabbouri, M. (2021, December). Prediction of moroccan stock price based on machine learning algorithms. In *International Conference on Intelligent Systems Design and Applications* (pp. 735-741). Cham: Springer International Publishing.

Ikhide, J. E., Timur, A. T., & Ogunmokun, O. A. (2023). A balanced perspective on the affordance of a gamified HRM system for employees' creative performance. *Personnel Review*, *52*(3), 631–648. DOI: 10.1108/PR-01-2021-0062

Ilicic, J., & Webster, C. M. (2016). Being true to oneself: Investigating celebrity brand authenticity. *Psychology and Marketing*, *33*(6), 410–420. DOI: 10.1002/mar.20887

Ilies, R., Morgeson, F. P., & Nahrgang, J. D. (2005). Authentic leadership and eudaemonic well-being: Understanding leader–follower outcomes. *The Leadership Quarterly*, *16*(3), 373–394. DOI: 10.1016/j.leaqua.2005.03.002

Independant.io. **(2024).** 25 statistiques & 5 tendances sur le marketing d'influence. *Independant.io*. https://independant.io/statistiques-marketing-influence/

Ingrams, A., Kaufmann, W., & Jacobs, D. (2022). In AI we trust? Citizen perceptions of AI in government decision making. *Policy and Internet*, *14*(2), 390–409. DOI: 10.1002/poi3.276

Isaac, H. (2020). 'Stratégie et intelligence artificielle'. Enjeux numériques, 12. Paris- Dauphine University Press.

Jabbour, A. B., Laguir, I., Stekelorum, R., & Gupta, S. (2025). The nexus of artificial intelligence and sustainability performance: Unveiling the impact of supply chain transparency and customer pressure on ethical conduct. *Journal of Environmental Management*, *379*(March), 124847. DOI: 10.1016/j.jenvman.2025.124847 PMID: 40054355

Jaldi, S. (2022). L' intelligence artificielle au Maroc : entre encadrement réglementaire et stratégie économique. Policy Brief, N°59/22.

Jamal, A., Aissaoui, K., & Kassal, S. (2024). Enhancing Recruitment Transparency and Efficiency with Explainable AI (XAI). In 2024 3rd International Conference on Embedded Systems and Artificial Intelligence (ESAI) (pp. 1-6). IEEE.

James, G., Witten, D., Hastie, T., & Tibshirani, R. (2013). *An introduction to statistical learning: With applications in R* (Vol. 103). Springer., DOI: 10.1007/978-1-4614-7138-7

Jarrahi, M. H. (2018). Artificial intelligence and the future of work: Human-AI symbiosis in organizationnal decision making. *Business Horizons*, *61*(4), 577–586. DOI: 10.1016/j.bushor.2018.03.007

Javed, A., Hussain, S., & Ali, M. (2022). Machine learning in automotive pricing: A case study from South Asia. *Applied Artificial Intelligence*, *36*(1), 1–17.

Jetha, A., Shamaee, A., Bonaccio, S., Gignac, M. A., Tucker, L. B., Tompa, E., Bültmann, U., Norman, C. D., Banks, C. G., & Smith, P. M. (2021). Fragmentation in the future of work: A horizon scan examining the impact of the changing nature of work on workers experiencing vulnerability. *American Journal of Industrial Medicine*, *64*(8), 649–666. DOI: 10.1002/ajim.23262 PMID: 34125433

Jhawar, A., Kumar, P., & Varshney, S. (2023). The emergence of virtual influencers: A shift in the influencer marketing paradigm. *Young Consumers*, *24*(4), 468–484. DOI: 10.1108/YC-05-2022-1529

Johnson, J. V., & Hall, E. M. (1988). Job strain, work place social support, and cardiovascular disease: A cross-sectional study of a random sample of the Swedish working population. *American Journal of Public Health*, *78*(10), 1336–1342. DOI: 10.2105/AJPH.78.10.1336 PMID: 3421392

Jordan, M. I., & Mitchell, T. M. (2015). Machine learning: Trends, perspectives, and prospects. *Science*, *349*(6245), 255–260. DOI: 10.1126/science.aaa8415 PMID: 26185243

Jorzik, P., Antonio, J. L., Kanbach, D. K., Kallmuenzer, A., & Kraus, S. (2024). Sowing the seeds for sustainability: A business model innovation perspective on artificial intelligence in green technology startups. *Technological Forecasting and Social Change*, *208*(August), 123653. DOI: 10.1016/j.techfore.2024.123653

Juchnowicz, M., & Kinowska, H. (2021). Employee well-being and digital work during the COVID-19 pandemic. *Information (Basel)*, *12*(8), 293. DOI: 10.3390/info12080293

Juliani, F., & Maciel, C. D. (2024). Bayesian networks supporting management practices: A multifaceted perspective based on the literature. *International Journal of Information Management Data Insights*, *4*(1), 100231. DOI: 10.1016/j.jjimei.2024.100231

Jun, S., & Yi, J. (2020). What makes followers loyal? The role of influencer interactivity in building influencer brand equity. *Journal of Product and Brand Management*, *29*(6), 803–814. DOI: 10.1108/JPBM-02-2019-2280

Kaaria, A. (2024). Artificial Intelligence and Employee Well-Being: Balancing Technological Progressions with Human-Centric Workplace Strategies, a Research Agenda. *East African Journal of Information Technology*, *7*(1), 355–365. DOI: 10.37284/eajit.7.1.2281

Kaiser, M. S., Mahmud, M., Noor, M. B. T., Zenia, N. Z., Al Mamun, S., Mahmud, K. A., & Hussain, A. (2021). iWorkSafe: Towards healthy workplaces during COVID-19 with an intelligent pHealth App for industrial settings. *IEEE Access : Practical Innovations, Open Solutions*, *9*, 13814–13828. DOI: 10.1109/ACCESS.2021.3050193

Kamoun, A., Boujelbane, R., & Boujelben, S. (2024). A prediction model to detect non-compliant taxpayers using a supervised machine learning approach: Evidence from Tunisia. *Journal of Business Analytics*, *8*(2), 116–133. DOI: 10.1080/2573234X.2024.2438195

Kane, G. C., Young, A. G., Majchrzak, A., & Ransbotham, S. (2021). Avoiding an oppressive future of machine learning: A design theory for emancipatory assistants. *Management Information Systems Quarterly*, *45*(1), 371–396. DOI: 10.25300/MISQ/2021/1578

Kang, W., & Shao, B. (2023). The impact of voice assistants' intelligent attributes on consumer well-being: Findings from PLS-SEM and fsQCA. *Journal of Retailing and Consumer Services, 70*(May 2022), 103130. https://doi.org/DOI: 10.1016/j.jretconser.2022.103130

Kaplan, A., & Haenlein, M. (2019). Siri, Siri, in my hand: Who's the fairest in the land? On the interpretations, illustrations, and implications of artificial intelligence. *Business Horizons*, *62*(1), 15–25. DOI: 10.1016/j.bushor.2018.08.004

Kawaguchi, T., Tsutsumi, T., Nakano, D., & Torimura, T. (2022). MAFLD: Renovation of clinical practice and disease awareness of fatty liver. *Hepatology Research*, *52*(5), 422–432. DOI: 10.1111/hepr.13706 PMID: 34472683

Kekez, I., Lauwaert, L., &Ređep, N. B. (2025). Is artificial intelligence (AI) research biased and conceptually vague? A systematic review of research on bias and discrimination in the context of using AI in human resource management. *Technology in Society*, *81*, 102818. DOI: 10.1016/j.techsoc.2025.102818

Kellogg, K. C., Valentine, M., & Christin, A. (2020). Algorithms at work: the new contested terrain of control academy of management annals algorithms at work: the new contested terrain of control. *The Academy of Management Annals*, *14*(1), 366–410. DOI: 10.5465/annals.2018.0174

Kernis, M. H., & Goldman, B. M. (2006). Une conceptualisation multidimensionnelle de l'authenticité: Théorie et recherche. *Advances in Experimental Social Psychology*, *38*, 283–357. DOI: 10.1016/S0065-2601(06)38006-9

Keyes, C. L. M. (2006). The subjective well-being of America's youth: Toward a comprehensive assessment. *Adolescent & Family Health*, *4*(1), 3–11.

Keyes, C. L. M., & Lopez, S. J. (2002). Toward a science of mental health: Positive directions in diagnosis and interventions. In Snyder, C. R., & Lopez, S. J. (Eds.), *Handbook of positive psychology* (pp. 45–59). Oxford University Press.

Khaw, D., & Kern, M. (2014). A cross-cultural comparison of the PERMA model of well-being. *Undergraduate Journal of Psychology at Berkeley, University of California*, *8*(1), 10–23.

Ki, C. W. C., & Kim, Y. K. (2019). Le mécanisme par lequel les influenceurs des médias sociaux persuadent les consommateurs: Le rôle du désir des consommateurs d'imiter. *Psychology and Marketing*, *36*(10), 905–922. DOI: 10.1002/mar.21244

Kieslich, K., Keller, B., & Starke, C. (2022). Artificial intelligence ethics by design. Evaluating public perception on the importance of ethical design principles of artificial intelligence. *Big Data & Society*, *9*(1), 20539517221092956. Advance online publication. DOI: 10.1177/20539517221092956

Kietzmann, J., Paschen, J., & Treen, E. (2018). Artificial intelligence in advertising: How marketers can leverage artificial intelligence along the consumer journey. 'Journal of Advertising Research, 58'(3), 263-267.

Kim, J. J.,Phua, J. et Jin, S. V. (2017). Utilisations et gratifications des sites de réseautage social pour rapprocher et lier le capital social: une comparaison de Facebook, Twitter, Instagram et Snapchat. *Les ordinateurs dans le comportement humain, 72*, 115-122.

Kim, M., & Baek, T. H. (2023). Are virtual influencers friends or foes? Uncovering the perceived creepiness and authenticity of virtual influencers in social media marketing in the United States. *International Journal of Human-Computer Interaction*, •••, 1–14. DOI: 10.1080/10447318.2023.2175575

Kirby, J., & Davenport, T. (2016). The knowledge jobs most likely to be automated. *Harvard Business Review*, 1–2.

Kirchler, E., Hoelzl, E., & Wahl, I. (2008). Enforced versus voluntary tax compliance: The "slippery slope" framework. *Journal of Economic Psychology*, *29*(2), 210–225. DOI: 10.1016/j.joep.2007.05.004

Kismawadi, E. R., Aditchere, J., & Libeesh, P. C. (2024). Integration of Artificial Intelligence Technology in Islamic Financial Risk Management for Sustainable Development. In *Applications of Block Chain technology and Artificial Intelligence: Lead-ins in Banking, Finance, and Capital Market* (pp. 53–71). Springer International Publishing. DOI: 10.1007/978-3-031-47324-1_4

Kleanthous, C., & Chatzis, S. (2019). Gated Mixture Variational Autoencoders for Value Added Tax audit case selection. *Knowledge-Based Systems, 188*, 105048. DOI: 10.1016/j.knosys.2019.105048

Kleven, H. J., Knudsen, M. B., Kreiner, C. T., Pedersen, S., & Saez, E. (2011). Unwilling or Unable to Cheat? Evidence From a Tax Audit Experiment in Denmark. *Econometrica, 79*(3), 651–692. DOI: 10.3982/ECTA9113

Koivula, K., Shamsuzzoha, A., & Shamsuzzaman, M. (2024). Application of artificial intelligence as a knowledge creation instrument in tax procedures. *Engineering Applications of Artificial Intelligence, 133*, 108417. DOI: 10.1016/j.engappai.2024.108417

Korzynski, P., Mazurek, G., Krzypkowska, P., & Kurasinski, A. (2023). Artificial intelligence prompt engineering as a new digital competence: Analysis of generative AI technologies such as ChatGPT. *Entrepreneurial Business and Economics Review, 11*(3), 25–37. DOI: 10.15678/EBER.2023.110302

Kotler, P., & Armstrong, G. (2017). *Principles of marketing* (17th ed.). Pearson Education.

Koubaa, A. (2023). GPT-4 vs. GPT-3.5: A concise showdown. *Preprints. org*, 2023030422.

Kowalczyk, C. M., & Pounders, K. R. (2016). Transforming celebrities through social media: The role of authenticity and emotional attachment. *Journal of Product and Brand Management, 25*(4), 345–356. DOI: 10.1108/JPBM-09-2015-0969

Kraut, R. E., & Johnston, R. E. (1979). Social and emotional messages of smiling: An ethological approach. *Journal of Personality and Social Psychology, 37*(9), 1539–1553. DOI: 10.1037/0022-3514.37.9.1539

Kshetri, N., & Hughes, L. (2023). "So what if ChatGPT wrote it?" Multidisciplinary perspectives on opportunities, challenges and implications of generative conversational AI for research, practice and policy. *International Journal of Information Management, 71*, 102642. DOI: 10.1016/j.ijinfomgt.2023.102642

Kumar, S., & Ashok, V. (2020). A comparative study on machine learning models for price prediction. *International Journal of Artificial Intelligence & Applications, 11*(2), 45–53. DOI: 10.5121/ijaia.2020.11204

Kuźniacki, B., Almada, M., Tyliński, K., Górski, L., Winogradska, B., & Zeldenrust, R. (2022). Towards eXplainable artificial intelligence (XAI) in tax law: The need for a minimum legal standard. *World Tax Journal, 14*(4). Advance online publication. DOI: 10.59403/2yhh9pa

Lafuente, E., Vaillant, Y., Vendrell-Herrero, F., & Gomes, E. (2019). Bouncing Back from Failure: Entrepreneurial Resilience and the Internationalisation of Subsequent Ventures Created by Serial Entrepreneurs. *Applied Psychology, 68*(4), 658–694. DOI: 10.1111/apps.12175

Lahrache, , RBekkaoui, , A. (2024). The impact of artificial intelligence on decision-making. *Revue Internationale des Sciences de Gestion, 7*(3).

Larkin, C., Drummond Otten, C., & Árvai, J. (2022). Paging Dr. JARVIS! Will people accept advice from artificial intelligence for consequential risk management decisions? *Journal of Risk Research, 25*(4), 407–422. DOI: 10.1080/13669877.2021.1958047

Larson, D. B., Doo, F. X., Allen, B.Jr, Mongan, J., Flanders, A. E., & Wald, C. (2024). Proceedings from the 2022 ACR-RSNA workshop on safety, effectiveness, reliability, and transparency in AI. *Journal of the American College of Radiology, 21*(7), 1119–1129. DOI: 10.1016/j.jacr.2024.01.024 PMID: 38354844

Le Tran, V., & Leirvik, T. (2019). A simple but powerful measure of market efficiency. *Finance Research Letters, 29*, 141–151. DOI: 10.1016/j.frl.2019.03.004

Le Tran, V., & Leirvik, T. (2020). Efficiency in the markets of crypto-currencies. *Finance Research Letters, 35*, 101382. DOI: 10.1016/j.frl.2019.101382

LeCun, Y., Bengio, Y., & Hinton, G. (2015). Deep learning. *Nature, 521*(7553), 436–444. DOI: 10.1038/nature14539 PMID: 26017442

Lee, I., Zhang, H., Moore, K., Zhou, X., Perret, B., Cheng, Y., Zheng, R., & Pu, G. (2022). AI Book Club: An Innovative Professional Development Model for AI Education. *SIGCSE 2022 - Proceedings of the 53rd ACM Technical Symposium on Computer Science Education, 1*, 202–208. https://doi.org/DOI: 10.1145/3478431.3499318

Lee, K., & Lee, S. (2013). Patterns of technological innovation and evolution in the energy sector: A patent-based approach. *Energy Policy, 59*, 415–432. DOI: 10.1016/j.enpol.2013.03.054

Lemon, K. N., & Verhoef, P. C. (2016). Understanding customer experience throughout the customer journey. 'Journal of Marketing, 80' (6), 69-96. DOI: 10.1509/jm.15.0420

Leonard, T. (2024). Understanding and predicting customer preferences in retail using AI: A literature review. 'International Journal of Economic Studies and Management, 4' (1), 45-62. https://doi.org/DOI: 10.1111/ijesm.2024.4.issue-1

Leray, P. (2006) 'Réseaux bayésiens: apprentissage et diagnostic de systèmes complexes. Modélisation et simulation', *Université de Rouen*. FFTEL-00485862.

Liang, T., Wang, F., Wang, S., Li, K., Ma, X., & Mo, X. (2024). Towards unified aleatory and epistemic uncertainty quantification for machinery health prognostic through sequential heteroscedastic Gaussian process regression. Advanced Engineering Informatics Volume 62. *Advanced Engineering Informatics*, *102719*, 102719. Advance online publication. DOI: 10.1016/j.aei.2024.102719

Li, B., Sun, Q., & Wei, Z. (2024). Implicit barriers, market integration and asset prices: Evidence from the inclusion of china a-shares in msci global indices. *Journal of International Financial Markets, Institutions and Money*, *93*, 101998. DOI: 10.1016/j.intfin.2024.101998

Lien, N.-H. (2001). Elaboration likelihood model in consumer research: A review. *Actes du National Science Council, Part C: Humanities and Social Sciences*, *11*(4), 301–310.

Lim, X.-J., Radzol, A., Cheah, J.-H., & Wong, M. (2017). The impact of Social Media Influencers on Purchase Intention and the Mediation Effect of Customer Attitude. *Asian Journal of Business Research*, *7*(2), 19–36. DOI: 10.14707/ajbr.170035

Lin, C. Y., & Marques, J. A. L. (2024). Stock market prediction using artificial intelligence: A systematic review of systematic reviews. *Social Sciences & Humanities Open*, *9*, 100864. DOI: 10.1016/j.ssaho.2024.100864

Lin, S. (2023). Based on the Two-factor Theory, The Influence of Artificial Intelligence on Employee Motivation Is Analyzed. *Frontiers in Business, Economics and Management*, *11*(3), 91–94. DOI: 10.54097/fbem.v11i3.13194

Lin, W., Zhang, H., & Xu, J. (2021). Predictive pricing of second-hand vehicles using XGBoost in emerging markets. *Journal of Intelligent Systems*, *30*(2), 205–220.

Li, X., Zhang, M., Liu, W., & Wang, Z. (2024). The impact of entrepreneurial co-founders' support on founders' entrepreneurial resilience in the high-tech industry: The roles of perceived digital technology and perceived failure-tolerant climate. *Technological Forecasting and Social Change*, *202*(March), 123320. DOI: 10.1016/j.techfore.2024.123320

Li, Z., & Montomoli, M. (2024). Aleatory uncertainty quantification based on multi-fidelity deep neural networks. *Reliability Engineering & System Safety*, *245*, 109975. DOI: 10.1016/j.ress.2024.109975

Lo, A. (2017). *Adaptive markets: Financial evolution at the speed of thought*. Princeton University Press.

Lo, A. W. (2004). The adaptive markets hypothesis: Market efficiency from an evolutionary perspective. *Journal of Portfolio Management*, *30*(5), 15–29. DOI: 10.3905/jpm.2004.442611

Lo, A. W. (2005). Reconciling efficient markets with behavioral finance: The adaptive markets hypothesis. *The Journal of Investment Consulting*, *7*(2), 21–44.

Longo, F., Mirabelli, G., Padovano, A., & Solina, V. (2023). The Digital Supply Chain Twin paradigm for enhancing resilience and sustainability against COVID-like crises. *Procedia Computer Science*, *217*, 1940–1947. DOI: 10.1016/j.procs.2022.12.394 PMID: 36687282

Lopez-Lira, A., & Tang, Y. (2023). Can chatgpt forecast stock price movements? return predictability and large language models. arXiv preprint arXiv:2304.07619.

Lou, C., Kiew, S. T. J., Chen, T., Lee, T. Y. M., Ong, J. E. C., & Phua, Z. (2023). Authentically fake? How consumers respond to the influence of virtual influencers. *Journal of Advertising*, *52*(4), 540–557. DOI: 10.1080/00913367.2022.2149641

Lou, C., & Yuan, S. (2019). Influencer marketing: How message value and credibility affect consumer trust of branded content on social media. *Journal of Interactive Advertising*, *19*(1), 58–73. DOI: 10.1080/15252019.2018.1533501

Lukianykhina, O., Suprunenko, S., Slavkova, A., Skorba, O., & Zavrazhnyi, K. (2024). Digital Innovations in the Fiscal Policy of Ukraine: Promoting Sustainable Economic Development. *International Journal of Economics and Financial Issues*, *14*(4), 77–86. DOI: 10.32479/ijefi.16202

Lund, B. D., Wang, T., Mannuru, N. R., Nie, B., Shimray, S., & Wang, Z. (2023). ChatGPT and a new academic reality: Artificial Intelligence-written research papers and the ethics of the large language models in scholarly publishing. *Journal of the Association for Information Science and Technology*, *74*(5), 570–581. DOI: 10.1002/asi.24750

Lundberg, S. M., & Lee, S. I. (2017). A unified approach to interpreting model predictions. *Advances in Neural Information Processing Systems*, *30*, 4765–4774. DOI: 10.48550/arXiv.1705.07874

Luthans, F., & Avolio, B. J. (2003). Authentic leadership development. *Positive organizational scholarship, 241*(258), 1-26.

Lu, Y. (2019). Artificial intelligence : A survey on evolution, models, applications and future trends. *Journal of Management Analytics, 6*(1), 1–29. DOI: 10.1080/23270012.2019.1570365

Ma, F., Lyu, Z., & Li, H. (2024). Can ChatGPT predict Chinese equity premiums? *Finance Research Letters, 65*, 105631. DOI: 10.1016/j.frl.2024.105631

Maghraoui, O., & Belghith, A. (2019). Ethical challenges of AI-driven personalization in digital marketing. 'Journal of Business Ethics, 156' (4), 747-763. DOI: 10.1007/s10551-019-04193-w

Malashin, I. P., Masich, I. S., Tynchenko, V. S., Gantimurov, A. P., Nelyub, V. A., & Borodulin, A. S. (2024a). Confidence-Aware Rejection Class Minimization in Indirect Tax Audit Classification. *IEEE Access : Practical Innovations, Open Solutions*, •••, 1–1. DOI: 10.1109/ACCESS.2024.3519333

Malashin, I. P., Masich, I. S., Tynchenko, V. S., Gantimurov, A. P., Nelyub, V. A., Borodulin, A. S., Tokarev, S. I., & Vasilev, D. I. (2024b). Anomaly Detection in Restaurant Receipts Data. *IEEE Access : Practical Innovations, Open Solutions, 12*, 145590–145607. DOI: 10.1109/ACCESS.2024.3471081

Malik, A., De Silva, M. T. T., Budhwar, P., & Srikanth, N. R. (2021). Elevating talents' experience through innovative artificial intelligence-mediated knowledge sharing: Evidence from an IT-multinational enterprise. *Journal of International Management, 27*(4), 100871. DOI: 10.1016/j.intman.2021.100871

Manickam, P., Mariappan, S. A., Murugesan, S. M., Hansda, S., Kaushik, A., Shinde, R., & Thipperudraswamy, S. P. (2022). Artificial intelligence (AI) and internet of medical things (IoMT) assisted biomedical systems for intelligent healthcare. *Biosensors (Basel), 12*(8), 562. DOI: 10.3390/bios12080562 PMID: 35892459

Manning C. (2020), *Artificial Intelligence Definitions*, Stanford University, Human-Centered Artificial Intelligence – HAI.

Mansouri, S. (2018). The personalization-privacy paradox in AI marketing. 'Marketing Science, 37' (5), 733-751. DOI: 10.1287/mksc.2018.1115

Mao, W., Chen, J., Liang, X., & Zhang, X. (2019). A new online detection approach for rolling bearing incipient fault via self-adaptive deep feature matching. *IEEE Transactions on Instrumentation and Measurement, 69*(2), 443–456. DOI: 10.1109/TIM.2019.2903699

Marabelli, M., Newell, S., & Handunge, V. (2021). The lifecycle of algorithmic decision-making systems: Organizational choices and ethical challenges. *The Journal of Strategic Information Systems*, *30*(3), 101683. Advance online publication. DOI: 10.1016/j.jsis.2021.101683

Marcus, E., & Teuwen, J. (2024). Artificial intelligence and explanation: How, why, and when to explain black boxes. *European Journal of Radiology*, *173*, 111393. DOI: 10.1016/j.ejrad.2024.111393 PMID: 38417186

Martín López, J. (2022). INTELIGENCIA ARTIFICIAL, SESGOS Y NO DISCRIMINACIÓN EN EL ÁMBITO DE LA INSPECCIÓN TRIBUTARIA. *Revista Crónica Tributaria*, *182*(1), 51–89. DOI: 10.47092/CT.22.1.2

Martin, K. (2018). Ethical implications and accountability of algorithms. 'Journal of Business Ethics, 160'(4), 835-850.

Martinez, L. F., & Ferreira, A. I. (2012). Sick at work: Presenteeism among nurses in a Portuguese public hospital. *Stress and Health*, *28*(4), 297–304. DOI: 10.1002/smi.1432 PMID: 22282226

Marwala, T. (2014). *Artificial intelligence techniques for rational decision making*. Springer. DOI: 10.1007/978-3-319-11424-8

Marwala, T. (Ed.). (2009). *Computational intelligence for missing data imputation, estimation, and management: Knowledge optimization techniques: Knowledge optimization techniques*. IGI Global.

Marwala, T., & Hurwitz, E. (2017). *Artificial intelligence and economic theory: Skynet in the market* (Vol. 1). Springer International Publishing.

Marwick, A. E. (2015). Instafame: selfies de luxe dans l'économie de l'attention. *Culture publique, 27*(1 (75)), 137-160.

Matamoros-Echeverria, K. L., Sanchez-Leon, E. R., & Toledo-Orozco, M. (2025). The Impact of Artificial Intelligence on the Digital Economy: A Review of Economic, Social and Technological Dimensions. *Journal of Posthumanism*, *3*(1), 23–38. DOI: 10.33182/joph.v3i1.3368

Mauro, M., Noto, G., Prenestini, A., & Sarto, F. (2024). Digital transformation in healthcare: Assessing the role of digital technologies for managerial support processes. *Technological Forecasting and Social Change*, *209*, 123781. Advance online publication. DOI: 10.1016/j.techfore.2024.123781

McCarthy, J., Minsky, M. L., Rochester, N., & Shannon, C. E. (2006). A proposal for the dartmouth summer research project on artificial intelligence, august 31, 1955. *AI Magazine*, *27*(4), 12–12.

McIntyre, K. M., Cooper, M., & Baylis, M. (2023). Capacity for One Health research in the Horn of Africa. *One Health*, *16*, 100549. DOI: 10.1016/j.onehlt.2023.100549 PMID: 37363254

Mckinsey, & Company. (2018). Notes From the Ai Frontier: Modeling the Impact of Ai on the World Economy. Modeling the Global Economic Impact of AI | McKinsey, September, 1–61. https://www.mckinsey.com/featured-insights/artificial-intelligence/notes-from-the-ai-frontier-modeling-the-impact-of-ai-on-the-world-economy

Mdarbi, S., & Belkebir, Z. (2024). La contribution de la littératie financière et de la résilience entrepreneuriale dans la survie des entreprises: Élaboration d'un cadre conceptuel. [REMAC]. *Revue de Management et Cultures*, *12*, 122–137.

Mehdiyev, N., Majlatow, M., & Fettke, P. (2025). Integrating permutation feature importance with conformal prediction for robust Explainable Artificial Intelligence in predictive process monitoring. *Engineering Applications of Artificial Intelligence*, *149*, 110363. DOI: 10.1016/j.engappai.2025.110363

Merkel, D. (2014). Docker: Lightweight Linux containers for consistent development and deployment. *Linux Journal*, *2014*(239), 2.

Mignenan, V. (2021). Collective Intelligence and Entrepreneurial Resilience in the Context of Covid-19. *International Business Research*, *14*(9), 1. DOI: 10.5539/ibr.v14n9p1

Miles, M., & Huberman, (2003). Analyse des données qualitatives. Bruxelles: De Boeck Université.

Milojević, N., & Redzepagic, S. (2021). Prospects of artificial intelligence and machine learning application in banking risk management. *Journal of Central Banking Theory and Practice*, *10*(3), 41–57. DOI: 10.2478/jcbtp-2021-0023

Mir, J., & Barka, H. (2024). L ' entrepreneuriat digital au Maroc : Zoom sur les startups digitales de la région de l ' Oriental. *International Journal of Accounting, Finance, Auditing. Management and Economics*, *5*(1), 51–67. DOI: 10.5281/zenodo.10547363

Misra, P., & Chaurasia, S. (2020). Data-driven trend forecasting in stock market using machine learning techniques. [JITR]. *Journal of Information Technology Research*, *13*(1), 130–149. DOI: 10.4018/JITR.2020010109

Misra, S. K., Sharma, S. K., Gupta, S., & Das, S. (2023). A framework to overcome challenges to the adoption of artificial intelligence in Indian Government Organizations. *Technological Forecasting and Social Change, 194*, 122721. DOI: 10.1016/j.techfore.2023.122721

Mitchell, R. (2015). *Web scraping with Python: Collecting more data from the modern web*. O'Reilly Media.

Mittelstadt, B. D., Allo, P., Taddeo, M., Wachter, S., & Floridi, L. (2016). The ethics of algorithms: Mapping the debate. *Big Data & Society, 3*(2), 1–21. DOI: 10.1177/2053951716679679

Mocanu, C., Matei, M. M. M., & Năstasă, A. (2024). Patterns of Artificial Intelligence Adoption in Small and Medium Businesses. In Fotea, S. L., Văduva, S. A., & Fotea, I. Ş. (Eds.), *Reimagining Capitalism in a Post-Globalization World. GSMAC 2023. Springer Proceedings in Business and Economics*. Springer., DOI: 10.1007/978-3-031-59858-6_26

Mohammad, W., Elomri, A., & Kerbache, L. (2022). The Global Semiconductor Chip Shortage: Causes, Implications, and Potential Remedies. *IFAC-PapersOnLine, 55*(10), 476–483. DOI: 10.1016/j.ifacol.2022.09.439

Mohanty, D. K., Parida, A. K., & Khuntia, S. S. (2021). Financial market prediction under deep learning framework using auto encoder and kernel extreme learning machine. *Applied Soft Computing, 99*, 106898. DOI: 10.1016/j.asoc.2020.106898

Mokni, K., El Montasser, G., Ajmi, A. N., & Bouri, E. (2024). On the efficiency and its drivers in the cryptocurrency market: The case of Bitcoin and Ethereum. *Financial Innovation, 10*(1), 39. DOI: 10.1186/s40854-023-00566-3

Moore, T. (2017). On the harms arising from the Equifax data breach of 2017. *International Journal of Critical Infrastructure Protection, 19*, 47–48. DOI: 10.1016/j.ijcip.2017.10.004

Morgan, T. R., Roath, A. S., & Richey, R. G. (2023). How risk, transparency, and knowledge influence the adaptability and flexibility dimensions of the responsiveness view. *Journal of Business Research, 158*, 113641. DOI: 10.1016/j.jbusres.2022.113641

Morocco World News. (2023, August). Automotive industry exports in Morocco soar to $11 billion in 2022. *Morocco World News*. https://www.moroccoworldnews.com/2023/08/357041/automotive-industry-exports-in-morocco-soar-to-11-billion-in-2022

Mosteanu, N. R. (2020). Digital Systems and New Challenges of Financial Management – FinTech, XBRL, Blockchain and Cryptocurrencies. *Quality - Access to Success, 21*(174).

Mouatif, M., & El Agy, M. (2023). Entrepreneur's resilience process and entrepreneurial rebound : A preliminary exploration of the Moroccan context. Innovative Space of Scientific Research Journals ISSN 2351-8014 69(2), 331–339.

Moura, E. O. D., & Bispo, M. D. S. (2020). Sociomateriality: Theories, methodology, and practice. Canadian Journal of Administrative Sciences/Revue Canadienne des Sciences de l'Administration, 37(3), 350-365.

Mourad, K., & Salahddine, A. (2023). The acceptance of SAP by the employees of the Regional Agricultural Valuation Office of Souss Massa: TAM2. *American Scientific Journal, 3*(16), 544–544.

Moustaid, E., & Moflih, Y. (2024). L'impact de l'introduction de l'intelligence artificielle sur le marché du travail. *Revue Française d'Economie et de Gestion, 5*(7), 249–271.

Mouti, S., Shukla, S. K., Althubiti, S. A., Ahmed, M. A., Alenezi, F., & Arumugam, M. (2022). Cyber security risk management with attack detection frameworks using multi-connect variational auto-encoder with probabilistic Bayesian networks. *Computers & Electrical Engineering, 103*, 108308. DOI: 10.1016/j.compeleceng.2022.108308

Munjeyi, E., & Schutte, D. (2024). Examining the critical success factors influencing the diffusion of AI in tax administration in Botswana. *Cogent Social Sciences, 10*(1), 2419537. DOI: 10.1080/23311886.2024.2419537

Munn, Z., Peters, M. D. J., Stern, C., Tufanaru, C., McArthur, A., & Aromataris, E. (2018). Systematic review or scoping review ? Guidance for authors when choosing between a systematic or scoping review approach. 'BMC Medical Research Methodology, 18' (1), 143. DOI: 10.1186/s12874-018-0611-x

Munnukka, J., Maity, D., Reinikainen, H., & Luoma-aho, V. (2019). "Thanks for watching". The effectiveness of YouTube vlog endorsements. *Computers in Human Behavior, 93*, 226–234. DOI: 10.1016/j.chb.2018.12.014

Munzert, S., Rubba, C., Meißner, P., & Nyhuis, D. (2015). *Automated data collection with R: A practical guide to web scraping and text mining*. Wiley.

Murorunkwere, B. F., Haughton, D., Nzabanita, J., Kipkogei, F., & Kabano, I. (2023). Predicting tax fraud using supervised machine learning approach. *African Journal of Science, Technology, Innovation and Development, 15*(6), 731–742. DOI: 10.1080/20421338.2023.2187930

Murorunkwere, B. F., Tuyishimire, O., Haughton, D., & Nzabanita, J. (2022). Fraud Detection Using Neural Networks: A Case Study of Income Tax. *Future Internet, 14*(6), 168. DOI: 10.3390/fi14060168

Mustafayev, M. (2024). The impact of artificial intelligence on the motivation of bank employees in Azerbaijan. In Lecture Notes in Networks and Systems. International Conference on Smart Environment and Green Technologies, 1252. Springer. DOI: 10.1007/978-3-031-81564-5_45

Nallakaruppan, K., Balusamy, B., Lawanya Shri, M., Malathi, V., & Bhattacharyya, S. (2024). An Explainable AI framework for credit evaluation and analysis. *Applied Soft Computing, 153*, 111307. DOI: 10.1016/j.asoc.2024.111307

Nawaz, N., Arunachalam, H., Pathi, B. K., & Gajenderan, V. (2024). The adoption of artificial intelligence in human resources management practices. *International Journal of Information Management Data Insights, 4*(1), 100208. Advance online publication. DOI: 10.1016/j.jjimei.2023.100208

Nazareno, L., & Schiff, D. S. (2021). The impact of automation and artificial intelligence on worker well-being. *Technology in Society, 67*, 101679. DOI: 10.1016/j.techsoc.2021.101679

Nelson, R. R., & Winter, S. G. (1982). An Evolutionary Theory of Economic Change (Cambridge, Massachusetts and London, Belknap Press of Harvard University Press). Vol.

Newell, S., & Marabelli, M. (2015). Strategic opportunities (and challenges) of algorithmic decision-making: A call for action on the long-term societal effects of 'datification. *The Journal of Strategic Information Systems, 24*(1), 3 14. DOI: 10.1016/j.jsis.2015.02.001

Ngah, R., & Salleh, Z. (2015). Emotional Intelligence and Entrepreneurs' innovativeness towards Entrepreneurial Success: A Preliminary Study. *American Journal of Economics, 2015*(2), 285–290. DOI: 10.5923/c.economics.201501.37

Nguyen, M., Malik, A., Sharma, P., Kingshott, R., & Gugnani, R. (2024). High involvement work system and organizational and employee resilience: Impact of digitalisation in crisis situations. *Technological Forecasting and Social Change, 205*(June), 123510. DOI: 10.1016/j.techfore.2024.123510

Nikiforidis, K., Kyrtsoglou, A., Vafeiadis, T., Kotsiopoulos, T., Nizamis, A., Ioannidis, D., & Sarigiannidis, P. (2024). Enhancing transparency and trust in AI-powered manufacturing: A survey of explainable AI (XAI) applications in smart manufacturing in the era of industry 4.0/5.0. *ICT Express*. Advance online publication. DOI: 10.1016/j.icte.2024.12.001

Nissenbaum, H. (2010). *Privacy in context: Technology, policy, and the integrity of social life*. Stanford University Press.

Niu, S., Yin, Q., Ma, J., Song, Y., Xu, Y., Bai, L., Pan, W., & Yang, X. (2024). Enhancing healthcare decision support through explainable AI models for risk prediction. *Decision Support Systems*, *181*, 114228. DOI: 10.1016/j.dss.2024.114228

Noble, S. U. (2018). *Algorithms of oppression: How search engines reinforce racism*. NYU Press.

O'Neil, C. (2016). *Weapons of math destruction: How big data increases inequality and threatens democracy*. Crown Publish.

OCDE. BCG & ING. (2024). The Adoption of Artificial Intelligence in Firms : New Evidence for policymaking. In OECD publishing. https://doi.org/https://doi.org/10.1787/f9ef33c3

OECD. (2017). *Tax Administration 2017: Comparative Information on OECD and Other Advanced and Emerging Economies*. OECD., DOI: 10.1787/tax_admin-2017-

OECD. (2021). *Tax Administration 2021: Comparative Information on OECD and other Advanced and Emerging Economies*. OECD., DOI: 10.1787/cef472b9-

Okoroafor, U. C., & Leirvik, T. (2022). Time varying market efficiency in the Brent and WTI crude market. *Finance Research Letters*, *45*, 102191. DOI: 10.1016/j.frl.2021.102191

Oladipo, E. K., Adeyemo, S. F., Oluwasanya, G. J., Oyinloye, O. R., Oyeyiola, O. H., Akinrinmade, I. D., Elutade, O. A., Areo, D. O., Hamzat, I. O., Olakanmi, O. D., Ayanronbi, I. I., Akanmu, A. J., Ajekiigbe, F. O., Taiwo, M. O., Ogunfidodo, V. M., Adekunle, C. A., Adeleke, P. O., Olubunmi, D. A., Adeogun, P. A., & Nnaji, N. D. (2024). Impact and Challenges of Artificial Intelligence Integration in the African Health Sector: A Review. *Trends in Medical Research*, *19*(1), 220–235. Advance online publication. DOI: 10.3923/tmr.2024.220.235

Omerani, D., & Oummou, Y. A. (2023). The effect of the Russian-Ukrainian Conflict on the main frontier Markets: An Event Study Approach. International Journal of Financial Studies. *Economics and Management*, *2*(2), 42–54.

Open, A. I. (2023). GPT-4 Technical Report. https://arxiv.org/pdf/2303.08774

Open, A. I. (2023). *GPT-4 technical report.* https://openai.com/research/gpt-4

Opesemowo, O. A. G. (2025). Artificial Intelligence in Mathematics Education: The Pros and Cons. In *Encyclopedia of Information Science and Technology, Sixth Edition* (pp. 1-18). IGI Global.

Orabi, M., & Bentaleb, C. (2020). Les pratiques de bien-être au travail dans les entreprises au Maroc: Enseignements d'une étude de cas. *Moroccan Journal of Quantitative and Qualitative Research*, *2*(1), 1–14.

Ordóñez-Placencia, J., Hallo, M., & Luján-Mora, S. (2024). A data mining model to predict the debts with risk of non-payment in tax administration. *International Journal of Information and Decision Sciences*. DOI: 10.1504/IJIDS.2024.140186

Oukhouya, H., & El Himdi, K. (2023, April). Comparing machine learning methods—svr, xgboost, lstm, and mlp—for forecasting the moroccan stock market. In Computer Sciences & Mathematics Forum (Vol. 7, No. 1, p. 39). MDPI.

Ourdani, N., Aknin, N., & Chrayah, M. (2024). Towards a new approach to maximize tax collection using machine learning algorithms. *IAES International Journal of Artificial Intelligence*, *13*(1), 737. Advance online publication. DOI: 10.11591/ijai.v13.i1.pp737-746

Ouyang, L., Wu, J., Jiang, X., Almeida, D., Wainwright, C., Mishkin, P., & Lowe, R. (2022). Training language models to follow instructions with human feedback. *Advances in Neural Information Processing Systems*, *35*, 27730–27744.

Palomino Guerrero, M. (2022). Inteligencia artificial: Un mecanismo para frenar la evasión fiscal sin vulnerar los derechos del contribuyente. *Cuestiones Constitucionales*, *46*, 213–236. DOI: 10.22201/iij.24484881e.2022.46.17053

Pang, S., & Hua, G. (2024). How does digital tax administration affect R&D manipulation? Evidence from dual machine learning. *Technological Forecasting and Social Change*, *208*(123691), 123691. DOI: 10.1016/j.techfore.2024.123691

Parent-Rocheleau, X., & Parker, S. K. (2022). Algorithms as work designers: How algorithmic management influences the design of jobs. *Human Resource Management Review*, *32*(3), 100838. Advance online publication. DOI: 10.1016/j.hrmr.2021.100838

Parker, S. K., & Grote, G. (2022). Automation, algorithms, and beyond: Why work design matters more than ever in a digital world. *Applied Psychology*, *71*(4), 1171–1204. DOI: 10.1111/apps.12241

Park, K., & Yoon, H. Y. (2024). Beyond the code: The impact of AI algorithm transparency signaling on user trust and relational satisfaction. *Public Relations Review, 50*(5), 102507. DOI: 10.1016/j.pubrev.2024.102507

Passalacqua, M., Pellerin, R., Yahia, E., Magnani, F., Rosin, F., Joblot, L., & Léger, P.-M. (2024). Practice with less AI makes perfect: Partially automated AI during training leads to better worker motivation, engagement, and skill acquisition. *International Journal of Human-Computer Interaction, 1*(21). Advance online publication. DOI: 10.1080/10447318.2024.2319914

Pedregosa, F., Varoquaux, G., Gramfort, A., Michel, V., Thirion, B., Grisel, O., & Duchesnay, E. (2011). Scikit-learn: Machine learning in Python. *Journal of Machine Learning Research, 12*, 2825–2830.

Peeters, B. (2024). Editorial: European law restrictions on tax authorities' use of artificial intelligence systems: Reflections on some recent developments. *EC Tax Review, 33*(2), 54–57. DOI: 10.54648/ECTA2024006

Pereira, L., Resio, M., Costa, R., Dias, Á., & Gonçalves, R. (2021). Artificial Intelligence in Strategic Business Management: The Case of Auditing. *International Journal of Business Information Systems, 1*(1), 10039269. Advance online publication. DOI: 10.1504/IJBIS.2021.10039269

Pereira, V., Hadjielias, E., Christofi, M., & Vrontis, D. (2023). A systematic literature review on the impact of artificial intelligence on workplace outcomes: A multi-process perspective. *Human Resource Management Review, 33*(1), 100857. DOI: 10.1016/j.hrmr.2021.100857

Pérez López, C., Delgado Rodríguez, M. J., & De Lucas Santos, S. (2019). Tax Fraud Detection through Neural Networks: An Application Using a Sample of Personal Income Taxpayers. *Future Internet, 11*(4), 86. DOI: 10.3390/fi11040086

Petty, R. E., Cacioppo, J. T., Petty, R. E., & Cacioppo, J. T. (1986). *The elaboration likelihood model of persuasion*. Springer New York.

Pinck, A. S., & Sonnentag, S. (2018). Leader mindfulness and employee well-being: The mediating role of transformational leadership. *Mindfulness, 9*(3), 884–896. DOI: 10.1007/s12671-017-0828-5

Podina, I. R., & Caculidis-Tudor, D. (2023). Increasing Well-Being and Mental Health Through Cutting-Edge Technology and Artificial Intelligence. In *Brain, Decision Making and Mental Health* (pp. 347–364). Springer International Publishing. DOI: 10.1007/978-3-031-15959-6_17

Pöyry, E., Pelkonen, M., Naumanen, E., & Laaksonen, S. (2019). Un appel à l'authenticité: réponses du public aux endossements des influenceurs des médias sociaux dans la communication stratégique. *Revue internationale de communication stratégique, 13*, 336 - 351.

Prokhorenkova, L., Gusev, G., Vorobev, A., Dorogush, A. V., & Gulin, A. (2018). CatBoost: Unbiased boosting with categorical features. *Advances in Neural Information Processing Systems, 31*, 6638–6648. https://proceedings.neurips.cc/paper/2018/hash/14491b756b449614c919e6a0a8682cd3-Abstract.html

Proulx, S., Millette, M., & Heaton, L. (2012). *Médias sociaux: enjeux pour la communication*. Puq.

Puspita, A. F., Palil, M. R. B., Puspaningrum, A., & Suman, A. (2024). Taxing artificial intelligence: Value impacts and governance in the tax sector (study in Indonesia and Malaysia). *Pakistan Journal of Life and Social Sciences, 22*(1). Advance online publication. DOI: 10.57239/PJLSS-2024-22.1.00343

Radford, A., Wu, J., Child, R., Luan, D., Amodei, D., & Sutskever, I. (2019). Language models are unsupervised multitask learners. OpenAI blog, 1(8), 9.

Raed, H., Qawasmeh, E., Alserhan, A., Ahmad, H., Hammouri, Q., Halim, M., & Darawsheh, D. (2023). Utilizing business intelligence and digital transformation and leadership to enhance employee job satisfaction and business added value in greater Amman municipality. *International Journal of Data and Network Science, 7*(3), 1077–1084. DOI: 10.5267/j.ijdns.2023.5.016

Ragu-Nathan, T. S., Tarafdar, M., Ragu-Nathan, B. S., & Tu, Q. (2008). The consequences of technostress for end users in organizations: Conceptual development and empirical validation. *Information Systems Research, 19*(4), 417–433. DOI: 10.1287/isre.1070.0165

Rahayu, S. K. (2021). Utilization of artificial intelligence in tax audit in Indonesia. *Management and Accounting Review (MAR), 20*(3). https://ir.uitm.edu.my/id/eprint/61675/

Ramanathan, S., Tang, S. G. H., Afzal, M. M., & Ker, P. J. (2024). Artificial Intelligence and Socioeconomic Impacts of Pandemic: Key Roles and Potentials. World Journal of Science. *Technology and Sustainable Development, 19*(3–4), 205–218. DOI: 10.1108/WJSTSD-01-2023-0002

Ransbotham, S., Kiron, D., Gerbert, P., & Reeves, M. (2017). Reshaping business with artificial intelligence: Closing the gap between ambition and action. *MIT Sloan Management Review, 59*(1).

Raschka, S. (2018). *Python machine learning: Machine learning and deep learning with Python, scikit-learn, and TensorFlow 2*. Packt Publishing.

Raz, J. (1979). *The authority of law: Essays on law and morality*. Oxford University Press., DOI: 10.1093/acprof:oso/9780198253457.001.0001

Ribeiro, M. T., Singh, S., & Guestrin, C. (2016). "Why should I trust you?" Explaining the predictions of any classifier. In *Proceedings of the 22nd ACM SIGKDD International Conference on Knowledge Discovery and Data Mining* (pp. 1135–1144). ACM.

Rogers, C. R. (1961). *Sur le fait de devenir une personne: le point de vue d'un thérapeute sur la psychothérapie*. Constable.

Ruddick, J., Ceusters, G., Van Kriekinge, G., Genov, E., De Cauwer, C., Coosemans, T., & Messagie, M. (2024). Real-world validation of safe reinforcement learning, model predictive control and decision tree-based home energy management systems. *Energy and AI, 18*, 100448. DOI: 10.1016/j.egyai.2024.100448

Russell, S. J., & Norvig, P. (2016). *Artificial Intelligence: A Modern Approach*. Pearson Education Limited.

Rust, R. T. (2020). The future of marketing. 'International Journal of Research in Marketing, 37'(1), 15-26.

Ryan, R. M., & Deci, E. L. (2001). On happiness and human potentials: A review of research on hedonic and eudaimonic well-being. *Annual Review of Psychology, 52*(1), 141–166. DOI: 10.1146/annurev.psych.52.1.141 PMID: 11148302

Ryff, C. D., & Keyes, C. L. M. (1995). The structure of psychological well-being revisited. *Journal of Personality and Social Psychology, 69*(4), 719–727. DOI: 10.1037/0022-3514.69.4.719 PMID: 7473027

Saad, S. M., Ubeywarna, D., & Zhang, H. (2024). Supply network risk mitigation—Industry 4.0 approach. *Procedia Computer Science, 232*, 3206–3215. DOI: 10.1016/j.procs.2024.02.136

Saboune, K. (2022). The deterioration of well-being at work in an EHPAD: An analysis based on the concept of the psychological contract and the job demands-resources model. @. *GRH, 42*(1), 35–58. DOI: 10.3917/grh.042.0035

Sadeghi, S. (2024). Employee well-being in the age of AI: Perceptions, concerns, behaviors, and outcomes. DOI: 10.48550/ARXIV.2412.04796

Saggu, A., & Ante, L. (2023). The influence of ChatGPT on artificial intelligence related crypto assets: Evidence from a synthetic control analysis. *Finance Research Letters, 55*, 103993. DOI: 10.1016/j.frl.2023.103993

Salanova, M., Llorens, S., & Ventura, M. (2014). Technostress: The Dark Side of Technologies. In Korunka, C., & Hoonakker, P. (Eds.), *The Impact of ICT on Quality of Working Life*. Springer., DOI: 10.1007/978-94-017-8854-0_6

Sang, N. M. (2024). Bibliometric insights into the evolution of digital marketing trends. *Innovative Marketing*, *20*(2), 1–14. DOI: 10.21511/im.20(2).2024.01

Santhi, R., Tang, S. G. H., Afzal, M. M., & Ker, P. J. (2023). The relevance of artificial intelligence in mitigating socio-economic impacts of COVID-19 and future epidemics. *World Sustainable Development Outlook*, *21*, 105–118.

Santoro, G., Bertoldi, B., Giachino, C., & Candelo, E. (2020). Exploring the relationship between entrepreneurial resilience and success: The moderating role of stakeholders' engagement. *Journal of Business Research*, *119*, 142–150. DOI: 10.1016/j.jbusres.2018.11.052

Saradhi, V. V., & Palshikar, G. K. (2011). Employee churn *prediction. Expert Systems with Applications*, *38*(3), 1999–2006. DOI: 10.1016/j.eswa.2010.07.134

Saragih, A. H., Reyhani, Q., Setyowati, M. S., & Hendrawan, A. (2023). The potential of an artificial intelligence (AI) application for the tax administration system's modernization: The case of Indonesia. *Artificial Intelligence and Law*, *31*(3), 491–514. DOI: 10.1007/s10506-022-09321-y

Satheeskumar, R. (2024). Enhancing drug discovery with AI: Predictive modeling of pharmacokinetics using graph neural networks and ensemble learning. Intelligent Pharmacy. Advance online publication. DOI: 10.1016/j.ipha.2024.11.002

Saulitis, A., & Chapkovski, P. (2024). Appealing, threatening or nudging? Assessing various communication strategies to promote tax compliance. *Public Choice*. Advance online publication. DOI: 10.1007/s11127-024-01194-w

Schächtele, S. (2023). Tax Responses at Low Taxable Incomes: Evidence from Germany*. *Fiscal Studies*, *41*(2), 411–439. DOI: 10.1111/1475-5890.12220

Schank, R. C. (1987). What is AI, anyway? *AI Magazine*, *8*(4), 59. DOI: 10.1609/aimag.v8i4.623

Schaufeli, W. B. (2017). Applying the Job Demands-Resources model: A 'how to' guide to measuring and tackling work engagement and burnout. *Organizational Dynamics*, *46*(2), 120–132. DOI: 10.1016/j.orgdyn.2017.04.008

Schumpeter, J. A. (1942). Capitalism, Socialism, and Democracy. *University of Illinois at Urbana-Champaign's Academy for Entrepreneurial Leadership Historical Research Reference in Entrepreneurship.*

Sedjari, S., Essaadi, U. A., Kebdani, H. E. L., & Moutaqi, B. E. L. (2025). Renforcer l ' accompagnement entrepreneurial des TPE et auto- entrepreneurs pour intégrer l ' économie informelle au Maroc. *International Journal of Accounting, Finance, Auditing. Management and Economics*, *6*(2), 194–216. DOI: 10.5281/zenodo.14788100

Senihji, M. (2023). *Ethical AI in marketing: Principles and practical implementation*. MIT Press.

Setzu, M., Guidotti, R., Monreale, A., Turini, F., Pedreschi, D., & Giannotti, F. (2021). GLocalX - From Local to Global Explanations of Black Box AI Models. *Artificial Intelligence*, *294*, 103457. DOI: 10.1016/j.artint.2021.103457

Sharma, M., Alkatheeri, H., Jabeen, F., & Sehrawat, R. (2022). Impact of COVID-19 pandemic on perishable food supply chain management: A contingent Resource-Based View (RBV) perspective. *International Journal of Logistics Management*, *33*(3), 796–817. DOI: 10.1108/IJLM-02-2021-0131

Sheldon, P., & Bryant, K. (2016). Instagram: Motives for its use and relationship with narcissism and contextual age. *Computers in Human Behavior*, *58*, 89–97. DOI: 10.1016/j.chb.2015.12.059

Shepherd, D. (2015). Party on! A call for entrepreneurship research that is more interactive, activity based, cognitively hot, compassionate, and pro-social. *Journal of Business Venturing*, *30*(4), 489–507. DOI: 10.1016/j.jbusvent.2015.02.001

Shepherd, D. A., & Majchrzak, A. (2022). Machines augmenting entrepreneurs: Opportunities (and threats) at the Nexus of artificial intelligence and entrepreneurship. *Journal of Business Venturing*, *37*(4), 106227. Advance online publication. DOI: 10.1016/j.jbusvent.2022.106227

Shepherd, D. A., Osofero, M., & Wincent, J. (2022). A personal adversity model of justifying the costs of entrepreneurial action: The case of oil thieves in the Niger DELTA. *Journal of Business Venturing*, *37*(1), 106163. DOI: 10.1016/j.jbusvent.2021.106163

Shi, B., Dong, B., Xu, Y., Wang, J., Wang, Y., & Zheng, Q. (2023). An edge feature aware heterogeneous graph neural network model to support tax evasion detection. *Expert Systems with Applications*, *213*, 118903. DOI: 10.1016/j.eswa.2022.118903

Shoenberger, H., Kim, E., & Sun, Y. (2021). Advertising during COVID-19: Exploring perceived brand message authenticity and potential psychological reactance. *Journal of Advertising*, *50*(3), 253–261. DOI: 10.1080/00913367.2021.1927914

Shujaaddeen, A., Ba-Alwi, F. M., & Al-Gaphari, G. (2024). A New Machine Learning Model for Detecting levels of Tax Evasion Based on Hybrid Neural Network. *International Journal of Intelligent Systems and Applications in Engineering, 2147–6799214.*

Siddik, A. B., Li, Y., Du, A. M., & Migliavacca, M. (2025). Fueling financial development: The crucial role of generative AI financing across nations. *Finance Research Letters*, *72*, 106519. DOI: 10.1016/j.frl.2024.106519

Siimon, Õ. R., & Lukason, O. (2021). A Decision Support System for Corporate Tax Arrears Prediction. *Sustainability (Basel)*, *13*(15), 8363. DOI: 10.3390/su13158363

Silva, E. S., & Bonetti, F. (2021). Digital humans in fashion: Will consumers interact? *Journal of Retailing and Consumer Services*, *60*, 102430. Advance online publication. DOI: 10.1016/j.jretconser.2020.102430

Simon, H. (1957). A Behavioral Model of Rational Choice. Models of Man, Social and Rational: Mathematical Essays on Rational Human Behavior in a Social Setting/Wiley.

Simon, H. (1982). *Models of bounded rationality* (Vol. 3).

Simwanda, L., Ikotun, B. D., Ilunga, F. M., & Onyari, E. K. (2025). Epistemic uncertainties in torque capacity prediction models for circular CFDST members. *Journal of Constructional Steel Research*, *226*, 109299. DOI: 10.1016/j.jcsr.2024.109299

Slemp, G. R., Kern, M. L., & Vella-Brodrick, D. A. (2015). Workplace well-being: The role of job crafting and autonomy support. *Psychology of Well-Being*, *5*(1), 1–17. DOI: 10.1186/s13612-015-0034-y

Sonnentag, S. (2018). The recovery paradox: Portraying the complex interplay between job stressors, lack of recovery, and poor well-being. *Research in Organizational Behavior*, *38*, 169–185. DOI: 10.1016/j.riob.2018.11.002

Stamate, A. N., Sauvé, G., & Denis, P. L. (2021). The rise of the machines and how they impact workers' psychological health: An empirical study. *Human Behavior and Emerging Technologies*, *3*(5), 942–955. DOI: 10.1002/hbe2.315

Statista. (2023, January 6). Virtual influencers—Statistics & facts. Statista. Retrieved from https://www.statista.com/topics/9805/virtual-influencers/#topicOverview

Statista. (2024). Instagram - Statistics & Facts. Available at: https://www.statista.com/topics/1882/instagram/#topicOverview (Accessed February 27, 2025).

Stein, J., Barton, K., & Pennington, J. (2022). Virtual influencers: More human than humans? *Journal of Digital and Social Media Marketing*, *10*(1), 15–26.

Stein, J.-P., Breves, P. L., & Anders, N. (2022). Parasocial interactions with real and virtual influencers: The role of perceived similarity and human-likeness. *New Media & Society*, *26*(6), 3433–3453. DOI: 10.1177/14614448221102900

Stone, M. (1974). Cross-validation: A review. *Mathematical Modeling and Statistical Computation*, *36*, 111–133.

Strauss, H., Fawcett, T., & Schutte, D. (2020). An evaluation of the digital response of tax authorities to optimise tax administration within the digitalised economy. *eJournal of Tax Research*.

Stubb, C. (2018). Story versus info: Tracking blog readers' online viewing time of sponsored blog posts based on content-specific elements. *Computers in Human Behavior*, *82*, 54–62. DOI: 10.1016/j.chb.2018.01.001

Sundararajan, M., & Najmi, A. (2020). The many Shapley values for model explanation. *Proceedings of the 37th International Conference on Machine Learning (ICML 2020)*. https://proceedings.mlr.press/v119/sundararajan20a.html

Sundaresan, S. (2014). Work-Life Balance – Implications for Working Women. Int. J. Sustain. Dev. 7 (7), 93–102. OIDA. *International Journal of Sustainable Development*, *7*(7), 93–102.

Sun, T. Q., & Medaglia, R. (2019). Mapping the challenges of Artificial Intelligence in the public sector: Evidence from public healthcare. *Government Information Quarterly*, *36*(2), 368–383. DOI: 10.1016/j.giq.2018.09.008

Taddeo, M., & Floridi, L. (2018). How AI can be a force for good. 'Science, 361'(6404), 751-752.

Tagliaferri, G., Scacciatelli, D., & Loro, P. A. D. (2020). VAT tax gap prediction: A 2-steps Gradient Boosting approach. *Statistical Methods & Applications*, *32*(1), 237–270. DOI: 10.1007/s10260-022-00643-4

Tak, C. C., Zulnaidi, H., & Eu, L. K. (2025). Factors influencing the attitude of undergraduate students towards mathematical reasoning: An approach using AMOS-structural equation modelling. *Infinity Journal*, *14*(1), 109–124. DOI: 10.22460/infinity.v14i1.p109-124

Tambe, P., Cappelli, P., & Yakubovich, V. (2019). Artificial Intelligence in Human Resources Management: Challenges and a Path Forward. SSRN *Electronic Journal, January 2018*. https://doi.org/DOI: 10.1177/0008125619867910

Tan, E., Petit Jean, M., Simonofski, A., Tombal, T., Kleizen, B., Sabbe, M., Bechoux, L., & Willem, P. (2023). Artificial intelligence and algorithmic decisions in fraud detection: An interpretive structural model. *Data & Policy*, *5*, e25. DOI: 10.1017/dap.2023.22

Tanner, S., Prayag, D. G., & Coelho Kuntz, D. J. (2022). Psychological capital, social capital and organizational resilience: A Herringbone Model perspective. *International Journal of Disaster Risk Reduction*, *78*(July), 103149. DOI: 10.1016/j.ijdrr.2022.103149

Tanujaya, B., Prahmana, R. C. I., & Mumu, J. (2022). Likert scale in social sciences research: Problems and difficulties. *FWU Journal of Social Sciences*, *16*(4), 89–101.

Tarafdar, M., Tu, Q., Ragu-Nathan, B. S., & Ragu-Nathan, T. S. (2007). The impact of technostress on role stress and productivity. *Journal of Management Information Systems*, *24*(1), 301–328. DOI: 10.2753/MIS0742-1222240109

Taylor, R., Brown, P., & Adams, S. (2019). Vehicle price prediction system using machine learning techniques. *International Journal of Advanced Computer Science and Applications*, *10*(4), 123–130. https://www.researchgate.net/publication/317608326_Vehicle_Price_Prediction_System_using_Machine_Learning_Techniques

Thiele, S. (2019). Detecting underestimates of risk in VaR models. *Journal of Banking & Finance*, *101*, 12–20. DOI: 10.1016/j.jbankfin.2019.01.018

Thiétart, R.-A. (2014). Méthodes de Recherche. In *Management. 4ème Édition*. Dunod., DOI: 10.3917/dunod.thiet.2014.01

Thomas, V. L., & Fowler, K. (2021). Close encounters of the AI kind: Use of AI influencers as brand endorsers. *Journal of Advertising*, *50*(1), 11–25. DOI: 10.1080/00913367.2020.1810595

Tian, Y., & Fan, X. (2014). Adversity quotients, environmental variables and career adaptability in student nurses. *Journal of Vocational Behavior*, *85*(3), 251–257. DOI: 10.1016/j.jvb.2014.07.006

Torres, P., Augusto, M., & Matos, M. (2019). Antecedents and outcomes of digital influencer endorsement: An exploratory study. *Psychology and Marketing*, *36*(12), 1267–1276. DOI: 10.1002/mar.21274

Townsend, D. M., & Hunt, R. A. (2019, January). Entrepreneurial action, creativity, & judgment in the age of artificial intelligence. *Journal of Business Venturing Insights*, *11*, e00126. DOI: 10.1016/j.jbvi.2019.e00126

Trenerry, B., Chng, S., Wang, Y., Suhaila, Z. S., Lim, S. S., Lu, H. Y., & Oh, P. H. (2021). Preparing workplaces for digital transformation: An integrative review and framework of multi-level factors.[. *Frontiers in Psychology*, *12*, 620766. Advance online publication. https://philpapers.org. DOI: 10.3389/fpsyg.2021.620766 PMID: 33833714

Tussyadiah, I., Li, S., & Miller, G. (2020). Privacy protection in tourism: Where we are and where we should be heading for. *Journal of Travel Research*, *59*(7), 1223–1234. DOI: 10.1177/0047287519883030

Ucbasaran, D., Shepherd, D. A., Lockett, A., & Lyon, S. J. (2013). Life After Business Failure: The Process and Consequences of Business Failure for Entrepreneurs. *Journal of Management* (Vol. 39, Issue 1, pp. 163–202). https://doi.org/DOI: 10.1177/0149206312457823

Ul Hassan, S., Abdulkadir, S. J., Zahid, M. S. M., & Al-Selwi, S. M. (2025). Local interpretable model-agnostic explanation approach for medical imaging analysis: A systematic literature review. *Computers in Biology and Medicine*, *185*, 109569. DOI: 10.1016/j.compbiomed.2024.109569 PMID: 39705792

UNESCO. (2024). *MAROC: Rapport d'évaluation de l'état de préparation à l'intelligence artificielle*. Place de Fontenoy.

Utami, T. L. W. (2021). Technology adoption on online learning during Covid-19 pandemic: Implementation of technology acceptance model (TAM). *Diponegoro International Journal of Business*, *4*(1), 8–19. DOI: 10.14710/dijb.4.1.2021.8-19

Uzunoğlu, E., & Kip, S. M. (2014). Brand communication through digital influencers: Leveraging blogger engagement. *International Journal of Information Management*, *34*(5), 592–602. DOI: 10.1016/j.ijinfomgt.2014.04.007

Vagnoli, M., & Remenyte-Prescott, R. (2022). Updating conditional probabilities of Bayesian belief networks by merging expert knowledge and system monitoring data. *Automation in Construction*, *140*, 104366. DOI: 10.1016/j.autcon.2022.104366

Van De Voorde, K., Paauwe, J., & Van Veldhoven, M. (2012). Employee well-being and the HRM–organizational performance relationship: A review of quantitative studies. *International Journal of Management Reviews*, *14*(4), 391–407. DOI: 10.1111/j.1468-2370.2011.00322.x

Van der Doef, M., & Maes, S. (1999). The job demand-control (-support) model and psychological well-being: A review of 20 years of empirical research. *Work and Stress*, *13*(2), 87–114. DOI: 10.1080/026783799296084

Vandenberghe, C., Stordeur, S., & d'Hoore, W. (2009). Une analyse des effets de la latitude de décision, de l'épuisement émotionnel et de la satisfaction au travail sur l'absentéisme au sein des unités de soins infirmiers. *Le Travail Humain*, *72*(3), 209–228. DOI: 10.3917/th.723.0209

Vansteenkiste, M., Ryan, R. M., & Soenens, B. (2020). Basic psychological need theory: Advancements, critical themes, and future directions. *Motivation and Emotion*, *44*(1), 1–31. DOI: 10.1007/s11031-019-09818-1

Vecchiarini, M., & Somià, T. (2023). Redefining entrepreneurship education in the age of artificial intelligence: An explorative analysis. *International Journal of Management Education*, *21*(3), 1–11. DOI: 10.1016/j.ijme.2023.100879

Verhoef, P. C., Broekhuizen, T., Bart, Y., Bhattacharya, A., Dong, J. Q., Fabian, N., & Haenlein, M. (2021). Digital transformation: A multidisciplinary reflection and research agenda. *Journal of Business Research*, *122*, 889–901. DOI: 10.1016/j.jbusres.2019.09.022

Vinichenko, M. V., Melnichuk, A. V., & Karácsony, P. (2020). Technologies of improving the university efficiency by using artificial intelligence: Motivational aspect. *Journal of Entrepreneurship and Sustainability Issues*, *7*(4), 2696–2714. DOI: 10.9770/jesi.2020.7.4(9)

Vogue Business. (2022). *Balmain's virtual army*. https://www.voguebusiness.com/fashion/balmains-virtual-army

Vogue Business. (2022). *Shudu Gram collaborates with Fenty Beauty*. https://www.voguebusiness.com/beauty/shudu-gram-collaborates-with-fenty-beauty

Volberda, H. W., Khanagha, S., Baden-Fuller, C., Mihalache, O. R., & Birkinshaw, J. (2021). Strategizing in a digital world: Overcoming cognitive barriers, reconfiguring routines and introducing new organizational forms. *Long Range Planning*, *54*(5), 102110. DOI: 10.1016/j.lrp.2021.102110

Vozár, A., & Bán, E. (2024). Digitalisation, digital transformation – In the practice of the National Tax and Customs Office. *Public Finance Quarterly*, *70*(1), 85–109. DOI: 10.35551/PFQ_2024_1_5

Wach, K., Duong, C. D., Ejdys, J., Kazlauskaitė, R., & Simionescu, M. (2023). The dark side of generative artificial intelligence: The risk of "technostress" among employees in Europe. *Entrepreneurial Business and Economics Review*, *11*(2), 7–24. DOI: 10.15678/EBER.2023.110201

Wahlström, M., Tammentie, B., Salonen, T. T., & Karvonen, A. (2024). AI and the transformation of industrial work: Hybrid intelligence vs double-black box effect. *Applied Ergonomics*, *118*, 104271. DOI: 10.1016/j.apergo.2024.104271 PMID: 38579495

Waltersdorfer, L., & Sabou, M. (2025). Leveraging knowledge graphs for AI system auditing and transparency. *Journal of Web Semantics*, *84*, 100849. DOI: 10.1016/j.websem.2024.100849

Walumbwa, F. O., Avolio, B. J., Gardner, W. L., Wernsing, T. S., & Peterson, S. J. (2008). Authentic leadership: Development and validation of a theory-based measure. *Journal of Management*, *34*(1), 89–126. DOI: 10.1177/0149206307308913

Wang, W., Yin, H., & Huang, S. (2016). The missing links between emotional job demand and exhaustion and satisfaction: Testing a moderated mediation model. *Journal of Management & Organization*, *22*(1), 80–95. DOI: 10.1017/jmo.2015.21

Wang, Y.-Y., & Su, X. (2021). Driving factors of digital transformation for manufacturing enterprises: A multi-case study from China. *International Journal of Technology Management*, *87*(2/3/4), 229. DOI: 10.1504/IJTM.2021.120932

Warr, P. (1990). The measurement of well-being and other aspects of mental health. *Journal of Occupational Psychology*, *63*(3), 193–210. DOI: 10.1111/j.2044-8325.1990.tb00521.x

Waterman, A. S. (1993). Two conceptions of happiness: Contrasts of personal expressiveness (eudaimonia) and hedonic enjoyment. *Journal of Personality and Social Psychology*, *64*(4), 678–691. DOI: 10.1037/0022-3514.64.4.678

Watson, D., Clark, L. A., & Tellegen, A. (1988). Development and validation of brief measures of positive and negative affect: The PANAS scales. *Journal of Personality and Social Psychology*, *54*(6), 1063–1070. DOI: 10.1037/0022-3514.54.6.1063 PMID: 3397865

Weber, P., Carl, K. V., & Hinz, O. (2024). Applications of explainable artificial intelligence in finance—A systematic review of finance, information systems, and computer science literature. *Management Review Quarterly*, *74*(2), 867–907. DOI: 10.1007/s11301-023-00320-0

Wedel, M., & Kannan, P. K. (2016). Marketing analytics for data-rich environments. 'Journal of Marketing, 80'(6), 97-121. DOI: 10.1509/jm.15.0413

Wei, Y., Hu, R., Zhang, J., & Wang, Q. (2024). Does the carbon market signal the market efficiency of clean and dirty cryptocurrencies? An analysis of quantile directional dependence. *Finance Research Letters*, *67*, 105913. DOI: 10.1016/j.frl.2024.105913

Wellman, M. L., Stoldt, R., Tully, M., & Ekdale, B. (2020). Ethics of authenticity: Social media influencers and the production of sponsored content. *Journal of Media Ethics*, *35*(2), 68–82. DOI: 10.1080/23736992.2020.1736078

West, A. B., Guo, Y. V., & Bucher, A. (2023). Leveraging behavioral science and artificial intelligence to support mental health in the workplace: A pilot study. *Frontiers in Psychiatry*, *14*, 14. DOI: 10.3389/fpsyt.2023.1219229 PMID: 37928926

Westin, A. F. (1967). *Privacy and freedom*. Atheneum Press.

Wibawa, R. C., Pratiwi, C. P., Wahyono, E., Hidayat, D., & Adiasari, W. (2022). Virtual Influencers: Is The Persona Trustworthy? [JAMIKA]. *Jurnal Manajemen Informatika*, *12*(1), 51–62. DOI: 10.34010/jamika.v12i1.6706

Wickens, C. D., & Carswell, C. M. (2021). Information processing. Handbook of human factors and ergonomics, 114-158.

Wilson, H. J., & Daugherty, P. R. (2018). Collaborative intelligence: Humans and AI are joining forces. *Harvard Business Review*, *96*(4), 114–123.

Wirtz, J., & Zeithaml, V. (2018). AI and machine learning in customer service. 'Journal of Service Management, 29'(5), 907-931.

Woellner, R. (2020). It Is a Bad Look. *eJournal of Tax Research, 18*(2), 508–530.

Wu, D., Zhang, T., Zhang, J., Lv, H., Yue, C., & Fu, M. (2024). Sensitivity analysis and multiobjective optimization for rural house retrofitting considering construction and occupant behavior uncertainty: A case study of Jiaxian, China. *Applied Energy*, *360*, 122835. DOI: 10.1016/j.apenergy.2024.122835

Wu, Y. (2024, June 30). Enterprise financial sharing and risk identification model combining recurrent neural networks with transformer model supported by blockchain. *Heliyon*, *10*(12), e32639. DOI: 10.1016/j.heliyon.2024.e32639 PMID: 38988581

Xiao, J. Xu, Z. Xiao, A. Wang, X. Skare, M. (2024);Overcoming barriers and seizing opportunities in the innovative adoption of next-generation digital technologies, Journal of Innovation & Knowledge, Volume 9, Issue 4, .DOI: 10.1016/j.jik.2024.100622

Xia, Z., & Shannon, R. (2025). Navigating the Digital Frontier. Exploring the Dynamics of Customer–Brand Relationships Through AI Chatbots. *Sustainability (Basel)*, *2025*(17), 2173. DOI: 10.3390/su17052173

Xie, Q., Han, W., Lai, Y., Peng, M., & Huang, J. (2023). The wall street neophyte: A zero-shot analysis of chatgpt over multimodal stock movement prediction challenges. arXiv preprint arXiv:2304.05351.

Xing, S., Lei, Y., Wang, S., & Jia, F. (2020). Distribution-invariant deep belief network for intelligent fault diagnosis of machines under new working conditions. *IEEE Transactions on Industrial Electronics*, *68*(3), 2617–2625. DOI: 10.1109/TIE.2020.2972461

Xiong, Y., & Kim, J. K. (2025). Who wants to be hired by AI? How message frames and AI transparency impact individuals' attitudes and behaviors toward companies using AI in hiring. *Computers in Human Behavior: Artificial Humans*, *3*, 100120. DOI: 10.1016/j.chbah.2025.100120

Yacoubi, L., & Tourabi, A. (2021). Résilience psychologique de l'entrepreneur et résilience organisationnelle de la PME : élaboration d'un cadre conceptuel. *Alternatives Managériales et Economiques*. E-ISSN: 2665-7511 Vol 3, No 2, 2020-238

Yadav, N., Kumar, R., Pandey, D. (2025). 12 - Impact of artificial intelligence bias in medical systems. Revolutionizing Medical Systems using Artificial Intelligence, A Breakthrough in Healthcare, 227-243. DOI: 10.1016/B978-0-443-32862-6.00012-2

Yakovenko, Y. Y., Bilyk, M. Y., & Oliinyk, Y. V. (2022). The transformative impact of the development of artificial intelligence on employment and work motivation in business in the conditions of the information economy. 2022 IEEE 4th International Conference on Modern Electrical and Energy System (MEES).

Yang, S., Demichela, M., Geng, J., Wang, L., & Ling, Z. (2024). A data-driven Bayesian network of management and organizational factors for human reliability analysis in the process industry. *Heliyon*, *10*(15), e35048. DOI: 10.1016/j.heliyon.2024.e35048 PMID: 39166060

Yang, X., & Yan, S. (2024). Encourage or reject employee involvement: Value creation in Human Resource Management in the AI era-an evolutionary game analysis of enterprises and employees. *Behavioral Sciences (Basel, Switzerland)*, *14*(12), 1220. Advance online publication. DOI: 10.3390/bs14121220 PMID: 39767361

Yang, Y., & Danes, S. M. (2015). Resiliency and resilience process of trepreneurs in new venture creation. *Entrepreneurship Research Journal*, *5*(1), 1–30. DOI: 10.1515/erj-2013-0076

Yao, K., Li, X., & Liang, B. (2021). Failure learning and entrepreneurial resilience: The moderating role of firms' knowledge breadth and knowledge depth. *Journal of Knowledge Management*, *25*(9), 2141–2160. DOI: 10.1108/JKM-10-2020-0772

Ye, Y., & Chen, K.-H. (2024). Hospitality employees and digital transformation: The mediating roles of alienation and motivation. *International Journal of Hospitality Management*, *119*(103731), 103731. Advance online publication. DOI: 10.1016/j.ijhm.2024.103731

Yilmaz, R., & Karaoglan Yilmaz, F. G. (2023). The effect of generative artificial intelligence (AI)-based tool use on students' computational thinking skills, programming self-efficacy and motivation. *Computers and Education: Artificial Intelligence.*, *4*, 100147. Advance online publication. DOI: 10.1016/j.caeai.2023.100147

Ying, X., Lu, A., Cai, Q., & Lu, J. (2024). Bayesian network modeling applied to food risks: Data from General Administration of Customs of China as an example. *Applied Food Research*, *4*(2), 100565. DOI: 10.1016/j.afres.2024.100565

Yoo, S.-K., & Kim, B.-Y. (2018). A Decision-Making Model for Adopting a Cloud Computing System. *Sustainability (Basel)*, *10*(8), 2952. Advance online publication. DOI: 10.3390/su10082952

Yuan, Y., Chaffart, D., Wu, T., & Zhu, J. (2024). Transparency: The Missing Link to Boosting AI Transformations in Chemical Engineering. *Engineering (Beijing)*, *39*, 45–60. DOI: 10.1016/j.eng.2023.11.024

Zaharia, M., Xin, R., Wendell, P., Das, T., Armbrust, M., Dave, A., & Ghodsi, A. (2018). MLflow: A platform for managing the machine learning lifecycle. In *Proceedings of the 27th International Conference on Machine Learning (ICML).*

Zaid, M., Farooqi, R., & Azmi, S. N. (2025). Driving sustainable supply chain performance through artificial intelligence and big data analytics. In *Handbook of Research on Big Data and Artificial Intelligence in the Supply Chain* (pp. xx–xx). IGI Global., DOI: 10.4018/978-1-6684-6810-3.ch011

Zhang, Y. (2018). *A used car price evaluation model based on neural network* [Master's thesis, Tianjin University].

Zhang, C., & Meng, Y. (2024). Bayesian deep learning: An enhanced AI framework for legal reasoning alignment. *Computer Law & Security Review*, *55*, 106073. DOI: 10.1016/j.clsr.2024.106073

Zhang, L., & Wei, W. (2021). Influencer Marketing: A Comparison of Traditional Celebrity, Social Media Influencer, and AI Influencer Endorsement. *Boston University Business Horizons*, *4*(3), 58–68.

Zhang, M., Wang, H., Conti, F., Manderbacka, T., Remes, H., & Hirdaris, S. (2025). A hybrid deep learning method for the real-time prediction of collision damage consequences in operational conditions. *Engineering Applications of Artificial Intelligence*, *145*, 110158. DOI: 10.1016/j.engappai.2025.110158

Zhang, R., Yang, Y., Fang, Q., Liu, Y., Zhu, X., Wang, M., & Su, L. (2020). Effect of indoors artificial lighting conditions on computer-based learning performance. *International Journal of Environmental Research and Public Health*, *17*(7), 2537. DOI: 10.3390/ijerph17072537 PMID: 32276306

Zhang, T., & Ahmed, S. (2022). Fair pricing through explainable machine learning. *AI & Society*, *37*(2), 456–470. DOI: 10.1007/s00146-021-01232-4

Zhang, W. (2025). Bank liquidity supply and corporate investment during the 2008–2009 financial crisis. *The North American Journal of Economics and Finance*, *76*, 102371. DOI: 10.1016/j.najef.2025.102371

Zhang, X., Nutakor, F., Minlah, M. K., & Li, J. (2023). Can digital transformation drive green transformation in manufacturing companies?—Based on socio-technical systems theory perspective. *Sustainability (Basel)*, *15*(3), 2840. DOI: 10.3390/su15032840

Zhang, X., Zheng, P., Peng, T., He, Q., Lee, C. K., & Tang, R. (2022). Promoting employee health in smart office: A survey. *Advanced Engineering Informatics*, *51*, 101518. DOI: 10.1016/j.aei.2021.101518

Zhang, X., Zheng, P., Peng, T., Li, D., Zhang, X., & Tang, R. (2023). Privacy-preserving activity recognition using multimodal sensors in smart office. *Future Generation Computer Systems*, *148*, 27–38. DOI: 10.1016/j.future.2023.05.023

Zhao, Y., Li, Y., Xiao, Y., Chang, H., & Liu, B. (2024). Factors influencing the acceptance of ChatGPT in higher education: A quantitative analysis of student attitudes and behavioral intentions. *SAGE Open*, *14*(1). Advance online publication. DOI: 10.1177/21582440241234567

Zhao, Z., Zhang, Q., Yu, X., Sun, C., Wang, S., Yan, R., & Chen, X. (2021). Applications of unsupervised deep transfer learning to intelligent fault diagnosis: A survey and comparative study. *IEEE Transactions on Instrumentation and Measurement*, *70*, 1–28. DOI: 10.1109/TIM.2021.3116309

Zhou, W., Wang, C., Liu, Y., Zhang, W., & Chen, Z. (2017). A Research of Influence on HR Management of Robots Used in a Large Scale. *J. Nanjing Univ. Philos. Humanit. Soc. Sci*, *54*, 23–34.

Zhou, Y., Wang, L., & Chen, W. (2023). The dark side of AI-enabled HRM on employees based on AI algorithmic features. *Journal of Organizational Change Management, 36*(7), 1222–1241. DOI: 10.1108/JOCM-10-2022-0308

Zhou, Y., & Yuen, K. F. (2024). A Bayesian network model for container shipping companies' organisational sustainability risk management. *Transportation Research Part D, Transport and Environment, 126*, 103999. DOI: 10.1016/j.trd.2023.103999

Zhu, J., Chen, N., & Shen, C. (2019). A new deep transfer learning method for bearing fault diagnosis under different working conditions. *IEEE Sensors Journal, 20*(15), 8394–8402. DOI: 10.1109/JSEN.2019.2936932

Zickmund, S. (2007). Deliberation, phronesis, and authenticity: Heidegger's early conception of rhetoric. *Philosophy & Rhetoric, 40*(4), 406–415. DOI: 10.2307/25655289

Zohuri, B., Mossavar-Rahmani, F., & Behgounia, F. (2022). Chapter 4 - Structured and unstructured data processing. Knowledge is Power in Four Dimensions: Models to Forecast Future Paradigm With Artificial Intelligence Integration in Energy and Other Use Cases, Pages 87-119. DOI: 10.1016/B978-0-323-95112-8.00004-0

Zuboff, S. (2019). *The Age of Surveillance Capitalism*. Profile Books Limited.

Zuboff, S. (2019). *The age of surveillance capitalism: The fight for a human future at the new frontier of power*. PublicAffairs.

About the Contributors

Abdelfattah Jamal is an Associate Professor with Habilitation in Management Sciences at the Faculty of Legal, Economic and Social Sciences, University Cadi Ayyad Marrakech, Morocco. He holds a Ph.D. in Economics and Management from Sidi Mohammed Ben Abdellah University Fez and a Habilitation to Direct Research. His research focuses on organizational change management, managerial and social innovation, agility and resilience, digital transformation, and the integration of artificial intelligence in HR management and marketing. A permanent researcher at the Laboratory of New Management Practices (NPG) at Cadi Ayyad University, he supervises doctoral theses on digital transformation, corporate social responsibility (CSR), and AI. He actively participates in national and international conferences on digital-era management. Author of scientific publications in peer-reviewed journals and conference proceedings, he is a member of several scientific committees of academic journals and professional associations. He also contributes as a reviewer for recognized journals in management and organizational psychology.

Karima Aissaoui is an Associate Professor at the Faculty of Sciences, University Mohammed I, Oujda, Morocco, specializing in Computer Science. With extensive expertise in Artificial Intelligence, e-Learning, Security, and Systems Engineering, Pr. Aissaoui has made significant contributions to these fields, focusing on innovative solutions and interdisciplinary approaches. Her research interests include developing intelligent systems, enhancing online learning platforms, improving cybersecurity measures, and optimizing complex systems. Pr. Aissaoui's work has contributed to advancing both academic knowledge and practical applications in these rapidly evolving areas of technology.

Lhoussaine Alla, professor in management sciences at the National School of Applied Sciences, researcher at the LAREMEF laboratory, Sidi Mohamed Ben Abdellah University, Fez, Morocco. Prof. Lhoussaine ALLA has invested more in scientific research in various themes inherent in marketing, finance, entrepreneurship, tourism, logistics. He is also editor of the journal “Management et Alternatives Economiques - AME” (https://revues.imist.ma/index.php/AME). Prof. Lhoussaine ALLA has accumulated as many educational and scientific experiences, which he constantly mobilizes to catalyze a large team of researchers and experts in analysis, reflexivity and application of innovative and intelligent solutions from Data Engineering and AI in various management dimensions. Prof. Lhoussaine ALLA is a co-editor of collective works published by IGI Global: InteIntegrating Intelligence and Sustainability in Supply Chains; Applying Qualitative Research Methods to Science and Management; Using Technology to Manage Territories.

Bouchra Alj is a professor and researcher in management sciences, with more than 22 years of experience, having gained international recognition through her contributions to the management of organizations, public finances and taxation. After obtaining her PhD at the Mohammed V University, Faculty of Legal, Economic and Social Sciences (FSJES) in Rabat-Agdal, she joined the Cadi Ayyad University in Marrakech before joining the Hassan II University in Casablanca, where she is currently working for the FSJES in Mohammedia. She coordinates the Accounting – Finance – Taxation course and teaches specialized modules covering bachelor’s, master’s and doctoral degrees, such as management of organizations, corporate taxation, tax audit, entrepreneurship and management science research methodology. Prof. Bouchra ALJ is also the head of a research team within the Research Laboratory in Economics, Management and Strategies of Organizations (LAREMSO), where she leads innovative research projects and supervises doctoral theses as well as graduate and master’s degree projects. Under his direction, the team explores a variety of topics related to finance, economics, management and econometrics, focusing on an interdisciplinary approach to address concrete and current issues. In addition to her academic responsibilities, Prof. Bouchra ALJ is the author of several books, including on income taxation in Morocco and management of organizations. As the Director of Publication for The Economics & Management Review (), a journal indexed on IMIST, she is actively contributing to the dissemination of original research, Strengthening links between Moroccan researchers and the international scientific community. She is also a member of several scientific and editorial committees for renowned academic journals. Her work as a private sector consultant allows her to integrate the latest developments in management and taxation into an international context, bridging the gap between theory and practice. Prof. Bouchra ALJ regularly publishes in national and international academic journals, and her research is presented at renowned conferences around the world. His research is oriented towards management, public finance and taxation, with a particular interest in tax psychology and tax justice. She is also co-author of articles published in English and French, thus broadening the scope of her contributions.

Very active on the national and international academic scene, Prof. Bouchra ALJ is frequently invited to sit on juries and panels of national and international conferences and plays a key role in organizing and hosting seminars, seminars and study days for committed researchers. She frequently participates in scientific and project evaluation committees, thus strengthening her influence in the field of management sciences.

Badr Bentalha teaches Supply Chain and Operations Management at National School Of Business and Management – Fez, Sidi Mohamed Ben Abdellah University – Morocco. Dr. Bentalha investigates the structural dynamics and control of complex networks, applying his findings to supply chain management, Industry 4.0, risk analysis, and digital supply chains. His pioneering research has established seminal academic and practical approaches for sustainable and intelligent supply chain optimization. Using optimization, simulation, control theory, and AI, he tackles real-world supply chain and operations challenges. His work emphasizes the intersection of supply chain management, operations research, industrial engineering, and digital technology. As a professor, he teaches undergraduate, graduate, and, doctoral courses in operations management, supply chain management, logistics, management information systems, and strategic management. Through guest lectures, webinars, and scholarly presentations, he engages students and fosters an active learning environment. He aims to equip future industry leaders with the management knowledge and technological skills to build more resilient, adaptable, and sustainable supply chain operations. Dr. Bentalha's academic background includes management and economics, operations research, and supply chain management. He studied management operations and supply chain management, graduating with honors. He earned PhD degrees and completed an aggregation in economics and management. Before entering academia, he primarily worked in industry and consulting, focusing on process optimization in manufacturing, logistics, and ERP systems. His practical experience includes numerous operations research and process optimization projects for operations design, logistics, scheduling, and supply chain management. Before joining the Fez National School of Business and Management, he was a professor of economics and management preparatory classes since 2009. Dr. Bentalha's influential research is cited in supply chain management and logistics. His publication record includes over 60 papers in prestigious academic journals such as the International Journal of Logistics Systems and Management, International Journal of Business Performance Management, International Journal of Business and Technology Studies, Journal of Environmental Issues and Climate Change, and Economical Managerial Alternatives. He is also the author of three books: Netnography: Principles, Method, and Ethics, Internal Audit of Treasury and Cash Management: Report on the Audit of Treasury and Integrating Intelligence and

Sustainability in Supply Chains. Professor Bentalha specializes in supply chain and operations management, operations research, and service management. He is passionate about integrating knowledge across disciplines to solve real-world problems. He has delivered numerous invited plenary talks, keynotes, and panel discussions at conferences and global webinars. He serves as Associate Editor of the Economical Managerial Alternatives journal and is on the editorial boards and advisory committees of several other publications. He regularly presents his research and has chaired organized program committees, and served on advisory boards for over 60 international conferences in supply chain management, operations, management studies, control theory, and information science. He is a member of numerous scientific committees of international journals and conferences. Since 2009, Mr. Bentalha has helped sundry companies implement an audit system, resolve issues, and improve performance.

***

Youness Ait Oummou is a junior researcher in finance, a PhD candidate, and a part-time lecturer at Cadi Ayyad University. His research interests include stock market dynamics, macroeconomic theory, and monetary and financial economics. With a focus on empirical analysis, he employs quantitative and econometric modeling to examine financial data and analyze complex economic phenomena.

Asmaa Farah holds a phd in management sciences from Cadi Ayyad University, where she began her academic career. She is currently a professor at ENCG Beni Melall - Sultan Moulay Slimane University and deputy director of the Research Laboratory in Economics and Management of Organizations (LAREMO). Her research interests include: work-life balance, quality of life at work, diversity and inclusion, and CSR. She is the author and co-author of several scientific articles in indexed journals and international conferences. She is a member of the scientific committees of several international conferences and coordinator of the International Conference on Human Capital, Organizations and Development

Mohamed Atounti is a distinguished academic affiliated with Mohammed First University in Oujda, Morocco. He serves as the Director of the Higher School of Technology of Nador (École Supérieure de Technologie de Nador - ESTN), a constituent institution of Mohammed First University . Dr. Atounti's scholarly work primarily focuses on areas such as numerical methods, antenna design, and ground-penetrating radar (GPR) systems. His research contributions include the development of novel patch antennas for 5G applications and the optimization of bowtie antennas for ground-penetrating radar systems . In addition to his research, Dr. Atounti has played a significant role in academic conference organization. He was a member of the organizing committee for the International Conference on Bio-Materials Science, Mechanical and Electrical Engineering (ICBMSM2E'24), held on December 11–12, 2024, in Nador, Morocco . Dr. Atounti has also contributed to the field of software engineering, with research on reverse engineering of web applications using the Architecture-Driven Modernization (ADM) approach . Through his extensive research and academic involvement, Dr. Mohamed Atounti has made significant contributions to his field and continues to influence the academic community at Mohammed First University and beyond.

Yassine Bamalk is an academic researcher. He is interested in various aspects of Human Resource Management, including the integration of emerging technologies, employee well-being, and leadership behavior.

Mohammed Ben Amar is a Professor Researcher in Marketing in the National School of Business and Management of Fez

Yasmine Benimma is a PhD candidate in management sciences at the University of Sidi Mohammed Ben Abdellah in Fès. Her research focuses on ethics, artificial intelligence, and marketing, with a particular interest in the impact of emerging technologies on responsible marketing practices. A graduate of the National School of Business and Management with a specialization in Marketing and Commercial Action, she has gained experience in marketing project management and digital strategies. Through her work, she explores issues related to transparency, responsibility, and consumer trust in an ever-evolving digital environment.

Bouchra Benraïss is a professor at the Faculty of Legal, Economic and Social Sciences of Fez (Sidi Mohamed Ben Abdellah University) and a member of the Research Team on Management of Organizations and Territories (ERMOT). She specializes in Human Resource Management and conducts research on workplace well-being, corporate social responsibility, and emerging forms of organizational engagement. She supervises numerous theses and dissertations, and regularly teaches in training programs for business professionals. She also contributes to projects on leadership and organizational change. She publishes in both French- and English-language academic journals, pursuing a rigorous and committed research agenda grounded in contemporary management challenges.

Hicham Chanqaoui is a PhD student at the LIRE-MD Research Laboratory, Faculty of Legal, Economic and Social Sciences, Cadi Ayyad University, Morocco. His doctoral research focuses on the integration of artificial intelligence into tax administration systems, with an emphasis on privacy, ethical considerations, and fraud detection. He is committed to exploring innovative, responsible approaches to digital governance and public sector modernization.

Abdelouahab El Boukhari is an Assistant Professor of Information Systems Management at Cadi Ayyad University and a core member of the Laboratoire Interdisciplinaire de Recherches et d'Études en Management et Droit des Organisations (LIRE-MD) in Marrakesh, Morocco. His research explores how advanced information technologies, particularly artificial intelligence, data analytics, and digital platforms, transform decision-making and value creation in tourism, social entrepreneurship, public administration, and governance. Dr. El Boukhari combines quantitative modeling, mixed-methods designs, and bibliometric analysis to investigate technology adoption, e-governance resilience, and inclusive regional development. He frequently presents his work at national and international conferences and collaborates on multi-institutional research projects.

Fouad Elotmani is a Moroccan researcher and engineer specializing in software engineering and model-driven development. He is affiliated with the Department of Mathematics and Computer Science at Université Mohammed Premier in Oujda, Morocco. Academic Background and Research Interests Dr. Elotmani holds a Doctorate in Engineering and is actively involved in research related to: • Model-Driven Architecture (MDA): Focusing on platform-independent models (PIM) and platform-specific models (PSM) to streamline software development processes. • NoSQL Databases in Big Data Contexts: Exploring the automatic generation and optimization of document-oriented, graph-based, and column-oriented NoSQL databases. • Energy Efficiency in Data Management: Investigating the impact of database architectures on energy consumption in large-scale data environments. His notable publications include: • Toward Automatic Generation of Document-Oriented NoSQL Databases in Big Data Context (2024) • Automating the Creation of Graph-Based NoSQL Databases in the Context of Big Data (2023) • Creation of Column-Oriented NoSQL Databases Automatically in Big Data Environments and Its Impact on Energy Consumption (2023) • The Reverse Engineering of a Web Application Struts Based in the ADM Approach (2020) Collaborations and Professional Network Dr. Elotmani frequently collaborates with researchers such as Redouane Esbai and Mohamed Atounti. He is associated with the Laboratoire de Mathématiques Appliquées et Systèmes d'Information (MASI) at Université Mohammed Premier.

Wissem Ennouri holds a Ph.D. in Management Sciences, specializing in Logistics and Production, with extensive expertise in risk management and supply chain optimization. He earned his doctorate with Highest Honors from the Faculty of

Economics and Management of Sfax, where his research focused on developing innovative models, including the use of Bayesian networks for risk management in supply chains. In addition to his academic pursuits, Wissem ENNOURI has significant experience in university teaching, delivering courses in production management, logistics, and operational research since 2008. He has also supervised several master's theses and final-year projects, covering diverse topics such as vehicle routing optimization and inventory management. His research has been published in international journals and presented at renowned conferences, addressing topics such as risk management, multicriteria analysis, and the impact of emerging technologies like the Internet of Things (IoT) in supply chain management. Additionally, he has contributed to practical case studies, particularly in the energy and transportation sectors in Tunisia. Committed to first aid and emergency response, Wissem ENNOURI has been a national trainer at the Tunisian Red Crescent since 2013 and a volunteer at the Tunisian Civil Protection since 2019. His professional journey also includes experience as a manager of an international trading company, further enhancing his skills in management and international trade. Wissem ENNOURI is a versatile professional, combining academic expertise, practical experience, and social engagement, with a passion for innovation and continuous improvement in the fields of logistics and risk management.

Wako Gelgelo is a Research scholar, Department of Management, Bule Hora University - (Ethiopia)

Wako Jio is a PhD Research Scholar, Department of Management, Bule Hora University, Ethiopia

Kamar Reda is a PhD student in Management Sciences at the New Management Practices Laboratory (NPG), Faculty of Legal, Economic and Social Sciences, Cadi Ayyad University, Marrakech (Morocco). She holds a Master's degree in Accounting, Control and Auditing and is a certified Data Analyst. Her research focuses on digital transformation, HRM, organizational behavior, and the integration of AI in managerial and marketing processes. She is an active author of several scientific publications and national and international scientific communication. She is actively involved in the organization of scientific symposiums and conferences as a member of organizing and steering committees for scientific studies.

Shashi Kant is an assistant professor Research scholar, Department of Management, Bule Hora University, Ethiopia

Sabah Laflafi is a Phd student in management science at Cadi Ayyad University, Marrakech, Faculty of Legal, Economic and Social Sciences -L-ERMESSAD

Driss Omerani is a professor of Management and Quantitative Methods at Cadi Ayyad University, specializing in finance and banking. He is currently Vice-Dean in charge of training at the Faculty of Legal, Economic and Social Sciences - Marrakech. Prof. Omerani holds a Ph.D. in Economics from the University of Social Sciences of Toulouse, obtained in 1991. His research focuses on resource economics, monopoly behavior, and the influence of uncertainty on economic decision-making.

Charaf Saidi is a research professor at cadi ayyad university, marrakech, Faculty of Legal, Economic and Social Sciences of Marrakech (LERMESSAD)

Index

A

B

C

O

P

R

S

T

U

W

www.ingramcontent.com/pod-product-compliance
Lightning Source LLC
LaVergne TN
LVHW080350011026
849161LV00009B/2258